READINGS IN MODERN WORLD CIVILIZATION

Readings in

COMPILED AND EDITED BY

Leon Bernard, PH.D.

UNIVERSITY OF NOTRE DAME

Theodore B. Hodges, PH.D.

UNITED STATES GOVERNMENT

MODERN WORLD CIVILIZATION

THE MACMILLAN COMPANY NEW YORK

MACMILLAN NEW YORK, LONDON

A DIVISION OF THE CROWELL-COLLIER PUBLISHING COMPANY

First Printing

Library of Congress catalog card number: 62-8564

The Macmillan Company, New York
Macmillan New York, London
Brett-Macmillan Ltd., Galt, Ontario

Printed in the United States of America

Designed by Mina Baylis

Foreword

THIS BOOK IS INTENDED PRIMARILY for college survey courses in modern civilization and modern European history. Its starting point is the Renaissance and Reformation. The first half is devoted almost exclusively to readings in European history to 1815, while the second half deals increasingly with Europe's world-wide ramifications.

The *raison d'être* of the work lies in our conviction that to study and understand history properly the text-book is not enough. A text-book by its very nature must confine itself largely to the presentation of the facts. Only by being introduced to contemporaneous literature can the student gain a sense of the spirit and feel of the past. Without developing such a sense of historical imagination, the student is likely to find history a rather misty and dull affair. A judicious sampling of historical readings not only enlivens the basic text-book but gives added meaning to it. Our aim has been to choose selections with this in mind. Even official documents, at first glance unappealing to the average freshman, can by careful editing be made both interesting and profitable to the student.

Each of the thirty-seven chapters contains about fifteen pages of historical selections, nearly all of which were written by men who either participated in or were contemporaneous to the events described. We have liberally exercised our editorial privilege to condense and to make extracts, always aiming, of course, to preserve the flavor and meaning of the original work. Editorial matter has been kept to a minimum, since it is our aim to supplement the text-book rather than to provide a second text. In selecting the material, we have sought a balance among political, military, intellectual, religious and economic elements in history. It appears to us that recent collections of readings have tended to become simply anthologies of the history of ideas, more suitable to "Great Books" seminars than to history classes. While not neglecting the great thinkers, this book does not place disproportionate emphasis on them. We believe that wars and revolutions, for example, have played a very important part in shaping the modern world, along with ideas, and to neglect them is to give a warped picture of the past.

We hope that this anthology of historical selections will prove useful to teacher and student alike.

Leon Bernard
T. B. Hodges

Contents

I

Renaissance and Reformation

A LONG-STANDING INTELLECTUAL pastime among historians is debating when the "modern world" began. The debate is relatively new. Historians of the nineteenth century and earlier would have, if asked, unhesitatingly replied that modern times started around 1500 with the Italian Renaissance and the Reformation. If pressed to justify their position, they would have patiently recounted what in their view seemed obvious. They would have explained how Europeans had for a thousand years been dominated by a clerical caste which had never permitted man to take his sights off the solitary objective of his soul's salvation. According to one notable representative of this school, John Addington Symonds, "During the Middle Ages man had lived enveloped in a cowl." Presumably, medieval man had not even been interested in the beauties of nature (one exception was allowed: St. Francis of Assisi), so intent was he on shunning all worldly pleasures. Held in a yoke by his church and society, his individuality always suppressed, his intellectual accomplishments limited to endless scholastic dialectic on such subjects as how many angels could dance on the head of a pin, medieval man could in the end point only to a thousand years of Gothic blackness as his legacy. From all this bleakness Europe was rescued towards the end of the 1400's. Classical antiquity was "rediscovered" and exciting new norms of beauty and truth drove first the Italians and then other Europeans to accomplishments unheard of in Europe for the past thousand years. The "middle ages" had ended, modernity begun.

Needless to say, such a black and white interpretation of European history is no longer reputable. Historical research has produced a picture of the Middle Ages far more flattering than once held. Today the generally held view tends to "evolution" from medieval civilization to modern, rather than "revolution." The only difference of opinion nowadays concerns the precise degree to which medievalism influenced Renaissance times. In general, those historians who have made the study of the Middle Ages their lifework see a great deal of continuity, while historians of the Renaissance tend to stress what is new, or relatively new, in culture, ideas, and institutions. In any case, the extreme interpretation of the Middle Ages has disappeared; a term such as the "Dark Ages" brands the user as quite ignorant of his past. Even the tenth century, generally acknowledged to have been the most dismal age in the history of western civilization, has yielded to the researches of historians and has been shown to have been not so dark after all.

There are those historians who argue that from a purely rational standpoint we should date the start of the "modern" epoch from the economic revival of the eleventh and twelfth centuries. The reappearance of interregional and long-distance commerce at that time led to the rebirth of urban life which in turn made possible the bourgeois class with which nearly all future material and cultural progress was to be identified. Here, it is argued, was a revolution worthy of the name, a far greater break with the past than that of the fifteenth century. While one can scoff at the concept of a "renaissance" in the tenth century, there is every justification for such a term applied to the twelfth and thirteenth centuries. These years, the so-called "High Middle Ages," mark the apogee of medieval Christian culture. They are the period of cathedral building, of the growth of towns and municipal institutions, of the "invention" of universities and parliaments—achievements which the later traditional Renaissance cannot match.

The culture of the Middle Ages rose to its zenith in the thirteenth century, faltered perceptibly at the end of the century, and then entered its long years of decay. The most obvious symptom of the decline was the weakening of the Church's spiritual and temporal authority. In the thirteenth century the Catholic Church had been the heart of European civilization. Virtually all aspects of life had been subordinated to or influenced by the Church. Kings and emperors recognized, at least theoretically, the superior authority of the popes. Europe was in truth a Catholic community.

Two centuries later that community had been shattered. The Church, which in its long history had successfully met so many challenges, was unable to deal with the secularism of the Renaissance and the heresy of Protestantism. In part, the explanation lies in the internal weakening of the Church stemming from the Babylonian Captivity, the Great Schism, the conciliar dispute, and the growing preoccupation of the popes with their temporal possessions. But equally important are the changes in the European political and social systems. The economic revolution of the High Middle Ages had resulted in the creation of a mercantile society upon which a whole new political edifice had gradually been built. With the taxes contributed by their subjects, monarchs were now able to raise armies and pay for administrative bureaucracies on a scale unknown since the days of Imperial Rome. The growth of monarchic absolutism posed a grave threat to the supranational Catholic Church. Since early medieval times, it had paid scant attention to political boundaries in carrying out its many duties. But now it found itself constantly frustrated by secular-minded rulers who brooked no encroachments upon their authority. Just as disturbing from the point of view of the Church was the steady growth in western Europe of a body of educated and cultured lay people, increasingly critical of the coarseness of many of the clergy and the crudity of popular religious practices. It was in this manner that the Renaissance touched upon the Reformation. The humanists played an important, although often unwitting, role in preparing the way for the latter.

1

The Renaissance in Italy

Traditionally, modern western history begins with the cultural awakening first discernible in Italy in the fourteenth century and clearly manifested in the fifteenth. Ironically, the new age sought progress by emulating the distant classical past. At the forefront of the movement were the literary figures known as the humanists, who rejected the "Gothic barbarism" of the Middle Ages and sought new standards of literary and artistic beauty in Graeco-Roman antiquity. Especially striking among the Italian humanists was their tendency to minimize the supernatural values of medieval man. Their importance in history does not lie in the musty classical manuscripts they "rediscovered" but rather in the new secular outlook they represented and publicized. As Petrarch declared, ". . . among mortals the care of things mortal should come first." Such a philosophy fitted in very nicely with the needs of the prosperous urbanized society of the age.

[1] *ITALIAN HUMANISTS DEBATE CICERO'S DIVINITY* *

The first great Italian humanist was Francesco Petrarch (1304–1374). In the following letter, he writes an account of a friendly controversy with an aged scholar

* J. H. Robinson and H. W. Rolfe, *Petrarch: The First Modern Scholar and Man of Letters* (New York and London: G. P. Putnam's Sons, 1909), pp. 244–247. Used by permission.

whom he met in the course of a journey. The letter illustrates the intense feeling of Petrarch and his contemporaries for antiquity.

. . . some one made mention of Cicero, as will very often happen among men of literary tastes. This name at once brought our desultory conversation to an end. We all turned our thoughts toward him. Nothing but Cicero was discussed after that. As we sat and feasted together we vied with one another in singing his praises. Still, there is nothing in this world that is absolutely perfect; never has the man existed in whom the critic, were he ever so lenient, would see nothing at all to reprehend. So it chanced that while I expressed admiration for Cicero, almost without reservation, as a man whom I loved and honoured above all others, and amazement too at his golden eloquence and his heavenly genius, I found at the same time a little fault with his fickleness and inconsistency, traits that are revealed everywhere in his life and works. At once I saw that all who were present were astonished at so unusual an opinion, and one among them especially so. I refer to the old man . . . whose name has gone from me, although his image is fresh in my memory, and I revere him, both for his years and for his scholarship.

Well, the circumstances seemed to demand that I fetch the manuscript of my correspondence with my friends, which I had with me in my chest. It was brought in, and added fuel to the flame. For among the letters that were written to my contemporaries there are a few, inserted with an eye to variety and for the sake of a little diversion in the midst of my more serious labours, that are addressed to some of the more illustrious men of ancient times. A reader who was not forewarned would be amazed at these, finding names so old and of such renown mingled with those of our own day. Two of them are to Cicero himself; one criticising his character, the other praising his genius. These two you read, while the others listened; and then the strife of words grew warmer. Some approved of what I had written, admitting that Cicero deserved my censure. But the old man stood his ground, more stubbornly even than before. He was so blinded by love of his hero and by the brightness of his name that he preferred to praise him even when he was in the wrong; to embrace faults and virtues together, rather than make any exceptions. He would not be thought to condemn anything at all in so great a man. . . . He would stretch out his hand and say imploringly, "Gently, I beg of you, gently with my Cicero." And when we asked him if he found it impossible to believe that Cicero had made mistakes, he would close his eyes and turn his face away and exclaim with a groan, as if he had been smitten, "Alas! alas! Is my beloved Cicero accused of doing wrong?" just as if we were speaking not of a man but of some god. I asked him, accordingly, whether in his opinion Tullius [Marcus Tullius Cicero] was a god, or a man like others. "A god," he replied; and then, realising what he had said, he added, "a god of eloquence." "Oh, very well" I answered; "if he is a god, he certainly could not have erred. However, I never heard him styled so before. And yet, if Cicero calls Plato his god, why should not you in turn speak of Cicero as yours?—except that it is not in harmony with our religious beliefs for men to fashion gods for themselves as they may fancy." "I am only jesting," said he; "I know that Tullius was a man, but he was a man of godlike genius." "That is better," I responded; "for when Quintilian called him heavenly he spoke no more than the truth. But then, if you admit that he was a man, it follows necessarily that he could make mistakes, and did so." As I spoke these words he shuddered and turned away, as if they were aimed not at another man's reputation but at his own life. What could I say, I who am myself so great an admirer of Cicero's genius? I felt that the old scholar was to be envied for his ardour and devotion, which had something of the Pythagorean savour. I rejoiced at finding such reverence for even one great man; such almost religious regard, so fervent that to suspect any touch of human weakness in its object seemed like sacrilege. I was amazed, too, at having discovered a person who cherished a love greater than mine for the man whom I always had loved beyond all others; a person who in old age still held, deeply rooted in his heart, the opinions concerning him which I remember to have entertained in my boyhood; and who, notwithstanding his advanced years, was incapable of arguing that if Cicero was a man it followed that in some cases, in many indeed, he must have erred, a conclusion that I have been forced, by common sense and by knowledge of his life, to accept at this earlier stage of my development,—although this conviction does not alter the fact that the beauty of his work delights me still, beyond that of any other writer. Why, Tullius himself, the very man of whom we are speaking, took this view, for he often bewailed his errors, bitterly. If, in our eagerness to praise him, we deny that he thus understood himself, we deprive him of a large part of his renown as a philosopher, the praise, namely, that is due to self-knowledge and modesty.

[2] *GREEK STUDIES ARE REVIVED IN THE WESTERN WORLD* *

The greatest accomplishment of the humanists was to rediscover Greek, virtually unknown during the Middle Ages. Major credit belongs to a Greek Byzantine,

* Bruni, *History of His Own Times in Italy*, as found in H. O. Taylor, *Thought and Expression in the Sixteenth Century*, Second Revised Edition (New York: The Macmillan Company, 1930), Vol. I, pp. 36–37.

Manuel Chrysoloras (1350?–1415), who was sent to Italy by his emperor to secure from the Latin West help against the Turks. He lingered in Florence for several years teaching the Greek classics to highly enthusiastic auditors, including the author of the following passage.

Then first came a knowledge of Greek, which had not been in use among us for seven hundred years. Chrysoloras the Byzantine, a man of noble birth and well versed in Greek letters, brought Greek learning to us. When his country was invaded by the Turks, he came by sea, first to Venice. The report of him soon spread, and he was cordially invited and besought and promised a public stipend, to come to Florence and open his store of riches to the youth. I was then studying Civil Law, but . . . I burned with love of academic studies, and had spent no little pains on dialectic and rhetoric. At the coming of Chrysoloras I was torn in mind, deeming it shameful to desert the law, and yet a crime to lose such a chance of studying Greek literature; and often with youthful impulse I would say to myself: "Thou, when it is permitted thee to gaze on Homer, Plato and Demosthenes, and the other poets, philosophers, orators, of whom such glorious things are spread abroad, and speak with them and be instructed in their admirable teaching, wilt thou desert and rob thyself? Wilt thou neglect this opportunity so divinely offered? For seven hundred years, no one in Italy has possessed Greek letters; and yet we confess that all knowledge is derived from them. How great advantage to your knowledge, enhancement of your fame, increase of your pleasure, will come from an understanding of this tongue? There are doctors of civil law everywhere; and the chance of learning will not fail thee. But if this one and only doctor of Greek letters disappears, no one can be found to teach thee." Overcome at length by these reasons, I gave myself to Chrysoloras, with such zeal to learn, that what through the wakeful day I gathered, I followed after in the night, even when asleep.

[3] *POPE NICHOLAS V CREATES A CLASSICAL LIBRARY* *

Popes had long collected books on theology and canon law for the papal library. To Pope Nicholas V (1447–1454) belongs the credit for adding an impressive collection of classical Greek and Latin works. Unfortunately, his immediate successors allowed the books to be scattered, so that the work had to begin anew towards the end of the fifteenth century. The author of the following passage was a contemporary bookseller and man of letters.

* Vespasiano da Bisticci, *Life of Nicholas V*, as found in Merrick Whitcomb, ed., *A Literary Source-Book of the Italian Renaissance* (Philadelphia: University of Pennsylvania, 1900), pp. 70–71.

At this time [1450] came the year of jubilee, and since it was the true jubilee, that is, at the end of a period of fifty years, according to the law of the Church, the concourse of people at Rome was such that no one had ever known a greater. It was a wonderful thing to see the great assemblage of people who came. In Rome and Florence the streets were so crowded that the people seemed like swarms of ants; and at the bridge of Sant' Angelo there was such a crowd of people of all nationalities, that they were jammed together, and unable to move in any direction. So great was the crowd, indeed, that in the struggle between those who came to seek indulgences and those who were already at the place, more than two hundred persons, male and female, lost their lives. When Pope Nicholas, who felt much anxiety in regard to these matters, heard of the accident, he was much displeased, took provisions to prevent its recurrence, and caused to be built at the approach to the bridge two small churches in memory of so great a disaster as was this destruction of so many men upon the occasion of the jubilee, and he provided for their burial.

A great quantity of money came by this means to the Apostolic See, and with this the pope commenced building in many places, and sent for Greek and Latin books, wherever he was able to find them, without regard to price. He gathered together a large band of writers, the best that he could find, and kept them in constant employment. He also summoned a number of learned men, both for the purpose of composing new works, and of translating such works as were not already translated, giving them most abundant provision for their needs meanwhile; and when the works were translated and brought to him, he gave them large sums of money, in order that they should do more willingly that which they undertook to do. He made great provision for the needs of learned men. He gathered together great numbers of books upon every subject, both Greek and Latin, to the number of 5000 volumes. So at his death it was found by inventory that never since the time of Ptolemy had half the number of books of every kind been brought together. All books he caused to be copied, without regard to what it cost him, and there were few places where his Holiness had not copiers at work. When he could not find a book, nor secure it in any way, he had it copied. After he had assembled at Rome, as I said above, many learned men at large salaries, he wrote to Florence to Messer Giannozzo Manetti, that he should come to Rome to translate and compose for him. And when Manetti left Florence and came to Rome, the pope, as was his custom, received him with honor, and assigned to him, in addition to his income as secretary, six hundred ducats, urging him to attempt the translation of the books of the Bible and of Aristotle and to complete the book already commenced by him, *Contra Judeos et gentes;* a wonderful work, if it had been completed, but he carried it only to the tenth book. Moreover.

he translated the New Testament, and the Psalter *De hebraica Veritate*, with five apologetical books in defense of this Psalter, showing that in the Holy Scriptures there is not one syllable that does not contain the greatest of mysteries.

[4] *LEONARDO DA VINCI PRESENTS HIS QUALIFICATIONS FOR EMPLOYMENT* *

Leonardo da Vinci (1452–1519), the universal genius of the Italian Renaissance, wandered for most of his life from one Italian city to another, offering to various patrons his remarkable talents. In the following letter, addressed to Ludovico Sforza (Il Moro), despot of Milan, Leonardo asked for a job and submitted his qualifications. The reader should observe the relative importance Leonardo attached to painting and sculpture.

Most Illustrious Lord,—Having now sufficiently considered the specimens of all those who proclaim themselves skilled contrivers of instruments of war, and that the invention and operation of the said instruments are nothing different to those in common use: I shall endeavor, without prejudice to anyone else, to explain myself to your Excellency, showing your Lordship my secrets, and then offering them to your best pleasure and approbation to work with effect at opportune moments on all those things which, in part, shall be briefly noted below.

I have . . . extremely light and strong bridges, adapted to be most easily carried, and with them you may pursue, and at any time flee from the enemy; . . . easy and convenient to lift and place. Also [a] method of burning and destroying those of the enemy.

I know how, when a place is besieged, to take water out of the trenches, and make endless variety of bridges, and covered ways and ladders, and other machines pertaining to such expeditions.

ITEM. If, by reason of the height of the banks, or the strength of the place and its position, it is impossible, when besieging a place, to avail oneself of the plan of bombardment, I have methods of destroying every rock or other fortress, even if it were founded on a rock, etc.

Again, I have kinds of mortars; most convenient and easy to carry; and with these I can fling small stones almost resembling a storm; and with the

* Letter of Leonardo da Vinci to Il Moro (Ludovico Sforza, despot of Milan), 1493, in J. P. and I. A. Richter, *The Literary Works of Leonardo da Vinci* (New York: Oxford University Press, Inc., 1939), Vol. II, pp. 325–327. Used by permission of Gisela M. A. Richter, the copyright owner.

smoke of these cause great terror to the enemy, to his great detriment and confusion.

And if the fight should be at sea I have kinds of many machines most efficient for offence and defence; and vessels which will resist the attack of the largest guns and powder and fumes.

ITEM. I have means by secret and tortuous mines and ways, made without noise to reach a designated [spot], even if it were needed to pass under a trench or a river.

ITEM. I will make covered chariots, safe and unattackable, which, entering among the enemy, with their artillery, there is no body of men so great but they would break them. And behind these, infantry could follow quite unhurt and without any hindrance.

ITEM. In case of need I will make big guns, mortars, and light ordnance of fine and useful forms, out of the common type.

Where the operation of bombardment might fall, I would contrive catapults, mangonels, *trabocchi* and other machines of marvellous efficacy and not in common use. And in short, according to the variety of cases, I can contrive various and endless means of offence and defence.

In time of peace I believe I can give perfect satisfaction and to the equal of any other in architecture and the composition of buildings, public and private; and in guiding water from one place to another.

ITEM. I can carry out sculpture in marble, bronze, or clay, and also I can do in painting whatever may be done, as well as any other, be he whom he may.

Again, the bronze horse may be taken in hand, which is to be the immortal glory and eternal honour of the prince your father of happy memory, and of the illustrious house of Sforza.

And if any one of the above-named things seems to anyone to be impossible or not feasible, I am most ready to make the experiment in your park, or in whatever place may please your Excellency, to whom I commend myself with the utmost humility.

[5] *CELLINI, TOO, SHOWS THE VERSATILITY OF THE RENAISSANCE MAN* *

One of the most colorful figures in an epoch replete with colorful personalities was Benvenuto Cellini (1500–1571), principally famous as a sculptor and gold-

* J. A. Symonds, trans., *The Autobiography of Benvenuto Cellini,* The Modern Library (New York: Random House, Inc., no date), pp. 81–83, 284–286.

smith. His Autobiography, *excerpts from which follow, reveals him as boastful and completely uninhibited. The first excerpt concerns an episode in the siege of Rome in 1526; the second has to do with the designing of one of Cellini's masterpieces, the gold salt cellar of King Francis I of France.*

[A] I pursued my business of artilleryman, and every day performed some extraordinary feat, whereby the credit and the favour I acquired with the Pope [Clement VII] was something indescribable. There never passed a day but what I killed one or another of our enemies in the besieging army. On one occasion the Pope was walking round the circular keep, when he observed a Spanish Colonel in the Prati; he recognised the man by certain indications, seeing that this officer had formerly been in his service; and while he fixed his eyes on him, he kept talking about him. I, above by the Angel, knew nothing of all this, but spied a fellow down there, busying himself about the trenches with a javelin in his hand; he was dressed entirely in rose-colour; and so, studying the worst that I could do against him, I selected a gerfalcon which I had at hand; it is a piece of ordnance larger and longer than a swivel, and about the size of a demiculverin. This I emptied, and loaded it again with a good charge of the fine powder mixed with the coarser sort; then I aimed it exactly at the man in red, elevating prodigiously, because a piece of that calibre could hardly be expected to carry true at such a distance. I fired, and hit my man exactly in the middle. He had trussed his sword in front, for swagger, after a way those Spaniards have; and my ball, when it struck him, broke upon the blade, and one could see the fellow cut in two fair halves. The Pope, who was expecting nothing of this kind, derived great pleasure and amazement from the sight, both because it seemed to him impossible that one should aim and hit the mark at such a distance, and also because the man was cut in two, and he could not comprehend how this should happen. He sent for me, and asked about it. I explained all the devices I had used in firing; but told him that why the man was cut in halves, neither he nor I could know. Upon my bended knees I then besought him to give me the pardon of his blessing for that homicide; and for all the others I had committed in the castle in the service of the Church. Thereat the Pope, raising his hand, and making a large open sign of the cross upon my face, told me that he blessed me, and that he gave me pardon for all murders I had ever perpetrated, or should ever perpetrate, in the service of the Apostolic Church. When I left him, I went aloft, and never stayed from firing to the utmost of my power; and few were the shots of mine that missed their mark. My drawing, and my fine studies in my craft, and my charming art of music, all were swallowed up in the din of that artillery; and if I were to relate in detail all the splendid things I did in that infernal work of cruelty, I should make the world stand by and wonder. But, not to be too prolix, I will pass them over. Only I must tell a few of the most remarkable, which are, as it were, forced in upon me.

To begin then: pondering day and night what I could render for my own part in defence of Holy Church, and having noticed that the enemy changed guard and marched past through the great gate of Santo Spirito, which was within a reasonable range, I thereupon directed my attention to that spot; but, having to shoot sideways, I could not do the damage that I wished, although I killed a fair percentage every day. This induced our adversaries, when they saw their passage covered by my guns, to load the roof of a certain house one night with thirty gabions, which obstructed the view I formerly enjoyed. Taking better thought than I had done of the whole situation, I now turned all my five pieces of artillery directly on the gabions, and waited till the evening hour, when they changed guard. Our enemies, thinking they were safe, came on at greater ease and in a closer body than usual; whereupon I set fire to my blow-pipes. Not merely did I dash to pieces the gabions which stood in my way; but, what was better, by that one blast I slaughtered more than thirty men. In consequence of this manoeuvre, which I repeated twice, the soldiers were thrown into such disorder, that being, moreover, encumbered with the spoils of that great sack, and some of them desirous of enjoying the fruits of their labour, they oftentimes showed a mind to mutiny and take themselves away from Rome. However after coming to terms with their valiant captain, Gian di Urbino, they were ultimately compelled, at their excessive inconvenience, to take another road when they changed guard. It cost them three miles of march, whereas before they had but half a mile. Having achieved this feat, I was entreated with prodigious favours by all the men of quality who were invested in the castle. This incident was so important that I thought it well to relate it, before finishing the history of things outside my art, the which is the real object of my writing: forsooth, if I wanted to ornament by biography with such matters, I should have far too much to tell. . . .

[B] . . . the Cardinal ordered me to make the model for a salt-cellar; but he said he should like me to leave the beaten track pursued by such as fabricated these things. Messer Luigi, apropos of this salt-cellar, made an eloquent description of his own idea; Messer Gabriello Cesano also spoke exceeedingly well to the same purpose. The Cardinal, who was a very kindly listener, showed extreme satisfaction with the designs which these two able men of letters had described in words. Then he turned to me and said: "My Benvenuto, the design of Messer Luigi and that of Messer Gabriello please me both so well that I know not how to choose between them, therefore I leave the choice to you, who will have to execute the work." I replied as follows: "It is apparent, my lords, of what vast consequence are the sons of kings and emperors, and what a marvellous brightness of divinity appears in them; nevertheless, if you ask some poor humble shepherd which he loves best, those royal children or his sons, he will certainly tell you that he loves his own sons best. Now I too have a great affection for the children which I bring forth from my art; consequently the first which I will show you, most reverend monsignor my good master, shall be of my own making and invention. There are many things beautiful enough in words which do not match together well when executed by an artist." Then I turned to the two scholars and said: "You have spoken, I will do." Upon this Messer Luigi Alamanni smiled, and added a great many witty things, with the greatest charm of manner, in my praise; they became him well, for he was handsome of face and figure, and had a gentle voice. Messer Gabriello Cesano was quite the opposite, as ugly and displeasing as the other was agreeable; accordingly he spoke as he looked.

Messer Luigi had suggested that I should fashion a Venus with Cupid, surrounded by a crowd of pretty emblems, all in proper keeping with the subject. Messer Gabriello proposed that I should model an Amphitrite, the wife of Neptune, together with those Tritons of the sea, and many such-like fancies, good enough to describe in words, but not to execute in metal.

I first laid down an oval framework, considerably longer than half a cubit—almost two-thirds, in fact; and upon this ground, wishing to suggest the interminglement of land and ocean, I modelled two figures, considerably taller than a palm in height, which were seated with their legs interlaced, suggesting those lengthier branches of the sea which run up into the continents. The sea was a man, and in his hand I placed a ship, elaborately wrought in all its details, and well adapted to hold a quantity of salt. Beneath him I grouped the four sea-horses, and in his right hand he held his trident. The earth I fashioned like a woman, with all the beauty of form, the grace, and charm of which my art was capable. She had a richly decorated temple firmly based upon the ground at one side; and here her hand rested. This I intended to receive the pepper. In her other hand I put a cornucopia, overflowing with all the natural treasures I could think of. Below this goddess, in the part which represented earth, I collected the fairest animals that haunt our globe. In the quarter presided over by the deity of ocean, I fashioned such choice kinds of fishes and shells as could be properly displayed in that small space. What remained of the oval I filled in with luxuriant ornamentation.

Then I waited for the Cardinal; and when he came, attended by the two accomplished gentlemen, I produced the model I had made in wax. On beholding it, Messer Gabriello Cesano was the first to lift his voice up, and to cry: "This is a piece which it will take the lives of ten men to finish: do not expect, most reverend monsignor, if you order it, to get it in your lifetime. Benvenuto, it seems, has chosen to display his children in a vision, but not to give them to the touch, as we did when we spoke of things that could be carried out, while he has shown a thing beyond the bounds of possibility." Messer Alamanni took my side; but the Cardinal said he did not care to undertake so important an affair. Then I turned to them and said: "Most reverend monsignor, and you, gentlemen, fulfilled with learning; I tell you that I hope to complete this piece for whosoever shall be destined to possess it; and each one of you shall live to see it executed a hundred times more richly than the model. Indeed, I hope that time will be left me to produce far greater things than this." The Cardinal replied in heat: "Unless you make it for the King [of France], to whom I mean to take you, I do not think that you will make it for another man alive. . . ."

[6] *MACHIAVELLI SETS NEW STANDARDS OF POLITICAL MORALITY* *

Niccolo Machiavelli (1469–1527), who rose no higher than a secretarial position in the government of Florence, presented in The Prince *a masterfully realistic and candid portrayal of Italian political behavior in the Renaissance. His model prince, Cesare Borgia, was an utterly immoral tyrant of the Papal States. Not without reason did Pope Paul IV in 1557 condemn* The Prince *and place it on the* Index.

[From the dedication to Lorenzo di Medici]

It is customary for those who wish to gain the favour of a prince to endeavour to do so by offering him gifts of those things which they hold most precious, or in which they know him to take especial delight. In this way princes are often presented with horses, arms, cloth of gold, gems, and such-like ornaments worthy of their grandeur. In my desire, however, to offer to Your Highness some humble testimony of my devotion, I have been unable to find among my possessions anything which I hold so dear or esteem so highly as that knowledge of the deeds of great men which I have acquired through a long experience of modern events and a constant study of the past.

* Niccolo Machiavelli, *The Prince and Other Discourses,* trans. by Luigi Ricci and revised by E. R. P. Vincent, The Modern Library (New York: Random House, Inc., 1940), pp. 3, 34–35, 53, 56–57, 59–60, 61, 63–64. Used by permission of Oxford University Press, London.

[Extracts from *The Prince*]

. . . cruelties [can be] exploited well or badly. Well committed may be called those (if it is permissible to use the word well of evil) which are perpetrated once for the need of securing one's self, and which afterwards are not persisted in, but are exchanged for measures as useful to the subjects as possible. Cruelties ill committed are those which, although at first few, increase rather than diminish with time. . . .

. . . in taking a state the conqueror must arrange to commit all his cruelties at once, so as not to have to recur to them every day, and so as to be able, by not making fresh changes, to reassure people and win them over by benefiting them. Whoever acts otherwise, either through timidity or bad counsels, is always obliged to stand with knife in hand, and can never depend on his subjects, because they, owing to continually fresh injuries are unable to depend upon him. For injuries should be done all together, so that being less tasted, they will give less offence. Benefits should be granted little by little, so that they may be better enjoyed. . . .

A prince should therefore have no other aim or thought, nor take up any other thing for his study, but war and its organisation and discipline, for that is the only art that is necessary to one who commands, and it is of such virtue that it not only maintains those who are born princes, but often enables men of private fortune to attain to that rank. And one sees, on the other hand, that when princes think more of luxury than of arms, they lose their state. The chief cause of the loss of states, is the contempt of this art, and the way to acquire them is to be well versed in the same.

. . . how we live is so far removed from how we ought to live, that he who abandons what is done for what ought to be done will rather learn to bring about his own ruin than his preservation. A man who wishes to make a profession of goodness in everything must necessarily come to grief among so many who are not good. Therefore it is necessary for a prince, who wishes to maintain himself, to learn how not to be good, and to use this knowledge and not use it, according to the necessity of the case.

. . . I know that every one will admit that it would be highly praiseworthy in a prince to possess all the . . . qualities that are reputed good, but as they cannot all be possessed or observed, human conditions not permitting of it, it is necessary that he should be prudent enough to avoid the scandal of those vices which would lose him the state, and guard himself if possible against those which will not lose it him, but if not able to, he can indulge them with less scruple. And yet he must not mind incurring the scandal of those vices, without which it would be difficult to save the state, for if one considers well, it will be found that some things which seem virtues would, if followed, lead to one's ruin, and some others which appear vices result in one's greater security and well-being.

. . . There is nothing which destroys itself so much as liberality, for by using it you lose the power of using it, and become either poor and despicable, or, to escape poverty, rapacious and hated. And of all things that a prince must guard against, the most important are being despicable or hated, and liberality will lead you to one or other of these conditions. It is, therefore, wiser to have the name of a miser, which produces disgrace without hatred, than to incur of necessity the name of being rapacious, which produces both disgrace and hatred.

. . . I say that every prince must desire to be considered merciful and not cruel. He must, however, take care not to misuse this mercifulness. Cesare Borgia was considered cruel, but his cruelty had brought order to the Romagna, united it, and reduced it to peace and fealty. If this is considered well, it will be seen that he was really much more merciful than the Florentine people, who, to avoid the name of cruelty, allowed Pistoia to be destroyed. A prince, therefore, must not mind incurring the charge of cruelty for the purpose of keeping his subjects united and faithful; for, with a very few examples, he will be more merciful than those who, from excess of tenderness, allow disorders to arise, from whence spring bloodshed and rapine; for these as a rule injure the whole community, while the executions carried out by the prince injure only individuals. . . .

. . . the question [arises] whether it is better to be loved more than feared, or feared more than loved. The reply is, that one ought to be both feared and loved, but as it is difficult for the two to go together, it is much safer to be feared than loved, if one of the two has to be wanting. For it may be said of men in general that they are ungrateful, voluble, dissemblers, anxious to avoid danger, and covetous of gain; as long as you benefit them, they are entirely yours; they offer you their blood, their goods, their life, and their children, as I have before said, when the necessity is remote; but when it approaches, they revolt. And the prince who has relied solely on their words, without making other preparations, is ruined; for the friendship which is gained by purchase and not through grandeur and nobility of spirit is bought but not secured, and at a pinch is not to be expended in your service. And men have less scruple in offending one who makes himself loved than one who makes himself feared; for love is held by a chain of obligation which, men being selfish, is broken whenever it serves their purpose; but fear is maintained by a dread of punishment which never fails.

How laudable it is for a prince to keep good faith and live with integrity, and not with astuteness, every one knows. Still the experience of our times shows those princes to have done great things who have had little regard for good faith, and have been able by astuteness to confuse men's brains, and who have ultimately overcome those who have made loyalty their foundation.

You must know, then, that there are two methods of fighting, the one by law, the other by force: the first method is that of men, the second of beasts; but as the first method is often insufficient, one must have recourse to the second. It is therefore necessary for a prince to know well how to use both the beast and the man. . . .

A prince being thus obliged to know well how to act as a beast must imitate the fox and the lion, for the lion cannot protect himself from traps, and the fox cannot defend himself from wolves. One must therefore be a fox to recognise traps, and a lion to frighten wolves. Those that wish to be only lions do not understand this. Therefore, a prudent ruler ought not to keep faith when by so doing it would be against his interest, and when the reasons which made him bind himself no longer exist. If men were all good, this precept would not be a good one; but as they are bad, and would not observe their faith with you, so you are not bound to keep faith with them. . . .

2

The Renaissance North of the Alps

By the end of the fifteenth century, Italian humanism and art were heavily influencing the "barbarian" regions to the north. "Out of the thick Gothic night our eyes are opened to the glorious torch of the sun," wrote Rabelais. The northern Renaissance was in some ways quite different from that of Italy. It was more conservative and less ready to overthrow the medieval past. The northern universities remained strongholds of the old traditions, to the vast disgust of the humanists. Most significant of all was the preoccupation of the northern Renaissance with theology and church reform, in glaring contrast to the indifferentism and even outright paganism of the Italian humanists.

[7] *HUMANIST LEARNING COMES TO ENGLAND* *

Polydore Vergil (1470?–1555), the author of the following passage, was a scholarly Italian who spent several years in England as collector of Peter's Pence. One

* Polydore Vergil, *Historia Anglica* (Basel, 1570), as found in C. Colby, ed., *Selections from the Sources of English History* (New York: Longmans, Green and Company, 1905), pp. 135–137. Used by permission.

must not conclude from his narrative that learning was non-existent in England before this time, but there is no gainsaying the great impetus which Italian humanism gave English letters.

During the same period [c. 1500–1520] the excellent literature of Greece and Rome, which had been excluded, shut out and banished from Italy by unholy wars, extended itself across the Alps throughout all Germany, France, England and Scotland. The Germans, although they had been formerly the least learned of all races, after they received it into their towns became especially erudite. The same boon was bestowed by a good and wise God upon the French, the English, the Scotch, to say nothing of others. Indeed it is by letters alone that our good deeds are immortalised and the memory of our name preserved. Therefore very many distinguished men and high-born women everywhere began to aid the study of liberal arts and of learning; to promote the more ardent pursuit of which among the English, Margaret the king's mother, a most saintly woman, at the instance of John Fisher, Bishop of Rochester, a man of the highest learning, grace and uprightness, reared at noble and famous Cambridge two splendid edifices. In them she established two bodies of students, and dedicated the one to Christ our Saviour, the other to St. John the Evangelist, and she provided large endowments for their maintenance. In this same university John Alcock, a father of shining righteousness and virtue, had founded a little while before a college which he consecrated to Jesus, so that with him for a leader those who should there devote themselves to study should not wander, but should by the straight way advance to receive the true reward of glory and praise which He has promised to well-doers.

At the same time William Smyth, Bishop of Lincoln, prompted by the example of Margaret, established a college at Oxford in Brasyn Nose Hall for youths who were following literary pursuits. This hall had its name from a statue with a huge brass face which stood just outside the gate. Moreover Richard, Bishop of Winchester, wrought a similar work at Oxford, and called his college Corpus Christi.

The same spur of virtue and glory incited John Colet, Dean of St. Paul's, to promote in the same wise the study of good literature. He, illustrious alike for merit of soul and mind and for uprightness of life and conduct, was deemed by his countrymen to be almost another Apostle Paul. Nature made him holy and devout, so that from the time when he left off his boyish studies he betook him to divinity, and chose Paul for his teacher, to such purpose both at Oxford and Cambridge and afterward in Italy that he became a man finished, as the saying is, to the nail. When he came home he began to lecture upon the Epistles of St. Paul at London, his birthplace, and often to preach in church: and since his life and teaching were at one, people assented in wonderful wise to his good precepts: since he was the most temperate of men, only eating once a day, not thirsting for honours nor seeking riches, which nevertheless followed him as he fled from them. He was the only survivor of the twenty-two children whom his father, Henry Colet, a citizen of the utmost modesty and weight, and his noble wife Christiana, had; and he inherited his father's estate.

Then John, seeing that many of his fellow citizens were in the habit of shunning quiet and serious men, thought that it would be much better for themselves if they were educated. Therefore at his own cost he determined to help the youth of London to get learning, and about this time established on the east of St. Paul's cemetery a splendid school. He made William Lily head master, and there was another master to teach the beginners, so that provision was made for literature, good morals and earnestness. . . . After passing some years in Italy to complete his education he came home, and was the first of the English to teach his countrymen good literature. Before him, Cornelius Vitellius, a noble Italian from the sea-coast town of Corneto in Etruria, first taught literature to the youth of Oxford. He was next followed by John Ritwyse, a good and learned man, and then by Richard Jones. Colet paid these masters from his own purse year after year, to the end that they and afterwards others to all time should give free instruction. And as, thanks to St. Paul's School, the youth of London is far more polished than it used to be, so throughout all England studies and students prosper.

[8] *THOMAS MORE DEPICTS LIFE IN UTOPIA* *

One of the greatest of the English humanists was Thomas More (1478–1535). His principal literary work was Utopia *(1516), an account of a perfect society where communism was practised, education was universal, and religious toleration recognized. The book illustrates the preoccupation of northern humanists with social questions, a matter of small import to the Italian humanists.*

. . . I have described to you, as truly as I could, the constitution of that commonwealth Utopia, which I think not only the best but the only one which can rightly claim the name of a commonwealth. For in all others men talk freely of the public good, but only look after their own. Here, where there is no private property, they seriously mind the affairs of state. Assuredly in both cases there is good reason. For elsewhere there are few who do not

* G. C. Richards, ed., *More's Utopia* (Oxford: Basil Blackwell, 1923), pp. 118–121. Used by permission.

understand that unless they make some separate provision for themselves, however much the commonwealth may flourish, they will themselves starve; so necessity compels them to think that they must take account of themselves rather than the people, that is, of others than themselves. On the other hand, here, where all things are common, no one doubts that the individual will always have plenty, provided the common granaries are well filled. For the distribution of good things is not niggardly; and there are no poor, and beggars: though no man has anything, yet all are rich. For what can be greater riches for a man than to live in joy and peace, with no anxieties as to the future, not troubled about food, nor harassed by the querulous demands of his wife, not fearing poverty for his son, not worrying about his daughter's dowry, and without anxiety about his own livelihood or that of his belongings, his wife, sons, grandsons, great-grandsons, great-great-grandsons and all the long succession of descendants that gentlefolk anticipate, but sure of their happiness? Then take into account the fact that there is no less provision for those who have been labourers but are now past work, than for those who are still labouring. Here I should like anyone to be so bold as to compare this fair system with the so-called justice practised in other nations, among whom, upon my word, I cannot discover any trace of justice and fairness. For what justice is it that a noble, or a goldsmith, or a money-lender, or in fact any other of the idle classes, whose work, if they do any, is not very essential to the commonwealth, should live in grandeur and luxury, doing nothing at all or only that which is superfluous? But in the meantime, the day labourer, the carter, the smith, the husbandman, by continuous toil, the beasts of burden could scarcely endure, and toil so essential, that no state could last for a year without it, get such a poor living, and lead such a miserable life, that the condition of beasts of burden might seem far preferable; for these have not to work so incessantly, they are not much worse fed, and they get more enjoyment out of it, and have no fear for the future. The labourers not only have to work without return or profit at the time, but are agonized by the thought of a helpless and indigent old age; for their daily wage is too scanty to suffice even for the day, much less can they spare or save anything that can be laid by for their needs when they are old.

Now is not this an unjust and ungrateful commonwealth, which lavishes such great rewards on gentle folk, as they call them, and goldsmiths and such other persons, who are either idle, or mere parasites and purveyors of empty pleasures, but has no kind care for husbandmen, colliers, day labourers, carters and smiths, without whom there would be no commonwealth at all? But after it has misused their labour in their prime, then, when they are weighed down with age and disease, and in utter want, it forgets all the benefits it has received at their hands, and ungratefully requites them with a most miserable death. And what is worse, the rich every day take away a part of the daily allowance of the poor not only by private fraud but by statute law, and thus they have now made worse what even before seemed unjust, that those who have deserved best of the commonwealth should have the worst return for their labours; and yet by the statutes they have passed, this becomes justice. So when I consider and turn over in my mind the state of all flourishing commonwealths to-day, so help me God, I can see nothing but a conspiracy of the rich, who are aiming at their own advantage under the name and title of the commonwealth. They invent and devise all ways and means, by which they may keep without fear of losing all that they have amassed by evil practices, and next to that may purchase as cheaply as possible, and misuse the labour and toil of the poor.

. . . When in Utopia all greed for money was entirely removed with its use, what a mass of troubles was lopped off, how great a crop of crimes was pulled up by the roots! For who does not know that fraud, theft, rapine, quarrels, disorders, strife, seditions, murders, treasons, poisonings, which are punished rather than restrained by daily executions, die out with the death of money, and that fear, anxiety, worries, toils and watchings will perish along with money? Poverty itself, which seemed only to lack money, would forthwith disappear and die out if money were removed. To make this more clear, consider in your thoughts some barren and unfruitful year, in which many thousands of men have been carried off by hunger. I am sure that at the end of that scarcity, if the rich man's granaries had been searched, so much corn might have been found as, if it had been divided among those who were killed off by hunger and disease, would have prevented anyone from feeling that meagre return of climate and soil. So easily might men get their living, if that much lauded money, that grand invention to open the way to a living, did not exist and form the only barrier in the way of our getting a living. I doubt not that even the rich perceive that it would be a much better state of things to lack no necessity than to have abundance of superfluities, to be released from such numerous troubles than to be hemmed in by great riches. Nor do I doubt that regard for a man's own advantage, or the authority of our Saviour Christ—Who, of His wisdom, could not fail to know what was best, and of His goodness could not advise what He knew not to be best—would long ago have brought the world to adopt the laws of this commonwealth, had not one single monster, the chief and progenitor of all plagues, Pride, stood in the way. She measures prosperity not by her own good, but by the harm of others. She would not even consent to be made a goddess, if no poor wretches were left for her to domineer over, over whose miseries her good fortune might shine in the comparison, whose poverty she might vex and torment by unfolding her own wealth. This serpent of Hell enters the hearts of men and stops them from entering on the better path of life, and is so deeply rooted in men that she cannot easily be plucked out. That this constitution, which I should be glad to see all enjoy, has been the good fortune of the Utopians, fills me with rejoicing. They have adopted such institutions of life as have laid the foundations of a commonwealth not only most happily, but also to last for ever, so far as human prescience can forecast. For when at home, along with other vices, ambition and factiousness have been uprooted, there is no danger of trouble from domestic discord, which has been the only cause of ruin to the well-established prosperity of many cities.

But while harmony is preserved at home and its institutions are in a healthy state, not all the envy of the neighbouring kings, though it has often attempted it and been repelled, can avail to shake or even to influence that realm.

[9] *A FRENCH HUMANIST LAUDS THE NEW LEARNING* *

An outstanding figure of the French Renaissance was François Rabelais (1494?–1553)—monk, doctor, vagabond, humorist. He is chiefly noted for two grotesque novels, Pantagruel *and* Gargantua, *both classics of satire and racy humor. The first excerpt, from* Gargantua, *is a description of Thélème, Rabelais' concept of a model religious community. The second is the famous letter of Gargantua to Pantagruel, a student at the University of Paris.*

[A] HOW THE THELEMITES WERE GOVERNED, AND OF THEIR MANNER OF LIVING

All their life [the Thelemites] was spent not in laws, statutes, or rules, but according to their own free will and pleasure. They rose out of their beds when they thought good: they did eat, drink, labour, sleep, when they had a mind to it, and were disposed for it. None did awake them, none did offer to constrain them to eat, drink, nor to do any other thing; for so had Gargantua established it. In all their rule, and strictest tie of their order, there was but this one clause to be observed,

DO WHAT THOU WILT

. . . men that are free, well-born, well-bred, and conversant in honest companies, have naturally an instinct and spur that prompteth them into virtuous actions, and withdraws them from vice, which is called honour.

* C. H. Page, ed., *Rabelais* (New York and London: G. P. Putnam's Sons, 1905), pp. 110–112, 149–153. Used by permission of Putnam & Co. Ltd. (London).

Those same men, when by base subjection and constraint they are brought under and kept down, turn aside from that noble disposition, by which they formerly were inclined to virtue, to shake off and break that bond of servitude, wherein they are so tyrannously enslaved; for it is agreeable with the nature of man to long after things forbidden, and to desire what is denied us.

By this liberty they entered into a very laudable emulation, to do all of them what they saw did please one. If any of the gallants or ladies should say, "Let us drink," they would all drink. If any one of them said, "Let us play," they all played. If one said, "Let us go a-walking into the fields," they went all. If it were to go a hawking, or a hunting, the ladies mounted upon dainty well-paced nags, seated in a stately palfrey saddle, carried on their lovely fists, miniardly begloved every one of them, either a sparhawk, or a laneret, or a merlin, and the young gallants carried the other kinds of hawks.

So nobly were they taught, that there was neither he nor she amongst them, but could read, write, sing, play upon several musical instruments, speak five or six . . . languages, and compose in them all very quaintly, both in verse and prose. Never were seen so valiant knights, so noble and worthy, so dextrous and skilful both on foot and a horseback, more brisk and lively, more nimble and quick, or better handling all manner of weapons, than were there. Never were seen ladies so proper and handsome, so miniard and dainty, less forward, or more ready with their hand, and with their needle, in every honest and free action belonging to that sex, than were there. For this reason, when the time came, that any man of the said abbey, either at the request of his parents, or for some other cause, had a mind to go out of it, he carried along with him one of the ladies, namely her whom he had before that chosen for his mistress, and they were married together. And if they had formerly in Thélème lived in good devotion and amity, they did continue therein and increase it to a greater height in their state of matrimony: and did entertain that mutual love till the very last day of their life, in no less vigour and fervency, than at the very day of their wedding.

[**B**] Most dear Son,

. . . although my deceased father of happy memory, Grangousier, had bent his best endeavours to make me profit in all perfection and political knowledge, . . . nevertheless, as thou mayest well understand, the time then was not so proper and fit for learning as it is at present, neither had I plenty of such good masters as thou hast had. For that time was darksome, obscured with clouds of ignorance, and savouring a little of the infelicity and calamity of the Goths, who had, wherever they set footing, destroyed all good literature, which in my age hath by the divine goodness been restored unto its former light and dignity, and that with such amendment and increase of the knowledge, that now hardly should I be admitted unto the first form of the little grammar-school-boys— . . . I, who in my youthful days was . . . reputed the most learned of that age. . . .

Now is it, that the minds of men are qualified with all manner of discipline, and the old sciences revived, which for many ages were extinct. Now it is, that the learned languages are to their pristine purity restored, viz., Greek, without which a man may be ashamed to account himself a scholar, Hebrew, Arabic, Chaldaean, and Latin. Printing likewise is now in use, so elegant and so correct, that better cannot be imagined, although it was found out but in my time by divine inspiration, as by a diabolical suggestion on the other side, was the invention of ordnance. All the world is full of knowing men, of most learned schoolmasters, and vast libraries; and it appears to me as a truth, that neither in Plato's time, nor Cicero's, nor Papinian's, there was ever such conveniency for study, as we see at this day there is. . . . I see robbers, hangmen, freebooters, tapsters, ostlers, and such like, of the very rubbish of the people, more learned now than the doctors and preachers were in my time.

. . . Wherefore, my son, I admonish thee to employ thy youth to profit as well as thou canst, both in thy studies and in virtue. Thou art at Paris, where the laudable examples of many brave men may stir up thy mind to gallant actions, and hast likewise for thy tutor and pedagogue the learned Epistemon, who, by his lively and vocal documents may instruct thee in the arts and sciences.

I intend, and will have it so, that thou learn the languages perfectly: first of all, the Greek, as Quintilian will have it; secondly, the Latin; and then the Hebrew, for the holy Scripture-sake; and then the Chaldee and Arabic likewise, and that thou frame thy style in Greek in imitation of Plato; and for the Latin, after Cicero. Let there be no history which thou shalt not have ready in thy memory. . . . Of the liberal arts of geometry, arithmetic, and music, I gave thee some taste when thou wert yet little, and not above five or six years old. Proceed further in them, and learn the remainder if thou canst. As for astronomy, study all the rules thereof. Let pass, nevertheless, the divining and judicial astrology, and the art of Lullius, as being nothing else but plain abuses and vanities. As for the civil law, of that I would have thee to know the texts by heart, and then to confer them with philosophy.

Now, in matter of the knowledge of the works of nature, I would have thee to study that exactly; and that so there be no sea, river, nor fountain, of which thou dost not know the fishes; all the fowls of the air; all the several kinds of shrubs and trees, whether in forests or orchards; all the sorts of herbs and flowers that grow upon the ground; all the various metals that are hid within the bowels of the earth; together with all the diversity of precious stones, that are to be seen in the orient and south parts of the world. Let nothing of all these be hidden from thee. Then fail not most carefully to peruse the books of the Greek, Arabian, and Latin physicians, not despising the Talmudists and Cabalists; and by frequent anatomies get thee the perfect knowledge of the other world, called the microcosm, which is man. And at some hours of the day apply thy mind to the study of the holy Scriptures; first in Greek, the New Testament, with the Epistles of the Apostles; and then the Old Testament in Hebrew. In brief, let me see an abyss and bottomless pit of knowledge: for from henceforward, as thou growest great and becomest a man, thou must part from this tranquillity and rest of study, thou must learn chivalry, warfare, and the exercises of the field, the better thereby to defend my house and our friends, and to succour and protect them at all their needs, against the invasion and assaults of evildoers.

. . . Suspect the abuses of the world. Set not thy heart upon vanity, for this life is transitory, but the Word of the Lord endureth for ever. Be serviceable to all thy neighbours, and love them as thyself. Reverence thy preceptors: shun the conversation of those whom thou desirest not to resemble; and receive not in vain the graces which God hath bestowed upon thee. And, when thou shalt see that thou hast attained to all the knowledge that is to be acquired in that part, return unto me, that I may see thee, and give thee my blessing before I die. My son, the peace and grace of our Lord be with thee, Amen.

From Utopia the 17 day of the month of March.

Thy father, Gargantua.

These letters being received and read, Pantagruel plucked up his heart, took a fresh courage to him, and was inflamed with a desire to profit in his studies more than ever, so that if you had seen him, how he took pains, and how he advanced in learning, you would have said that the vivacity of his spirit amidst the books was like a great fire amongst dry wood, so active it was, vigorous, and indefatigable.

[10] *THE "OBSCURE MEN" ARE PUZZLED BY THE INTRICACIES OF CHURCH LAW* *

A great controversy raged in Germany on the eve of the Reformation over the efforts of the humanist John Reuchlin to introduce the study of Hebrew in the

* Francis G. Stokes, trans. and ed., *Epistolae Obscurorum Virorum* (London: Chatto and Windus, 1925), pp. 445–447. Used by permission.

universities. Certain of his friends championed his cause by publishing The Letters of Obscure Men, *supposedly letters exchanged among the clerical opponents of Reuchlin, but in fact a pure hoax designed to show up the ignorance and pomposity of Reuchlin's Dominican opponents.*

Heinrich Schafmaul [Sheep's Mouth] to Magister Ortuinus Gratius

Inasmuch as before I journeyed to [the Roman] Court you charged me to write to you oft, and propose from time to time knotty points in Theology, which you would straightway resolve better than the Courticians [members of the Papal Court] at *Rome:* therefore, I now write to ask your reverence what opinion you hold concerning one who on a Friday, that is on the sixth day of the week—or on any other fast-day—should eat an egg with a chicken in it?

For you must know that we were lately sitting in an inn in the *Campo dei Fiori,* having our supper, and were eating eggs, when on opening one I saw that there was a young chicken within.

This I showed to a comrade; whereupon quoth he to me, "Eat it up speedily, before the taverner sees it, for if he mark it, you will have to pay a Carline or a Julius for a fowl. For it is the rule of the house that once the landlord has put anything on the table you must pay for it—he won't take it back. And if he sees that there is a young fowl in that egg, he will say 'Pay me for that fowl!' Little or big, 'tis all one."

In a trice I gulped down the egg, chicken and all.

And then I remembered that it was Friday!

Whereupon I said to my crony, "You have made me commit a mortal sin, in eating flesh on the sixth day of the week!"

But he averred that it was not a mortal sin—nor even a venial one, seeing that such a chickling is accounted merely as an egg, until it is born.

He told me, too, that it is just the same in the case of cheese, in which there are sometimes grubs, as there are in cherries, peas, and new beans: yet all these may be eaten on Fridays, and even on Apostolic Vigils. But taverners are such rascals that they call them flesh, to get the more money.

Then I departed, and thought the matter over.

And by the Lord, Master *Ortwin,* I am in a mighty quandary, and know not what to do.

I would willingly seek counsel of one of the Courticians, but they are not devout men.

It seemeth to me that these young fowls in eggs are flesh, because their substance is formed and fashioned into the limbs and body of an animal, and possesseth a vital principle.

It is different in the case of grubs in cheese, and suchlike, because grubs are accounted fish, as I learnt from a physician who is also skilled in Natural Philosophy.

Most earnestly do I entreat you to resolve the question that I have propounded. For if you hold that the sin is mortal, then, I would fain get shrift here, ere I return to Germany.

[11] *POPE JULIUS II APPEARS AT THE GATE OF HEAVEN* *

The dialogue Julius II Exclusus *appeared anonymously in Paris in 1513. Erasmus denied having written it, but most of his contemporaries attributed it to him, and, although the authorship has never been thoroughly established, it is generally assumed to be his work.*

[POPE] JULIUS. What the devil is this? The gates not opened! Something is wrong with the lock.

SPIRIT. You have brought the wrong key perhaps. The key of your money-box will not open the door here. You should have brought both keys. This is the key of power, not of knowledge.

JULIUS. I never had any but this, and I don't see the use of another. Hey there, porter! I say, are you asleep or drunk?

PETER. Well that the gates are adamant, or this fellow would have broken in. He must be some giant, or conqueror. Heaven, what a stench! Who are you? What do you want here?

JULIUS. Open the gates, I say. Why is there no one to receive me?

PETER. Here is fine talk. Who are you, I say?

JULIUS. You know this key, I suppose, and the triple crown, and the pallium?

PETER. I see a key, but not the key which Christ gave to me a long time since. The crown? I don't recognize the crown. No heathen king ever wore such a thing, certainly none who expected to be let in here. The pallium is strange too. And see, there are marks on all three of that rogue and impostor Simon Magus, that I turned out of office.

JULIUS. Enough of this. I am Julius the Ligurian, P.M., as you can see by the letters if you can read.

PETER. P.M.! What is that? Pestis Maxima? [Greatest Plague.]

JULIUS. Pontifex Maximus, you rascal.

PETER. If you are three times Maximus, if you are Mercury Trismegistus, you can't come in unless you are Optimus too.

* "Julius II Exclusus," in J. A. Froude, *Life and Letters of Erasmus* (New York: Charles Scribner's Sons, 1895), pp. 149–151, 168.

JULIUS. Impertinence! You, who have been no more than Sanctus all these ages—and I Sanctissimus, Sanctissimus Dominus, Sanctitas, Holiness itself, with Bulls to show it.

PETER. Is there no difference between being Holy and being called Holy? Ask your flatterers who called you these fine names to give you admittance. Let me look at you a little closer. Hum! Signs of impiety in plenty, and none of the other thing. Who are these fellows behind you? Faugh! They smell of stews, drink-shops, and gunpowder. Have you brought goblins out of Tartarus to make war with heaven? Yourself, too, are not precisely like an apostle. Priest's cassock and bloody armour below it, eyes savage, mouth insolent, forehead brazen, body scarred with sins all over, breath loaded with wine, health broken with debauchery. Ay, threaten as you will, I will tell you what you are for all your bold looks. You are Julius the Emperor come back from hell. . . .

JULIUS. Will you make an end of your talking and open the gates? We will break them down else. You see these followers of mine.

PETER. I see a lot of precious rogues, but they won't break in here.

JULIUS. Make an end, I say, or I will fling a thunderbolt at you. I will excommunicate you. I have done as much to kings before this. Here are the Bulls ready.

PETER. Thunderbolts! Bulls! I beseech you, we had no thunderbolts or Bulls from Christ.

JULIUS. You shall feel them if you don't behave yourself. . . .

PETER. You must show your merits first; no admission without merits.

JULIUS. What do you mean by merits?

PETER. Have you taught true doctrine?

JULIUS. Not I. I have been too busy fighting. There are monks to look after doctrine, if that is of any consequence.

PETER. Have you gained souls to Christ by pious example?

JULIUS. I have sent a good many to Tartarus.

PETER. Have you worked any miracles?

JULIUS. Pshaw! miracles are out of date.

PETER. Have you been diligent in your prayers?

SPIRIT. You waste your breath. This is mockery.

PETER. These are the qualities which make a respectable pope. If he has others better, let him produce them. . . .

JULIUS. Then you won't open the gates?

PETER. Sooner to anyone than to such as you. We are not of your communion in this place. You have an army of sturdy rogues behind you, you have money, and you are a famous architect. Go build a paradise of your own, and fortify it, lest the devils break in on you.

[12] *ERASMUS SATIRIZES THE FOIBLES OF MAN* *

Desiderius Erasmus (1466–1536) was the greatest of the northern humanists. He occupied a position in the intellectual life of his times which has probably never been equalled. His most entertaining work is the Praise of Folly, *a typically gentle but highly effective satire exposing the silliness of virtually every class and profession.*

. . . let us examine the behavior of men, and it will become evident how much they owe me [Dame Folly is speaking], and how widely I am imitated by all classes of society. Since it would take too long to review the lives of everyone, let us choose only distinguished persons. It will be easy enough to infer from them what the others are like. Besides, everyone admits that ordinary citizens are fools. . . .

Men put on a superb daily performance for the gods. In the morning, of course, when they are sober, the gods are busy settling quarrels and hearing prayers; but later in the day, after they have had several drinks and are tired of the office, they find a seat in the grandstand and look down at the human spectacle. It's the greatest show on earth! No theater has as many comic acts. I sometimes take a seat alongside the gods myself. Here is a fellow pining away for a sweet young thing, and the less she responds, the more helplessly he falls in love. This one marries a dowry rather than a girl. That one prostitutes his own wife. Another husband is insanely jealous. See how foolishly this grief-stricken person behaves. Hiring mourners as if they were actors, to put on a show of sorrow! And that fellow squeezes out a tear at the tomb of his mother-in-law. Everything this man can scrape together he spends on his belly, and presently he is just as hungry as ever. Another is convinced that nothing excels sleep and idleness. There are those who stew over other people's business, while they neglect their own. There is also the bankrupt broker who thinks he is rich because he handles so much money. Another is happy living like a pauper in order to enrich his heirs. This man, for the sake of a small and uncertain profit, risks his priceless life at sea. His friend goes to war for riches, when he might live in ease and safety at home. Some think that playing up to childless old men is the highroad to wealth. There is no lack, either, of those who chase after rich old women. Both are entertaining to watch, because they are usually fooled by their intended victims.

* Desiderius Erasmus, *The Praise of Folly,* trans. by Leonard Dean (Chicago: Packard and Company, 1946), pp. 88–96. Used by permission of the copyright holder, Farrar, Straus & Cudahy, Inc.

The merchants, however, are the biggest fools of all. They carry on the most sordid business and by the most corrupt methods. Whenever it is necessary, they will lie, perjure themselves, steal, cheat, and mislead the public. Nevertheless, they are highly respected because of their money. There is no lack of flattering friars to kowtow to them and call them Right Honorable in public. The motive of the friars is clear enough: they are after some of the loot. . . .

. . . let us turn to those who have a reputation for wisdom and who seek the golden bough. Among these stand first the grammarians, a tormented, calamity-ridden, God-forsaken body of men. Their wretched profession would be unbearable if I did not relieve it with folly. Grammarians are subject not only to the five curses of the *Iliad* but to six hundred more, considering their starving and dirty schools. I said "schools," but I should have said "prisons," or "factories," or even "slaughter-houses" for boys. There the grammarians grow old at their labors, become deafened with noise, and waste away in the midst of the stench and filth. Yet with my assistance they consider themselves superior to everyone else. Their complacency and feeling of importance grow as they terrify their trembling classes with menacing words and looks. They beat the wretches with ferrules, rods, or straps; and, like Aesop's ass, they rage dogmatically in all directions at once. . . .

The poets owe less to me, although the license they proverbially claim for themselves would seem to identify them with my party. Their whole business is to soothe the ears of fools with airy trifles and ridiculous stories. With a marvelous confidence they promise themselves immortality and a life equal to that of the gods, and they even assure the same thing to others. Poets are notorious for self-love and flattery; no one else cultivates me in that respect more sincerely and constantly. . . .

This is the place to speak of those who seek fame by writing books. They all owe much to me, although the scribblers of nonsense are of course the chief debtors. Scholars who write for a few learned judges, like Persius and Laelius, seem to me to be miserable rather than happy. They torture themselves by making endless additions and changes. They strike something out and then put it back in. They revise their work, show it to friends, keep it for nine years, and are still not satisfied. Their empty reward is the praise of a handful, and it is obtained only at the cost of ceaseless study and sacrifice, and of sleep, which is even more important. Add the loss of health and good looks, strained eyes or even blindness, poverty, envy, lack of pleasures, premature old age, early death—extend the list as far as you can. For all such hardships the learned writer considers himself compensated if he gains the approval of one or two other near-sighted scholars. . . .

Among professional men, the lawyers claim first place. No others are so satisfied with themselves, . . . By stirring together six hundred statutes at once, regardless of their relevance, and by piling gloss on gloss and opinion on opinion, they create the impression that their work is extremely difficult. They confuse tediousness with brilliance. . . . Any one of them can out-talk twenty picked women. They would be happier if they were only wordy, and were not in addition so quarrelsome that they will fight over goat's wool and lose the truth in the midst of disputing. Self-love restores their happiness, however. Armed with three syllogisms, they will argue with any man about any subject. . . .

After the lawyers come the philosophers, who are reverenced for their beards and the fur on their gowns. They announce that they alone are wise, and that the rest of men are only passing shadows. Their folly is a pleasant one. They frame countless worlds, and measure the sun, moon, stars, and spheres as with thumb and line. They unhesitatingly explain the causes of lightning, winds, eclipses, and other inexplicable things. One would think that they had access to the secrets of nature, who is the maker of all things, or that they had just come from a council of the gods. Actually, nature laughs uproariously at them all the time. The fact that they can never explain why they constantly disagree with each other is sufficient proof that they do not know the truth about anything. They know nothing at all, yet profess to know everything. . . .

Perhaps it would be wise to pass over the theologians in silence. That short-tempered and supercilious crew is as unpleasant to deal with as Lake Camarina [a notoriously malodorous swamp in Sicily] . . . They may attack me with an army of six hundred syllogisms; and if I do not recant, they will proclaim me a heretic. With this thunderbolt they terrify the people they don't like. They are extremely reluctant to acknowledge my benefits to them, which are nevertheless considerable. Their opinion of themselves is so great that they behave as if they were already in heaven; they look down pityingly on other men as so many worms. A wall of imposing definitions, conclusions, corollaries, and explicit and implicit propositions protects them. They have so many hideouts that even Vulcan could not catch them with his net. They escape through distinctions, and cut knots as easily as with a double-bitted axe from Tenedos. They are full of big words and newly-invented terms.

3

The Expansion of European Civilization

The Age of the Renaissance is distinguished by more than a new intellectual outlook. It is the period of the greatest geographical discoveries in the history of man. For two centuries, voyage followed upon voyage until European man had succeeded in constructing a world map only the details of which remained to be filled in. The incentives for this work of discovery and exploration were many: the search for gold, the quest for a northwest passage to the riches of Asia, the desire to spread the Christian faith, the sheer love of adventure. Furthermore, Europe was not content merely to discover; it began to "export" its institutions and way of life, a fateful development which would seemingly terminate only in our own day.

[13] *JOHN HAWKINS ROUNDS UP A LUCRATIVE CARGO OF SLAVES* *

Before becoming a rear admiral in the English navy and a leader in the defeat of the Spanish Armada, John Hawkins (1532–1595) engaged in the less exalted but

* E. J. Payne, ed., *Voyages of the Elizabethan Seamen* (London, 1880), pp. 52–53.

highly lucrative African slave trade. The operations of this notorious trade are well illustrated in Hawkins' own account of the voyage of 1567–1568.

The Third troublesome Voyage made with the *Jesus of Lubeck,* the *Minion,* and four other ships, to the parts of Guinea and the West Indies, in the years 1567 and 1568, by Master John Hawkins.

The ships departed from Plymouth, the 2nd day of October, Anno 1567, . . . and arrived at Cape Verde on the 18th day of November: where we landed 150 men, hoping to obtain some negroes, where we got but few, and those with great hurt and damage to our men, which chiefly proceeded of their envenomed arrows. And although in the beginning they seemed to be but small hurts, yet there hardly escaped any that had blood drawn of them, but died in strange sort, with their mouths shut some ten days before they died, and after their wounds were whole; where I myself had one of the greatest wounds, yet, thanks be to God, escaped. From thence we passed the time upon the coast of Guinea, searching with all diligence the rivers from Rio Grande unto Sierra Leone, till the 12th of January, in which time we had not gotten together a hundred and fifty negroes. Yet notwithstanding, the sickness of our men and the late time of the year commanded us away: and thus having nothing wherewith to seek the coast of the West Indies, I was with the rest of our company in consultation to go to the coast of the Mine, hoping there to have obtained some gold for our wares, and thereby to have defrayed our charge. But even in that present instant, there came to us a negro, sent from a king, oppressed by other kings his neighbours, desiring our aid, with promise that as many negroes as by these wars might be obtained, as well of his part as of ours, should be at our pleasure. Whereupon we concluded to give aid, and sent 120 of our men, which on the 15th of January assaulted a town of the negroes of our ally's adversaries, which had in it 8,000 inhabitants, being very strongly impaled and fenced after their manner. But it was so well defended, that our men prevailed not, but lost six men and forty hurt: so that our men sent forthwith to me for more help. Whereupon, considering that the good success of this enterprise might highly further the commodity of our voyage, I went myself, and with the help of the king of our side, assaulted the town, both by land and by sea and very hardly with fire (their houses being covered with dry palm leaves) obtained the town and put the inhabitants to flight, where we took 250 persons, men, women, and children, and by our friend the king of our side, there were taken 600 prisoners, whereof we hoped to have had our choice. But the negro (in which nation is seldom or never found truth) meant nothing less: for that night he removed his camp and prisoners, so that we were fain to content us with those few which we had gotten ourselves.

Now had we obtained between four and five hundred negroes, wherewith we thought it somewhat reasonable to seek the coast of the West Indies; and there, for our negroes, and our other merchandise, we hoped to obtain whereof to countervail our charges with some gains. Whereunto we proceeded with all diligence, furnished our watering, took fuel, and departed the coast of Guinea on the 3d of February, continuing at the sea with a passsage more hard than before hath been accustomed till the 27th day of March, which day we had sight of an island, called Dominica, upon the coast of the West Indies, in fourteen degrees. From thence we coasted from place to place, making our traffic with the Spaniards as we might, somewhat hardly, because the king had straitly commanded all his governors in those parts by no means to suffer any trade to be made with us. Notwithstanding, we had reasonable trade, and courteous entertainment, from the Isle of Margarita unto Cartagena, without anything greatly worth the noting, saving at Capo de la Vela, in a town called Rio de la Hacha, from whence come all the pearls. The treasurer, who had the charge there, would by no means agree to any trade, or suffer us to take water. He had fortified his town with divers bulwarks in all places where it might be entered, and furnished himself with an hundred arquebusiers, so that he thought by famine to have enforced us to have put on land our negroes. Of which purpose he had not greatly failed, unless we had by force entered the town; which (after we could by no means obtain his favour) we were enforced to do, and so with two hundred men brake in upon their bulwarks, and entered the town with the loss only of two men of our part, and no hurt done to the Spaniards, because after their volley of shot discharged, they all fled. Thus having the town with some circumstance, as partly by the Spaniards' desire of negroes, and partly by friendship of the treasurer, we obtained a secret trade: whereupon the Spaniards resorted to us by night, and bought of us to the number of 200 negroes. In all other places where we traded the Spanish inhabitants were glad of us and traded willingly.

[14] *MARTIN FROBISHER SEEKS THE NORTHWEST PASSAGE* *

The navigator most closely associated with the search for the Northwest Passage to the East Indies is Martin Frobisher (1537?–1594). He made an epochal voyage

* Richard Hakluyt, *The Principal Navigations, Voyages, Traffiques and Discoveries of the English Nation* (Glasgow: James MacLehose and Sons; New York: The Macmillan Company, 1904), Vol. VII, pp. 234–237.

past the Labrador coast in 1576 and two more voyages in 1577 and 1578. The following vivid account of the third voyage was written by Thomas Ellis, a member of the expedition.

At the first entring into the ice in the mouth of the Straights, our passage was very narrow, and difficult but being once gotten in, we had a faire open place without any ice for the most part, being a league in compasse, the ice being round about us and inclosing us, as it were, within the pales of a parke. In which place (because it was almost night), we minded to take in our sailes, and lie a hull all that night. But the storme so increased, and the waves began to mount aloft, which brought the ice so neere us, and comming on so fast upon us, that we were faine to beare in and out, where we might espie an open place. Thus the ice comming on us so fast, we were in great danger, looking every houre for death. And thus passed we on in that great danger, seeing both our selves and the rest of our ships so troubled and tossed amongst the ice, that it would make the strongest heart to relent.

At the last the Barke Dionyse being but a weake ship, and bruised afore amongst the ice, being so leake that no longer she could tarry above the water, sanke without saving any of the goods which were within her: which sight so abashed the whole Fleete, that we thought verily we should have tasted of the same sauce. But nevertheless we seeing them in such danger, manned our boates and saved all the men in such wise, that not one perished: God be thanked.

The storme still increased and the ice inclosed us, so that we were faine to take downe top and top mastes: for the ice had so invironed us, that we could see neither land nor sea, as farre as we could kenne: so that we were faine to cut our cables to hang over boord for fenders, somewhat to ease the ships sides from the great and driry strokes of the ice: some with Capstan barres, some fending off with oares, some with plancks of two inches thicke, which were broken immediately with the force of the ice, some going out upon the ice to beare it off with their shoulders from the ships. But the rigorousness of the tempest was such, and the force of the ice so great, that not onely they burst and spoyled the foresaid provision, but likewise so rased the sides of the ships, that it was pitifull to behold, and caused the hearts of many to faint.

Thus we continued all that dismall and lamentable night plunged in this perplexity, looking for instant death: but our God (who never leaveth them destitute which faithfully call upon him, although he often punisheth for amendements sake) in the morning caused the winds to cease, and the fogge which all that night lay on the face of the water to cleare: so that we might perceive about a mile from us, a certaine place cleare from any ice, to the which with an easie breath of wind which our God sent us, we bent our selves. And furthermore, hee provided better for us then we deserved or hoped for: for when we were in the foresaid cleare place, he sent us a fresh gale at West or at West Southwest, which set us cleare without all the ice. And further he added more: for he sent us so pleasant a day as the like we had not of a long time before, as after punishment consolation.

Thus we joyfull wights being at libertie, tooke in all our sailes and lay a hull, praysing God for our deliverance, and stayed to gather together our Fleete: which once being done, we seeing that none of them had any great hurt, neither any of them wanted, saving onely they of whom I spake before and the ship which was lost, then at the last wee hoisted our sailes, and lay bulting off and on, till such time as it would please God to take away the ice that wee might get into the Straights.

And as we thus lay off and on we came by a marveilous huge mountaine of ice, which surpassed all the rest that ever we saw: for we judged it to be neere fourescore fathomes above water, and we thought it to be a ground for anything that we could perceive, being there nine score fathoms deepe, and of compasse about halfe a mile.

Also the fifth of July there fell a hidious fogge and mist, that continued till the nineteenth of the same: so that one shippe could not see another. Therefore we were faine to beare a small sayle and to observe the time: but there ran such a current of a tide, that it set us to the Northwest of the Queenes foreland the backside of all the Straights: where (through the contagious fogge having no sight either of Sunne or Starre) we scarce knew where we were. In this fogge the tenth of July we lost the company of the Viceadmirall, the *Anne Francis*, the *Busse of Bridgewater*, and the *Francis of Foy*.

The 16. day one of our small Barkes named the *Gabriel* was sent by our Generall to beare in with the land to descrie it, where being on land, they met with the people of the Countrey, which seemed very humane and civill, and offered to traffike with our men, profering them foules and skins for knives, and other trifles: whose courtesie caused us to thinke, that they had small conversation with other of the Straights.

Then we bare backe againe to goe with the Queenes foreland: and the eighteenth day wee came by two Islands whereon we went on shore, and found where the people had bene: but we saw none of them. This day wee were againe in the ice, and like to be in as great perill as we were at the first. For through the darknesse and obscuritie of the foggie mist, we were almost run on rocks and Islands before we saw them: but God (even miraculously) provided for us, opening the fogges that we might see clearely both where and in what danger we presently were, and also the way to escape: or els without faile we had ruinously runne upon the rocks.

When we knew perfectly our instant case, wee cast about to get againe on Sea-bord, which (God be thanked) by night we obtained and praised God. The cleare continued scarce an houre, but the fogge fell againe as thicke as ever it was.

Then the Rearadmirall and the *Beare* got themselves cleare without danger of ice and rocks, strooke their sailes and lay a hull, staying to have the rest of the Fleete come forth: which as yet had not found the right way to cleare themselves from the danger of rockes and ice, untill the next morning, at what time the Rearadmirall discharged certaine warning pieces to give notice that she had escaped, and that the rest (by following of her) might set themselves free, which they did that day.

[15] *A DOMINICAN FRIAR DESCRIBES THE CHRISTIAN PENETRATION OF ASIA* *

The expansion of the European world was not marked solely by greed and violence. In the sixteenth century, while the Catholic Church was losing millions of adherents in the Old World, Catholic missionaries were partially making up for these losses by their work in Asia and the New World. A convenient cataloguing of the gains was made in 1569 by Fr. Gaspar da Cruz in the prologue of the first book printed in Europe dealing specifically with China.

In order that the peoples might be summoned to hear the gospel as they ought to be before the end of the world (according to Saint Paul and according to Christ through Saint Matthew), God ordained the discoveries made by the Spaniards in the New World, and that done by the Portugals in the navigation of India. By these means God through his servants has converted many peoples newly to the faith, and continues converting and will convert them, until the coming (as Saint Paul the Apostle says) of the overflowing of the peoples; Israel being saved by conversion, Jews and Gentiles forming one flock, and thus all will be in one pale of one holy and catholic Church, and under one pastor as Christ says. The peoples that the Portugals have summoned, and of whom many have been converted to the faith, are the Brasis, [Brazilians] and those of all the Guinee coast, where there are many multitudes of Christians made in diverse ways beyond the Cape of Good Hope, and all along the coast to Milinde, including Sofala

* "The Narration of Fr. Gaspar da Cruz, O.P.," as found in C. R. Boxer, ed., *South China in the Sixteenth Century* (London: The Hakluyt Society, 1953), p. 51–55. Used by permission.

and Mocambique. There are many Christians dwelling among the Portugals in Ormuz and its lands (which are in the coasts of Arabia and Persia), for Ormuz is an island wherein is a very noble and wealthy city, and this island is in the midst of the sea. There are also many Christians on the borders of Persia and Arabia, but as these peoples are Moors, fewer of them are converted than are of idolaters. Along all the coast of India, namely from Diu to Cape Camorim, [at the extremity of the Indian peninsula] where are the principal strongholds of the Portugals and their principal habitations, there are many thousands of Christians in all the regions possessed by the Portugals, where many temples of idols have been demolished, and where idolatry has been largely destroyed; many churches have been founded (many of them very noble) and many monasteries of religious. In all these lands baptism is carried on unceasingly; and even though many of the peoples who are converted in these parts are bad Christians or apostates who leave the faith, yet I can affirm from my own experience that many of them live better than commonly do the Portugals who frequent those regions. The principal Christian communities are those in the lands of Bacana and at the end of the island of Tana opposite Bacaim, called Salsete, where the fathers of Saint Francis [Franciscans] have churches in various places, and fathers who take care of them for doctrine and adminstration of the Sacraments, which are well cultivated and taught in doctrine. The fathers of the Company [Jesuits] have likewise contributed their share in the christianising of the city proper. And now that those of Saint Dominic [Dominicans] have founded a house there, they have likewise begun to lend a hand with the others, both in baptising as in catechising.

The fathers of the Company have also a good harvest of new Christianity in Tana, where they have a dignified house and church. And the said fathers have under their charge an island near Goa called Chorao, a little island, where they have a good church and a good and populous Christian community. They have made in the course of time many thousands of Christians in their noble house in the city of Goa, and they instruct well those of their converts who are under their wing. The fathers of Saint Dominic have made many thousands of Christians, both in their house at Goa as in five churches which are entrusted to them, and wherein they teach and administer the Sacraments, teaching their converts thoroughly. The fathers of Saint Francis have made many Christians in Cranganor, five leagues from Cochim, and in other places such as Vaipi and Our Lady of Grace, but chiefly in Cranganor, where they have a good breed of youths in an institution. The fathers of Saint Dominic have made many Christians in Cochim at Reis Magos, which is at the end of the island where the Portugals have a fortress. They have also increased the cult and devotion of Our Lady in the said Cochim, through a confraternity of Our Lady of the Rosary, founded there by Malabar nobles, very rich and noble, whereby her devotion is increased and the faith augmented. The fathers of Saint Francis at Coulao have likewise made great fruit in the new Christian community there, helped by those of the Company. These are the chief and new fruits of the coast of India, besides which there are many Christians everywhere in great number. . . .

. . . those who read this work should give praise to God for His greatness and likewise feel compassion for such a vast multitude of lost souls who are ignorant of the truth,—praying God to spread His holy Catholic faith among this people as the others, rescuing them from their ignorance and blindness in which they live idolatrously, and opening up a road for His servants to lead these (and the others whom we have mentioned) by way of baptism into the fold of His church. And above all, because seeing so many and such blind peoples, being withal so politic, the reader may give thanks to his Redeemer because although He has not called these, or not brought them into the fold of His Church (because this is the gift of God) He has yet brought the reader and given him the light of faith and knowledge of Himself; and so the reader while making an act of grace may feel inspired to further His love and service.

[16] *CORTES GATHERS A FABULOUS TREASURE FOR THE KING OF SPAIN* *

One of the great incentives of the voyagers was the plunder of the New World. Some notion of the loot awaiting the western conquerors can be obtained from the following description of Montezuma's treasure. The passage is from a letter written in 1520 by Hernando Cortes to his sovereign.

Some days after [the] formal acknowledgment of service to your Majesty I was speaking to Muteczuma and told him that your Majesty was in need of gold for certain works which he had in hand; I asked him to send some of his own men, to whom I would add an equal number of Spaniards, to the estates and houses of those nobles who had publicly offered themselves as vassals of your Majesty, asking them to do your Majesty some service with what riches they might possess; for over and above your Majesty's need of gold, it would be made manifest that they were beginning to serve him, and your Majesty would perceive more surely the zeal they had in his

* Hernando Cortes, *Five Letters: 1519–1526,* trans. by J. Bayard Morris (London: George Routledge and Sons, Ltd., 1928), pp. 83–85. Used by permission.

service: moreover I requested that he himself might give me some portion of his treasure that I might send it to Spain as I had already sent gold and other articles to your Majesty with my previous messengers. He thereupon asked me to send him the Spaniards whom I had chosen and immediately divided them two by two and five by five between the several cities and provinces, whose names (since they were numerous and my manuscripts have been lost) I cannot recollect, save that some of them were as much as eighty and a hundred leagues from the capital. With my men he sent his own, ordering them to visit the rulers of those cities and to require of each one of them in my name a certain measure of gold. And so it came about that each one of those lords to whom he sent gave very freely when he was asked, whether jewels, small bars and plates of gold and silver, or other valuables which he possessed; of all this treasure gathered together the fifth due to your Majesty amounted to over two thousand four hundred *pesos* of gold, exclusive of all the ornaments in gold, silver and featherwork, the precious stones and other costly articles which I set aside for your Majesty, which would be worth some hundred thousand ducats and more; and which apart from their value were so marvellous on account of their novelty and strangeness as to be almost without price, for it is doubtful whether any of all the known princes of the world posseses such treasures and in such quantity. And let this not appear fabulous to your Majesty, for in truth there was not a living thing on land or sea of which Muteczuma could have knowledge which was not so cunningly represented in gold, silver, precious stones or featherwork as almost to seem the thing itself: of all of which Muteczuma gave me great store for your Majesty, not to mention others of which I gave him examples to copy, and he had them reproduced in gold, such as images, crucifixes, medallions, carved jewels and necklaces, and many other ornaments belonging to us which I persuaded him to have copied. There fell likewise to your Majesty as a fifth part of the silver which was obtained over a hundred marks, which I bid the natives work up into dishes large and small, porringers, cups and spoons, the which they did as perfectly as we were able to give them instructions. In addition to this Muteczuma gave me many garments belonging to himself which, considering that they were woven of cotton without any admixture of silk, could not, I think, be matched in all the world: among them were both men's and women's clothes and bedspreads such as could not be bettered had they been of silk: there were also hangings resembling tapestrywork which could be used in large rooms and churches, together with counterpanes and other coverings for the bed both of feathers and of cotton, variously coloured and likewise exquisitely made, and many other things so numerous and so ingenious that I cannot describe them to your Majesty.

He also gave me a dozen blowpipes . . . which he used to shoot arrows, the workmanship of which I am again as little able to describe to your Majesty, for they were decorated all over with excellent little paintings in natural colours of birds, animals, trees, flowers, and other objects, and the mouthpieces and tips of gold extending some six inches as also a band in the middle of the same metal elaborately worked. He also gave me a gilded pouch of netting for pellets (such as they shoot with) which he told me he would also provide me with in gold, moulds of gold for making the same, and many other things too numerous to mention. For to give your Majesty a full account of all the strange and marvellous things to be found in this great city of Tenochtitlan would demand much time and many and skilled writers, and I shall be able to describe but a hundredth part of all the many things which are worthy of description.

[17] *RICHARD HAKLUYT PROMOTES NORTH AMERICAN COLONIZATION* *

Most sixteenth century Europeans, when they thought about America at all, thought in terms of its quick and easy exploitation. An exception was the Englishman, Richard Hakluyt, who devoted much of his life to enlightening his countrymen on the merits of North America as a site of English colonization. The following excerpt is from one of his propaganda pieces, written in 1584.

A brefe collection of certaine reasons to induce her Majestie and the state to take in hande the westerne voyadge and the plantinge there.—

1. The soyle yeldeth, and may be made to yelde, all the severall comodities of Europe, and of all kingdomes, domynions, and territories that England tradeth withe, that by trade of merchandize cometh into this realme.

2. The passage thither and home is neither to longe nor to shorte, but easie, and to be made twise in the yere.

3. The passage cutteth not nere the trade of any prince, nor nere any of their contries or territories, and is a safe passage, and not easie to be annoyed by prince or potentate whatsoever.

4. The passage is to be perfourmed at all times of the yere, and in that respecte passeth our trades in the Levant Seas within the Straites of Juberalter, and the trades in the seas within the Kinge of Denmarkes Straite, and the trades to the portes of Norwey and of Russia, & c.; for as in

* Richard Hakluyt, "Discourse Concerning Westerne Planting," Chapter XX, as found in *Old South Leaflets* (Boston: The Old South Association, n.d.), Vol. V, pp. 444–449.

the south weste Straite there is no passage in somer by lacke of windes, so within the other places there is no passage in winter by yse and extreme colde.

6. This enterprise may staye the Spanishe Kinge from flowinge over all the face of . . . America, if wee seate and plante there in time, in tyme I say, . . . And England posessinge the purposed place of plantinge, her Majestie may, by the benefete of the seate, havinge wonne good and royall havens, have plentie of excellent trees for mastes, of goodly timber to builde shippes and to make good navies, of pitche, tarr, hempe, and all things incident for a navie royall, and that for no price, and withoute money or request. Howe easie a matter may it be to this realme, swarminge at this day with valiant youthes, rustinge and hurtfull by lacke of employment, and havinge good makers of cable and of all sortes of cordage, and the best and moste connynge shipwrights of the worlde, to be lordes of all those sees, and to spoile Phillipps Indian navye, and to deprive him of yerely passage of his treasure into Europe, and consequently to abate the pride of Spaine and of the supporter of the greate Ante-christe of Rome, and to pull him downe in equallitie to his neighbour princes, and consequently to cutt of the common mischefes that come to all Europe by the peculiar aboundaunce of his Indian treasure, and thiss withoute difficultie.

9. The greate masse of wealthe of the realme imbarqued in the marchantes shippes, caried oute in this newe course, shall not lightly, in so farr distant a course from the coaste of Europe, be driven by windes and tempestes into portes of any forren princes, as the Spanishe shippes of late yeres have bene into our portes of the Weste Contries, & c.; and so our marchantes in respecte of private state, and of the realme in respecte of a generall safetie from venture of losse, are by this voyadge oute of one greate mischefe.

10. No forren commoditie that comes into England comes withoute payment of custome once, twise, or thrise, . . . and so all forren comodities become derer to the subjectes of this realme; . . . nowe the realme become the poore by the purchasinge of forreine comodties in so greate a masse at so excessive prices.

11. At the firste traficque with the people of those partes, the subjectes of this realme for many yeres shall chaunge many cheape comodities of these partes for thinges of highe valor there not estemed; and this to the greate inrichinge of the realme, if common use faile not.

13. By makinge of shippes and by preparinge of thinges for the same, by makinge of cables and cordage, by plantinge of vines and olive trees, and by makinge of wyne and oyle, by husbandrie, and by thousandes of thinges there to be done, infinite nombers of the Englishe nation may be set

on worke, to the unburdenynge of the realme with many that nowe lyve chardgeable to the state at home.

16. Wee shall by plantinge there inlarge the glory of the gospell, and from England plante sincere relligion, and provide a safe and a sure place to receave people from all partes of the worlde that are forced to flee for the truthe of Gods worde.

18. The Spaniardes governe in the Indies with all pride and tyranie; and like as when people of contrarie nature at the sea enter into gallies, where men are tied as slaves, all yell and crye with one voice, *Liberta, liberta,* as desirous of libertie and freedome, so no doubte whensoever the Queene of England, a prince of such clemencie, shall seate upon that firme of America, and shal be reported throughe oute all that tracte to use the naturall people there with all humanitie, curtesie, and freedome, they will yelde themselves to her government, and revolte cleane from the Spaniarde, and specially when they shall understande that she hathe a noble navie, and that she aboundeth with a people moste valiaunte for theyr defence. . . .

20. Many men of excellent wittes and of divers singular giftes, overthrowen by . . . some folly of youthe, that are not able to live in England, may there be raised againe, and doe their contrie goodd service; and many nedefull uses there may (to greate purpose) require the savinge of greate nombers, that for trifles may otherwise be devoured by the gallowes.

21. Many souldiers and servitours, in the ende of the warres, that mighte be hurtfull to this realme, may there be unladen, to the common profite and quiet of this realme, and to our forreine benefite there, as they may be employed.

22. The frye of the wandringe beggars of England, that growe upp idly, and hurtefull and burdenous to this realme, may there be unladen, better bredd upp, . . .

[18] *ENGLAND MAKES HERSELF "ODIOUS TO ALL NATIONS"* *

For many Englishmen, Hakluyt's long-sighted plea for peaceful colonization had little appeal. Privateering—plundering the plunderers—was much more attractive. Such piratical methods were hardly calculated to endear England to other nations, as is evident in the following despatch (1603) of a Venetian diplomat in London to the Venetian Senate.

While on this topic I must not omit to say that the English through their

* Horatio F. Brown, ed., *Calendar of State Papers and Manuscripts Relating to English Affairs Existing in Venice* (London, 1897), Vol. IX (1592–1603), pp. 556–557.

rapacity and cruelty have become odious to all nations. With Spain they are at open war and are already plundering her and upsetting the India trade; they are continually robbing with violence the French, whom they encounter on the long stretches of the open sea. They cannot sail at present to Poland and Prussia, because the Danish Straits are blocked against them. In Germany, at Hamburg, Lubeck, and other ports, for example, they are detested; because the German merchants still claim their ancient privileges of their exchange house in London, of which they were deprived by the Queen a few years ago, merely with the view to foster English and restrict foreign commerce. The Venetians have suffered in the same way. With the Flemish they have little accord on account of the Spanish war, but also for natural reasons; for the Flemish trade in the Levant has grown to such proportions that the English trade is considerably diminished; and the same has taken place between the Flemish and the Venetians; for they are working away to ruin the German Exchange in Venice by opening another route for the import not only of spices but of cotton into Germany; and although the English exaggerate this topic out of rivalry with the Flemish, I nevertheless feel bound to represent these considerations to your Serenity, on account of their great importance. Then inside the Straits of Gibraltar, how can the English be endured, seeing that under the guise of merchants they plunder in the very vitals of foreign dominions all the shipping they find? On this I need not enlarge further, except to say that in despatches of December last the English Ambassador at Constantinople enclosed a decree passed by the Turks, drawn up by the Mufti on religious grounds at the instance of the French Ambassador, that English vessels shall always render an account of all goods bought and sold in Barbary and elsewhere within Turkish dominions; and the English Ambassador is charged to see the order carried out. This information is extremely disliked.

Hence both those who command, and those who execute here in England, see quite clearly how great, how universal, and how just is the hatred which all nations, nay all peoples we might say, bear to the English, for they are the disturbers of the whole world. And yet with all this they not only do not take any steps to remedy the mischief, but in a certain sense they glory that the English name should become formidable just in this way. For whereas the Kings of England, down to Henry VII. and Henry VIII., were wont to keep up a fleet of one hundred ships in full pay as a defence, now the Queen's ships do not amount to more than fifteen or sixteen, as her revenue cannot support a greater charge; and so the whole of the strength and repute of the nation rests on the vast number of small privateers, which are supported and increase to that dangerous extent which everyone recognises; and to ensure this support, the privateers make the ministers partners in the profits, without the risk of a penny in the fitting out, but only a share in the prizes, which are adjudged by judges placed there by the ministers themselves. To such a state has this unhappy Kingdom come that from a lofty religion has fallen into the abyss of infidelity.

London, 20th March 1603.

[19] *A SIXTEENTH CENTURY ECONOMIST PONDERS THE CAUSE OF RISING PRICES* *

One of the results of the influx of gold and silver into Europe in the sixteenth century was a marked rise in the price level. Probably the first to recognize this fact was the French political economist, Jean Bodin (1530–1596).

I find that the high prices we see today are due to some four or five causes. The principal & almost the only one (which no one has referred to until now) is the abundance of gold & silver . . . in this Kingdom. . . . That there was not as much gold & silver in this Kingdom three hundred years ago . . . is evident at a glance. For if there is money in a country, it cannot be so well hidden that Princes will not find it, when they are in straits. Now the fact is that King John was unable to obtain a loan of sixty thousand francs . . . in his extreme need; & during the eight years he was held prisoner by the English, after the battle of Poitiers, neither his children, nor his friends, nor his people, nor he himself, who came in person, could find his ransom, & he was compelled to go back to England, to wait till money was made for him. . . . Moreover, we read in our old histories that, because of a lack of silver, money was made of leather with a silver nail in it, which shows well the extreme need of gold & silver at that time in France.

Now if we come down to our own times, we shall find that in six months the King obtained in Paris, without going outside, more than three million four hundred thousand *livres,* besides the household charges, which were also obtained in Paris, as well as the subsidies & domainal revenues.

But, someone will say, where did so much gold & silver come from since that time? I find that the merchant & the artisan, who cause the gold & silver to come, were inactive at that time; for the Frenchman, having one of the most fertile countries in the world, devoted himself to tilling the soil

* Jean Bodin, "Concerning the Dearness of all Things and the Remedy Therefor," as found in A. E. Monroe, ed., *Early Economic Thought* (Cambridge, Mass.: Harvard University Press, 1945), pp. 127–132. Used by permission.

& feeding his cattle, which is the greatest industry in France, neglecting thé trade with the Levant, because of fear of the Barbary pirates, who hold the coast of Africa, & of the Arabs, whom our fathers called Saracens, who controlled the whole Mediterranean sea, treating the Christians they captured like galley slaves. And as for the trade with the West, it was entirely unknown before Spain had sailed the Indian sea. . . . A hundred fifty years ago . . . the Portugese, sailing the high seas by the compass, made himself master of the Gulf of Persia, & to some extent of the red sea, & by this means filled his vessels with the wealth of the Indies & of fruitful Arabia, outwitting the Venetians & Genoese, who obtained the merchandise from Egypt & from Syria, whither it was brought by the caravans of the Arabs & Persians, to sell it to us in small lots & for its weight in gold. At the same time the Castilian, having gained control of the new lands full of gold & silver, filled Spain with them, & prompted our Citizens to make the trip around Africa with a marvelous profit. It is incredible, and yet true, that there have come from Peru since the year 1533, when it was conquered by the Spaniards, more than a hundred millions of gold, & twice as much silver. The ransom of King Atubalira brought 1,326,000 *pesans* of gold. . . .

. . . There is much more [gold and silver] in Spain & Italy than in France, owing to the fact that in Italy even the nobility engage in trade, & the people of Spain have no other occupation; & so everything is dearer in Spain & in Italy than in France, & dearer in Spain than in Italy. This is true even of servants & artisans, which attracts our Auvergnats & Limousins into Spain, as I learned from them myself, because they earn three times as much as they do in France; for the rich, proud, & indolent Spaniard sells his labor very dear . . . It is therefore the abundance of gold & silver which causes, in part, the high prices of things.

4

The Reformation on the Continent

The starting point of the Protestant Revolt was a spiritual crisis in the life of an obscure German monk which led him to repudiate Church doctrine on indulgences. But behind Martin Luther was a whole complex of currents going back into the Middle Ages which made the times propitious for a revolt against Rome. The development of national monarchies created many sources of friction between kings and popes. The growth of commerce and townlife helped produce a secular state of mind. Increased lay education and humanism often undermined the prestige of the Church. Most important of all, the discipline and spiritual health of the Church declined greatly in the century before Luther, and a purely secularized Papacy showed no inclination toward reform.

[20] *LUTHER LAYS DOWN SOME FUNDAMENTAL PRINCIPLES OF THE REFORMATION* *

The two selections below are from Luther's great reform tracts of 1520. They were provoked by the publication of the pope's bull of excommunication in June,

* Martin Luther, "Address to the German Nobility" and "Concerning Christian Liberty," in *The Harvard Classics,* ed. by Charles W. Eliot (New York: P. F. Collier & Son Corp., 1910), Vol. XXXVI, pp. 276–352. Used by permission.

1520. In them are beautifully summarized the basic religious, political, and economic principles of the reform movement. The "Address to the German Nobility" shows Luther's utilization of German nationalism against Rome. The second pamphlet, "Of Christian Liberty," gives the theological basis of the revolt.

[A] To his most Serene and Mighty Imperial Majesty and to the Christian Nobility of the German Nation

The Romanists have, with great adroitness, drawn three walls round themselves, with which they have hitherto protected themselves, so that no one could reform them, whereby all Christendom has fallen terribly.

Firstly, if pressed by the temporal power, they have affirmed and maintained that the temporal power has no jurisdiction over them, but, on the contrary, that the spiritual power is above the temporal.

Secondly, if it were proposed to admonish them with the Scriptures, they objected that no one may interpret the Scriptures but the Pope.

Thirdly, if they are threatened with a council, they pretend that no one may call a council but the Pope.

Let us, in the first place, attack the first wall.

It has been devised that the Pope, bishops, priests, and monks are called the *spiritual estate*, princes, lords, artificers, and peasants are the *temporal estate*. This is an artful lie and hypocritical device, but let no one be made afraid by it, and that for this reason: that all Christians are truly of the spiritual estate, and there is no difference among them, save of office alone. . . . We are all consecrated as priests by baptism, as St. Peter says: "Ye are a royal priesthood, a holy nation;" . . . to put the matter even more plainly, if a little company of pious Christian laymen were taken prisoners and carried away to a desert, and had not among them a priest consecrated by a bishop, and were there to agree to elect one of them, born in wedlock or not, and were to order him to baptise, to celebrate the mass, to absolve, and to preach, this man would as truly be a priest, as if all the bishops and all the popes had consecrated him. . . .

The second wall is even more tottering and weak: that they alone pretend to be considered masters of the Scriptures; although they learn nothing of them all their life. . . . It is a wickedly devised fable—and they cannot quote a single letter to confirm it—that it is for the Pope alone to interpret the Scriptures or to confirm the interpretation of them. They have assumed the authority of their own selves. And though they say that this authority was given to St. Peter when the keys were given to him, it is plain enough that the keys were not given to St. Peter alone, but to the whole community. Besides, the keys were not ordained for doctrine or authority, but for sin, to bind or loose; and what they claim besides this from the keys is mere invention. But what Christ said to St. Peter: "I have prayed for thee that thy faith fail not" (St. Luke xxii. 32), cannot relate to the Pope, inasmuch as the greater part of the Popes have been without faith, as they are themselves forced to acknowledge; nor did Christ pray for Peter alone, but for all the Apostles and all Christians. . . .

The third wall falls of itself, as soon as the first two have fallen; for if the Pope acts contrary to the Scriptures, we are bound to stand by the Scriptures, to punish and to constrain him. . . . When need requires, and the Pope is a cause of offence to Christendom, in these cases whoever can best do so, as a faithful member of the whole body, must do what he can to procure a true free council. This no one can do so well as the temporal authorities, especially since they are fellow-Christians, fellow-priests, sharing one spirit and one power in all things, and since they should exercise the office that they have received from God without hindrance. . . .

And now I hope the false, lying spectre will be laid with which the Romanists have long terrified and stupefied our consciences. . . .

Now though I am too lowly to submit articles that could serve for the reformation of these fearful evils, I will yet sing out my fool's song, and will show, as well as my wit will allow, what might and should be done by the temporal authorities or by a general council.

1. Princes, nobles, and cities should promptly forbid their subjects to pay the *annates* [a papal tax developed in the fourteenth century by which a newly elected bishop or abbot had to pay the Papacy the first year's income of his office] to Rome and should even abolish them altogether. . . .

2. [The nobility] should ordain, order, and decree that henceforth no benefice shall be drawn away to Rome. . . . And if a courtling came from Rome, he should receive the strict command to withdraw, or to leap into the Rhine, or whatever river be nearest, and to administer a cold bath to the Interdict, seal and letters and all. . . .

4. Let it be decreed that no temporal matter shall be submitted to Rome, but all shall be left to the jurisdiction of the temporal authorities. . . . .

7. The Roman See must abolish the papal offices, and diminish the crowd of crawling vermin at Rome, so that the Pope's servants may be supported out of the Pope's own pocket, and that his court may cease to surpass all royal courts in its pomp and extravagance; . . .

9. The Pope should have no power over the Emperor, except to anoint and crown him at the altar, as a bishop crowns a king; . . .

11. The custom of kissing the Pope's feet must cease. It is an unchristian, or rather an anti-Christian, example that a poor sinful man should suffer his feet to be kissed by one who is a hundred times better than he. . . .

12. Pilgrimages to Rome must be abolished. . . . This I say, not because

pilgrimages are bad in themselves, but because at the present time they lead to mischief; for at Rome a pilgrim sees no good examples, but only offence. They themselves have made a proverb, "The nearer to Rome, the farther from Christ." . . .

13. Now we come to the great crowd that promises much and performs little. . . . Let no more mendicant monasteries be built! [The principal mendicant orders were the Franciscans, Dominicans, and Luther's own order, the Augustinians.] God help us! there are too many as it is. Would to God they were all abolished, or at least made over to two or three orders! It has never done good, it will never do good, to go wandering about over the country. . . . For their preaching and confession has led to nought but mere hatred and envy between priests and monks, to the great offence and hindrance of the people. . . . It does not look at all improbable that the Holy Roman See had its own reasons for encouraging all this crowd of monks: the Pope perhaps feared that priests and bishops, growing weary of his tyranny, might become too strong for him, and begin a reformation unendurable to his Holiness.

14. We see also how the priesthood is fallen, and how many a poor priest is encumbered with a woman and children and burdened in his conscience. . . . My advice is to restore liberty, and to leave every man free to marry or not to marry. . . .

16. It were also right to abolish annual festivals, processions, and masses for the dead, or at least to diminish their number; for we evidently see that they have become no better than a mockery, exciting the anger of God and having no object but money-getting gluttony, and carousals. . . .

17. One should also abolish certain punishments inflicted by the canon law, especially the interdict, which is doubtless the invention of the evil one. . . .

18. One should abolish all saints' days, keeping only Sunday. But if it were desired to keep the festivals of Our Lady and the greater saints, they should all be held on Sundays, or only in the morning with the mass; the rest of the day being a working day. My reason is this: with our present abuses of drinking, gambling, idling, and all manner of sin, we vex God more on holy days than on others. . . .

21. It is one of the most urgent necessities to abolish all begging in Christendom. No one should go about begging among Christians. . . .

24. It is high time to take up earnestly and truthfully the cause of the Bohemians. . . . First of all, we must honestly confess the truth, without attempting self-justification, and own one thing to the Bohemians, namely that John Huss and Jerome of Prague were burnt at Constance in violation of the papal, Christian and imperial oath and safe-conduct, and that thus

God's commandment was broken and the Bohemians excited to great anger. . . .

25. The universities also require a good, sound reformation. . . . What are the universities, as at present ordered, but, as the book of Maccabees says, "schools of 'Greek fashion' and 'heathenish manners'" . . . full of dissolute living, where very little is taught of the Holy Scriptures and of the Christian faith, and the blind heathen teacher, Aristotle, rules even further than Christ? Now, my advice would be that the books of Aristotle, the *Physics,* the *Metaphysics, Of the Soul, Ethics,* which have hitherto been considered the best, be altogether abolished. . . .

. . . I daresay I have sung a lofty strain, that I have proposed many things that will be thought impossible, and attacked many points too sharply. But what was I to do? . . . I have hitherto made many offers of peace to my adversaries; but, as I see, God has forced me through them to open my mouth wider and wider, and, because they do not keep quiet, to give them enough cause for speaking, barking, shouting, and writing. Well, then, I have another song still to sing concerning them and Rome; if they wish to hear it, I will sing it to them, and sing with all my might. Do you understand, my friend Rome, what I mean?

[B] From "Of Christian Liberty"

. . . Man is composed of a two-fold nature, a spiritual and a bodily. As regards the spiritual nature, which they name the soul, he is called the spiritual, inward, new man; as regards the bodily nature, which they name the flesh, he is called the fleshly, outward, old man. . . .

. . . One thing, and one alone, is necessary for life, justification, and Christian liberty; and that is the most holy word of God, the Gospel of Christ, as He says: "I am the resurrection and the life; he that believeth in me shall not die eternally" (John xi. 25); and also (John viii. 36) "If the Son shall make you free, ye shall be free indeed"; and (Matt. iv. 4) "Man shall not live by bread alone, but by every word that proceedeth out of the mouth of God."

Let us therefore hold it for certain and firmly established that the soul can do without everything, except the word of God, without which none at all of its wants are provided for. . . .

The first care of every Christian ought to be, to lay aside all reliance on works, and strengthen his faith alone more and more, and by it grow in the knowledge, not of works, but of Christ Jesus, who has suffered and risen again for him, as Peter teaches, when he makes no other work to be a Christian one. . . .

Now let us turn to the other part, to the outward man. Here we shall give an answer to all those who, taking offence at the word of faith and at what I have asserted, say: "If faith does everything, and by itself suffices for justification, why then are good works commanded? Are we then to take our ease and do no works, content with faith?" Not so, impious men, I reply; not so. . . .

Although, as I have said, inwardly, and according to the spirit, a man is amply enough justified by faith, having all that he requires to have, except that this very faith and abundance ought to increase from day to day, even till the future life; still he remains in this mortal life upon earth, in which it is necessary that he should rule his own body, and have intercourse with men. Here then works begin; here he must not take his ease; here he must give heed to exercise his body by fastings, watchings, labor, and other moderate discipline, so that it may be subdued to the spirit, and obey and conform itself to the inner man and faith, and not rebel against them nor hinder them, as is its nature to do if it is not kept under. . . .

These works, however, must not be done with any notion that by them a man can be justified before God—for faith, which alone is righteousness before God, will not bear with this false notion—but solely with this purpose, that the body may be brought into subjection, and be purified from its evil lusts, so that our eyes may be turned only to purging away those lusts. . . .

True then are these two sayings: Good works do not make a good man, but a good man does good works. Bad works do not make a bad man, but a bad man does bad works. . . .

[21] *THE LOWER CLASSES IN GERMANY REBEL AND ARE DENOUNCED BY LUTHER* *

Until the Peasants' War, Luther was hailed by the great majority of Germans as a national hero. His position changed radically, however, after his violent denunciation of the peasants and artisans in 1525. He thereby alienated the lower classes in Germany and became the leader of only a faction. The first selection below is from a diary of a citizen of Rothenburg in Bavaria; the second is from Luther's famous denunciation of the rebels.

[A] From the Diary of Michael Eisenhart, 1525

On March 21, a Tuesday, thirty or forty peasants got together in a mob

* J. H. Robinson, *Readings in European History* (New York: Ginn and Company, 1904), Vol. II, pp. 101–108.

in Rothenburg, bought a kettledrum, and marched about the town, a part going to Pretheim and a part toward Orenbach. . . .

The working classes in the town now begin to revolt. . . .

March 24. This evening between five and six o'clock some one knocked off the head of Christ's image on a crucifix and struck off the arms.

March 26. Chrischainz, the baker, knocked the missal out of the priest's hand in the chapel of our Lady and drove away the priest from mass. . . .

On Tuesday eight hundred peasants came together. Those who would not join them willingly they forced to do so or took their property, as happened to a peasant at Wettring.

On this same day all the artisans were to lay all their complaints and demands before a committee. The taxes, wages, and methods of weighing were discussed. . . .

On Saturday the blind monk, Hans Rotfuchs, spoke contemptuously of the holy sacrament, calling it idolatry and heresy.

April 19. The peasants take three casks of wine from the priests at Scheckenpach and drink it up.

On Wednesday (April 26) Lorenz Knobloch was hewn to pieces by the peasants at Ostheim, and then they pelted one another with the fragments. They said he was a traitor and that he wanted to mislead them. Divine retribution! He had said he would not die until he had killed three priests, but, thank God, not one fell into his hands.

In Rothenburg the citizens are summoned to decide whether, like the neighboring towns of Heilbronn, Dinkelsbühl, and Wimfen, they will aid the peasants. The majority decide to send them guns and pikes, powder and lead.

May 15. The bell summoned the community. In spite of the protests of the old Christians, they are forced to obey the majority, and Rothenburg that day fell away from the empire and joined the peasants. . . .

May 21. Certain Hohenlohe peasants burn their lord's castle.

On the next Monday Margrave Casimir proceeds with his forces to subdue and punish the peasants. . . .

On Monday after Whitsunday eight thousand peasants are slaughtered by the troops of the League [the Swabian League under Casimir] near Büttart and Sulzdorf. In all these battles the League lost not over one hundred and fifty men.

On June 6 messengers are sent from Rothenburg to Casimir to ask for pardon. Next day others are sent to the League, but they are told that they must surrender unconditionally.

On Thursday following, after the League had retaken the town of Wurzburg, they beheaded sixty-two.

After the League had attacked Bamberg they beheaded twenty-one.

On Friday after Corpus Christi, mass was once more chanted in Rothenburg, as formerly.

On the eve of Peter and Paul's day Margrave Casimir rides into Rothenburg with four hundred horsemen, a thousand footmen, and two hundred wagons full of arms and equipments.

June 30. The citizens of Rothenburg are summoned to the market place by a herald and surrounded by pikemen. They are accused of deserting the empire and joining the peasants, and are threatened with the vengeance they deserve.

The names of a number of citizens are read off, and they are beheaded on the spot. Their bodies are left on the market place all day. Some got away through the ring of soldiers: Lorenz Diem, the sexton, Joseph Schad, a tanner, Fritz Dalck, a butcher, and others, but were nevertheless executed.

July 1. Fifteen more are beheaded in the market place, including the blind monk. All the bodies are left on the market place all day, then buried. All of these died without confession or the last sacrament, and did not even ask for it.

[B] From Luther, "Against the Murdering and Robbing Bands of the Peasants"

With threefold horrible sins against God and men have these peasants loaded themselves, for which they have deserved a manifold death of body and soul.

First, they have sworn to their true and gracious rulers to be submissive and obedient, in accord with God's command (Matt. xxii. 21), "Render therefore unto Caesar the things which are Caesar's," and (Rom. xiii. 1), "Let every soul be subject unto the higher powers." But since they have deliberately and sacrilegiously abandoned their obedience, and in addition have dared to oppose their lords, they have thereby forfeited body and soul, as perfidious, perjured, lying, disobedient wretches and scoundrels are wont to do. . . .

Second, they cause uproar and sacrilegiously rob and pillage monasteries and castles that do not belong to them, for which, like public highwaymen and murderers, they deserve the twofold death of body and soul. It is right and lawful to slay at the first opportunity a rebellious person, who is known as such, for he is already under God's and the emperor's ban. Every man is at once judge and executioner of a public rebel; just as, when a fire starts, he who can extinguish it first is the best fellow. Rebellion is not simply vile murder, but is like a great fire that kindles and devastates a country; it fills the land with murder and bloodshed, makes widows and orphans, and destroys everything, like the greatest calamity. Therefore, whosoever can, should smite, strangle, and stab, secretly or publicly, and should remember that there is nothing more poisonous, pernicious, and devilish than a rebellious man. Just as one must slay a mad dog, so, if you do not fight the rebels, they will fight you, and the whole country with you.

Third, they cloak their frightful and revolting sins with the gospel, call themselves Christian brethren, swear allegiance, and compel people to join them in such abominations. Thereby they become the greatest blasphemers and violators of God's holy name, and serve and honor the devil under the semblance of the gospel, so that they have ten times deserved death of body and soul, for never have I heard of uglier sins. . . . Lo, how mighty a prince is the devil, how he holds the world in his hands and can put it to confusion: who else could so soon capture so many thousands of peasants, lead them astray, blind and deceive them, stir them to revolt, and make them the willing executioners of his malice. . . .

[22] *ERASMUS IS "PELTED ON BOTH SIDES"* *

Both the Catholic and Lutheran camps made strenuous efforts to gain the support of Erasmus, the foremost intellectual figure of his time. Luther had publicly acknowledged the indebtedness of the reformers for the literary ground-work laid by Erasmus. But Luther's hopes for a clear avowal of support were quickly dashed, as the following letters of the great humanist reveal.

Erasmus to Nicholas Beraldus, Louvain, Feb. 16, 1521

. . . Luther is bringing the greatest odium both upon me and on liberal studies. Everybody knew that the Church was oppressed by tyranny and burdened with ceremonies and human decrees invented to make money; and many were already wishing for or devising a remedy, but remedies unskilfully applied are often worse than the disease, and it generally happens that those who try to throw off the yoke, but fail in the attempt, are carried back into still more cruel slavery. I wish that man had either kept out of it altogether, or made the attempt more moderately and circumspectly. For Luther I do not trouble myself, but I feel concerned for Christ's glory; for I see some are of such a temper that if they should succeed nothing will be left but to write the epitaph of the Gospel.

Erasmus to Jodocus Jonas, Louvain, May 10, 1521

. . . At first Luther received more applause than I fancy has fallen to the lot of any mortal for several centuries past. For, as we easily believe what

* Robert B. Drummond, *Erasmus, His Life and Character* (London: Smith, Elder, and Co., 1873), pp. 70–73, 79–80.

we desire very much, it was supposed that a man had arisen free from all the passions of this world, who could apply a remedy to the great evils under which we were groaning. Nor was I altogether without hope that it might be so, except that at my first glance into the works which had begun to appear in Luther's name. I feared that the matter would end in tumult and in a universal revolution. Accordingly I wrote letters, warning both Luther himself and friends of his, whose influence I thought was likely to weigh with him; what advice they may have given him I know not—this only is certain, that there is danger lest through want of skill in the use of remedies the mischief may be doubled. And I greatly wonder, my dear Jonas, what demon inspires Luther to inveigh as he does against the Roman Pontiff, all the Universities, philosophy itself, and the mendicant orders. Now, if all he says were true—which they who take it on them to criticise his writings say is by no means the case—what other issue could be expected by the provocation of so many than that which we actually see?

Certain offensive passages, which were thought to have a close relationship with some of Luther's dogmas, have been extracted from my books, which I wrote before I had the least idea that Luther would ever arise, and have been published in German. And the men who act thus wish to be regarded as my friends, though my deadliest enemy could not well do anything worse. Those who wished me most evil never displayed so much ingenuity in devising methods of hurting me. It is they who have put this weapon into the hands of my enemies, so that they can now declare in their sermons what are the points on which I agree with Luther; as if, forsooth, falsehood did not border upon truth on both sides if you never pass the boundary line. I somewhere recommend, it may be, that vows should not be made rashly, or I express my disapproval of the conduct of those who run away to the shrine of St. James, or to Jerusalem, where they have no business whatever, leaving at home their wife and children, whose maintenance and protection from evil ought to have been their first care. I recommend that young men should not be enticed into submitting to the restraints of religious vows, before they know their own mind, and understand the meaning of the word religion. Luther, it is said, condemns all vows without restriction. I complain somewhere that the duty of confession is made doubly onerous by the subtleties with which it is frequently complicated. Luther, it is said, teaches that confession should be altogether abandoned as dangerous. I have somewhere taught that the best authors should be read first of all, adding that so much profit cannot be gained from the works of Dionysius as the titles seem to promise. Luther, I understand, calls this author a fool, and not deserving of being read at all. A fine agreement truly, if somebody else must corrupt and carry to the most extravagant lengths what I have said incidentally and with strict regard to truth and modesty! . . .

Erasmus to Peter Barbirius, Bruges, August 13, 1521

. . . In truth, I am well rewarded for all my labours by being pelted on both sides! Among ourselves I am most falsely accused of being a Lutheran, while among the Germans I am evil spoken of as an adversary of the Lutheran faction. I would, however, gladly give up not only my good name, but my life itself, to calm this most disastrous storm! I see no end to it . . .

[23] *CALVIN ASSERTS A NEW THEOLOGY* *

In a manner completely foreign to Martin Luther, Calvin gathered up all the scattered and unsystematic reformed opinions of his time, added some distinctive interpretations of his own, and produced the theological chef d'oeuvre *of the Reformation, the* Institutes of the Christian Religion *(1536).*

On the Calling

. . . We must . . . administer [our earthly blessings] as if we constantly heard the words sounding in our ears, "Give an account of your stewardship." At the same time, let us remember by whom the account is to be taken—that is, by him who, while he so highly commends abstinence, sobriety, frugality, and moderation, abominates luxury, pride, ostentation, and vanity; who approves of no administration but that which is combined with charity, who with his own lips has already condemned all those pleasures which withdraw the heart from chastity and purity, or darken the intellect.

. . . the Lord enjoins every one of us, in all the actions of life, to have respect to our own calling. He knows the boiling restlessness of the human mind, the fickleness with which it is borne hither and thither, its eagerness to hold opposites at one time in its grasp, its ambition. Therefore, lest all things should be thrown into confusion by our folly and rashness, he has assigned distinct duties to each in the different modes of life. And that no one may presume to overstep his proper limits, he has distinguished the different modes of life by the name of callings. Every man's mode of life, therefore, is a kind of station assigned him by the Lord, that he may not be always driven about at random. So necessary is this distinction, that all our actions are thereby estimated in his sight, and often in a very different way from that in which human reason or philosophy would estimate them. . . . in all our cares, toils, annoyances, and other burdens, it will be no small alleviation to know that all these are under the superintendence of God. The

* John Calvin, *Institutes of the Christian Religion,* trans. by Henry Beveridge (London: James Clark and Co. Ltd., 1949), Vol. II, pp. 34, 98–99, 206–207, 210–211, 652–657. Used by permission.

magistrate will more willingly perform his office, and the father of a family confine himself to his proper sphere. Every one in his particular mode of life will, without repining, suffer its inconveniences, cares, uneasiness, and anxiety, persuaded that God has laid on the burden. This, too, will afford admirable consolation, that in following your proper calling, no work will be so mean and sordid as not to have a splendour and value in the eye of God.

On Good Works

. . . The allegation is, that justification by faith destroys good works. I will not describe what kind of zealots for good works the persons are who thus charge us. We leave them as much liberty to bring the charge, as they take license to taint the whole world with the pollution of their lives. They pretend to lament that when faith is so highly extolled, works are deprived of their proper place. But what if they are rather ennobled and established? We dream not of a faith which is devoid of good works, nor of a justification which can exist without them: the only difference is, that while we acknowledge that faith and works are necessarily connected, we, however, place justification in faith, not in works. . . . Christ . . . justifies no man without also sanctifying him. These blessings are conjoined by a perpetual and inseparable tie. Those whom he enlightens by his wisdom he redeems; whom he redeems he justifies; whom he justifies he sanctifies. . . .

On Predestination

The predestination by which God adopts some to the hope of life, and adjudges others to eternal death, no man who would be thought pious ventures simply to deny; but it is greatly cavilled at, especially by those who make prescience its cause. We, indeed, ascribe both prescience and predestination to God; but we say that it is absurd to make the latter subordinate to the former. When we attribute prescience to God, we mean that all things always were, and ever continue, under his eye; that to his knowledge there is no past or future, but all things are present, and indeed so present, that it is not merely the idea of them that is before him (as those objects are which we retain in our memory), but that he truly sees and contemplates them as actually under his immediate inspection. This prescience extends to the whole circuit of the world, and to all creatures. By predestination we mean the eternal decree of God, by which he determined with himself whatever he wished to happen with regard to every man. All are not created on equal terms, but some are preordained to eternal life, others to eternal damnation; and, accordingly, as each has been created for one or other of these ends, we say that he has been predestinated to life or to death. This God has testified, not only in the case of single individuals; he has also given a specimen of it in the whole posterity of Abraham, to make it plain that the future condition of each nation was entirely at his disposal . . .

. . . We say, then, that Scripture clearly proves this much, that God by his eternal and immutable counsel determined once for all those whom it was his pleasure one day to admit to salvation, and those whom, on the other hand, it was his pleasure to doom to destruction. We maintain that this counsel, as regards the elect, is founded on his free mercy, without any respect to human worth, while those whom he dooms to destruction are excluded from access to life by a just and blameless, but at the same time incomprehensible judgment. In regard to the elect, we regard calling as the evidence of election, and justification as another symbol of its manifestation, until it is fully accomplished by the attainment of glory. But as the Lord seals his elect by calling and justification, so by excluding the reprobate either from the knowledge of his name or the sanctification of his Spirit, he by these marks in a manner discloses the judgment which awaits them. . . .

On Civil Government

. . . it is perfect barbarism to think of exterminating [civil government], its use among men being not less than that of bread and water, light and air, while its dignity is much more excellent. Its object is not merely, like those things, to enable men to breathe, eat, drink, and be warmed (though it certainly includes all these, while it enables them to live together); this, I say, is not its only object, but it is, that no idolatry, no blasphemy against the name of God, no calumnies against his truth, nor other offences to religion, break out and be disseminated among the people; that the public quiet be not disturbed, that every man's property be kept secure, that men may carry on innocent commerce with each other, that honesty and modesty be cultivated; in short, that a public form of religion may exist among Christians, and humanity among men. . . . I approve of civil order which is directed to this end—that is, to prevent the true religion, which is contained in the law of God, from being with impunity openly violated and polluted by public blasphemy. . . .

. . . There are three kinds of civil government; namely, Monarchy, which is the domination of one only, whether he be called King or Duke, or otherwise; Aristocracy, which is a government composed of the chiefs and people of note; and Democracy, which is a popular government, in which each of the people has power.

. . . When these three forms of government, of which philosophers treat, are considered in themselves, I, for my part, am far from denying that the form which greatly surpasses the others is aristocracy, either pure or modified by popular government, not indeed in itself, but because it very rarely happens that kings so rule themselves as never to dissent from what is just and right, or are possessed of so much acuteness and prudence as always to see correctly. Owing, therefore, to the vices or defects of men, it is safer and more tolerable when several bear rule, that they may thus mutually assist, instruct, and admonish each other, and should any one be disposed to go too far, the others are censors and masters to curb his excess. . . . And as I willingly admit that there is no kind of government happier than where liberty is framed with becoming moderation, and duly constituted so as to be durable, so I deem those very happy who are permitted to enjoy that form, and I admit that they do nothing at variance with their duty when they strenuously and constantly labour to preserve and maintain it. . . . But should those to whom the Lord has assigned one form of government, take it upon them anxiously to long for a change, the wish would not only be foolish and superfluous, but very pernicious. If you fix your eyes not on one state merėly, but look around the world, or at least direct your view to regions widely separated from each other, you will perceive that Divine Providence has not, without good cause, arranged that different countries should be governed by different forms of polity. For as only elements of unequal temperature adhere together, so in different regions a similar inequality in the form of government is best. All this, however, is said unnecessarily to those to whom the will of God is a sufficient reason. For if it has pleased him to appoint kings over kingdoms, and senates or burgomasters over free states, whatever be the form which he has appointed in the places in which we live, our duty is to obey and submit.

[24] *CALVIN ATTEMPTS TO LEGISLATE MORALITY IN GENEVA* *

Between 1541 and his death in 1564, Calvin strove to make Geneva a model of Christian government. A group of elders or presbyters, "persons of upright life and good repute," were assigned to all parts of the city to keep watch over the life and conduct of each individual. The regulations the elders were enjoined to enforce were embodied in a long list of ordinances, excerpts from which follow.

* John Calvin, *Opera*, Vol. X, pp. 51 *et. seq.*, in *Translations and Reprints from the Original Sources of European History* (Philadelphia: University of Pennsylvania, 1902), Series II, Vol. III, No. 3, pp. 10–11.

CONCERNING THE TIME OF ASSEMBLING AT CHURCH. That the temples be closed for the rest of the time, in order that no one shall enter therein out of hours, impelled thereto by superstition; and if any one be found engaged in any special act of devotion therein or nearby he shall be admonished for it: if it be found to be of a superstitious nature for which simple correction is inadequate, then he shall be chastised.

BLASPHEMY. Whoever shall have blasphemed, swearing by the body or by the blood of our Lord, or in similar manner, he shall be made to kiss the earth for the first offence; for the second to pay 5 *sous,* and for the third 6 *sous,* and for the last offence be put in the pillory for one hour.

DRUNKENNESS. 1. That no one shall invite another to drink under penalty of 3 *sous.*

2. That taverns shall be closed during the sermon, under penalty that the tavern-keeper shall pay 3 *sous,* and whoever may be found therein shall pay the same amount.

3. If any one be found intoxicated he shall pay for the first offence 3 *sous* and shall be remanded to the consistory; for the second offence he shall be held to pay the sum of 6 *sous,* and for the third 10 *sous* and be put in prison.

SONGS AND DANCES. If any one sing immoral, dissolute or outrageous songs, or dance the *virollet* or other dance, he shall be put in prison for three days and then sent to the consistory.

USURY. That no one shall take upon interest or profit more than five per cent. upon penalty of confiscation of the principal and of being condemned to make restitution as the case may demand.

GAMES. That no one shall play at any dissolute game or at any game whatsoever it may be, neither for gold nor silver nor for any excessive stake, upon penalty of 5 *sous* and forfeiture of stake played for.

5

The Reformation in England

The Protestant Revolt in England took a form quite different from that of the Continent. Personal and national issues, rather than doctrinal, caused the break with the traditional authority of Rome. Henry VIII prided himself on his Catholic orthodoxy and persecuted with equal severity followers of the Continental Reformers and Catholics who refused to recognize the King as "Protector and Only Supreme Head of the Church and Clergy of England." But in the reigns of succeeding monarchs the demand for doctrinal changes became irresistible. Well before the end of the century, many characteristically Protestant beliefs and practices had been permanently incorporated into the Church of England.

[25] *CATHERINE OF ARAGON DEFENDS HERSELF BEFORE THE PAPAL LEGATE, 1529* *

When Henry VIII insisted on an annulment of his seventeen-year marriage with Catherine of Aragon, Pope Clement VII appointed Cardinals Campeggio and

* Hall, *Chronicle,* as found in Edward P. Cheyney, ed., *Readings in English History* (New York: Ginn and Company, 1908), pp. 337–339. Used by permission.

Wolsey to examine Henry's claims. It was before these prelates that Catherine made the following pitiful plea for justice. No decision was reached at this time, and the case was transferred to the Pope himself. The selection is from the Chronicle of Edward Hall (*d. 1547*).

The court being thus furnished and ordered, the judges commanded the crier to proclaim silence; then was the judges' commission, which they had of the pope, published and read openly before all the audience there assembled. That done, the crier called the king, by the name of "King Henry of England, come into the court," etc. With that the king answered and said, "Here, my lords!" Then he called also the queen, by the name of "Catherine Queen of England, come into the court," etc.; who made no answer to the same, but rose up incontinent out of her chair, where as she sat, and because she could not come directly to the king for the distance which severed them, she took pain to go about unto the king, kneeling down at his feet in the sight of all the court and assembly, to whom she said in effect, in broken English, as followeth:

"Sir," quoth she, "I beseech you for all the loves that hath been between us, and for the love of God, let me have justice and right; take of me some pity and compassion, for I am a poor woman and a stranger born out of your dominion; I have here no assured friend, and much less impartial counsel; I flee to you as to the head of justice within this realm. Alas! sir, wherein have I offended you, or what occasion of displeasure have I designed against your will and pleasure, intending, as I perceive, to put me from you? I take God and all the world to witness, that I have been to you a true, humble, and obedient wife. . . .

"This twenty years I have been your true wife or more, and by me ye have had divers children, although it hath pleased God to call them out of this world, which hath been no default in me. And when ye had me at the first, I take God to be my judge, I was a true maid, without touch of man; and whether this be true or no, I put it to your conscience. If there be any just cause by the law that ye can allege against me, either of dishonesty or any other impediment, to banish and put me from you, I am well content to depart to my great shame and dishonor; and if there be none, then here I most lowly beseech you let me remain in my former estate, and receive justice at your hands. . . .

". . . I most humbly require you, in the way of charity, and for the love of God, who is the just judge, to spare me the extremity of this new court, until I may be advertised what way and order my friends in Spain will advise me to take. And if ye will not extend to me so much indifferent favor, your pleasure then be fulfilled, and to God I commit my cause!"

And with that she rose up, making a low courtesy to the king, and so departed from thence. Many supposed that she would have resorted again to her former place; but she took her way straight out of the house, leaning (as she was wont always to do) upon the arm of her general receiver, called Master Griffith. And the king being advertised of her departure, commanded the crier to call her again, who called her by the name of "Catherine Queen of England, come into the court," etc. With that quoth Master Griffith, "Madam, ye be called again." "On, on," quoth she; "it maketh no matter, for it is no impartial court for me, therefore I will not tarry. Go on your ways." And thus she departed out of that court, without any farther answer at that time, or at any other, nor would ever appear at any other court after.

[26] *THE ENGLISH CHURCH BREAKS OFF FROM ROME* *

The English Reformation is usually said to have begun with the Submission of the Clergy, made in clerical Convocation in 1532. During the next two years, a series of momentous acts was passed by Parliament renouncing one aspect or another of the authority of Rome. The logical conclusion was reached with the Act of Supremacy of 1534. High lights of these laws follow.

[A] The Submission of the Clergy, 1532

We your most humble subjects, daily orators and bedesmen of your clergy of England, having our special trust and confidence in your most excellent wisdom, your princely goodness and fervent zeal to the promotion of God's honour and Christian religion, and also in your learning, far exceeding, in our judgement, the learning of all other kings and princes that we have read of, and doubting nothing but that the same shall still continue and daily increase in your majesty—

First, do offer and promise, *in verbo sacerdotii,* here unto your highness, submitting ourselves most humbly to the same, that we will never from henceforth enact, put in ure, promulge, or execute, any new canons or constitutions provincial, or any other new ordinance, provincial or synodal, in our Convocation or synod in time coming, which Convocation is, always has been, and must be, assembled only by your highness' commandment of writ, unless your highness by your royal assent shall license us to assemble our Convocation, and to make, promulge, and execute such constitutions and ordinances as shall be made in the same; and thereto give your royal assent and authority.

* [A] and [E] from Henry Bettenson, ed., *Documents of the Christian Church* (London: Oxford University Press, 1943), pp. 305–306, 319. Used by permission. [B], [C], and [D] from Henry Gee and William Hardy, eds., *Documents Illustrative of English Church History* (London: Macmillan and Co., Ltd., 1921), pp. 179–181, 188–189, 204. Used by permission.

Secondly, that whereas divers of the constitutions, ordinances, and canons, provincial or synodal, which have been heretofore enacted, be thought to be not only much prejudicial to your royal prerogative, but also overmuch onerous to your highness' subjects, your clergy aforesaid is contented, if it may stand so with your highness' pleasure, that it be committed to the examination and judgement of your grace, and of thirty-two persons, whereof sixteen to be of the upper and nether house of the temporalty, and other sixteen of the clergy, all to be chosen and appointed by your most noble grace. So that, finally, whichsoever of the said constitutions, ordinances, or canons, provincial or synodal, shall be thought and determined by your grace and by the most part of the said thirty-two persons not to stand with God's laws and the laws of your realm, the same to be abrogated and repealed by your grace and the clergy; and such of them as shall seem to your grace, and by the most part of the said thirty-two persons, to stand with God's laws and the laws of your realm, to stand in full strength and power, your grace's most royal assent and authority once impetrate and fully given to the same.

[B] The Restraint of Annates, 1532

The noblemen . . . of the realm, and the wise, sage, politic Commons of the same, assembled in this present Parliament, considering that the Court of Rome ceases not to tax, take, and exact the said great sums of money, under the title of annates, or first-fruits, . . . to the great damage of the said prelates and this realm; which annates, or first-fruits, were first suffered to be taken within the same realm, for the only defence of Christian people against the infidels, and now they be claimed and demanded as mere duty, only for lucre, against all right and conscience: insomuch that it is evidently known, that there has passed out of this realm unto the Court of Rome, since the second year of the reign of the most noble prince of famous memory, King Henry VII, unto this present time, under the name of annates, or first-fruits, paid for the expedition of bulls of archbishoprics, and bishoprics, the sum of eight hundred thousand ducats, amounting in sterling money, at the least, to eight score thousand pounds, besides other great and intolerable sums which have yearly been conveyed to the said Court of Rome, by many other ways and means, to the great impoverishment of this realm:

And albeit that our said sovereign the king, and all his natural subjects, as well spiritual as temporal, be as obedient, devout, catholic, and humble children of God and Holy Church, as any people be within any realm christened; yet the said exactions of annates, or first-fruits, be so intolerable and importable to this realm, that it is considered and declared . . . that the king's highness before Almighty God is bound . . . to do all that in him is to obviate, repress, and redress the said abuses and exactions of annates, or first-fruits: and because that divers prelates of this realm be now in extreme age, and in other debilities of their bodies, so that of likelihood bodily death in short time shall or may succeed unto them; by reason whereof great sums of money shall shortly after their deaths be conveyed into the Court of Rome, for the unreasonable and uncharitable causes above-said, to the universal damage, prejudice, and impoverishment of this realm, if speedy remedy be not in due time provided:

It is therefore ordained, established, and enacted, by authority of this present Parliament, that the unlawful payments of annates, or first-fruits, and all manner contributions for the same, for any archbishopric or bishopric, or for any bulls hereafter to be obtained from the Court of Rome, to or for the aforesaid purpose and intent, shall from henceforth utterly cease, and no such hereafter to be paid for any archbishopric, or bishopric, within this realm, . . .

[C] The Restraint of Appeals, 1533

. . . whereas the king, his most noble progenitors, and the nobility and Commons of this said realm, at divers and sundry Parliaments, as well in the time of King Edward I, Edward III, Richard II, Henry IV, and other noble kings of this realm, made sundry ordinances, laws, statutes, and provisions for the entire and sure conservation of the prerogatives, liberties, and preeminences of the said imperial crown of this realm, and of the jurisdiction spiritual and temporal of the same, to keep it from the annoyance . . . of the see of Rome: . . .

. . . yet nevertheless since the making of the said good statutes and ordinances, divers and sundry inconveniences and dangers, not provided for plainly by the said former acts, statutes, and ordinances, have arisen and sprung by reason of appeals sued out of this realm to the see of Rome . . . not only to the great inquietation, vexation, trouble, cost and charges of the king's highness, but also to the great delay of the said causes, for so much as the parties appealing to the said Court of Rome most commonly do the same for the delay of justice.

In consideration whereof the king's highness, his nobles and Commons, considering the great enormities, dangers, long delays and hurts, that as well to his highness, as to his said nobles, subjects, commons, and residents of this his realm, . . . does therefore by his royal assent, and by the assent of the lords spiritual and temporal, and the Commons, in this present Parliament assembled, and by authority of the same, enact, establish, and ordain, that all causes testamentary, causes of matrimony and divorces, rights of tithes, oblations and obventions . . . shall be from henceforth heard, examined, discussed, clearly, finally, and definitively adjudged . . . within the king's jurisdiction and authority, and not elsewhere; . . . any foreign inhibition, appeals, sentences, summons, citations, suspensions, interdictions, excommunications, restraints, judgments . . . from the see of Rome . . . notwithstanding.

[D] The Ecclesiastical Appointments Act, 1534

. . . be it now therefore enacted by the king our sovereign lord, by the assent of the Lords spiritual and temporal, and the commons, in this present Parliament assembled, and by the authority of the same, that . . . no person or persons hereafter shall be presented, nominated, or commended to the said Bishop of Rome, otherwise called the pope, or to the see of Rome, to or for the dignity or office of any archbishop or bishop within this realm, or in any other the king's dominions, nor shall send nor procure there for any manner of bulls, briefs, palls, or other things requisite for an archbishop or bishop, . . .

And furthermore be it ordained and established by the authority aforesaid, that at every avoidance of every archbishopric or bishopric within this realm, or in any other the king's dominions, the king our sovereign lord, his heirs and successors, may grant to the prior and convent, or the dean and chapter of the cathedral churches or monasteries where the see of such archbishopric or bishopric shall happen to be void, a licence under the great seal, as of old time has been accustomed, to proceed to election of an archbishop or bishop of the see so being void, with a letter missive, containing the name of the person which they shall elect and choose . . .

[E] The Supremacy Act, 1534

Albeit the king's majesty justly and rightfully is and ought to be the supreme head of the Church of England, and so is recognized by the clergy of this realm in their Convocations, yet nevertheless for corroboration and confirmation thereof, and for increase of virtue in Christ's religion within this realm of England, and to repress and extirp all errors, heresies, and other enormities and abuses heretofore used in the same; be it enacted by authority of this present Parliament, that the king our sovereign lord, his heirs and successors, kings of this realm, shall be taken, accepted, and reputed the only supreme head in earth of the Church of England, called *Anglicana Ecclesia;* . . . and that our said sovereign lord, his heirs and successors, kings of this realm, shall have full power and authority from time to time to visit, repress, redress, reform, order, correct, restrain, and amend all such errors, heresies, abuses, offences, contempts, and enormities, whatsoever they be, which by any manner spiritual authority or jurisdiction ought or may lawfully be reformed, repressed, ordered, redressed, corrected, restrained, or amended, most to the pleasure of Almighty God, the increase of virtue in Christ's religion, and for the conservation of the peace, unity, and tranquillity of this realm; . . .

[27] *SIR THOMAS MORE IS BEHEADED FOR TREASON* *

Among the Englishmen who refused to accept the foregoing Act of Supremacy was the brilliant humanist and ex-Chancellor, Sir Thomas More. He was committed to the Tower of London, indicted for high treason, found guilty and beheaded in 1535. His head was exhibited on London Bridge. More's last days are described in the following pages of William Roper's notable biography.

. . . early in the morning [of his day of execution] came to him Sir Thomas Pope, his singular friend, on message from the King and his Council, that he should before nine of the clock in the same morning suffer death, and that therefore forthwith he should prepare himself thereto. "Mr. Pope," saith he, "for your good tidings I most heartily thank you. I have been always bounden much to the King's Highness for the benefits and honours which he hath still from time to time most bountifully heaped upon me, and yet more bounded I am to his Grace for putting me into this place, where I have had convenient time and space to have remembrance of my end, and so help me God most of all, Mr. Pope, am I bound to his Highness, that it pleased him so shortly to rid me of the miseries of this wretched world. And therefore will I not fail most earnestly to pray for his Grace both here, and also in another world." "The King's pleasure is further," quoth Mr. Pope, "that at your execution you shall not use many words." "Mr. Pope" (quoth he), "you do well that you give me warning of his Grace's pleasure. For otherwise had I purposed at that time somewhat to have spoken, but of no matter wherewith his Grace, or any other should have had cause to be offended. Nevertheless, whatsoever I intend I am ready obediently to conform myself to his Grace's commandment. . . ."

Wherewithal Mr. Pope taking his leave of him could not refrain from weeping, which Sir Thomas More perceiving, comforted him in this wise, "Quiet yourself, good Mr. Pope, and be not discomforted. For I trust that we shall once in heaven see each other full merrily, where we shall be sure to live and love together in joyful bliss eternally." Upon whose departure Sir Thomas More, as one that had been invited to a solemn feast, changed himself into his best apparel; which Mr. Lieutenant espying, advised him to put it off, saying, That he that should have it was but a worthless fellow. "What

* William Roper, *The Life of Sir Thomas More,* in *The Harvard Classics,* ed. by Charles W. Eliot (New York: P. F. Collier & Son Corp., 1910), Vol. XXXVI, pp. 138–141. Used by permission.

Mr. Lieutenant" (quoth he), "shall I account him a worthless fellow, that will do me this day so singular a benefit? Nay, I assure you, were it cloth of gold I would account it well bestowed on him, as St. Cyprian did, who gave his executioner thirty pieces of gold." And albeit at length, through Mr. Lieutenant's persuasions, he altered his apparel, yet, after the example of that holy martyr St. Cyprian, did he of that little money that was left him, send one angel of gold to his executioner. And so was he brought by Mr. Lieutenant out of the Tower, and from thence led towards the place of execution, where going up the scaffold, which was so weak that it was ready to fall, he said to Mr. Lieutenant, "I pray you, I pray you, Mr. Lieutenant, see me safe up, and for my coming down left me shift for myself." Then desired he all the people thereabouts to pray for him, and to bear witness with him, that he should then suffer death in and for the faith of the holy Catholic Church, which done he kneeled down, and after his prayers said, he turned to the executioner, and with a cheerful countenance spake unto him. "Pluck up thy spirits, man, and be not afraid to do thine office, my neck is very short. Take heed therefore thou shoot not awry for saving thine honesty." So passed Sir Thomas More out of this world to God upon the very same day in which himself had most desired.

Soon after whose death came intelligence thereof to the Emperor Charles, whereupon he sent for Sir Thomas Eliott, our English Ambassador, and said unto him, "My Lord Ambassador, we understand that the King your master hath put his faithful servant and grave wise councillor Sir Thomas More to death." Whereunto Sir Thomas Eliott answered, that he understood nothing thereof. "Well," said the Emperor, "it is very true, and this will we say, that if we had been master of such a servant, of whose doings ourselves have had these many years no small experience, we would rather have lost the best city of our dominions, than have lost such a worthy councillor." Which matter was by Sir Thomas Eliott to myself, to my wife, to Mr. Clement and his wife, to Mr. John Haywood and his wife, and divers others of his friends accordingly reported.

[28] *HENRY VIII FINDS SIN IN THE MONASTERIES AND DISSOLVES THEM* *

In 1536 Henry VIII secured from Parliament the first act for the dissolution of the monasteries [A]. *Affected were only the smaller monasteries. Three years later, Henry seized the greater monasteries, resulting in the spoliation of Glastonbury*

* [A] Henry Gee and William Hardy, eds., *Documents Illustrative of English Church History* (London: Macmillan and Company, Ltd., 1921), pp. 257–259. Used by permission. [B] and [C] T. Wright, ed., *Letters Relating to the Suppression of Monasteries* (London: Camden Society, 1843), pp. 255–256, 261–262.

[B] *in southwest England, one of the oldest and most famous English monastic houses. Its abbot, Richard Whiting, refused to surrender the property when Cromwell's agents appeared. He, too, was charged with high treason and executed.*

[A] Act for the Dissolution of the Lesser Monasteries, 1536

Forasmuch as manifest sin, vicious, carnal and abominable living is daily used and committed among the little and small abbeys, priories, and other religious houses of monks, canons, and nuns, where the congregation of such religious persons is under the number of twelve persons, whereby the governors of such religious houses, and their convent, spoil, destroy, consume, and utterly waste, as well their churches, monasteries, priories, principal houses, farms, granges, lands, tenements, and hereditaments, as the ornaments of their churches, and their goods and chattels, to the high displeasure of Almighty God, slander of good religion, and to the great infamy of the king's highness and the realm, if redress should not be had thereof. And albeit that many continual visitations hath been heretofore had, by the space of two hundred years and more, for an honest and charitable reformation of such unthrifty, carnal, and abominable living, yet nevertheless little or none amendment is hitherto had, but their vicious living shamelessly increases and augments, and by a cursed custom so rooted and infested, that a great multitude of the religious persons in such small houses do rather choose to rove abroad in apostasy, than to conform themselves to the observation of good religion; so that without such small houses be utterly suppressed, and the religious persons therein committed to great and honourable monasteries of religion in this realm, where they may be compelled to live religiously, for reformation of their lives, there cannot else be no reformation in this behalf:

In consideration whereof, the king's most royal majesty—being supreme head on earth, under God, of the Church of England, daily finding and devising the increase, advancement, and exaltation of true doctrine and virtue in the said Church, to the only glory and honour of God, and the total extirping and destruction of vice and sin, having knowledge that the premises be true, as well by the accounts of his late visitations, as by sundry credible informations, considering also that divers and great solemn monasteries of this realm, wherein (thanks be to God) religion is right well kept and observed, be destitute of such full numbers of religious persons, as they ought and may keep—has thought good that a plain declaration should be made of the premises, as well to the Lords spiritual and temporal, as to other his loving subjects, the Commons, in this present Parliament assembled: whereupon the said Lords and Commons, by a great deliberation, finally be resolved, that it is and shall be much more to the pleasure of Almighty God, and for the honour of this his realm, that the possessions of such small religious houses, now being spent, spoiled, and wasted for increase and maintenance of sin, should be used and converted to better uses, and the unthrifty religious persons, so spending the same, to be compelled to reform their lives: and thereupon most humbly desire the king's highness that it may be enacted by authority of this present Parliament, that his majesty shall have and enjoy to him and to his heirs for ever, all and singular such monasteries, priories, and other religious houses of monks, canons, and nuns, of what kinds or diversities of habits, rules, or orders soever they be called or named, which have not in lands, tenements, rents, tithes, portions, and other hereditaments, above the clear yearly value of two hundred pounds. And in like manner shall have and enjoy all the sites and circuits of every such religious houses, and all and singular the manors, granges, meases, lands, tenements, rents, reversions, services, tithes, pensions, portions, churches, chapels, advowsons, patronages, annuities, rights, entries, conditions, and other hereditaments appertaining or belonging to every such monastery, priory, or other religious house, not having, as is aforesaid, above the said clear yearly value of two hundred pounds, in as large and ample manner as the abbots, priors, abbesses, prioresses, or other governors of such monasteries, priories, and other religious houses now have, or ought to have the same in the right of their houses. . . .

[B] Letter of the Visitors Sent to Examine the Abbot of Glastonbury to Thomas Cromwell, September 22, 1539

Please it your lordship to be advertised, that we came to Glastonbury on Friday last past, about ten of the clock in the forenoon: and [because] . . . the Abbot was then at Sharpham, a place of his, a mile and somewhat more from the abbey, we, without any delay, went unto the same place; and there . . . examined him upon certain articles. And [because] . . . his answer was not then to our purpose, we advised him to call to his remembrance that which he had as then forgotten, and so declare the truth, and then came with him the same day to the abbey; and there of new proceeded that night to search his study for letters and books: and found in his study . . . a written book of arguments against the divorce of his king's majesty and the lady dowager, as also divers pardons, copies of bulls, and the counterfeit life of Thomas Becket in print; but we could not find any letter that was material. And so we proceeded again to his examination concerning the articles we received from your lordship, in the answers whereof, as we take it, shall appear his cankered and traitorous heart and mind against the king's majesty and his succession; as by the same answers, signed with his hand, and sent to your lordship by this bearer, more plainly shall appear. And so, with as fair words as we could, we have conveyed him from hence into the tower, being but a very weak man and sickly. . . . We have in money 300 l. and above; but the certainty of plate and other stuff there as yet we know not, for we have not had opportunity for the same, but shortly we intend (God willing) to proceed to the same; whereof we shall ascertain your lordship so shortly as we may. This is also to advertise your lordship, that we have found a fair chalice of gold, and divers other parcels of plate, which the abbot had hid secretly from all such commissioners as have been there in times past; . . . It may please your lordship to advertise us of the king's pleasure by this bearer, to whom we shall deliver the custody and keeping of the house, with such stuff as we intend to leave there convenient to the king's use. We assure your lordship it is the goodliest house of that sort that ever we have seen. We would that your lordship did know it as we do; then we doubt not but your lordship would judge it a house meet for the king's majesty, and for no man else: which is to our great comfort; and we trust verily that there shall never come any double hood within that house again. Also this is to advertise your lordship, that there is never a one doctor within that house; but there be three bachelors of divinity, which be but meanly learned, as we can perceive. And thus our Lord preserve your good lordship.

[C] Letter of One of the Visitors, Richard Pollard, to Cromwell, November 16, 1539

Pleaseth it your lordship to be advertised, that . . . [on November 15] the late abbot of Glastonbury went from Wells to Glastonbury, and there was drawn through the town upon a hurdle to the hill called the Torre, where he was put to execution; at which time he asked God mercy and the king for his great offences towards his highness. . . . Afore his execution, [he] was examined upon divers articles and interrogatories to him ministered by me, but he could accuse no man but himself of any offence against the king's highness, nor he would confess no more gold nor silver nor any other thing more than he did before your lordship in the Tower. . . . I suppose it will be near Christmas before I shall have surveyed the lands at Glastonbury, and taken the audit there. . . .

[29] *POPE PIUS V DECLARES QUEEN ELIZABETH A HERETIC (1570)* *

The papal bull directed against Queen Elizabeth carried enormous political implications. From this moment, more or less open warfare existed between England and the Counter-Reformation, spearheaded by Spain. For generations to come, Englishmen would equate Catholicism with treason.

* Henry Bettenson, ed., *Documents of the Christian Church* (London: Oxford University Press, 1943), pp. 338–339. Used by permission.

He that reigns in the highest, to whom has been given all power in heaven and earth, entrusted the government of the one Holy Catholic and Apostolic Church (outside which there is no salvation) to one man alone on the earth, namely to Peter, the chief of the Apostles, and to Peter's successor, the Roman pontiff, in fullness of power [*potestatis plenitudo*]. This one man he set up as chief over all nations and all kingdoms, to pluck up, destroy, scatter, dispose, plant and build. . . .

. . . Resting then upon the authority of him who has willed to place us (albeit unequal to such a burden) in this supreme throne of justice, we declare the aforesaid Elizabeth a heretic and an abettor of heretics, and those that cleave to her . . . to have incurred the sentence of anathema, and to be cut off from the unity of Christ's body.

Moreover we declare her to be deprived of her pretended right to the aforesaid realm, and from all dominion, dignity and privilege whatsoever.

And the nobles, subjects and peoples of the said realm, and all others who have taken an oath of any kind to her we declare to be absolved for ever from such oath and from all dues of dominion, fidelity and obedience, as by the authority of these presents we do so absolve them; and we deprive the said Elizabeth of her pretended right to the realm and all other things aforesaid: and we enjoin and forbid all and several the nobles, etc. . . . that they presume not to obey her and her admonitions, commands, and laws. All who disobey our command we involve in the same sentence of anathema.

[30] *ELIZABETH'S RELIGIOUS SETTLEMENT AROUSES OPPOSITION* *

The Queen was interested primarily in a religious settlement which would unify her realm. In a spirit of compromise she fostered a church largely Protestant in doctrine and Catholic in ritual and hierarchy. The Thirty-nine Articles [A], *an adaptation of the Forty-two Articles of Edward VI, were adopted as the official profession of faith in 1563. They quickly aroused the opposition of the powerful Puritan elements* [B], *as well as that of the more radical Independents* [C].

[A] Excerpts from the Thirty-nine Articles

VI. OF THE SUFFICIENCY OF THE HOLY SCRIPTURES FOR SALVATION

Holy Scripture containeth all things necessary to salvation: so that whatsoever is not read therein, nor may be proved thereby, is not to be required

* [A] Philip Schaff, ed., *The Creeds of Christendom* (New York: Harper Bros., 1877), Vol. III, pp. 489–507. [B] and [C] G. W. Prothero, ed., *Select Statutes and Other Constitutional Documents* (Oxford: The Clarendon Press, 1894), pp. 219–221, 223.

of any man, that it should be believed as an article of the Faith, or be thought requisite or necessary to salvation.

XI. OF THE JUSTIFICATION OF MAN

We are accounted righteous before God only for the merit of our Lord and Saviour Jesus Christ by Faith, and not for our own works or deservings. Wherefore, that we are justified by Faith only, is a most wholesome Doctrine, and very full of comfort, as more largely is expressed in the Homily of Justification.

XII. OF GOOD WORKS

Albeit that Good Works, which are the fruits of Faith, and follow after Justification, can not put away our sins, and endure the severity of God's judgment; yet are they pleasing and acceptable to God in Christ, and do spring out necessarily of a true and lively Faith; insomuch that by them a lively Faith may be as evidently known as a tree discerned by the fruit.

XVII. OF PREDESTINATION AND ELECTION

Predestination to Life is the everlasting purpose of God, whereby (before the foundations of the world were laid) he hath constantly decreed by his counsel secret to us, to deliver from curse and damnation those whom he hath chosen in Christ out of mankind, and to bring them by Christ to everlasting salvation, as vessels made to honour. Wherefore, they which be endued with so excellent a benefit of God, be called according to God's purpose by his Spirit working in due season; they through Grace obey the calling: they be justified freely: they be made sons of God by adoption: they be made like the image of his only-begotten Son Jesus Christ: they walk religiously in good works, and at length, by God's mercy, they attain to everlasting felicity.

As the godly consideration of Predestination, and our Election in Christ, is full of sweet, pleasant, and unspeakable comfort to godly persons, and such as feel in themselves the working of the Spirit of Christ, mortifying the works of the flesh, and their earthly members, and drawing up their mind to high and heavenly things, as well because it doth greatly establish and confirm their faith of eternal Salvation to be enjoyed through Christ, as because it doth fervently kindle their love towards God: So, for curious and carnal persons, lacking the Spirit of Christ, to have continually before their eyes the sentence of God's Predestination, is a most dangerous downfall, whereby the Devil doth thrust them either into desperation, or into wretchedness of most unclean living, no less perilous than desperation.

XIX. OF THE CHURCH

The visible Church of Christ is a congregation of faithful men, in the which the pure Word of God is preached, and the Sacraments be duly ministered according to Christ's ordinance, in all those things that of necessity are requisite to the same.

As the Church of Jerusalem, Alexandria, and Antioch, have erred; so also the Church of Rome hath erred, not only in their living and manner of Ceremonies, but also in matters of Faith.

XXII. OF PURGATORY

The Romish Doctrine concerning Purgatory, Pardons, Worshipping and Adoration, as well of Images as of Relics, and also Invocation of Saints, is a fond [silly] thing, vainly invented, and grounded upon no warranty of Scripture, but rather repugnant to the Word of God.

XXIV. OF SPEAKING IN THE CONGREGATION IN SUCH A TONGUE AS THE PEOPLE UNDERSTANDETH

It is a thing plainly repugnant to the Word of God, and the custom of the Primitive Church, to have public Prayer in the Church, or to minister the Sacraments, in a tongue not understanded of the people.

XXV. OF THE SACRAMENTS

Sacraments ordained of Christ be not only badges or tokens of Christian men's profession, but rather they be certain sure witnesses, and effectual signs of grace, and God's good will towards us, by the which he doth work invisibly in us, and doth not only quicken, but also strengthen and confirm our Faith in him.

There are two Sacraments ordained of Christ our Lord in the Gospel, that is to say, Baptism, and the Supper of the Lord.

Those five commonly called Sacraments, that is to say, Confirmation, Penance, Orders, Matrimony, and Extreme Unction, are not to be counted for Sacraments of the Gospel, . . .

XXVIII. OF THE LORD'S SUPPER

The Supper of the Lord is not only a sign of the love that Christians ought to have among themselves one to another; but rather it is a Sacrament of our Redemption by Christ's death: insomuch that to such as rightly, worthily, and with faith, receive the same, the Bread which we break is a partaking of the Body of Christ; and likewise the Cup of Blessing is a partaking of the Blood of Christ.

Transubstantiation (or the change of the substance of Bread and Wine) in the Supper of the Lord, can not be proved by Holy Writ; but is repugnant to the plain words of Scripture, overthroweth the nature of a Sacrament, and hath given occasion to many superstitions.

The Body of Christ is given, taken, and eaten, in the Supper, only after an heavenly and spiritual manner. And the mean whereby the Body of Christ is received and eaten in the Supper is Faith.

The Sacrament of the Lord's Supper was not by Christ's ordinance reserved, carried about, lifted up, or worshiped.

XXX. OF BOTH KINDS

The Cup of the Lord is not to be denied to the Lay-people: for both the parts of the Lord's Sacrament, by Christ's ordinance and commandment, ought to be ministered to all Christian men alike.

[B] Puritan Petition to the Queen, 1585

Certain humble petitions, which are in most humble manner to be presented to the godly consideration of our sovereign lady Queen Elizabeth . . .

IX. . . . That every archbishop and bishop of this Church . . . , if it be found . . . that the office of the archbishop or bishop, as it is now, is both necessary and profitable for the Church . . . , shall . . . have assigned . . . unto him, by the same authority by which he is chosen archbishop or bishop, eight, ten, twelve, or more preaching pastors, doctors and deacons, such as are resident on their own parishes and charges, within his and their diocese, together with some other grave and godly men of worship or justices of peace within that shire, in such a certain number as shall be thought good to the Queen and her council, which may be assistant to him . . . ; and that the said archbishop and bishop shall, with them and by their counsel, advise and consent, hear and determine every cause ecclesiastical which is now used to be heard before any archbishop and bishop or ordinary . . .

X. And that . . . every pastor resident on his charge . . . shall by the advice and direction of the bishop of the diocese, and of his associates, present to the said bishop and his associates, four, six or eight inhabitants of his parish, such as shall be thought . . . meet to be the associates and seniors . . . with the said pastor, to govern his said parish with him; to hear and order with him such quarrels, offences, and disorders in life and manners, as should be among the same parishioners. And if the causes and quarrels . . . be such that the same pastor and his associates or seniors cannot determine the same, . . . then shall the said pastor . . . bring the said cause before the bishop of the diocese and the elders, which are to him associate . . .

XIII. That no one bishop do hereafter proceed in admitting or depriving of any pastor by his sole authority, nor in excommunicating any faulty person, nor in absolving any person that is excommunicated, nor in the deciding and determining of any cause ecclesiastical, without the advice and consent of the aforesaid seniors and associates joined with him . . .

XVIII. . . . That neither the said archbishops . . . nor the bishops . . . do hereafter, by their sole and private authority, make and publish any injunctions touching religion or church government . . .

XXIV. That . . . in every synod hereafter to be called, . . . the bishops, deans, archdeacons, clerks, and such as shall be called by order to the synod, do all sit together brotherly in one house; and that they do choose one of themselves to be the *moderator* or *prolocutor* of the synod . . . That there may be also by the appointment of the Queen and her council, joined to them, to sit with them in the synod or convocation, some other godly learned men which are not in the order of the ministry, . . . to give their consent to the conclusions which shall be made.

XXIX. . . . And to the end that the said bishops may hereafter do that office which shall be committed to them the more sincerely, we desire that they . . . may be delivered from the burden of all worldly pomp, honour and charge; . . . and that they also be set so free from the administration of all civil causes and offices, that they may wisely apply themselves to the labour of the gospel and ecclesiastical function in diligence and sincerity . . .

[C] Doctrines of the Independents (from a contemporary history)

. . . [Among the accused were] Henry Barrow, gentleman, and John Greenwood, clerk, who were [brought] before the High Commissioner for Causes Ecclesiastical in November, 1587 for their schismatical and seditious opinions, namely, that [the Anglican] Church is no Church, or at the least no true Church; yielding these reasons therefore, That the worship of the English Church is flat idolatry: that we admit into our Church persons unsanctified: that our preachers have no lawful calling: that our government is ungodly: that no bishop or preacher preacheth Christ sincerely and truly: that the people of every parish ought to choose their bishop, and that every elder, though he be no doctor nor pastor, is a bishop: that all [who] refuse the ceremonies of the Church and yet preach in the same Church, strain a gnat and swallow a camel and are close hypocrites and walk in a left-handed policy: . . . that set prayer is blasphemous.

6

The Catholic Reformation

By the time of Luther's death in 1546 Roman Catholicism gave the appearance of a dying institution. Northern and central Germany, Scandinavia, England, and part of Switzerland were lost to the old faith. Protestants were making steady gains in the Lowlands, France, Poland, and Hungary. The Catholic Church was on the defensive nearly everywhere. But a generation later the situation had been reversed. The growth of the Protestant churches had been checked, and Catholicism was recouping many of its earlier losses. Thanks to a reformed Papacy, the Council of Trent, new religious orders like the Jesuits, and strong political support, the Roman Catholic Church was reinvigorated.

[31] *A YOUNG CLERIC IS WARNED OF ROMAN CORRUPTION* *

The letter in this selection was written by Lorenzo the Magnificent, ruler of Florence, to his son Giovanni shortly after the latter was created cardinal at the age

* Merrick Whitcomb, ed., *A Literary Source-Book of the Italian Renaissance* (Philadelphia: University of Pennsylvania, 1900), pp. 80–82.

of thirteen. There is a good deal of unconscious hypocrisy in Lorenzo's words: the Medicis' insistence on using the Papacy to further family interests was the sort of thing which caused the very corruption Lorenzo piously deplores.

You, and all of us who are interested in your welfare, ought to esteem ourselves highly favored by Providence, not only for the many honours and benefits bestowed upon our house, but more particularly for having conferred upon us, in your person, the greatest dignity we have ever enjoyed. This favor, in itself so important, is rendered still more so by the circumstances with which it is accompanied, and especially by the consideration of your youth and of our situation in the world. The first that I would therefore suggest to you is that you ought to be grateful to God, and continually to recollect that it is not through your merits, your prudence, or your solicitude, that this event has taken place, but through his favour, which you can only repay by a pious, chaste and exemplary life; and that your obligations to the performance of these duties are so much the greater, as in your early years you have given some reasonable expectations that your riper age may produce such fruits. . . .

I well know, that as you are now to reside at Rome, that sink of all iniquity, the difficulty of conducting yourself by these admonitions will be increased. The influence of example is itself prevalent; but you will probably meet with those who will particularly endeavor to corrupt and incite you to vice; because, as you may yourself perceive, your early attainment to so great a dignity is not observed without envy, and those who could not prevent your receiving that honour will secretly endeavor to diminish it, by inducing you to forfeit the good estimation of the public; thereby precipitating you into that gulf into which they had themselves fallen; in which attempt, the consideration of your youth will give them a confidence of success. To these difficulties you ought to oppose yourself with the greater firmness, as there is at present less virtue amongst your brethren of the college. I acknowledge indeed that several of them are good and learned men, whose lives are exemplary, and whom I would recommend to you as patterns of your conduct. By emulating them you will be so much the more known and esteemed, in proportion as your age and the peculiarity of your situation will distinguish you from your colleagues. Avoid, however, as you would Scylla or Charybdis, the imputation of hypocrisy; guard against all ostentation, either in your conduct or your discourse; affect not austerity, nor even appear too serious. This advice, you will, I hope, in time understand and practice better than I can express it.

Yet you are not unacquainted with the great importance of the character which you have to sustain, for you well know that all the Christian world would prosper if the cardinals were what they ought to be; because in such a case there would always be a good pope, upon which the tranquility of Christendom so materially depends. Endeavor then to render yourself such, that if all the rest resemble you, we might expect this universal blessing. To give you particular directions as to your behaviour and conversation would be a matter of no small difficulty. I shall therefore only recommend, that in your intercourse with the cardinals and other men of rank, your language be unassuming and respectful, guiding yourself, however, by your own reason, and not submitting to be impelled by the passions of others, who, actuated by improper motives, may pervert the use of their reasons. . . .

[32] *A PAPAL COMMISSION SPEAKS FRANKLY OF CHURCH ABUSES* *

In 1537 the reform-minded Pope Paul III selected a commission of nine cardinals to investigate the ills of the Church. A year later the commission rendered a remarkably candid report, a condensation of which is given below. Although intended to be secret, the report fell into the hands of the Lutherans. It was widely disseminated and regarded by Protestants as justification for their rebellion against Rome.

You [the Pope] have summoned us to yourself, unskilled as we are and unequal to such a great task . . . and with the most serious words you have enjoined that we collect all these abuses and report them to you. . . .

(1) The first abuse is that in the ordination of clerics and even of priests . . . no diligence is employed: the most ignorant men, those born of the most worthless family, reprobates, and adolescents are admitted to Holy Orders and even to the priesthood. . . . In some places the divine worship has not only diminished, but is even already extinct. . . . Your Holiness should not allow anyone to be ordained except by his bishop, or with the permission of his bishop or of the deputies in the city: in addition, each bishop should have in his diocese a teacher to instruct clerics in minor orders in both letters and morals. . . .

(2) Another abuse of great seriousness is in the granting of ecclesiastical benefices, especially of parishes, and above all of bishoprics, in which it has become customary that the persons to whom benefices are granted are provided for, and not the flock of Christ and the Church. Therefore, bene-

* B. J. Kidd, ed., *Documents Illustrative of the Continental Reformation* (Oxford: The Clarendon Press, 1921), pp. 307–318. Used by permission of the publisher. An original translation by Peter Ford.

fices, parishes, and especially bishoprics should be granted . . . to holy and learned men: . . . Nor should a benefice in Spain or Britain be granted to an Italian, or vice versa. . . .

(3) When benefices are conferred on or granted to others, another abuse has crept in by the fixing of payments on their fruits: . . . A great abuse which should be reformed is the granting of payments to rich clerics, who can live quite comfortably and honestly on the revenues they already have.

(4) Another such abuse is in the exchanging of benefices by simoniacal bargains with no consideration except profit.

(5) . . . Although the law of the Church prohibits the bequeathing of benefices by will, because they belong not to the testator but to the Church, . . . human . . . ingenuity finds many ways of evading this law. . . .

(6) Another abuse is in regard to expectations . . . of benefices whereby the occasion is presented that the death of another might be desired and eagerly listened for. . . .

. . . bishops . . . and curates should not absent themselves from their churches and parishes, except for some serious reason. . . . What more wretched sight is there visible to a Christian man traveling through the Christian world than this desertion of churches? Almost all pastors have left their flocks, almost all parishes have been entrusted to hirelings. . . .

(9) Another abuse is that so many . . . cardinals absent themselves from this Curia, and perform no part of their duties. . . .

(11) Another abuse which ought to be corrected is in the orders of religious, because so many are corrupt that they injure the seculars by great scandal and bad example. . . .

(13) Another abuse troubles the Christian people, namely in regard to nuns who are under the care of conventual friars, for in many monasteries public sacrileges are committed, to the great scandal of all. . . .

(14) Another great and dangerous abuse is in the public schools, especially in Italy, in which professors of philosophy teach impiety. . . .

(15) . . . friars and religious . . . after a solemn vow leave their orders and obtain permission not to be obliged to wear their habits. . . .

(17) Another abuse is . . . a dispensation granted to a person in Holy Orders to marry. . . .

(18) An abuse is in regard to dispensation from marital impediments of consanguinity and affinity. Certainly a dispensation in the second degree should not be granted except for a serious public cause. . . .

(19) Another abuse is in the absolution of a simoniac. . . . This deadly disease reigns in the Church of God to such a degree that certain men are not afraid to commit simony, then immediately seek absolution from punishment . . . and in this way keep the benefice which they bought. . . .

(23) . . . many foreigners are scandalized who go into the Church of St. Peter where there are filthy, ignorant priests . . . celebrating Mass. . . .

(24) In this city public prostitutes walk or ride on mule as honorable women followed . . . by clerics and noble retinues of cardinals. . . .

These, Holy father, are the abuses . . . which would seem to us ought to be corrected. . . . We have satisfied our consciences, not without a great hope that under your leadership we may see the Church of God purged, beautiful as a dove . . . with the eternal memory of your name. You have taken the name of Paul: we hope that you will imitate the love of Paul: chosen as he was as the vessel to carry the name of Christ to the Gentiles: we hope that you have been chosen, that you might restore the name of Christ which has been so forgotten by the people and us clergy.

[33] *A GENERAL COUNCIL LEADS THE WAY TO CATHOLIC REVIVAL* *

The Council of Trent met in twenty-five sessions from 1545 to 1563. Its work was two-fold: to restate and clarify the doctrines of the Church, particularly those tenets which had been repudiated by Luther, Calvin, and other Protestant leaders; and, secondly, to reform the discipline of the Church [C]. *The doctrinal work took two forms: definitions of doctrine* [A] *and anathemas against specific heretical opinions* [B].

[A] Excerpts from the Formulation of Doctrine

ON THE INSTITUTION OF THE SACRIFICE OF THE MASS. . . . He, therefore, our God and Lord, though He was about to offer Himself once on the altar of the cross unto God the Father by means of His death there to operate an eternal redemption; nevertheless, [so] that His priesthood [would] not be extinguished by His death, in the last supper, on the night in which He was betrayed . . . offered up to God the Father His own body and blood under the species of bread and wine; and, under the symbols of those same things, He delivered (His own body and blood) to be received by His apostles, whom He then constituted priests of the New Testament; and by those words, *Do this in commemoration of me,* He commanded them and their successors in the priesthood, to offer (them); even as the Catholic Church has always understood and taught. . . . [Twenty-second Session, 1562.]

ON THE INSTITUTION OF THE PRIESTHOOD. Sacrifice and priesthood are, by

* J. Waterworth, trans., *The Canons and Decrees of the Sacred and Oecumenical Council of Trent* (London: C. Dolman, 1848), *passim.*

the ordinance of God, in such wise conjoined, as that both have existed in every law. Whereas, therefore, in the New Testament, the Catholic Church has received, from the institution of Christ, the holy visible sacrifice of the Eucharist; it must needs also be confessed, that there is, in that Church, a new, visible, and external priesthood, into which the old has been translated. And the sacred Scriptures show, and the tradition of the Catholic Church has always taught, that this priesthood was instituted by the same Lord our Saviour, and that to the apostles, and their successors in the priesthood, was the power delivered of consecrating, offering, and administering His Body and Blood, as also of forgiving and of retaining sins. [Twenty-third Session, 1563.]

ON TRANSUBSTANTIATION. And because that Christ, our Redeemer, declared that which He offered under the species of bread to be truly His own body, therefore has it ever been a firm belief in the Church of God, and this holy Synod doth now declare it anew, that, by the consecration of the bread and of the wine, a conversion is made of the whole substance of the bread into the substance of the body of Christ our Lord, and of the whole substance of the wine into the substance of His blood; which conversion is, by the holy Catholic Church, suitably and properly called Transubstantiation. [Thirteenth Session, 1551.]

DECREE CONCERNING THE USE OF THE SACRED BOOKS. The same sacred and holy Synod,—considering that no small utility may accrue to the Church of God, if it be made known which out of all the Latin editions, now in circulation, of the sacred books, is to be held as authentic,—ordains and declares, that the said old and vulgate edition, which, by the lengthened usage of so many ages, has been approved of in the Church, be, in public lectures, disputations, sermons and expositions, held as authentic; and that no one is to dare, or presume to reject it under any pretext whatever. Furthermore, in order to restrain petulant spirits, It decrees, that no one, relying on his own skill, shall,—in matters of faith, and of morals pertaining to the edification of Christian doctrine,—wresting the sacred Scripture to his own senses, presume to interpret the said sacred Scripture contrary to that sense which holy mother Church . . . hath held and doth hold; . . . [Fourth Session, 1546.]

ON THE INVOCATION AND RELICS OF SAINTS. The holy Synod enjoins on all bishops, and others who sustain the office and charge of teaching, that, agreeably to the usage of the Catholic and Apostolic Church, received from the primitive times of the Christian religion, and agreeably to the consent of the holy Fathers, and to the decrees of sacred Councils, they especially instruct the faithful diligently concerning the intercession and invocation of saints; the honour (paid) to relics; and the legitimate use of images:

teaching them, that the saints, who reign together with Christ, offer up their own prayers to God for men; that it is good and useful suppliantly to invoke them, and to have recourse to their prayers, aid, (and) help for obtaining benefits from God, through His Son, Jesus Christ our Lord, who is our alone Redeemer and Saviour; . . . [Twenty-fifth Session, 1563.]

[B] Excerpts from the Anathemas

ON JUSTIFICATION. If any one saith, that man may be justified before God by his own works, whether done through the teaching of human nature, or that of the law, without the grace of God through Jesus Christ; let him be anathema. . . . [Sixth Session, 1547.]

ON THE SACRIFICE OF THE MASS. If any one saith, that in the mass a true and proper sacrifice is not offered to God; or, that to be offered is nothing else but that Christ is given us to eat; let him be anathema.

If any one saith, that by those words, *Do this for the commemoration of me* (Luke xxii. 19), Christ did not institute the apostles priests; or, did not ordain that they, and other priests should offer His own body and blood; let him be anathema. . . .

If any one saith, that the rite of the Roman Church, according to which a part of the canon and the words of consecration are pronounced in a low tone, is to be condemned; or, that the mass ought to be celebrated in the vulgar tongue only; . . . let him be anathema. . . . [Twenty-second Session, 1562.]

ON THE SACRAMENTS IN GENERAL. If any one saith, that the sacraments of the New Law were not all instituted by Jesus Christ, our Lord; or, that they are more, or less, than seven, to wit, Baptism, Confirmation, the Eucharist, Penance, Extreme Unction, Order, and Matrimony; or even that any one of these seven is not truly and properly a sacrament; let him be anathema. . . .

If any one saith, that the sacraments of the New Law are not necessary unto salvation, but superfluous; and that, without them, or without the desire thereof, men obtain of God, through faith alone, the grace of justification;—though all (the sacraments) are not indeed necessary for every individual; let him be anathema. . . .

If any one saith, that all Christians have power to administer the word, and all the sacraments; let him be anathema. . . .

If any one saith, that a minister, being in mortal sin,—if so be that he observe all the essentials which belong to the effecting, or conferring of, the sacrament,—neither effects, nor confers the sacrament; let him be anathema. . . . [Seventh Session, 1547.]

ON THE EUCHARIST. If any one saith, that Christ, given in the Eucharist, is eaten spiritually only, and not also sacramentally and really; let him be anathema. . . . [Thirteenth Session, 1551.]

ON THE SACRAMENT OF MATRIMONY. If any one saith, that the Church has erred, in that she hath taught, and doth teach, in accordance with the evangelical and apostolical doctrine, that the bond of matrimony cannot be dissolved on account of the adultery of one of the married parties; . . . let him be anathema. . . .

If any one saith, that the marriage state is to be placed above the state of virginity, or of celibacy, and that it is not better and more blessed to remain in virginity, or in celibacy, than to be united in matrimony; let him be anathema. . . . [Twenty-fourth Session, 1563.]

[C] Excerpts from the Reformatory Decrees

ON THE ESTABLISHMENT OF SEMINARIES FOR CLERICS. . . . the holy Synod ordains, that all cathedral, metropolitan, and other churches greater than these, shall be bound, each according to its means and the extent of the diocese, to maintain, to educate religiously, and to train in ecclesiastical discipline, a certain number of youths of their city and diocese. . . . [Twenty-third Session, 1563.]

ON THE NECESSITY FOR PREACHING. The holy Synod, desirous that the office of preaching . . . may be exercised as frequently as possible . . . ordains, that the bishops shall themselves in person, each in his own church, announce the sacred Scriptures and the divine law . . . and in the other churches the parish priests . . . and this at least on all Lord's Days and solemn festivals; but, during the season of the fasts, of Lent and of the Advent of the Lord, daily. . . . [Twenty-fourth Session, 1563.]

ON THE FURNITURE AND TABLE OF PRELATES. . . . [The Synod] not only orders that bishops be content with modest furniture, and a frugal table and diet, but that they also give heed that in the rest of their manner of living, and in their whole house, there be nothing seen that is alien from this holy institution, and which does not manifest simplicity, zeal towards God, and a contempt of vanities. Also, It wholly forbids them to strive to enrich their own kindred or domestics out of the revenues of the church: . . . [Twenty-fifth Session, 1563.]

ON THE USE OF THE POWER OF EXCOMMUNICATION. Although the sword of excommunication is the very sinews of ecclesiastical discipline, and very salutary for keeping the people in their duty, yet is it to be used with sobriety and great circumspection; seeing that experience teaches, that if it be rashly or for slight causes wielded, it is more despised than feared, and produces ruin rather than safety. . . . nor shall [the bishops] be induced to grant the said excommunications by the authority of any Secular person whatever, even though a magistrate; . . . [Twenty-fifth Session, 1563.]

ON INDULGENCES. Whereas the power of conferring Indulgences was granted by Christ to the Church; and she has, even in the most ancient times, used the said power, delivered unto her of God; the sacred holy Synod teaches, and enjoins, that the use of Indulgences . . . is to be retained in the Church; and It condemns with anathema those who either assert, that they are useless; or who deny that there is in the Church the power of granting them. In granting them, however, It desires that, in accordance with the ancient and approved custom in the Church, moderation be observed; . . . [Twenty-fifth Session, 1563.]

ON DUELLING. The detestable custom of duelling, introduced by the contrivance of the devil, that by the bloody death of the body, he may accomplish the ruin of the soul, shall be utterly exterminated from the Christian world. . . . [Twenty-fifth Session, 1563.]

[34] *TRENT FORMULATES A PROFESSION OF FAITH* *

The doctrinal work of the Council of Trent was summed up in an uncompromising Profession of Faith issued by Pope Pius IV in 1564. All bishops and beneficed clergy were directed to recite it publicly. It is still imposed today on all converts to Roman Catholicism.

I, *N*, with steadfast faith believe and profess each and all the things contained in the Symbol of faith which the holy Roman Church uses, namely "I believe in One God, etc. [The Nicene Creed]."

I most firmly acknowledge and embrace the Apostolical and ecclesiastical traditions and other observances and constitutions of the same Church. I acknowledge the sacred Scripture according to that sense which Holy Mother Church has held and holds, to whom it belongs to decide upon the true sense and interpretation of the holy Scriptures, nor will I ever receive and interpret the Scripture except according to the unanimous consent of the Fathers.

I profess also that there are seven sacraments. . . . I embrace and receive each and all of the definitions and declarations of the sacred Council of Trent on Original Sin and Justification.

I profess likewise that true God is offered in the Mass, a proper and

* Henry Bettenson, ed., *Documents of the Christian Church* (London: Oxford University Press, 1943), pp. 372–374. Used by permission of the publisher.

propitiatory sacrifice for the living and the dead, and that in the most Holy Eucharist there are truly, really and substantially the body and blood, together with the soul and divinity of Our Lord Jesus Christ, and that a conversion is made of the whole substance of bread into his body and of the whole substance of wine into his blood, which conversion the Catholic Church calls transubstantiation. I also confess that the whole and entire Christ and the true sacrament is taken under the one species alone.

I hold unswervingly that there is a purgatory and that the souls there detained are helped by the intercessions of the faithful; likewise also that the Saints who reign with Christ are to be venerated and invoked; that they offer prayers to God for us and that their relics are to be venerated. I firmly assert that the images of Christ and of the ever-Virgin Mother of God, as also those of other Saints, are to be kept and retained, and that due honour and veneration is to be accorded them; and I affirm that the power of indulgences has been left by Christ in the Church, and that their use is very salutary for Christian people.

I recognize the Holy Catholic and Apostolic Roman Church as the mother and mistress of all churches; and I vow and swear true obedience to the Roman Pontiff, the successor of blessed Peter, the chief of Apostles and the representative [*vicarius*] of Jesus Christ.

I accept and profess, without doubting, the traditions, definitions and declarations of the sacred Canons and Oecumenical Councils and especially those of the holy Council of Trent; and at the same time I condemn, reject and anathematize all things contrary thereto, and all heresies condemned, rejected and anathematized by the Church. This true Catholic Faith (without which no one can be in a state of salvation), which at this time I of my own will profess and truly hold, I, *N*, vow and swear, God helping me, most constantly to keep and confess entire and undefiled to my life's last breath, and that I will endeavour, as far as in me shall lie, that it be held, taught and preached by my subordinates or by those who shall be placed under my care: so help me God and these Holy Gospels of God.

[35] *ROME OBTAINS AN INVALUABLE NEW WEAPON AGAINST PROTESTANTISM* *

Leading the Catholic counter-offensive against Protestantism was a remarkable new order, the Society of Jesus (Jesuits), founded in 1534 by Ignatius Loyola and recognized by Pope Paul III in 1540. It soon became the single most effective

* Henry Bettenson, ed., *Documents of the Christian Church* (London: Oxford University Press, 1943), pp. 361–364. Used by permission of the publisher.

weapon available to the Papacy. The following extracts illustrate the spirit of the new order.

[A] Loyola's "Rules for Thinking With the Church," from the *Spiritual Exercises*

1. Always to be ready to obey with mind and heart, setting aside all judgement of one's own, the true spouse of Jesus Christ, our holy mother, our infallible and orthodox mistress, the Catholic Church, whose authority is exercised over us by the hierarchy.

2. To commend the confession of sins to a priest as it is practised in the Church; the reception of the Holy Eucharist once a year, or better still every week, or at least every month, with the necessary preparation.

3. To commend to the faithful frequent and devout assistance at the holy sacrifice of the Mass, the ecclesiastical hymns, the divine office, and in general the prayers and devotions practised at stated times, whether in public in the churches or in private.

4. To have a great esteem for the religious orders, and to give the preference to celibacy or virginity over the married state.

5. To approve of the religious vows of chastity, poverty, perpetual obedience, as well as the other works of perfection and supererogation. . . .

6. To praise relics, the veneration and invocation of Saints: also the stations, and pious pilgrimages, indulgences, jubilees, the custom of lighting candles in the Churches, and other such aids to piety and devotion.

7. To praise the use of abstinence and fasts as those of Lent, of Ember Days, of Vigils, of Friday, of Saturday, and of others undertaken out of pure devotion: also voluntary mortifications, which we call penances, not merely interior, but exterior also.

9. To uphold especially all the precepts of the Church, and not censure them in any manner; but, on the contrary, to defend them promptly, with reasons drawn from all sources, against those who criticise them.

13. That we may be altogether of the same mind and in conformity with the Church herself, if she shall have defined anything to be black which to our eyes appears to be white, we ought in like manner to pronounce it to be black. For we must undoubtedly believe, that the Spirit of our Lord Jesus Christ, and the Spirit of the Orthodox Church His Spouse, by which Spirit we are governed and directed to Salvation, is the same; . . .

14. It must also be borne in mind, that although it be most true, that no one is saved but he that is predestinated, yet we must speak with circumspection concerning this matter, lest perchance, stressing too much the grace or predestination of God, we should seem to wish to shut out the force of free will and the merits of good works; or on the other hand, attributing to

these latter more than belongs to them, we derogate meanwhile from the power of grace.

15. For the like reason we should not speak on the subject of predestination frequently; if by chance we do so speak, we ought so to temper what we say as to give the people who hear no occasion of erring and saying, "If my salvation or damnation is already decreed, my good or evil actions are predetermined"; whence many are wont to neglect good works, and the means of salvation.

17. Nor any more must we push to such a point the preaching and inculcating of the grace of God, as that there may creep thence into the minds of the hearers the deadly error of denying our faculty of free will. We must speak of it as the glory of God requires . . . that we may not raise doubts as to liberty and the efficacy of good works.

18. Although it is very praiseworthy and useful to serve God through the motive of pure charity, yet we must also recommend the fear of God; and not only filial fear, but servile fear, which is very useful and often even necessary to raise man from sin. . . . Once risen from the state, and free from the affection of mortal sin, we may then speak of that filial fear which is truly worthy of God, and which gives and preserves the union of pure love.

[B] "Obedience of the Jesuits" from the Order's *Constitution*

Let us with the utmost pains strain every nerve of our strength to exhibit this virtue of obedience, firstly to the Highest Pontiff, then to the Superiors of the Society; so that in all things, to which obedience can be extended with charity, we may be most ready to obey his voice, just as if it issued from Christ our Lord . . . , leaving any word, even a letter, that we have begun and have not yet finished; by directing to this goal all our strength and intention in the Lord, that holy obedience may be made perfect in us in every respect, in performance, in will, in intellect; by submitting to whatever may be enjoined on us with great readiness, with spiritual joy and perseverence; by persuading ourselves that all things [commanded] are just; by rejecting with a kind of blind obedience all opposing opinion or judgement of our own; and that in all things which are ordained by the Superior where it cannot be clearly held that any kind of sin intervenes. And let each one persuade himself that they that live under obedience ought to allow themselves to be borne and ruled by divine providence working through their Superiors exactly as if they were a corpse which suffers itself to be borne and handled in any way whatsoever; or just as an old man's stick which serves him who holds it in his hand wherever and for whatever purpose he wish to use it. . . .

[36] *THE VENETIAN AMBASSADOR DESCRIBES PHILIP II* *

The Papacy's most reliable lay ally in the crucial second half of the 16th century was the king of Spain, Philip II. English historians have traditionally pictured him in a most unsympathetic light. A less biased description can be found in the following report of the Venetian ambassador to Madrid.

The Catholic king was born in Spain, in the month of May, 1527, and spent a great part of his youth in that kingdom. Here, in accordance with the customs of the country and the wishes of his father and mother,—who belonged to the house of Portugal,—he was treated with all the deference and respect which seemed due to the son of the greatest emperor whom Christendom had ever had, and to the heir to such a number of realms and to such grandeur. As a result of this education, when the king left Spain for the first time and visited Flanders, passing on his way through Italy and Germany, he everywhere made an impression of haughtiness and severity, so that the Italians liked him but little, the Flemings were quite disgusted with him, and the Germans hated him heartily. But when he had been warned by the cardinal of Trent and Queen Mary [of Hungary, his aunt], and above all by his father, that this haughtiness was not in place in a prince destined to rule over a number of nations so different in manners and sentiment, he altered his manner so completely that on his second journey, when he went to England, he everywhere exhibited such distinguished mildness and affability that no prince has ever surpassed him in these traits. Although his actions display that royal dignity and gravity which are natural and habitual to him, he is none the less agreeable for this; on the contrary, his courtesy toward all seems only the more striking. His pleasing figure, his manly air, and his suavity of speech and manner serve to enhance the pleasing effect. He is slight in stature, but so well built, so admirably proportioned, and dressed with such taste and discernment that one could hardly imagine anything more perfect. . . .

Although the king resembles his father in his face and speech, in his attention to his religious duties, and in his habitual kindness and good faith, he nevertheless differs from him in several of those respects in which the greatness of rulers, after all, lies. The emperor was addicted to war, which he well understood; the king knows but little of it and has no love for it. The emperor undertook great enterprises with enthusiasm; his son avoids them. The father was fond of planning great things and would in the end

* James Harvey Robinson, *Readings in European History* (New York: Ginn and Company, 1906), pp. 168–169. Used by permission.

realize his wishes by his skill; his son, on the contrary, pays less attention to augmenting his own greatness than to hindering that of others. The emperor never allowed himself to be influenced by threats or fear, while the king has lost some of his dominions owing to unreasonable apprehensions. The father was guided in all matters by his own opinion, the son follows the opinions of others.

In the king's eyes no nation is superior to the Spaniards. It is among them that he lives, it is they that he consults, and it is they that direct his policy; in all this he is acting quite contrary to the habit of his father. He thinks little of the Italians and Flemish and still less of the Germans. Although he may employ the chief men of all the countries over which he rules, he admits none of them to his secret counsels, but utilizes their services only in military affairs, and then perhaps not so much because he really esteems them, as in the hope that he will in this way prevent his enemies from making use of them.

[37] *AUSTERITY BECOMES THE KEYNOTE AT ROME* *

In the years after the Council of Trent, the popes set the example for all Catholic clerics. Characteristic of the new moral tone of the Papacy is the description sent in 1600 by the Fugger correspondent in that city.

The Pope is quite determined to lead a monastic life as an example to the whole world. On account of this he has already ordered all carpets and ornaments to be removed from his rooms and especially from his sleeping chamber, allowing nothing to remain therein except a bedstead, a table and several skulls, as he wishes only to lie between four walls. Near him sleep two Benedictine monks, who stand in very good repute. He has summoned them to his presence, in order to pass his time with them and only to think of spiritual matters.

Last Saturday the Pope sat in the chair of the Chief Penitentiary in the Church of St. Peter with a white rod in his hand, and heard confessions there for three hours, granting the people absolution. Among these were many pilgrims, such as the Viceroy of Naples and the Duke of Sessa, as well as the bandit chief and the former most intimate advisor of the Sciarra. . . .

* Victor von Karwill, ed., *The Fugger News-Letters* (New York: G. P. Putnam's Sons, 1924), p. 227.

7

The Wars of Religion

For over a century before the Peace of Westphalia (1648), Europeans slaughtered one another in a series of civil and international wars having to do mainly with religion. These were the "ideological" wars of early modern history and were fought with all the savagery characteristic of modern wars between "rightists" and "leftists." But as the era of religious wars drew to a close, the religious issues became more and more blurred. In the Thirty Years' War, for example, Catholic France lined up with the German Protestants against the Catholic Emperor in order to achieve long-standing political objectives. The inevitable result of such conflict was the triumph of the spirit of religious indifferentism, or, more rarely, of genuine religious toleration. In the Peace of Westphalia political considerations scored a clear-cut victory over religious.

[38] *THE VENETIAN AMBASSADOR PREDICTS CIVIL WAR IN FRANCE* *

The first theater of the religious wars was Germany, where from 1546 to 1555 Charles V made belated and indecisive attempts to destroy Protestantism. An

* Rawdon Brown and G. C. Bentinck, eds., *Calendar of State Papers and Manuscripts Relating to English Affairs Existing in Venice* (London, 1890), Vol. VII (1558–1580), pp. 322–323.

uneasy compromise was attained by the Peace of Augsburg (1555). The scene of religious conflict shifted a few years later to France. There Calvinists (Huguenots) made remarkable strides in the 1550's under the guidance of Geneva. In the following selection the Venetian ambassador assesses the situation in France in 1561. A year later almost four decades of civil war began.

Unless it otherwise pleases the Almighty, religious affairs will soon be in an evil case in France, because there is not one single province uncontaminated. Indeed in some provinces, such as Normandy, almost the whole of Brittany, Touraine, Poitou, Gascony, and a great part of Languedoc, of Dauphiny, and of Provence, comprising three-fourths of the kingdom, congregations and meetings, which they call assemblies, are held; and in these assemblies they read and preach, according to the rites and uses of Geneva, without any respect either for the ministers of the King or the commandments of the King himself. This contagion has penetrated so deeply that it affects every class of persons, and, what appears more strange, even the ecclesiastical body itself. I do not mean only priests, friars, and nuns, for there are but few monasteries that are not corrupted, but even bishops and many of the principal prelates; who hitherto had not shown any such disposition; and it is only on account of the rigorous execution of the law that other persons besides the populace have not disclosed themselves, because they have restrained themselves for the time being from fear of the loss of their property and lives. But your Serenity must learn that while the people and the populace show fervent devotion by frequenting the churches and observing the Catholic rites, all other classes are supposed to be disaffected, and the nobility perhaps more than any other class, and, particularly, persons of forty years of age and under. If these disaffected individuals continue to attend mass and the Divine offices, and externally to practise Catholic rites, they do so for show and from fear; because when they either are, or believe themselves to be, unobserved, they avoid and even fly from the mass above all things, and also from the churches as far as they are able, and more so since it became known that by imprisonment, chastisement, and burnings, no remedy was found. It has now been determined not to proceed against any disaffected persons unless they venture to preach, persuade, and to take part publicly in congregations and assemblies. All other such persons are allowed to live, and some have been set at liberty, and released from the prisons of Paris and of other parts of the kingdom. A great number of these last have still remained in the kingdom, preaching and speaking publicly, and boasting that they have gained their cause against the Papists, as they delight to style their adversaries; so that, now, every one of them is assured against the fear of being questioned; and there exists thus a silent truce, because whilst formerly all suspected persons had to quit the kingdom, and to retire some to Geneva, some to Germany, and some to England, now they not only do not leave the country, but a large number of those who had already emigrated have returned. . . . Your Serenity will hardly believe the influence and the great power which the principal minister of Geneva, by name Calvin, a Frenchman, and a native of Picardy, possesses in this kingdom; he is a man of extraordinary authority, who by his mode of life, his doctrines, and his writings, rises superior to all the rest; and it is almost impossible to believe the enormous sums of money which are secretly sent to him from France to maintain his power. It is sufficient to add that if God does not interfere, there is great and imminent danger that one of two things will happen in this kingdom: either that the truce, which is desired and sought publicly, will end by the heretics having churches wherein they can preach, read, and perform their rites, according to their doctrine, without hindrance, and in like manner as they obtained churches by command of the late King, given at Fontainebleau, at the end of August, in compliance with a petition presented to him by the Admiral [Coligny]; or, else, that we shall see an obedience to the Pope and to the Catholic rites enforced, and shall have resort to violence and imbrue our hands in noble blood. For these reasons I foresee a manifest and certain division in the kingdom, and civil war as a consequence; and this will be the cause of the ruin both of the kingdom and of religion, because upon a change in religion a change in the State necessarily follows.

[39] *COLIGNY BECOMES THE FIRST VICTIM OF THE MASSACRE OF ST. BARTHOLOMEW* *

The bloodiest single episode in the French religious wars was the massacre of several thousand Protestants in Paris on St. Bartholomew's Day, 1572. First to be murdered was the Huguenot leader, Admiral Coligny. The following description is by the contemporary historian, de Thou.

Meanwhile Coligny awoke and recognized from the noise that a riot was taking place. Nevertheless he remained assured of the king's good will, of which he was persuaded by his credulity or by Teligny, his son-in-law; and he believed the populace had been stirred up by the Guises and that quiet would be restored as soon as it was seen that soldiers of the guard under the command of Cosseins had been detailed to protect him and guard his property.

* Jacques de Thou, *Histoire de Mon Temps,* Vol. III, as found in *Translations and Reprints from the Original Sources of European History* (Philadelphia: University of Pennsylvania Press, 1897), Vol. III, No. 3, pp. 24–26.

But when he perceived that the noise increased and that some one had fired an arquebuse in the courtyard of his dwelling, then at length conjecturing what it might be, but too late, he arose from his bed and having put on his dressing-gown he said his prayers, leaning against the wall. Labonne held the key of the chamber, and when Cosseins commanded him in the king's name to open the door he obeyed at once without fear and apprehending nothing. But scarcely was Cosseins in the room when Labonne, who stood in his way, was killed with a dagger-thrust. The Swiss, who were in the courtyard, when they saw this, fled into the house and closed the door, piling against it tables and all the furniture they could find. It was in the first scrimmage that a Swiss was killed with a ball from an arquebuse fired by one of Cosseins' people. But finally the conspirators broke through the door and mounted the stairway, Cosseins, Attin, Corberan de Cordillac, Seigneur de Sarlabous, first captains of the regiment of the guards, Achilles Petrucci of Sienna, all armed with cuirasses, and Besme the German, who had been brought up as a page in the house of Guise; for the duke of Guise was lodged at court, together with the great nobles and others who accompanied him.

After Coligny had said his prayers with Merlin the minister, he said without any appearance of alarm to those who were present, and almost all were surgeons, for few of them were of his retinue: "I see clearly that which they seek, and I am ready steadfastly to suffer that death which I have never feared and which for a long time past I have pictured to myself. I consider myself happy in feeling the approach of death and in being ready to die in God, by whose grace I hope for the life everlasting. I have no further need of human succor. Go then from this place, my friends, as quickly as you may, for fear lest you shall be involved in my misfortune, and that some day your wives shall curse me as the author of your loss. For me it is enough that God is here, to whose goodness I commend my soul, which is so soon to issue from my body." After these words they ascended to an upper room whence they sought safety in flight here and there upon the tiles.

Meanwhile the conspirators, having burst through the door of the chamber, entered, and when Besme, sword in hand, had demanded of Coligny, who stood near the door, "Are you Coligny?" Coligny replied, "Yes, I am he," with fearless countenance. "But you, young man, respect these white hairs. What is it you would do? You cannot shorten by many days this life of mine." As he spoke Besme gave him a sword thrust through the body, and having withdrawn his sword, another thrust in the mouth, by which his countenance was disfigured. So Coligny fell, killed with many thrusts. Others have written that Coligny in dying pronounced as though in anger these words: "Would that I at least might die at the hands of a soldier and not a valet." But Attin, one of the murderers, has reported as I have written, and added that he never saw anyone less afraid in so great a peril, nor die more steadfastly.

Then the duke of Guise inquired of Besme from the courtyard if the thing were done, and when Besme answered him that it was, the duke replied that the Chevalier d'Angoulême was unable to believe it unless he saw it; and at the same time that he made the inquiry they threw the body through the window into the courtyard, disfigured as it was with blood. When the Chevalier d'Angoulême, who could scarcely believe his eyes, had wiped away with a cloth the blood which overran the face and finally had recognized him, some say that he spurned the body with his foot. However this may be, when he left the house with his followers he said: "Cheer up, my friends! Let us do thoroughly that which we had begun. The king commands it." He frequently repeated these words and as soon as they had caused the palace clock to strike, on every side arose the cry "To arms," and the people ran to the house of Coligny. After his body had been insultingly treated in every way, they threw it into a neighboring stable and finally cut off his head, which they sent to Rome. They also cut off his privates and his hands and feet and dragged his body through the streets to the bank of the Seine, a thing which he had formerly almost prophesied, although he did not think of anything like this.

As the children were throwing the body into the river, it was dragged out and placed upon the gibbet of Montfaucon, where it hung by the feet in chains of iron; and then they built a fire beneath, by which he was burned without being consumed; so that he was, so to speak, tortured with all the elements, since he was killed upon the earth, thrown into the water, placed upon the fire, and finally put to hang in the air. After he had served for several days as a spectacle to gratify the hate of many and arouse the just indignation of many others, who reckoned that this fury of the people would cost the king and France many a sorrowful day, Francois de Montmorency, who was nearly related to the dead man, and still more his friend, and who moreover had escaped in time the danger, had him taken by night from the gibbet by trusty men and carried to Chantilly, where he was buried in the chapel.

[40] *THE EDICT OF NANTES RESTORES PEACE IN FRANCE* *

The wars of religion in France were terminated by the ascent to the throne in 1589 of the Huguenot Henry IV and his subsequent conversion to Catholicism in 1593.

* Sidney Ehler and John Morrall, eds., *Church and State Through the Centuries* (Westminster, Md.: The Newman Press, 1954), pp. 184–188. Used by permission of the publisher.

The Edict of Nantes was issued to calm the fears of the Huguenots and assure their political loyalty. Never before in European history had the principle of religious liberty been invoked on such a large scale.

Henry, by the grace of God King of France and of Navarre, to all present and future greeting.

Among the infinite graces which it pleased God to bestow upon us, one of the most significant and remarkable is that He gave us the strength and power not to succumb to terrifying troubles, confusions and disorders which existed at our accession to the kingdom, which was divided into so many parts and factions that the most just of them was in the minority; nevertheless He so strengthened us against this vexation that we finally overcame it and now have reached the harbour of salvation and repose of this State.—

Having truly and happily triumphed by the grace of God (in the civil war), and as arms and hostilities have been given up by all in the whole of the kingdom, we hope that there will be equal success in the other matters which remain to be settled therein, and that by this means we shall arrive at the establishment of a good peace and quiet repose, which has always been the goal of all our vows and intentions and the prize which we desire for the many trials and labours through which we have passed in the course of our life. . . .

. . . now that it has pleased God to begin to make us enjoy better quiet, we have judged that we could not employ it better than in attending to that which concerns the glory of His Holy Name and His service, and in ensuring that he can be worshipped and prayed to by all our subjects; and if it has not pleased Him yet to allow that there should be a single common religion, let there at least be a single intention, with an arrangement so that there is no more trouble or tumult between our subjects.

For these reasons, having well and carefully weighed and considered this whole problem with the advice of the princes of our blood, other princes and officers of the Crown, and other great and prominent persons of our Council of State being present with us,

We have by this perpetual and irrevocable Edict pronounced, declared, and ordained and we pronounce, declare and ordain: . . .

Art. II. We forbid all our subjects, of whatever rank and quality they may be, . . . to attack, be hostile to, injure or provoke each other in revenge for the past, whatever may be the reason and pretext; or to dispute, argue or quarrel about it, or to do violence, or to give offence in deed or word, but let them restrain themselves and live peaceably together as brothers, friends and fellow-citizens, on pain of being liable to punishment as disturbers of the peace and troublers of public quiet.

Art. III. We ordain that the Catholic, Apostolic and Roman religion shall be restored and re-established in all places and districts of this our kingdom and the countries under our rule, where its practice has been interrupted, so that it can be peacefully and freely practiced there, without any disturbance or hindrance. . . .

Art. VI. And in order not to leave any cause for discords and disputes between our subjects, we have permitted and we permit those of the so-called Reformed religion to live and dwell in all the towns and districts of this our kingdom and the countries under our rule, without being annoyed, disturbed, molested or constrained to do anything against their conscience, or for this cause to be sought out in their houses and districts where they wish to live, provided that they conduct themselves in other respects according to the provisions of our present Edict.—

Art. XXII. We ordain that there shall be no difference or distinction, because of the aforesaid religion, in the reception of students to be instructed in Universities, Colleges and schools, or of the sick and poor into hospitals, infirmaries and public charitable institutions.—

Art. XXVII. In order to reunite more effectively the wills of our subjects, as is our intention, and to remove all future complaints, we declare that all those who profess or shall profess the aforesaid so-called Reformed religion are capable of holding and exercising all public positions, honours, offices, and duties whatsoever, Royal, seigneurial, or offices in the towns of our kingdom, countries, lands and lordships subject to us, notwithstanding all contrary oaths, and of being admitted and received into them without distinction; it shall be sufficient for our courts of Parliament and other judges to ascertain and enquire concerning the life, morals, religion and honest behaviour of those who are or shall be appointed to offices, whether of one religion or the other, without exacting from them any oath other than that of well and faithfully serving the King in the exercise of their functions and keeping the ordinances, as has been perpetually the custom. . . .

Art. XCII. And for greater security of the behaviour and conduct which we expect with regard to it (sc. the Edict), we will, command and desire that all the Governors and Lieutenants-General of our provinces, Bailiffs, Seneschals and other ordinary judges in towns in our aforesaid kingdom, immediately after the reception of this Edict, swear to cause it to be kept and observed, each one in his own district; likewise the mayors, sheriffs, captains, consuls and magistrates of the towns, annual and perpetual. . . .

For such is our pleasure. As witness thereof we have signed the present enactment with our own hand, and in order that it may be sure and stable permanently, we have placed and affixed our Seal to it.

Given at Nantes in the month of April, in the year of grace 1598, the ninth year of our reign.

[41] *THE DUTCH DECLARE THEIR INDEPENDENCE FROM SPAIN, 1581* *

In what is often called the first declaration of independence on the part of a modern people, the seven predominantly Calvinist counties of the northern Netherlands formally renounced their allegiance to Spain in 1581. Although other issues were involved, the primary one was religion. Spain did not recognize Dutch independence and sporadic fighting continued until 1648 when the Treaty of Westphalia formally recognized Dutch freedom.

. . . it is apparent to all, that a prince is constituted by God to be ruler of a people, to defend them from oppression and violence, as the shepherd his sheep; and [that] God did not create the people slaves to their prince, to obey his commands, whether right or wrong, but rather the prince for the sake of the subjects (without which he could be no prince), to govern them according to equity, to love and support them as a father his children, or a shepherd his flock, and even at the hazard of life to defend and preserve them. And when he does not behave thus, but, on the contrary, oppresses them, seeking opportunities to infringe their ancient customs and privileges, exacting from them slavish compliance, then he is no longer a prince, but a tyrant, and the subjects are to consider him in no other view. And particularly when this is done deliberately, unauthorized by the States, they may not only disallow his authority, but legally proceed to the choice of another prince for their defence.

This is the only method left for subjects, whose humble petitions and remonstrances could never soften their prince, or dissuade him from his tyrannical proceedings; and this is what the law of nature dictates for the defence of liberty, which we ought to transmit to posterity, even at the hazard of our lives; and this we have seen done frequently in several countries, upon the like occasion, whereof there are notorious instances, and more justifiable, in our land, which has been always governed according to their ancient privileges, which are expressed in the oath taken by the prince at his admission to the government; for most of the Provinces receive their prince upon certain conditions, which he swears to maintain, which, if the prince violates, he is no longer sovereign. Now thus it was with the king of Spain [Philip II] after the demise of the emperor his father, Charles the Fifth, of glorious memory (of whom he received all these Provinces). . . .

Notwithstanding these discouragements, we used all possible means, by petitions in writing, and the good offices of the greatest princes in Christen-

* Hutton Webster, ed., *Historical Selections* (New York: D. C. Heath and Company, 1929), pp. 629–631. Used by permission of the publisher.

dom, to be reconciled to our king. . . . At last we found by experience that nothing would be obtained of the king by prayers and treaties, which latter he made use of to divide and weaken the Provinces, that he might the easier execute his plan rigorously, by subduing them one by one, which afterwards plainly appeared by certain proclamations and proscriptions published by the king's orders, by virtue of which we and all officers and inhabitants of the United Provinces, with all our friends, are declared rebels, and as such, to have forfeited our lives and estates; thus, by rendering us odious to all, he might interrupt our commerce, likewise reducing us to dispair, offering a great sum to any that would assassinate the Prince of Orange. So having no hope of reconciliation, and finding no other remedy, we have, agreeable to the law of nature, in our own defence, and for maintaining the rights, privileges, and liberties of our countrymen, wives, and children, and latest posterity, from being enslaved by the Spaniards, been constrained to renounce allegiance to the king of Spain, and pursue such methods as appear to us most likely to secure our ancient liberties and privileges.

Know all men by these presents, that, being reduced to the last extremity, as above-mentioned, we have unanimously and deliberately declared, and do by these presents declare, that the King of Spain has forfeited, *ipso jure,* all hereditary right to the sovereignty of those countries, and are determined from henceforward not to acknowledge his sovereignty or jurisdiction, nor any act of his relating to the domains of the Low Countries, nor make use of his name as prince, nor suffer others to do it. In consequence whereof we also declare all officers, judges, lords, gentlemen, vassals, and all other the inhabitants of this country of what condition or quality soever, to be henceforth discharged from all oaths and obligations whatsoever made to the king of Spain, as sovereign of those countries.

[42] *PHILIP II SENDS THE ARMADA AGAINST THE ENGLISH HERETICS, 1588* *

Philip II of Spain, painfully aware of the help that England was giving the Dutch rebels and the French Huguenots and incensed by the constant English raids on Spanish shipping, determined to invade the island kingdom. His expedition was the most massive naval assemblage ever collected up to that time. The following narrative is by a young English courtier, Robert Carey.

The next yeare the king of Spain's great Armado came upon our coast,

* Edward P. Cheyney, *Readings in English History* (New York: Ginn and Company, 1908), pp. 406–408. Used by permission of the publisher.

thinking to devour us all. Upon the newes sent to court from Plimouth of their certain arrivall, my Lord Cumberland and myselfe tooke post horse, and rode streight to Portsmouth, where we found a frigot that carried us to sea; and having sought for the fleets a whole day, the night after wee fell amongst them: where it was our fortune to light first on the Spanish fleet; and finding ourselves in the wrong, we tackt about, and in short time gott to our own fleet, which was not farre from the other. At our coming aboord our Admirall, wee stay'd there awhile; but finding the ship much pestered and scant of cabins, we left the Admirall and went aboord Captain Reyman, where wee stay'd and were very welcome, and much made of.

It was on Thursday that wee came to the fleet. All that day wee followed close the Spanish Armado, and nothing was attempted on either side: the same course wee held all Friday and Saturday, by which time the Spanish fleet cast anchor just before Calais. We likewise did the same, a very small distance behind them, and so continued till Munday morning about two of the clocke; in which time our counsaile of warre had provided six old hulkes and stuffed them full of all combustible matter fitt for burning, and on Monday at two in the morning they were lett loose, with each of them a man in her to direct them. The tide serving they brought them very near the Spanish fleet, so that they could not misse to come amongst the midest of them; then they set fire on them, and came off themselves, having each of them a little boate to bring him off. The ships set on fire, came so directly to the Spanish fleet, as they had no way to avoid them, but to cut all their halsers, and so escape; and their haste was such that they left one of their four great galeasses on ground before Calais, which our men took and had the spoil of, where many of the Spaniards were slaine with the governour thereof, but most of them were saved with wading ashore to Calais.

They being in this disorder, wee made ready to follow them, where began a cruell fight, and wee had such advantage both of wind and tide as wee had a glorious day of them; continuing fight from foure o'clocke in the morning, till almost five or six at night, where they lost a douzen or fourteene of their best shippes, some sunke, and the rest ranne ashore in diverse parts to keep themselves from sinking. After God had given us this great victory, they made all the hast they could away, and wee followed them Tuesday and Wednesday, by which time they were gotten as farre as Flamboroughhead. It was resolved on Wednesday at night, that by four o'clocke on Thursday, wee should have a new fight with them for a farewell; but by two in the morning, there was a flagge of counsaile hung out in our Vice-Admirall, when it was found that in the whole fleet there was not munition sufficient to make halfe a fight; and therefore it was concluded that we should let them passe, and our fleet to return to the Downes. That night wee parted with them, wee had a mighty storme. Our fleet cast anchor, and endured it; but the Spanish fleet, wanting their anchors, were many of them cast ashore on the west of Ireland, where they had all their throates cutt by the kernes; and some of them on Scotland, where they were no better used; and the rest (with much adoe) gott into Spaine againe. Thus did God blesse us, and gave victory over this invincible navy; the sea calmed, and all our shippes came to the Downes on Friday in safety.

On Saturday my lord of Cumberland and myselfe came on shore, and took post horse and found the queene in her army at Tilbury campe, where I fell sick of a burning fever and was carried in a litter to London.

[43] *A DEFENESTRATION AT PRAGUE TOUCHES OFF THE THIRTY YEARS' WAR* *

On May 23, 1618, certain rabid Bohemian Protestants led by Count Matthias of Thurn showed their determination to maintain their religious and political independence by throwing two imperial governors out of a palace window. The scene is described by a modern historian, C. V. Wedgwood.

Thurn called a meeting of Protestant officials and deputies from all over Bohemia and appealed for the release of the prisoners. When this demonstration proved useless, he urged . . . a yet larger assembly of Protestants. This second meeting was fixed for May 1618; it was now March. In the intervening time both parties set themselves to work up the feelings of the people and of the townsfolk of Prague in particular. In spite of Catholic propaganda the Protestant meeting assembled on May 21st, a formidable gathering of noblemen, gentry and burghers from all over the province. The imperial governors in vain commanded them to dissolve. Only then did Slavata and Martinitz grasp the danger in which they stood, and on the evening of the 22nd a secretary of state escaped in disguise towards Vienna to implore immediate help.

It was too late. That very night Thurn called on the leading nobility to form a plan of action. . . . He demanded death for Slavata and Martinitz and the establishment of a Protestant emergency government. The city was already alive with excitement and when on the following morning the Protestant deputies were seen making their way towards the royal castle of the Hradschin an immense crowd followed in their wake. Through the

* C. V. Wedgwood, *The Thirty Years' War* (New Haven, Conn.: Yale University Press, 1949), pp. 78–80. Used by permission of Jonathan Cape Limited, London, copyright holder.

portals surmounted by the outspread eagle of the Hapsburg they surged into the courtyard; up the staircase the deputies led the way, through the audience hall and into the small room where the governors sat. Trapped between the council table and the wall, the crowd before and the blank stones behind, Slavata and Martinitz stood at bay. Neither doubted that his last hour had come.

A hundred hands dragged them towards the high window, flung back the casement and hoisted them upwards. Martinitz went first. "Jesu Maria! Help!" he screamed and crashed over the sill. Slavata fought longer, calling on the Blessed Virgin and clawing at the window frame under a rain of blows until someone knocked him senseless and the bleeding hands relaxed. Their shivering secretary clung to Schlick for protection; out of sheer intoxication the crowd hoisted him up and sent him to join his masters.

One of the rebels leant over the ledge, jeering: "We will see if your Mary can help you!" A second later, between exasperation and amazement, "By God, his Mary has helped," he exclaimed, for Martinitz was already stirring. Suddenly a ladder protruded from a neighbouring window; Martinitz and the secretary made for it under a hail of misdirected missiles. Some of Slavata's servants, braving the mob, went down to his help and carried him after the others, unconscious but alive.

The extraordinary chance which had saved three lives was a holy miracle or a comic accident according to the religion of the beholder, but it had no political significance. Martinitz fled that night in disguise and Slavata continued, ill and a prisoner, in the house whither he had been carried. That evening his wife knelt before the Countess Thurn entreating some guarantee for her husband's life, a request which the lady granted with the pessimistic stipulation that the Countess Slavata should do her a like service after the next Bohemian revolution.

Murder or no murder, the *coup d'état* was complete, and since Thurn had overruled many of his supporters in demanding death it was as well for the conscience of his allies that a pile of mouldering filth in the courtyard of the Hradschin had made soft falling for the governors.

[44] *WESTPHALIA ACHIEVES A COMPROMISE SETTLEMENT OF THE RELIGIOUS ISSUES* *

The religious clauses of the Peace of Westphalia are to be found in the Treaty of Osnabrueck (Oct. 24, 1648), one of the treaties which make up the Peace of

* Sidney Ehler and John Morrall, eds. *Church and State Through the Centuries* (Westminster, Md.: The Newman Press, 1954), pp. 190–192. Used by permission of the publisher.

Westphalia. Reflected therein is a clear awareness that neither side could hope to achieve a decisive victory. The settlement is noteworthy for its spirit of political expediency—which explains the Pope's subsequent condemnation of the treaty.

Art. V, sec. 1. The arrangement initiated at Passau in 1552 and the religious peace confirming it in 1555, as also those things agreed upon at Augsburg in 1566 and afterwards in various general assemblies of the Holy Roman Empire, have been confirmed in all their details by the unanimous consent of the Emperor, Electors, Princes and Estates of each religion; they are to be considered as being ratified from beginning to end and are to be observed in a faithful and inviolable manner. Therefore those things which have been decreed by this common agreement of the parties on certain disputed articles of the previously mentioned arrangements shall be observed in legal and other matters, until by God's grace unity shall be reached in religion; (this agreement shall apply) notwithstanding gainsaying or protest put forward by any authority whatever, ecclesiastical or political, inside or outside the Empire at any time; all such protests are proclaimed to be null and void by virtue of the present statement. In all other matters there shall be exact and mutual equality among all the Electors, Princes and Estates of each religion, as far as is conformable to the interests of the commonwealth, the constitutions of the Empire and the present agreement, so that what is just for one party shall also be just for the other; and all violence and physical force in these as in other matters shall be perpetually forbidden for either side.

Art. V, sec. 2. The point from which should be commenced the restitution of ecclesiastical possessions and the reversal of any political changes which have been made in their regard shall be the first day of January, 1624.

Art. V, sec. 14. As for ecclesiastical possessions, whether they be Archbishoprics, Bishoprics, Prelacies, Abbeys, Bailiwicks, Provostships, Commanderies, or free secular foundations, or any others, with the revenues, rents and all other things of whatever description, situated inside or outside the towns; the Catholic Estates or those following the Augsburg Confession, whichever possessed them on the first day of January, 1624, shall possess them entirely, unreservedly, peacefully and without disturbance, until a settlement is reached (which may it be God's Will to bring about) over the conflicts concerning religion; and it shall not be lawful for either of the parties to disturb the other judicially or by any other means, nor cause it any trouble or annoyance. And in the event that it may not be possible to settle amicably the religious differences (which may it not be God's Will to allow), the present agreement shall serve as a permanent law and the Peace shall have perpetual validity.

Art. V, sec. 34. It has also been decided that those adherents to the Confession of Augsburg who are subjects of Catholics, as also Catholics who are subjects of Estates of the Confession of Augsburg, who did not enjoy before 1624 at any time the public or private practice of their religion, or who after the publication of peace at any time in the future shall profess and embrace a different religion from the lord of their territory, shall be allowed patiently and with a free conscience to frequent privately their place of worship without being subjected to enquiry or disturbed; and they shall not be prevented from taking part in the public exercise of their religion in their neighbourhood. . . . or to send their children for education in schools belonging to their religion or to private tutors at home.

Art. V, sec. 48. Let diocesan law and all ecclesiastical jurisdiction in all its forms directed against the Electors, Princes, Estates (including the free nobility of the Empire) and subjects espousing the Confession of Augsburg be suspended pending the Christian settlement of the religious differences both between the Catholics and the followers of the Confession of Augsburg and also between the Estates themselves of the Confession of Augsburg, and let diocesan law and ecclesiastical jurisdiction limit themselves to the boundaries of their own territory.

Art. VII, sec. 1 and 2. By the unanimous consent of His Imperial Majesty and of all the Estates of the Empire, it has been found good that the same right or privilege which all the other Imperial constitutions, the religious peace, the present public treaty, and the settlement of grievances contained therein, accord to Catholic Estates and subjects and to those of the Confession of Augsburg, be also accorded to those who call themselves the Reformed; . . . And since the differences of religion between the Protestants have not been ended so far, being reserved for a future settlement, and since for this reason they form two parties, it has been accordingly agreed between both parties with regard to the law of the Reformation that if any prince or any lord of territory, or patron of any church, would pass hereafter to the religion of another party, or if he should have acquired or recovered by right of succession, or by virtue of the present treaty, or by any other title, a principality or lordship where the religion of another party is at present professed publicly, he shall be permitted without hindrance to have near him and in his residence special preachers of his own confession for his court; this, however, shall not be at the expense and to the prejudice of his subjects. But it shall not be lawful for him to change the religion officially practised or the ecclesiastical laws or constitutions which were in force previously, or to take away from this religion their temples, schools, hospitals, or the revenues, pensions and salaries thereof and grant them to the members of his own religion; still less to compel his subjects to receive as ministers those of another religion under pretext . . .

II

Absolutism and Revolution (1648-1815)

After waging religious warfare for a century or more, European monarchs turned to a more constructive task, the systematic and rational modernization of their states. The domestic policies of the European states in the seventeenth and eighteenth centuries were strikingly similar. From the steppes of Russia to the shores of Normandy the aim of the monarchs was to sweep away the accumulated clutter of the feudal past and to create modern armies, tax-collecting bureaucracies, and administrative systems answerable to their will. In modern parlance, the monarchs were bent upon streamlining their states.

The main obstacle was the nobles, who since the end of the Middle Ages had consistently resisted the centralist policies of the national monarchs. They did so with good reason, since any movement to centralize inevitably reduced their traditional control over local affairs. The ancient rivalry between kings and nobles now entered a new and decisive stage. The monarchs could usually count on the support of the bourgeoisie—the men of commerce, of productive enterprise, and of the professions—who by the eighteenth century had grown greatly in numbers and in strength. The bourgeoisie generally identified the cause of centralization and reform with their own, since a semi-feudal state was not the type of political organization best suited to the needs of the business community. Bourgeois support of the monarch rested on self-interest, not veneration of royal institutions. It was largely a matter of what the bourgeosie disliked the most, royal absolutism or aristocratic control. Since they came into daily contact with the often rapacious nobility and felt the weight of the Crown much less, the bourgeoisie inclined to the latter.

In central and eastern Europe, where a flourishing middle class had not yet come into prominence, the monarchs carried on their conflict with the aristocracy without the help of the bourgeoisie. Peter the Great, for example, in his bloody encounters with the Muscovite nobility, neither sought nor received help from whatever middle class existed in Moscow. He relied instead on his army and loyal nobles. In Prussia, the bourgeoisie were subordinated to the Crown, just as effectively as the nobility. An alliance with the commoners against the Junkers was never attractive to the Hohenzollern rulers of Prussia.

As the model of the modern, centralized, secular state, rulers in the seventeenth and early eighteenth centuries were nearly unanimous in their choice of Louis XIV's France. Rarely has a country been so honored by its imitators. Even rulers who found themselves repeatedly at odds with the aggressive foreign policy of the *Roi Soleil* could not help but admire and emulate his well-ordered and relatively rational government. What could be more attractive to a foreign ruler than Bossuet's dictum that all power and authority resided in the king and that he was responsible to God alone for the conduct of the state? Louis' well-equipped and disciplined army, his rational codes of law, his loyal bureaucracy staffed by men of bourgeois origin, his control of national economic activity, all these and much more were the envy of his fellow-monarchs. One admiring ruler, the elector of Brandenburg, intent upon following the example of Louis XIV's court, took an official mistress in the manner of the Sun King despite the fact he was happily married and entirely faithful to his wife.

The attack on the old feudal order by monarchs such as Louis XIV was only a preliminary to a much broader attack by the intellectuals of the eighteenth century, the *philosophes*. These men, inspired by the achievements of the physical scientists of the preceding century and using what they construed to be their methodology, confidently turned to the total rationalization of society—politics, education, laws, economics, religion, *et. al.* By the use of reason, the *philosophes* were convinced they could establish the same kind of order in the world of man that Newton had established in the physical universe. The result would be an earthly Utopia. "Happiness is a new idea in Europe," exulted one representative of the new school.

The political embodiment of the Age of Reason was Enlightened Despotism, represented by such rulers as Frederick the Great of Prussia, Joseph II of Austria, and Catherine II of Russia. In actuality, the Enlightened Despots were no whit different from the divine-right absolutists of the previous century. Their aims were precisely the same: unification, centralization, rationalization. By subscribing to the fashionable beliefs of the intellectuals and loftily proclaiming themselves the "servants of the state," the Enlightened Despots earned new support among their subjects and thereby made their task less difficult. However, the times were against the concept of enlightened despotism. Influenced by the Glorious Revolution of 1688 and the libertarian thought of the Age of Reason, Europeans concluded that they wanted an end to absolutism, enlightened or otherwise. The most "advanced" state for such thinking was France. Here in 1789 broke out a revolution of the bourgeoisie, backed by the peasants, against the feudal aristocracy. Louis XVI, forgetting the historic association of monarchy and bourgeoisie in French history, impelled by a combination of sentiment and fear, cast his lot with the utterly discredited nobility. As a consequence, three years later he lost his throne and shortly thereafter his head. The era of liberal and democratic revolution had begun in Europe.

8

The Age of Louis XIV

Louis XIV's reign began at an auspicious moment in the history of France. For the first time in a century and a half, thanks largely to Richelieu, the monarchy could feel secure against both internal and foreign foes: feudal nobility, Huguenots, and Hapsburgs. Young Louis XIV recognized his opportunity. With Colbert, he launched an era of reform without equal in the history of the Old Regime. Unfortunately, the King's mounting devotion to military glory and conquest terminated his ambitious plans for internal reform. The latter part of the reign is a depressing chronicle of wars, religious fanaticism, and economic woes.

[45] *LOUIS XIV REVIEWS THE FUNCTIONS OF A MONARCH* *

Early in his reign Louis XIV began to write memoirs for the future instruction of his son. The following was probably written in 1666. In describing himself as a hard-working, reform-minded monarch, he was telling no more than the truth. Note the obvious pleasure he derives from ruling.

* *A King's Lessons in Statecraft: Louis XIV*, trans. by Herbert Wilson (New York: Albert and Charles Boni, 1925), pp. 48–50. Used by permission of Routledge & Kegan Paul Ltd., London.

Two things without doubt were absolutely necessary: very hard work on my part, and a wise choice of persons capable of seconding it.

As for work, it may be, my son, that you will begin to read these Memoirs at an age when one is far more in the habit of dreading than loving it, only too happy to have escaped subjection to tutors and to have your hours regulated no longer, nor lengthy and prescribed study laid down for you.

. . . it is . . . toil *by which* one reigns, and *for which* one reigns. . . .

I laid a rule on myself to work regularly twice every day, and for two or three hours each time with different persons, without counting the hours which I passed privately and alone, nor the time which I was able to give on particular occasions to any special affairs that might arise. There was no moment when I did not permit people to talk to me about them, provided that they were urgent; with the exception of foreign ministers who sometimes find too favourable moments in the familiarity allowed to them, either to obtain or to discover something, and whom one should not hear without being previously prepared.

I cannot tell you what fruit I gathered immediately I had taken this resolution. I felt myself, as it were, uplifted in thought and courage; I found myself quite another man, and with joy reproached myself for having been too long unaware of it. This first timidity, which a little self-judgment always produces and which at the beginning gave me pain, especially on occasions when I had to speak in public, disappeared in less than no time. The only thing I felt then was that I was King, and born to be one. I experienced next a delicious feeling, hard to express, and which you will not know yourself except by tasting it as I have done. For you must not imagine, my son, that the affairs of State are like some obscure and thorny path of learning which may possibly have already wearied you, wherein the mind strives to raise itself with effort above its purview, more often to arrive at no conclusion, and whose utility or apparent utility is repugnant to us as much as its difficulty. The function of Kings consists principally in allowing good sense to act, which always acts naturally and without effort. What we apply ourselves to is sometimes less difficult than what we do only for our amusement. Its usefulness always follows. A King, however skilful and enlightened be his ministers, cannot put his own hand to the work without its effect being seen. Success, which is agreeable in everything, even in the smallest matters, gratifies us in these as well as in the greatest, and there is no satisfaction to equal that of noting every day some progress in glorious and lofty enterprises, and in the happiness of the people which has been planned and thought out by oneself. All that is most necessary to this work is at the same time agreeable; for, in a word, my son, it is to have one's eyes open to the whole earth; to learn each hour the news concerning every province and every nation, the secrets of every court, the mood and the weaknesses of each Prince and of every foreign minister; to be well-informed on an infinite number of matters about which we are supposed to know nothing; to elicit from our subjects what they hide from us with the greatest care; to discover the most remote opinions of our own courtiers and the most hidden interests of those who come to us with quite contrary professions. I do not know of any other pleasure we would not renounce for that, even if curiosity alone gave us the opportunity. . . .

[46] *SAINT-SIMON DESCRIBES THE SUN KING* *

One of Europe's greatest memoirists was the Duke of Saint-Simon. For thirty years he recorded the detailed "inside story" of the reigns of Louis XIV and Louis XV. His memoirs are of great historical value but must be used with caution since the author is consistently hostile to Louis XIV. Among other things, Saint-Simon, a member of the old aristocracy, would not forgive the King for choosing his ministers from the bourgeoisie.

At eight o'clock the chief *valet de chambre* on duty, who alone had slept in the royal chamber, and who had dressed himself, awoke the King. The chief physician, the chief surgeon, and the nurse (as long as she lived), entered at the same time. The latter kissed the King; the others rubbed and changed his shirt, because he was in the habit of sweating a great deal. At the quarter, the grand chamberlain was called (or, in his absence, the first gentleman of the chamber), and those who had what was called the *grandes entrées*. The chamberlain (or chief gentleman) drew back the curtains which had been closed again, and presented the holy water from the vase, at the head of the bed. These gentlemen stayed but a moment, and that was the time to speak to the King, if anvone had anything to ask of him; in which case the rest stood aside. . . . Then all passed into the cabinet of the council. A very short religious service being over, the King called, they re-entered. The same officer gave him his dressing gown; immediately after, other priviliged courtiers entered, and then everybody, in time to find the King putting on his shoes and stockings, for he did almost everything himself and with address and grace. Every other day we saw the King shave himself; and he had a little short wig in which he always appeared, even in bed, and on medicine days. He often spoke of the chase, and sometimes said

* Saint-Simon, *Memoirs of Louis XIV and the Regency*, trans. by Bayle St. John (New York: M. Walter Dunne, 1901), Vol. III, pp. 30–37; *Memoirs of the Duke of Saint-Simon on the Reign of Louis XIV and the Regency*, trans. by Bayle St. John (London: Chatto and Windus, 1876), Vol. II, pp. 367–369.

a word to somebody. No toilet table was near him; he had simply a mirror held before him.

As soon as he was dressed, he prayed to God, at the side of his bed, where all the clergy present knelt, the cardinals without cushions, all the laity remaining standing; and the captain of the guards came to the balustrade during the prayer, after which the King passed into his cabinet.

He found there, or was followed by all who had the *entrée,* a very numerous company, for it included everybody in any office. He gave orders to each for the day; thus within a half a quarter of an hour it was known what he meant to do; and then all this crowd left directly. The bastards, a few favorites, and the valets alone were left. It was then a good opportunity for talking with the King; for example, about plans of gardens and buildings; and conversation lasted more or less according to the person engaged in it. . . .

The King went to mass, where his musicians always sang an anthem. . . . During the mass the ministers assembled in the King's chamber where distinguished people could go and speak or chat with them. The King amused himself a little upon returning from mass and asked almost immediately for the Council. Then the morning was finished. . . .

The dinner was always *au petit couvert,* that is, the King ate by himself in his chamber upon a square table in front of the middle window. It was more or less abundant, for he ordered in the morning whether it was to be "a little," or "very little" service. . . .

Upon leaving the table the King immediately entered his cabinet. That was the time for distinguished people to speak to him. He stopped at the door a moment to listen, then entered; very rarely did anyone follow him, never without asking him for permission to do so; and for this few had the courage. If followed he placed himself in the embrasure of the window nearest to the door of the cabinet, which immediately closed of itself, and which you were obliged to open yourself on quitting the King. This also was the time for the bastards and the valets.

The King amused himself by feeding his dogs, and remained with them more or less time, then asked for his wardrobe, changed before the very few distinguished people it pleased the first gentleman of the chamber to admit there, and immediately went out by the back stairs into the court of marble to get into his coach. . . .

The King was fond of air, and when deprived of it his health suffered; he had headaches and vapors caused by the undue use he had formerly made of perfumes, so that for many years he could not endure any, except the odor of orange flowers; therefore if you had to approach anywhere near him you did well not to carry them.

As he was but little sensitive to heat or cold, or even rain, the weather was seldom sufficiently bad to prevent his going abroad. He went out for three objects: stag hunting, once or more each week; shooting in his parks (and no man handled a gun with more grace and skill), once or twice each week; and walking in his gardens for exercise, and to see his workmen. Sometimes he made picnics with ladies in the forest at Marly or at Fontainebleau, and in this last place, promenades with all the Court around the canal, which was a magnificent spectacle. . . .

Upon returning home from walks or drives, anybody, as I have said, might speak to the King from the moment he left his coach till he reached the foot of his staircase. He changed his dress again, and rested in his cabinet an hour or more, then went to Madame de Maintenon's and on the way anyone who wished might speak to him.

At ten o'clock his supper was served. . . . This supper was always on a grand scale. . . .

After supper the King stood some moments, his back to the balustrade of the foot of his bed, encircled by all his Court; then, with bows to the ladies, passed into his cabinet, where on arriving, he gave his orders. He passed a little less than an hour there, seated in an armchair, with his legitimate children and bastards, his grandchildren, legitimate and otherwise, and their husbands or wives. . . .

The King, wishing to retire, went and fed his dogs; then said good night, passed into his chamber to the *ruelle* of his bed, where he said his prayers, as in the morning, then undressed. He said good night with an inclination of the head, and while everybody was leaving the room stood at the corner of the mantlepiece, where he gave the order to the colonel of the guards alone. Then commenced what was called the *petit coucher,* at which only the specially privileged remained. That was short. They did not leave until he got into bed. It was a moment to speak to him. . . .

On medicine days, which occurred about once a month, the King remained in bed, then heard mass. The royal household came to see him for a moment, and Madame de Maintenon seated herself in the airmchair at the head of his bed. The King dined in bed about three o'clock, everybody being allowed to enter the room, then rose, and the privileged alone remained. . . .

Never did man give with better grace than Louis XIV, or augmented so much, in this way, the price of his benefits. Never did man sell to better profit his words, even his smiles,—nay, his looks. Never did disobliging words escape him; and if he had to blame, to reprimand, or correct, which was very rare, it was nearly always with goodness, never, except on one occasion . . . , with anger or severity. Never was man so naturally polite, or of a politeness so measured, so graduated, so adapted to person, time, and place. Towards women his politeness was without parallel. Never did he pass the humblest petticoat without raising his hat; even to chambermaids, that he knew to be such, as often happened at Marly. For ladies he took his hat off completely, but to a greater or less extent; for titled people half off, holding it in his hand or against his ear some instants, more or less marked. For the nobility he contented himself by putting his hand to his hat. He took it off for the princes of the blood, as for the ladies. If he accosted ladies he did not cover himself until he had quitted them. All this was out of doors, for in the house he was never covered. His reverences, more or less marked, but always light, were incomparable for their grace and manner; even his mode of half raising himself at supper for each lady who arrived at table. Though at last this fatigued him, yet he never ceased it; the ladies who were to sit down, however, took care not to enter after supper had commenced.

If he was made to wait for anything while dressing, it was always with patience. He was exact to the hours that he gave for all his day, with a precision clear and brief in his orders. If in the bad weather of winter, when he could not go out, he went to Madame de Maintenon's a quarter of an hour earlier than he had arranged (which seldom happened), and the captain of the guards was not on duty, he did not fail afterwards to say that it was his own fault for anticipating the hour, not that of the captain of the guards for being absent. Thus, with this regularity which he never deviated from, he was served with the utmost exactitude.

The King loved air and exercise very much, as long as he could make use of them. He had excelled in dancing, and at tennis and mall. On horseback he was admirable, even at a late age. He liked to see everything done with grace and address. To acquit yourself well or ill before him was a merit or a fault. He said that with things not necessary it was best not to meddle, unless they were done well. He was very fond of shooting, and there was not a better or more graceful shot than he. He had always in his cabinet seven or eight pointer bitches, and was fond of feeding them, to make himself known to them. He was very fond, too, of stag hunting; but in a *calèche,* since he broke his arm, while hunting at Fontainebleau, immediately after the death of the Queen. He rode alone in a species of "box," drawn by four little horses—with five or six relays, and drove himself with an address and accuracy unknown to the best coachmen. His postillions were children from ten to fifteen years of age, and he directed them.

He liked splendour, magnificence, and profusion in everything: you pleased him if you shone through the brilliancy of your houses, your clothes, your table, your equipages. Thus a taste for extravagance and luxury was disseminated through all classes of society; causing infinite harm, and leading to general confusion of rank and to ruin.

As for the King himself, nobody ever approached his magnificence. His buildings, who could number them? At the same time, who was there who did not deplore the pride, the caprice, the bad taste seen in them? He built nothing useful or ornamental in Paris, except the Pont Royal, and that simply by necessity; so that despite its incomparable extent, Paris is inferior to many cities of Europe. St. Germain, a lovely spot, with a marvellous view, rich forest, terraces, gardens, and water he abandoned for Versailles; the dullest and most ungrateful of all places, without prospect, without wood, without water, without soil; for the ground is all shifting sand or swamp, the air accordingly bad. But he liked to subjugate nature by art and treasure. He built at Versailles, on, on, without any general design, the beautiful and the ugly, the vast and the mean, all jumbled together. . . .

[47] *COLBERT REGULATES INDUSTRY AND SCOLDS BUSINESSMEN* *

An essential feature of the mercantilism which Colbert symbolized was the minute regulation of private industry, the principal aim being to raise production standards and thereby increase the demand for French goods abroad. In 1669 a sort of master code was drawn up for the textile industry. Suspecting that manufacturers were not paying much attention to the code, Colbert in 1670 created inspectors to enforce the law, as we read in the first selection below. The second selection illustrates Colbert's hostile attitude towards businessmen.

[A] Ordinance of 1670 Creating Textile Inspectors

TO THE INTENDANTS: The King, desiring to remedy the abuses which are committed in the . . . manufactures of France . . . had the goodness to have drawn up general regulations and to have them registered in his presence in his *parlement* of Paris, August 13, 1669. His Majesty has resolved to send inspectors into all the provinces of his kingdom . . . to inform the judges, the merchants, and the workers of his wishes. . . . That is why, on the express order of His Majesty, we have prepared the following directive. . . . Signed, Colbert.

1. The said inspector shall report to Monsieur ——, [intendant] of His Majesty. . . .

2. The said inspector, having received his orders from the intendant, will betake himself immediately to the nearest manufacturing center and con-

* [A] *Lettres, Instructions, et Mémoires de Colbert,* edited by Pierre Clément (Paris: Imprimerie Impériale, 1863), Vol. II, pp. 832–837. Our translation. [B] Charles W. Cole, *Colbert and a Century of French Mercantilism* (New York: Columbia University Press, 1939), Vol. I, pp. 334–335.

sult with the mayor and aldermen; . . . he will ascertain from them if the regulation for manufactures . . . has been registered and published. . . .

3. There will be established a community room in the City Hall . . . where the examiners can see, inspect, and mark the merchandise which will be taken there at set times by the cloth-workers, where they can settle on the spot disputes which might develop because of defects in the said manufactures and instil fear [of the laws] in the minds of the said cloth-workers. . . . And since the merchants have a particular knowledge of the good quality or defects of merchandise, and since it is in their interest that the merchandise be perfect, it will also be necessary that the aldermen elect one of the more prominent merchants to be present at the said inspections and markings. . . .

11. The said inspector will assemble all the . . . [guild] masters in the community room, and will read the said regulation to them [the general regulation concerning textile manufacture of 1669], explaining to them article by article what they must do to carry it out properly, and informing them that if they contravene it that their ruin will surely follow, because their goods will be confiscated and the selvedges torn to bits [causing the cloth to unravel]. . . . Do not neglect to inform [the masters] that the goods of the same name, kind, and quality must be uniform throughout the kingdom in length, width, and strength. . . .

18. The said inspector will inform himself . . . of all the important fairs which will be held in his department and will betake himself there . . . to inspect the said merchandise, to see whether it has been marked at the place of manufacture and meets the quality called for by the regulation; if not, to seize and confiscate it and tear the selvedge publicly on the spot. . . . But as it is very important not to disturb the fairs . . . this must be carried out with much prudence . . . on the days and hours most convenient to the sellers and buyers. . . .

27. The said inspectors will give the greatest encouragement to all the masters and cloth-workers . . . to make their cloth the most perfect possible in order to strengthen the commerce and manufactures of France and to outstrip foreign competitors. . . .

[B] Extracts from Colbert's Correspondence

For a long time I have been convinced that you only have to let the merchants know that you want to do something to help them, to have them dislike it. . . .

Especially, I beg you to be on guard against the advice you will get from merchants because you well know that they always consult only their individual interests without examining what would be for the public good and the advantage of commerce in general. . . .

Merchants . . . nearly always understand merely their own little commerce and not the great forces which make commerce go. . . .

The merchants of Marseilles . . . are folk who live only from day to day and see only the small profit that they can make immediately. . . .

There are no greater enemies of general commerce and of the order which should be established than the merchants of Marseilles. . . . The little merchants of Marseilles, not believing that there is any commerce other than that which passes through their shops, would willingly overturn all general commerce in the hope of a little immediate profit, which would ruin them in the end. . . .

It will be necessary for you to act with care because all merchants as a rule wish to have complete liberty in all that has to do with their trade, and particularly in manufactures of which they wish always to change and reduce the lengths, widths, and qualities for considerations of some small profit that they make, and which tends to the ruin of manufactures, of which the principle consists, in a state as flourishing and as great as this, in making them always equal in length, width, and goodness. To attain this degree of fidelity, it is necessary to go entirely beyond the motives of little individual interests, which do not deserve consideration in connection with the general motives of the good of the state.

[48] *LOUIS XIV DEALS WITH GALLICANS, PROTESTANTS, AND JANSENISTS* *

Like all absolute monarchs, Louis XIV aimed at religious uniformity submissive to his authority. His religious policy has three facets: the limitation of the practical authority of the Papacy in France; the elimination of the French Protestants (Huguenots); and the repression of the mildly heretical sect known as the Jansenists. The following selections illustrate each of these in turn.

[A] The Gallican Articles, 1682

Many are endeavouring to subvert the decrees of the Gallican Church

* [A] and [B] Sidney Ehler and John Morrall, eds., *Church and State Through the Centuries* (Westminster, Md.: The Newman Press, 1954), pp. 207–208, 211–213; [C] *Pascal's Pensées,* Everyman's Library Edition with an introduction by T. S. Eliot (New York: E. P. Dutton and Co., Inc., 1958), pp. 60, 61, 66–67, 146, 153, 162, 198. Used by permission.

and the liberties for which our forefathers fought with such zeal, and their foundations based on the holy Canons and the tradition of the Fathers; nor are those people absent who, in the pretended defence of these liberties do not lack the daring to assault the primacy conferred by Christ on blessed Peter and his successors, the Roman Pontiffs, and the obedience owed to them by all Christians, and the Majesty of the Apostolic See, by which the Faith is taught and the unity of the Church is preserved and revered by all the nations. The heretics also leave nothing undone to show that this authority, which preserves the peace of the Church, is hostile and oppressive to kings and peoples and they detach simple minds by such trickery from Mother Church and from the visible communion of Christ. In order that we may repulse such undesirable notions, we, the archbishops and bishops gathered in Paris by royal command, representing the Gallican Church, together with other churchmen deputed to be with us, have given exhaustive consideration to the matter and have decided that the following articles should be promulgated and declared:

1. Power has been conferred by God on blessed Peter and his successors, Vicars of Christ Himself, a power over the spiritual things of the Church and those which pertain to eternal salvation, but not over civil and temporal matters. For the Lord Himself said: "My kingdom is not of this world," and again: "Render therefore to Caesar the things that are Caesar's and to God the things that are God's." The Apostle also states his opinion as follows: "Let every soul be subject to higher powers, for there is no power but from God, and those that are ordained by God. Therefore he that resisteth the power resisteth the ordinance of God." Consequently kings and princes are not subjected by the ordinance of God to any ecclesiastical authority in temporal affairs; nor by the authority of the keys of the Church can they be deposed, directly or indirectly, nor can their subjects be dispensed from loyalty and obedience or absolved from the oath of fidelity which they have taken. This judgment is to be universally held as necessary to public quietness, useful to the Church as well as to secular authority and agreeable to the word of God, the tradition of the Fathers, and the examples of the Saints.

2. Full authority in spiritual matters is, however, inherent in the Apostolic See and the successors of Peter the Vicar of Christ, while at the same time the decrees of the Holy General Council of Constance (passed in its fourth and fifth sessions), concerning the authority of General Councils, are to remain valid and unchanged, approved, as they are, by the Apostolic See and by the practice of the Roman Pontiffs themselves and of the whole Church; nor may the Gallican Church give approval to those who minimize the force of those decrees, as if they were of doubtful authority and little

backing, or who disparage the statements of the Council as referring only to the time of schism.

3. Hence the exercise of the Apostolic authority should be moderated by the Canons established by the Holy Spirit and consecrated by the respect of the whole world. Also the rules, customs and institutions accepted in the French kingdom and Church are to keep their force and the bounds fixed by our fathers are to remain undisturbed; for it is essential for the dignity of the Apostolic See, that the statutes and customs, confirmed by the consent of that See itself and of the churches, should enjoy their rightful stability.

4. In questions of faith the leading role is to be that of the Supreme Pontiff; and his decrees apply to all churches in general and to each of them in particular. But his judgment is not unchangeable, unless it receives the consent of the Church.

These are the maxims which we have received from our fathers and which we have decided to send to all the Gallican churches and to the bishops whom the Holy Spirit has installed there to govern them, in order that we may all say the same thing, that we may share the same opinions and all hold the same doctrine.

[B] The Revocation of the Edict of Nantes, 1685

Article 1. Know that we, . . . with our certain knowledge, full power and royal authority, have by this present, perpetual and irrevocable edict, suppressed and revoked the edict of the aforesaid king our grandfather, given at Nantes in the month of April, 1598, . . .

Article 2. We forbid our subjects of the so-called Reformed religion to assemble any more for public worship of the above-mentioned religion, in any place or private house, under whatever pretext, . . .

Article 3. We likewise forbid all lords, of whatever rank they may be, to carry out heretical services in houses and fiefs, of whatever type these fiefs may be, the penalty for all our subjects who shall carry out the said worship being confiscation of their bodies and possessions.

Article 4. We order all ministers of the aforesaid so-called Reformed religion who do not wish to be converted and to embrace the Catholic, Apostolic and Roman religion, to depart from our kingdom and the lands subject to us within fifteen days from the publication of our present edict, . . .

Article 7. We prohibit private schools for the instruction of children of the so-called Reformed religion and everything in general which can make any concession, whatever it may be, in favour of this religion.

Article 8. With regard to children who shall be born to those of the aforesaid so-called Reformed religion, we desire that they be baptized by their parish priests. We command the fathers and mothers to send them to the churches for that purpose, on penalty of a fine of 500 *livres* or more if they fail to do so; and afterwards, the children shall be brought up in the Catholic, Apostolic and Roman religion, for which purpose we very expressly command the supervision of the magistrates of the districts.

Article 10. All our subjects of the so-called Reformed religion, with their wives and children, are to be strongly and repeatedly prohibited from leaving our aforesaid kingdom, countries and the lands subject to us, or of taking out of them their possessions and effects, under penalty, for the men, of the galleys, and for the women, confiscation of bodies and possessions.

For the rest, the members of the so-called Reformed religion, while awaiting God's pleasure to enlighten them like the others, can live in the towns and districts of our kingdom, countries and lands subject to us, and continue their occupation there, and enjoy their possessions, without any one having the power to trouble or interfere with them, by reason of the aforesaid so-called Reformed religion, on condition, as has been said, that they do not make public profession of it, or assemble for prayers or for the worship, whatever it may be, of their religion, under the above-mentioned penalties of body and possessions.

[C] A Sampling of Jansenist Thought: Pascal's *Pensées*

Let us imagine a number of men in chains, and all condemned to death, where some are killed each day in the sight of the others, and those who remain see their own fate in that of their fellows, and wait their turn, looking at each other sorrowfully and without hope. It is an image of the condition of men.

The eternal silence of these infinite spaces frightens me.

. . . Let us then examine this point, and say, "God is, or He is not." But to which side shall we incline? Reason can decide nothing here. There is an infinite chaos which separated us. A game is being played at the extremity of this infinite distance where heads or tails will turn up. What will you wager? According to reason, you can do neither the one thing nor the other; according to reason, you can defend neither of the propositions.

Do not then reprove for error those who have made a choice; for you know nothing about it. "No, but I blame them for having made, not this choice, but a choice; for again both he who chooses heads and he who chooses tails are equally at fault, they are both in the wrong. The true course is not to wager at all."

Yes; but you must wager. It is not optional. You are embarked. Which will you choose then? Let us see. Since you must choose, let us see which interests you least. You have two things to lose, the true and the good; and two things to stake, your reason and your will, your knowledge and your happiness; and your nature has two things to shun, error and misery. Your reason is no more shocked in choosing one rather than the other, since you must of necessity choose. This is one point settled. But your happiness? Let us weigh the gain and the loss in wagering that God is. Let us estimate these two chances. If you gain, you gain all; if you lose, you lose nothing. Wager, then, without hesitation that He is. . . .

. . . through Jesus Christ, and in Jesus Christ, we prove God, and teach morality and doctrine. Jesus Christ is then the true God of men.

But we know at the same time our wretchedness; for this God is none other than the Saviour of our wretchedness. So we can only know God well by knowing our iniquities. Therefore those who have known God, without knowing their wretchedness, have not glorified Him, but have glorified themselves. . . .

The Christian religion teaches men these two truths; that there is a God whom men can know, and that there is a corruption in their nature which renders them unworthy of Him. It is equally important to men to know both these points; and it is equally dangerous for man to know God without knowing his own wretchedness, and to know his own wretchedness without knowing the Redeemer who can free him from it. The knowledge of only one of these points gives rise either to the pride of philosophers, who have known God, and not their own wretchedness, or to the despair of atheists, who know their own wretchedness, but not the Redeemer.

If there were no obscurity, man would not be sensible of his corruption; if there were no light, man would not hope for a remedy. Thus, it is not only fair, but advantageous to us, that God be partly hidden and partly revealed; since it is equally dangerous to man to know God without knowing his own wretchedness, and to know his own wretchedness without knowing God.

When I see the blindness and the wretchedness of man, when I regard the whole silent universe, and man without light, left to himself, and, as it were, lost in this corner of the universe, without knowing who has put him there, what he has come to do, what will become of him at death, and incapable of all knowledge, I become terrified, like a man who should be carried in his sleep to a dreadful desert island, and should awake without knowing where he is, and without means of escape. And thereupon I wonder how people in a condition so wretched do not fall into despair. I see other persons around me of a like nature. I ask them if they are better informed than I am. They tell me that they are not. . . .

[49] *LOUIS XIV ACCEPTS THE THRONE OF SPAIN FOR HIS GRANDSON* *

When Charles II, the last of the Spanish Hapsburgs, died in 1700, he left a will making the grandson of Louis XIV his successor. The French King knew full well that acceptance meant war with most of Europe. Nevertheless, he accepted, and the greatest war the world had known up to that time began. Saint-Simon describes this historic moment.

. . . The news arrived at Court (Fontainebleau) in the month of November. The King was going out shooting that day; but, upon learning what had taken place, at once countermanded the sport, announced the death of the King of Spain, and at three o'clock held a council of the ministers in the apartments of Madame de Maintenon. This council lasted until past seven o'clock in the evening. Monseigneur [the Dauphin], who had been out wolf hunting, returned in time to attend it. On the next morning, Wednesday, another council was held, and in the evening a third, in the apartments of Madame de Maintenon. . . .

At the first receipt of the news the King and his ministers had been overwhelmed with a surprise that they could not recover from for several days. When the news was spread abroad, the Court was equally surprised. The foreign ministers passed whole nights deliberating upon the course the King would adopt. Nothing else was spoken of but this matter. The King, one evening, to divert himself, asked the princesses their opinion. They replied that he should send M. le Duc d'Anjou (the second son of Monseigneur) into Spain, and that this was the general sentiment. "I am sure," replied the King, "that whatever course I adopt many people will condemn me."

At last, on Tuesday, the 16th of November, the King publicly declared himself. The Spanish ambassador had received intelligence which proved the eagerness of Spain to welcome the Duc d'Anjou as its King. There seemed to be no doubt of the matter. The King, immediately after getting up, called the ambassador into his cabinet, where M. le Duc d'Anjou had already arrived. Then, pointing to the Duke, he told the ambassador he might salute him as King of Spain. The ambassador threw himself upon his knees after the fashion of his country, and addressed to the Duke a tolerable long compliment in the Spanish language. Immediately afterward, the King, contrary to all custom, opened the two folding doors of his cabinet, and commanded everybody to enter. It was a very full Court that day. The King,

* Saint-Simon, *Memoirs of Louis XIV and the Regency*, trans. by Bayle St. John (New York: M. Walter Dunne, 1901), Vol. I, pp. 198–200.

majestically turning his eyes toward the numerous company, and showing them M. le Duc d'Anjou said: "Gentlemen, behold the King of Spain. His birth called him to that crown; the late King also has called him to it by his will; the whole nation wished for him, and has asked me for him eagerly; it is the will of heaven; I have obeyed it with pleasure." And then, turning toward his grandson, he said, "Be a good Spaniard, that is your first duty; but remember that you are a Frenchman born, in order that the union between the two nations may be preserved; it will be the means of rendering both happy, and of preserving the peace of Europe. . . ."

[50] *VOLTAIRE LAUDS LOUIS XIV* *

Few historians have had kinder things to say about Louis XIV than Voltaire, who in his great historical study, The Century of Louis XIV, *credited Louis with doing "more good for his country than twenty of his predecessors together." Needless to say, many historians disagree with this view.*

Every age has produced its heroes and statesmen; every nation has experienced revolutions; every history is the same to one who wishes merely to remember facts. But the thinking man, and what is still rarer, the man of taste, numbers only four ages in the history of the world; four happy ages when the arts were brought to perfection and which, marking an era of the greatness of the human mind, are an example to posterity.

The first of these ages, to which true glory belongs, is that of Philip and Alexander, or rather of Pericles, Demosthenes, Aristotle, Plato, . . .

The second age is that of Caesar and Augustus, distinguished moreover by the names of Lucretius, Cicero, Livy, Virgil, Horace, Ovid, Varro and Vitruvius.

The third is that which followed the taking of Constantinople by Mohamet II. The reader may remember that the spectacle was then witnessed of a family of mere citizens in Italy accomplishing what should have been undertaken by the kings of Europe. The scholars whom the Turks had driven from Greece were summoned by the Medici to Florence; it was the hour of Italy's glory. . . .

The fourth age is that which we call the age of Louis XIV; and it is perhaps of the four the one which most nearly approaches perfection. Enriched with the discoveries of the other three, it accomplished in certain departments more than the three together. All the arts, it is true, did not progress

* Voltaire, *The Age of Louis XIV*, trans. by M. P. Pollock, Everyman's Library Edition (New York: E. P. Dutton and Co., Inc.), pp. 1–2.

further than they did under the Medici, under Augustus or under Alexander; but human reason in general was brought to perfection.

Rational philosophy only came to light in this period; and it is true to say that from the last years of Cardinal Richelieu to those which followed the death of Louis XIV, a general revolution took place in our arts, minds and customs, as in our government, which will serve as an eternal token of the true glory of our country. This beneficent influence was not merely confined to France; it passed over into England, and inspired a profitable rivalry in that intellectual and fearless nation; it imported good taste into Germany, and the sciences into Russia; it even revived Italy, who had begun to languish, and Europe has owed both her manners and the social spirit to the court of Louis XIV. . . .

9

The English Revolutions of the Seventeenth Century

The political stability which we have come to associate with the English nation was definitely not characteristic of its seventeenth century history. To the Continental of that period, the English people must have seemed extremely fickle and excitable. Two revolutions, a royal execution, and a prolonged civil war, among other things, disturbed the tranquility of the English scene. But by the end of the century England had obtained the type of liberal, parliamentary, and Protestant monarchy that most of her citizens desired. So "advanced" did the English form of government become that many enlightened Europeans began to think of it as a model which all progressive states might well emulate.

[51] *THE DIFFICULTIES OF THE EARLY STUARTS: CONSTITUTIONAL, RELIGIOUS, FINANCIAL* *

The first two Stuarts, James I (1603–1625) and Charles I (1625–1649) managed to estrange a large part of the English people for one reason or another. Their

* G. W. Prothero, ed., *Select Statutes and Other Constitutional Documents Illustrative of the Reigns of Elizabeth and James I* (Oxford: The Clarendon Press, 1913), pp. 293–295, 420–421, 359–360. Used by permission of the publisher.

high-handed interpretation of monarchy as an institution responsible only to God [A] *brought them into conflict with powerful parliamentary interests. Their insistence upon religious uniformity* [B] *alienated Puritans and non-conformists. Finally, their financial embarrassments caused them to resort to extra-legal taxes such as benevolences* [C].

[A] Speech of James I Before Parliament, March 21, 1610

. . . The state of monarchy is the supremest thing upon earth: for kings are not only God's lieutenants upon earth and sit upon God's throne, but even by God himself they are called gods. There be three principal similitudes that illustrate the state of monarchy: one taken out of the word of God, and the two other out of the grounds of policy and philosophy. In the Scriptures kings are called gods, and so their power after a certain relation compared to the Divine power. Kings are also compared to fathers of families: for a king is truly *parens patriae,* the politic father of his people. And lastly, kings are compared to the head of this microcosm of the body of man. . . .

I conclude then this point touching the power of kings with this axiom of divinity, That as to dispute what God may do is blasphemy, . . . so is it sedition in subjects to dispute what a king may do in the height of his power. But just kings will ever be willing to declare what they will do, if they will not incur the curse of God. I will not be content that my power be disputed upon; but I shall ever be willing to make the reason appear of all my doings, and rule my actions according to my laws . . .

Now the second general ground whereof I am to speak concerns the matter of grievances. . . . First then, I am not to find fault that you inform yourselves of the particular just grievances of the people; nay I must tell you, ye can neither be just nor faithful to me or to your countries that trust and employ you, if you do it not . . . But I would wish you to be careful to avoid three things in the matter of grievances.

First, that you do not meddle with the main points of government: that is my craft: *tractent fabrilia fabri;* to meddle with that, were to lesson me. I am now an old king . . . ; therefore there should not be too many Phormios to teach Hannibal: I must not be taught my office.

Secondly, I would not have you meddle with such ancient rights of mine as I have received from my predecessors, possessing them *more majorum:* such things I would be sorry should be accounted for grievances. All novelties are dangerous as well in a politic as in a natural body: and therefore I would be loath to be quarrelled in my ancient rights and possessions: for that were to judge me unworthy of that which my predecessors had and left me.

And lastly I pray you, beware to exhibit for grievance anything that is established by a settled law, and whereunto (as you have already had a proof) you know I will never give a plausible answer: for it is an undutiful part in subjects to press their king, wherein they know beforehand he will refuse them. Now if any law or statute be not convenient, let it be amended by Parliament, but in the meantime term it not a grievance; for to be grieved with the law is to be grieved with the king, who is sworn to be the patron and maintainer thereof. . . .

[B] Proclamation Enjoining Conformity to the Established Church, July 1604

The care which we have had and pains which we have taken to settle the affairs of this Church of England in an uniformity as well of doctrine as of government, both of them agreeable to the word of God, the doctrine of the primitive church and the laws heretofore established for those matters in this realm, may sufficiently appear by our former actions. For no sooner did the infection of the plague reigning immediately after our entry into this kingdom give us leave to have any assembly, but we held at our honour of Hampton Court for that purpose a conference between some principal bishops and deans of this church, and such other learned men as understood or favoured the opinions of those that seek alteration, before ourself and our council. Of which conference the issue was, that no well grounded matter appeared to us or our said council why the state of the church here by law established should in any material point be altered . . . Not withstanding at the late assembly of our parliament there wanted not many that renewed with no little earnestness the questions before determined and many more, as well about the Book of Common Prayer as other matters of church government, and importuned us for our assent to many alterations therein. But . . . the end of all their motions and overtures falling out to be none other in substance than was before at the conference at Hampton Court, . . . we have thought good once again to give notice thereof to all our subjects by public declaration, . . . and consequently to admonish them all in general to conform themselves thereunto, without listening to the troublesome spirits of some persons, who never receive contentment either in civil or ecclesiastical matters but in their own fantasies, especially of certain ministers who under pretended zeal of reformation are the chief authors of divisions and sects among our people. Of many of which we hope that now when they shall see that such things as they have proposed for alteration prove upon trial so weakly grounded as deserve not admittance, they will out of their own judgment conform themselves . . . But if our hope herein fail us, we must advertise them that our duty towards God requireth at our hands, that what untractable men do not perform upon admonition, they must be compelled unto by authority . . . And yet by advice of our council and opinion of the bishops, we have thought good to give time to all ministers disobedient to the orders of the church and to ecclesiastical authority here by law established, and who for such disobedience, either in the days of the Queen our sister of famous memory deceased or since our reign, have incurred any censures of the church or penalties of laws, until the last of November now next ensuing to bethink themselves of the course they will hold therein, . . . assuring them that after that day we shall not fail to do that which princely providence requireth at our hands; that is, to put into execution all ways and means that may take from among our people all grounds and occasions of sects, divisions and unquietness . . .

[C] Circular Letter for a Benevolence, 1622

What endeavours his Majesty hath used by treaty and by all fair and amiable ways to recover the patrimony of his children in Germany, now for the most part withholden from them by force, is not unknown to all his loving subjects, since his Majesty was pleased to communicate to them in parliament his whole proceedings in that business: of which treaty, being of late frustrate, he was enforced to take other resolutions, namely, to recover that by the sword which by other means he saw no likelihood to compass. For which purpose it was expected by his Majesty that his people in parliament would (in a cause so nearly concerning his and his children's interest) have cheerfully contributed thereunto. But the same unfortunately failing, his Majesty is constrained, in a case of so great necessity, to try the dutiful affections of his loving subjects in another way, as his predecessors have done in former times, by propounding unto them a voluntary contribution. And therefore, as yourselves have already given a liberal and worthy example (which his Majesty doth take in very gracious part), so his pleasure is, and we do accordingly hereby authorize and require your lordships, as well to countenance and assist the service by your best means, in your next circuits, in the several counties where you hold general assizes, as also now presently with all convenient expedition to call before you all the officers and attorneys belonging to any his Majesty's courts of justice, and also all such others of the houses and societies of court or that otherwise have dependence upon the law, as are meet to be treated withall in this kind and have not already contributed; and to move them to join willingly in this contribution in some good measure, answerable to that yourselves and others have done before, according to their means and fortunes; wherein his Majesty doubteth not, but beside the interest of his children and his own crown and dignity, the religion professed by his Majesty and happily flourishing under him within his kingdom (having a great part in the success of this business) will be a special motive to incite and persuade them thereunto. Nevertheless, if any person shall, out of obstinacy or disaffection, refuse to contribute herein proportionably to their estates and means, you are to certify their names unto this board.

[52] *CHARLES I SACRIFICES THE EARL OF STRAFFORD* *

One of Charles I's ablest ministers was the Earl of Strafford. Accused of an assortment of despotic acts, he was the object of a bill of attainder passed by Parliament and approved by a frightened monarch in 1641. Conscience-stricken, Charles addressed the following half-hearted appeal for clemency to the House of Lords.

My Lords, I did yesterday satisfy the justice of the kingdom, by passing of the bill of attainder against the earl of Strafford; but mercy being as inherent and inseparable to a king as justice, I desire at this time in some measure, to show that likewise, by suffering that unfortunate man to fulfil the natural course of his life in a close imprisonment, yet so that, if ever he make the least offer to escape, or offer, directly or indirectly, to meddle with any sort of public business, especially with me, either by message or letter, it shall cost him his life, without further press.

This, if it may be done without the discontent of my people, will be an unspeakable comfort to me; to which end, as in the first place, I by this letter do earnestly desire your approbation; and to endear it the more, have chosen him to carry, that of all your house is most dear to me [the Prince of Wales]; so I do desire, that by a conference you will endeavour to give the House of Commons contentment; likewise assuring you, that the exercise is no more pleasing to me than to see both Houses of Parliament consent, for my sake, that I should moderate the severity of the law in so important a case. I will not say, that your complying with me in this my pretended mercy, shall make me more willing, but certainly it will make me more cheerful in granting your just grievances; but, if no less than his life can satisfy my people, I must say, *fiat justitia.*

Thus again earnestly recommending the consideration of my intentions to you, I rest,

Your unalterable and affectionate friend,

CHARLES R.

Whitehall, 11th May, 1641

If he *must* die, it were charity to reprieve him till Saturday.

* Harleian Ms. 1769, Art. 12, as found in Elizabeth Kimball Kendall, ed., *Source-Book of English History* (New York: The Macmillan Company, 1900), pp. 236–237.

[53] *CHARLES I INVADES PARLIAMENT TO ARREST FIVE "ROGUES"* *

Relations between monarch and Parliament steadily worsened between 1640 and 1642. Matters came to a climax when Charles strode into Parliament at the head of an armed escort to arrest five troublesome members. The following account of this tumultuous scene (1642) is provided by John Rushworth, a member of the parliamentary faction.

. . . The said five accused Members this day *after dinner* came into the House. . . .

They were no sooner sate in their places, but the House was informed . . . that his Majesty was coming with a Guard of Military Men, Commanders and Souldiers, to the House of Commons. . . . Whereupon a certain Member of the House having also private Intimation . . . that endeavours would be used this day to apprehend the five Members, the House required the five Members to depart the House forthwith, to the end to avoid Combustion in the House, if the said Souldiers should use Violence to pull any of them out. To which Command of the House, four of the said Members yielded ready Obedience, but Mr. Stroud was obstinate, till Sir Walter Earle (his ancient acquaintance) pulled him out by force, the King being at that time entering into the New Pallace-yard, in Westminster: And as his Majesty came through Westminster Hall, the Commanders, Reformadoes, &c. that attended him, made a Lane on both sides the Hall (through which his Majesty passed and came up the Stairs to the House of Commons) and stood before the Guard of Pentioners, and Halberteers, (who also attended the Kings Person,) and the door of the House of Commons being thrown open, his Majesty entered the House, and as he passed up towards the Chair he cast his eye on the Right-hand near the Bar of the House, where Mr. Pym used to sit, but his Majesty not seeing him there (knowing him well) went up to the Chair, and said, "By your leave, (Mr. Speaker) I must borrow your Chair a little," whereupon the Speaker came out of the Chair, and his Majesty stept up into it, after he had stood in the Chair a while, casting his Eye upon the Members as they stood up uncovered, but could not discern any of the five Members to be there, nor indeed were they easie to be discerned (had they been there) among so many bare Faces all standing up together.

* John Rushworth, *Historical Collections* (London: 1691), Vol. IV, pp. 477–478, as found in Elizabeth Kimball Kendall, ed., *Source-Book of English History* (New York: The Macmillan Company, 1900), pp. 237–240.

Then his Majesty made this Speech,

"Gentlemen,

"I am sorry for this occasion of coming unto you: Yesterday I sent a Serjeant at Arms upon a very Important occasion to apprehend some that by my command were accused of High Treason, whereunto I did expect Obedience and not a Message. And I must declare unto you here, that albeit, no King that ever was in England, shall be more careful of your Priviledges, to maintain them to the uttermost of his power then I shall be; yet you must know that in Cases of Treason, no person hath a priviledge. And therefore I am come to know if any of these persons that were accused are here: For I must tell you Gentlemen, that so long as these persons that I have accused (for no slight Crime but for Treason) are here, I cannot expect that this House will be in the Right way that I do heartily wish it; Therefore I am come to tell you that I must have them wheresoever I find them. Well since I see all the Birds are Flown, I do expect from you, that you shall send them unto me, as soon as they return hither. But I assure you, in the word of a King, I never did intend any Force, but shall proceed against them in a legal and fair way, for I never meant any other.

"And now since I see I cannot do what I came for, I think this no unfit occasion to repeat what I have said formerly, That whatsoever I have done in favour, and to the good of my Subjects, I do mean to maintain it.

"I will trouble you no more, but tell you I do expect as soon as they come to the House, you will send them to me; otherwise I must take my own Course to find them."

When the King was looking about the House, the Speaker standing, below by the Chair, his Majesty ask'd him, whether any of these persons were in the House? Whether he saw any of them? and where they were? To which the Speaker falling on his Knee, thus Answered.

"May it please your Majesty, I Have neither Eyes to see, nor Tongue to speak in this place, but as the House is pleased to direct me, whose Servant I am here, and humbly beg your Majesties Pardon, that I cannot give any other Answer than this, to what your Majesty is pleased to demand of me."

The King having Concluded his Speech, went out of the House again which was in great disorder, and many Members, cried out, aloud so as he might hear them, "Priviledge! Priviledge!" and forthwith Adjourned till the next Day at One of the Clock. . . .

[54] *CROMWELL PUTS THE "BARBAROUS" IRISH TO THE SWORD* *

After the execution of Charles I in 1649, Cromwell was faced with a rebellion in Ireland of Roman Catholics allied with Protestant royalists. His savage suppression of the rebellion has left a stain on his memory, but in his view, he was doing God's work in exterminating the Catholic Irish. The following account of the storming of Drogheda is from one of Cromwell's letters to Parliament.

Upon Tuesday the 10th of this instant, about five o'clock in the evening, we began the storm, and after some hot dispute we entered about seven or eight hundred men, the enemy disputing it very stiffly with us. And indeed, through the advantages of the place, and the courage God was pleased to give the defenders, our men were forced to retreat quite out of the breach, not without some considerable loss; . . .

Although our men that stormed the breaches were forced to recoil . . . yet, being encouraged to recover their loss, they made a second attempt, wherein God was pleased [so] to animate them that they got ground of the enemy, and by the goodness of God, forced him to quit his entrenchments. And after a very hot dispute, the enemy having both horse and foot, and we only foot, within the wall, they gave ground, and our men became masters of their retrenchments and the church; . . .

The enemy retreated, divers of them, into the Mill-Mount: a place very strong and of difficult access, being exceedingly high, having a good graft, and strongly palisadoed. The Governor, Sir Arthur Ashton, and divers considerable Officers being there, our men getting up to them, were ordered by me to put them all to the sword. And indeed, being in the heat of action, I forbade them to spare any that were in arms in the town, and, I think, that night they put to the sword about 2,000 men, divers of the officers and soldiers being fled over the Bridge into the other part of the Town, where about one hundred of them possessed St. Peter's church-steeple, some the west gate, and others a strong round tower next the gate called St. Sunday's. These being summoned to yield to mercy, refused, whereupon I ordered the steeple of St. Peter's Church to be fired, where one of them was heard to say in the midst of the flames: "God damn me, God confound me; I burn, I burn."

* Reprinted by permission of the publishers from Wilbur Cortez Abbot, ed., *The Writings and Speeches of Oliver Cromwell* (Cambridge, Mass.: Harvard University Press, 1939), Vol. II, pp. 126–127. Copyright 1939 by the President and Fellows of Harvard College.

The next day, the other two towers were summoned, in one of which was about six or seven score; but they refused to yield themselves, and we knowing that hunger must compel them, set only good guards to secure them from running away until their stomachs were come down. From one of the said towers, notwithstanding their condition, they killed and wounded some of our men. When they submitted, their officers were knocked on the head, and every tenth man of the soldiers killed, and the rest shipped for the Barbadoes. The soldiers in the other tower were all spared, as to their lives only, and shipped likewise for the Barbadoes. . . .

And now give me leave to say how it comes to pass that this work is wrought. It was set upon some of our hearts, That a great thing should be done, not by power or might, but by the Spirit of God. And is it not so clear? That which caused your men to storm so courageously, it was the Spirit of God, who gave your men courage, and took it away again; and gave the enemy courage, and took it away again; and gave your men courage again, and therewith this happy success. And therefore it is good that God alone have all the glory. . . .

[55] *SAMUEL PEPYS DESCRIBES CHARLES II'S RETURN* *

One of the best known English diarists is Samuel Pepys, who between 1660 and 1669 kept a colorful and highly informative record of his activities as a civilian naval official. So frank were his observations that the author prudently employed a complicated shorthand which was not deciphered until more than a century later. Here is Pepys' account of Charles II's triumphant return to England in 1660.

May 22nd. News brought that the two Dukes are coming on board, which, by and by, they did, in a Dutch boat, the Duke of York in yellow trimmings, the Duke of Gloucester in grey and red. My Lord went in a boat to meet them, the Captain, myself, and others, standing at the entering port. So soon as they were entered we shot the guns off around the fleet. After that they went to view the ship all over, and were most exceedingly pleased with it. They seem to be very fine gentlemen. . . . news is sent us that the King is on shore; so my Lord fired all his guns round twice, and all the fleet after him. The gun over against my cabbin I fired myself to the King, which was the first time that he had been saluted by his own ships since this change; but holding my head too much over the gun, I had almost spoiled my right eye. Nothing in the world but giving of guns almost all

* *The Diary of Samuel Pepys* (London: Library of Classics, n.d.), pp. 46–50.

this day. In the evening we began to remove cabbins; I to the carpenter's cabbin, and Dr. Clerke with me. Many of the King's servants come on board to-night; and so many Dutch of all sorts come to see the ship till it was quite dark, that we could not pass by one another, which was a great trouble to us all.

23rd. In the morning some infinity of people on board from the King to go along with him. My Lord, Mr. Crewe, and others, go on shore to meet the King as he comes off from shore, . . . The King, with the two Dukes and Queen of Bohemia, Princesse Royalle, and Prince of Orange, come on board, where I in their coming in kissed the King's, Queen's and Princesse's hands, having done the other before. Infinite shooting off of the guns, and that in a disorder on purpose, which was better than if it had been otherwise. All day nothing but Lords and persons of honour on board, that we were exceeding full. Dined in a great deal of state, the Royalle company by themselves in the coach, which was a blessed sight to see. After dinner the King and Duke altered the name of some of the ships, viz. the *Naseby* into *Charles;* the *Richard, James;* the *Speaker, Mary;* the *Dunbar* (which was not in company with us), the *Henry; Winsly, Happy Return; Wakefield, Richmond; Lambert,* the *Henrietta; Cheriton,* the *Speedwell; Bradford,* the *Successe.* That done, the Queen, Princess Royalle, and Prince of Orange, took leave of the King, and the Duke of York went on board the *London,* and the Duke of Gloucester, the *Swiftsure.* Which done, we weighed anchor, and with a fresh gale and most happy weather we set sail for England. All the afternoon the King walked here and there, up and down (quite contrary to what I thought him to have been) very active and stirring. Upon the quarter-deck he fell into discourse of his escape from Worcester, where it made me ready to weep to hear the stories that he told of his difficulties that he had passed through, as his travelling four days and three nights on foot, every step up to his knees in dirt, with nothing but a green coat and a pair of country breeches on, and a pair of country shoes that made him so sore all over his feet, that he could scarce stir. Yet he was forced to run away from a miller and other company, that took them for rogues. His sitting at table at one place, where the master of the house, that had not seen him in eight years, did know him, but kept it private; when at the same table there was one that had been of his own regiment at Worcester, could not know him, but made him drink the King's health, and said that the King was at least four fingers higher than he. At another place he was by some servants of the house made to drink, that they might know that he was not a Roundhead, which they swore he was. In another place at his inn, the master of the house, as the King was standing with his hands upon the back of a chair by the fireside, kneeled down and kissed his hand, privately, saying, that he would not ask him who he was, but bid God bless him whither he was going. . . .

. . . Under sail all night, and most glorious weather.

24th. Up, and made myself as fine as I could, . . . Extraordinary press of noble company, and great mirth all the day. . . . Walking upon the decks, where persons of honour all the afternoon, among others, Thomas Killigrew, (a merry droll, but a gentleman of great esteem with the King,) who told us many merry stories. . . . To bed, coming in sight of land a little before night.

25th. By the morning we were come close to the land, and every body made ready to get on shore. The King and the two Dukes did eat their breakfast before they went, and there being set some ship's diet, they eat of nothing else but pease and pork, and boiled beef. . . . Great expectation of the King's making some Knights, but there was none. . . .

. . . got on shore when the King did, who was received by General Monk with all imaginable love and respect at his entrance upon the land of Dover. Infinite the crowd of people and the horsemen, citizens, and noblemen of all sorts. The Mayor of the town come and gave him his white staffe, the badge of his place, which the King did give him again. The Mayor also presented him from the town a very rich Bible, which he took and said it was the thing that he loved above all things in the world. A canopy was provided for him to stand under, which he did, and talked awhile with General Monk and others, and so into a stately coach there set for him, and so away through the towne towards Canterbury, without making any stay at Dover. The shouting and joy expressed by all is past imagination. . . .

[56] *ENGLAND EXCHANGES CATHOLIC KING FOR PROTESTANT* *

Although political and constitutional issues played a role, the main reason for the Glorious Revolution of 1688 was religious. James II's open espousal of Roman Catholicism was extremely distasteful to the great majority of Englishmen. John Evelyn's Diary, *excerpts from which follow, reflects the state of public opinion in England.*

29th December, 1686. I went to hear the music of the Italians in the new chapel, now first opened publicly at Whitehall for the Popish Service. . . .

* *The Diary of John Evelyn,* in the Universal Classics Library (Washington and London: M. Walter Dunne, 1901), pp. 258–284.

Here we saw the Bishop in his mitre and rich copes, with six or seven Jesuits and others in rich copes, sumptuously habited, often taking off and putting on the Bishop's mitre, who sat in a chair with arms pontifically, was adored and censed by three Jesuits in their copes; . . . I could not have believed I should ever have seen such things in the King of England's palace, after it had pleased God to enlighten this nation; . . .

20th March, 1687. . . . His Majesty again prorogued the Parliament, foreseeing it would not remit the laws against Papists. . . .

15th January, 1688. There was a solemn and particular office used at our, and all the churches of London and ten miles round, for a thanksgiving to God, for her Majesty being with child. . . .

18th May, 1688. The King enjoining the ministers to read his Declaration for giving liberty of conscience (as it was styled) in all churches of England, this evening, six Bishops . . . in the name of all the rest of the Bishops, came to his Majesty to petition him, that he would not impose the reading of it to the several congregations within their dioceses; . . .

8th June, 1688. This day, the Archbishop of Canterbury, with the Bishops of Ely, Chichester, St. Asaph, Bristol, Peterborough, and Bath and Wells, were sent from the Privy Council prisoners to the Tower. . . .

10th June, 1688. A YOUNG PRINCE born, which will cause disputes.

About two o'clock, we heard the Tower ordnance discharged, and the bells ring for the birth of a Prince of Wales. This was very surprising, it having been universally given out that her Majesty did not look till the next month. . . .

29th June, 1688. They [the bishops] appeared; the trial lasted from nine in the morning to past six in the evening. . . . The jury were locked up till that time, eleven of them being for an acquittal; but one (Arnold, a brewer) would not consent. At length he agreed with the others. . . . When this was heard, there was great rejoicing; and there was a lane of people from the King's Bench to the water side, on their knees, as the Bishops passed and repassed, to beg their blessing. Bonfires were made that night, and bells rung, which was taken very ill at Court. . . .

10th August, 1688. Dr. Tenison now told me there would suddenly be some great thing discovered. This was the Prince of Orange intending to come over. . . .

30th September, 1688. The Court in extraordinary a consternation, on assurance of the Prince of Orange's intention to land. . . .

28th October, 1688. A tumult in London on the rabble demolishing a Popish chapel, that had been set up in the city. . . .

5th November, 1688. I went to London; heard the news of the Prince having landed at Torbay, coming with a fleet of near 700 sail, passing through the Channel with so favorable a wind, that our navy could not intercept, or molest them. This put the King and Court into great consternation. . . .

14th November, 1688. The Prince increases every day in force. Several Lords go in to him. Lord Cornbury carries some regiments, and marches to Honiton, the Prince's headquarters. The city of London in disorder; the rabble pulled down the nunnery newly bought by the Papists of Lord Berkeley, at St. John's. . . .

2nd December, 1688. . . . The great favorites at Court, Priests and Jesuits, fly or abscond. . . . The Papists in offices lay down their commissions, and fly. Universal consternation among them; it looks like a revolution. . . .

13th December, 1688. The King flies to sea, puts in at Faversham for ballast; is rudely treated by the people; comes back to Whitehall. . . .

18th December, 1688. I saw the King take barge to Gravesend at twelve o'clock– a sad sight! The Prince comes to St. James's, and fills Whitehall with Dutch guards. . . .

All the world go to see the Prince at St. James's, where there is a great Court. There I saw him, and several of my acquaintance who came over with him. He is very stately, serious and reserved. The English soldiers sent out of town to disband them; not well pleased.

24th December, 1688. The King passes into France, whither the Queen and child were gone a few days before. . . .

[57] *A CENTURY OF CONFLICT ENDS WITH THE BILL OF RIGHTS, 1689* *

A document of basic importance in the constitutional development of England is the Bill of Rights, passed immediately after the Revolution of 1688 and promptly accepted by William and Mary. It sums up the points at issue during the century and, along with a long list of enactments in the next fifteen years, established the permanent supremacy of Parliament over Crown.

Whereas the said late King James II having abdicated the government, and the throne being thereby vacant, his Highness the prince of Orange (whom it hath pleased Almighty God to make the glorious instrument of delivering this kingdom from popery and arbitrary power) did (by the advice of the lords spiritual and temporal, and diverse principal persons

* Edward P. Cheyney, *Readings in English History* (New York: Ginn and Company, 1908), pp. 545–547. Used by permission of the publisher.

of the Commons) cause letters to be written to the lords spiritual and temporal, being Protestants, and other letters to the several counties, cities, universities, boroughs, and Cinque Ports, for the choosing of such persons to represent them, as were of right to be sent to parliament, to meet and sit at Westminster upon the two-and-twentieth day of January, in this year 1689, in order to [provide] such an establishment as that their religion, laws, and liberties might not again be in danger of being subverted; upon which letters elections have been accordingly made.

And thereupon the said lords spiritual and temporal and Commons, pursuant to their respective letters and elections, being now assembled in a full and free representation of this nation, taking into their most serious consideration the best means for attaining the ends aforesaid, do in the first place (as their ancestors in like case have usually done), for the vindicating and asserting their ancient rights and liberties, declare:

1. That the pretended power of suspending laws, or the execution of laws, by regal authority, without consent of parliament, is illegal.

2. That the pretended power of dispensing with laws, or the execution of laws, by regal authority, as it hath been assumed and exercised of late, is illegal.

3. That the commission for erecting the late court of commissioners for ecclesiastical causes, and all other commissions and courts of like nature, are illegal and pernicious.

4. That levying money for or to the use of the crown by pretense of prerogative, without grant of parliament, for longer time or in other manner than the same is or shall be granted, is illegal.

5. That it is the right of the subjects to petition the king, and all commitments and prosecutions for such petitioning are illegal.

6. That the raising or keeping a standing army within the kingdom in time of peace, unless it be with consent of parliament, is against law.

7. That the subjects which are Protestants may have arms for their defense suitable to their conditions, and as allowed by law.

8. That election of members of parliament ought to be free.

9. That the freedom of speech, and debates or proceedings in parliament, ought not to be impeached or questioned in any court or place out of parliament.

10. That excessive bail ought not to be required, nor excessive fines imposed, nor cruel and unusual punishments inflicted.

11. That jurors ought to be duly impaneled and returned, and jurors which pass upon men in trials for high treason ought to be freeholders.

12. That all grants and promises of fines and forfeitures of particular persons before conviction are illegal and void.

13. And that for redress of all grievances, and for the amending, strengthening, and preserving of the laws, parliament ought to be held frequently.

And they do claim, demand, and insist upon all and singular the premises, as their undoubted rights and liberties; and that no declarations, judgments, doings, or proceedings, to the prejudice of the people in any of the said premises, ought in any wise to be drawn hereafter into consequence or example.

To which demand of their rights they are particularly encouraged by the declaration of his Highness the prince of Orange, as being the only means for obtaining a full redress and remedy therein.

Having therefore an entire confidence that his said Highness the prince of Orange will perfect the deliverance so far advanced by him, and will still preserve them from the violation of their rights, which they have here asserted, and from all other attempts upon their religion, rights, and liberties:

The said lords spiritual and temporal, and commons, assembled at Westminster, do resolve that William and Mary, prince and princess of Orange, be, and be declared king and queen of England, France, and Ireland, and the dominions thereunto belonging, to hold the crown and royal dignity of the said kingdoms and dominions to them and said prince and princess during their lives, and the life of the survivor of them; and that the sole and full exercise of the regal power be only in, and executed by, the said prince of Orange, in the names of the said prince and princess, during their joint lives; and after their deceases, the said crown and royal dignity of the said kingdoms and dominions to be to the heirs of the body of the said princess; and for default of such issue to the princess Anne of Denmark, and the heirs of her body; and for default of such issue to the heirs of the body of the said prince of Orange. And the lords spiritual and temporal, and commons, do pray the said prince and princess to accept the same accordingly. . . .

Upon which their said Majesties did accept the crown and royal dignity of the kingdoms of England, France, Ireland, and the dominions thereunto belonging, according to the resolution and desire of the said lords and commons contained in the said declaration. . . .

10

Political Thought in the Sixteenth and Seventeenth Centuries

The sixteenth and seventeenth centuries produced a great fermentation in political thought. Such disturbing developments as the decline of the medieval super-authorities (the Holy Roman Empire and the Roman Catholic Church), the rise of the new national monarchies, and changes in the European social structure led to intensive rethinking of mankind's political relationships. In general, theory followed upon fact; ideas were shaped by history rather than vice versa. The abstract thought of the period cannot be understood without constant reference to the historical milieu. Bodin's ideas, for example, stemmed from the chaos of the French religious wars, as a consequence of which Bodin sought a principle of authority capable of maintaining order. In England, Milton, Hobbes, and Locke, all of whom had taken part in the English civil wars, were led thereby to formulate masterly vindications of their positions, authoritarian or constitutional.

[58] *JEAN BODIN DEFINES SOVEREIGNTY* *

One of the most important political theorists of early modern Europe was the Frenchman, Jean Bodin (1530–1596). By nature a political moderate, he was driven by the exigencies of the religious wars into becoming an apologist for royal absolutism. His view of the nature of man was so pessimistic as to lead him to conclude that there was no alternative to absolutism. The doctrine of sovereignty as a power above all limitation by positive law forms Bodin's great contribution to modern political thought.

Sovereignty is supreme power over citizens and subjects, unrestrained by laws. . . . Suppose that supreme power, unlimited by laws, and without protest or appeal, be granted by the people to some one or few, shall we say that the latter have sovereignty? For he has sovereignty who, after God, acknowledges no one greater than himself. I hold that sovereignty resides not in such persons, but in the people, at whose pleasure they hold their power, or to whom they must return their authority at the expiration of the period designated. The people cannot be considered as having divested themselves of their power when they intrust supreme authority, unrestrained by laws, to one or a few, if the commitment is for a certain period of time, or at the pleasure of the people; for in either case the holders of the supreme authority must render account of their doings to the prince or people, who, being sovereign, are required to give account to no one, save immortal God. . . .

But what if the people have given supreme and perpetual power to any one for life? If the power is given unlimited by laws, and without the name of magistrate, deputy, governor, or guardian, and not at the pleasure of any one, certainly it must be confessed that sovereign rights have been conceded to such a one. The people in such case have despoiled themselves of their authority, in order to give to another all the privileges of sovereignty, without conditions; in like manner as any one might by pure gift surrender to another the ownership and possession of his property; such a perfect donation contains no conditions.

The sovereignty of a prince is manifest in the fact that when the estates and orders of the people, with humble mien, present their requests to him they are exercising no authority of commanding, forbidding, or concurring; but the prince by his own judgment and will directs everything; whatever he desires and orders has the force of law. The opinion of those who in

* Jean Bodin, *Six Books Concerning the State,* Book I, ch. viii, as found in Francis William Coker, ed., *Readings in Political Philosophy* (New York: The Macmillan Company, 1914), pp. 230–234.

books scattered broadcast have written that the king is bound by the popular command, must be disregarded; such doctrine furnishes seditious men with material for revolutionary plots, and leads to disturbance in the commonwealth. No reasonable ground can be adduced why subjects should control princes, or why power should be attributed to popular assemblies—except in the infancy, madness, or captivity of the prince, when a guardian or deputy may be created by the suffrages of the people. If princes were restrained by laws made by these assemblies or by the commands of the people, the power of the prince would be worthless and the royal name a vain thing.

The approval and promulgation of laws, which is commonly done in an assembly or senate, does not imply that the sovereignty of the realm resides in such assembly or senate, but only a species of authority without which laws issued by the king might be called in question at his death, or before the senate when it acts judicially. I hold, therefore, that the sovereignty of the prince is in no degree diminished by calling together the assemblies or estates, though indeed a prince grants many things to the assembled people which he would not so readily grant to individuals; this is because the voices of individuals are not heard so clearly as the voice of the multitude; or it is because the prince, accustomed to use the eyes and ears of others, in the assembly sees and hears the people directly, and so, impelled by shame, religious fear, or his own good disposition, he grants their requests. But the highest privilege of sovereignty consists primarily in giving laws not only to individuals but also to the people as a whole, without their consent.

[59] *GROTIUS EXAMINES SOVEREIGN POWER* *

Hugo Grotius (1583–1645) was a Dutch jurist remembered for his great pioneer work in international law, The Law of War and Peace. *While this treatise deals primarily with the laws governing intercourse among states, the author first examines the problem of sovereignty within the state.*

That power is called sovereign, whose actions are not subject to the control of any other power, so as to be annulled at the pleasure of any other human will. The term ANY OTHER HUMAN WILL exempts the sovereign himself from this restriction, who may annul his own acts, as may also his successor, who enjoys the same right, having the same power and no other. We are

* Hugo Grotius, *The Rights of War and Peace* (Washington, D.C.: M. Walter Dunne, 1901), Bk. I, ch. 3, pp. 62–63, 67–68.

to consider then what is the subject in which this sovereign power exists. Now the subject is in one respect common, and in another proper, as the body is the common subject of sight, the eye the proper, so the common subject of sovereign power is the state, which has already been said to be a perfect society of men. . . . The proper subject is one or more persons according to the laws and customs of each nation. . . .

And here is the proper place for refuting the opinion of those who maintain that everywhere and without exception, the sovereign power is vested in the people, so that they have a right to restrain and punish kings for an abuse of their power. However there is no man of sober wisdom who does not see the incalculable mischiefs which such opinions have occasioned, and may still occasion; and upon the following grounds they may be refuted.

From the Jewish, as well as the Roman Law, it appears that any one might engage himself in private servitude to whom he pleased. Now if an individual may do so, why may not a whole people, for the benefit of better government and more certain protection, completely transfer their sovereign rights to one or more persons, without reserving any portion to themselves? Neither can it be alleged that such a thing is not to be presumed in a doubtful case, but what may lawfully be done. Nor is it any more to the purpose to object to the inconveniences, which may, and actually do arise from a people's thus surrendering their rights. For it is not in the power of man to devise any form of government free from imperfections and dangers. . . .

. . . the assertion that the constituent always retains a control over the sovereign power, which he has contributed to establish, is only true in those cases where the continuance and existence of that power depends upon the will and pleasure of the constituent: but not in cases where the power, though it might derive its origin from that constituent, becomes a necessary and fundamental part of the established law. Of this nature is that authority to which a woman submits when she gives herself to a husband. Valentinian the Emperor, when the soldiers who had raised him to the throne made a demand of which he did not approve, replied; "Soldiers, your election of me for your emperor was your own voluntary choice; but since you have elected me, it depends upon my pleasure to grant your request. It becomes you to obey as subjects, and me to consider what is proper to be done."

. . . though guardianship were invented for the benefit of wards, yet the guardian has a right to authority over the ward. Nor, though a guardian may for mismanagement be removed from his trust, does it follow that a king may for the same reason be deposed. The cases are quite different, the guardian has a superior to judge him; but in governments, as there must be some *dernier ressort,* it must be vested either in an individual, or in some public body, whose misconduct, as there is no superior tribunal before which they can be called, God declares that he himself will judge. He either punishes their offences, should he deem it necessary; or permits them for the chastisement of his people.

This is well expressed by Tacitus: he says, "you should bear with the rapacity or luxury of rulers, as you would bear with drought, or excessive rains, or any other calamities of nature. For as long as men exist there will be faults and imperfections; but these are not of uninterrupted continuance, and they are often repaired by the succession of better times. . . ."

[60] *MILTON PLACES SEVERE LIMITATIONS ON ROYAL SOVEREIGNTY* *

Like Bodin and Grotius, John Milton (1608–1674) lived in a period of civil conflict which impelled him to reflect on the nature of the state and of sovereignty. His conclusions were radically different, however, as we read in the following extract from his political tract, The Tenure of Kings and Magistrates, *written in justification of the execution of Charles I in 1649.*

No man, who knows aught, can be so stupid to deny that all men naturally were born free, being the image and resemblance of God himself, and were by privilege above all the creatures, born to command and not to obey. And that they lived so, till from the root of Adam's transgression falling among themselves to do wrong and violence, and foreseeing that such courses must needs tend to the destruction of them all, they agreed by common league to bind each other from mutual injury, and jointly to defend themselves against any that gave disturbance or opposition to such agreement. Hence came cities, towns, and commonwealths. And because no faith in all was found sufficiently binding, they saw it needful to ordain some authority that might restrain by force and punishment what was violated against peace and common right.

This authority and power of self-defence and preservation being originally and naturally in every one of them, and unitedly in them all; for ease, for order, and lest each man should be his own partial judge, they communicated and derived either to one whom for the eminence of his wisdom and integrity they chose above the rest, or to more than one, whom they thought of equal deserving: the first was called a king; the other magistrates:

* John Milton, *The Tenure of Kings and Magistrates* (London: George Routledge and Sons, 1889), pp. 358–362.

not to be their lords and masters—though afterwards those names in some places were given voluntarily to such as had been authors of inestimable good to the people—but to be their deputies and commissioners, to execute, by virtue of their intrusted power, that justice, which else every man by the bond of nature and of covenant must have executed for himself, and for one another. And to him that shall consider well why among free persons one man by civil right should bear authority and jurisdiction over another, no other end or reason can be imaginable.

It being thus manifest that the power of Kings and Magistrates is nothing else but what is only derivative, transferred, and committed to them in trust from the People to the common good of them all, in whom the power yet remains fundamentally and cannot be taken from them without a violation of their natural birthright; and seeing that from hence Aristotle and the best of political writers have defined a king, "him who governs to the good and profit of his people, and not for his own ends"; it follows from necessary causes, that the titles of sovereign lord, natural lord and the like are either arrogancies or flatteries, not admitted by emperors and kings of best note, and disliked by the church both of Jews (Isa. xxvi, 13) and ancient Christians, as appears by Tertullian and others. . . .

Secondly, that to say, as is usual, the king hath as good right to his crown and dignity as any man to his inheritance, is to make the subject no better than the king's slave, his chattel, or his possession that may be bought and sold: and doubtless, if hereditary title were sufficiently inquired, the best foundation of it would be found but either in courtesy or convenience. . . .

Thirdly, it follows, that to say kings are accountable to none but God, is the overcoming of all law and government. For if they may refuse to give account, then all covenants made with them at coronation, all oaths, are in vain, and mere mockeries; all laws which they swear to keep made to no purpose: for if the king fear not God—as how many of them do not—we hold then our lives and estates by the tenure of his mere grace and mercy, as from a god, not a mortal magistrate; a position that none but court parasites or men besotted would maintain. Aristotle, therefore, whom we commonly allow for one of the best interpreters of nature and morality, writes in the fourth of his *Politics,* chap. x, that "monarchy unaccountable is the worst sort of tyranny, and least of all to be endured by free-born men."

It follows, lastly, that since the King or Magistrate holds his authority of the People, both originally and naturally for their good, in the first place, and not his own, then may the people, as oft as they shall judge it for the best, either choose him or reject him, retain him or despose him, though no tyrant, merely by the liberty and right of free-born men to be governed as seems to them best.

[61] *HOBBES DEPICTS NATURAL MAN: "SOLITARY, POOR, NASTY, BRUTISH"* *

Thomas Hobbes (1588–1679) is the author of one of the great master-works of political philosophy in English, the Leviathan *(1651). It, too, was the product of tumultous civil strife. An enthusiastic royalist, Hobbes sought philosophic justification for kingly prerogative. The result was the following unpleasant view of man and society.*

. . . in the nature of man we find three principal causes of quarrel. First, competition; secondly, diffidence; thirdly, glory.

The first maketh men invade for gain; the second, for safety; and the third, for reputation. The first use violence, to make themselves masters of other men's persons, wives, children, and cattle; the second, to defend them; the third, for trifles, as a word, a smile, a different opinion and any other sign of undervalue, either direct in their persons, or by reflection in their kindred, their friends, their nation, their profession, or their name.

Hereby it is manifest that during the time men live without a common power to keep them all in awe, they are in that condition which is called war; and such a war, as is of every man against every man. For war consisteth not in battle only, or the act of fighting; but in a tract of time, wherein the will to contend by battle is sufficiently known: and therefore the notion of time is to be considered in the nature of war, as it is in the nature of weather. For as the nature of foul weather lieth not in a shower or two of rain, but in an inclination thereto of many days together; so the nature of war consisteth not in actual fighting, but in the known disposition thereto during all the time there is no assurance to the contrary. All other time is peace.

Whatsoever therefore is consequent to a time of war, where every man is enemy to every man, the same is consequent to the time wherein men live without other security than what their own strength and their own invention shall furnish them withal. In such condition there is no place for industry, because the fruit thereof is uncertain, and consequently no culture of the earth; no navigation, nor use of the commodities that may be im-

* W. Molesworth, ed., *The English Works of Thomas Hobbes* (London, 1839), Vol. III, Part 1, ch. 13; Part 2, chs. 17 and 18.

ported by sea; no commodious building; no instruments of moving and removing such things as require much force; no knowledge of the face of the earth; no account of time; no arts; no letters; no society; and, which is worst of all, continual fear and danger of violent death; and the life of man, solitary, poor, nasty, brutish, and short.

The only way to erect a common power . . . to defend them from the invasion of foreigners and the injuries of one another, and thereby to secure them in such sort as that by their own industry, and by the fruits of the earth, they may nourish themselves and live contentedly, is to confer all their power and strength upon one man, or upon one assembly of men, that may reduce all their wills, by plurality of voices, unto one will: which is as much as to say, to appoint one man, or assembly of men, to bear their person; and every one to own and acknowledge himself to be author of whatsoever he that so beareth their person shall act, or cause to be acted, in those things which concern the common peace and safety; and therein to submit their wills, every one to his will, and their judgments to his judgment. This is more than consent, or concord; it is a real unity of them all in one and the same person, made by covenant of every man with every man, in such manner as if every man should say to every man, "I authorize and give up my right of governing myself, to this man or to this assembly of men, on this condition, that thou give up thy right to him and authorize all his actions in like manner." This done, the multitude so united in one person is called a "commonwealth," in Latin *civitas*. This is the generation of that great leviathan, or rather, to speak more reverently, of that mortal god, to which we owe under the immortal God, our peace and defence. For by this authority, given him by every particular man in the commonwealth, he hath the use of so much power and strength conferred on him, that by terror thereof, he is enabled to perform the wills of them all, to peace at home, and mutual aid against their enemies abroad. And in him consisteth the essence of the commonwealth; which, to define it, is "one person, of whose acts a great multitude, by mutual covenants one with another, have made themselves every one the author, to the end he may use the strength and means of them all, as he shall think expedient, for their peace and common defence."

And he that carrieth this person is called sovereign, and said to have sovereign power; and every one besides, his subject.

. . . as the power, so also the honor of the sovereign, ought to be greater than that of any or all the subjects. For in the sovereignty is the fountain of honor. The dignities of lord, earl, duke, and prince are his creatures. As in the presence of the master the servants are equal, and without any honor at all; so are the subjects in the presence of the sovereign. And though they shine some more, some less, when they are out of his sight; yet in his presence, they shine no more than the stars in the presence of the sun.

But a man may here object that the condition of subjects is very miserable; as being obnoxious to the lusts, and other irregular passions of him or them that have so unlimited a power in their hands. And commonly they that live under a monarch, think it the fault of monarchy; and they that live under the government of democracy, or other sovereign assembly, attribute all the inconvenience to that form of commonwealth; whereas the power in all forms, if they be perfect enough to protect them, is the same: not considering that the state of man can never be without some incommodity or other; and that the greatest, that in any form of government can possibly happen to the people in general, is scarce sensible, in respect of the miseries and horrible calamities that accompany a civil war, or that dissolute condition of masterless men, without subjection to laws and a coercive power to tie their hands from rapine and revenge: nor considering that the greatest pressure of sovereign governors proceedeth not from any delight or profit they can expect in the damage or weakening of their subjects, in whose vigor consisteth their own strength and glory; but in the restiveness of themselves, that unwillingly contributing to their own defence, make it necessary for their governors to draw from them what they can in time of peace, that they may have means on any emergent occasion, or sudden need, to resist, or take advantage on their enemies. For all men are by nature provided of notable multiplying glasses, that is their passions and self-love, through which every little payment appeareth a great grievance; but are destitute of those prospective glasses, namely, moral and civil science, to see afar off the miseries that hang over them, and cannot without such payments be avoided.

[62] *BOSSUET EXPLAINS KINGSHIP "BY GRACE OF GOD"* *

The author of the following classic defense of divine-right monarchy is the distinguished bishop, orator, and theologian of the reign of Louis XIV, Bossuet (1627–1704). He and Hobbes have one thing in common: a belief in monarchic absolutism. There the resemblance ends, however. Hobbes' Leviathan *rests on a foundation of philosophic materialism, while Bossuet looked to Scripture for his theories of government.*

We have already seen that all power is of God. The ruler, adds St. Paul,

* Bossuet, *Politics Drawn from the Very Words of Holy Scripture,* as found in James Harvey Robinson, *Readings in European History* (New York: Ginn and Company, 1906), pp. 273–277.

"is the minister of God to thee for good. But if thou do that which is evil, be afraid; for he beareth not the sword in vain: for he is the minister of God, a revenger to execute wrath upon him that doeth evil." Rulers then act as the ministers of God and as his lieutenants on earth. It is through them that God exercises his empire. Think ye "to withstand the kingdom of the Lord in the hand of the sons of David?" Consequently, as we have seen, the royal throne is not the throne of a man, but the throne of God himself. The Lord "hath chosen Solomon my son to sit upon the throne of the kingdom of the Lord over Israel." And again, "Solomon sat on the throne of the Lord."

Moreover, that no one may assume that the Israelites were peculiar in having kings over them who were established by God, note what is said in Ecclesiasticus: "God has given to every people its ruler, and Israel is manifestly reserved to him." He therefore governs all peoples and gives them their kings, although he governed Israel in a more intimate and obvious manner.

It appears from all this that the person of the king is sacred, and that to attack him in any way is sacrilege. God has the kings anointed by his prophets with the holy unction in like manner as he has bishops and altars anointed. But even without the external application in thus being anointed, they are by their very office the representatives of the divine majesty deputed by Providence for the execution of his purposes. . . . Kings should be guarded as holy things, and whosoever neglects to protect them is worthy of death. . . .

There is something religious in the respect accorded to a prince. The service of God and the respect for kings are bound together. St. Peter unites these two duties when he says, "Fear God. Honour the king. . . ."

But kings, although their power comes from on high, as has been said, should not regard themselves as masters of that power to use it at their pleasure; . . . they must employ it with fear and self-restraint, as a thing coming from God and of which God will demand an account. "Hear, O kings, and take heed, understand, judges of the earth, lend your ears, ye who hold the peoples under your sway, and delight to see the multitude that surround you. It is God who gives you the power. Your strength comes from the Most High, who will question your works and penetrate the depths of your thoughts, for, being ministers of his kingdom, ye have not given righteous judgments nor have ye walked according to his will. He will straightway appear to you in a terrible manner, for to those who command is the heaviest punishment reserved. The humble and the weak shall receive mercy, but the mighty shall be mightily tormented. For God fears not the power of any one, because he made both great and small and he has care for both. . . ."

Kings should tremble then as they use the power God has granted them; and let them think how horrible is the sacrilege if they use for evil a power which comes from God. We behold kings seated upon the throne of the Lord, bearing in their hand the sword which God himself has given them. What profanation, what arrogance, for the unjust king to sit on God's throne to render decrees contrary to his laws and to use the sword which God has put in his hand for deeds of violence and to slay his children! . . .

The royal power is absolute. With the aim of making this truth hateful and insufferable, many writers have tried to confound absolute government with arbitrary government. But no two things could be more unlike, . . .

O kings, exercise your power then boldly, for it is divine and salutary for human kind, but exercise it with humility. You are endowed with it from without. At bottom it leaves you feeble, it leaves you mortal, it leaves you sinners, and charges you before God with a very heavy account.

[63] *LOCKE DISCUSSES THE ORIGIN AND CHARACTER OF GOVERNMENT* *

Far more influential than any of the preceding authors, particularly for the leaders of the American Revolution, was John Locke (1632–1704). The author of a great metaphysical work, the Essay Concerning Human Understanding, *Locke in 1690 published his* Two Treatises of Government. *The first treatise is rather negative in the sense that it simply refutes the doctrine of divine right; the second, extracts from which appear below, is the first philosophical statement of the doctrine which will later be called liberalism.*

Political power, then, I take to be a right of making laws, with penalties of death, and consequently all less penalties for the regulating and preserving of property, and of employing the force of the community in the execution of such laws, and in the defense of the commonwealth from foreign injury, and all this only for the public good.

To understand political power right, and derive it from its original, we must consider what state all men are naturally in, and that is a state of perfect freedom to order their actions and dispose of their possessions and persons as they think fit, within the bounds of the law of nature, without asking leave or depending upon the will of any other man.

A state also of equality, wherein all the power and jurisdiction is reciprocal, no one having more than another, there being nothing more evident

* *Of Civil Government*, in *The Works of John Locke* (London, 1824), 12th edition, Vol. IV, Bk. II, chs. 1, 2, 9, 19.

than that creatures of the same species and rank, promiscuously born to all the same advantages of nature, and the use of the same faculties, should also be equal one amongst another, without subordination or subjection, unless the lord and master of them all should, by any manifest declaration of his will, set one above another, and confer on him, by an evident and clear appointment, an undoubted right to dominion and sovereignty.

But though this be a state of liberty, yet it is not a state of license; though man in that state have an uncontrollable liberty to dispose of his person or possessions, yet he has not liberty to destroy himself, or so much as any creature in his possession, but where some nobler use than its bare preservation calls for it. The state of nature has a law of nature to govern it, which obliges every one; and reason, which is that law, teaches all mankind who will but consult it, that being all equal and independent, no one ought to harm another in his life, health, liberty or possessions; . . .

And that all men may be restrained from invading others' rights, and from doing hurt to one another, and the law of nature be observed, which willeth the peace and preservation of all mankind, the execution of the law of nature is in that state put into every man's hands, whereby every one has a right to punish the transgressors of that law to such a degree as may hinder its violation. For the law of nature would, as all other laws that concern man in this world, be in vain if there were nobody that in the state of nature had a power to execute that law, . . .

If man in the state of nature be so free as has been said, if he be absolute lord of his own person and possessions, equal to the greatest and subject to nobody, why will he part with his freedom, why will he give up his empire, and subject himself to the dominion and control of any other power? To which it is obvious to answer, that though in the state of nature he hath such a right, yet the enjoyment of it is very uncertain and constantly exposed to the invasion of others; for all being kings as much as he, every man his equal, and the greater part no strict observers of equity and justice, the enjoyment of the property he has in this state is very unsafe, very insecure. This makes him willing to quit a condition which, however free, is full of fears and continual dangers; and it is not without reason that he seeks out and is willing to join in society with others who are already united, or have a mind to unite for the mutual preservation of their lives, liberties and estates, which I call by the general name—property.

The great and chief end, therefore, of men uniting into commonwealths, and putting themselves under government, is the preservation of their property; to which in the state of nature there are many things wanting.

First: there wants an established, settled, known law, received and allowed by common consent to be the standard of right and wrong, and the common measure to decide all controversies between them. For though the law of nature be plain and intelligible to all rational creatures, yet men, being biased by their interest, as well as ignorant for want of study of it, are not apt to allow of it as a law binding to them in the application of it to their particular cases.

Secondly: in the state of nature there wants a known and indifferent judge, with authority to determine all differences according to the established law. For every one in that state being both judge and executioner of the law of nature, men being partial to themselves, passion and revenge is very apt to carry them too far, and with too much heat in their own cases, as well as negligence and unconcernedness to make them too remiss in other men's.

Thirdly: in the state of nature there often wants power to back and support the sentence when right, and to give it due execution. They who by any injustice offend will seldom fail, where they are able, by force to make good their injustice. Such resistance many times makes the punishment dangerous, and frequently destructive to those who attempt it.

Thus mankind, notwithstanding all the privileges of the state of nature, being but in an ill condition while they remain in it, are quickly driven into society. Hence it comes to pass, that we seldom find any number of men live any time together in this state. The inconveniences that they are therein exposed to by the irregular and uncertain exercise of the power every man has of punishing the transgressions of others, make them take sanctuary under the established laws of government, and therein seek the preservation of their property. . . .

The reason why men enter into society is the preservation of their property; and the end while they choose and authorize a legislative is that there may be laws made, and rules set, as guards and fences to the properties of all the society, to limit the power, and moderate the dominion of every part and member of the society. For since it can never be supposed to be the will of the society that the legislative should have a power to destroy that which every one designs to secure by entering into society, and for which the people submitted themselves to legislators of their own making; whenever the legislators endeavor to take away and destroy the property of the people, or to reduce them to slavery under arbitrary power, they put themselves into a state of war with the people, who are thereupon absolved from any farther obedience, and are left to the common refuge which God hath provided for all men against force and violence. Whensoever, therefore, the legislative shall transgress this fundamental rule of society, and either by ambition, fear, folly, or corruption, endeavor to grasp themselves, or put into the hands of any other, an absolute power over the lives, liberties, and estates of the people, by this breach of trust they forfeit the power the people had put into their hands for quite contrary ends, and it devolves to the people, who have a right to resume their original liberty, and by the establishment of a new legislative (such as they shall think fit), provide for their own safety and security, which is the end for which they are in society. What I have said here concerning the legislative in general holds true also concerning the supreme executor, who having a double trust put in him, both to have a part in the legislative and the supreme execution of the law, acts against both, when he goes about to set up his own arbitrary will as the law of the society. . . .

11

The Beginnings of Modern Science

The seventeenth century is often called the century of genius. The intellectual giants of the period are not only numerous but form a new breed; their fields of interest are no longer the traditional ones of theology, letters, and the arts. The geniuses of this century are in large part preoccupied with the facts of the physical universe ascertained by means of observation and experimentation. Practitioners of experimental science could be found in earlier centuries, but men like Roger Bacon and da Vinci were simply isolated precursors of modern science. In the seventeenth century science became an institution. Scientific academies and journals were founded so that scientists could work together towards a common goal. For increasing numbers of thinking men, science became the key to human progress, to the creation of a better world here on earth.

[64] *COPERNICUS REVIVES THE HELIOCENTRIC THEORY OF THE UNIVERSE* *

Niklas Koppernigk (Nicolaus Copernicus) was born in Poland in 1473. He obtained doctorates of both canon law and medicine in Italian universities but on

* Nicolaus Copernicus, *De Revolutionibus*, trans. by John F. Dobson and Selig Brodetsky (London: Royal Astronomical Society, 1947), Preface and Book I, pp. 3–6. Used by permission of the publisher.

his return to Poland became increasingly interested in astronomy. His great work, Concerning the Revolutions of Heavenly Bodies *(1543), is often said to mark the birth of modern science. The preface, slightly condensed, follows.*

TO THE MOST HOLY LORD, POPE PAUL III

I may well presume, most Holy Father, that certain people, as soon as they hear that in this book I ascribe movement to the earthly globe, will cry out that, holding such views, I should at once be hissed off the stage. For I am not so pleased with my own work that I should fail duly to weigh the judgment which others may pass thereon; and though I know that the speculations of a philosopher are far removed from the judgment of the multitude—for his aim is to seek truth in all things as far as God has permitted human reason so to do—yet I hold that opinions which are quite erroneous should be avoided.

Thinking therefore within myself that to ascribe movement to the Earth must indeed seem an absurd performance on my part to those who know that many centuries have consented to the establishment of the contrary judgment, namely that the Earth is placed immovably as the central point in the middle of the Universe, I hesitated long whether, on the one hand, I should give to the light these my Commentaries written to prove the Earth's motion, or whether, on the other hand, it were better to follow the example of the Pythagoreans and others who were wont to impart their philosophic mysteries only to intimates and friends, and then not in writing but by word of mouth, as the letter of Lysis to Hipparchus witnesses. . . . the thought of the scorn which I had to fear on account of the novelty and incongruity of my theory, well-nigh induced me to abandon my project.

These misgivings and actual protests have been overcome by my friends. First among these was Nicolaus Schonberg, Cardinal of Capua, a man renowned in every department of learning. Next was one who loved me well, Tiedemann Giese, Bishop of Kulm, a devoted student of sacred and all other good literature, who often urged and even importuned me to publish this work which I had kept in store not for nine years only, but to a fourth period of nine years. The same request was made to me by many other eminent and learned men. They urged that I should not, on account of my fears, refuse any longer to contribute the fruits of my labours to the common advantage of those interested in mathematics. They insisted that, though my theory of the Earth's movement might at first seem strange, yet it would appear admirable and acceptable when the publication of my elucidatory comments should dispel the mists of paradox. Yielding then to their persuasion I at last permitted my friends to publish that work which they have so long demanded. . . .

I pondered long upon [the] uncertainty of mathematical tradition in establishing the motions of the system of the spheres. At last I began to chafe that philosophers could by no means agree on any one certain theory of the mechanism of the Universe, wrought for us by a supremely good and orderly Creator, though in other respects they investigated with meticulous care the minutest points relating to its orbits. I therefore took pains to read again the works of all the philosophers on whom I could lay hand to seek out whether any of them had ever supposed that the motions of the spheres were other than those demanded by the mathematical schools. I found first in Cicero that Hicetas had realized that the Earth moved. Afterwards I found in Plutarch that certain others had held the like opinion. . . .

Taking advantage of this I too began to think of the mobility of the Earth; and though the opinion seemed absurd, yet knowing now that others before me had been granted freedom to imagine such circles as they chose to explain the phenomena of the stars, I considered that I also might easily be allowed to try whether, by assuming some motion of the Earth, sounder explanations than theirs for the revolution of the celestial spheres might so be discovered.

Thus assuming motions, which in my work I ascribe to the Earth, by long and frequent observations I have at last discovered that, if the motions of the rest of the planets be brought into relation with the circulation of the Earth and be reckoned in proportion to the orbit of each planet, not only do their phenomena presently ensue, but the orders and magnitudes of all stars and spheres, nay the heavens themselves, become so bound together that nothing in any part thereof could be moved from its place without producing confusion of all the other parts and of the Universe as a whole.

In the course of the work the order which I have pursued is as here follows. In the first book I describe all positions of the spheres together with such movements as I ascribe to Earth; so that this book contains, as it were, the general system of the Universe. Afterwards, in the remaining books, I relate the motions of the other planets and all the spheres to the mobility of Earth, that we may gather thereby how far the motions and appearances of the rest of the planets and spheres may be preserved, if related to the motions of the Earth.

I doubt not that gifted and learned mathematicians will agree with me if they are willing to comprehend and appreciate, not superficially but thoroughly, according to the demands of this science, such reasoning as I bring to bear in support of my judgment. But that learned and unlearned alike may see that I shrink not from any man's criticism, it is to your Holiness rather than anyone else that I have chosen to dedicate these studies of mine, since in this remote corner of Earth in which I live you are regarded as the most eminent by virtue alike of the dignity of your Office and of your love of letters and science. You by your influence and judgment can readily hold the slanders from biting, though the proverb hath it that there is no remedy against a sycophant's tooth. It may fall out, too, that idle babblers, ignorant of mathematics, may claim a right to pronounce a judgment on my work, by reason of a certain passage of Scripture basely twisted to suit their purpose. Should any such venture to criticize and carp at my project, I make no account of them; I consider their judgment rash, and utterly despise it. I well know that even Lactantius, a writer in other ways distinguished but in no sense a mathematician, discourses in a most childish fashion touching the shape of the Earth, ridiculing even those who have stated the Earth to be a sphere. Thus my supporters need not be amazed if some people of like sort ridicule me too.

[65] *GALILEO ORIGINATES TELESCOPIC ASTRONOMY* *

Copernicus' heliocentric theory gained little acceptance until the astronomers of later generations began to produce data which made it incontrovertible. Galileo Galilei (1564–1642), making use of the telescope, furnished such proof. Following is his account (1610) of his early observations.

In the present small treatise I set forth some matters of great interest for all observers of natural phenomena to look at and consider. They are of great interest, I think, first, from their intrinsic excellence; secondly, from their absolute novelty; and lastly, also on account of the instrument by the aid of which they have been presented to my apprehension.

The number of the fixed Stars which observers have been able to see without artificial powers of sight up to this day can be counted. It is therefore decidely a great feat to add to their number, and to set distinctly before the eyes other stars in myriads, which have never been seen before, and which surpass the old, previously known, stars in number more than ten times.

Again, it is a most beautiful and delightful sight to behold the body of the Moon, which is distant from us nearly sixty semidiameters of the Earth, as near as if it was at a distance of only two of the same measures; so that the diameter of this same Moon appears about thirty times larger, its surface about nine hundred times, and its solid mass nearly 27,000 times larger than when it is viewed only with the naked eye: and consequently any one may

* Galileo Galilei, "The Siderial Messenger," as found in Harlow Shapley and Helen Howarth, eds., *A Source Book in Astronomy* (New York: McGraw-Hill Book Co., Inc., 1929), pp. 41–43. Used by permission of Harvard University Press, the copyright owner.

know with the certainty that is due to the use of our senses, that the Moon certainly does not possess a smooth and polished surface, but one rough and uneven, and, just like the face of the Earth itself, is everywhere full of vast protuberances, deep chasms, and sinuosities.

Then to have got rid of disputes about the Galaxy or Milky Way, and to have made its nature clear to the very senses, not to say to the understanding, seems by no means a matter which ought to be considered of slight importance. In addition to this, to point out, as with one's finger, the nature of those stars which every one of the astronomers up to this time has called *nebulous,* and to demonstrate that it is very different from what has hitherto been believed, will be pleasant, and very fine. But that which will excite the greatest astonishment by far, and which indeed especially moved me to call to the attention of all astronomers and philosophers, is this, namely, that I have discovered four planets, neither known nor observed by any one of the astronomers before my time, which have their orbits round a certain bright star, one of those previously known, like Venus and Mercury round the Sun, and are sometimes in front of it, sometimes behind it, though they never depart from it beyond certain limits. All which facts were discovered and observed a few days ago by the help of a telescope devised by me, through God's grace first enlightening my mind.

Perchance, other discoveries still more excellent will be made from time to time by me or by other observers, with the assistance of a similar instrument, so I will first briefly record its shape and preparation, as well as the occasion of its being devised, and then I will give an account of the observations made by me.

About ten months ago a report reached my ears that a Dutchman had constructed a telescope, by the aid of which visible objects, although at a great distance from the eye of the observer, were seen distinctly as if near; and some proofs of its most wonderful performances were reported, which some gave credence to, but others contradicted. A few days after, I received confirmation of the report in a letter written from Paris by a noble Frenchman, Jaques Badovere, which finally determined me to give myself up first to inquire into the principle of the telescope, and then to consider the means by which I might compass the invention of a similar instrument, which after a little while I succeeded in doing, through deep study of the theory of Refraction; and I prepared a tube, at first of lead, in the ends of which I fitted two glass lenses, both plane on one side, but on the other side one spherically convex, and the other concave. Then bringing my eye to the concave lens I saw objects satisfactorily large and near, for they appeared one-third of the distance off and nine times larger than when they are seen with the natural eye alone. I shortly afterwards constructed another telescope with more nicety, which magnified objects more than sixty times. At length, by sparing neither labour nor expense, I succeeded in constructing for myself an instrument so superior that objects seen through it appear magnified nearly a thousand times, and more than thirty times nearer than if viewed by the natural powers of sight alone.

It would be altogether a waste of time to enumerate the number and importance of the benefits which this instrument may be expected to confer, when used by land or sea. But without paying attention to its use for terrestrial objects, I betook myself to observations of the heavenly bodies; and first of all, I viewed the Moon as near as if it was scarcely two semidiameters of the Earth distant. After the Moon, I frequently observed other heavenly bodies, both fixed stars and planets, with incredible delight; and, when I saw their very great number, I began to consider about a method by which I might be able to measure their distances apart, and at length I found one. And here it is fitting that all who intend to turn their attention to observations of this kind should receive certain cautions. For, in the first place, it is absolutely necessary for them to prepare a most perfect telescope, one which will show very bright objects distinct and free from any mistiness, and will magnify them at least 400 times, for then it will show them as if only one-twentieth of their distance off. For, unless the instrument be of such power, it will be in vain to attempt to view all the things which have been seen by me in the heavens, or which will be enumerated hereafter . . .

[66] *FRANCIS BACON PLEADS FOR THE "TRUE INTERPRETATION OF NATURE"* *

One of the most vigorous proponents of the new scientific learning was Fráncis Bacon (1561–1626). In his Novum Organum, *selections from which follow, and many other lengthy works, he argued for knowledge derived from observation of phenomena rather than from religious authority or the ancients.*

. . . There are . . . three sources of error and three species of false philosophy; the sophistic, empiric, and superstitious.

Aristotle affords the most eminent instance of the first; for he corrupted natural philosophy by logic—thus he formed the world of categories, assigned to the human soul, the noblest of substances, a genus determined by words of secondary operation, treated of density and rarity (by which bodies occupy a greater or lesser space), by the frigid distinctions of action

* Francis Bacon, *Advancement of Learning and Novum Organum* (New York and London: The Co-Operative Publication Society, 1900), pp. 327–328, 332–333, 341, 366.

and power, asserted that there was a peculiar and proper motion in all bodies, and that if they shared in any other motion, it was owing to an external moving cause, and imposed innumerable arbitrary distinctions upon the nature of things; being everywhere more anxious as to definitions in teaching and the accuracy of the wording of his propositions, than the internal truth of things. . . . Nor is much stress to be laid on his frequent recourse to experiment in his books on animals, his problems, and other treatises; for he had already decided, without having properly consulted experience as the basis of his decisions and axioms, and after having so decided, he drags experiment along as a captive constrained to accommodate herself to his decisions; so that he is even more to be blamed than his modern followers (of the scholastic school) who have deserted her altogether.

The empiric school produces dogmas of a more deformed and monstrous nature than the sophistic or theoretic school; not being founded in the light of common notions (which, however poor and superstitious, is yet in a manner universal, and of a general tendency), but in the confined obscurity of a few experiments. Hence this species of philosophy appears probable, and almost certain to those who are daily practised in such experiments, and have thus corrupted their imagination, but incredible and futile to others. We have a strong instance of this in the alchemists and their dogmas; . . .

The corruption of philosophy by the mixing of it up with superstition and theology, is of a much wider extent, and is most injurious to it both as a whole and in parts. For the human understanding is no less exposed to the impressions of fancy, than to those of vulgar notions. The disputatious and sophistic school entraps the understanding, whilst the fanciful, bombastic, and, as it were, poetical school, rather flatters it. There is a clear example of this among the Greeks, especially in Pythagoras, where, however, the superstition is coarse and overcharged, but it is more dangerous and refined in Plato and his school. This evil is found also in some branches of other systems of philosophy, where it introduces abstracted forms, final and first causes, omitting frequently the intermediate and the like. Against it we must use the greatest caution; for the apotheosis of error is the greatest evil of all, and when folly is worshipped, it is, as it were, a plague spot upon the understanding. Yet some of the moderns have indulged this folly with such consummate inconsiderateness, that they have endeavored to build a system of natural philosophy on the first chapter of Genesis, the book of Job, and other parts of Scripture; seeking thus the dead amongst the living. And this folly is the more to be prevented and restrained, because not only fantastical philosophy, but heretical religion spring from the absurd mixture of matters divine and human. It is therefore most wise soberly to render unto faith the things that are faith's.

The sciences we possess have been principally derived from the Greeks; for the additions of the Roman, Arabic, or more modern writers, are but few and of small importance, and such as they are, are founded on the basis of Greek invention. But the wisdom of the Greeks was professional and disputatious, and thus most adverse to the investigation of truth. The name, therefore, of sophists, which the contemptuous spirit of those who deemed themselves philosophers, rejected and transferred to the rhetoricians—Gorgias, Protagoras, Hippias, Polus—might well suit the whole tribe, such as Plato, Aristotle, Zeno, Epicurus, Theophrastus, and their successors—Chrysippus, Carneades, and the rest. There was only this difference between them—the former were mercenary vagabonds, travelling about to different states, making a show of their wisdom, and requiring pay; the latter more dignified and noble, in possession of fixed habitations, opening schools, and teaching philosophy gratuitously. Both, however (though differing in other respects), were professorial, and reduced every subject to controversy, establishing and defending certain sects and dogmas of philosophy, so that their doctrines were nearly (what Dionysius not unaptly objected to Plato) the talk of idle old men to ignorant youths. . . .

No one has yet been found possessed of sufficient firmness and severity to resolve upon and undertake the task of entirely abolishing common theories and notions, and applying the mind afresh, when thus cleared and leveled, to particular researches; hence our human reasoning is a mere farrago and crude mass made up of a great deal of credulity and accident, and the puerile notions it originally contracted.

It will, perhaps, be as well to distinguish three species and degrees of ambition. First, that of men who are anxious to enlarge their own power in their country, which is a vulgar and degenerate kind; next, that of men who strive to enlarge the power and empire of their country over mankind, which is more dignified but not less covetous; but if one were to endeavor to renew and enlarge the power and empire of mankind in general over the universe, such ambition (if it may be so termed) is both more sound and more noble than the other two. Now the empire of man over things is founded on the arts and sciences alone, for nature is only to be commanded by obeying her.

Lastly, let none be alarmed at the objection of the arts and sciences becoming depraved to malevolent or luxurious purposes and the like, for the same can be said of every worldly good; talent, courage, strength, beauty, riches, light itself, and the rest. Only let mankind regain their rights over nature, assigned to them by the gift of God, and obtain that power, whose exercise will be governed by right reason and true religion.

[67] *HARVEY PLOTS A "NEW ROUTE" FOR THE BLOOD* *

William Harvey's epoch-making treatise, On the Motion of the Heart and Blood in Animals, *first appeared in 1628 in a Latin edition published in Germany. The notion of the circulation of the blood stirred up violent controversy in the medical profession but was generally accepted within a generation after Harvey's death in 1657. The dedication of the treatise to Harvey's colleagues in the Royal College of Physicians is given here.*

I have already and repeatedly presented you, my learned friends, with my new views of the motion and function of the heart, in my anatomcial lectures; but having now for more than nine years confirmed these views by multiplied demonstrations in your presence, illustrated them by arguments, and freed them from the objections of the most learned and skilful anatomists, I at length yield to the requests, I might say entreaties, of many, and here present them for general consideration in this treatise.

Were not the work indeed presented through you, my learned friends, I should scarce hope that it could come out scatheless and complete; for you have in general been the faithful witnesses of almost all the instances from which I have either collected the truth or confuted error. You have seen my dissections, and at my demonstrations of all that I maintain to be objects of sense, you have been accustomed to stand by and bear me out with your testimony. And as this book alone declares the blood to course and revolve by a new route, very different from the ancient and beaten pathway trodden for so many ages, and illustrated by such a host of learned and distinguished men, I was greatly afraid lest I might be charged with presumption did I lay my work before the public at home, or send it beyond seas for impression, unless I had first proposed the subject to you, had confirmed its conclusions by ocular demonstrations in your presence, had replied to your doubts and objections, and secured the assent and support of our distinguished President. For I was most intimately persuaded, that if I could make good my proposition before you and our College, illustrious by its numerous body of learned individuals, I had less to fear from others. I even

* William Harvey, *On the Motion of the Heart and Blood in Animals,* as found in *The Harvard Classics* (New York: P. F. Collier Son Corp., 1910), Vol. XXXVIII, pp. 65–67. Used by permission of the publisher.

ventured to hope that I should have the comfort of finding all that you had granted me in your sheer love of truth, conceded by others who were philosophers like yourselves. True philosophers, who are only eager for truth and knowledge, never regard themselves as already so thoroughly informed, but that they welcome further information from whomsoever and from wheresoever it may come; nor are they so narrow-minded as to imagine any of the arts or sciences transmitted to us by the ancients, in such a state of forwardness or completeness, that nothing is left for the ingenuity and industry of others. On the contrary, very many maintain that all we know is still infinitely less than all that still remains unknown; nor do philosophers pin their faith to others' precepts in such wise that they lose their liberty, and cease to give credence to the conclusions of their proper senses. Neither do they swear such fealty to their mistress Antiquity, that they openly, and in sight of all, deny and desert their friend Truth. But even as they see that the credulous and vain are disposed at the first blush to accept and believe everything that is proposed to them, so do they observe that the dull and unintellectual are indisposed to see what lies before their eyes, and even deny the light of the noonday sun. They teach us in our course of philosophy to sedulously avoid the fables of the poets and the fancies of the vulgar, as the false conclusions of the sceptics. And then the studious and good and true, never suffer their minds to be warped by the passions of hatred and envy, which unfit men duly to weigh the arguments that are advanced in behalf of truth, or to appreciate the proposition that is even fairly demonstrated. Neither do they think it unworthy of them to change their opinion if truth and undoubted demonstration require them to do so. They do not esteem it discreditable to desert error, though sanctioned by the highest antiquity, for they know full well that to err, to be deceived, is human; that many things are discovered by accident and that many may be learned indifferently from any quarter, by an old man from a youth, by a person of understanding from one of inferior capacity.

My dear colleagues, I had no purpose to swell this treatise into a large volume by quoting the names and writings of anatomists, or to make a parade of the strength of my memory, the extent of my reading, and the amount of my pains; because I profess both to learn and to teach anatomy, not from books but from dissections; not from the positions of philosophers but from the fabric of nature; and then because I do not think it right or proper to strive to take from the ancients any honor that is their due, nor yet to dispute with the moderns, and enter into controversy with those who have excelled in anatomy and been my teachers. I would not charge with wilful falsehood any one who was sincerely anxious for truth, nor lay it to any one's door as a crime that he had fallen into error. I avow myself the partisan of truth alone; and I can indeed say that I have used all my endeavours, bestowed all my pains on an attempt to produce something that should be agreeable to the good, profitable to the learned, and useful to letters.

[68] *MOLIÈRE SATIRIZES THE MEDICAL PROFESSION* *

In the seventeenth century by no means all medical practitioners emulated Harvey in their approach to medical problems. The authority of the ancient Greeks still remained very strong. Many doctors were more intent on showing their classical learning than on curing their patients. No one has more effectively satirized the pretentiousness of the profession than Molière (1622–1673). Here is a scene from one of his plays, The Physician in Spite of Himself.

SGANARELLE. Is this the patient?

GÉRONTE. Yes, I have but one daughter; and I would never get over it if she were to die.

SGANARELLE. Do not let her do anything of the kind. She must not die without a prescription of the physician. . . .

GÉRONTE. . . . She has become dumb, without our having been able till now to discover the cause. This accident has obliged us to postpone her marriage.

SGANARELLE. And why so?

GÉRONTE. He whom she is going to marry wishes to wait for her recovery to conclude the marriage.

SGANARELLE. And who is this fool that does not want his wife to be dumb? Would to Heaven that mine had that complaint! I should take particular care not to have her cured. . . . (*Turning to the patient.*) Give me your hand. (*To Géronte.*) The pulse tells me that your daughter is dumb.

GÉRONTE. Sir, that is what is the matter with her; ah! yes, you have found it out at the first touch.

SGANARELLE. Of course!

JACQUELINE. See how he has guessed her complaint.

SGANARELLE. We great physicians, we know matters at once. An ignoramus would have been nonplussed, and would have told you: it is this, that or the other; but I hit the nail on the head from the very first, and I tell you that your daughter is dumb.

GÉRONTE. Yes, but I should like you to tell me whence it arises.

* Molière, *The Physician in Spite of Himself,* Act II, Scene vi, in *The Dramatic Works of Molière* (Philadelphia: Gebbie and Barrie, 1878), pp. 276–280.

SGANARELLE. Nothing is easier; it arises from loss of speech.

GÉRONTE. Very good. But the reason of her having lost her speech, pray?

SGANARELLE. Our best authorities will tell you that it is because there is an impediment in the action of her tongue.

GÉRONTE. But, once more, your opinion upon this impediment in the action of her tongue.

SGANARELLE. Aristotle on this subjects says . . . a great many clever things.

GÉRONTE. I dare say.

SGANARELLE. Ah! He was a great man!

GÉRONTE. No doubt.

SGANARELLE. Yes, a very great man. (*Holding out his arm, and putting a finger of the other hand in the bend.*) A man who was, by this, much greater than I. But to come back to our argument: I am of opinion that this impediment in the action of her tongue is caused by certain humours, which among us learned men, we call peccant humours; peccant—that is to say . . . peccant humours; inasmuch as the vapours formed by the exhalations of the influences which rise in the very region of diseases, coming . . . as we may say to . . . Do you understand Latin?

GÉRONTE. Not in the least.

SGANARELLE. (*Suddenly rising.*) You do not understand Latin?

GÉRONTE. No.

SGANARELLE. (*Assuming various comic attitudes.*) *Cabricias arci thuram, catalamus, singulariter, nominativo, haec musa,* the muse, *bonus, bona, bonum. Deus sanctus, estne oratio latinas? Etiam,* Yes. *Quare?* Why. *Quia substantivo et adjectivum, concordat in generi, numerum, et casus.*

GÉRONTE. Ah! Why did I not study?

JACQUELINE. What a clever man!

LUCAS. Yes, it is so beautiful that I do not understand a word of it.

SGANARELLE. Thus these vapours which I speak of, passing from the left side, where the liver is, to the right side, where we find the heart, it so happens that the lungs, which in Latin we call *armyan,* having communication with the brain, which in Greek we style *nasmus,* by means of the *vena cava,* which in Hebrew, is termed *cubile,* meet in their course the said vapours, which fill the ventricles of the omoplata; and because the said vapours . . . now understand well this argument, pray . . . and because these said vapours are endowed with a certain malignity . . . listen well to this, I beseech you.

GÉRONTE. Yes.

SGANARELLE. Are endowed with a certain malignity which is caused . . . pay attention here, if you please.

GÉRONTE. I do.

SGANARELLE. Which is caused by the acridity of these humours engendered in the concavity of the diaphragm, it happens that these vapours . . . *Ossabandus, nequeis, nequer, potarinum, puipsa milus.* That is exactly the reason that your daughter is dumb.

JACQUELINE. Ah! How well this gentleman explains all this.

LUCAS. Why does not my tongue wag as well as his?

GÉRONTE. It is undoubtedly impossible to argue better. There is but one thing that I cannot exactly make out: that is the whereabouts of the liver and the heart. It appears to me that you place them differently from what they are; that the heart is on the left side, and the liver on the right.

SGANARELLE. Yes; this was so formerly; but we have changed all that, and we now-a-days practise the medical art on an entirely new system.

GÉRONTE. I did not know that, and I pray you pardon my ignorance.

SGANARELLE. There is no harm done; and you are not obliged to be so clever as we are.

GÉRONTE. Certainly not. But what think you, Sir, ought to be done for this complaint?

SGANARELLE. What do I think ought to be done?

GÉRONTE. Yes.

SGANARELLE. My advice is to put her to bed again, and make her, as a remedy, take plenty of bread soaked in wine.

GÉRONTE. Why so, sir?

SGANARELLE. Because there is in bread and wine mixed together a sympathetic virtue which produces speech. Do you not see that they give nothing else to parrots, and that, by eating it, they learn to speak?

GÉRONTE. That is true. Oh! the great man! Quick, plenty of bread and wine.

SGANARELLE. I shall come back tonight to see how the patient is getting along. . . .

[69] *NEWTON OFFERS THE* PRINCIPIA *TO THE WORLD* *

Easily the most famous scientist of his time was Isaac Newton (1642–1727). His greatest work was Mathematical Principles of Natural Philosophy, *usually referred to as Newton's* Principia, *which appeared in 1687. In this book Newton proved that the entire physical universe is subject to the same laws of gravitation*

* Sir Isaac Newton, *Mathematical Principles of Natural Philosophy and His System of the World,* trans. by Andrew Motte (1729) and revised by Florian Cajori (Berkeley, Cal.: University of California Press, 1947), pp. xvii, xviii, 398–400. Used by permission.

and motion we observe on earth. His conception of the universe remained unchallenged until scientists of our own day placed certain limitations on his design. Here is Newton's preface to his monumental treatise and a short extract therefrom.

[A] Newton's Preface to the First Edition of the *Principia*

Since the ancients . . . esteemed the science of mechanics of greatest importance in the investigation of natural things, and the moderns, rejecting substantial forms and occult qualities, have endeavored to subject the phenomena of nature to the laws of mathematics, I have in this treatise cultivated mathematics as far as it relates to philosophy. The ancients considered mechanics in a twofold respect; as rational, which proceeds accurately by demonstration, and practical. To practical mechanics all the manual arts belong, from which mechanics took its name. But as artificers do not work with perfect accuracy, it comes to pass that mechanics is so distinguished from geometry that what is perfectly accurate is called geometrical; what is less so, is called mechanical. However, the errors are not in the art, but in the artificers. He that works with less accuracy is an imperfect mechanic; and if any could work with perfect accuracy, he would be the most perfect mechanic of all, for the description of right lines and circles, upon which geometry is founded, belongs to mechanics. Geometry does not teach us to draw these lines, but requires them to be drawn, for it requires that the learners should first be taught to describe these accurately before he enters upon geometry, then it shows how by these operations problems may be solved. To describe right lines and circles are problems, but not geometrical problems. The solution of these problems is required from mechanics, and by geometry the use of them, when so solved is shown; and it is the glory of geometry that from those few principles, brought from without, it is able to produce so many things. Therefore geometry is founded in mechanical practice, and is nothing but that part of universal mechanics which accurately proposes and demonstrates the art of measuring. But since the manual arts are chiefly employed in the moving of bodies, it happens that geometry is commonly referred to their magnitude, and mechanics to their motion. In this sense rational mechanics will be the science of motions resulting from any forces whatsoever, and of the forces required to produce any motions, accurately proposed and demonstrated. This part of mechanics, as far as it extended to the five powers which relate to manual arts, was cultivated by the ancients, who considered gravity (it not being a manual power) no otherwise than in moving weights by those powers. But I consider philosophy rather than arts and write not concerning manual but natural powers, and considering chiefly those things which relate to gravity, levity, elastic force, the resistance of fluids, and the like forces, whether attractive or impulsive; and therefore I offer this work as the mathematical principles of philosophy, for the whole burden of philosophy seems to consist in this—from the phenomena of motions to investigate the forces of nature, and then from these forces to demonstrate the other phenomena; and to this end the general propositions in the first and second Books are directed. In the third Book I give an example of this in the explication of the System of the World; for by the propositions mathematically demonstrated in the former Books, in the Third I derive from the celestical phenomena the forces of gravity with which bodies tend to the sun and the several planets. Then from these forces, by other propositions which are also mathematical, I deduce the motions of the planets, the comets, the moon, and the sea. I wish we could derive the rest of the phenomena of Nature by the same kind of reasoning from mechanical principles, for I am induced by many reasons to suspect that they may all depend upon certain forces by which the particles of bodies, by some causes hitherto unknown, are either mutually impelled towards one another, and cohere in regular figures, or are repelled and recede from one another. These forces being unknown, philosophers have hitherto attempted the search of Nature in vain; but I hope the principles here laid down will afford some light either to this or some truer method of philosophy.

. . . I heartily beg that what I have here done may be read with forebearance; and that my labors in a subject so difficult may be examined, not so much with a view to censure, as to remedy their defects.

[B] Rules of Reasoning in Philosophy

RULE I

We are to admit no more causes of natural things than such as are both true and sufficient to explain their appearance.

To this purpose the philosophers say that Nature does nothing in vain, and more is in vain when less will serve; for Nature is pleased with simplicity, and affects not the pomp of superfluous causes.

RULE II

Therefore to the same natural effects we must, as far as possible, assign the same causes.

As to respiration in a man and in a beast; the descent of stones in Europe and in America; the light of our culinary fire and of the sun; the reflection of light in the earth, and in the planets.

RULE III

The qualities of bodies, which admit neither intensification nor remission of degrees, and which are found to belong to all bodies within the reach of our experiments, are to be esteemed the universal qualities of all bodies whatsoever.

For since the qualities of bodies are only known to us by experiments, we are to hold for universal all such as universally agree with experiments; and such as are not liable to diminution can never be quite taken away. We are certainly not to relinquish the evidence of experiments for the sake of dreams and vain fictions of our own devising; nor are we to recede from the analogy of Nature, which is wont to be simple, and always consonant to it-self. We no other way know the extension of bodies than by our senses, nor do these reach it in all bodies; but because we perceive extension in all that are sensible, therefore we ascribe it universally to all others also. That abundance of bodies are hard, we learn by experience; and because the hardness of the whole arises from the hardness of the parts, we therefore justly infer the hardness of the undivided particles not only of the bodies we feel but of all others. That all bodies are impenetrable, we gather not from reason, but from sensation. The bodies which we handle we find im-penetrable and thence conclude impenetrability to be an universal property of all bodies whatsoever. That all bodies are movable, and endowed with certain powers (which we call inertia) of persevering in their motion, or in their rest, we only infer from the like properties observed in the bodies which we have seen. The extension, hardness, impenetrability, mobility, and inertia of the whole, result from the extension, hardness, impenetrability, mobility, and inertia of the parts; and hence we conclude the least particles of all bodies to be also all extended, and hard and impenetrable, and mov-able, and endowed with their proper inertia. And this is the foundation of all philosophy. . . .

RULE IV

In experimental philosophy we are to look upon propositions inferred by gen-eral inductions from phenomena as accurately or very nearly true, notwith-standing any contrary hypotheses that may be imagined, till such time as other phenomena occur, by which they may either be made more accurate, or liable to exceptions.

This rule we must follow, that the argument of induction may not be evaded by hypotheses.

[70] COLBERT COMBINES ASTRONOMY AND ICHTHYOLOGY *

By the second half of the 17th century, science had become what it is now, a measure of national prestige. In France, Colbert in particular took a lively interest in the patronage of scientific work, as can be seen in these two typical letters found in his correspondence.

Colbert to Abbé Picard, on Mission at Brest, September 21, 1679

I am very happy to hear that you have taken some fine [astronomical] observations which will perhaps be very advantageous. Continue your work with great care. However, I have deemed it very necessary to send the sieur du Verney to find you, my intention being that the sieur de La Hire stay with him and that the two of them investigate all the fish life which they can find on the coast of Brittany and that of Normandy, in order to dissect it and make drawings, in the conviction that this will be a very pleasant and singular work and one which will even be of practical value.

It is essential then that, as soon as the said sieur du Verney has joined you, and while you are taking your observations, that they work together investigating [and] fishing in all the harbors and following the coasts of these two provinces. If they consider it necessary to go even as far as Picardy, there should be no hesitation about doing so; and in case expense is incurred, for fishing or for the purchase of the said fish, the sieur de La Hire will take care of it and will render an account to me punctually every week. In case he needs money, if he will let me know I will not fail to get it to him.

When the astronomical observations are completed, you may return and let them complete the expedition along the coasts of these two provinces.

Colbert to Sieur de La Hire, Member of the Academy of Sciences, on Mission in Brittany, Nov. 10, 1679

I have received the letter informing me of the dissections which you have made of several fish. Continue in this research and be assured that there is no time better spent than this, because this work will be very useful joined to the other dissections which have been made and which will continue to be made in the Academy [of Sciences].

* Pierre Clément, ed., *Lettres, Instructions, et Mémoires de Colbert* (Paris: Imprimerie Impériale, 1868), Vol. V, pp. 403–404, 407–408. Our translation.

12

The Expansion and Europeanization of Russia

To Europeans of medieval and early modern times, Russia seemed as remote and barbaric as it was inconsequential to the continental balance of power. But from the early 18th century on, although most Europeans continued to regard Russians as people of doubtful civilization, no longer could Russia be disregarded by western governments. The man responsible for the emergence of Russia onto the stage of history was the extraordinary Tsar Peter the Great (1689–1725). By supreme strength of will, and despite the strenuous opposition of the great majority of his subjects, he partially modernized and Europeanized Russian institutions. Russia was never quite the same again. For two centuries Russians remained gravely divided between those who were willing to accept westernization—mainly the upper classes—and those who rejected it—the common people.

[71] *AN ENGLISHMAN DESCRIBES THE RUSSIA OF IVAN THE TERRIBLE* *

Ivan III (1533–1584) was the first grand duke of Muscovy to assume the title tsar. *He suffered from insanity, which manifested itself in a pathological fear of*

* Richard Hakluyt, *The Principal Navigations, Voyages, Traffiques and Discoveries of the English Nation* (New York: The Macmillan Company, 1903, Vol. II, pp. 438–448.

the boyars, or old nobility. Everyone he suspected of disloyalty he had murdered or executed, including his own son. The following description of Russian society in his day was written in 1557 by the English traveller, Anthony Jenkinson.

THE MANERS, USAGES, AND CEREMONIES OF THE RUSSES

OF THE EMPEROUR

The Emperours name in their tongue is Ivan Vasilivich, . . . Before his father they were neither called Emperours nor kings but onely Ruese Velike, that is to say, great Duke. And as this Emperor which now is Ivan Vasilivich, doeth exceede his predecessors in name, that is, from a Duke to an Emperour, even so much by report he doeth exceede them in stoutnesse of courage and valiantnesse, and a great deale more: for he is no more afraid of his enemies which are not few, then the Hobbie of the larks.

This Emperour useth great familiaritie, as wel unto all his nobles and subjects, as also unto strangers which serve him either in his warres, or in occupations: for his pleasure is that they shall dine oftentimes in the yeere in his presence, and besides that he is oftentimes abroad, either at one Church or another, and walking with his noble men abroad. And by this meanes he is not onely beloved of his nobles and commons, but also had in great dread and feare through all his dominions, so that I thinke no prince in Christendome is more feared of his owne then he is, nor yet better beloved. For if he bid any of his Dukes goe, they will runne, if he give any evil or angrie worde to any of them, the partie will not come into his majesties presence againe of a long time if he be not sent for, but will faine him to be very sicke, and will let the haire of his head grow very long, without either cutting or shaving, which is an evident token that hee is in the Emperours displeasure: for when they be in their prosperity, they account it a shame to weare long haire, in consideration whereof, they use to have their heads shaven.

His majesty heareth all complaints himselfe, and with his owne mouth giveth sentence, and judgement of all matters, and that with expedition: but religious matters he medleth not withall, but referreth them wholly unto the Metropolitane.

OF THEIR RELIGIOUS MEN

The Metropolitane is next unto God, our Lady and S. Nicholas excepted . . . All matters of religion are reformed by the Metropolitane, he heareth the causes and giveth sentence as himselfe listeth, and is authorized so to doe, whether it be to whip, hang or burne, his will must needs be fulfilled.

They have both monks, friers and nunnes, with a great number of great & rich monasteries: they keepe great hospitalitie, and doe relieve much poore people day by day. . . . They shewed me a coffin covered with cloth of gold which stoode upon one side within their church, in which they told me lay a holy man, who never eate or dranke, and yet that he liveth. And they told me (supposing that I had beleeved them) that he healeth many diseases, and giveth the blind their sight, with many other miracles, but I was hard of belief because I saw him worke no miracle whilest I was there.

They have no preachers no not one in al the land to instruct the people, so that there are many, & the most part of the poore in the country, who if one aske them how many gods there be, they wil say a great many, meaning that every image which they have is a god: for all the countrey and the Emperours majesty himselfe wil blesse and bowe, and knocke their heads before their images, in so much that they will crie earnestly unto their images to helpe them to the things which they need. Al men are bound by their law to have those images in their houses, and over every gate in all their townes and cities are images set up, unto which the people bow and bend, and knocke their heads against the ground before them: as often as they come by any church or crosse they do in like maner. And when they come to any house, they blesse themselves 3. or 4. times before they will salute any man in the house.

All their service is in the Russe tongue, and they and the common people have no other praiers but this, Ghospodi Jesus Christos esine voze ponuloi nashe. That is to say, O Lorde Jesus Christ, sonne of God have mercy upon us: and this is their prayer, so that the most part of the unlearned know neither Pater noster, nor the Beliefe, nor Ten commandements, nor scarcely understand the one halfe of their service which is read in their Churches.

Their matrimonie is nothing solemnized, but rather in most points abhominable, and as neere as I can learne, in this wise following. When [the parties] are agreed, and the day of marriage appointed, when they shall goe towardes the Church, the bride will in no wise consent to go out of the house, but resisteth and striveth with them that would have her out, and faineth her selfe to weepe, yet in the end, two women get her out, and lead her towards the church, her face being covered close, because of her dissimulation, that it should not be openly perceived: for she maketh a great noise, as though she were sobbing and weeping, until she come at the Church, and then her face is uncovered. The man commeth after among other of his friends, and they carry with them to the church a great pot with wine or mead: then the priest coupleth them together much after our order, one promising to love and serve the other during their lives together, &c.

which being done, they begin to drinke, and first the woman drinketh to the man, and when he hath drunke he letteth the cuppe fall to the ground, hasting immediately to tread upon it, and so doth she, and whether of them tread first upon it must have the victorie and be master at all times after, which commonly happeneth to the man, for he is readiest to set his foot on it, because he letteth it fall himselfe, then they goe home againe, the womans face beeing uncovered. The boyes in the streetes crie out and make a noyse in the meane time, with very dishonest wordes.

When they come home, the wife is set at the upper end of the table, and the husband next unto her: they fall then to drinking till they bee all drunke, they perchance have a minstrell or two, and two naked men, which led her from the Church daunce naked a long time before all the companie. When they are wearie of drinking, the bride and the bridegrome get them to bed, for it is in the evening alwayes when any of them are married: and when they are going to bedde, the bridegrome putteth certain money both golde and silver, if he have it, into one of his boots, and then sitteth down in the chamber, crossing his legges, and then the bride must plucke off one of his boots, which she will, and if she happen on the boote wherein the money is, she hath not onely the money for her labor, but is also at such choyse, as she need not ever from that day forth to pul off his boots, but if she misse the boot wherein the money is, she doth not onely loose the money, but is also bound from that day forwards to pull off his boots continually.

Then they continue in drinking and making good cheere three daies following, being accompanied with certaine of their friends, and during the same three daies he is called a Duke, & shee a dutches, although they be very poore persons, and this is as much as I have learned of their matrimony: but one common rule is amoengst them, if the woman be not beaten with the whip once a weeke, she will not be good, and therefore they looke for it orderly, & the women say, that if their husbands did not beate them, they should not love them.

OF THEIR BURIALL

When any man or woman dieth, they stretch him out, and put a new paire of shooes on his feete, because he hath a great journey to goe: then doe they winde him in a sheet, as we doe, but they forget not to put a testimonie in his right hand, which the priest giveth him, to testifie unto S. Nicholas that he died a Christian man or woman. And they put the coarse alwayes in a coffin of wood, although the partie be very poore: and when they goe towards the Church, the friends and kinsemen of the partie departed carrie in their hands small waxe candles, and they weepe and howle, and make much lamentation.

They that be hanged or beheaded, or such like, have no testimonie with them: how they are received into heaven, it is a wonder, without their pasport.

There are a great number of poore people among them which die daily for lacke of sustenance, which is a pitifull case to beholde: for there hath beene buried in a small time, within these two yeeres, above 80 persons young and old, which have died onely for lacke of sustenance . . . a great many are forced in the winter to drie straw and stampe it, and to make bread thereof, or at the least they eate it in stead of bread. . . . barks of trees are good meat with them at all times. There is no people in the world, as I suppose, that live so miserably as do the poverty in those parts: and the most part of them that have sufficient for themselves, and also to relieve others that need, are so unmerciful that they care not how many they see die of famine or hunger in the streets.

It is a countrey full of diseases, divers, and evill, . . .

[72] *PETER THE GREAT VISITS WESTERN EUROPE* *

In 1697 and 1698 Peter paid his historic visit to the West. Traveling in a foolishly elaborate incognito, he carefully inspected western institutions with the expectation of transplanting them to his backward empire. The following accounts of his visit were written by [A] *the great French memoirist, Saint-Simon, and* [B] *the Anglican bishop and historian, Gilbert Burnet.*

[A] The Czar, Peter the Great, Emperor of Russia, had at this time [arrived] in Holland, learning shipbuilding. Although incognito, he wished to be recognised, but after his own fashion; and was annoyed that, being so near to England, no embassy was sent to him from that country, which he wished to ally himself with for commercial reasons.

At last an embassy arrived; he delayed for some time to give it an audience, but in the end fixed the day and hour at which he would see it. The reception, however, was to take place on board a large Dutch vessel that he was going to examine. There were two ambassadors; they thought the meeting-place rather an odd one, but were obliged to go there. When they arrived on board the Czar sent word that he was in the "top," and that it was there he would see them. The ambassadors, whose feet were unaccustomed to rope-ladders, tried to excuse themselves from mounting; but it was all in vain. The Czar would receive them in the "top" or not at all. At last they

* [A] Bayle St. John, trans., *The Memoirs of the Duke of Saint-Simon* (London: Chatto and Windus, 1876), Vol. I, p. 113. [B] Bishop Burnet, *History of His Own Time* (London, 1753), Vol. III, pp. 306–308.

were compelled to ascend, and the meeting took place on that narrow place high up in the air. The Czar received them there with as much majesty as though he had been upon his throne, listened to their harangue, replied very graciously, and then laughed at the fear painted upon their faces, and good-humouredly gave them to understand that he had punished them thus for arriving so late.

After this the Czar passed into England, curious to see and learn as much as possible; and, having well fulfilled his views repaired into Holland. He wished to visit France, but the King civilly declined to receive him. He went, therefore, much mortified, to Vienna instead. Three weeks after his arrival he was informed of a conspiracy that had been formed against him in Moscow. He hastened there at once, and found that it was headed by his own sister; he put her in prison, and hanged her most guilty accomplices to the bars of his windows, as many each day as the bars would hold. . . .

[B] . . . The Czar came this winter over to England, and stayed some Months among us; I waited often on him, and was ordered, both by the King and the Archbishop and Bishops, to attend upon him, and to offer him such Informations of our Religion and Constitution, as he was willing to receive: I had good Interpreters, so I had much free discourse with him. He is a man of a very hot temper, soon inflamed, and very brutal in his Passion; he raises his natural heat by drinking much Brandy, which he rectifies himself with great application: He is subject to convulsive Motions all over his Body, and his Head seems to be affected with these; he wants not Capacity, and has a larger measure of Knowledge than might be expected from his Education, which was very indifferent: A want of Judgment, with an instability of Temper, appear in him too often and too evidently; he is mechanically turned, and seems designed by Nature rather to be a Ship Carpenter, than a great Prince: this was his chief study and exercise while he stayed here: He wrought much with his own hands, and made all about him work at the Models of Ships: He told me, he designed a great Fleet at Azov, and with it to attack the Turkish Empire; but he did not seem desirous to mend matters in Muscovy: He was indeed resolved to encourage Learning, and to polish his People, by sending some of them to travel in other Countries, and to draw Strangers to come and live among them. He seemed apprehensive still of his Sister's Intrigues. There was a mixture both of Passion and Severity in his temper. He is resolute, but understands little of War, and seemed not at all inquisitive that way. After I had seen him often, and had conversed much with him, I could not but adore the depth of the Providence of God, that had raised up such a furious man, to so absolute an Authority over so great a part of the World. . . .

. . . He went from hence to the Court of Vienna, where he purposed to have stayed some time, but he was called home sooner than he had intended, upon a discovery or a suspicion of Intrigues managed by his Sister: The Strangers to whom he trusted most, were so true to him, that those designs were crushed before he came back; but on this occasion, he let loose his fury on all whom he suspected; some hundred of them were hanged all round Moscow, and it was said, that he cut off many Heads with his own hand, and so far was he from relenting or showing any sort of tenderness, that he seemed delighted with it. How long he is to be the Scourge of that Nation, or of his Neighbours, God only knows: . . .

[73] *THE CZAR TAKES BLOODY VENGEANCE ON THE STRELITZI* *

To his unbounded annoyance, Peter's European visit was interrupted by news of the revolt of the strelitzi, *the elite Moscow garrison. Quickly returning to his capital, he proceeded to punish the conspirators with a savagery which suggested that he had learned more about Western technology than humanitarianism. The ensuing eye-witness description is from the pen of John Korb, secretary of the Austrian legation at Peter's court.*

. . . Peter was still tarrying at Vienna, quite full of the desire of setting out for Italy; but, fervid as was this curiosity of rambling abroad, it was, nevertheless, speedily extinguished on the announcement of the troubles that had broken out in the bowels of his realm. . . . He took the quick post, as his ambassador suggested, and in four weeks time, he had got over about three hundred miles without accident, and arrived on the 4th of September,—a monarch for the well-disposed, but an avenger for the wicked. His first anxiety, after his arrival, was about the rebellion. In what it consisted? What the insurgents meant? Who had dared to instigate such a crime? And as nobody could answer accurately upon all points, and some pleaded their own ignorance, others the obstinacy of the Strelitz, he began to have suspicions of everybody's loyalty, and began to cogitate about a fresh investigation. The rebels that were kept in custody, in various places in the environs, were all brought in by four regiments of the guards, to a fresh investigation and fresh tortures. Prison, tribunal, and rack, for those that were brought in, was in Bebraschentsko. No day, holy or profane, were the

* Count MacDonnell, ed., *Diary of an Austrian Secretary of Legation at the Court of Czar Peter the Great* (London: Bradbury and Evans, 1863), Vol. II, pp. 85–107.

inquisitors idle; every day was deemed fit and lawful for torturing. As many as there were accused there were knouts, and every inquisitor was a butcher. Prince Feodor Jurowicz Romadonowski showed himself by so much more fitted for his inquiry, as he surpassed the rest in cruelty. The very Grand Duke himself, in consequence of the distrust he had conceived of his subjects, performed the office of inquisitor. He put the interrogatories, he examined the criminals, he urged those that were not confessing, he ordered such Strelitz as were more pertinaciously silent, to be subjected to more cruel tortures; those that had already confessed about many things were questioned about more; those who were bereft of strength and reason, and almost of their senses, by excess of torment, were handed over to the skill of the doctors, who were compelled to restore them to strength, in order that they might be broken down by fresh excruciations. The whole month of October was spent in butchering the backs of the culprits with knout and with flames: no day were those that were left alive exempt from scourging or scorching, or else they were broken upon the wheel, or driven to the gibbet, or slain with the axe—the penalties which were inflicted upon them as soon as their confessions had sufficiently revealed the heads of the rebellion.

To this exhibition of avenging justice the Czar's Majesty invited all the ambassadors of foreign sovereigns, as it were to assert anew on his return that sovereign prerogative of life and death which the rebels had disputed with him.

The barracks in Bebraschentsko end in a bare field which rises to the summit of a rather steep hill. This was the place appointed for the executions. Here were planted the gibbet stakes, on which the foul heads of these confessedly guilty wretches were to be set, to protract their ignominy beyond death. . . . The strangers that had gathered to the spectacle were kept aloof from too close approach; the whole regiment of guards was drawn up in array under arms. A little further off, on a high *tumulus* in the area of the place, there was a multitude of Muscovites, crowded and crushing together in a dense circle. . . .

. . . There was a cart for every criminal, and a soldier to guard each. No priestly office was to be seen; as if the condemned were unworthy of that pious compassion. But they all bore lighted tapers in their hands, not to die without light and cross. The horrors of impending death were increased by the piteous lamentations of their women, the sobbing on every side, and the shrieks of the dying that rung upon the sad array. . . .

To prove to all the people how holy and inviolable are those walls of the city, which the Strelitz rashly meditated scaling in a sudden assault, beams were run out from all the embrasures in the walls near the gates, on each of which two rebels were hanged. . . . There are few cities fortified with as many palisades as Moscow has given gibbets to her guardian Strelitz.

[74] *AN ENGLISH ENGINEER DESCRIBES PETER THE GREAT'S RUSSIA* *

During his visit to England, Peter the Great arranged to have a number of English technicians return with him to Russia to help modernize the country. One of these men was the hydraulic engineer John Perry, who spent fourteen frustrating and unrewarded years in Russia. Finally, in grave peril of his life, he managed to escape in 1712. His book on Russia was widely read and influential in western Europe in the eighteenth century.

It was a very rare thing in Russia before this present Czar's time to have found any man, even among the highest and most learned of the clergy, to have understood any language but their own; and as they were themselves void of learning, so they were wary and cautious to keep out all means that might bring it in, lest their ignorance should be discovered . . . for which reason the learning of foreign languages and books were always formerly discouraged; even as they are to this day in the Turkish Empire. . . .

There came once a press and letters out of Poland to Mosco, where a printing-house was set up with the approbation of one of the former Czars; but not long after the house was fir'd in the night-time, and the press and letters were burnt, as was thought by the procurement of the priests, they looking upon all other books except the history of their own countrey, and the exploits and victories of their Czars, and the lives and miracles of their saints, to be as dangerous as witchcraft.

This ignorance was not so much to be wonder'd at when it is consider'd that they neither suffer'd their sons to travel, nor was there ever any university in the countrey, or considerable school of any learning, till this Czar's time. . . .

. . . notwithstanding their pretended purity in keeping their fasts, and abstaining from flesh, there is nothing more common than to have both the people and the priest, too, go to church on a holiday in the morning, and get drunk in the afternoon long before night; especially the greater the holiday, the more it is excusable, and the custom, to be drunk. It is very ordinary at such times, if you ride through Mosco in the evening on a great holiday, to see the priests, as well as other men, lie drunk about the streets

* John Perry, "The State of Russia under the Present Czar," in *Seven Britons in Imperial Russia, 1698–1812*, ed. by Peter Putnam (Princeton, N.J.: Princeton University Press, 1952), pp. 31–62. Used by permission.

. . . and so far from it being accounted a scandal to be drunk, that the very women, not only the meaner sort, but even women of distinction and fashion, will make no scruple to own, that they have been very drunk; and in publick company will thank them for the civility and kindness, as they call it, of making them drunk, when they have been entertained any place, the next time they meet them. And, indeed, when I first went into the countrey, and for some years after, it was the common way, not only at all great entertainments where the court was invited and present, but even among private friends, to make their visitants drunk before they parted, or it was not accounted that they had been made welcome; . . .

It had been the manner of the Russes, like the Patriarchs of old, to wear long beards hanging down upon their bosoms, which they comb'd out with pride, and kept smooth and fine, without one hair to be diminish'd. . . . The Czar, therefore, to reform this foolish custom, and to make them look like other Europeans, ordered a tax to be laid, on all gentlemen, merchants, and others of his subjects (excepting the priests and common peasants, or slaves) that they should each of them pay a hundred rubles per annum, for the wearing of their beards, and that even the common people should pay a copeck at the entrance of the gates of any of the towns or cities of Russia. . . .

. . . the Czar came down to Veronize, where I was then on service, and a great many of my men that had worn their beards all their lives, were now obliged to part with them, amongst which . . . was an old Russ carpenter that had been with me at Camishinka. . . . I jested a little with him on this occasion, telling him that he was become a young man, and asked him what he had done with his beard? Upon which he put his hand in his bosom and pull'd it out, and shed'd it to me: farther telling me, that when he came home, he would lay it up to have it put in his coffin and buried along with him, that he might be able to give an account of it to St. Nicholas, when he came to the other world; and that all his brothers (meaning his fellow-workmen, who had been shaved that day) had taken the same care. . . .

The Czar . . . gave orders that all his boyars and people whatsoever, that came near his court, and that were in his pay should . . . equip themselves with handsome cloathes made after the English fashion. . . . And next he commanded, that a pattern of cloathes of the English fashion should be hung up at all the gates of the city of Mosco, and that publication should be made, that all persons (excepting the common peasants who brought goods and provisions into the city) should make their cloathes according to the said patterns; and that whosoever should disobey the said orders, and should be found passing any of the gates of the city in their long habits, should either pay two grevens (which is 20 pence) or be obliged to kneel down at the gates of the city, and to have their coats cut off just even with the ground. . . .

It had been the custom of Russia, in case of marriages, that the match always be made up between the parents on each side, without any previous meeting, consent or liking of one another. . . . It [is] a thing common in Russia to beat wives in a most barbarous manner, very often so unhumanly that they die with the blows; the wives being thus many times made desperate, murther their husbands in revenge for the ill usage they receive; on which occasion there is a law made, that when they murther their husbands, they are set alive in the ground, standing upright, with the earth fill'd about them, and only their heads left just above the earth, and a watch set over them, that they shall not be relieved till they are starved to death; which is a common sight in that countrey, and I have known them live sometimes seven or eight days in that posture.

. . . among some other causes, one of the chief which makes the generality of the nobility at present uneasy, is, that the Czar obliges them against their will, to come and live at Petersburgh, with their wives and their families, where they are oblig'd to build new houses for themselves, and where all manner of provisions are usually three or four times as dear, and forage for their horses, etc. at least six or eight times as dear as it is at Mosco; which happens from the small quantity which the countrey thereabouts produces, being more than two thirds woods and bogs; and not only the nobility, but merchants and tradesmen of all sorts, are oblig'd to go and live there. . . .

As for the Czar, he is a great lover of the water, and entirely delights in ships and boats, and in sailing. . . . But his lords have no relish nor pleasure in those things, and though they seemingly compliment the Czar whenever he talks to them of the beauties and delights of Petersburgh; yet when they get together by themselves, they complain and say that there are tears and water enough at Petersburgh, but they pray God to send them to live again at Mosco.

[75] *CATHERINE THE GREAT TELLS HOW SHE ROSE TO POWER* *

The following account of the palace revolution which overthrew Czar Peter III in 1762 and put his wife Catherine on the throne is taken from a letter written by

* Letter of Catherine to Stanislaw Poniatowski, August, 1762, as found in R. N. Bain, *Peter III, Emperor of Russia* (New York: E. P. Dutton and Co., Inc., 1902), pp. 263–265.

Catherine to her lover Stanislaw Poniatowski, later king of Poland. Catherine's explanation of her husband's death can hardly be taken literally; there is little doubt that he was murdered.

. . . It is six months ago since my accession to the throne was first put in hand. Peter III had lost the little wit he had. He ran his head against everything. He wanted to break up the Guards. . . . He wanted to change his religion, marry Elizabeth Vorontsov and shut me up.

The day of the celebration of the peace with [Prussia,] after having publicly insulted me at table, he ordered my arrest the same evening. My uncle, Prince George, got this order retracted, and from thenceforth I lent an ear to the propositions which had been made to me [ever] since the death of the Empress [Elizabeth].

The [original] design was to seize him in his apartments and shut him up as was done with the Princess Anne and her children. He went off [however] to Oranienbaum. We were sure of a great number of the captains of the Guards. The fate of the secret was in the hands of the three brothers Orlov. . . . They are extremely determined people and much beloved by the common soldiers, having served in the Guards. I am under great obligation to these people, all Petersburg is my witness. . . .

I was at Peterhof. Peter III was making merry and dwelling at Oranienbaum. . . . I was sleeping calmly. . . . At 6 o'clock in the morning of the 28th . . . Alexius Orlov enters my room and says quite gently: "It is time to get up; all is ready for your proclamation." . . . I dressed myself quickly without making my toilet and got into the carriage which he had brought with him. . . .

Five versts from the town I met the elder Orlov with the younger Prince Bariatinsky. Orlov gave up his carriage to me, for my horses were done up, and we got out at the barracks of the Ismailovsky Regiment. [At the gates] were only twelve men, and a drummer, who began sounding an alarm, when the soldiers came running out, kissing me, embracing my hands and feet and clothes, and calling me their deliverer. Then they began swearing allegiance to me. When this had been done, they begged me to get into the carriage, and the priest, cross in hand, walked on in front. We went [first] to the [barracks of the] Semenovsky Regiment, but the regiment came marching out to meet us, crying, "Vivat!" Then we went to the church of Kazan, where I got out. Then the Preobrazhensky Regiment arrived, crying, "Vivat!" "We beg your pardon," they said to me, "for being the last. Our officers stopped us, but here are four of them whom we have arrested to show you our zeal. We want what our brothers want." Then the horse-guards arrived frantic with joy, I never saw anything like it, weeping and crying at the deliverance of their country. . . . I went to the new Winter Palace where the Synod and the Senate were assembled. A manifesto and a form of oath were hastily drawn up. Then I went down and received the troops on foot. There were more than 14,000 men, guards and country regiments. As soon as they saw me they uttered cries of joy which were taken up by an innumerable crowd. . . . it was resolved to go to Peterhof. . . . On leaving town, three soldiers of the Guards . . . came to me and said: "Here! take what Peter III has entrusted us with [a manifesto], we give it to you. We are very glad of the opportunity of joining our brethren."

After the first letter came a second, the bearer whereof, General Michal Ismailov, threw himself at my feet and said: "Do you take me for an honest man?" On my replying, "Yes!" "Well," says he, "it is pleasant to have to do with sensible folk. The Emperor offers to resign. I will bring to you [a form of abdication] after a very few alterations. I will save my country from a civil war without any difficulty."

I charged him with this commission, and off he went to accomplish it. Peter III abdicated, at Oranienbaum, in full liberty, surrounded by 5000 Holsteiners, and came with Elizabeth Vorontsov, Gudovich and Ismailov to Peterhof, where, to protect his person, I gave him five officers and some soldiers. . . . Thereupon I sent the deposed Emperor to a remote and very agreeable place called Ropsha, 25 versts from Peterhof, under the command of Alexius Orlov, with four officers and a detachment of picked, good-natured men, whilst decent and convenient rooms were being prepared for him at Schlusselburg. But God disposed otherwise. Fear had given him a diarrhoea which lasted three days and passed away on the fourth; in this [fourth] day he drank excessively, for he had all he wanted except liberty. Nevertheless, the only things he asked me for were his mistress, his dog, his Negro and his violin; but for fear of scandal and increasing the agitation of the persons who guarded him, I only sent him the last three things.

The hemorrhoidal colic which seized him affected his brain: two days he was delirious, and the delirium was followed by very great exhaustion, and despite all the assistance of the doctors, he expired whilst demanding a Lutheran priest. I feared that the officers might have poisoned him, so I had him opened, but it is an absolute fact that not the slightest trace of poison was found inside him. The stomach was quite sound, but inflammation of the bowels and a stroke of apoplexy had carried him off. His heart was extraordinarily small and quite decayed. . . .

At last, then God has brought everything to pass according to His predisposition. The whole thing is rather a miracle than a fact foreseen and arranged beforehand, for so many felicitous combinations could not have coincided unless God's hand had been over it all.

. . . Be assured, too, that hatred of foreigners was the leading principle of the whole affair, and that Peter III himself passed for a foreigner.

Adieu, there are some very strange situations in this world.

[76] *CATHERINE THE GREAT WRITES HER WILL* *

When Catherine II died in 1796 the following will was made public. The document is remarkably curt considering her lifelong propensity for long-winded prose. It also reflects the thorough-going Russianism of the German-born Empress.

If I should die in Tsarskoe Selo, I wish to be buried in the Sophien town cemetery.

If in the town of St. Peter—in the Nevsky monastery in the cathedral or funereal church.

If in Pella—to be brought by sea to the Nevsky monastery.

If in Moscow—in the Don monastery or the nearest town cemetery.

If in Peterhof—in the Troitza-Sergiev monastery.

If in any other place—in the nearest cemetery.

The coffin should be carried by Chevalier Guards and nobody else.

My body should be dressed in white and a golden crown bearing my name should be placed on my head.

The mourning to last six months, not more and even better if less.

After the first six weeks all public entertainments to be resumed.

Marriages and music to be allowed immediately after the burial. . . .

My desire is to bring Constantine to the throne of the Great Eastern Empire.

For the good of the Russian and Greek Empires I advise that the Princes of Wurtemberg should be banished from the affairs of these Empires and have as little to do with them as possible; I also advise avoiding consulting all Germans of both sexes.

* Dominique Maroger, ed., *The Memoirs of Catherine the Great,* trans. by Baroness Moura Budberg (New York: The Macmillan Company [1955]), pp. 377–378.

13

The Rise of Brandenburg-Prussia

Until the middle of the seventeenth century, the history of Brandenburg had been quite undistinguished. Originally established as a military outpost against the Slavs, and ruled since 1415 by the house of Hohenzollern, little had occurred to suggest future greatness. In the Thirty Years' War, Brandenburg attempted to remain neutral and was overrun and devastated by both sides. Then in 1640 Elector Frederick William became margrave and with him the greatness of the state began. Thereafter, a succession of able and single-minded Hohenzollerns guided the destinies of the realm, and despite meager economic resources, unfavorable geography, and a very small population, transformed Brandenburg-Prussia into a state to be reckoned with among the powers of Europe.

[77] *THE GREAT ELECTOR SETS NEW GOALS FOR BRANDENBURG* *

The man whose determination and ability launched a hitherto obscure German state on the road to greatness was Frederick William, the Great Elector (1620–

* Ferdinand Schevill, *The Great Elector* (Chicago: The University of Chicago Press, 1947), pp. 406–409. Used by permission of the publisher.

1688). Following is an evaluation of his work by a modern—and sympathetic—American historian.

. . . An accident of birth made [the Great Elector] ruler of a polity which at his accession had already been in existence for five hundred years. If we accept Albrecht the Bear as the first designer of Brandenburg, we cannot but agree that for the mark to have survived along the dangerously exposed eastern frontier of Germany, Albrecht must have been followed by a number of builders in no way inferior to himself; and this was indeed the case. On the extinction of Albrecht's dynasty we encountered two lines of absentee margraves, shameless shirkers of their responsibilities, under whom Brandenburg was threatened with dissolution. But the anarchy which they precipitated was overcome when Emperor Sigismund took pity on the disordered province and enfeoffed Frederick of Hohenzollern with the margraviate. On the strength of his labors of rehabilitation Frederick may fairly be assigned a place as founder at the side of Albrecht. While among the first Hohenzollern's descendants his son, Frederick II, and his great-grandson, Joachim I, invite acceptance as contributory architects of the rising state, we encountered in the first Joachim's successors an unbroken string of feckless rulers until from their painful mediocrity there sprang [the Great Elector], who by every reasonable measuring-scale overtops all his founding predecessors including Albrecht, the initiator of the work.

. . . the towering of Frederick William above the long file of his predecessors does not admit of dispute. These forerunners built, and he inherited from them, a German territorial state which, as an electorate of the Reich, had achieved a certain power and dignity but which in a span of five centuries had not succeeded in reaching a position enabling it in any decisive way to influence German destiny. With Frederick William's arrival on the scene a period of Brandenburg history came to a close which, apart from an animated early chapter of conquest and settlement, presents itself by contrast as, in the main, a kind of harmless vegetating in unenterprising complacency. Although but a twenty-year-old youth at his accession and a fugitive, besides, from Brandenburg, which a foreign state had taken over, he managed, within a few years and in spite of his continued helplessness among the warring powers that were tearing Germany apart, to win sufficient consideration not only to oblige these powers to cease pushing him about at their pleasure but also to play a part out of all proportion to his strength at the Westphalian congress that finally brought peace to the tortured land.

Granted that his success at Westphalia was partly attributable to the small army with which he had succeeded in providing himself, it sprang in far greater measure from a spiritual quality which he had brought into play and which had not failed to make an impression on the armed masters of Europe. They noted and responded with involuntary respect to the unabashed and daring manner in which the young ruler of the war-ruined mark moved among them. While they did not understand at what precisely he was driving or consider it important enough greatly to bother, the ruler himself was visited by no doubts as to his purpose. He was resolved to hold fast to his own, his passionately cherished and imperiled own, consisting of the three groups of inherited territories strung across the broad north German plain. Widely separated from one another, they constituted an almost unsolvable problem of defense and were, in addition, even after the German civil broils had ended, in practically unrelieved jeopardy.

Let us glance at this inheritance as it presented itself to his eyes and begin with the duchy of Prussia, in which he was residing at the time of his accession: It was completely surrounded by the kingdom of Poland, of which, moreover, in terms of feudal law it was a component part. To the west, all the way, indeed, to the utmost German west, lay the Rhinelands of Cleve-Mark; they had been all but alienated from their ruler during the Thirty Years' War and even after the coming of peace looked a good deal like a morsel the nearby Dutch republic was merely awaiting a favorable opportunity to swallow. As for the remaining Hohenzollern possession, Brandenburg, while it had been cleared of the occupying Swedes at the Westphalian turning point, it continued to dwell beneath the mailed fist of these invaders by reason of the devastating decision at the peace settlement which allotted the immediately adjoining territory of western Pomerania to the Scandinavian power.

While the elector's decision firmly and at all costs to maintain his hold on his threatened territories constituted the core of his early policy and while any one of his predecessors, including his distracted, ill-starred father, might be conceived as setting himself in the same circumstances an identical goal, it is unbelievable, in the face of their record, that they would have stuck to their purpose with anything approaching the obstinacy and resourcefulness of their living representative. His pre-eminent endowment was a passionate will to live, and, lustily indulging it, he discovered that it expanded by its own energy into the more massive will to grow. . . .

. . . hardly had Frederick William begun the struggle to keep his own when he became convinced that, in order to keep it, he would have to bring it to greater vigor; and the accomplishment of this purpose, through either winning a broader territorial base or achieving a more compact organization of whatever he held or through both of these developments together, became the gist of his labors throughout his long reign. Regarding the territorial program, moreover, a glance at the map sufficed to show him that the logical procedure would be to attempt to bridge the gaps between his three isolated footholds. But overwhelmed with the sheer problem of day-to-day living that never at any time eased its pressure, very early in his reign he had to abandon this objective as outside the realm of practical politics. And when he died the Hohenzollern realm was still, as at his accession, flung in scattered fragments across northern Germany. Nonetheless, he had indicated, if not in quotable passages of his correspondence, by the whole tenor of his striving, that the proper and inescapable concern of a ruler vulnerable, like himself, by reason of the unhappy dispersion and consequent multiplied contacts of his separate units was to draw them together, or at least to begin the work of drawing them together, into an unbroken territorial mass.

So insurmountable were the obstacles piled in the path of a policy of territorial consolidation in Frederick William's time that it would be an error to suggest that he ever regarded it as other than a vague and tantalizing dream. Indeed, for so hardheaded a realist as he it was so entirely impracticable as to have been not even tantalizing. All we can safely say is that the dream came into existence in his day and that it was a direct reflection of his purposeful activity. . . .

With this conclusion in mind the issue of Frederick William's preeminence among the succession of Brandenburg margraves settles itself without further debate. While the unimportant state which he inherited was their work, it was he who gave it a new solidity and set it a new goal. Even his none-too-capable son was able to improve its European status by transforming it into the kingdom of Prussia. Then, under his unusually gifted grandson and great-grandson the forces which he had set in motion vastly expanded their field of operation until through further consistent advances in the nineteenth century a new German empire was brought to birth. In last analysis Frederick William not only created the kingdom of Prussia but was the unconscious projector of a renovated Germany.

[78] *BRANDENBURG GIVES REFUGE TO THE FRENCH HUGUENOTS* *

In his anxiety to build up his sparsely populated and scattered territories, Frederick William announced that he would welcome French religious refugees after the Revocation of the Edict of Nantes in 1685.

* James Harvey Robinson, *Readings in European History* (New York: Ginn and Company, 1906), Vol. II, pp. 316–317. Used by permission of the publisher.

In view of the sympathy which we ought to, and do, feel for our brethren of the reformed evangelical religion in France, who have been driven by persecution to leave their homes and settle in other countries, we, Frederick William, etc., desire by this edict to offer them a free and safe refuge in all our lands and possessions and to specify what rights, privileges, and prerogatives we are graciously minded to grant them. . . .

We particularly specify the towns of Stendal, Werben, Rathenow, Brandenburg, and Frankfurt in the electorate of Brandenburg, Magdeburg, Halle, and Calbe in the duchy of Magdeburg, and Königsberg in Prussia, as places where living is cheap and opportunities for trade and other means of support abundant; and we command herewith that when any of the said French people of the reformed evangelical religion make their appearance, they shall be well received in the said towns, and that every opportunity and assistance shall be given them in establishing themselves there. They shall, moreover, be free to establish themselves in any other place in our lands and dominions outside the above-mentioned towns which shall seem to them more convenient for the purposes of their trade or calling.

They shall be permitted to bring with them any furniture, merchandise, or other movable property free of all duties or imposts of any kind whatever. . . .

In towns or other places where there are unoccupied or waste lands or properties, we ordain that these shall be given over to our said French brethren of the reformed evangelical religion, free of all and every incumbrance, to hold and enjoy for themselves and their posterity. We further ordain that the necessary materials for the cultivation of these lands shall be furnished them gratis. . . .

So soon as any of our said French brethren of the reformed evangelical religion shall have settled themselves in any town or village, they shall be invested, without payment of any kind, with all the rights, benefits, and privileges of citizenship enjoyed or exercised by our subjects who live and were born in said town or village.

If any of them shall desire to establish manufactories of cloth, stuffs, hats, or other articles, we will not only bestow on them all the necessary permissions, rights, and privileges, but will further aid them, so far as is in our power, with money and requisite materials.

Those who wish to settle in the country shall be given a certain amount of land to cultivate, shall be furnished with the requisite utensils and materials and encouraged in every way, as has been done in the case of certain families who have come from Switzerland to settle in our country.

In every town where our said French brethren in the faith are established, we will support a special preacher and set apart a proper place where they may hold their services in the French language, and with such usages and ceremonies as are customary in the reformed evangelical churches in France.

As for the members of the French nobility who have placed themselves under our protection and entered our service, they enjoy the same honors, dignities, and prerogatives as our own subjects of noble birth, and several of them have been given some of the most important offices at our court as well as in our army; and we are graciously disposed to show like favor to all such of the French nobility as may in future present themselves to us.

Given at Potsdam, the 29th of October, 1685.

FREDERICK WILLIAM, Elector

[79] *THE ELECTOR OF BRANDENBURG BECOMES KING OF PRUSSIA, 1701* *

The great achievement of the otherwise mediocre son of the Great Elector was the acquisition of a royal title. Negotiations on Frederick's behalf were carried on by two Jesuit priests, Vota and Wolff, who hoped thereby to secure the Elector's conversion to Roman Catholicism. Following is a letter written by Father Vota to Frederick from Warsaw in 1700 and the Pope's angry reaction to the crowning as expressed in a letter to the Holy Roman Emperor.

[A] Father Vota to the Elector of Brandenburg, Warsaw, April 27, 1700

I can no longer restrain my ardor . . . for the successful outcome of the crowning of Your Electoral Highness. People talk about it here as a closed matter. It gives me inexpressible joy. But there is no occasion for idleness; I have had to answer those who are informed neither on the right nor the might of Your Electoral Highness, . . . I have made them understand by a hundred examples that it is not necessary to possess an entire country in order to assume its title, and consequently that to be King of Prussia is not the same as declaring oneself master of the two Prussias to the prejudice of Poland. That is the fantasy to which ignorance leads some. I have convinced the others that the Republic [Poland] will lose nothing but will gain considerably in recognizing Your Electoral Highness among the Kings, since that detracts nothing from the Kingdom of Poland, as it will detract nothing from the kingdoms of France, Spain, etc., . . .

* **[A]** Albert Waddington, *L'acquisition de la Couronne Royale de Prusse par les Hohenzollern* (Paris: Ernest Leroux, 1888), pp. 434–436. Our translation. **[B]** James Harvey Robinson, *Readings in European History* (New York: Ginn and Company, 1906), Vol. II, p. 318. Used by permission.

I have stressed that since Your Electoral Highness does not need to beg the crown from anyone . . . it is hardly necessary for the King of Poland to await the example of any other monarch to give Him the marks of his esteem and his true fraternal affection by recognizing his crown first. I have said that it could redound to the glory of the king of Poland to give an example rather than to follow it, that his merit in the eyes of His Electoral Highness would be greatly augmented, and that considering the military position of His Majesty it would be very advantageous to His Majesty to give this illustrious testimony to Your Electoral Highness of his true and sincere friendship. I have made people here see that nearly all the kings of the Universe have set themselves up by their own efforts and by the acclamation of their peoples. . . . Finally I concluded that those who would want to deal with Your Electoral Highness and would have need of him should accommodate themselves accordingly in order not to do harm to themselves. Your friends would do this with pleasure. About the enemies we would not worry.

Nevertheless, Monseigneur, my zeal tells me that where things now stand there is no time to lose. The King, after the *Senatus Consilium* on May 10 will shortly leave for Prussia. I would be overjoyed if he himself attended the acclamation. He only has to listen to his own best interests and to repudiate those with false scruples who quibble about everything. I do not doubt that the other monarchs will follow the example of His Majesty after a short while . . .

[B] We, Clement XI, send to our beloved son in Christ our good wishes and apostolic blessing.

Although it is well known to us that your Majesty [the Emperor] in no way approves the bad example which has been given to all Christendom by the behavior of Frederick, margrave of Brandenburg, in daring to openly assume the title of king; nevertheless, lest we seem to fail in upholding our office, we cannot pass over this matter in silence; for a non-Catholic person cannot, without affront to the Church, assume the sacred title of king, and the said margrave has not hesitated to call himself king of a part of Prussia which has from of old belonged to the German knights.

Wherefore, in view of this our admonition, we require your Majesty (whose magnanimity is well known to us) to refrain from according to the said margrave the kingly dignity which he has so rashly ventured to assume. Such as he are condemned and cast out by the word of God, which says, "Ye have ruled, but not through me; ye have become princes and I have not known ye."

Our reverend brother, Philip Anthony, archbishop of Athens, will further communicate our views on this matter to your Majesty, to whom, in

God's name, we wish all happiness and graciously send our apostolic blessing.

Given at Rome, at St. Peter's, under the seal of the fisherman's ring, the 16th of April, 1701.

[80] *CROWN PRINCE FREDERICK IS TAUGHT PRUSSIAN DISCIPLINE* *

Few princes have been brought up with greater rigor than was Frederick the Great by his father, Frederick William I. The first two selections below are an exchange of letters between the sixteen-year-old Frederick and his father. The third selection tells the unhappy consequences of an attempt by Frederick (eighteen at the time) to run away to England. He and his companion, Lieutenant Katte, were apprehended, tried by a court-martial acting under the King's thumb, and condemned to death.

[A] Frederick to His Father, September 11, 1728

I have not ventured for a long time to present myself before my dear papa, partly because I was advised against it, but chiefly because I anticipated an even worse reception than usual and feared to vex my dear papa still further by the favor I have now to ask; so I have preferred to put it in writing.

I beg my dear papa that he will be kindly disposed toward me. I do assure him that after long examination of my conscience I do not find the slightest thing with which to reproach myself; but if, against my wish and will, I have vexed my dear papa, I hereby beg most humbly for forgiveness, and hope that my dear papa will give over the fearful hate which has appeared so plainly in his whole behavior and to which I cannot accustom myself. I have always thought hitherto that I had a kind father, but now I see the contrary. However, I will take courage and hope that my dear papa will think this all over and take me again into his favor. Meantime I assure him that I will never, my life long, willingly fail him, and in spite of his disfavor I am still, with most dutiful and childlike respect, my dear papa's

Most obedient and faithful servant and son,

FREDERICK

[B] Frederick William in Reply

A bad, obstinate boy, who does not love his father; for when one does

* [A] and [B] J. H. Robinson, *Readings in European History* (New York: Ginn and Company, 1904), Vol. II, pp. 321–322. Copyright 1904 by James Harvey Robinson. Used by permission of the publisher. [C] *Memoirs of Frederica Sophia Wilhelmina,* edited by W. D. Howells (Boston: James R. Osgood, 1877), Vol. I, pp. 239–245.

one's best, and especially when one loves one's father, one does what he wishes not only when he is standing by but when he is not there to see. Moreover you know very well that I cannot stand an effeminate fellow who has no manly tastes, who cannot ride or shoot (to his shame be it said!), is untidy about his person, and wears his hair curled like a fool instead of cutting it; and that I have condemned all these things a thousand times, and yet there is no sign of improvement. For the rest, haughty, offish as a country lout, conversing with none but a favored few instead of being affable and popular, grimacing like a fool, and never following my wishes out of love for me but only when forced into it, caring for nothing but to have his own way, and thinking nothing else is of any importance. This is my answer. . . .

[C] Frederick's Sister Tells of Katte's Execution

The king would have suffered the sentence [i.e., the death sentence of Prince Frederick] to be executed had not all the foreign powers interceded for the prince, and particularly the emperor and the states-general. Seckendorff exerted himself very much; as he had caused the mischief, he wished to repair it. He told the king that though the prince royal was his son, he belonged to the empire, and that his Majesty had no right over him. It was with very great difficulty he obtained his pardon. His continual solicitations, however, gradually weakened the sanguinary intentions of the king. Grumkow, who became aware of this change, sought to take to himself the merit of it with my brother. He went to Cüstrin, and prevailed with the prince to write and make his submission to the king.

Seckendorff also attempted to save Katte; but the king remained inflexible. . . .

Major Schenk now came to inform him [Katte] that his execution was to take place at Cüstrin, and that the coach, which was to convey him thither, was waiting for him. He appeared somewhat surprised at this intelligence; but soon resuming his tranquillity, he with a smiling countenance followed M. de Schenk, who got into the coach with him, besides two other officers of the horse-guards. . . . He arrived at Cüstrin at nine o'clock in the morning, and was taken directly to the scaffold.

The day before, General Lepel, governor of the fortress, and President Munchow had conducted my brother to an apartment that had been purposely prepared for him on the floor above that where he had lodged. He there found a bed and some furniture. The window-curtains were let down, which at first prevented his seeing what was going on without. A plain brown coat was brought to him, in which he was obliged to dress himself. I forgot to state that a similar coat had been given to Katte. The general, having then drawn up the curtains, pointed out to the prince a scaffold covered with black, and as high as the window, which had been widened and the bars of which had been removed. After this, both the general and Munchow retired. This sight, and the downcast look of Munchow, induced my brother to think that sentence of death was going to be passed upon him, and that these preparations regarded himself, which caused him a violent agitation.

General Lepel and President Munchow entered the prince's room in the morning a little before Katte appeared, and endeavored to prepare the prince in the best manner they could for this horrible scene. It is said that he was in such a state of despair and grief as had never before been witnessed. In the meantime Schenk was rendering the like friendly office to Katte. On entering the fortress he said to him: "Continue firm, my dear Katte; you are going to undergo a severe trial; you are at Cüstrin, and you will see the prince royal." "Rather say," answered Katte, "that I am going to have the greatest consolation that could have been granted to me." With these words he ascended the scaffold. My unfortunate brother was then forced to stand at the window. He attempted to throw himself out of it, but was prevented. "I entreat you, for Heaven's sake," said the prince to those who were around him, "delay the execution; I shall inform the king that I am ready to renounce my right to the crown, if his Majesty will pardon Katte." M. de Munchow stopped the prince's mouth with a handkerchief. When the prince saw Katte, he exclaimed: "How wretched I am, my dear Katte! I am the cause of your death. Would to Heaven I were in your place!" "Ah!" replied Katte, "if I had a thousand lives, I would sacrifice them all for your royal highness." At the same time he dropped on his knees. One of his servants attempted to blindfold him, but he would not suffer it, and elevating his thoughts to Heaven, he ejaculated: "My God! I commit my soul into thy hands!" Scarcely had he pronounced these words, when his head, cut off at one blow, rolled at his feet. . . . [My brother] fainted away, and the gentlemen about him had laid him on his bed, where he remained senseless for some hours. . . . M. de Munchow, in spite of the orders of the king, let the curtains down, and sent for physicians, who found the prince in a very dangerous state. He would not take anything that was given him. His mind was so bewildered, and his agitation so great, that he would have destroyed himself had he not been prevented. Religious considerations, it was thought, would soften him; a clergyman was sent for to comfort him: but all in vain; the violent convulsions ceased only when his strength was exhausted. Tears succeeded to these dreadful agitations. It was with extreme difficulty that he was prevailed upon to take medicine. Nothing could induce him to do it, but the representation that he would also cause the queen's death and mine, if he persisted in his own destruction. A profound melancholy fastened upon him for a long time, and for three successive days his life was in imminent danger. The body of Katte remained exposed on the scaffold until sunset. It was buried in one of the bastions of the fortress. . . .

[81] *FREDERICK THE GREAT IN WINTER QUARTERS INDULGES IN FLUTE AND PHILOSOPHY* *

One of the best characterizations of Frederick the Great is to be found in the memoirs of his secretary, librarian, and long-time confidant, Henri de Catt. Here is an excerpt from these memoirs written in winter quarters at Breslau during the Seven Years' War, when Prussia was fighting for its very existence against overwhelming odds.

The life of the King at Breslau during the three months that he remained there [1759] was as well filled and as melancholy as it had been in these two respects at Dresden. . . . Rising during the first two months of his stay at six o'clock, in the morning, he rose during the last month at five o'clock, and towards the end at four, to accustom himself, he said, and to be prepared in time, when he should begin his campaign. . . .

When the King was dressed, he read his despatches, tearing up or throwing into the fire the letters to which he did not wish to reply, and played for a quarter of an hour on his flute, either *solfeggi* which he had noted down for himself, or others which he invented. His cabinet secretaries were next called; the King dictated to them what they had to reply to each letter dealing with civil or military affairs. There were few replies to make on the first, and he allowed them to take their own course.

"The military side alone, in these critical moments, should be the object of all my attention. If I am happy enough to end this unfortunate war, I shall then busy myself with all my departments, in order to amend the abuses which may have cropped up, the errors which may have been committed, and the negligences whose multitude I suspect. But what can I do? I am not left with enough time to attend to and counter everything. I must give myself to the most urgent."

Having sent off his letters, he composed either in prose or epistles in verse, and this work lasted until eleven o'clock, when he gave the parole [the watch-word]. He returned again to his work until dinner-time. The dinner did not last long. He used to invite a few generals and Sir Andrew

* *Frederick the Great: The Memoirs of His Reader: Henri de Catt (1758–1760)*, trans. by F. S. Flint (London: Constable and Company Ltd., 1916), Vol. II, pp. 93–102. Used by permission of the publisher.

Mitchell, with whom he talked more than with the others. After the meal, the King played for a quarter of an hour on the flute, and he played, he used to say, to aid digestion. He then sat down again to his composition of the morning, or he corrected his earlier works and the pieces he had composed during the campaign. I will speak in what follows of his compositions during this hibernation and of the works he read. I was called at five o'clock and remained until seven. During this sitting of two hours, the King spoke to me of his morning and afternoon's work, and afterwards read to me some funeral orations or from some philosophical works, which gave rise to observations, and sometimes to disputes. The rules of the dispute were not often too well observed, and although I was permitted an entire liberty, he permitted himself a greater, which sometimes annihilated that which he had the kindness to permit; or he would not define the terms, or he would say that the definitions were bad, when they showed a contradiction into which he would fall in arguing as he did, or, finally, he cut the discussion short by saying that you were wrong; and yet, on another occasion and on the same matters, he put forward as judicious and logical what he had condemned as being pure sophistries. I have already shown, at the beginning of these memoirs, this method of arguing which royalty permitted itself. He then seemed gratified to have the pleasure of instructing me, and of bringing me round to logical arguments; and I was careful not to spoil this pleasure, which enabled me to follow in all its ramifications the turn of this singular and superior mind. . . .

At seven o'clock the King would play until half-past eight a concerto and several solos by Quantz, . . .

. . . After his concert, he read alone until ten o'clock, and went to bed. During the last month, he went to bed at nine o'clock, to accustom himself to going to bed earlier still during the campaign. . . .

Seeing the King one day with a more tranquil expression than usual, I said to him:

"Why, Sire, all this serious reading which you have been doing for so long will certainly make you devout. These funeral orations, these sermons, these holy tragedies announce an approaching conversion."

He did not reply, looked at me fixedly, but with a smile, and spoke to me of indifferent things. Six days afterwards, he came up to me when I entered his apartment; he had a paper in his hand, which he kept behind his back.

"You asked me, sir, why I did so much serious reading." Presenting the paper to me which he held: "See and judge."

It was a funeral oration which he had written on Matthew Reinhart, master shoemaker.

"That, my dear sir, is the fruit of the readings which astonished you. Bossuet and Fléchier made funeral orations to celebrate the life and death of illustrious heads. As for me, not worthy to untie the latchet of the shoes of these great preachers—I have written the funeral praise of a poor shoemaker, who by his abilities, his virtue and his piety was more deserving than kings and princes to pass to the most distant posterity. Flattery, that unworthy flattery of which it is impossible to rid yourself when you speak of these 'illustrious ingrates,' has not soiled my pen in composing the praise of my shoemaker. I have depicted him with truth, a worthy man, all the greater for his real virtues, which he owed only to himself. Now, sir, are you pleased, and do you think that my gloomy readings were useless to me?"

At the end of four days, the King came towards me, having, like the first time, his hands behind his back.

"When you saw me so attached to my preachers, you seemed to me to fear that I might become devout. Alas, sir, your fears were but too well founded; I am devout according to all the rules. Read this title; that is the subject on which I have just been working."

It was a sermon on the Last Judgment.

"Do not think, sir" (he kept up the sir), "that my devotion dates from this present moment. A few months after the battle of Kolin, I had composed the half of my edifying piece. Since then, carried away by the diversity and multitude of my affairs, I thought no more of my sermon, lukewarmness having again come upon me; and now, returned to the better path, I have finished it for your edification. When you fear to be carried away by the torrent of bad examples, alas! the flesh is so weak, read my sermon. Accept these last efforts of a voice which is known to you, these last words of a dying voice, and a vanishing ardour."

He terminated his compositions by this sermon on the Last Judgment, which he corrected several times.

"As the matter is serious," he said, "I have written it on black-edged paper."

His conversations, during his stay at Breslau, were usually serious and sad. I seldom saw him give way to a little gaiety. Hardly a day passed on which he did not speak to me of his sister's death. He often re-read the epistle he had composed for her. In reading it, he seized on everything which might have some relation to the immateriality and the immortality of the soul, and he argued about it as he had done previously. One evening, he was speaking on this subject which he seemed to have so much at heart that he always spoke with great warmth about it, and his little favourite dog which he had sent for from Potsdam kept jumping at him.

"Down, Frolic, finish your jumps and your caresses. Why will you interrupt a philosopher who is arguing on such serious things?"

[82] *THE DEATH OF THE CZARINA (1762) SAVES FREDERICK II AND PRUSSIA* *

After his spectacular victories in the opening years of the Seven Years' War, Frederick II was worn down by the weight of his enemies and forced to stage a long and exhausting defensive war. By the beginning of 1762, as the following correspondence indicates, Frederick was in a despairing mood. He was saved in the nick of time by the death of the Czarina and the accession of the mad but friendly Peter III.

Frederick to Prince Henry, His Brother, January 9, 1762

. . . you want me to tell you what course should be followed in an extremity like this. I suggest that we gather all our forces and employ this mass to strike at our enemies by turn. That is the best thing to do. It is not enough, and I can already hear all the obstacles and objections you are going to present. But think it over; after all, to perish by bits or to perish *en masse,* is it not all the same?

Prince Henry to Frederick, January 16, 1762

You had the kindness to reply, on the subject of the next campaign, that you intend to assemble all your forces and strike against one after another of the enemy. . . . The solution you have decided upon seems to me very desperate. . . . I admit all the difficulties which result from dividing our forces; but since it is only a question of perishing, it is merely necessary to know what is the slowest way to die. If the end is prolonged there is some hope that some unforseen event will take place. . . . A skillful doctor tries to drag out the life of his patient, if he cannot cure him, so that, when he dies, he at least has the consolation that it is according to the rule of Galen and the precepts of Hippocrates, and I consequently think that regiments placed opposite the enemy would at least check them, and that is all that can be done and hoped for. . . .

Frederick to Prince Henry, January 19, 1762

I have just received your letter of the sixteenth of this month. You know that there are two doctors in Molière, Dr. So-Much-the-Worse and Dr. So-

* *Oeuvres de Frédéric le Grand* (Berlin: Rodolphe Decker, 1855), Vol. XXVI, pp. 234–237. Our translation.

Much-the-Better, and it is impossible for them to agree. [The King is confusing Molière with La Fontaine's *Fables.*] I have a sick person to treat who has a violent fever. Despairing, I order an emetic for him, and you want to give him an anodyne. . . . I will say no more about the situation in which I find myself here, neither of all that I fear. I hope to keep going until the month of March. . . .

To Prince Henry, January 20, 1762

I did not want to leave you uninformed of the important news which I have just received of the death of the Empress of Russia, which took place the fifth of this month.

I would not as yet be able to tell you the consequences of this event, and we will have to be patient for a couple of weeks to see where this will lead . . . but what I fully expect is that it will not turn out at all badly for us.

To Prince Henry, January 31, 1762

I have to tell you the good news that Czernichew leaves for Poland with his Russians. We have nothing more to fear, for the moment, from those people. Here we are, thank heavens, with no one on our back. . . .

I hope this news will cause you to cheer up.

14

Foundation of the British Empire

Historians sometimes give the label, "Second Hundred Years' War," to the period from 1689 to 1815. During these years France and England fought six major wars totalling more than six decades. They were wars of a new type, fought on a world-wide scale and having as their main stake not the acquisition of patches of European real estate or some narrow dynastic advantage but rather the achievement of naval and colonial supremacy. England had the advantage in that her leaders had a better understanding of the underlying economic issues, while France tended to be "distracted" by old-fashioned continental interests. The decisive Treaty of Paris of 1763, by driving France out of North America and India, effectively destroyed French dreams of empire for at least a century. The subsequent French victory in the War of American Independence only salved the pride of some patriotic Frenchmen.

[83] *THE SPANISH SUCCESSION TOUCHES OFF WORLD CONFLICT* *

The War of the Spanish Succession, fought from 1701 to 1713, was the first of the "world wars." It culminated in the Treaty of Utrecht, key extracts from which appear below [B]. *Selection* [A] *consists of some revealing letters dashed off in the field by the Duke of Marlborough, commander of the British forces on the Continent, after the great victory at Blenheim in 1704.*

[A] Letters of Marlborough to His Wife after Blenheim

August 13, 1704

I have not time to say more, but to beg you will give my duty to the queen, and let her know her army has had a glorious victory. M. Tallard and two other generals are in my coach, and I am following the rest. The bearer, my aide-de-camp, colonel Parke, will give her an account of what has passed. I shall do it in a day or two, by another more at large.

August 14

. . . Before the battle was quite done yesterday, I writ to my dearest soul to let her know that I was well, and that God had blessed her majesty's arms with as great a victory as has ever been known; for prisoners I have the marshal de Tallard, and the greatest part of his general officers, above 8,000 men, and near 1,500 officers. In short the army of M. de Tallard, which was that which I fought with, is quite ruined; that of the elector of Bavaria and the marshal de Marsin, which prince Eugene fought against, I am afraid has not had much loss, for I can't find that he has many prisoners. As soon as the elector knew that monsieur de Tallard was like to be beaten, he marched off, so that I came only in time enough to see him retire. As all these prisoners are taken by the troops I command, it is in my power to send as many of them to England as her majesty shall think for her honour and service. My own opinion in this matter is, that the marshal de Tallard, and the general officers, should be sent or brought to her majesty when I come to England; but should all the officers be brought, it would be a very great expence, and I think the honour is in having the marshal and such other officers as her majesty pleases. But I shall do in this, as in all things, that which shall be most agreeable to her. I am so very much out of order with having been 17 hours on horseback yesterday, and not having been

* [A] William Coxe, *Memoirs of John Duke of Marlborough with His Original Correspondence* (London, 1818), Vol. I, pp. 305, 315, 316. [B] William Macdonald, ed., *Documentary Source Book of American History, 1606–1898* (New York: The Macmillan Company, 1909), pp. 93–94.

able to sleep above three hours last night, that I can write to none of my friends. However I am so pleased with this action, that I can't end my letter without being so vain as to tell my dearest soul, that within the memory of man there has been no victory so great as this; and as I am sure you love me entirely well, you will be infinitely pleased with what has been done, upon my account as well as the great benefit the public will have. For had the success of prince Eugene been equal to his merit, we should in that day's action have made an end of the war.

August 18

I have been so very much out of order for these four or five days, that I have been obliged this morning to be let blood, which I hope will set me right; for I should be very much troubled not to be able to follow the blow we have given, which appears greater every day than another, for we have now above 11,000 prisoners. I have also this day a deputation from the town of Augsburg to let me know that the french were marched out of it yesterday morning, by which they have abandoned the country of Bavaria, so that the orders are already given for the putting a garrison into it. If we can be so lucky as to force them from Ulm, where they are now all together, we shall certainly then drive them to the other side of the Rhine. After which we flatter ourselves that the world will think we have done all that could have been expected from us. This day the whole army has returned their thanks to almighty God for the late success, and I have done it with all my heart; for never victory was so complete, notwithstanding that they were stronger than we, and very advantageously posted. But believe me, my dear soul, there was an absolute necessity for the good of the common cause to make this venture, which God has so blessed. I am told the elector has sent for his wife and children to come to Ulm. If it be true, he will not then quit the french interest, which I had much rather he should do, if it might be upon reasonable terms; but the imperialists are for his entire ruin. My dearest life, if we could have another such a day as Wednesday last, I should then hope we might have such a peace as that I might enjoy the remaining part of my life with you. The elector has this minute sent a gentleman to me, I think only to amuse us; we shall see the truth in a day or two, for we march to-morrow. The blood they have taken from me has done me a great deal of good, which is very necessary, for I have not time to be sick.

[B] Extracts from the Treaty of Utrecht, 1713

X. The said most Christian King [Louis XIV] shall restore to the kingdom and Queen of Great Britain, to be possessed in full right for ever, the bay and streights of Hudson, together with all lands, seas, sea-coasts, rivers, and places situate in the said bay and streights, and which belong thereunto, no tracts of land or of sea being excepted, which are at present possessed by the subjects of France. . . . But it is agreed on both sides, to determine within a year, by commissaries to be forthwith named by each party, the limits which are to be fixed between the said Bay of Hudson and the places appertaining to the French. . . . The same commissaries shall also have orders to describe and settle, in like manner, the boundaries between the other British and French colonies in those parts.

XII. The most Christian King shall take care to have delivered to the Queen of Great Britain, on the same day that the ratifications of this treaty shall be exchanged, solemn and authentic letters, or instruments, by virtue whereof it shall appear, that the island of St. Christopher's is to be possessed alone hereafter by British subjects, likewise all Nova Scotia or Acadie, with its ancient boundaries, as also the city of Port Royal, now called Annapolis Royal, and all other things in those parts, which depend on the said lands and islands . . . ; and that in such ample manner and form, that the subjects of the most Christian King shall hereafter be excluded from all kind of fishing in the said seas, bays, and other places, on the coasts of Nova Scotia, that is to say, on those which lie towards the east, within 30 leagues, beginning from the island commonly called Sable, inclusively, and thence stretching along towards the south-west.

XIII. The island called Newfoundland, with the adjacent islands, shall from this time forward belong of right wholly to Britain; and to that end the town and fortress of Placentia, and whatever other places in the said island are in the possession of the French, shall be yielded and given up, within seven months from the exchange of the ratifications of this treaty, or sooner, if possible, by the most Christian King, to those who have a commission from the Queen of Great Britain for that purpose. . . .

[84] *THE AFRICAN SLAVE TRADE: "PILLAR" OF BRITISH TRADE* *

In the eighteenth century, as the "plantation" system developed in the Americas, the African slave trade became of basic importance to British imperial interests. Not only were Negroes sold to the French and Spanish at great profit, but the

* D. B. Horn and Mary Ransome, eds., *English Historical Documents, 1714–1783* in *English Historical Documents*, ed. by David C. Douglas (New York: Oxford University Press, 1957), Vol. X, pp. 824–826. Used by permission of the publisher, Eyre and Spottiswoode (London).

Africans furnished most of the man-power to produce the goods imported by the British from the New World. Here are extracts from an anonymous pamphlet of 1745 propagandizing the African slave trade.

. . . Had not too long Experience proved the contrary, one would think it impossible, that the obvious Connection and Dependency subsisting between our *Plantation* and *Guinea Trades* should be so notoriously disregarded; and remain as much unobserved as if there really were no such Relation between those Branches of our Commerce. Yet this has been the Case; we have suffered our *African Company,* the sole Guardian of our *Guinea Trade,* to moulder and dwindle away almost to Nothing; and then vainly have expected that our *Plantation Commerce,* not only first founded on that Trade, but still daily upheld thereby, should stand alone without its fundamental Prop and Support!

The Policy of our dangerous Rivals has been quite otherwise. *France* has long seen the essential Dependency between those Trades, and that the *one* cannot subsist or prosper without giving all due Encouragement to the *other.* Wherefore, while this Nation has accountably suffered our *African Company* to labour under every Difficulty and Discouragement, (as will appear) *France* has wisely cherished and encouraged *Theirs;* Is it to be wondered therefore, that our Enemies should raise a magnificent Superstructure of *American Commerce* and *Naval Power* on an *African Foundation,* while ours has been for many Years past neglected, and suffered to decline. . . .

Whoever will take upon him to suggest that the same reciprocal Connection, the same mutual Dependency does not subsist in as essential a Manner between the *British Plantation* and *British Guinea Trades,* as between these Trades belonging to *France,* let him discriminate, and shew wherein the Difference consists.

But is it not notorious to the whole World, that the Business of *Planting* in our *British Colonies,* as well as in the *French,* is carried on by the Labour of *Negroes,* imported thither from *Africa?* Are we not indebted to that valuable People, the *Africans,* for our *Sugars, Tobaccoes, Rice, Rum,* and all other *Plantation Produce?* And the greater the Number of *Negroes* imported into our *Colonies,* from *Africa,* will not the Exportation of *British* Manufactures among the *Africans* be in Proportion; they being paid for in such Commodities only? The more likewise our Plantations abound in *Negroes,* will not more Land become cultivated, and both *better* and greater *Variety* of *Plantation Commodities* be produced? As those Trades are subservient to the Well Being and Prosperity of each other; so the more either flourishes or declines, the other must be necessarily affected; and the general Trade and Navigation of their *Mother Country,* will be proportionably benefited or injured. May we not therefore say, with equal Truth, as the *French* do . . . that the general NAVIGATION of *Great Britain* owes all its *Encrease* and *Splendor* to the Commerce of its *American* and *African Colonies;* and that it cannot be maintained and enlarged otherwise than from the constant Prosperity of both those Branches, *whose Interests are mutual and inseparable?*

Whatever *other* Causes may have conspired to enable the *French* to beat us out of all the Markets in Europe in the *Sugar* and *Indigo Trades,* etc. the great and extraordinary Care they have taken to cherish and encourage their *African Company,* to the End that their *Plantations* might be cheaply and plentifully stocked with Negroe Husbandmen, is amply sufficient of itself to Account for the Effect; for this Policy, they wisely judged, would enable them to produce those Commodities cheaper than we, who have suffered the *British* Interest to decline in *Africa,* as that of the *French* has advanced; and when they could produce the Commodities cheaper, is it at all to be admired that they have undersold us at all the foreign Markets in *Europe,* and hereby got that most beneficial Part of our Trade into their own Hands?

As their great Care and our great Neglect of the *African Trade,* has for many Years past given *France* the Advantage over us in *Planting;* so while the same *Cause* continues, Is it not impossible, in the Nature of Things that the *Effect* should cease, and our Trade return to its former flourishing State? All other Measures as they hitherto have, so always will prove only *temporary Expedients,* not *effectual Restoratives:* They have none of them struck at the Root of the Evil; nor is it possible to work a thorough Cure any other way, but by enabling the *African Company* effectually to maintain and support *British* Rights and Privileges on the Coast of *Africa* against the Encroachments of the *French,* and all other Rivals; and in Consequence thereof, by stocking our own Plantations with greater Plenty of *Negroes,* and at *cheaper Rates* than our Rivals would, in such Case, be able to do. . . .

But if the whole *Negroe Trade* be thrown into the Hands of our Rivals, and our Colonies are to depend on the Labour of *White Men* to supply their Place, they will either soon be undone, or shake off their Dependency on the Crown of *England.* For *White Men* cannot be obtained near so cheap, or the Labour of a sufficient Number be had for the Expence of their Maintenance only, as we have of the *Africans.* Has not long Experience also shewn that *White Men* are not constitutionally qualified to sustain the Toil of Planting in the Climates of our *Island Colonies* like the Blacks?

Were it possible however, for *White Men* to answer the End of *Negroes* in Planting, must we not drain our own Country of *Husbandmen, Mechanicks* and *Manufacturers* too? Might not the latter be the Cause of our Colonies interfering with the Manufactures of these Kingdoms, as the *Palatines* attempted in *Pensilvania?* In such Case indeed, we might have just Reason to dread the Prosperity of our Colonies; but while we can be well supplied with *Negroes,* we can be under no such Apprehensions; their Labour will confine the Plantations to *Planting* only; which will render our *Colonies* more beneficial to these Kingdoms than the *Mines* of *Peru* and *Mexico* are to the *Spaniards.*

Doctor Davenant tells us, that in the Time of King CHARLES II. our *Merchants,* interested in the *American Trade,* made a Representation to that King, setting forth, that by a just Medium, they made it appear, that the Labour of an hundred *Negroes* was, at that Time of Day, £1600 *per Annum* Profit to this Nation, deducting therefrom the Amount of the Value of what we consume in Plantation Produce. It was then estimated there were no more than 100,000 *Negroes* in *America;* but the most experienced Judges now do not rate them at less than 300,000; So that if we reckon them of no more Worth to *Great Britain* now than at that Time, and estimate the Value of our Home Consumption of Plantation Commodities at the highest Rate, the annual Gain of the Nation by *Negroe Labour* will fall little short of Three Million [pounds] *per Annum:* And it is to be hoped we shall not sacrifice such an Annuity rather than give all just and reasonable Encouragement for the due Support of our *African Company,* which has been the FOUNDATION of such Profit to these Kingdoms! . . .

[85] *A SURVIVOR TELLS OF THE BLACK HOLE OF CALCUTTA* *

In 1756 the Newab of the Bengal region captured British headquarters at Calcutta and placed 146 prisoners in the "Black Hole." What ensued in the course of one terrible night is described by one of the survivors, J. Z. Holwell.

Figure to yourself, my friend, if possible, the situation of a hundred and forty-six wretches, exhausted by continual fatigue and action, crammed together in a cube of eighteen feet, in a close sultry night, in Bengal, shut up to the eastward and southward (the only quarters from whence air could reach us) by dead walls, and by a wall and door to the north, open only to the westward by two windows, strongly barred with iron, from which we could receive scarce any circulation of fresh air. . . .

We had been but a few minutes confined before every one fell into a

* Narrative of J. Z. Holwell in *The Annual Register . . . for the Year 1758,* pp. 279–285.

perspiration so profuse, you can form no idea of it. This brought on a raging thirst, which increased in proportion as the body was drained of its moisture.

Various expedients were thought of to give more room and air. To obtain the former, it was moved to put off their cloaths; this was approved as a happy motion, and in a few minutes I believe every man was stripped (myself, Mr. Court, and the two young gentlemen by me excepted.) For a little time they flattered themselves with having gained a mighty advantage; every hat was put in motion to produce a circulation of air, and Mr. Baillie proposed that every man should sit down on his hams. This expedient was several times put in practice, and at each time many of the poor creatures, whose natural strength was less than that of others, or who had been more exhausted and could not immediately recover their legs, as others did when the word was given to rise, fell to rise no more; for they were instantly trod to death or suffocated. When the whole body sat down, they were so closely wedged together, that they were obliged to use many efforts before they could put themselves in motion to get up again. . . .

Now every body, excepting those situated in and near the windows, began to grow outrageous, and many delirious: *Water, water,* became the general cry. And the old Jemmautdaar before mentioned, taking pity on us, ordered the people to bring some skins of water. This was what I dreaded. I foresaw it would prove the ruin of the small chance left us, and essayed many times to speak to him privately to forbid its being brought; but the clamour was so loud, it became impossible. The water appeared. Words cannot paint to you the universal agitation and raving the sight of it threw us into. I flattered myself that some, by preserving an equal temper of mind, might outlive the night; but now the reflection, which gave me the greatest pain, was, that I saw no possibility of one escaping to tell the dismal tale.

Until the water came, I had myself not suffered much from thirst, which instantly grew excessive. We had no means of conveying it into the prison, but by hats forced through the bars; and thus myself and Messieurs Coles and Scott (notwithstanding the pains they suffered from their wounds) supplied them as fast as possible. But those who have experienced intense thirst, or are acquainted with the cause and nature of this appetite, will be sufficiently sensible it could receive no more than a momentary alleviation; the cause still subsisted. Though we brought full hats within the bars, there ensued such violent struggles, and frequent contests to get at it, that before it reached the lips of any one, there would be scarcely a small tea cup full left in them. These supplies, like sprinkling water on fire, only served to feed and raise the flame. . . .

By half an hour past eleven, the much greater number of those living were in an outrageous delirium, and the others quite ungovernable; few retaining any calmness, but the ranks next the windows. They all now found, that water, instead of relieving, rather heightened their uneasiness; and, *Air, air,* was the general cry. Every insult that could be devised against the guard, all the opprobrious names and abuse that the suba, Monickchund, &c. could be loaded with, were repeated to provoke the guard to fire upon us, every man that could, rushing tumultuously towards the windows, with eager hopes of meeting the first shot. Then a general prayer to heaven to hasten the approach of the flames to the right and left of us, and put a period to our misery. But these failing, they whose strength and spirits were quite exhausted, laid themselves down and expired quietly upon their fellows: others who had yet some strength and vigour left, made a last effort for the windows, and several succeeded by leaping and scrambling over the backs and heads of those in the first ranks; and got hold of the bars, from which there was no removing them. Many to the right and left sunk with the violent pressure, and were soon suffocated; for now a steam arose from the living and the dead. . . .

I need not, my dear friend, ask your commiseration, when I tell you, that in this plight, from half an hour after eleven till near two in the morning, I sustained the weight of a heavy man, with his knees on my back, and the pressure of his whole body on my head; a Dutch serjeant, who had taken his seat upon my left shoulder, and a Topaz [a black Christian soldier] bearing on my right: all which, nothing could have enabled me long to support, but the props and pressure equally sustaining me all around. The two latter I frequently dislodged, by shifting my hold on the bars, and driving my knuckles into their ribs; but my friend above stuck fast, and, as he held by two bars, was immoveable. . . .

When the day broke, and the gentlemen found that no entreaties could prevail to get the door opened, it occurred to one of them (I think to Mr. Secretary Cooke) to make a search for me, in hopes I might have influence enough to gain a release from this scene of misery. Accordingly Messrs. Lushington and Walcot undertook the search, and by my shirt discovered me under the dead upon the platform. They took me from thence, and imagining I had some signs of life, brought me towards the window I had first possession of.

But as life was equally dear to every man (and the stench arising from the dead bodies was grown so intolerable) no one would give up his station in or near the window: so they were obliged to carry me back again. But soon after Captain Mills, (now captain of the company's yacht) who was in possession of a seat in the window, had the humanity to offer to resign it. I was again brought by the same gentlemen and placed in the window.

At this juncture the suba, who had received an account of the havoc death had made amongst us, sent one of his Jemmautdaars to enquire if the chief survived. They showed me to him; told I had appearance of life remaining; and believed I might recover if the door was opened very soon. This answer being returned to the suba, an order came immediately for our release, it being then near six in the morning.

As the door opened inwards, and as the dead were piled up against it, and covered all the rest of the floor, it was impossible to open it by any efforts from without; it was therefore necessary that the dead should be removed by the few that were within, who were become so feeble, that the task, though it was the condition of life, was not performed without the utmost difficulty, and it was 20 minutes after the order came, before the door could be opened.

About a quarter after six in the morning, the poor remains of 146 souls, being no more than three and twenty, came out of the Blackhole alive, but in a condition which made it very doubtful whether they would see the morning of the next day; among the living was Mrs. Carey, but poor Leech was among the dead. The bodies were dragged out of the hole by the soldiers, and thrown promiscuously into the ditch of an unfinished ravelin, which was afterwards filled with earth. . . .

[86] *THE FRENCH LOSE QUEBEC, 1759* *

The key to Canada was the city of Quebec. When Wolfe forced its surrender it was the beginning of the end of the French empire in North America. This episode in the Seven Years' War is told by Captain John Knox, who took part in the battle he describes.

Before daybreak this morning we made a descent upon the north shore, about half a quarter of a mile to the eastward of Sillery, and the light troops were fortunately, by the rapidity of the current, carried lower down, between us and Cape Diamond; we had, in this debarkation, thirty flat-bottomed boats, containing about sixteen hundred men. This was a great surprise on the enemy, who, from the natural strength of the place, did not suspect, and consequently were not prepared against, so bold an attempt. The chain

* John Knox, *Historical Journal,* Vol. II, pp. 66–79, as found in Edward P. Cheyney, ed., *Readings in English History* (New York: Ginn and Company, 1908), pp. 598–600. Used by permission of the publisher.

of sentries, which they had posted along the summit of the heights, galled us a little, and picked off several men, and some officers, before our light infantry got up to dislodge them.

This grand enterprise was conducted and executed with great good order and discretion; as fast as we landed, the boats put off for reënforcements, and the troops formed with much regularity: the general, with Brigadiers Monckton and Murray, were ashore with the first division. We lost no time here, but clambered up one of the steepest precipices that can be conceived, being almost a perpendicular, and of an incredible height. As soon as we gained the summit all was quiet, and not a shot was heard, owing to the excellent conduct of the light infantry under Colonel Howe; it was by this time clear daylight. Here we formed again, the river and the south country in our rear, our right extending to the town, our left to Sillery, and halted a few minutes. The general then detached the light troops to our left to rout the enemy from their battery and to disable their guns, except they could be rendered serviceable to the party who were to remain there; and this service was soon performed. We then faced to the right, and marched towards the town by files, till we came to the Plains of Abraham: an even piece of ground which Mr. Wolfe had made choice of, while we stood forming upon the hill. Weather showery; about six o'clock the enemy first made their appearance upon the heights, between us and the town; whereupon we halted, and wheeled to the right, thereby forming the line of battle.

About eight o'clock we had two pieces of short brass six-pounders playing on the enemy, which threw them into some confusion, and obliged them to alter their disposition, and Montcalm formed them into three large columns; about nine the two armies moved a little nearer each other. The light cavalry made a faint attempt upon our parties at the battery of Sillery, but were soon beat off, and Monsieur de Bougainville, with his troops from Cape Rouge, came down to attack the flank of our second line, hoping to penetrate there; but, by a masterly disposition of Brigadier Townshend, they were forced to desist, and the third battalion of Royal Americans was then detached to the first ground we had formed on after we gained the heights, to preserve the communication with the beach and our boats.

About ten o'clock the enemy began to advance briskly in three columns, with loud shouts and recovered arms, two of them inclining to the left of our army, and the third towards our right, firing obliquely at the two extremities of our line, from the distance of one hundred and thirty, until they came within forty, yards; which our troops withstood with the greatest intrepidity and firmness, still reserving their fire, and paying the strictest obedience to their officers. This uncommon steadiness, together with the havoc which the grapeshot from our fieldpieces made among them, threw them into some disorder, and was most critically maintained by a well-timed, regular, and heavy discharge of our small arms, such as they could no longer oppose. Hereupon they gave way, and fled with precipitation, so that, by the time the cloud of smoke was vanished, our men were again loaded, and, profiting by the advantage we had over them, pursued them almost to the gates of the town and the bridge over the little river, redoubling our fire with great eagerness, making many officers and men prisoners. . . .

Our joy at this success is inexpressibly damped by the loss we sustained of one of the greatest heroes which this or any other age can boast of,—General James Wolfe, who received his mortal wound as he was exerting himself at the head of the grenadiers of Louisbourg.

. . . The Sieur de Montcalm died late last night: when his wound was dressed, and he settled in bed, the surgeons who attended him were desired to acquaint him ingenuously with their sentiments of him, and being answered that his wound was mortal, he calmly replied that he was glad of it. His excellency then demanded whether he could survive it long, and how long. He was told, "about a dozen hours, perhaps more, peradvanture less." "So much the better," rejoined this eminent warrior; "I am happy I shall not live to see the surrender of Quebec. . . ."

After our late worthy general, of renowned memory, was carried off wounded to the rear of the front line, he desired those who were about him to lay him down; being asked if he would have a surgeon he replied, "It is needless; it is all over with me." One of them cried out, "They run, see how they run!" "Who runs?" demanded our hero with great earnestness, like a person aroused from sleep. The officer answered, "The enemy, sir; egad, they give way everywhere." Thereupon the general rejoined, "Go one of you, my lads, to Colonel Burton; tell him to march Webb's regiment with all speed down to Charles's river, to cut off the retreat of the fugitives from the bridge." Then, turning on his side, he added, "Now, God be praised, I will die in peace"; and thus expired. . . .

[87] *FRANCE IS EVICTED FROM NORTH AMERICA* *

Between 1758 and 1760, with the surrender to the English of such key positions as Louisburg, Niagara, Fort Duquesne, Quebec, and Montreal, French power in North America came to an end. The Seven Years' War dragged on in Europe for three more years, but in 1763 the Treaty of Paris recognized British control of

* William Macdonald, ed., *Documentary Source Book of American History, 1606–1898* (New York: The Macmillan Company, 1909), pp. 109–112.

North America east of the Mississippi. (France surrendered as much of Louisiana as lay west of the Mississippi to Spain.) The chief articles of the Treaty relating to America are given here.

IV. His most Christian Majesty [Louis XV] renounces all pretensions, which he has heretofore formed, or might form, to Nova Scotia or Acadia, in all its parts, and guaranties the whole of it, and with all its dependencies, to the King of Great Britain: moreover, his most Christian Majesty cedes and guaranties to his said Britannic Majesty, in full right, Canada, with all its dependencies, as well as the Island of Cape Breton, and all the other islands and coasts in the gulph and river St. Laurence, and, in general, every thing that depends on the said countries, lands, islands, and coasts, with the sovereignty, property, possession, and all rights, acquired by treaty or otherwise, which the most Christian King, and the crown of France, have had till now over the said countries, islands, lands, places, coasts, and their inhabitants . . .

V. The subjects of France shall have the liberty of fishing and drying, on a part of the coasts of the Island of Newfoundland, such as it is specified in the XIIIth article of the treaty of Utrecht; which article is renewed and confirmed by the present treaty (except what relates to the island of Cape Breton, as well as to the other islands and coasts in the mouth and in the gulph of St. Laurence:) and his Britannic Majesty consents to leave to the subjects of the most Christian King the liberty of fishing in the gulph St. Laurence, on condition that the subjects of France do not exercise the said fishery but at the distance of three leagues from all the coasts belonging to Great Britain, as well those of the continent, as those of the islands situated in the said gulph of St. Laurence. . . .

VI. The King of Great Britain cedes the islands of St. Pierre and Miquelon, in full right, to his most Christian Majesty, to serve as a shelter to the French fishermen: and his said most Christian Majesty engages not to fortify the said islands; to erect no building upon them, but merely for the convenience of the fishery; and to keep upon them a guard of fifty men only for the police.

VII. . . . it is agreed, that, for the future, the confines between the dominions of his Britannic Majesty, and those of his most Christian Majesty, in that part of the world, shall be fixed irrevocably by a line drawn along the middle of the river Mississippi, from its source to the river Iberville, and from thence, by a line drawn along the middle of this river, and the lakes Maurepas and Pontchartrain, to the sea; and for this purpose, the most Christian King cedes in full right, and guaranties to his Britannic Majesty, the river and port of the Mobile, and everything which he possesses, or ought to possess, on the left side of the river Mississippi, except the town of New Orleans, and the island on which it is situated, which shall remain to France; provided that the navigation of the river Mississippi shall be equally free, as well to the subjects of Great Britain as to those of France, in its whole breadth and length, from its source to the sea, . . .

VIII. The King of Great Britain shall restore to France the islands of Guadeloupe, of Marie Galante, of Desirade, of Martinico, and of Belleisle; and the fortresses of these islands shall be restored in the same condition they were in when they were conquered by the British arms . . .

[88] *A CONVICT SETTLEMENT IS ESTABLISHED IN AUSTRALIA* *

The British had long shipped the overflow from their jails to North America. The loss of the Thirteen Colonies led to a search for new penal settlements. In 1786 the government decided to make use of Botany Bay on the eastern coast of Australia, and in 1788 the first convoy of prisoners arrived, marking the establishment of England's Australian colony.

[A] The Home Secretary Announces H. M.'s Decision

The several gaols and places for the confinement of felons in this kingdom being in so crowded a state that the greatest danger is to be apprehended, not only from their escape, but from infectious distempers, which may hourly be expected to break out amongst them, his Majesty, desirous of preventing by every possible means the ill consequences which might happen from either of these causes, has been pleased to signify to me his royal commands that measures should immediately be pursued for sending out of this kingdom such of the convicts as are under sentence or order of transportation.

The Nautilus, sloop, which, upon the recommendation of a Committee of the House of Commons, had been sent to explore the southern coast of Africa, in order to find out an eligible situation for the reception of the said convicts, where from their industry they might soon be likely to obtain means of subsistence, having lately returned, and it appearing by the report of her officers that the several parts of the coast which they examined . . . are sandy and barren, and from other causes unfit for a settlement of that description, H. M. has thought it advisable to fix upon Botany Bay

* A. Aspinwall and E. Anthony Smith, eds., *English Historical Documents, 1783–1832* in *English Historical Documents*, ed. by David C. Douglas (New York: Oxford University Press, 1959), Vol. XI, pp. 781, 787–788. Used by permission of the publisher, Eyre and Spottiswoode (London).

. . . which, according to the accounts given by the late Captain Cook, as well as the representations of persons who accompanied him during his last voyage, and who have been consulted upon the subject, is looked upon as a place likely to answer the above purposes.

I am, therefore, commanded to signify to your Lordships H. M.'s pleasure that you do forthwith take such measures as may be necessary for providing a proper number of vessels for the conveyance of 750 convicts to Botany Bay, together with such provisions, necessaries, and implements for agriculture as may be necessary for their use after arrival. . . .

According to the best opinions that can be obtained, it is supposed that a quantity of provisions equal to two years' consumption should be provided. . . .

In the meantime, I have only to recommend it to your Lordships to cause every possible expedition to be used in preparing the shipping for the reception of the said convicts, and for transporting the supplies of provisions and necessaries for their use to the place of their destination.

[B] Letter from a Woman Convict in Australia, November 14, 1788

I take the first opportunity that has been given us, to acquaint you with our disconsolate situation in this solitary waste of the creation. Our passage, you may have heard by the first ships, was tolerably favourable; but the inconveniences since suffered for want of shelter, bedding &c. are not to be imagined by any stranger. However, we have now two streets, if four rows of the most miserable huts you can possibly conceive of, deserve that name: windows they have none, as from the Governor's house, &c. now nearly finished, no glass could be spared; so that lattices of twigs are made by our people to supply their places. At the extremity of the lines, where, since our arrival, the dead are buried there is a place called the church-yard, but we hear as soon as a sufficient quantity of bricks can be made, a church is to be built, and named St. Philip, after the Governor. Notwithstanding all our presents, the savages continue to do us all the injury they can, which makes the soldiers' duty very hard, and much disaffection among the officers. I know not how many of our people have been killed. As for the distresses of the women, they are past description, as they are deprived of tea and other things they were indulged in, in the voyage, by the seamen: and as they are all totally unprovided with clothes, those who have young children are quite wretched. Besides this, though a number of marriages have taken place, several women who became pregnant on the voyage, and are since left by their partners, who have returned to England, are not likely even here to form any fresh connections. We are comforted with the hopes of a supply of tea from China, and flattered with getting riches when the settlement is complete, and the hemp which the place produces is brought to perfection. Our kangaroo cats are like mutton, but much leaner; and here is a kind of chickweed so much in taste like our spinage, that no difference can be discerned. Something like ground ivy is used for tea; but a scarcity of salt and sugar makes our best meals insipid. The separation of several of us to an uninhabited island was like a second transportation. In short, everyone is so taken up with their own misfortunes, that they have no pity to bestow upon others. All our letters are examined by an officer; but a friend takes this for me privately. The ships sail tonight.

15

The Enlightenment

Inspired by the scientific revolution of the seventeenth century, and making use of what was confidently supposed to be the methodology of the natural scientists, the eighteenth century embarked on a momentous intellectual and moral revolution known as the "Enlightenment." By the application of reason to all problems—political, religious, social, and economic—man would lift himself from the alleged superstition and darkness of the past and create a perfect world here below. All that was necessary was to permit Nature and Nature's Laws to rule. Man's social universe was as well ordered, it was thought, as the physical; the trouble had always been that man had constantly exercised irrational interference in the working of the "Laws." The principal practitioners of the new ideas were a class of writers and thinkers called *philosophes* (who were often anything but philosophical) and a group of rulers and ministers styled "enlightened despots" (who were usually more despotic than enlightened).

[89] *DIDEROT DEFINES A* PHILOSOPHE *

While Diderot does not possess the stature of Montesquieu, Rousseau, or Voltaire, his importance in the "Enlightenment" is considerable. He was the principal editor

* *Translations and Reprints from the Original Sources of European History* (Philadelphia: University of Pennsylvania, 1900), Series I, Vol. VI, No. 1, pp. 20–22.

of the great literary monument of the century, the Encyclopédie, *and the author of several influential philosophical works. The excerpt below is from the* Encyclopédie.

There is nothing which costs less to acquire nowadays than the name of *Philosopher;* an obscure and retired life, some outward signs of wisdom, with a little reading, suffice to attach this name to persons who enjoy the honor without meriting it.

Others in whom freedom of thought takes the place of reasoning, regard themselves as the only true philosophers, because they have dared to overturn the consecrated limits placed by religion, and have broken the fetters which faith laid upon their reason. Proud of having gotten rid of the prejudices of education, in the matter of religion, they look upon others with scorn as feeble souls, servile and pusillanimous spirits, who allow themselves to be frightened by the consequences to which irreligion leads, and who, not daring to emerge for an instant from the circle of established verities, nor to proceed along unaccustomed paths, sink to sleep under the yoke of superstition. But one ought to have a more adequate idea of the philosopher, and here is the character which we give him:

Other men make up their minds to act without thinking, nor are they conscious of the causes which move them, not even knowing that such exist. The philosopher, on the contrary, distinguishes the causes to what extent he may, and often anticipates them, and knowingly surrenders himself to them. In this manner he avoids objects that may cause him sensations that are not conducive to his well being or his rational existence, and seeks those which may excite in him affections agreeable with the state in which he finds himself. Reason is in the estimation of the philosopher what grace is to the Christian. Grace determines the Christian's action; reason the philosopher's.

Other men are carried away by their passions, so that the acts which they produce do not proceed from reflection. These are the men who move in darkness; while the philosopher, even in his passions, moves only after reflection. He marches at night, but a torch goes on ahead.

The philosopher forms his principles upon an infinity of individual observations. The people adopt the principle without a thought of the observations which have produced it, believing that the maxim exists, so to speak, of itself; but the philosopher takes the maxim at its source, he examines its origin, he knows its real value, and only makes use of it, if it seems to him satisfactory.

Truth is not for the philosopher a mistress who vitiates his imagination, and whom he believes to find everywhere. He contents himself with being able to discover it wherever he may chance to find it. He does not confound it with its semblance; but takes for true that which is true, for false that which is false, for doubtful that which is doubtful, and for probable that which is only probable. He does more—and this is the great perfection of philosophy; that when he has no real grounds for passing judgment, he knows how to remain undetermined.

The philosopher is then an honest man, actuated in everything by reason. . . .

[90] *NATURAL RELIGION AND IRRELIGION IN THE AGE OF REASON* *

One point on which all philosophes *were in agreement was that reason and revealed religion were incompatible. Some of the more conservative* philosophes *deduced a "natural religion" which vaguely acknowledged a Supreme Being, immortality, reward for good and punishment for evil, but repudiated virtually all else in traditional Christianity. These were the Deists. But as the Age of Reason progressed, religious radicalism grew and outright atheism became an increasingly common "creed." These two positions appear below as exemplified in the writings of Rousseau and d'Holbach.*

[A] Extracts from Rousseau's *Emile*

In what I have said [the fictitious Vicar is explaining his religious views to Rousseau] you see Natural Religion alone; it is indeed strange that there need be any other. How can I know that such a necessity exists? Of what can I be guilty, when I serve God according to the lights which He bestows upon my mind, and according to the feelings with which He inspires my heart? What purity in morals, or what dogma at once useful to man and honourable to his Maker, can I get from a positive doctrine, which I could not get, without it, from a good use of my own faculties? For the glory of God, for the good of society, and for my own profit, show me what can be added to the duties of the natural law, and show me what virtue can be produced from a new cult, which is not already a result of mine. Our greatest ideas about the Godhead reach us through reason alone. Observe Nature. Listen to the voice within. Has not God told us everything through our eyes, our conscience, our judgement? What more will men say to us? Their

* [A] "Profession of Faith of a Savoyard Vicar," Part II, chs. 2 and 7 in John Martin Creed and John Sandwith Boys Smith, eds., *Religious Thought in the Eighteenth Century* (London: Cambridge University Press, 1934), pp. 169–170. [B] *Translations and Reprints from the Original Sources of European History* (Philadelphia: The University of Pennsylvania, 1900), Vol. VI, No. 1, pp. 26–27.

revelations, by ascribing to God human passions, only degrade Him. Far from making clearer our conceptions of the Eternal Being, I notice that particular doctrines confuse those conceptions; instead of ennobling them, they cheapen them; to the unsearchable mysteries which already surround Him, they add absurd contradictions. These dogmas make man proud, intolerant, cruel; instead of establishing peace upon the earth, they bring fire and sword. I ask myself what is the good of it all, and I do not know what answer to give. I see there nothing but the crimes of men and the miseries of the human race.

All the theology which I am able to acquire for myself by contemplation of the universe, and by the good use of my faculties is confined to what I have already explained to you. To know more, one must have recourse to extraordinary means. These means cannot be human authority, for, since no man is of a different species from me, all that a man may know by nature, I too may know, and another man may be deceived as much as I. When I believe what he says, it is not because he says it, but because he proves it. The testimony of men is in the end then only that of my own reason, and adds nothing to the natural means which God has given me whereby I may know the truth.

[B] Extracts from d'Holbach, *The System of Nature*

Man's ignorance has endured so long, he has taken such slow, irresolute steps to ameliorate his condition, only because he has neglected to study nature, to scrutinize her laws, to search out her resources, to discover her properties. His sluggishness finds its account in permitting himself to be guided by precedent, rather than to follow experience which demands activity; to be led by routine, rather than by his reason which exacts reflection. Hence may be traced the aversion man betrays for everything that swerves from these rules to which he has been accustomed; hence his stupid, his scrupulous respect for antiquity, for the most silly, the most absurd institutions of his fathers; hence those fears that seize him, when the most advantageous changes are proposed to him, or the most probable attempts are made to better his condition. He dreads to examine, because he has been taught to hold it a profanation of something immediately connected with his welfare; he credulously believes the interested advice, and spurns those who wish to show him the danger of the road he is traveling.

This is the reason why nations linger on in the most scandalous lethargy, groaning under abuses transmitted from century to century, trembling at the very idea of that which alone can remedy their misfortunes.

The more man reflects, the more he will be convinced that the soul, very far from being distinguished from the body, is only the body itself considered relatively to some of its functions, or to some of the modes of existing or acting of which it is susceptible whilst it enjoys life. Thus, the soul in man is considered relatively to the faculty he has of feeling, of thinking, and of acting in a mode resulting from his peculiar nature; that is to say, from his properties, from his particular organization, from the modifications, whether durable or transitory, which the beings who act upon him cause his machine to undergo.

An organized being may be compared to a clock, which, once broken, is no longer suitable to the use for which it was designed. To say that the soul shall feel, shall think, shall enjoy, shall suffer after the death of the body, is to pretend that a clock, shivered into a thousand pieces, will continue to strike the hour and have the faculty of marking the progress of time. Those who say that the soul of man is able to subsist notwithstanding the destruction of the body, evidently support the position that the modification of a body will be enabled to conserve itself after the subject is destroyed; but this is completely absurd.

[91] A PHILOSOPHE *FLAYS TRADITIONAL EDUCATION* *

The following selection is an extract from Diderot's Plan of a University, *submitted to Catherine the Great upon her request. The author was no more qualified to write on higher education than was Rousseau to write on child rearing. He never attended a university and his teaching experience was limited to a few months, which made him nervously ill to the point of madness. But it was the conviction of the* philosophes *that the "reasonable" mind could cope with any problem.*

The only advantage that is derived from our schools is one that was never intended; that is the habit of application, of continuous application to futile but difficult things. This habit gives a marvelous aptitude for subjects that are of greater importance for all the functions of society. It is a habit that particularly distinguishes one man from another, especially if the usages of society cure him of the tendency to cavil; which, however, does not always happen.

This is the result of seven years of hard work and continuous imprisonment.

At the end of this long and barren avenue, which is called the Faculty of Arts, and along which seven or eight tedious, wearying and fruitless years

* By permission from *French Liberalism and Education in the Eighteenth Century*, ed. by F. de la Fontainerie, pp. 209–212. Copyright, 1932, McGraw-Hill Book Co., Inc.

are spent, open three vestibules which lead to the Faculty of Theology, the Faculty of Law and the Faculty of Medicine.

Questions and Replies

—But do all those who have followed this Avenue of the Arts to the end enter one of the schools of these three faculties?

—No.

—Then, what becomes of them?

—As they are lazy, ignorant and too old to begin to learn some mechanical art, they become actors, soldiers, pick-pockets, gamblers, rogues, swindlers and vagabonds.

—And those who quit along the way?

—Though they know absolutely nothing that can be of use to them, still they have lost less time and are not incapable of following some useful calling. This is their resource.

Without doubt it is not the intention of her Imperial Majesty that her university should be copied from this model. May she permit me to add that neither is it mine.

OUR FACULTY OF LAW

Our Faculty of Law is wretched. Not a word of French law is read; no more of international law than if there were none at all; nothing about our civil or criminal codes, our legal procedures, our laws, our statutes, the constitutions of the State, the rights of sovereigns, those of subjects; nothing about liberty or property, and no more about obligations and contracts.

—What is done there then?

—Roman law is studied in all its branches. A Law which has almost no relation to ours. Thus, he who has just been decorated with the cap of a Doctor of Laws is about as helpless, if someone seduces his daughter, abducts his wife or disputes his right to his field, as the least of the citizens. All this fine knowledge would be of great use to him if he were called Moevius or Sempronius, and if we returned to the times of Honorius or of Arcadius. Then he would plead his case magnificently. Under Louis XVI, he is as stupid as a villager from Chaillot or a peasant from lower Normandy. The Faculty of Law no longer occupies an old Gothic building, but it continues, nevertheless, to speak Gothic under the superb arcade of the modern edifice erected for it.

OUR FACULTY OF THEOLOGY

The Faculty of Theology has regulated its studies according to the present circumstances. They are all directed towards the controversies with Protestants, Lutherans, Socinians, deists and the host of modern unbelievers. It is, itself, an excellent school of unbelief, and there are few Sorbonists who do not conceal under their furred robes either deism or atheism. They are only the more intolerant and interfering, either by disposition, or through ambition, self-interest or hypocrisy. They are the least useful, the most intractable and the most dangerous subjects of the State. They and their adherents, priests or monks, have often abused the right of addressing public assemblies. If I were a sovereign, and I thought that, on every holy day and every Sunday, between eleven o'clock and noon, a hundred and fifty thousand of my subjects say to all the others and make them believe, in the name of God, all that suits the demon of fanaticism and pride which possesses them, I should shudder with terror.

Her Imperial Majesty certainly does not wish any of this kind of people, and, if she must have priests, she will without doubt demand that they be edifying, enlightened and peaceable.

OUR FACULTY OF MEDICINE

Our Faculty of Medicine is the best of the four. There is little that needs to be rectified. Anatomy, surgery, the treatment of diseases in all its branches, the elements of natural history, botany, chemistry and pharmacy are all taught. There is need only of fixing the order and the duration of these studies. Besides, there is no practical experience, which is a great defect. How many things there are pertaining to the science of healing that cannot be learned either from books or lectures! Can the discourse of a professor teach how to recognize whether a pulse is strong or weak, slow or rapid, regular or irregular, normal or abnormal? What description can be accurate enough to give a precise notion of certain wounds, discharges, fractures, etc.? A young physician then makes his first experiments on us, and he becomes skillful only through murder.

[92] *BECCARIA PLEADS FOR HUMANE LAWS* *

The best-known Italian philosophe *was the Marquis of Beccaria (1735?–1794). His* Essay on Crimes and Punishments *(1764) condemned torture, capital punishment, and much else in contemporary legal procedure. Like all* philosophes, *he placed great faith in education as a means of preventing crime. His ideas had much effect on the French revolutionary code.*

* Beccaria, *An Essay on Crimes and Punishments,* American edition of 1819 (Stanford, Cal.: Academic Reprints, 1953), Ch. XVI, pp. 59–62.

The torture of a criminal during the course of his trial is a cruelty consecrated by custom in most nations. It is used with an intent either to make him confess his crime, or to explain some contradictions into which he had been led during his examination, or discover his accomplices, or for some kind of metaphysical and incomprehensible purgation of infamy, or, finally, in order to discover other crimes of which he is not accused, but of which he may be guilty.

No man can be judged a criminal until he be found guilty; nor can society take from him the public protection until it has been proved that he has violated the conditions on which it was granted. What right, then, but that of power, can authorise the punishment of a citizen so long as there remains any doubt of his guilt? This dilemma is frequent. Either he is guilty, or not guilty. If guilty, he should only suffer the punishment ordained by the laws, and torture becomes useless, as his confession is unnecessary. If he be not guilty, you torture the innocent; for, in the eye of the law, every man is innocent whose crime has not been proved. Besides, it is confounding all relations to expect that a man should be both the accuser and accused; and that pain should be the test of truth, as if truth resided in the muscles and fibres of a wretch in torture. By this method the robust will escape, and the feeble be condemned. These are the inconveniencies of this pretended test of truth, worthy only of a cannibal, and which the Romans, in many respects barbarous, and whose savage virtue has been too much admired, reserved for the slaves alone.

What is the political intention of punishments? To terrify and be an example to others. Is this intention answered by thus privately torturing the guilty and the innocent? It is doubtless of importance that no crime should remain unpunished; but it is useless to make a public example of the author of a crime hid in darkness. A crime already committed, and for which there can be no remedy, can only be punished by a political society with an intention that no hopes of impunity should induce others to commit the same. If it be true, that the number of those who from fear or virtue respect the laws is greater than of those by whom they are violated, the risk of torturing an innocent person is greater, as there is a greater probability that, *coeteris paribus,* an individual hath observed, than that he hath infringed the laws.

There is another ridiculous motive for torture, namely, *to purge a man from infamy.* Ought such an abuse to be tolerated in the eighteenth century? Can pain, which is a sensation, have any connection with a moral sentiment, a matter of opinion? Perhaps the rack may be considered as the refiner's furnace.

It is not difficult to trace this senseless law to its origin; for an absurdity, adopted by a whole nation, must have some affinity with other ideas established and respected by the same nation. This custom seems to be the offspring of religion, by which mankind, in all nations and in all ages, are so generally influenced. We are taught by our infallible church, that those stains of sin contracted through human frailty, and which have not deserved the eternal anger of the Almighty, are to be purged away in another life by an incomprehensible fire. Now infamy is a stain, and if the punishments and fire of purgatory can take away all spiritual stains, why should not the pain of torture take away those of a civil nature? I imagine, that the confession of a criminal, which in some tribunals is required as being essential to his condemnation, has a similar origin, and has been taken from the mysterious tribunal of penitence, where the confession of sins is a necessary part of the sacrament. Thus have men abused the unerring light of revelation; and, in the times of tractable ignorance, having no other, they naturally had recourse to it on every occasion, making the most remote and absurd applications. Moreover, infamy is a sentiment regulated neither by the laws nor by reason, but entirely by opinion; but torture renders the victim infamous, and therefore cannot take infamy away.

[93] *POLITICAL AND SOCIAL INSTITUTIONS COME UNDER ATTACK* *

One of the principal targets of the philosophes *was contemporary political institutions, which were deemed as irrational as dogmatic religion. In this selection will be found extracts from three noted attacks on eighteenth century politics. The first is from Montesquieu's fictitious* Persian Letters *(1721), a book written in the form of letters exchanged by two mythical Persian visitors to France with their friends at home. The second extract presents Rousseau's version of contractual government, one both democratic and authoritarian in its implications. The last extract is from Beaumarchais' comedy,* The Marriage of Figaro *(1784), which clearly foreshadows the French Revolution.*

[A] Rica to Ibben, Paris, the 4th of the Second Moon of Rebiab, 1712

We have now been a month at Paris, and all the time constantly moving about. There is much to do before one can get settled, find out the people with whom one has business, and procure the many requisites which are all wanted at the same time.

Paris is quite as large as Ispahan. The houses are so high that you

* [A] *The Persian Letters* (New York and London: M. Walter Dunne, 1901), Letter XXIV, pp. 65–68. [B] *The Social Contract,* I, 6, trans. by Gerard Hopkins, The World's Classics series (London and New York: Oxford University Press, 1945), pp. 254–257. Used by permission of the publisher. [C] *Le Marriage de Figaro,* trans. by Crane Brinton, ed., *The Portable Age of Reason Reader* (New York: The Viking Press, 1956), pp. 506–508. Reprinted by permission of the publisher.

would swear they must be inhabited by astrologers. You can easily imagine that a city built in the air, with six or seven houses one above the other, is densely peopled; and that when everybody is abroad, there is a mighty bustle.

You will scarcely believe that during the month I have been here I have not yet seen any one walking. There is no people in the world who hold more by their vehicles than the French: they run; they fly: the slow carriages of Asia, the measured step of our camels, would put them into a state of coma. As for me, who am not made for such hurry, and who often go a-foot without changing my pace, I am sometimes as mad as a Christian; for, passing over splashing from head to foot, I cannot pardon the elbowings I meet with regularly and periodically. A man, coming up behind me, passes me, and turns me half round; then another, crossing me on the opposite side, spins me suddenly round to my first position. Before I have walked a hundred paces, I am more bruised than if I had gone ten leagues.

You must not expect from me an exhaustive account of the manners and customs of the Europeans: I have myself but a faint notion of them yet, and have hardly had time to recover from my astonishment.

The King of France [Louis XIV] is the most powerful of European potentates. He has no mines of gold like his neighbor, the King of Spain; but he is much wealthier than that prince, because his riches are drawn from a more inexhaustible source, the vanity of his subjects. He has undertaken and carried on great wars, without any other supplies than those derived from the sale of titles of honor; and it is by a prodigy of human pride that his troops are paid, his towns fortified, and his fleets equipped.

Then again, the king is a great magician, for his dominion extends to the minds of his subjects; he makes them think what he wishes. . . . If he has a costly war on hand, and is short of money, he simply suggests to his subjects that a piece of paper is coin of the realm, and they are straightway convinced of it. He has even succeeded in persuading them that his touch is a sovereign cure for all sorts of diseases, so great is the power and influence he has over their minds.

What I have told you of this prince need not astonish you: there is another magician more powerful still, who is master of the king's mind, as absolutely as the king is master of the minds of his subjects. This magician is called the Pope. Sometimes he makes the king believe that three are no more than one; that the bread which he eats is not bread; the wine which he drinks not wine; and a thousand things of a like nature.

I will continue to write you, and acquaint you with matters differing widely from the Persian character and genius. We tread, indeed, the same earth; but it seems incredible, remembering in the presence of the men of this country those of the country in which you are.

[B] Rousseau's *Social Contract*

I assume, for the sake of argument, that a point was reached in the history of mankind when the obstacles to continuing in a state of Nature were stronger than the forces which each individual could employ to the end of continuing in it. The original state of Nature, therefore, could no longer endure, and the human race would have perished had it not changed its manner of existence.

Now, since men can by no means engender new powers, but can only unite and control those of which they are already possessed, there is no way in which they can maintain themselves save by coming together and pooling their strength in a way that will enable them to withstand any resistance exerted upon them from without. They must develop some sort of central direction and learn to act in concert.

Such a concentration of powers can be brought about only as the consequence of an agreement reached between individuals. But the self-preservation of each single man derives primarily from his own freedom. How, then, can he limit these without, at the same time, doing himself an injury and neglecting that care which it is his duty to devote to his own concerns? This difficulty, in so far as it is relevant to my subject, can be expressed as follows:

"Some form of association must be found as a result of which the whole strength of the community will be enlisted for the protection of the person and property of each constituent member, in such a way that each, when united to his fellows, renders obedience to his own will, and remains as free as he was before." That is the basic problem of which the Social Contract provides the solution.

The clauses of this Contract are determined by the Act of Association in such a way that the least modification must render them null and void. Even though they may never have been formally enunciated, they must be everywhere the same, and everywhere tacitly admitted and recognized. So completely must this be the case that, should the social compact be violated, each associated individual would at once resume all the rights which once were his, and regain his natural liberty, by the mere fact of losing the agreed liberty for which he renounced it.

It must be clearly understood that the clauses in question can be reduced, in the last analysis, to one only, to wit, the complete alienation by each associate member to the community of *all his rights*. For, in the first place, since each has made surrender of himself without reservation, the resultant conditions are the same for all: and, because they are the same for all, it is in the interest of none to make them onerous to his fellows.

Furthermore, this alienation having been made unreservedly, the union of individuals is as perfect as it well can be, none of the associated members having any claim against the community. For should there be any rights left to individuals, and no common authority be empowered to pronounce as between them and the public, then each, being in some things his own judge, would soon claim to be so in all. Were that so, a state of Nature would still remain in being, the conditions of association becoming either despotic or ineffective.

In short, whoso gives himself to all gives himself to none. And, since there is no member of the social group over whom we do not acquire precisely the same rights as those over ourselves which we have surrendered to him, it follows that we gain the exact equivalent of what we lose, as well as an added power to conserve what we already have.

If, then, we take from the social pact everything which is not essential to it, we shall find it to be reduced to the following terms: "each of us contributes to the group his person and the powers which he wields as a person, and we receive into the body politic each individual as forming an indivisible part of the whole."

As soon as the act of association becomes a reality, it substitutes for the person of each of the contracting parties a moral and collective body made up of as many members as the constituting assembly has votes, which body receives from this very act of constitution its unity, its dispersed *self*, and its will. . . .

[C] Soliloquy from *The Marriage of Figaro*

FIGARO (*Alone, walking in the darkness, speaks in sombre tones*): . . . No, Monsieur le Comte, you shan't have her! You shan't have her. Because you are a great noble, you think you are a great genius! Nobility, a fortune, a rank, appointments to office: all this makes a man so proud! What did you do to earn all this? You took the trouble to get born—nothing more. Moreover, you're really a pretty ordinary fellow! While as for me, lost in the crowd, I've had to use more knowledge, more brains, just to keep alive than your likes have had to spend on governing Spain and the Empire for a century. And you want to contest with me—Someone's coming, it's she—no, nobody—The night is black as the devil, and here I am plying the silly trade of husband, though I'm only half a husband. (*He sits down on a bench*) Is there anything stranger than my fate? Son of I don't know whom, kidnapped by robbers, brought up in their ways, I got disgusted with them, and tried to follow an honest career; and everywhere I met with rebuffs. I learned chemistry, pharmacy, surgery, and all the credit of a great noble barely succeeded in putting a veterinary's lancet in my hand! Tired of making sick beasts sadder, I turned to a very different trade, and threw myself into the life of the theatre. What a stone I hung around my neck that time! I sketched a comedy about harem life; being a Spanish writer, I assumed I could be irreverent towards Mohammed without any scruples: but at once an Envoy from somewhere complained that my verses offended the Sublime Porte, Persia, a part of India, all Egypt, the kingdoms of Barca, Tripoli, Tunis, Algiers and Morocco; and there was my comedy burned, to please some Mohammedan princes not one of whom I suppose knows how to read, and who keep cursing away at us all as "Christian dogs"—not being able to degrade the human spirit, they take revenge by abusing it. A question came up about the nature of wealth: and since it isn't necessary to own a thing to reason about it, I, penniless, wrote on the value of money and the *produit net:* at once I saw, from the inside of a cab, the lowered drawbridge of a fortress prison at the entrance to which I left hope and liberty! (*He gets up*) How I'd love to get one of these powerful men of four days' standing, so ready with such penalties, just after some good disgrace had fermented his pride! I'd tell him—that printed foolishness has no importance, except for those who try to suppress it; that without freedom to blame, there can be no flattering eulogies; and that only little men fear little writings. (*He sits down again*) Tired of feeding an obscure boarder, they let me out of prison. I was told that during my economic retreat, there had been established in Madrid a system of free sale of products which included even the press. To profit by this sweet liberty, I announced a periodical, and, thinking to offend no one, I called it *The Useless Journal.* Whew! I had a thousand poor devils of scribblers rise up against me: I was suppressed; and there I was once more among the unemployed. I began almost to despair; I was thought of for a government post, but unfortunately I was qualified for it. They needed an accountant: a dancer got the job. All that was left for me was stealing; I set up a faro game; and now, good folk, I supped in society, and people known as *comme il faut* opened their houses to me politely, on condition they kept three-quarters of the profits. I might have gone pretty far, for I was beginning to understand that to gain wealth it is better to have know-how [*savoir-faire*] than to have knowledge [*savoir*]. But as everybody about me stole, while insisting I stay honest, I should have failed once more. I should have left this world and put a watery grave between me and it, but a kindly God recalled me to my first condition. I took up once more my barber's case and my English leather strop. I travelled about, shaving, from town to town, living at last a carefree life.

[94] *CONDORCET PREDICTS AN ELYSIUM OF REASON* *

The eighteenth century could well be called the Age of Optimism. Never had man been so confident that perfection was attainable here on earth. Simply by letting Reason and the Laws prevail, complete happiness was thought to be within the reach of man. An eloquent expression of this optimism is to be found in the Marquis of Condorcet's Sketch for a Historical Picture of the Human Mind, *written, ironically, in 1793–1794 while the author was hiding for his life in Paris.*

. . . No one can doubt that, as preventive medicine improves and food and housing becomes healthier, as a way of life is established that develops our physical powers by exercise without ruining them by excess, as the two most virulent causes of deterioration, misery and excessive wealth, are eliminated, the average length of human life will be increased and a better health and a stronger physical constitution will be ensured. The improvement of medical practice, which will become more efficacious with the progress of reason and of the social order, will mean the end of infectious and hereditary diseases and illnesses brought on by climate, food, or working conditions. It is reasonable to hope that all other diseases may likewise disappear as their distant causes are discovered. Would it be absurd, then, to suppose that this perfection of the human species might be capable of indefinite progress; that the day will come when death will be due only to extraordinary accidents or to the decay of the vital forces, and that ultimately the average span between birth and decay will have no assignable value? Certainly man will not become immortal, but will not the interval between the first breath that he draws and the time when in the natural course of events, without disease or accident, he expires, increase indefinitely? . . .

. . . are not our physical faculties and the strength, dexterity and acuteness of our senses, to be numbered among the qualities whose perfection in the individual may be transmitted? Observation of the various breeds of domestic animals inclines us to believe that they are, and we can confirm this by direct observation of the human race.

Finally may we not extend such hopes to the intellectual and moral faculties? May not our parents, who transmit to us the benefits or disadvantages of their constitution, and from whom we receive our shape and features, as well as our tendencies to certain physical affections, hand on to us also that

* Marquis de Condorcet, *Sketch for a Historical Picture of the Human Mind,* trans. by June Barraclough (New York: Meridian Books, Inc., 1955), pp. 197–202. Reprinted by permission of the publisher.

part of the physical organization which determines the intellect, the power of the brain, the ardour of the soul or the moral sensibility? Is it not probable that education, in perfecting these qualities, will at the same time influence, modify and perfect the organization itself? Analogy, investigation of the human faculties and the study of certain facts, all seem to give substance to such conjectures, which would further push back the boundaries of our hopes.

These are the questions with which we shall conclude this final stage. How consoling for the philosopher, who laments the errors, the crimes, the injustices which still pollute the earth, and of which he is often the victim, is this view of the human race, emancipated from its shackles, released from the empire of fate and from that of the enemies of its progress, advancing with a firm and sure step along the path of truth, virtue and happiness! It is the contemplation of this prospect that rewards him for all his efforts to assist the progress of reason and the defence of liberty. He dares to regard these strivings as part of the eternal chain of human destiny; and in this persuasion he is filled with the true delight of virtue and the pleasure of having done some lasting good, which fate can never destroy by a sinister stroke of revenge, by calling back the reign of slavery and prejudice. Such contemplation is for him an asylum, in which memory of his persecutors cannot pursue him; there he lives in thought with man restored to his natural rights and dignity, forgets man tormented and corrupted by greed, fear, or envy; there he lives with his peers in an Elysium created by reason and graced by the purest pleasures known to the love of mankind.

16

The American Revolution

Coinciding with the climax of the European Enlightenment, the American Revolution broke out in 1775. It is tempting to seek a logical connection between the intellectual currents of the Old World and the political upheavals in the New. Some historians interpret the American revolt as simply the first manifestation of a sweeping revolutionary movement—a sort of "bourgeois internationale"—affecting the entire Atlantic World at the close of the eighteenth century. The mission of the *philosophes,* according to this theory, had been to lay the intellectual groundwork for the ensuing events. That the American Revolution employed the language of the Enlightenment is evident in the wording of such basic documents as the Declaration of Independence, the Constitution, and the Bill of Rights. But, basically, the revolt of the colonists was motivated, not by the desire to put into practice the abstractions of the eighteenth century thinkers, but rather to secure redress of specific and often local grievances. America, by providing a viable example of liberal democracy, probably influenced Europe more than it had been influenced by the intellectuals of the Age of Reason.

[95] *THE STAMP ACT STIRS UP LIVELY OPPOSITION* *

Even before the formal conclusion of the Seven Years' War, the English government decided that henceforth the American colonies must pay an increased share of the cost of defending North America. The new colonial policy was implemented by the Revenue Act of 1764 and, in even more onerous form, by the Stamp Act of 1765. Stamp duties had long prevailed in England but such a direct internal tax levied without consent was both novel and oppressive in the view of the colonists. A storm of protest greeted the imposition and sympathetic voices were heard in England as well.

[A] Extracts from the Stamp Act

Whereas by an Act made in the last session of Parliament, several duties were granted, continued, and appropriated towards defraying the expenses of defending, protecting, and securing the British colonies and plantations in America; and whereas it is just and necessary that provision be made for raising a further revenue within your Majesty's dominions in America towards defraying the said expenses; . . . be it enacted . . . that from and after the first day of November, one thousand seven hundred and sixty-five, there shall be raised, levied, collected, and paid unto his Majesty, his heirs, and successors, throughout the colonies and plantations in America which now are, or hereafter may be, under the dominion of his Majesty, his heirs and successors . . . [stamp duties on newspapers, pamphlets, cards, dice, and on each sheet of an extensive, varied, and complicated list of legal papers such as court proceedings and associated papers, wills, certificates of academic degrees, licences, bills of lading, clearances, appointments to public office, licences for selling spirits, letters of administration, surveys, warrants, grants or conveyances of land, indentures, leases, conveyances, bills of sale, contracts, notarial acts, deeds, and letters of attorney.]

LIV. And be it further enacted by the authority aforesaid, that all the moneys which shall arise by the several rates and duties hereby granted (except the necessary charges of raising, collecting, recovering, answering, paying, and accounting for the same, and the necessary charges from time to time incurred in relation to this Act, and the execution thereof) shall be paid into the receipt of his Majesty's Exchequer, and shall be entered separate and apart from all other moneys, and shall be there reserved to be

* [A] and [B] Merrill Jensen, ed., *American Colonial Documents to 1776* in *English Historical Documents*, ed. by David C. Douglas (New York: Oxford University Press, 1955), Vol. IX, pp. 655–656, 674–675. Used by permission of the publisher, Eyre and Spottiswoode (London). [C] Edward P. Cheyney, *Readings in English History* (New York: Ginn and Company, 1908), pp. 623–625. Used by permission of the publisher.

from time to time disposed of by Parliament, towards further defraying the necessary expenses of defending, protecting, and securing the said colonies and plantations.

[B] Letter of a Citizen of Newport, Rhode Island, April 29, 1765

In my last I promised to give you the particulars of our transactions here concerning the stamp affair, which I now shall endeavour to do. In the first place I'll just inform you concerning Mr. Martin Howard Jr. and Doctor Moffatt, who was hung in effigy with the Stamp Master. Mr. Howard and the doctor, you must know, have made themselves very busy with their pen (by all accounts) in writing against the colonies and in favour of the Stamp Act, etc.

In the morning of the 27 instant between five and six a mob assembled and erected a gallows near the Town House and then dispersed, and about ten o'clock reassembled and took the effigies of the above men and the Stamp Master and carted them up Thames Street, then up King Street to the said gallows where they was hung up by the neck and suspended near 15 feet in the air; and on the breast of the Stamp Master was this inscription, THE STAMP MAN, and holding in his right hand the Stamp Act. And upon the breast of the Doctor was wrote: THAT INFAMOUS, MISCREATED, LEERING JACOBITE DOCTOR MURFY. In his right hand was a folded letter with this direction: To that Mawgazeene of Knowledge Doct'r Muffy in Rhode Island; and on the same arm was wrote: If I had but rec'd this Letter from the Earl of Bute But One Week sooner. And upon a strip of paper hanging out of his mouth was wrote: It is too late Martinius to Retract, for we are all Aground.

And upon Mr. Howard's breast was wrote: THAT FAWNING, INSIDIOUS, INFAMOUS MISCREANT AND PARACIDE MARTINIUS SCRIBLERIUS; and upon his right arm was wrote: THE ONLY FILIAL PEN. Upon his left arm was wrote: CURS'D AMBITION AND YOUR CURSED CLAN HAS RUIN'D ME and upon the same arm a little below was this: WHAT THO' I BOAST OF INDEPENDENCE POSTERITY WILL CURSE MY MEMORY. And upon one of the posts of the gallows was wrote: We have an Heriditary Indefeasible Right to a Halter, Besides we Encourag'd the Growth of Hemp you know. And underneath that was a new song (made upon the occasion) which I have here enclosed. And upon the other post was wrote: That Person who shall Efface this Publick Mark of Resentment will be Deem'd an Enemy to liberty and Accordingly meet with Proper Chastisement. And about five o'clock in the afternoon they made a fire under the gallows which consumed the effigies, gallows and all, to ashes. I forgot to tell you that a boot hung over the doctor's shoulder with the devil peeping out of it, etc. I've enclosed you a piece that was stuck up in the Town House at the same time. And after the effigies were burnt the mob dispersed and we thought it was all over. But last night about dusk they all mustered again, and first they went to Martin Howard's and broke every window in his house, frames and all; likewise chairs, tables, pictures, and everything they could come across. They also sawed down two trees which stood before his door and brought them and stuck them up in two great guns which have been fixed at the bottom of the Parade some years as posts. When they found they had entirely demolished all his furniture and done what damage they could, they left his house and proceeded to Dr. Moffatts where they behaved much in the same manner. I can't say which came off the worst for all the furniture of both houses were entirely destroyed; . . .

A NEW SONG

He who for a Post or Base sordid Pelf
His Country Betrays, Makes a Rope for himself.
Of this an Example, Before you we Bring
In these Infamous Rogues, Who in Effigy Swing.

Huzza my Brave Boys, Ev'ry man Stand his Ground
With Liberty's Praise, Let the Welkin Resound
Eternal Disgrace On those Miscreants Fall
Who Through Pride or for Wealth, Wou'd Ruin us All.

Let us Make wise Resolves and to them stand strong
Your Puffs and your Vapours will Ne'er last Long
To Ma[i]ntain Our Just Rights, Every Measure Pursue
To Our King we'll be Loyal, To Ourselves we'll be True.

Those Blessings Our Fathers, Obtain'd by their Blood
We are Justly Oblig'd to Our Sons to make Good
All internal Taxes let us then Nobly spurn
These Effigy's First, The Next The Stamp Papers Burn.

Chorus

Sing Tantarara, Burn All, Burn All
Sing Tantarara, Burn All.

[C] Speech of William Pitt in Parliament, January 14, 1766

Gentlemen:

Sir, I have been charged with giving birth to sedition in America. They have spoken their sentiments with freedom against this unhappy act, and that freedom has become their crime. Sorry I am to hear the liberty of speech in this House imputed as a crime. But the imputation shall not discourage me. It is a liberty I mean to exercise. No gentleman ought to be afraid to exercise it. It is a liberty by which the gentleman who calumniates it might have profited. He ought to have desisted from his project. The gentleman tells us America is obstinate; America is almost in open rebellion. I rejoice that America has resisted. Three millions of people so dead to all the feelings of liberty as voluntarily to submit to be slaves, would have been fit instruments to make slaves of the rest. I come not here armed at all points, with law cases and acts of parliament, with the statute book doubled down in dog's-ears, to defend the cause of liberty; if I had, I myself would have cited the two cases of Chester and Durham. I would have cited them to have shown that, even under former arbitrary reigns, parliaments were ashamed of taxing a people without their consent, and allowed them representatives. . . .

I am no courtier of America. I stand up for this kingdom. I maintain that the parliament has the right to bind,—to restrain America. Our legislative power over the colonies is sovereign and supreme. When it ceases to be sovereign and supreme, I would advise every gentleman to sell his lands, if he can, and embark for that country. When two countries are connected together, like England and her colonies, without being incorporated, the one must necessarily govern; the greater must rule the less; but so rule it as not to contradict the fundamental principles that are common to both. . . .

The Americans have not acted in all things with prudence and temper. The Americans have been wronged. They have been driven to madness by injustice. Will you punish them for the madness you have occasioned? Rather let prudence and temper come first from this side. I will undertake for America that she will follow the example. There are two lines in a ballad of Prior's, of a man's behaviour to his wife, so applicable to you and your colonies that I cannot help repeating them:

> "Be to her faults a little blind:
> Be to her virtues very kind."

Upon the whole, I will beg leave to tell the House what is really my opinion. It is, that the Stamp Act be repealed absolutely, totally, and immediately. That the reason for the repeal be assigned, because it was founded on an erroneous principle. At the same time let the sovereign authority of this country over the colonies be asserted in as strong terms as can be devised, and be made to extend to every point of legislation whatsoever; that we may bind their trade, confine their manufactures, and exercise every power whatsoever, except that of taking their money out of their pockets without their consent.

[96] *REVOLUTIONARY PARTIES DEFEND COLONIAL LIBERTIES* *

In the decade after 1763, as Britain tried to clamp on ever-stricter controls, popular parties dedicated to the defense of colonial liberties developed in each of the colonies. The following extracts from John Adams' diary illustrate this political evolution. It should be noted that the author stood somewhat aloof from the popular elements; he approved their aims but not their methods.

Diary, February 1763

Boston. This day learned that the Caucus Club meets at certain times in the garret of Tom Dawes, the adjutant of the Boston Regiment. He has a large house, and he has a movable partition in his garret which he takes down, and the whole club meets in one room. There they smoke tobacco till you cannot see from one end of the garret to the other. There they drink flip, I suppose, and there they choose a moderator who puts questions to the vote regularly; and selectmen, assessors, collectors, wardens, fire-wards, and representatives are regularly chosen before they are chosen in the town. Uncle Fairfield, Story, Ruddock, Adams, Cooper, and a *rudis indigestaque moles* of others are members. They send committees to wait on the merchant's club, and to propose and join in the choice of man and measures. Captain Cunnungham says they have often solicited him to go to those caucuses; they have assured him benefit in his business, etc.

Diary, 28 May 1766

General election. At Boston. After lecture, dined at Mr. Austin's, the wine-cooper, with the Rev. Messrs. Prentice of Charlestown and Adams of Roxbury. Adams and Austin were the disputants in politics. Prentice a moderator.

This morning [Samuel] Adams was chosen clerk, and Otis speaker. Governor Bernard negatived him. Cushing was chosen. In the afternoon they proceeded to choose councillors when Hutchinson and the two Olivers were dropped, and Trowbridge was dropped, and Mr. Pitts, Colonel Gerrish, Colonel White, Bowers, Powell, and Mr. Saunders, and Dexter were chosen.

* Merrill Jensen, ed., *American Colonial Documents to 1776* in *English Historical Documents,* ed. by David C. Douglas (New York: Oxford University Press, 1955), Vol. IX, pp. 740–741. Used by permission of the publisher, Eyre and Spottiswoode (London).

What a change! This day seems to be the literal accomplishment of a prophecy of Mr. Otis, published two or three winters ago in the newspaper: "The day is hastening on with large strides when a dirty, very dirty, witless rabble, I mean the great vulgar, shall go down with deserved infamy to all posterity." Thus the triumph of Otis and his party are complete. But what changes are yet to come? Will not the other party soon be uppermost?

Diary, 29 May 1766

The governor negatived Otis, Sparhawk, Dexter, Saunders, Gerrish, and Bowers, and made the two Houses a most nitrous, sulphureous speech.

What will be the consequence?

Diary, 14 August 1769

Dined with three hundred and fifty Sons of Liberty at Robinson's, the sign of Liberty Tree, in Dorchester. We had two tables laid in the open field, by the barn, with between three and four hundred plates and an awning of sailcloth over head, and should have spent a most agreeable day had not the rain made some abatement in our pleasures. Mr. Dickinson, the Farmer's brother, and Mr. Reed, the secretary of New Jersey, were there; both cool, reserved, and guarded all day. After dinner was over and the toasts drunk, we were diverted with Mr. Balch's mimicry. He gave us the lawyer's head, and the hunting of a bitch fox. We had also the Liberty Song —that by the farmer and that by Dr. Church, and the whole company joined in the chorus. This is cultivating the sensations of freedom. There was a large collection of good company. Otis and Adams are politic in promoting these festivals; for they tinge the minds of the people; they impregnate them with the sentiments of liberty; they render the people fond of their leaders in the cause and averse and bitter against all opposers. To the honour of the Sons, I did not see one person intoxicated or near it.

Between four and five o'clock the carriages were all got ready, and the company rode off in procession, Mr. Hancock first, in his chariot, and another chariot bringing up the rear. I took my leave of the gentlemen and turned off for Taunton, oated at Doty's, and arrived long after dark at Noice's; there I put up. I should have been at Taunton if I had not turned back in the morning from Roxbury, but I felt as if I ought not to lose this feast; as if it was my duty to be there. I am not able to conjecture of what consequence it was whether I was there or not. Jealousies arise from little causes, and many might suspect that I was not hearty in the cause if I had been absent, whereas none of them are more sincere and steadfast than I am.

Diary, 3 September 1769

Heard Dr. Cooper in the forenoon, Mr. Champion of Connecticut in the afternoon, and Mr. Pemberton in the evening at the charity lecture. Spent the remainder of the evening and supped with Mr. Otis in company with Mr. Adams, Mr. William Davis, and Mr. John Gill. The evening spent in preparing for the next day's newspaper, a curious employment, cooking up paragraphs, articles, occurrences, &c., working the political engine! Otis talks all; he grows the most talkative man alive; no other gentleman in company can find a space to put in a word; as Dr. Swift expressed it, he leaves no elbow room. There is much sense, knowledge, spirit, and humour in his conversation; but he grows narrative like an old man; abounds with stories.

[97] *CONFLICTING ACCOUNTS OF LEXINGTON AND CONCORD* *

The early 1770's were a period of steadily mounting tension in the American colonies. Finally, in 1775, the inevitable occurred and actual fighting commenced. A British detachment, on its way from Boston to Concord to seize unauthorized stores of weapons, met opposition at Lexington. Who fired the first shot became a bone of contention, but in any case the war was on.

[A] An American Account

Last Wednesday the 19th of April, [1775] the Troops of His Britannick Majesty commenced hostilities upon the people of this Province . . . The particulars relative to this interesting event, . . . we have endeavoured to collect as well as the present confused state of affairs will admit.

On Tuesday evening a detachment from the Army, . . . proceeded with silence and expedition on their way to Concord, about eighteen miles from Boston. The people were soon alarmed, and began to assemble in several Towns, before daylight, in order to watch the motion of the Troops. At Lexington, six miles below Concord, a company of Militia, of about one hundred men, mustered near the Meeting-House; the Troops came in sight of them just before sunrise; and running within a few rods of them, the Commanding Officer accosted the Militia in words to this effect: "Disperse, you rebels—damn you, throw down your arms and disperse"; upon which the Troops huzzaed, and immediately one or two officers discharged their pistols, which were instantaneously followed by the firing of four or five of the soldiers, and then there seemed to be a general discharge from the

* Force, *American Archives*, 4th Series, Vol. II, pp. 391–392, 945–946, as found in Theodore Calvin Pease and A. Sellew Roberts, eds., *Selected Readings in American History* (New York: Harcourt, Brace and Company, 1928), pp. 124–127.

whole body: eight of our men were killed, and nine wounded. In a few minutes after this action the enemy renewed their march for Concord; at which place they destroyed several Carriages, Carriage Wheels, and about twenty barrels of Flour, all belonging to the Province. Here about one hundred and fifty men going towards a bridge, of which the enemy were in possession, the latter fired and killed two of our men, who then returned the fire, and obliged the enemy to retreat back to Lexington, where they met Lord Percy, with a large reinforcement, with two pieces of cannon. The enemy now having a body of about eighteen hundred men, made a halt, picked up many of their dead, and took care of their wounded. At Menotomy, a few of our men attacked a party of twelve of the enemy (carrying stores and provisions to the Troops), killed one of them, wounded several, made the rest prisoners, and took possession of all their arms, stores, provisions, &c., without any loss on our side. The enemy having halted one or two hours at Lexington, found it necessary to make a second retreat, carrying with them many of their dead and wounded, who they put into chaises and on horses that they found standing in the road. . . . notwithstanding their field-pieces, our people continued the pursuit, firing at them till they got to Charlestown Neck (which they reached a little after sunset) over which the enemy passed, proceeded up Breed's Hill, and soon afterwards went into the Town, under the protection of the *Somerset* Man-of-War of sixty-four guns . . . The savage barbarity exercised upon the bodies of our unfortunate brethren who fell is almost incredible: not contented with shooting down the unarmed, aged, and infirm, they disregarded the cries of the wounded, killing them without mercy, and mangling their bodies in the most shocking manner.

We have the pleasure to say, that, notwithstanding the highest provocations given by the enemy, not one instance of cruelty, that we have heard of, was committed by our victorious Militia; but, listening to the merciful dictates of the Christian religion, they "breathed higher sentiments of humanity. . . ."

[B] A British Account

. . . General Gage having received intelligence of a quantity of military stores being collected at Concord, for the avowed purpose of supplying a body of troops to act in opposition to His Majesty's Government, detached, on the eighteenth of April at night, the Grenadiers of his Army, and the Light-Infantry, under the command of Lieutenant-Colonel Smith, of the Tenth Regiment, and Major Pitcairn, of the Marines, with orders to destroy the said stores; . . .

Lieutenant-Colonel Smith finding, after he had advanced some miles on his march, that the country had been alarmed by the firing of guns and ringing of bells, despatched six Companies of Light-Infantry, in order to secure two bridges on different roads beyond Concord, who, upon their arrival at Lexington, found a body of the country people under arms, on a green close to the road; and upon the King's Troops marching up to them, in order to inquire the reason of their being so assembled, they went off in great confusion, and several guns were fired upon the King's Troops from behind a stone wall, and also from the meeting-house and other houses, by which one man was wounded, and Major Pitcairn's horse shot in two places. In consequence of this attack by the rebels, the troops returned the fire and killed several of them. After which the detachment marched on to Concord without any thing further happening, where they effected the purpose for which they were sent, having knocked off the trunnions of three pieces of iron ordnance, burnt some new gun carriages and a great number of carriage-wheels, and thrown into the river a considerable quantity of flour, gunpowder, musket-balls, and other articles. Whilst this service was performing, great numbers of the rebels assembled in many parts, and a considerable body of them attacked the Light-Infantry, posted at one of the bridges, on which an action ensued, and some few were killed and wounded.

On the return of the Troops from Concord, they were very much annoyed, and had several men killed and wounded by the rebels firing from behind walls, ditches, trees, and other ambushes; but the brigade, under the command of Lord Percy, having joined them at Lexington with two pieces of cannon, the rebels were for a while dispersed; but as soon as the troops resumed their march, they began to fire upon them from behind stone walls and houses, and kept up in that manner a scattering fire during the whole of their march of fifteen miles, by which means several were killed and wounded; and such was the cruelty and barbarity of the rebels, that they scalped and cut off the ears of some of the wounded men who fell into their hands.

It is not known what numbers of the rebels were killed and wounded, but it is supposed that their loss was considerable. . . .

[98] *CONGRESS DECLARES THE CAUSES FOR TAKING UP ARMS* *

A few months after Lexington and Concord, George Washington was sent to Massachusetts by the Continental Congress to take charge of the militia besieging

* Merrill Jensen, ed., *American Colonial Documents to 1776* in *English Historical Documents,* ed. by David C. Douglas (New York: Oxford University Press, 1955), Vol. IX, pp. 843–847. Used by permission of the publisher, Eyre and Spottiswoode (London).

Boston. At the same time, Congress issued the "Declaration of the Causes and necessity for taking up arms," the joint production of the radical Jefferson and the conservative Dickenson. The Declaration follows, somewhat abridged.

Our forefathers, inhabitants of the island of Great Britain, left their native land, to seek on these shores a residence for civil and religious freedom. At the expense of their blood, at the hazard of their fortunes, without the least charge to the country from which they removed, by unceasing labour, and an unconquerable spirit, they effected settlements in the distant and inhospitable wilds of America, then filled with numerous and warlike nations of barbarians. Societies or governments, vested with perfect legislatures, were formed under charters from the Crown, and an harmonious intercourse was established between the colonies and the kingdom from which they derived their origin. The mutual benefits of this union became in a short time so extraordinary as to excite astonishment. It is universally confessed that the amazing increase of the wealth, strength, and navigation of the realm arose from this source; and the minister who so wisely and successfully directed the measures of Great Britain in the late war, publicly declared that these colonies enabled her to triumph over her enemies.

Towards the conclusion of that war it pleased our sovereign to make a change in his counsels. From that fatal moment, the affairs of the British empire began to fall into confusion, and gradually sliding from the summit of glorious prosperity, to which they had been advanced by the virtues and abilities of one man, are at length distracted by the convulsions that now shake it to its deepest foundations. . . .

. . . We for ten years incessantly and ineffectually besieged the throne as supplicants; we reasoned, we remonstrated with Parliament, in the most mild and decent language. But [England] sent over fleets and armies. . . . The indignation of the Americans was roused, it is true; but it was the indignation of a virtuous, loyal, and affectionate people. A congress of delegates from the united colonies was assembled at Philadelphia on the fifth day of last September. We resolved again to offer an humble and dutiful petition to the king, and also addressed our fellow-subjects of Great Britain. We have pursued every temperate, every respectful measure: we have even proceeded to break off our commercial intercourse with our fellow-subjects, as the last peaceable admonition, that our attachment to no nation upon earth should supplant our attachment to liberty. This, we flattered ourselves, was the ultimate step of the controversy: But subsequent events have shown how vain was this hope of finding moderation in our enemies.

Fruitless were all the entreaties, arguments and eloquence of an illustrious band of the most distinguished peers and commoners who nobly and strenuously asserted the justice of our cause, to stay, or even to mitigate the heedless fury with which these accumulated and unexampled outrages were hurried on. Equally fruitless was the interference of the city of London, of Bristol, and many other respectable towns in our favour. Parliament adopted an insidious manoeuvre calculated to divide us, to establish a perpetual auction of taxations where colony should bid against colony, all of them uninformed what ransom would redeem their lives; and thus to extort from us, at the point of the bayonet, the unknown sums that should be sufficient to gratify, if possible to gratify, ministerial rapacity, with the miserable indulgence left to us of raising, in our own mode, the prescribed tribute. What terms more rigid and humiliating could have been dictated by remorseless victors to conquered enemies? In our circumstances to accept them would be to deserve them.

Soon after the intelligence of these proceedings arrived on this continent, General Gage, who in the course of the last year had taken possession of the town of Boston in the province of Massachusetts Bay, and still occupied it as a garrison, on the 19th day of April, sent out from that place a large detachment of his army, who made an unprovoked assault on the inhabitants of the said province, at the town of Lexington, as appears by the affidavits of a great number of persons, some of whom were officers and soldiers of that detachment, murdered eight of the inhabitants, and wounded many others. From thence the troops proceeded in warlike array to the town of Concord, where they set upon another party of the inhabitants of the same province, killing several and wounding more, until compelled to retreat by the country people suddenly assembled to repel this cruel aggression. Hostilities, thus commenced by the British troops, have been since prosecuted by them without regard to faith or reputation. . . .

We have received certain intelligence that General Carleton, the governor of Canada, is instigating the people of that province and the Indians to fall upon us; and we have but too much reason to apprehend that schemes have been formed to excite domestic enemies against us. In brief, a part of these colonies now feels, and all of them are sure of feeling, as far as the vengeance of administration can inflict them, the complicated calamities of fire, sword and famine. We are reduced to the alternative of choosing an unconditional submission to the tyranny of irritated ministers, or resistance by force. The latter is our choice. We have counted the cost of this contest and find nothing so dreadful as voluntary slavery. Honour, justice, and humanity forbid us tamely to surrender that freedom which we received from our gallant ancestors, and which our innocent posterity have a right to receive from us. We cannot endure the infamy and guilt of resigning succeeding generations to that wretchedness which inevitably awaits them, if we basely entail hereditary bondage upon them.

Our cause is just. Our union is perfect. Our internal resources are great, and, if necessary, foreign assistance is undoubtedly attainable. We gratefully acknowledge, as signal instances of the Divine favour towards us, that his Providence would not permit us to be called into this severe controversy, until we were grown up to our present strength, had been previously exercised in warlike operation, and possessed of the means of defending ourselves. With hearts fortified with these animating reflections, we must solemnly, before God and the world, declare, that, exerting the utmost energy of those powers which our beneficent Creator hath graciously bestowed upon us, the arms we have been compelled by our enemies to assume, we will in defiance of every hazard, with unabating firmness and perseverance, employ for the preservation of our liberties; being with our [one] mind resolved to die free men rather than live slaves.

Lest this declaration should disquiet the minds of our friends and fellow-subjects in any part of the empire, we assure them that we mean not to dissolve that union which has so long and so happily subsisted between us, and which we sincerely wish to see restored. Necessity has not yet driven us into that desperate measure, or induced us to excite any other nation to war against them. We have not raised armies with ambitious designs of separating from Great Britain, and establishing independent states. We fight not for glory or for conquest. . . .

With an humble confidence in the mercies of the supreme and impartial Judge and Ruler of the universe, we most devoutly implore his divine goodness to protect us happily through this great conflict, to dispose our adversaries to reconciliation on reasonable terms, and thereby to relieve the empire from the calamities of civil war.

[99] *A HESSIAN OFFICER WRITES OF THE WAR* *

Adjutant General Major Baurmeister was a Hessian officer who participated in the War of the American Revolution from 1776 to 1784. His letters and journal recounting his experiences came to light in recent years. Being affected by neither American nor British patriotism, his writings are unbiased and on the whole reliable. Here is an excerpt from a letter written in Philadelphia to his superior in Germany, January 20, 1776.

My last account covered the events up to the 16th of December, when

* *Revolution in America. Confidential Letters and Journals 1776–1784 of Adjutant General Major Baurmeister of the Hessian Forces,* trans. by Bernard A. Uhlendorf (New Brunswick, N. J.: Rutgers University Press, 1957), pp. 145–153. Used by permission of the publisher.

Lord Cornwallis departed for England. By this packet I send a continuation, which will show how little has been accomplished in the present war in spite of considerable losses, on both sides.

The last campaign furnished sufficient proof that the stubborn and inexperienced rebels are too lucky. The English army, active as it is, has got no farther than Philadelphia, is master of only some parts of the banks of the Delaware and Schuylkill, and has no foothold whatsoever in Jersey, from where, as well as from Germantown in front and from Wilmington, Darby, and Chester in the rear, it is being watched and constantly harassed by the enemy's main posts.

General Washington not only cautiously supports these posts from time to time, but also covers Lancaster, Reading, and the bank of the Susquehanna. With the greater part of his army he occupies a stationary camp at Valley Forge, where the soldiers have been encouraged with cash rewards to build solid huts. They have been told, moreover, that their steadfastness and patience through one more campaign will secure their independence once and for all. They also enjoy the generous support of foreign powers, who have their staple in Boston. Furthermore, they have more means of their own to keep up this war than was at first supposed.

The Americans are bold, unyielding, and fearless. They have always lived in plenty, and we cannot block their resources. Then their indomitable ideas of liberty, the main springs of which are held and guided by every hand in Congress! Good for nothing and unimportant as most of these men may have been before these disturbances (because they were incompetent and without wealth) they now resort to every means, for more than one reason, to weaken the rich and the loyalists within and stubbornly resist the English without.

This short exposition is meant only to show the state of things here, and that England, though she has not lost the game so far, nevertheless may lose everything. With little show, the Americans will exert themselves to the utmost to gain complete freedom, and they are by no means conquered. If only one province, for example, Jersey, could be subdued and a tolerable government set up without interference, then, everyone believes, all provinces would prefer peace to war.

Reports agree that Washington's force is less than seven thousand strong, for the standing militia in Jersey have been reinforced with some troops, including the greater part of the dragoons, and General Sullivan has been detached to Wilmington with two thousand men to cover Darby and Chester. Springfield has been occupied from Valley Forge. Scouting parties of dragoons come from all three places to the opposite bank of the Schuylkill.

During the month of December, 256 deserters came in, and so far in January, 63. It is not so much their lack of clothing as homesickness that drives them to desertion. This is such a dominant passion with them that General Washington keeps his troops constantly moving.

Congress is now holding its sessions in York Town, on the other side of the Susquehanna. General Wayne with his brigade is now in that region to protect Congress and enforce its orders more quickly among the inhabitants, for the plans of Congress, whose members are no longer all in attendance, meet with endless resistance. Even the people of New England are tired of contributing so much in man power, money, and provisions. I still believe that if we could subdue only one province, the rest would surrender. The rebels are spending enough money, but I have never heard of a generous, and therefore alluring, reward being given. If any people worships money, it is the Americans, for everyone is in business; even the most pious Quaker can give lessons to a Feidell [probably a shrewd merchant of Cassel].

Some time ago Major St. Ouary, a Frenchman whom we captured while scouting, assured us that forty-two French officers were looking forward to leaving the rebels forever. However, neither the Boston nor the Albany newspapers, which frequently come to us in a roundabout way, say a single word about their returning to France. . . .

The spectacle of Hessian troops on watch, church, and pay parades in completely new uniforms is applauded by everyone. The English troops also have new equipment, although several regiments lost theirs when the rebels stopped some ships, which they unloaded and burned. This must be blamed on the ships' masters, who were heedless and chose a poor time for their passage.

[100] *JOHN ADAMS IS RECEIVED AT THE COURT OF ST. JAMES* *

Almost two years after the signing of the Definitive Treaty of Peace between Great Britain and the United States (September 3, 1783), the first American envoy presented his credentials to the court of George III. This tense and dramatic scene is described in the correspondence of the United States' representative, John Adams.

Letter of Adams to John Jay, Westminister, June 2, 1785

On Tuesday evening, the Baron de Lynden called upon me, and said he came from the Baron de Nolken, and they had been conversing upon the

* *The Works of John Adams* (Boston: Little, Brown and Company, 1853), Vol. VIII, pp. 255–259.

singular situation I was in, and they agreed in opinion that it was indispensable that I should make a speech, and that that speech should be as complimentary as possible. All this was conformable to the advice lately given by the Count de Vergennes to Mr. Jefferson; so that, finding it was a custom established at both these great Courts, and that this Court and the foreign ministers expected it, I thought I could not avoid it, although my first thought and inclination had been to deliver my credentials silently and retire.

At one, on Wednesday, the master of ceremonies called at my house, and went with me to the secretary of state's office, . . . When we arrived in the antechamber . . . of St. James's, the master of the ceremonies met me and attended me, while the secretary of state went to take the commands of the King. While I stood in this place, where it seems all ministers stand upon such occasions, always attended by the master of ceremonies, the room very full of ministers of state, lords, and bishops, and all sorts of courtiers, as well as the next room, which is the King's bedchamber, you may well suppose I was the focus of all eyes. I was relieved, however, from the embarassment of it by the Swedish and Dutch ministers, who came to me, and entertained me in a very agreeable conversation during the whole time. . . . the Marquis of Carmarthen returned and desired me to go with him to his Majesty. I went with his Lordship through the levee room into the King's closet. The door was shut, and I was left with his Majesty and the secretary of state alone. I made the three reverences,—one at the door, another about half way, and a third before the presence,—according to the usage established at this and all the northern Courts of Europe, and then addressed myself to his Majesty in the following words:—

"Sir,—The United States of America have appointed me their minister plenipotentiary to your Majesty, and have directed me to deliver to your Majesty this letter which contains the evidence of it. It is in obedience to their express commands, that I have the honor to assure your Majesty of their unanimous disposition and desire to cultivate the most friendly and liberal intercourse between your Majesty's subjects and their citizens, and of their best wishes for your Majesty's health and happiness, and for that of your royal family. The appointment of a minister from the United States to your Majesty's Court will form an epoch in the history of England and of America. I think myself more fortunate than all my fellow-citizens, in having the distinguished honor to be the first to stand in your Majesty's royal presence in a diplomatic character; and I shall esteem myself the happiest of men, if I can be instrumental in recommending my country more and more to your Majesty's royal benevolence, and of restoring an entire esteem, confidence, and affection, or, in better words, the old good nature and the old good humor between people, who, though separated by an ocean, and under different governments, have the same language, a similar religion, and kindred blood.

"I beg your Majesty's permission to add, that, although I have some time before been intrusted by my country, it was never in my whole life in a manner so agreeable to myself."

The king listened to every word I said, with dignity, but with an apparent emotion. Whether it was the nature of the interview, or whether it was my visible agitation, for I felt more than I did or could express, that touched him, I cannot say. But he was much affected, and answered me with more tremor than I had spoken with, and said:—

"SIR,—The circumstances of this audience are so extraordinary, the language you have now held is so extremely proper, and the feelings you have discovered so justly adapted to the occasion, that I must say that I not only receive with pleasure the assurance of the friendly dispositions of the United States, but that I am very glad the choice has fallen upon you to be their minister. I wish you, sir, to believe, and that it may be understood in America, that I have done nothing in the late contest but what I thought myself indispensably bound to do, by the duty which I owed to my people. I will be very frank with you. I was the last to consent to the separation; but the separation having been made, and having become inevitable, I have always said, as I say now, that I would be the first to meet the friendship of the United States as an independent power. The moment I see such sentiments and language as yours prevail, and a disposition to give to this country the preference, that moment I shall say, let the circumstances of language, religion, and blood have their natural and full effect."

. . . He was indeed much affected, and I confess I was not less so, and, therefore I cannot be certain that I was so cool and attentive, heard so clearly, and understood so perfectly, as to be confident of all his words or sense; and, I think, that all which he said to me should at present be kept secret in America, unless his Majesty or his secretary of state, who alone was present, should judge proper to report it. . . .

The King then said a word or two to the secretary of state, which, being between them, I did not hear, and then turned round and bowed to me, as is customary with all kings and princes when they give the signal to retire. I retreated, stepping backward, as is the etiquette, and, making my last reverence at the door of the chamber, I went my way. The master of ceremonies joined me the moment of my coming out of the King's closet, and accompanied me through the apartments down to my carriage, several stages of servants, gentlemen-porters and under-porters, roaring out like thunder, as I went along, "Mr. Adams's servants, Mr. Adams's carriage, &c. . . ."

There are a train of other ceremonies yet to go through, in presentations to the Queen, and visits to and from ministers and ambassadors, which will take up much time, and interrupt me in my endeavors to obtain all that I have at heart,—the objects of my instructions. It is thus the essence of things is lost in ceremony in every country of Europe. We must submit to what we cannot alter. Patience is the only remedy.

17

The French Revolution

The French Revolution is an event of transcendent importance in both French and world history. Many of the basic movements which have determined nineteenth and twentieth century history stem in whole or in part from the French Revolution: liberalism, radicalism, nationalism, among others. The men of 1789 and 1792 pointed the way to the type of liberal, democratic, and secular state which is today taken for granted in the Western World. Until the Bolshevik Revolution of 1917 evoked a whole new set of competing and contradictory values, no event in European history could compare in world importance with the French Revolution.

[101] *THE NATIONAL (CONSTITUENT) ASSEMBLY RECONSTRUCTS FRANCE* *

From July, 1789, until its dissolution in September, 1791, the Assembly worked to "regenerate" France. The principles of the Age of Reason began to be trans-

* [A], [B], [C], and [D] J. H. Stewart, *A Documentary Survey of the French Revolution* (New York: The Macmillan Company, 1951), pp. 107–110, 113–115, 142–143, and 174–176. Used by permission. [E] Ferrières, *Mémoires,* as found in E. L. Higgins, ed., *The French Revolution as Told by Contemporaries* (Boston: Houghton Mifflin Company, 1939), pp. 153–155. Used by permission.

lated into reality. Time-sanctioned customs and institutions were given short shrift. Following are some of the more important acts of the Assembly.

[A] Feudalism Abolished, August 4, 1789

1. The National Assembly . . . decrees that feudal rights and dues deriving from real or personal *mainmorte* and personal servitude, and those representative thereof, are abolished without indemnity, and all others declared redeemable; . . .

2. . . . pigeons shall be confined at times determined by the communities; and during such periods they shall be regarded as game, and everyone shall have the right to kill them on his own land.

3. The exclusive right of hunting and open warrens is likewise abolished; and every proprietor has the right to destroy and to have destroyed, on his own property only, every kind of game. . . .

4. All seigneurial courts of justice are suppressed without any indemnity; . . .

5. Tithes of every kind and dues which take the place thereof . . . are abolished. . . .

7. Venality of judicial and municipal offices is suppressed henceforth. Justice shall be rendered gratuitously; . . .

9. Pecuniary privileges, personal or real, in matters of taxation are abolished forever. . . .

11. All citizens may be admitted, without distinction of birth, to all ecclesiastical, civil, and military employments and offices, and no useful profession shall entail forfeiture.

12. In the future no *deniers* for annates or for any other cause whatsoever shall be dispatched to the court of Rome. . . .

14. Plurality of benefices shall no longer exist when the revenues of the benefice or benefices of an incumbent exceed the sum of 3,000 *livres*. . . .

16. The National Assembly decrees that, in memory of the impressive and momentous deliberations just held for the welfare of France, a medal shall be struck, and that, as an expression of gratitude, a *Te Deum* shall be sung in all parishes and churches of the kingdom.

17. The National Assembly solemnly proclaims King Louis XVI *Restorer of French Liberty.*

18. The National Assembly shall repair *en masse* to the King to present to His Majesty the decree just pronounced, to bear him the homage of its most respectful gratitude, and to supplicate him to permit the *Te Deum* to be sung in his chapel, and to be present there himself. . . .

[B] Declaration of the Rights of Man, August 27, 1789

The National Assembly recognizes and proclaims in the presence and under the auspices of the Supreme Being, the following rights of man and citizen.

1. Men are born and remain free and equal in rights; social distinctions may be based only upon general usefulness.

2. The aim of every political association is the preservation of the natural and inalienable rights of man; these rights are liberty, property, security, and resistance to oppression.

3. The source of all sovereignty resides essentially in the nation; no group, no individual may exercise authority not emanating expressly therefrom.

4. Liberty consists of the power to do whatever is not injurious to others; thus the enjoyment of the natural rights of every man has for its limits only those that assure other members of society the enjoyment of those same rights; such limits may be determined only by law.

5. The law has the right to forbid only actions which are injurious to society. Whatever is not forbidden by law may not be prevented, and no one may be constrained to do what it does not prescribe.

6. Law is the expression of the general will; all citizens have the right to concur personally, or through their representatives, in its formation; it must be the same for all, whether it protects or punishes. All citizens, being equal before it, are equally admissible to all public offices, positions, and employments, according to their capacity, and without other distinction than that of virtues and talents.

7. No man may be accused, arrested, or detained except in the cases determined by law, and according to the forms prescribed thereby. . . .

8. The law is to establish only penalties that are absolutely and obviously necessary; and no one may be punished except by virtue of a law established and promulgated prior to the offence and legally applied.

9. Since every man is presumed innocent until declared guilty, if arrest be deemed indispensable, all unnecessary severity for securing the person of the accused must be severely repressed by law.

10. No one is to be disquieted because of his opinions, even religious, provided their manifestation does not disturb the public order established by law.

11. Free communication of ideas and opinions is one of the most precious of the rights of man. Consequently, every citizen may speak, write, and print freely, subject to responsibility for the abuse of such liberty in the cases determined by law. . . .

14. Citizens have the right to ascertain, by themselves or through their representatives, the necessity of the public tax, to consent to it freely, to supervise its use, and to determine its quota, assessment, payment, and duration. . . .

17. Since property is a sacred and inviolable right, no one may be deprived thereof unless a legally established public necessity obviously requires it, and upon condition of a just and previous indemnity.

[C] Hereditary Nobility and Titles Abolished, June 19, 1790

1. Hereditary nobility is abolished forever; accordingly, the titles of prince, duke, count, marquis, viscount, *vidame,* baron, knight, *messire,* squire, noble, and all other similar titles shall neither be accepted by nor bestowed upon anyone whomsoever.

2. A citizen may assume only his real family name; no one may wear liveries or have them worn, or have coats of arms; incense shall be burned in the churches only to honor the Divinity, and shall not be offered to any person whomsoever.

3. The titles of *monseigneur* and *messeigneurs* shall not be bestowed upon any group or individual; likewise, the titles of excellency, highness, eminence, grace, etc.; . . .

[D] Extracts from the Civil Constitution of the Clergy, July 12, 1790

1. Dating from the day of publication of the present decree, appointments to bishoprics and cures are to be made by election only.

2. All elections shall be by ballot and absolute majority of votes.

3. The election of bishops shall take place according to the form prescribed by . . . the decree of 22 December, 1789, for the appointment of members of the departmental assembly. . . .

7. To be eligible for a bishopric, one must have performed for at least fifteen years the duties of ecclesiastical ministry in the diocese, in the capacity of *curé,* officiating minister or vicar, or as superior or directing vicar of the seminary. . . .

16. Not later than a month subsequent to his election, the bishop-elect shall present himself in person to his metropolitan bishop; and if elected to the metropolitan see, to the oldest bishop of the *arrondissement,* with the *procès-verbal* of the election and proclamation, and shall request him to grant canonical confirmation.

17. The metropolitan or the senior bishop shall have the right to examine the bishop-elect, in the presence of his council, concerning his doctrine and morals. If he considers him qualified, he shall give him canonical institution; if he believes it his duty to refuse, the reasons for such refusal shall be given in writing, signed by the metropolitan bishop and his council, reserving to the interested parties the right to appeal by writ of error as provided hereinafter. . . .

19. The new bishop may not apply to the Pope for confirmation, but

shall write to him as the Visible Head of the Universal Church, in testimony of the unity of faith and communion which he is to maintain therewith. . . .

21. Before the ceremony of consecration begins, the bishop-elect shall take a solemn oath, in the presence of the municipal officials, the people, and the clergy, to watch with care over the faithful of the diocese entrusted to him, to be faithful to the nation, to the law, and to the King, and to maintain with all his power the Constitution decreed by the National Assembly and accepted by the King. . . .

25. The election of *curés* shall be conducted according to the forms prescribed by, and by the electors designated in, the decree of 22 December, 1789, for the election of members of the district administrative assembly. . . .

[E] The New National Spirit: the Festival of July 14, 1790

More than three hundred thousand people of both sexes, from Paris and the environs, had been assembled since six in the morning at the Champ-de-Mars. Sitting on turf seats, which formed an immense circus, drenched, draggled, sheltering themselves with parasols from the torrents of rain which descended upon them, and at the least ray of sunshine adjusting their dresses, they waited, laughing and chatting, for the federates and the National Assembly. A spacious amphitheater had been erected for the king, the royal family, the ambassadors, and the deputies. The federates, who first arrived, began to dance *farandoles;* those who followed joined them, forming a round which soon embraced part of the Champ-de-Mars. A sight worthy of the philosophic observer was that exhibited by this host of men, who had come from the most opposite parts of France, hurried away by the impulse of the national character, banishing all remembrance of the past, all idea of the present, all fear of the future, and indulging in a delicious thoughtlessness. Three hundred thousand spectators, of all ages and of both sexes, followed their motions, beating time with their hands, forgetting the rain, hunger, and the weariness of long waiting. At length, the whole procession having entered the Champ-de-Mars, the dance ceased, each federate repaired to his banner. The Bishop of Autun prepared to perform mass at an altar in the antique style, erected in the center of the Champ-de-Mars. Three hundred priests in white surplices, girt with broad tri-colored scarfs, ranged themselves at the four corners of the altar. The Bishop of Autun blessed the oriflamme and the eighty-three banners: he struck up the *Te Deum.* Twelve hundred musicians played that hymn. . . .

. . . The federates, before they quitted the capital, went to pay homage to the king: all of them testified the most profound respect, the warmest attachment. The chief of the Bretons dropped on his knee, and presented his sword to Louis XVI. "Sire," said he, "I deliver to you, pure and sacred, the sword of the faithful Bretons: it shall never be stained but with the blood of your enemies." "That sword cannot be in better hands than those of my dear Bretons," replied Louis XVI, raising the chief of the Bretons, and returning him his sword. . . . A mutual emotion prolonged for some moments this touching scene. The chief of the Bretons was the first to speak. "Sire," said he, "all the French, if I may judge from our hearts, love and will love you, because you are a citizen king."

[102] *THE CONSTITUTIONAL MONARCHY IS OVERTHROWN, AUGUST 10, 1792* *

The constitutional monarchy created in September, 1791, lasted less than a year. For one thing, Louis XVI was widely, and rightly, suspected of treasonous activity. For another, despite the "free and equal" clause of the Declaration of the Rights of Man, the Constitution of 1791 denied full political rights to about half the adult males of France. On August 10, 1792, occurred the "Second French Revolution" which led to the deposition of the King and the proclamation of a democratic republic. The following accounts of the attack on the King's palace and the September Massacres are by eyewitnesses.

[A] The Attack on the Tuileries

Nobles and persons attached to the king had come in great numbers to the palace, armed with swords and pistols. Their intention can only be praised; it was excellent; but one must disapprove of their action and avow that armed as they were they could only embarrass the defense and inspire distrust in the national guard.

At eleven o'clock in the evening [August 9, 1792], the information was received that the tocsin would sound at midnight. A little later it was known at the palace that the Faubourg Saint-Antoine had passed a resolution of which the principal articles were "to attack the palace; exterminate everybody, with particular attention to the Swiss; force the king to abdicate; and conduct the king, queen, and royal family to Vincennes to serve as hostages in case the foreigners launched themselves upon Paris."

At midnight, the tocsin was heard to sound. . . .

. . . At two in the morning, four battalions from the faubourgs had already arrived on the Place du Carrousel. They were ready to execute their horrible projects and only awaited their comrades.

* [A] Colonel Pfyffer d'Altishoffen, *Récit*, and [B] Ferrières, *Mémoires*, both as found in E. L. Higgins, *The French Revolution as Told by Contemporaries* (Boston: Houghton Mifflin Company, 1939), pp. 238–240, 249–250. Used by permission.

Between four and five o'clock, M. Mandat [in charge of the defense of the Tuileries] received an order to go to the commune. They were waiting to cut his throat on the steps of the Hôtel de Ville. They knew that he had in his pocket an order signed by Pétion [mayor of Paris] authorizing him to repel force with force, and were willing to employ murder to keep this written document from becoming public. . . .

Between eight and nine o'clock, the king decided to repair to the midst of the National Assembly. He was accompanied by all the royal family and some of the nobles. . . .

The army of Santerre put itself into movement, preceded by cannon, and soon was seen advancing towards the gates of the palace. . . .

Here is the state of things at the moment the combat was about to begin. There were seven hundred and fifty Swiss distributed over more than twenty posts, two hundred noblemen without arms, and some national guards who had remained faithful. Without commander-in-chief, without munitions, and without cannon, they were attacked from all sides by nearly a hundred thousand furious people having with them fifty pieces of artillery. This mob felt that it was encouraged by the legislative body, and that it was in control of the municipality.

The troops of Santerre let loose a discharge that wounded several soldiers. The Filles-Saint-Thomas grenadiers replied, followed by the Swiss. . . .

The action became general. It was soon decided in favor of the Swiss; the fire from the windows and that of M. de Durler's reserve had been deadly. In a short time the court found itself evacuated, heaped with dead, dying, and wounded. . . .

But the Swiss saw with anxiety that the moment was approaching when lack of munitions would leave them exposed to the fire of the enemy, without means of responding to it.

At this critical moment, M. d'Hervilly (since dead for the royal cause at Quiberon) arrived without arms, hatless, through musket and cannon fire. The officers wished to show him the dispositions that had just been made on the side of the garden. "Never mind that," he said. "You have to betake yourselves to the Assembly. . . ."

Finally they arrived in the corridors of the National Assembly. The deputies there cried out, "The Swiss, the Swiss!" and several sought to escape through the windows.

A deputy came to order the commander to lay down his arms; he refused to do so. M. de Durler was brought before His Majesty. He said to the king, "Sire, they want us to lay down our arms." The king replied, "Yield them to the national guard; I do not want brave men like you to perish." A moment afterwards, the king sent him a note in his own writing conceived in these terms: "The king orders the Swiss to lay down their arms and retire to the barracks." This order was a thunderbolt to these brave soldiers. They cried out that they could still defend themselves with the bayonet. Several cried with rage, but in this frightful extremity discipline and fidelity prevailed. All obeyed.

This order to abandon their weapons and deliver themselves over defenseless to tigers thirsting for their blood was the final sacrifice demanded of the Swiss. . . .

The palace being no longer defended, the army of Santerre entered it, and began a cowardly massacring of the wounded and those who had lost their way in the immensity of the palace. . . .

[B] The September Massacres Begin

While the commissaries of the commune inflame the populace by recitals of imaginary facts, and inspire all hearts with the fury which animates them, two or three hundred scoundrels repair to Les Carmes and to Saint-Germain to murder four hundred priests. They go next to the Abbaye, and soon the cries of the dying, mingled with the shrieks of the people as they call incessantly for new victims, bring terror to the souls of the prisoners. Each awaits in tortured anxiety the instant that is to mark his fate. . . .

The commune, seeking to give this horrible butchery the semblance of popular justice, hastily organizes a tribunal in each prison. He who presides [Maillard] has a long sword at his side; he sits before a table strewn with papers, pipes, and bottles. A dozen men compose the monstrous jury. Some, in workmen's blouses, remain standing. Others lie upon benches, dozing with fatigue and drunkenness. Three cutthroats bring in each prisoner. Their sabers cross his breast and he is warned that at the least movement he will be pierced. Two butchers with naked swords and their sleeves rolled up, their shirts spotted with blood, guard the door. The jailer has his hand on the bolts that secure it. A candle in the middle of the table adds shadowed somberness to the scene. Its wavering light is reflected on the sinister faces of the judges, and reveals their fierce and hideous features. "Your name and your profession," comes in harsh tones from the president. "Take çare; a lie will be your ruin."

No plea can save the designated victim. A man of sixty is presented as the president consults his jail-book. Two national guards appear to speak for the accused in the name of the Croix-Rouge section. They insist that he has always been a good citizen. "Recommendations are useless in the case of traitors," says the president shortly. "But that is horrible," the man cries out. "Your trial is an assassination." "My hands have been washed of it," the president replies. "Please conduct the gentleman." He is hustled out into the court and slaughtered.

[103] *TERROR DECLARED THE ORDER OF THE DAY* *

The Reign of Terror extended from September, 1793, to the overthrow of Robespierre, July 27, 1794. It was motivated by many considerations: the intrigues of the emigres; the imminent danger of invasion by the foreign coalition; civil war in several parts of France; a desperate economic situation which demanded scapegoats. At least 15,000 people were put to death during the Terror.

[A] A Parisian Newspaper Justifies the Principle of Terror

Yes, terror is the order of the day, and ought to be for the selfish, for the federalists, for the heartless rich, for dishonest opportunists, for shameless intriguers, for unpatriotic cowards, for all who do not feel the dignity of being free men and pure republicans. Rivers of blood have been shed for the gold of Peru and the diamonds of Golconda. Well! Does not liberty, that inestimable blessing which one would surely not tarnish by comparing it with the vile metals of the Indies, have the same right to sacrifice lives, fortunes, and even, for a time, individual liberties? In the thick of battle is there any foolish wailing over the soldiers fallen from the ranks? They are promptly replaced by others, and with the perfidious aggressor repulsed, one is free to weep over the unfortunate victims mowed down on the field of battle. Is not the French Revolution just such a deadly combat, a war to the death between those who want to be free and those content to be slaves? This is the situation, and the French people have gone too far to retreat with honor and safety. There is no middle ground; France must be entirely free or perish in the attempt, and any means are justifiable in fighting for so fine a cause. But our resources are being exhausted, say some. Well, when the Revolution is finished, they will be replenished by peace. A free people, as long as they have weapons and hands, can fight their enemies and plow their fields. . . .

[B] Defense of the Republic: the Levy *en masse*, August 23, 1793

1. Henceforth, until the enemies have been driven from the territory of the Republic, the French people are in permanent requisition for army service.

* [A] *Révolutions de Paris, No. 212,* as found in E. L. Higgins, *The French Revolution as Told by Contemporaries* (Boston: Houghton Mifflin Company, 1939), pp. 306–307. Used by permission. [B] and [C] J. H. Stewart, *A Documentary Survey of the French Revolution* (New York: The Macmillan Company, 1951), pp. 472–474 and pp. 447–478. Used by permission.

The young men shall go to battle; the married men shall forge arms and transport provisions; the women shall make tents and clothes, and shall serve in the hospitals; the children shall turn old linen into lint; the old men shall repair to the public places, to stimulate the courage of the warriors and preach the unity of the Republic and hatred of kings.

2. National buildings shall be converted into barracks; public places into armament workshops; the soil of cellars shall be washed in lye to extract saltpeter therefrom.

3. Arms of caliber shall be turned over exclusively to those who march against the enemy; the service of the interior shall be carried on with fowling pieces and sabers.

5. The Committee of Public Safety is charged with taking all measures necessary for establishing, without delay, a special manufacture of arms of all kinds, in harmony with the *élan* and the energy of the French people. . . .

11. The battalion organized in each district shall be united under a banner bearing the inscription: *The French people risen against tyrants*. . . .

[C] The Law of Suspects, September 17, 1793

1. Immediately after the publication of the present decree, all suspected persons within the territory of the Republic and still at liberty shall be placed in custody.

2. The following are deemed suspected persons: 1st, those who, by their conduct, associations, talk, or writings have shown themselves partisans of tyranny or federalism and enemies of liberty; 2nd, those who are unable to justify, in the manner prescribed by the decree of 21 March last, their means of existence and the performance of their civic duties; 3rd, those to whom certificates of patriotism have been refused; 4th, public functionaries suspended or dismissed from their positions by the National Convention or by its commissioners, and not reinstated, especially those who have been or are to be dismissed by virtue of the decree of 14 August last; 5th, those former nobles, husbands, wives, fathers, mothers, sons or daughters, brothers or sisters, and agents of the *émigrés*, who have not steadily manifested their devotion to the Revolution; 6th, those who have emigrated during the interval between 1 July, 1789, and the publication of the decree of 30 March –8 April, 1792, even though they have returned to France within the period established by said decree or prior thereto. . . .

5. Individuals arrested as suspects shall be taken first to the jails of the place of their detention; in default of jails, they shall be kept under surveillance in their respective dwellings.

6. Within the following week, they shall be transferred to national buildings, which the departmental administrations shall be required to

designate and to have prepared for such purpose immediately after the receipt of the present decree. . . .

[104] *THE GREAT DEBATE BEGINS* *

For more than a century and a half, historians and others have debated the merits of the French Revolution. The facts of the events of 1789–1794 are pretty well agreed upon, but there has long been violent difference of opinion on whether the total effect was "good" or "bad" for France and the world. The debate was given an early and brilliant start by Edmund Burke (Reflections on the French Revolution) *and Tom Paine* (The Rights of Man). *Burke's work appeared in November 1790; Paine's passionate rebuttal only three months later.*

[A] Excerpts from *Reflections on the French Revolution*

. . . from Magna Charta to the Declaration of Rights, it has been the uniform policy of our constitution to claim and assert our liberties, as an *entailed inheritance* derived to us from our forefathers, and to be transmitted to our posterity; as an estate specially belonging to the people of this kingdom, without any reference whatever to any other more general or prior right. By this means our constitution preserves a unity in so great a diversity of its parts. We have an inheritable crown; an inheritable peerage; and a House of Commons and a people inheriting privileges, franchises, and liberties, from a long line of ancestors.

This policy appears to me to be the result of profound reflection; or rather the happy effect of following nature, which is wisdom without reflection, and above it. A spirit of innovation is generally the result of a selfish temper and confined views. People will not look forward to posterity, who never look backward to their ancestors. Besides, the people of England well know, that the idea of inheritance furnishes a sure principle of conservation and a sure principle of transmission; without at all excluding a principle of improvement. . . .

After I had read over the list of the persons and descriptions selected into the *Tiers Etat,* nothing which they afterwards did could appear astonishing. Among them, indeed, I saw some of known rank; some of shining talents; but of any practical experience in the state, not one man was to be

* [A] Edmund Burke, *Reflections on the French Revolution,* Everyman's Library (London: J. M. Dent and Sons, Ltd.; New York: E. P. Dutton and Co., Inc., 1910), pp. 31, 38, 46–47, 49–50, 57–58, 73. Used by permission of the publishers. [B] Thomas Paine, *The Rights of Man,* Everyman's Library (London: J. M. Dent and Sons, Ltd.; New York: E. P. Dutton and Co., Inc., 1915), pp. 9, 12, 18–19, 31–32, 101–104. Used by permission of the publishers.

found. The best were only men of theory. But whatever the distinguished few may have been, it is the substance and mass of the body which constitutes its character, and must finally determine its direction. . . .

. . . Believe me, Sir, those who attempt to level, never equalise. In all societies, consisting of various descriptions of citizens, some descriptions must be uppermost. The levellers therefore only change and pervert the natural order of things; they load the edifice of society, by setting up in the air what the solidity of the structure requires to be on the ground. The associations of tailors and carpenters, of which the republic (of Paris, for instance) is composed, cannot be equal to the situation, into which, by the worst of usurpations, an usurpation on the prerogatives of nature, you attempt to force them.

The Chancellor of France at the opening of the States, said, in a tone of oratorical flourish, that all occupations were honourable. If he meant only, that no honest employment was disgraceful, he would not have gone beyond the truth. But in asserting that anything is honourable, we imply some distinction in its favour. The occupation of a hair-dresser, or of a working tallow-chandler, cannot be a matter of honour to any person—to say nothing of a number of other more servile employments. Such descriptions of men ought not to suffer oppression from the state; but the state suffers oppression, if such as they, either individually or collectively, are permitted to rule. . . .

It is said, that twenty-four millions ought to prevail over two hundred thousand. True; if the constitution of a kingdom be a problem of arithmetic. This sort of discourse does well enough with the lamp-post for its second: to men who *may* reason calmly, it is ridiculous. The will of the many and their interest must very often differ; and great will be the difference when they make an evil choice. A government of five hundred country attorneys and obscure curates is not good for twenty-four millions of men, though it were chosen by eight-and-forty millions; nor is it the better for being guided by a dozen of persons of quality, who have betrayed their trust in order to obtain that power. At present, you seem in everything to have strayed out of the high road of nature. The property of France does not govern it. Of course property is destroyed, and rational liberty has no existence. All you have got for the present is a paper circulation and a stock-jobbing constitution; and, as to the future, do you seriously think that the territory of France, upon the republican system of eighty-three independent municipalities (to say nothing of the parts that compose them), can ever be governed as one body, or can ever be set in motion by the impulse of one mind? When the National Assembly has completed its work, it will have accomplished its ruin. . . .

Government is not made in virtue of natural rights, which may and do exist in total independence of it; and exist in much greater clearness, and in a much greater degree of abstract perfection: but their abstract perfection is their practical defect. By having a right to everything they want everything. Government is a contrivance of human wisdom to provide for human *wants.* Men have a right that these wants should be provided for by this wisdom. Among these wants is to be reckoned the want, out of civil society, of a sufficient restraint upon their passions. Society requires not only that the passions of individuals should be subjected, but that even in the mass and body, as well as in the individuals, the inclinations of men should frequently be thwarted, their will controlled, and their passions brought into subjection. This can only be done *by a power out of themselves;* and not, in the exercise of its function, subject to that will and to those passions which it is its office to bridle and subdue. In this sense the restraints on men, as well as their liberties, are to be reckoned among their rights. . . .

It is now sixteen or seventeen years since I saw the queen of France, then the dauphiness, at Versailles; and surely never lighted on this orb, which she hardly seemed to touch, a more delightful vision. I saw her just above the horizon, decorating and cheering the elevated sphere she just began to move in,—glittering like the morning-star, full of life, and splendour, and joy. Oh! what a revolution! and what a heart must I have to contemplate without emotion that elevation and that fall! Little did I dream when she added titles of veneration to those of enthusiastic, distant, respectful love, that she should ever be obliged to carry the sharp antidote against disgrace concealed in that bosom; little did I dream that I should have lived to see such disasters fallen upon her in a nation of gallant men, in a nation of men of honour, and of cavaliers. I thought ten thousand swords must have leaped from their scabbards to avenge even a look that threatened her with insult. But the age of chivalry is gone. That of sophisters, economists, and calculators, has succeeded; and the glory of Europe is extinguished for ever. . . .

[B] Excerpts from *The Rights of Man*

Among the incivilities by which nations or individuals provoke and irritate each other, Mr. Burke's pamphlet on the French Revolution is an extraordinary instance. Neither the people of France, nor the National

Assembly, were troubling themselves about the affairs of England, or the English Parliament; and why Mr. Burke should commence an unprovoked attack upon them, both in Parliament and in public, is a conduct that cannot be pardoned on the score of manners, nor justified on that of policy.

There never did, there never will, and there never can, exist a Parliament, or any description of men, or any generation of men, in any country, possessed of the right or the power of binding and controuling posterity to the *"end of time,"* or of commanding for ever how the world shall be governed, or who shall govern it; and therefore all such clauses, acts or declarations by which the makers of them attempt to do what they have neither the right nor the power to do, nor the power to execute, are in themselves null and void. . . . The Parliament or the people of 1688, or of any other period, had no more right to dispose of the people of the present day, or to bind or to controul them *in any shape whatever,* than the Parliament or the people of the present day have to dispose of, bind or controul those who are to live a hundred or a thousand years hence. Every generation is, and must be, competent to all the purposes which its occasions require. It is the living, and not the dead, that are to be accommodated. . . .

"We have seen," says Mr. Burke, "the French rebel against a mild and lawful Monarch, with more fury, outrage, and insult, than any people has been known to rise against the most illegal usurper, or the most sanguinary tyrant." This is one among a thousand other instances, in which Mr. Burke shows that he is ignorant of the springs and principles of the French Revolution.

It was not against Louis XVI., but against the despotic principles of the government, that the Nation revolted. These principles had not their origin in him, but in the original establishment, many centuries back; and they were become too deeply rooted to be removed, and the Augean stable of parasites and plunderers too abominably filthy to be cleansed, by anything short of a complete and universal Revolution. . . . The Monarch and the Monarchy were distinct and separate things; and it was against the established despotism of the latter, and not against the person or principles of the former, that the revolt commenced, and the Revolution has been carried.

. . . four or five persons were seized by the populace and instantly put to death; . . . Their heads were stuck upon spikes, and carried about the city; and it is upon this mode of punishment that Mr. Burke builds a great part of his tragic scenes. Let us therefore examine how men came by the idea of punishing in this manner.

They learn it from the Governments they live under, and retaliate the punishments they have been accustomed to behold. . . .

Lay then the axe to the root, and teach Governments humanity. It is their sanguinary punishments which corrupt mankind. In England the punishment in certain cases is by *hanging, drawing* and *quartering;* the heart of the sufferer is cut out and held up to the view of the populace. In France, under the former Government, the punishments were not less barbarous. . . . The effect of those cruel spectacles exhibited to the populace is to destroy tenderness or excite revenge; and by the base and false idea of governing men by terror, instead of reason, they become precedents. . . .

"Government," says [Burke], "is a contrivance of human wisdom."

Admitting that Government is a contrivance of human *wisdom,* it must necessarily follow, that hereditary succession and hereditary rights (as they are called), can make no part of it, because it is impossible to make wisdom hereditary; and on the other hand, that cannot be a wise contrivance, which in its operation may commit the Government of a Nation to the wisdom of an idiot.

The ground which Mr. Burke now takes is fatal to every part of his cause. The argument changes from hereditary rights to hereditary wisdom; and the question is, Who is the wisest man?

He must now shew that every one in the line of hereditary succession was a Solomon, or his title is not good to be a King.

What a stroke has Mr. Burke now made! To use a sailor's phrase, he has swabbed the deck, and scarcely left a name legible in the list of Kings; and he has mowed down and thinned the House of Peers, with a scythe as formidable as Death and Time.

. . . A thousand years hence, those who shall live in America or in France, will look back with contemplative pride on the origin of their Governments, and say, *This was the work of our glorious ancestors!* But what can a monarchical talker say? What has he to exult in? Alas! he has nothing. A certain something forbids him to look back to a beginning, lest some robber, or some Robin Hood, should rise from the long obscurity of time and say, *I am the origin.* Hard as Mr. Burke laboured the Regency Bill and hereditary succession two years ago, and much as he dived for precedents, he still had not boldness enough to bring up William of Normandy, and say, *There is the head of the list, there is the fountain of honour;* the son of a prostitute and the plunderer of the English Nation.

18

Napoleon

The period from 1799 to 1814 is usually labelled the "Napoleonic Era." In France Napoleon instituted a government based on the new catchwords of order, stability, and moderation. The individual liberties guaranteed in 1789 by the Declaration of the Rights of Man were largely disregarded, but the social gains of the Revolution—notably equality before the law and the abolition of feudalism—were preserved. Outside of France he made use of the national patriotism and the national armies inherited from the Revolution to spread many of the ideas and institutions of revolutionary France to occupied states. In still other countries—notably Prussia—rulers were compelled at least partly to liberalize their governments in order to enlist the popular support necessary to withstand the Emperor of the French.

[105] *NAPOLEON GIVES HIS VERSION OF THE COUP OF BRUMAIRE* *

The following account of the coup d'état *of November 10, 1799, which put Napoleon in power as consul, is taken from Napoleon's* Memoirs *written at St.*

* *Memoirs of the History of France During the Reign of Napoleon, Dictated by the Emperor* (London, 1823), Vol. I, pp. 92–98.

Helena. It is a somewhat colored version of the occurrence. Instead of remaining the calm master of the situation, as he claims, Napoleon lost his nerve completely and was carried half-fainting from the Council of Five Hundred, the lower house of the legislature. It was his brother Lucien, the president of the Council, who saved the day for Napoleon.

Napoleon [he writes in the third person] entered the Council of Ancients [the upper house of the legislature], and placed himself at the bar, opposite to the president:

"You stand," said he, "upon a volcano; the Republic no longer possesses a government; the Directory is dissolved; factions are at work; the hour of decision is come. You have called in my arm, and the arms of my comrades, to the support of your wisdom: but the moments are precious: . . . I desire nothing but the safety of the Republic. . . ."

Upon this a member (Linglet) rose and said with a loud voice, "General, we applaud what you say; swear then, with us, obedience to the Constitution of the year III which alone can preserve the Republic."

The astonishment caused by these words produced the most profound silence.

Napoleon recollected himself for a moment; and then went on again emphatically: "The Constitution of the year III—you have it no longer—you violated it on the eighteenth of Fructidor, when the Government infringed on the independence of the Legislative Body; you violated it on the thirtieth of Prairial, in the year VII, when the Legislative Body struck at the independence of the Government; you violated it on the twenty-second of Floréal, when, by a sacrilegious decree, the Government and the Legislative Body invaded the sovereignty of the people, by annulling the elections made by them. The Constitution being violated, there must be a new compact, new guarantees."

The force of this speech, and the energy of the General, brought over three-fourths of the members of Council, who rose to indicate their approbation. . . . At this moment Napoleon was informed that [the Council of Five Hundred was] endeavouring to force the president Lucien to put the outlawry of his brother to the vote. Napoleon immediately hastened to the Five Hundred, entered the chamber with his hat off, and ordered the officers and soldiers who accompanied him to remain at the doors: he was desirous to present himself at the bar, to rally his party, which was numerous, but which had lost all unity and resolution. But to get to the bar, it was necessary to cross half the chamber, because the President had his seat on one of the wings. When Napoleon had advanced alone across one-third of the orangery, two or three hundred members suddenly rose, crying, "Death to the tyrant! down with the dictator!"

Two grenadiers, who, by the order of the General, had remained at the door, and who had reluctantly obeyed, saying to him, "You do not know them, they are capable of anything!" rushed in, sabre in hand, overthrowing all that opposed their passage, to join the General, and cover him with their bodies. All the other grenadiers followed this example, and forced Napoleon out of the chamber. . . .

The General descended into the court-yard, called the troops into a circle by beat of drum, got on horseback, and harangued them: "I was about," said he, "to point out to them the means of saving the Republic, and restoring our glory. They answered me with their daggers. It was thus they would have accomplished the wishes of the Allied Kings. What more could England have done? Soldiers, may I rely upon you?"

Unanimous acclamations formed the reply to this speech. Napoleon instantly ordered a captain to go with ten men into the chamber of the Five Hundred, and to liberate the President.

. . . The officer of grenadiers then presented himself at the door of the chamber, exclaiming, "*Vive la République!* . . ."

. . . No opposition was offered to the departure of the President, who left the chamber, rushed into the court-yard, mounted a horse, and cried out in his stentorian voice, "General—and you, soldiers—the President of the Council of Five Hundred proclaims to you that factious men, with drawn daggers, have interrupted the deliberations of that assembly. He calls upon you to employ force against these disturbers. The Council of Five Hundred is dissolved."

"President," replied the General, "it shall be done."

He then ordered Murat into the chamber, at the head of a detachment in close column. At this crisis General B—ventured to ask him for fifty men, in order to place himself in ambuscade upon the way, and fire upon the fugitives. Napoleon replied to this request only by enjoining the grenadiers to commit no excesses. "It is my wish," said he, "that not one drop of blood may be shed."

Murat presented himself at the door, and summoned the Council to disperse. The shouts and vociferations continued. Colonel Moulins, Brune's aide-de-camp, who had just arrived from Holland, ordered the charge to be beaten. The drum put an end to the clamour. The soldiers entered the chamber charging bayonets. The deputies leaped out at the windows, and dispersed, leaving their gowns, caps, &c.: in one moment the chamber was empty.

[106] *NAPOLEON GAINS ABSOLUTE CONTROL OVER THE ADMINISTRATIVE SYSTEM* *

One of Napoleon's first acts (February 17, 1800) was the reorganization of the French administrative system so as to give the First Consul dictatorial control over all the departments and local authority. Old Regime centralizers like Richelieu and Louis XIV would have envied and applauded him, but many Frenchmen who held the principles of '89 at heart felt that the Revolution had been betrayed by this despotic destruction of local liberties. Excerpts from the law follow.

1. The European territory of the Republic shall be divided into departments and communal districts, in conformity with the table annexed to the present law. [This table made but one change in the existing departments.]

2. There shall be in each department a prefect, a council of prefecture, and a department general council, which shall discharge the functions now performed by the administrations and department commissioners.

3. The prefect alone shall be charged with the administration.

8. In each communal district there shall be a sub-prefect and a district council composed of eleven members.

12. In the cities . . . whose population shall not exceed two thousand five hundred inhabitants, there shall be a mayor and a deputy; in the cities or towns of two thousand five hundred to five thousand inhabitants, a mayor and two deputies; in the cities of five thousand to ten thousand inhabitants, a mayor, two deputies, and a commissioner of police; in the cities whose population shall exceed ten thousand inhabitants, besides the mayor, two deputies and a commissioner of police, there shall be a deputy for each twenty thousand inhabitants in excess and a commissioner for each ten thousand in excess.

18. The First Consul shall appoint the prefects, the councillors of prefecture, the members of the general councils of the departments, the general secretary for the prefecture, the sub-prefects, the members of the district councils, the mayors and deputies of the cities of more than five thousand inhabitants, the commissioners-general of police and prefects of police in the cities in which they shall be established.

20. The prefects shall appoint and can suspend from their functions the members of the municipal councils; they shall appoint and can suspend the mayors and deputies in cities whose population is less than five thousand

* Frank M. Anderson, *The Constitutions and Other Select Documents Illustrative of the History of France, 1789–1901* (Minneapolis: H. W. Wilson, 1904), pp. 283–287.

inhabitants. The members of the municipal councils shall be appointed for three years: they can be continued.

[107] *RELIGION IS REORGANIZED* *

In 1802 Napoleon signed a concordat with the Catholic Church restoring normal relations with Rome after twelve years of conflict. To the dismay of Pope Pius VII, the First Consul unilaterally appended a series of reservations and interpretations to the Concordat which completely altered its meaning and effectively subordinated the Church to the State. Key provisions of these "Organic Articles" follow, as well as a passage from the Imperial Catechism which further illustrates how Napoleon made religion serve his needs.

[A] Excerpts from the Organic Articles (1802)

1. No bull, brief, rescript, decree, injunction, provision, signature serving as a provision, nor other documents from the court of Rome, even concerning individuals only, can be received, published, printed, or otherwise put into effect, without the authorisation of the Government.

2. No person calling himself nuncio, legate, vicar or apostolic commissioner, or taking advantage of any other denomination can, without the same authorisation, exercise upon French soil or elsewhere any function relative to the affairs of the Gallican Church.

3. The decrees of foreign synods, even those of general councils, cannot be published in France before the Government has examined their form, their conformity with the laws, rights, and liberties of the French Republic, and everything which, in their publication, may alter or affect the public tranquility.

4. No national or metropolitan council, no diocesan synod, no deliberative assembly, shall take place without the express permission of the Government.

11. The archbishops and bishops shall be able, with the authorisation of the Government, to establish cathedral chapters and seminaries in their dioceses. All other ecclesiastical establishments are suppressed.

12. The archbishops and bishops shall be free to add to their name the title of *Citizen* or that of *Monsieur*. All other designations are forbidden.

16. No one can be appointed bishop before reaching thirty years of age, nor unless he is of French origin.

19. The bishops shall appoint and install the *curés;* nevertheless, they

* Frank M. Anderson, *The Constitutions and Other Select Documents Illustrative of the History of France, 1789–1901* (Minneapolis: H. W. Wilson, 1904), pp. 299–303, 313–314.

shall not make known their appointment and they shall not give them the canonical investiture until after this appointment shall have been agreed to by the First Consul.

20. They shall be required to reside in their dioceses; they cannot leave them, except with the permission of the First Consul.

23. The bishops shall be charged with the organization of their seminaries, and the regulations for this organization shall be submitted to the approbation of the First Consul.

24. Those who shall be chosen to give instruction in the seminaries shall subscribe to the declaration made by the clergy of France in 1682 and published in an edict of the same year; they shall consent to teach in them the doctrine contained therein, and the bishops shall address a copy in due form to the Councillor of State charged with all matters relating to worship.

39. There shall be only one liturgy and one catechism for all the Catholic churches of France.

41. No religious festival, with the exception of the Sabbath, can be established without the permission of the Government.

43. All the ecclesiastics shall be dressed in French fashion and in black. The bishops can add to this costume the pastoral cross and violet stockings.

44. Family chapels and private oratories cannot be established without the express permission of the Government, granted upon the request of the bishop.

51. The *curés* at the sermons of the parochial masses shall pray and cause prayer to be offered for the French Republic and for the Consuls.

[B] Excerpt from the Imperial Catechism (1807)

Lesson VII. Continuation of the Fourth Commandment.

Q. What are the duties of Christians with respect to the princes who govern them, and what in particular are our duties towards Napoleon I, our Emperor?

A. Christians owe to the princes who govern them, and we owe in particular to Napoleon I, our Emperor, *love, respect, obedience, fidelity, military service* and the tributes laid for the preservation and defence of the Empire and of his throne; we also owe to him fervent prayers for his safety and the spiritual and temporal prosperity of the State.

Q. Why are we bound to all these duties towards our Emperor?

A. First of all, because God, who creates empires and distributes them according to His will, in loading our Emperor with gifts, both in peace and in war, has established him as our sovereign and has made him the minister of His power and His image upon the earth. *To honor and to serve our Emperor is then to honor and to serve God himself.* Secondly, because our

Lord Jesus Christ by His doctrine as well as by His example, has Himself taught us what we owe to our sovereign: He was born the subject of Caesar Augustus; He paid the prescribed impost; and just as He ordered to render to God that which belongs to God, so He ordered to render to Caesar that which belongs to Caesar.

Q. Are there no particular reasons which ought to attach us more strongly to Napoleon I, our Emperor?

A. Yes; for it is he whom God has raised up under difficult circumstances to re-establish the public worship of the holy religion of our fathers and to be the protector of it. He has restored and preserved public order by his profound and active wisdom; he defends the State by his powerful arm; he has become the anointed of the Lord through the consecration which he received from the sovereign pontiff, Head of the Universal Church.

Q. What ought to be thought of those who may be lacking in their duty towards our Emperor?

A. According to the Apostle Saint Paul, they would be resisting the order established by God himself and would render themselves *worthy of eternal damnation.*

Q. Will the duties which are required of us towards our Emperor be equally binding with respect to his lawful successors in the order established by the constitutions of the Empire?

A. Yes, without doubt; for we read in the Holy Scriptures, that God, Lord of heaven and earth, by an order of His supreme will and through His providence, gives empires not only to one person in particular, but also to his family.

[108] *NAPOLEON REGULATES PUBLIC OPINION* *

Like all dictators, Napoleon felt it essential to manufacture public opinion favorable to his regime. The great majority of newspapers in Paris were suppressed within a few months of Napoleon's advent to power. Theatrical and literary censorship quickly followed. The importance Napoleon attached to these matters is shown in the ensuing letters.

To Citizen Ripault, Napoleon's Librarian, July 23, 1801

Citizen Ripault is to see that he is supplied every day with all the papers

* The first four letters are from *Correspondance de Napoléon I* (Paris: 1854–1869), Vol. VII, p. 5647; Vol. X, p. 8821; Vol. XI, p. 9243; Vol. XII, p. 10209. The last letter is from L. Lecestre, *Lettres Inédites de Napoléon I* (Paris: 1897), Vol. I, p. 150. Our translation.

that come out, except the eleven political papers. He will read them carefully, make an abstract of everything they contain likely to influence public opinion, especially with regard to religion, philosophy, and political opinion. He will send me this abstract daily between five and six o'clock.

Once every ten days he will send me an analysis of all the books or pamphlets which have appeared during that period, calling attention to any passages on moral questions. . . .

He will take pains to procure copies of all the plays which are produced, and to analyse them for me, with observations of the same character as those mentioned above. This analysis must be made, at the least, within forty-eight hours of the production of the plays.

He is to send me every first and sixth day, between five and six o'clock, a list of all the bills, advertisements, etc. which deserve attention, as well as anything that has come to his knowledge, and anything that has been done or said in the various institutes, or important trials, that might be of interest from a political and moral point of view.

To Fouché, June 1, 1805

I would like newspaper editors [to have] enough sense not to publish news harmful to the nation. The attention of the papers ought to be directed toward attacking England—English fashions, English customs, English literature, the English constitution. . . . Voltaire did us great harm by his constant essays in Anglomania.

It seems to me that the success of the tragedy *The Templars* is turning attention to that incident in French history. That is good, but I don't think we ought to allow plays on subjects of too recent a date. I see in one of the papers that there is talk of putting on a tragedy about Henry IV [d. 1610]. That period is not distant enough to rouse no passions. The stage needs a touch of antiquity: and I think that, without interfering with the theater too much, you ought to veto this paricular play: but don't make your intervention public. . . .

To Portalis, September 19, 1805

Inform M. Robert, a priest at Bourges, of my displeasure at the extremely bad sermon on August 15.

To Fouché, May 7, 1806

A fourth volume of Millot has just been published, containing all kinds of ridiculous nonsense and harmful to the glory of our arms. It is the height of indecency that such an ignoramus should write in the grand manner about contemporary events. Have the book suppressed. . . .

To Fouché, April 21, 1807

I want you to get up a great agitation . . . against the persecution which the Irish Catholics are suffering at the hands of the Anglican Church. . . . I will get M. Portalis to make private arrangements with some of the bishops, so that, when these newspaper articles have had time to produce their effect, prayers will be offered entreating an end to the persecutions. But the administration must move very delicately and make use of the newspapers without their realizing what the government is driving at. . . . You must make people realize the cruelties and indignities committed by England against the Irish Catholics, whom they have been massacring in St. Bartholomew's Eve fashion for the last hundred years. Don't talk of "Protestants": say "the Anglican Church"; for there are Protestants in France, but there are no Anglicans.

[109] *NAPOLEON BESTOWS A CONSTITUTION ON THE KINGDOM OF WESTPHALIA* *

What Napoleonic rule implied to satellite German states like Westphalia can be seen in the following letter from the Emperor to his youngest brother, Jerome. The latter, deprived of his Baltimore bride and married to a German princess by order of the Emperor, assumed the throne of Westphalia a few weeks after this letter and the accompanying constitution were handed him.

Napoleon to Jerome, Fontainebleau, November 15, 1807

I enclose the Constitution for your Kingdom. It embodies the conditions on which I renounce all my rights of conquest, and all the claims I have acquired over your state. You must faithfully observe it. I am concerned for the happiness of your subjects, not only as it affects your reputation, and my own, but also for its influence on the whole European situation. Don't listen to those who say that your subjects are so accustomed to slavery that they will feel no gratitude for the benefits you give them. There is more intelligence in the Kingdom of Westphalia than they would have you believe; and your throne will never be firmly established except upon the trust and affection of the common people. What German opinion impatiently demands is that men of no rank, but of marked ability, shall have an equal claim upon your favour and your employment, and that every trace of serfdom, or of a feudal hierarchy between the sovereign and the lowest class of his subjects, shall be done away. The benefits of the Code Napoleon,

* J. M. Thompson, ed., *Napoleon Self-Revealed* (Boston: Houghton Mifflin Company, 1934), pp. 207–208. Used by permission of the publisher.

public trial, and the introduction of juries, will be the leading features of your government. And to tell you the truth, I count more upon their effects, for the extension and consolidation of your rule, than upon the most resounding victories. I want your subjects to enjoy a degree of liberty, equality, and prosperity hitherto unknown to the German people. I want this liberal regime to produce, one way or another, changes which will be of the utmost benefit to the system of the Confederation, and to the strength of your monarchy. Such a method of government will be a stronger barrier between you and Prussia than the Elbe, the fortresses, and the protection of France. What people will want to return under the arbitrary Prussian rule, once it has tasted the benefits of a wise and liberal administration? In Germany, as in France, Italy, and Spain, people long for equality and liberalism. I have been managing the affairs of Europe long enough now to know that the burden of the privileged classes was resented everywhere. Rule constitutionally. Even if reason, and the enlightenment of the age, were not sufficient cause, it would be good policy for one in your position; and you will find that the backing of public opinion gives you a great natural advantage over the absolute Kings who are your neighbours.

[110] *NAPOLEON WINS A CLASSIC VICTORY: AUSTERLITZ, 1805* *

The battle from which Napoleon professed to take the greatest satisfaction was one fought on December 2, 1805, near the small Austrian village of Austerlitz. Employing masterful tactics, Napoleon cut in half and routed an Austro-Russian force. The ensuing account is taken from Napoleon's battle orders, official bulletins, and proclamations on the battle.

General Dispositions for the Day of Battle, Issued from the Emperor's Bivouac, 8:30 P.M., December 1, 1805

Marshal Soult will give orders so that his three divisions shall be placed beyond the ravine (Bösenitz Brook) at seven o'clock in the morning, in such a manner as to be ready to commence the manoeuvre of the day, which is to be a march forward by echelons, the right wing leading. Marshal Soult will be personally at half-past seven in the morning near the emperor at his bivouac.

His Highness Prince Murat will give orders to the cavalry of General Kellermann, to that of Generals Walther, Beaumont, Nansouty and Hautpoul,

* T. A. Dodge, *Napoleon* (Boston: Houghton Mifflin Company, 1904), Vol. II, pp. 275–307.

so that the divisions may be placed at seven o'clock in the morning between the left of Marshal Soult and the right of Marshal Lannes, in a manner to occupy the least possible space, and so that at the moment when Marshal Soult shall begin his march, all the cavalry under the orders of Prince Murat shall pass the brook, and find itself placed in the centre of the army.

General Caffarelli is ordered to move at seven o'clock in the morning with his divisions so as to place himself on the right of Suchet's divisions, after having passed the brook. . . .

Marshal Bernadotte with his two infantry divisions will move at seven o'clock in the morning into the same position which is occupied to-day, the 10th, by Caffarelli's division, except that his left shall be close to and behind the Santon (hill), and will remain there in column by regiments.

Marshal Lannes will order a division of grenadiers to place itself in line in front of his present position, the left behind the right of General Caffarelli. . . .

Marshal Davout, with Friant's division and the division of dragoons of General Bourcier, will start at five o'clock in the morning from the Raigern Abbey, to reach the right of Marshal Soult. . . .

At half-past seven the marshals will be near the emperor in his bivouac, so that, according to the movements the enemy may have made during the night, he may give new orders. . . .

All the troops will remain in the dispositions indicated above until new orders. . . .

Each of the marshals will give the orders which apply to him in consequence of the present dispositions.

NAPOLEON

Proclamation Read to Each Battalion, December 1

Soldiers, a Russian army presents itself before you to avenge the Austrian army of Ulm. These are the same battalions which you beat at Hollabrünn, and which you have constantly pursued to this place. The positions we occupy are formidable, and while they are marching to turn my right, they will present me their flank.

Soldiers, I shall myself direct all your battalions. I shall hold myself distant from the fire, if with your accustomed bravery you carry disorder and confusion into the enemy's ranks; but should victory for a moment be uncertain, you would see your emperor expose himself to the first strokes; for victory ought not to hesitate, in this day especially where there is at stake the honor of the French infantry, which means so much to the honor of all the nation.

On pretext of carrying off the wounded, let not the ranks be disgarnished, and let each one be fully penetrated with this idea, that we must vanquish these stipendiaries of England, who are animated with so great a hatred against our nation.

This victory will finish our campaign, and we can retake our winter quarters, where we shall be joined by new armies which are forming in France; and then the peace I shall make will be worthy of my people, of you and of me.

NAPOLEON

Napoleon Visits His Troops (from the *Moniteur*)

In the evening [December 1st] the emperor desired to visit on foot and *incognito* all the bivouacs, but he had scarcely taken a few steps when he was recognized. It would be impossible to paint the enthusiasm of the soldiers on seeing him. Torches of straw were put in an instant at the tops of thousands of poles, and eighty thousand men presented themselves before the emperor, and saluted him with exclamations, some to feast the anniversary of the crowning, others saying that the army would tomorrow give its bouquet to the emperor. One of the old grenadiers approached him and said: "Sire, thou hast no need to expose thyself. I promise thee in the name of the grenadiers of the army that thou shalt have to fight but with thine eyes, and that we will bring thee to-morrow the flags and the artillery of the Russian army to celebrate the anniversary of thy crowning." The emperor said in returning to his bivouac, which consisted of a poor cabin of straw without a roof, which the grenadiers had made him, "This is the finest evening of my life . . . but I regret to think that I shall lose a great number of these brave men. I feel, by the way it hurts me, that these are really my children, and in truth I sometimes reproach myself with the sentiment, for I fear that it may end by making me unable to carry on war."

Excerpts from the Thirtieth Bulletin of the Grand Army, December 3, 1805

Never battlefield was more horrible. From the middle of the immense ponds one yet hears the cries of thousands of men whom one cannot save. It will take three days to send all the enemy's wounded to Brünn. One's heart bleeds; may so much blood shed, may so many misfortunes, finally fall on the perfidious islanders who are its cause: may the oligarchs of London bear the load of so many evils. . . . The Russian troops are brave, but much less brave than the French troops. . . . The Russians in fighting have the habit of leaving behind their haversacks. As the whole Russian army was routed, our soldiers took all the haversacks. We also took a great part of the baggage, and the men found a great deal of money. The French soldiers picked up a large quantity of medals and decorations. . . . General

Valhubert had his leg carried off by a cannonball. Four soldiers came to pick him up. Remembering the order of the day, he cried in a voice of thunder. "Join your ranks. If you come back victors, you can take me up after the battle. If you are vanquished, I attach no price to my life."

Napoleon's Proclamation to the Army, December 3

Soldiers, I am satisfied with you. You have in the day of Austerlitz justified all that I expected of your intrepidity. You have decorated your eagles with an immemorial glory. An army of one hundred thousand men, commanded by the Emperors of Austria and Russia, has been, in less than four hours, either cut off or dispersed. Those who escaped your steel were drowned in the ponds; forty flags, the standards of the Imperial Guard of Russia, one hundred and twenty pieces of cannon, twenty generals, more than thirty thousand prisoners, are the result of this day forever celebrated. This so much vaunted infantry in superior numbers was unable to resist your shock, and from now on you have no rivals to fear. Thus in two months this Third Coalition has been vanquished and dissolved. Peace cannot be distant. . . . Soldiers, when all that is necessary to assure the happiness and the prosperity of our country shall be accomplished, I will lead you back to France. There you will be the object of my most tender solicitude. My people will see you back with joy, and it will suffice you to say, "I was at the battle of Austerlitz," for people to answer, "There stands a brave man."

NAPOLEON

Napoleon's Decree of December 7

1. We adopt all the children of the French generals, officers and soldiers killed at the battle of Austerlitz. 2. They shall be kept and educated at our expense, the boys in our Imperial Palace of Rambouillet, and the girls in our Imperial Palace of St. Germain. The boys shall be placed in situations and the girls married by us. 3. Independently of their names of baptism and family, they shall have the right to join thereto the name of Napoleon.

Napoleon's Proclamation of December 27

Soldiers! Peace between me and the Emperor of Austria is signed. You have in this late season made two campaigns. You have performed everything that I expected of you. I am leaving to go to my capital. I have given promotion and rewards to those who most distinguished themselves. I will do all that I have promised you. You have seen your emperor partake your perils and fatigues. I also wish you to come and see me surrounded by the grandeur and the splendor which belong to the sovereign of the first people of the universe. I will give a great Fete in the first days of May in Paris.

You shall all be there, and after that we shall see where the happiness of our country and the interests of our glory will call us.

NAPOLEON

Bestowal of Awards to the Marshals, April 26, 1806, to Be Paid by the Italian Provinces Designated

To	May	from	Dalmatia	100,000 francs
"	Lannes	"	Istria	100,000 "
"	Soult	"	Friuli	60,000 "
"	Bessières	"	Cadore	60,000 "
"	Serurier	"	Belluno	60,000 "
"	Perignon	"	Conegliano	60,000 "
"	Moncey	"	Treviso	60,000 "
"	Mortier	"	Feltre	60,000 "
"	Dejean	"	Bassano	60,000 "
"	Champagny	"	Vicenza	60,000 "
"	Davout	"	Padua	60,000 "
"	Fouché	"	Rovigo	60,000 "

[111] *METTERNICH DRAWS THE PORTRAIT OF NAPOLEON* *

One of the men best qualified to judge Napoleon was the Austrian statesman and diplomat Prince Metternich. He was Austrian ambassador at Paris between 1806 and 1809 and was influential in securing Marie Louise as Napoleon's second wife. He came to know Napoleon as few other foreigners knew him.

I had never seen Napoleon till the audience which he gave me at St. Cloud, when I delivered my credentials. I found him standing in the middle of one of the rooms, with the Minister for Foreign Affairs and six other members of the Court. He wore the Guards uniform, and had his hat on his head. This latter circumstance, improper in any case, for the audience was not a public one, struck me as misplaced pretension, showing the *parvenu;* I even hesitated for a moment, whether I too should not cover. . . .

His attitude seemed to me to show constraint and even embarrassment. His short, broad figure, negligent dress, and marked endeavour to make an imposing effect, combined to weaken in me the feeling of grandeur naturally attached to the idea of a man before whom the world trembled. This im-

* *Memoirs of Prince Metternich,* trans. by Mrs. Alexander Napier (New York: Charles Scribner's Sons, 1880), Vol. I, pp. 270–286.

pression has never been entirely effaced from my mind; it was present with me in the most important interviews which I have had with Napoleon, at different epochs in his career. Possibly it helped to show me the man as he was, behind the masks with which he knew how to cover himself. In his freaks, in his fits of passion, in his brusque interpellations, I saw prepared scenes, studied and calculated to produce a certain effect on the person to whom he was speaking.

. . . The turn of his mind always led him towards the positive; he disliked vague ideas, and hated equally the dreams of visionaries and the abstraction of idealists, and treated as mere nonsense everything that was not clearly and practically presented to him. He valued only those sciences which can be controlled and verified by the senses or which rest on observation and experience. He had the greatest contempt for the false philosophy and the false philanthropy of the eighteenth century. Among the chief teachers of these doctrines, Voltaire was the special object of his aversion, and he even went so far as to attack, whenever he had the opportunity, the general opinion as to his literary power. . . .

In private life, without being amiable, he was good-natured, and even carried indulgence to the point of weakness. . . . His sisters, in particular, got from him everything that they wanted.

Neither of his wives had ever anything to complain of from Napoleon's personal manners. Although the fact is well known already, a saying of the Archduchesse Marie Louise will put it in a new light. "I am sure," she said to me some time after her marriage, "that they think a great deal about me in Vienna, and that the general opinion is that I live a life of daily suffering. So true is it that truth is often not probable. I have no fear of Napoleon, but I begin to think that he is afraid of me."

Simple and even easy as he was in private life, he showed himself to little advantage in the great world. It is difficult to imagine anything more awkward than Napoleon's manner in a drawing-room. The pains which he took to correct the faults of his nature and education only served to make his deficiencies more evident. I am satisfied that he would have made great sacrifices to add to his height and give dignity to his appearance, which became more common in proportion as his *embonpoint* increased. He walked by preference on tiptoe. His costumes were studied to form a contrast by comparison with the circle which surrounded him, either by their extreme simplicity or by their extreme magnificence. . . . Out of his mouth there never came one graceful or even a well-turned speech to a woman, although the effort to make one was often expressed on his face and in the sound of his voice. He spoke to ladies only of their dress, of which he declared himself a severe judge, or perhaps of the number of their children, and one of his usual questions was if they had nursed their children themselves, a question which he commonly made in terms seldom used in good society. . . .

The opinion of the world is still divided, and perhaps will always be, on the question, Whether Napoleon did in fact deserve to be called a great man? It would be impossible to dispute the great qualities of one who, rising from obscurity, has become in a few years the strongest and most powerful of his contemporaries. But strength, power, and superiority are more or less relative terms. To appreciate properly the degree of genius which has been required for a man to dominate his age, it is necessary to have the measure of that age. This is the point from which opinions with regard to Napoleon diverge so essentially. If the era of the Revolution was, as its admirers think, the most brilliant, the most glorious epoch of modern history, Napoleon, who has been able to take the first place in it, and to keep it for fifteen years, was, certainly, one of the greatest men who have ever appeared. If, on the contrary, he has only had to move like a meteor above the mists of a general dissolution; if he has found nothing around him but the *débris* of a social condition ruined by the excess of false civilisation; if he has only had to combat a resistance weakened by universal lassitude, feeble rivalries, ignoble passions, in fact, adversaries everywhere disunited and paralysed by their disagreements, the splendour of his success diminishes with the facility with which he obtained it. . . .

III

From Waterloo to Sarajevo

THE PERIOD OF NEARLY 100 YEARS between the downfall of Napoleon and the outbreak of World War I differed from previous historical eras in (1) the absence of prolonged or wide-spread wars; (2) the rise and spread of intense nationalism in Europe; (3) the increasing political, military, and economic domination of Europeans over the rest of the world; (4) the development and application of revolutionary industrial techniques; and (5) the emergence of the masses and the undermining of the aristocratic social structure of European society.

Peace prevailed during most of the period 1815–1914, mainly because the political leaders of the major powers of Europe preferred peace. In the early part of this era, universal exhaustion after the long Napoleonic Wars and the generally satisfactory arrangements made at the Congress of Vienna accounted for the absence of hostilities. Until the Crimean War of the 1850's, most of the armed conflicts were internal revolts by discontented liberals and nationalists against the prevailing conservative social and political order. The widespread revolutions of 1848 effected few permanent changes in the European scene. In France, however, the hitherto little-known Louis Napoleon Bonaparte, nephew of Napoleon I, won the presidential election of 1848. Subsequently, in transforming the Second French Republic into an Empire, Louis Napoleon announced that the Empire meant peace. Events proved otherwise, for in the decade of the 1860's, France played key roles in the wars of unification of Italy and Germany, assisting the former movement and opposing the latter. Bismarck's unification of Germany upset the old order in Europe and established a new structure for maining the peace thereafter—the alliance system.

After taking Alsace-Lorraine from France in 1871, Bismarck assumed that future French policy would be based upon the regaining of these provinces. Hence, the German Chancellor's policy was to keep France isolated from powerful potential allies. Germany formed an alliance with Austria-Hungary and Italy, the Triple Alliance, and maintained a "Reinsurance" Treaty with Russia until 1890. This complex system worked well under Bismarck, but fell apart during 1890–1907 under less capable direction. In succession, the "Reinsurance" Treaty was allowed to lapse; Russia and France reached agreement on a Dual Alliance; Great Britain, which had held aloof in "splendid isolation," felt the need for allies at the time of the Boer War, and, therefore, formed an alliance with Japan and reached a friendly agreement with France; Great Britain and Russia settled a number of outstanding colonial disputes in 1907, and joined with France in the Triple Entente. By 1907 German domination of European international affairs had disintegrated. A delicate balance of power was precariously maintained for the next seven years, but each minor conflict of interests among the major powers became a serious issue. Each succeeding crisis was more difficult to resolve.

The armed peace exploded into war in 1914 as a result of an act of violence committed by a frustrated Serb nationalist group. Nationalism in the late nineteenth century had become more intense than ever before. In the case of Serbia, nationalistic Serbs held great aspirations of expanding their tiny independent kingdom into a South Slavic state, much as Sardinia had served as the nucleus of a united Italy. The Serbs were not alone in feeling a sense of frustration in the attainment of their "destiny." Other national groups, as the Irish, Czechs, and Poles, were struggling to attain independence or autonomy. Those national groups which had earlier achieved independence and unification, were no less fervent in their adherence to nationalism.

Nationalism was essentially a product of European civilization, unfelt and unknown, as yet, in most of Africa, Asia, and the lands of the Pacific.

Largely because of nationalistic pride, Europeans embarked upon the scramble for colonial possessions which brought Europe into closer contact than ever before with the "backward" peoples of the world. A number of reasons have been advanced to explain the sudden wave of imperialism of the late nineteenth century: a need for raw materials for European factories and of protected markets for European manufactured products; a need for new areas for the investment of capital; a duty to Christianize and civilize "backward" peoples; and particularly the satisfaction of nationalist feeling by planting the flag in new areas of the world. This scramble for colonies, spheres of influence, and protectorates resulted in a global extension of European political, military, and economic power. The non-European great powers, Japan and the United States, joined in the imperialist expansion, in limited fashion.

The Europeanization of the world was made possible by the great increases in the technological and military power of Europe during the course of the nineteenth century. The industrial revolution, beginning in England in the eighteenth century, and spreading to the United States, Western Europe, and Japan during the nineteenth century, created an economic gulf between the industrialized and the non-industrialized regions. Power-driven machinery installed in factories formed the bases for great industrial cities. Improved transportation by railroad and steamship, and new techniques in agriculture eliminated the chronic threat of famine. As the masses in Europe and America became urbanized, literacy increased and class distinctions became blurred. Industrialization brought in its train a vast upheaval of the traditional agricultural-commercial basis of society.

19

Reaction and Reform, 1815-1832

With the exile of Napoleon to Elba in 1814, the rulers of Europe faced a rare opportunity to negotiate a lasting peace. Meeting at Vienna in 1814 and 1815, the monarchs and their advisers applied the principles of "legitimacy" and "compensation" in restoring former dynasties and settling territorial disputes. Metternich, Austrian chief minister, created the Concert of Europe, an arrangement for periodic consultation among the conservative powers belonging to the Quadruple Alliance for the purpose of suppressing any future liberal or national revolution. Metternich's conservative order was challenged by spotty local revolts in 1820 and 1821, shaken by the revolutions of 1830, and destroyed by the European-wide revolutions of 1848. In England, Tory reaction was overcome by Liberals and Whigs who carried through the Reform Bill of 1832. In the Monroe Doctrine of 1823 the United States expressed its desire to keep the Western Hemisphere free from all European entanglements.

[112] *TALLEYRAND GAINS INFLUENCE AT THE CONGRESS OF VIENNA* *

Behind the brilliant pageantry of the Congress of Vienna, the actual work was undertaken by representatives of the "Big Four" powers. A fifth power, defeated France, was represented by Talleyrand. He had been a bishop before the French Revolution and had served successively the governments of the Revolution, Napoleon, and Louis XVIII. Talleyrand possessed the rare talent of being able to anticipate political changes, and he capped his career by serving after 1830 as Louis Philippe's ambassador to England.

. . . at the opening of the negotiations, all the cabinets regarded themselves as being, notwithstanding the peace, in an attitude which, if not hostile, was at least very equivocal, with France! They all thought, more or less, that it would have been to their interest that she should have been more enfeebled still. Unable to do anything in that direction, they endeavored to diminish, at least, her influence. I saw that they all agreed on those various points.

It remained for me to hope that there would be among the powers some divergence of opinion, when they came to distribute the numerous territories that the war had put at their disposal, each one desiring, either to obtain for himself, or to give to the states dependent upon her, a considerable portion of the conquered territories. It was specially desired, at the same time, to exclude from the division those countries which it was feared would prove too independent. That variety of contest, however, offered me but scant opportunity to interfere with matters; for previous arrangements, by which the disposal of the most important territories had been regulated, existed beween the powers. To succeed in modifying those arrangements, or to have them completely renounced, according to the dictates of justice, there were more than prejudices to remove, more than pretensions to check, more than ambition to defeat. It was necessary to annul all that had been done without France. For if they consented to admit us to take a share in the acts of the congress, it was for the sake of form only, and in order to deprive us of the means of contesting their validity; but it was pretended that France should have nothing to say in the resolutions already settled, and that were looked upon as accomplished facts.

The opening of congress had been fixed for the 1st of October. I had been at Vienna since September 23, but I had been preceded there by several days, by the ministers who, having directed the war, and repented of peace,

* *Memoires of the Prince de Talleyrand,* ed. by the Duc de Broglie and trans. by R. L. de Beaufort (New York and London: G. P. Putnam's Sons, 1891), Vol. II, pp. 200–205.

wished to take up their advantages again at the congress. It was not long before I was informed that they had already formed a committee, and were holding conferences among themselves, of which a protocol had been prepared. Their object was to decide alone, what ought to be submitted to the deliberations of the congress, and that too, without the assistance of either France, Spain, or any power of the second order; to these however they would afterwards communicate, in the form of a proposition what would in reality be a resolution, viz., the different articles they should have determined upon. I made no remonstrances. I continued to see them, without speaking of business. I limited myself to communicating to the ministers of the secondary powers, who had a common interest with me, the dissatisfaction I felt. Discovering also, in the past policy of their countries, traces of confidence in France, they very soon looked upon me as their support, and once assured of their assent in all that I was about to do, I officially pressed the opening of the congress. In my first requests I acted as though I had no knowledge of the conferences that had been held. The opening of the congress was fixed for a certain day. That day passed; I entreated that another should be fixed in the near future. I gave it to be understood that it was necessary that I should not remain too long absent from France. A few replies, evasive at first, caused me to repeat my entreaties. I even went so far as to complain a little, but was finally obliged to make use of the personal influence that I had fortunately acquired in the previous negotiations, over the principal personages of the congress. Prince Metternich, and the Count Nesselrode, not wishing to be disobliging to me, both had me invited to a conference which was to have been held at the office of the minister of foreign affairs. Count de Labrador, minister of Spain, with whom I had the honour to support a common cause in the deliberations of the congress, received the same invitation.

I went to the office of the minister of state at the hour indicated, and found there, Lord Castlereagh, Prince von Hardenberg, Herr von Humboldt, and Herr von Gentz, a man of distinguished talents, who fulfilled the function of secretary. The protocol of the preceding sittings was on the table. I mention all the details of that first sitting, because it decided the position of France at the congress. Prince Metternich opened it by a few sentences on the duty of the congress to give solidity to the peace which had just been restored to Europe. The Prince von Hardenberg added, that in order to consolidate the peace it was indispensable that the engagements that followed perforce from the war should be religiously kept, and that such was the intention of the allied powers.

Placed by the side of Prince von Hardenberg, I was naturally forced to speak after him, and after having said a few words on the good fortune of

France in finding herself in relations of confidence and friendship with all the cabinets of Europe, I remarked that the Prince von Hardenberg had let fall an expression that appeared to me to belong to other times, for that they had both of them spoken of the intentions of the *allied powers.* I declared that *allied powers,* and a *congress* in which powers that were not allied were to be found, were in my eyes very little able to arrange affairs loyally together. I repeated with some astonishment and even warmth, the word *allied powers . . . "allied,"* I said, "and against whom? It is no longer against Napoleon—he is on the isle of Elba . . . it is no longer against France; for peace has been made . . . it is surely not against the King of France; he is a guarantee of the duration of that peace. Gentlemen, let us speak frankly; if there are still *allied powers,* I am one too many here."—I perceived that I had produced some impression, and especially on Herr von Gentz. I continued: "And nevertheless if I were not here, I should decidedly be missed. Gentlemen, I am perhaps the only one who asks nothing. Great esteem is all I would have for France. She is sufficiently powerful by her resources, her extent of territory, by the number and intelligence of her inhabitants, by the contiguity of her provinces, by the unity of her administration, by the defences with which nature and art have guaranteed her frontiers. I want nothing, I repeat it, but I bring you a great deal. The presence of a minister of Louis XVIII consecrates here the principle upon which all social order rests. The first need of Europe is to banish for ever the opinion that right can be acquired by conquest alone, and to cause the revival of that sacred principle of legitimacy from which all order and stability spring."

After a few moments' silence, Count Labrador (of Spain) made, in his proud and piquant language, a declaration almost identical with my own. Embarrassment was depicted on every face. They denied and explained in the same breath all that had taken place before this meeting. I profited by this moment in order to make a few concessions to the pride that I saw thus hurt. I said that in an assembly as numerous as the congress, where one was obliged to occupy oneself with so many different matters, to regulate questions of the first importance, and to decide a host of secondary interests, it was very difficult, nay even impossible, to reach any result by treating of all these subjects in general assemblies, but that some means of distributing and classifying all the business could be found without wounding either the interest or the dignity of any of the powers.

This language, though vague, yet pointed out the possibility of a particular direction being given to general business, and thus permitted the assembled ministers to reconsider what they had done, and to regard it all as null; while Herr von Gentz drew up the protocols of the previous sittings, and arranged one for that day. That protocol constituted the reports of the first sitting, and, in order to officially date our arrival at the congress, I signed it. From that time there was no conference among the great powers in which France did not take a part.

Thus, at the end of the month of October, 1814, I was able to write to Paris, that the house of Bourbon, which had only returned to France five months ago, and France herself, who had been conquered five months previously, found themselves already replaced to their proper place in Europe, and had again regained that influence that belonged to them, in the most important deliberations of the congress.

[113] *CZAR ALEXANDER PROPOSES A HOLY ALLIANCE* *

Czar Alexander I, the creator of the Holy Alliance, was probably the only ruler who took the document seriously. Yet, the Holy Alliance was so well publicized that to many liberals it seemed to symbolize reactionary repression. Actually, the basis for the Concert of Europe was the more effective bond of the Quadruple Alliance.

In the Name of the Very Holy and Indivisible Trinity.

Their majesties, the Emperor of Austria, the King of Prussia and the Emperor of Russia, in view of the great events which the last three years have brought to pass in Europe and in view especially of the benefits which it has pleased Divine Providence to confer upon those states whose governments have placed their confidence and their hope in Him alone, having reached the profound conviction that the policy of the powers, in their mutual relations, ought to be guided by the sublime truths taught by the eternal religion of God our Saviour, solemnly declare that the present act has no other aim than to manifest to the world their unchangeable determination to adopt no other rule of conduct, either in the government of their respective countries or in their political relations with other governments, than the precepts of that holy religion, the precepts of justice, charity and peace. These, far from being applicable exclusively to private life, ought on the contrary directly to control the resolutions of princes and to guide their steps as the sole means of establishing human institutions and of remedying their imperfections. Hence their majesties have agreed upon the following articles:

Article I. Conformably to the words of Holy Scripture which command all men to look upon each other as brothers, the three contracting monarchs will continue united by the bonds of a true and indissoluble fraternity and,

* *Translations and Reprints from the Original Sources of European History* (Philadelphia: University of Pennsylvania, 1894), Series I, Vol. I, No. 3, pp. 9–10.

regarding themselves as compatriots, they shall lend aid and assistance to each other on all occasions and in all places, [and] viewing themselves, in their relations to their subjects and to their armies, as fathers of families, they shall direct them in the same spirit of fraternity by which they are animated for the protection of religion, peace and justice.

Article II. Hence the sole principle of conduct, be it between the said government or their subjects, shall be that of rendering mutual service, and testifying by unceasing good-will, the mutual affection with which they should be animated. Considering themselves all as members of one great Christian nation, the three allied princes look upon themselves as delegates of Providence called upon to govern three branches of the same family, viz: Austria, Russia and Prussia. They thus confess that the Christian nation, of which they and their people form a part, has in reality no other sovereign than He alone to whom belongs by right the power, for in Him alone are to be found all the treasures of love, of knowledge, and of infinite wisdom, that is to say God, our Divine Saviour Jesus Christ, the word of the Most High, the word of life. Their majesties recommend, therefore, to their peoples, as the sole means of enjoying that peace which springs from a good conscience and is alone enduring, to fortify themselves each day in the principles and practice of those duties which the Divine Saviour has taught to men.

Article III. All those powers who wish solemnly to make avowal of the sacred principles which have dictated the present act, and who would recognize how important it is to the happiness of nations, too long agitated, that these truths should hereafter exercise upon human destiny all the influence belonging to them, shall be received into this Holy Alliance with as much cordiality as affection.

Engrossed in three copies and signed at Paris, year of grace, 1815, September 14/26.

FRANCIS
Signed FREDERICK WILLIAM
ALEXANDER

[114] *METTERNICH EXPLAINS HIS POLITICAL FAITH* *

Prince Clemens von Metternich (1773–1859), Austrian chief minister for nearly forty years, established within the vast Austrian Empire a model conservative

* *Memoires of Prince Metternich,* ed. by Prince Richard Metternich and trans. by Mrs. Alexander Napier (New York: Charles Scribner's Sons, 1881), Vol. III, pp. 455, 462–463, 465–467, 469–471, 475.

state. In Germany, Metternich used the mechanism of the Germanic Confederation to enforce a program of reaction. The same policy was imposed on most of Italy by the presence of Austrian troops and Hapsburg princes. The selection below forms part of a secret memorandum of 1820 from Metternich to Czar Alexander.

Kings have to calculate the chances of their very existence in the immediate future; passions are let loose, and league together to overthrow everything which society respects as the basis of its existence; religion, public morality, laws, customs, rights, and duties, all are attacked, confounded, overthrown, or called in question. The great mass of the people are tranquil spectators of these attacks and revolutions, and of the absolute want of all means of defence. A few are carried off by the torrent, but the wishes of the immense majority are to maintain a repose which exists no longer, and of which even the first elements seem to be lost.

The scenes of horror which accompanied the first phases of the French Revolution prevented the rapid propagation of its subversive principles beyond the frontiers of France, and the wars of conquest which succeeded them gave to the public mind a direction little favourable to revolutionary principles. Thus the Jacobin propaganda failed entirely to realise criminal hopes.

Nevertheless the revolutionary seed had penetrated into every country and spread more or less. It was greatly developed under the *régime* of the military despotism of Bonaparte. His conquests displaced a number of laws, institutions, and customs; broke through bonds sacred among all nations, strong enough to resist time itself; which is more than can be said of certain benefits conferred by these innovators. From these perturbations it followed that the revolutionary spirit could in Germany, Italy, and later on in Spain, easily hide itself under the veil of patriotism.

The evil exists and it is enormous. We do not think we can better define it and its cause at all times and in all places than we have already done by the word "presumption," that inseparable companion of the half-educated, that spring of an unmeasured ambition, and yet easy to satisfy in times of trouble and confusion.

It is principally the middle classes of society which this moral gangrene has affected, and it is only among them that the real heads of the party are found.

For the great mass of the people it has no attraction and can have none. The labours to which this class—the real people—are obliged to devote themselves, are too continuous and too positive to allow them to throw themselves into vague abstractions and ambitions. The people know what is the happiest thing for them: namely, to be able to count on the morrow, for it is the morrow which will repay them for the cares and sorrows of to-day. The laws which afford a just protection to individuals, to families, and to property, are quite simple in their essence. The people dread any movement which injures industry and brings new burdens in its train.

There is besides scarcely any epoch which does not offer a rallying cry to some particular faction. This cry, since 1815, has been *Constitution.* But do not let us deceive ourselves: this word, susceptible of great latitude of interpretation, would be but imperfectly understood if we supposed that the factions attached quite the same meaning to it under the different *régimes.* Such is certainly not the case. In pure monarchies it is qualified by the name of "national representation." In countries which have lately been brought under the representative *régime* it is called "development," and promises charters and fundamental laws. In the only State which possesses an ancient national representation it takes "reform" as its object. Everywhere it means change and trouble.

We are convinced that society can no longer be saved without strong and vigorous resolutions on the part of the Governments still free in their opinions and actions.

We are also convinced that this may yet be, if the Governments face the truth, if they free themselves from all illusion, if they join their ranks and take their stand on a line of correct, unambiguous, and frankly announced principles.

By this course the monarchs will fulfil the duties imposed upon them by Him, who, by entrusting them with power, has charged them to watch over the maintenance of justice, and the rights of all, to avoid the paths of error, and tread firmly in the way of truth.

Union between the monarchs is the basis of the policy which must now be followed to save society from total ruin.

In short, let the great monarchs strengthen their union, and prove to the world that if it exists, it is beneficent, and ensures the political peace of Europe: that it is powerful only for the maintenance of tranquility at a time when so many attacks are directed against it; that the principles which they profess are paternal and protective, menacing only the disturbers of public tranquility.

[115] *THE CARLSBAD DECREES MARK THE CONSERVATIVE TRIUMPH IN GERMANY* *

August von Kotzebue, a German dramatist and propagandist in the pay of the Russian Czar, was murdered in 1819 by a liberal university student. Metternich, thoroughly alarmed by the spread of liberalism among German professors, students, and journalists, called other German conservative statesmen to an emergency conference at Carlsbad, where the following resolutions were agreed upon. They were subsequently approved by the Diet of the Germanic Confederation.

Provisional Decree Relating to the Universities, Unanimously Adopted September 20, 1819

1. A special representative of the ruler of each state shall be appointed for each university with appropriate instructions and extended powers, and who shall reside in the place where the university is situated. This office may devolve upon the existing Curator or upon any other individual whom the government may deem qualified.

The function of this agent shall be to see to the strictest enforcement of existing laws and disciplinary regulations; to observe carefully the spirit which is shown by the instructors in the university in their public lectures and regular courses, and without directly interfering in scientific matters or in the methods of teaching, to give a salutary direction to the instruction, having in view the future attitude of the students. Lastly, they shall devote unceasing attention to everything that may promote morality, good order and outward propriety among the students.

The relation of these special agents to the Senate of the university, as well as all details relating to the extent of their duties and to their manner of action, shall be included in the instructions furnished by the superior government officials. These instructions shall be as precise as the circumstances which have dictated the appointment of the agents in question shall permit.

2. The confederated governments mutually pledge themselves to remove from the universities or other public educational institutions all teachers who, by obvious deviation from their duty or by exceeding the limits of their functions, or by the abuse of their legitimate influence over the youthful minds, or by propagating harmful doctrines hostile to the public order or subversive of existing governmental institutions, shall have unmistakably proved their unfitness for the important office intrusted to them. No obstacle

* *Translations and Reprints from the Original Sources of European History* (Philadelphia: University of Pennsylvania, 1894), Series I, Vol. I, No. 3, pp. 16–20.

whatever shall prevent the execution of this provision so long as it shall remain in force and until such time as this matter shall be definitely regulated. Removals of this character shall, however, never be made except upon the recommendation, accompanied with full reasons, of the aforesaid special agent of the government at the university or in view of a report previously required from him.

No teacher who shall have been removed in this manner shall be again appointed to a position in any public institution of learning in another state of the Union.

3. Those laws which have for a long period been directed against secret and unauthorized societies in the universities, shall be strictly enforced. These laws apply especially to that association established some years since under the name Universal Students' Union (*Allgemeine Burschenschaft*), since the very conception of the society implies the utterly unallowable plan of permanent fellowship and constant communication between the various universities. The duty of especial watchfulness in this matter should be impressed upon the special agents of the government.

The governments mutually agree that such persons as shall, after the publication of the present decree, be shown to have remained in secret or unauthorized associations or shall have entered such associations, shall not be admitted to any public office.

4. No student, who shall be expelled from a university by a decision of the University Senate, which was ratified or prompted by the agent of the government, or who shall have left the institution in order to escape expulsion, shall be received in any other university. Nor, in general, shall any student be admitted to another university without a satisfactory certificate of his good conduct at the university he has left.

Press Laws for Five Years

1. So long as this decree shall remain in force no publication which appears in the form of daily issues or as a serial not exceeding twenty sheets of printed matter shall go to press in any state of the Union without the previous knowledge and approval of the state officials.

Establishment of an Investigating Committee at Mainz

Article I. Within a fortnight, reckoning from the passage of this decree, there shall convene, under the auspices of the Confederation, in the city and federal fortress of Mainz, an Extraordinary Commission of Investigation to consist of seven members including the chairman.

Article II. The object of the Commission shall be a joint investigation, as thorough and extensive as possible, of the facts relating to the origin and manifold ramifications of the revolutionary plots and demagogical associations directed against the existing Constitution and internal peace both of the Union and of the individual states: of the existence of which plots more or less clear evidence is to be had already, or may be produced in the course of the investigation.

[116] *LORD JOHN RUSSELL PRESENTS THE REFORM BILL* *

While Metternich's system of rigid reaction prevailed in most of Europe, Liberals and Radicals in England successfully overthrew the repressive Tory regime by concentrating their attacks on the inequality of voting districts. The Great Reform Act of 1832 eliminated rotten boroughs, gave representation to the new industrial cities, and enfranchised a few additional voters.

. . . parliament met . . . on the 3rd of February. Ministers had hitherto veiled in profound secrecy the plan of Reform which they intended to introduce. . . . it was not until the 1st of March, that it was introduced into the House of Commons. It was introduced by lord John Russell, to whom, although not a cabinet minister, this duty had been intrusted, in consideration of his lordship having made, on many occasions, many motions for many partial changes in the existing state of the representation.

His lordship declared in the outset that the measure which he was about to propose had been formed in the mind of earl Grey himself: the world believed that the greater portion of the premier's mind, had been found, on this occasion, to reside within the body of his son-in-law, lord Durham. His lordship farther declared, that the object of ministers had been . . . to frame a measure with which every reasonable man in the country would be satisfied: that they wished to take their stand between two hostile parties, neither agreeing with the fanaticism of others, that only one particular reform could be wholesome or saisfactory, but taking a firm and steadfast ground between abuses which were to be amended, and convulsions which were to be averted. These were all most excellent general expressions.

His lordship next laid it down as one principle on which he and his colleagues agreed, that the question of *right* was in favour of the reformers; for the ancient constitution of the country declared that no man should be taxed for the support of the state who had not consented, by himself or his representative to the imposition of the taxes. The statute *de Tallagio non concedendo* spoke of the same language; and, although some historical

* "History," *The Annual Register, 1831* (London, 1832), pp. 5–7.

doubts had been thrown upon it, its legal meaning had never been questioned. It included "all the freemen of the land"; and it provided that each county should send to the Commons two knights, each city two burgesses, and each borough two members. About an 100 places sent representatives, and thirty or forty others occasionally enjoyed the privilege; but it was discontinued or revived as they rose or fell in the scale of wealth, and importance. No doubt, at that early period, the House of Commons did represent the people of England; but, added his lordship, there is likewise no doubt, that the House of Commons, as it presently subsists, does not represent the people of England.

The right being thus in favour of reform, the house would find that the result would be the same, when they looked to what was reasonable; for it would be impossible to keep the constitution of the House as it at present existed. Who had not heard of the fame of this country, that in wealth it was unparalleled, in civilization unrivalled, and in freedom unequalled, in the history of the empires of the world? Now suppose that a foreigner, well acquainted with these facts, were told that in this most wealthy, most civilized, and most free country, the representatives of the people, the guardians of her liberties, were chosen only every six years, would he not be very curious and very anxious to hear in what way that operation was performed, by which this great and wise nation selected the members who were to represent them, and upon whom depended their fortunes and their rights? Would not such a foreigner be much astonished if he were taken to a green mound and informed that it sent two members to the British parliament?—if he were shown a stone wall, and told that it also sent two members to the British parliament? . . . He would be still more astonished were he to go into the northern part of the country, and were to see flourishing towns, containing immense manufactories and depositories of every sort of merchandize, and be informed that these places sent no representatives to parliament. He would be still more astonished, were he taken to a great and opulent town—Liverpool for instance—and were to observe the manner in which general elections were there conducted. He would see bribery prevail to the greatest extent; he would see men openly paid for their votes; and he would be astonished that a nation, whose representatives were so chosen, should be at all competent to perform the functions of legislation. The people called loudly for reform, saying that whatever good existed in the constitution of this House—whatever confidence was placed in it by the people, was completely gone. Whatever might be thought of particular acts, the confidence of the country in the constitution of the House had long ceased; and so long as towns like Leeds and Manchester elected no representatives, while such places as Gatton and Old Sarum did, it was impossible to say that the representation was fairly and properly carried on. From these premises his lordship arrived at this conclusion—if the case be one of right, it is in favour of reform—if it be a question of reason it is in favour of reform—if it be a question of expediency, expedience calls loudly for it.

His lordship then stated the plan by which ministers proposed to meet and satisfy the demand for reform which they averred themselves to believe could no longer be resisted. That plan had been so framed as to remove the reasonable complaints of the people, and these complaints again were principally directed, first, against nomination by individuals; secondly, elections by close corporations; thirdly, the expenses of elections. In so far as concerned the first two grounds of complaint, the plan of ministers consisted first of disfranchisement, in order to get rid of places which had hitherto sent members to parliament: secondly, of enfranchisement, in order to enable places which had hitherto been unrepresented, to elect members: thirdly, of an extension of the franchise, in order to increase the number of electors in those places which were to be allowed to retain in whole, or in part, their existing privilege of sending members to the House of Commons.

[117] *PRESIDENT MONROE PROPOSES A NEW PRINCIPLE OF AMERICAN FOREIGN POLICY* *

Following the Latin American wars of independence of 1810–1822, the United States offered recognition to the new nations to the south, but feared European intervention in the Western Hemisphere. The Monroe Doctrine was contained in an address to Congress by President Monroe on December 2, 1823.

At the proposal of the Russian Imperial Government, made through the minister of the Emperor, residing here, a full power and instructions have been transmitted to the minister of the United States at St. Petersburg to arrange by amicable negotiation the respective rights and interests of the two nations on the northwest coast of this continent. A similar proposal has been made by His Imperial Majesty, to the Government of Great Britain, which has likewise been acceded to. The Government of the United States has been desirous by this friendly proceeding of manifesting the great value which they have invariably attached to the friendship of the Emperor and their solicitude to cultivate the best understanding with his Government. In the discussions to which this interest has given rise and in the arrangements by which they may terminate the occasion has been judged proper

* James D. Richardson, ed., *A Compilation of the Messages and Papers of the Presidents* (New York, 1897), Vol. II, pp. 207 ff.

for asserting as a principle in which the rights and interests of the United States are involved, that the American continents, by the free and independent condition which they have assumed and maintain, are henceforth not to be considered as subjects for future colonization by any European powers. . . .

It was stated at the commencement of the last session that a great effort was then making in Spain and Portugal to improve the condition of the people of those countries, and that it appeared to be conducted with extraordinary moderation. It need scarcely be remarked that the result has been so far very different from what was then anticipated. Of events in that quarter of the globe, with which we have so much intercourse, and from which we derive our origin, we have always been anxious and interested spectators. The citizens of the United States cherish sentiments the most friendly in favor of the liberty and happiness of their fellowmen on that side of the Atlantic. In the wars of the European powers in matters relating to themselves we have never taken any part, nor does it comport with our policy so to do. It is only when our rights are invaded or seriously menaced that we resent injuries or make preparation for our defense. With the movements in this hemisphere we are of necessity more immediately connected, and by causes which must be obvious to all enlightened and impartial observers. The political system of the allied powers is essentially different in this respect from that of America. This difference proceeds from that which exists in their respective Governments, and to the defence of our own, which has been achieved by the loss of so much blood and treasure, and matured by the wisdom of their most enlightened citizens, and under which we have enjoyed unexampled felicity, this whole nation is devoted We owe it, therefore, to candor and to the amicable relations existing between the United States and those powers to declare that we should consider any attempt on their part to extend their system to any portions of this hemisphere as dangerous to our peace and safety. With the existing colonies or dependencies of any European power we have not interfered and shall not interfere. But with the Governments who have declared their independence and maintained it, and whose independence we have, on great consideration and on just principles, acknowledged, we could not view any interposition for the purpose of oppressing them, or controlling in any other manner their destiny, by any European power in any other light than as the manifestation of an unfriendly disposition towards the United States. In the war between those new Governments and Spain we declared our neutrality at the time of their recognition, and to this we have adhered, and shall continue to adhere, provided no change shall occur which, in the judgment of the competent authorities of this Government, shall make a corresponding change on the part of the United States indispensable to their security.

The late events in Spain and Portugal shew [*sic*] that Europe is still unsettled. Of this important fact, no stronger proof can be adduced, than that the allied powers should have thought it proper, on any principle satisfactory to themselves, to have interposed by force in the internal concerns of Spain. To what extent such interposition may be carried, on the same principle, is a question, in which all independent powers whose governments differ from theirs are interested, even those most remote, and surely none more so than the United States. Our policy in regard to Europe, which was adopted at an early stage of the wars which have so long agitated that quarter of the globe, nevertheless remains the same, which is, not to interfere in the internal concerns of any of its powers; to consider the Government *de facto* as the legitimate government for us; to cultivate friendly relations with it, and to preserve those relations by a frank, firm, and manly policy, meeting in all instances the just claims of every power, submitting to injuries from none. But in regard to those continents circumstances are eminently and conspicuously different. It is impossible that the allied powers should extend their political systems to any portion of either continent without endangering our peace and happiness; nor can anyone believe, that our southern brethren, if left to themselves, would adopt it of their own accord. It is equally impossible, therefore, that we should behold such interposition in any form with indifference. If we look to the comparative strength and resources of Spain and those new governments, and their distance from each other, it must be obvious that she can never subdue them. It is still the true policy of the United States to leave the parties to themselves, in the hope that other powers will pursue the same course.

20

Romanticism and Science

Classicism, which had dominated European culture since the Renaissance, gave way in the late eighteenth and early nineteenth centuries to the Romantic movement. Romantic writers and artists stressed emotion and sentiment rather than pure reason, studied the individual instead of society, and sought originality and diversity rather than conformity to fixed standards. In religion, Methodists and Baptists increased their numbers, while a group of English intellectuals followed John Henry Newman as converts to Catholicism. Romanticism harmonized well with the growing surge of nationalism, and such a writer as Mazzini was both a Romanticist and a liberal nationalist. Quite apart from the world of Romanticism, individual scientists produced valuable new theories based on personal observation, experiment, and reason.

[118] *CLASSICISM IS OVERTHROWN BY THE ROMANTIC REVOLUTION* *

The Romantic movement is difficult to define and has been frequently misunderstood and misinterpreted by its critics. Jacques Barzun, the perceptive author of

* Jacques Barzun, *Romanticism and the Modern Ego* (Boston: Little, Brown and Company, 1943), pp. 82–84. Copyright 1943 by Jacques Barzun. Reprinted by permission of Little, Brown and Company.

the following selection, sees Romanticism as a form of realism and finds that Romantic writers were not only creative and imaginative, but were vigorously realistic as well.

Before we come to particulars, the general setting may be put in a few words: classicism perished from an excess of abstraction and generality. This was most visibly true in the several arts, and nothing shows more clearly the romanticists' realistic purpose than their refusal to go on imitating forms whose contents had evaporated. Seeing this refusal, we believe too readily in the miscalled "romantic revolt." We imagine a sudden and irresponsible rebellion of brash young men against the wisdom and experience of their elders. It was nothing of the kind. The breaking away was reluctant, painful, and deliberate. A whole generation of geniuses came to see that to continue writing in the manner of Paley, and Pye, Gottsched, Lebrun, and Delille, was intellectually impossible.

I use literary instances, but the other arts would furnish exact parallels. There was no choice but to begin afresh. The romanticist was in the position of a primitive with the seven arts to create out of nothing. At the same time, he labored under the handicap of having "inimitable" classical masterpieces held up to him to imitate, even though the substance of these great works had already been spread thin over fifty years of copying. This was like asking someone to produce the finest champagne by further diluting the weakest grape juice; the romantic revolt consisted solely in refusing to do the undoable.

Having perforce given up conventional abstractions, clichés, diction, and rules, what did the romanticists turn to? The answer can be generalized: for substance they turned to the world about them; they tried to meet the claims of every existing reality, both internal and external. For form, they relied on earlier romantic periods and on their own inventive genius.

The characteristics of romanticism which the textbooks list as if they were whimsical and isolated preferences are merely the embodiment of what I have just said. As against poetic diction and "noble" words, the romanticists admitted all words, especially the neglected host of common words; as against the exclusive use of a selected Graeco-Roman mythology, they took in the Celtic and Germanic; as against the uniform setting and tone of classical tragedy, they studied and reproduced the real diversities known as "local color." As against the antique subjects and the set scale of pictorial merits prescribed by the Academy, they took in the whole world, seen and unseen, and the whole range of colors. As against the academic rules prohibiting the use of certain chords, tonalities, and modulations, they sought to use and give shape to all manageable combinations of sound. As against the assumption that no civilization had existed since the fall of Rome, they rediscovered the Middle Ages and the sixteenth century, and made history their dominant avocation. As against the provincial belief that Paris and London were the sole centers of civilized life, they traveled to remote places such as America and the Near East, and earned the name of "exotic" for their pains. As against the snobbish idea that the products of sophistication and refined living are the only topics worth treating, they began to treasure folk literature and folk music, and to draw the subject matter of their art from every class and condition of men. As against the materialistic view that whatever is must be tangible, they made room in their notion of reality for the world of dreams, the mysterious in man and nature, and the supernatural.

All this they did knowingly, deliberately, with the patience and tenacity of pioneers and explorers. So that to those who speak sneeringly of the "romantic revolt" one may offer the answer of Liancourt to Louis XVI, "No Sire, it is a revolution."

[119] *BYRON CONDEMNS NAPOLEONIC TYRANNY AND EXTOLLS GREEK LIBERTY* *

Enthusiastically Romantic in both his poetry and his private life, George Gordon, Lord Byron (1788–1824), was also a fervent advocate of freedom. Two aspects of Byron's Romantic liberalism are revealed here: In the first selection his hero, Harold, muses at the battlefield of Waterloo on the passing of Napoleonic tyranny; in the second, Harold encourages the Greeks to cast off Turkish domination.

XVII

Stop! for thy tread is on an Empire's dust!
An Earthquake's spoil is sepulchred below!
Is the spot marked with no colossal bust?
Nor column trophied for triumphal show?
None; but the moral's truth tells simpler so,
As the ground was before, thus let it be;—
How that red rain hath made the harvest grow!
And is this all the world has gained by thee,
Thou first and last of fields! king-making Victory?

XVIII

And Harold stands upon this place of skulls,
The grave of France, the deadly Waterloo!

* George Gordon, Lord Byron, *Childe Harold's Pilgrimage,* Canto II, Stanzas Lxxiii–Lxxvi; Canto III, Stanzas Xvii–Xx.

How in an hour the power which gave annuls
Its gifts, transferring fame as fleeting too!
In "pride of place" here last the eagle flew,
Then tore with bloody talon the rent plain,
Pierced by the shaft of banded nations through;
Ambition's life and labours all were vain;
He wears the shattered links of the world's broken chain.

XIX

Fit retribution! Gaul may champ the bit
And foam in fetters;—but is Earth more free?
Did nations combat to make *One* submit;
Or league to teach all kings true sovereignty?
What! shall reviving thraldom again be
The patched-up idol of enlightened days?
Shall we, who struck the Lion down, shall we
Pay the Wolf homage? proffering lowly gaze
And servile knees to thrones? No; prove before ye praise!

XX

If not, o'er one fallen despot boast no more!
In vain fair cheeks were furrowed with hot tears
For Europe's flowers long rooted up before
The trampler of her vineyards; in vain years
Of death, depopulation, bondage, fears,
Have all been borne, and broken by the accord
Of roused-up millions: all that most endears
Glory, is when the myrtle wreathes a sword
Such as Harmodius drew on Athens' tyrant lord.

* * * *

LXXIII

Fair Greece! sad relic of departed worth!
Immortal, though no more; though fallen, great;
Who now shall lead thy scattered children forth,
And long accustomed bondage uncreate?
Not such thy sons who whilome did await,
The hopeless warriors of a willing doom,
In bleak Thermopylae's sepulchral strait—
Oh! who that gallant spirit shall resume,
Leap from Eurotas' banks, and call thee from the tomb?

LXXIV

Spirit of Freedom! when on Phyle's brow
Thou sat'st with Trasybulus and his train,
Couldst thou forebode the dismal hour which now
Dims the green beauties of thine Attic plain?
Not thirty tyrants now enforce the chain,
But every carle can lord it o'er thy land;
Nor rise thy sons, but idly rail in vain,
Trembling beneath the scourge of Turkish hand,
From birth till death enslaved; in word, in deed, unmanned.

LXXV

In all save form alone, how changed! and who
That marks the fire still sparkling in each eye,
Who but would deem their bosoms burned anew
With thy unquenchèd beam, lost Liberty!
And many dream withal the hour is nigh
That gives them back their father's heritage:
For foreign arms and aid they fondly sigh,
Nor solely dare encounter hostile rage,
Or tear their name defiled from Slavery's mournful page.

LXXVI

Hereditary bondsmen! know ye not
Who would be free themselves must strike the blow?
By their right arms the conquest must be wrought?
Will Gaul or Moscovite redress ye? no!
True, they may lay your proud despoilers low,
But not for you will Freedom's altars flame.
Shades of the Helots! triumph o'er your foe:
Greece! change thy lords, thy state is still the same;
Thy glorious day is o'er, but not thine years of shame.

[120] *DON CARLOS VISITS THE TOMB OF CHARLEMAGNE* *

Victor Hugo (1802–1885), the greatest of the French Romantic writers, was equally at home in the fields of drama, poetry, essay, satire, novel, or literary

* Victor Hugo, *Hernani,* Act IV, in *Dramas* (Boston and New York: University Press Co., n.d.), Vol. I, pp. 60–63.

criticism. Hernani, *his most famous play, is intensely emotional and thoroughly Romantic. At its opening performance in Paris in 1830, angry Classicists staged a riot. In this scene from* Hernani, *Don Carlos (Emperor Charles V) visits the tomb of Charlemagne, while awaiting his election as Holy Roman Emperor.*

Scene. *The monumental caverns of Aix-la-Chapelle. Spacious vaults of Lombard architecture, low and massy pillars, with ornamental capitals. On the right the tomb of Charlemagne, with a small low door of brass, the inscription "Karolo Magno" rendered conspicuous by the light of a lamp, which is suspended singly from the centre of the vaults. The eye is lost in the undefined depths of the Arcades.*

Enter Carlos and Ricardo, the latter leading the way with a lantern.

DON RICARDO. We have now, my liege, wound through the murky labyrinth. Here, no doubt, the traitors will assemble; and here is your chosen concealment.

DON CARLOS. We'll use it anon. Thanks to our diligence and the speed of our horses, we are far in advance of their appointed hour. And this, then, is to be the council hall of conspiracy? They'll sharpen their daggers on the tomb of Charlemagne, as if Carlos of Castile were unworthy to succeed him. Your list of these formidable conspirators.

DON RICARDO. 'T is here my liege, with the exception of two who have lately reinforced them, and who appear to be father and son; but their names I know not.

DON CARLOS. We may soon engrave them on their monument for public information. But in thus disposing of our pygmy foes, what is our dependence on our friends? The empire, Count, the empire! The crisis of its fate is near at hand.

DON RICARDO. The council, sire, is at this moment deliberating. You will succeed.

DON CARLOS. Three voices, as I think, would secure me. Three suffrages! Could I but purchase them for as many cities,—Ghent, Toledo, Salamanca. In Spain or Flanders let them make their choice, and they shall have the richest and the proudest.

DON RICARDO. 'T were a tempting bribe, sire.

DON CARLOS. 'T is nothing, Count,—a trifle. (*Tapping him familiarly.*) Cities, my sagacious friend, may be recovered; the empire once lost becomes a forlorn hope. (*Ricardo puts on his hat.*) Your hat, sir!

DON RICARDO. My liege, you have touched and familiarly accosted me. I am a grandee of Spain, *ipso facto.*

DON CARLOS. Ha, ha, ha! You are learned in the law, Count, and prompt at illustration. We venture not to litigate your claim, and therefore, grandee, we must admit you. Our Donna Zanthe, how has she sustained her journey?

DON RICARDO. Marvellously well, sire, since the worthy duchess you gave her in charge to, and her own experience, have assured her of your Highness's chivalrous forbearance.

DON CARLOS. Therein she flatters not *my* love, my lord.
But she is woman still, and should I triumph—
Have you considered our impatience, Count?
How shall we quickliest know the council's choice?

DON RICARDO. From the cannon's mouth, my liege. The discharge of one only will announce the election of the Duke of Saxony; two will report for Francis; and three will thunder for your Highness.

DON CARLOS. 'T is well devised. They'll boldly speak the worst, unminced with flattery. And now to prepare for our conspirators,—these self-elected guardians of the state and empire! Forget not my instructions.

DON RICARDO. I do not, my liege.

DON CARLOS. The key of the monument.

DON RICARDO. 'T is here! (*Gives it.*)

DON CARLOS. Now leave us, and obey our orders strictly.

(*Exit Ricardo, R.*)

DON CARLOS (*remains for a time in profound abstraction, then turns toward the tomb of Charlemagne*).

Charlemagne! mighty spirit! now enthroned
Above this coil and buzz of mortal passions,
Oh, let me commune with thee! Say, is all
Thy power, the wisdom and the mastery
Of soul, that with thy mortal nature came
On earth, gone with it,—perished, marbled up
With that poor dust, which balanced with the vilest
Nor weighs, nor values more? Let them be dumb
Who deem so, while a heart is swelling here,
That unrebuked, even in this awful presence,
Dares hope to track thee in thy giant path,
And do thy mighty deeds. Oh, empire! empire!
Winning thee fairly shall I not desire thee?
And having won thee, when I spot thy purple
With sloth or slavish passion, to my bosom
Take other counsellors than truth and justice,
Then strip it from me, Heaven, and degrade
The mightiest monarch to the meanest man.
And thou, immortal spirit! by my strength;

Sustain me; poise me on my height, and yield me
Awhile thy sanctuary. Dare I enter?
Should I in shadowy majesty behold him,
How would he palsy my presumption? Hark!
What step, save mine, profanes thy sacred rest?
(*Smiling.*) I had forgot. I wait for my assassins.
They come.

(*He enters the tomb and closes it. Several men enter with cautious step, enveloped in their mantles, finally meet each other, and speak in a low voice.*)

[121] *MAZZINI FOUNDS THE YOUNG ITALY MOVEMENT* *

Joseph (or Giuseppe) Mazzini (1805–1872), an unsuccessful revolutionary but a gifted writer, lifted the Italian movement for political unity to a high spiritual plane. He lived most of his life as an exile from his homeland and founded Young Italy in 1831 to inspire his fellow Italians to work for a united democratic republic.

It was during these months of imprisonment in Savona that I conceived the plan of the association of Young Italy (*La Giovina Italia*). I meditated deeply upon the principles upon which to base the organisation of the party, the aim and purpose of its labours—which I intended should be publicly declared—the method of its formation, the individuals to be selected to aid me in its creation, and the possibility of linking its operations with those of the existing revolutionary elements of Europe.

We were few in number, young in years, and of limited means and influence; but I believed the whole problem to consist in appealing to the true instincts and tendencies of the Italian heart, mute at that time, but revealed to us both by history and our own previsions of the future. Our strength must lie in our right appreciation of what those instincts and tendencies really were.

All great national enterprises have ever been originated by men of the people, whose sole strength lay in that power of *faith* and of *will,* which neither counts obstacles nor measures time. Men of means and influence follow after, either to support and carry on the movement created by the first, or, as too often happens, to divert it from its original aim.

I was not influenced by any mere political conception, nor idea of ele-

* *The Living Thoughts of Mazzini,* presented by Ignazio Silone (New York: Longmans, Green and Company, 1939), pp. 47–50. Used by permission of David McKay Company, Inc., New York, and Cassell and Company, Ltd., London.

vating the condition of the single people whom I saw thus dismembered, degraded, and oppressed; the parent thought of my every design was a presentiment that regenerated Italy was destined to arise the *initiatrix* of a new life, and a new and powerful Unity to all the nations of Europe.

Even at that time, in spite of the fascination exercised over my mind by the fervid words in which France at that day asserted her right of leadership amid the general silence, the idea was dimly stirring within me to which I gave expression six years later—the sense of a void, a want in Europe.

I felt that authority—true righteous and holy authority—the search after which, whether conscious or not, is in fact the secret of our human life, and which is only irrationally denied by those who confound it with its false semblance or shadow, and imagine they have abolished God Himself, when they have but abolished an idol;—I felt that authority had vanished, and become extinct in Europe; and that for this reason no power of *initiative* existed in any of the peoples of Europe.

The labours, studies, and sorrows of my life have not only justified and confirmed this idea, but have transformed it into a *faith.* And if ever—though I may not think it—I should live to see Italy One, and to pass one year of solitude in some corner of my own land, or of this land where I now write, and which affection has rendered a second country to me, I shall endeavor to develop and reduce the consequences which flow from this idea, and are of far greater importance than most men believe.

At that time even the immature conception inspired me with a mighty hope that flashed before my spirit like a star. I saw regenerate Italy becoming at one bound the missionary of a religion of progress and fraternity, far grander and vaster than that she gave to humanity in the past.

The worship of Rome was a part of my being. The great Unity, the One Life of the world, had twice been elaborated within her walls. Other peoples—their brief mission fulfilled—disappeared for ever. To none save to her had it been given twice to guide and direct the world. There, life was eternal, death unknown. There, upon the vestiges of an epoch of civilisation anterior to the Grecian, which had had its seat in Italy, and which the historical science of the future will show to have had a far wider external influence than the learned of our own day imagine—the Rome of the Republic, concluded by the Caesars, had arisen to consign the former world to oblivion, and borne her eagles over the known world, carrying with them the idea of right, the source of liberty.

In later days, while men were mourning over her as the sepulchre of the living, she had again arisen, greater than before, and at once constituted herself, through her Popes—as venerable once as abject now—the accepted centre of a new Unity, elevating the law from earth to heaven, and substituting to the idea of right an idea of duty—a duty common to all men, and therefore source of their equality.

Why should not a new Rome, the Rome of the Italian people—portents of whose coming I deemed I saw—arise to create a third and still vaster unity; to link together and harmonize earth and heaven, right and duty; and utter, not to individuals but to peoples, the great word Association—to make known to free men and equals their mission here below?

The immediate result of these ideas was to convince me that the labour to be undertaken was not merely a political, but above all a moral work; not negative, but religious; not founded upon any theory of self-interest, or well-being, but upon principles and upon duty.

During the first months of my university life my mind had been somewhat tainted by the doctrines of the foreign materialist school; but the study of history and the intuition of conscience—the only tests of truth—soon led me back to the spiritualism of our Italian fathers.

[122] *MICHAEL FARADAY DISCOVERS ELECTRO-MAGNETISM* *

Michael Faraday (1791–1867) was a brilliant, self-educated scientist, who had served early in his career as assistant to the great Sir Humphrey Davy. The assistant soon surpassed the master in originality and versatility. Faraday's discovery of electro-magnetic induction in 1831 and his subsequent invention of the dynamo provided the bases for most later developments of electrical machinery. He also discovered the anaesthetic properties of ether, developed the electroplating industrial process, and proposed a theory of electrons which was ignored for decades.

His mode of attacking any problem was intuitive rather than logical, though when on the track of a solution his reasoning, proceeding by process of elimination, of trial and error, was sound and logical enough. . . . Helmholtz, in his Faraday Lecture of 1881, said: "It is in the highest degree astonishing to see what a large number of general theorems, the methodical deduction of which requires the highest powers of mathematical analysis, he found by a kind of intuition, with the security of instinct, without the help of a single mathematical formula." He repeats this, evidently impressed by such a gift: "With a quite wonderful sagacity and intellectual precision, Faraday performed in his brain the work of a great mathematician without using a single mathematical formula. . . . The fundamental con-

* Wilfred L. Randell, *Michael Faraday* (London: Leonard Parsons, 1924), pp. 14, 15–16, 105–110.

ceptions by which Faraday was led to these much admired discoveries have not received an equal amount of consideration. They were very divergent from the trodden path of scientific theory, and appeared rather startling to his contemporaries. His principal aim was to express in his new conceptions only facts, with the least possible use of hypothetical substances and forces. This was really an advance in general scientific method, destined to purify science from the last remnants of metaphysics. Faraday was not the first, and not the only man, who had worked in this direction, but perhaps nobody else at his time did it so radically."

Since 1824 he had held the belief that as a current of electricity can cause a piece of soft iron to become a magnet, so, somehow, a magnet *ought* to be able to cause a current of electricity, or in some way, at any rate, to affect an existing current. But, try as he would—and he tried several times during the intervening years—the expected, the logical event, would not happen. In 1831 he succeeded. Ampere had caused electricity to produce magnetic effects and magnets; Faraday now, by means of magnets, elicited electrical action. This foreshadowed another crowning feat, the exposition of the inductive effects of electrical currents—that is, more simply worded, the fact that a current flowing through one wire causes or "induces" another current to flow through another wire near it, but not in any way directly connected with it. In December, 1824, he tried to obtain an electric current by means of a magnet closely approached to a wire, and on three occasions had made elaborate but unsuccessful attempts to produce a current in one wire either by means of a current in another wire or by a magnet.

He persevered in spite of his disappointments, and on August 29, 1831, he obtained the first evidence that an electric current can induce another current in a different and unconnected circuit. Writing to a friend, on September 23, he says: "I am busy just now again on electro-magnetism, and think I have got hold of a good thing, but can't say. It may be a weed instead of a fish that, after all my labours, I may at last pull up." Had he been able to foresee how these comparatively few weeks of work would revolutionize the world of electrical science and of industry in general, even his unfailing modesty might have been pardoned for yielding, for once, to a sense of pride and elation. In nine more days he arrived at definite results, and he described the whole series of epoch-making experiments in his first "Experimental Researches," read before the Royal Society on November 24 of the same year.

I give here, for their historical interest, a few sentences from two paragraphs in which he describes electrical induction and the experiment with a magnet:

"1. When an electric current is passed through one of two parallel wires, it causes at first a current in the same direction through the other, but this induced current does not last a moment, notwithstanding the inducing current (from the Voltaic battery) is continued; all seems unchanged, except that the principal current continues its course. But when the current is stopped, then a return current occurs in the wire under induction, of about the same intensity and momentary duration, but in the opposite direction to that first formed. . . .

"2. Then I found that magnets would induce just like voltaic currents, and by bringing helices and wires up to the poles of magnets, electrical currents were produced in them; these currents were able to deflect the galvanometer, or to make, by means of the helix, magnetic needles, or in one case even to give a spark. Hence the evolution of *electricity from magnetism.* The currents were not permanent. They ceased the moment the wires ceased to approach the magnet, because the new and apparently quiescent state was assumed, just as in the case of the induction of currents. But when the magnet was removed, and its induction therefore ceased, the return currents appeared as before."

[123] *NEWMAN DESCRIBES HIS EARLY RELIGIOUS BELIEFS* *

John Henry Newman was an Oxford scholar who felt greatly disturbed by the intellectual dominance of liberalism and its effect on religion in England. Newman was ordained in the Church of England in 1824, but his study of the theological bases of his church led him to Catholicism in 1845. Several other members of the "Oxford Movement" were also converted to Catholicism, and Newman himself was created a cardinal in 1879.

I have spoken of my firm confidence in my position; and now let me state more definitely what the position was which I took up, and the propositions about which I was so confident. These were three:—

1. First was the principle of dogma: my battle was with liberalism; by liberalism I meant the anti-dogmatic principle and its developments. This was the first point on which I was certain. Here I make a remark: persistence in a given belief is no sufficient test of its truth; but departure from it is at least a slur upon the man who has felt so certain about it. In proportion then as I had in 1832 a strong persuasion in beliefs which I have since given up, so far a sort of guilt attaches to me, not only for that vain confi-

* John Henry Newman, *Apologia Pro Vita Sua,* Third Edition (New York: D. Appleton and Company, 1865), pp. 95–99.

dence, but for my multiform conduct in consequence of it. But here I have the satisfaction of feeling that I have nothing to retract, and nothing to repent of. The main principle of the [Oxford] Movement is as dear to me now as it ever was. I have changed in many things: in this I have not. From the age of fifteen, dogma has been the fundamental principle of my religion: I know no other religion; I cannot enter into the idea of any other sort of religion; religion, as a mere sentiment, is to me a dream and a mockery. As well can there be filial love without the fact of a father, as devotion without the fact of a Supreme Being. What I held in 1816, I held in 1833, and I hold in 1864. Please God, I shall hold it to the end. . . .

2. Secondly, I was confident in the truth of a certain definite religious teaching, based upon this foundation of dogma; viz., that there was a visible Church with sacraments and rites which are the channels of invisible grace. I thought that this was the doctrine of Scripture, of the early Church, and of the Anglican Church. Here again, I have not changed in opinion; I am as certain now on this point as I was in 1833, and have never ceased to be certain. In 1834 and the following years I put this ecclesiastical doctrine on a broader basis, after reading Laud, Bramhall, and Stillingfleet and other Anglican divines on the one hand, and after prosecuting the study of the Fathers on the other; but the doctrine of 1833 was strengthened in me, not changed. . . .

And further, as to the Episcopal system, I founded it upon the Epistles of St. Ignatius, which inculcated it in various ways. One passage especially impressed itself upon me: speaking of cases of disobedience to ecclesiastical authority, he says, "A man does not deceive that Bishop whom he sees, but he practises rather upon the Bishop Invisible, and so the question is not with flesh, but with God, who knows the secret heart." I wished to act on this principle to the letter, and I may say with confidence that I never consciously transgressed it. I loved to act in the sight of my Bishop, as if I was, as it were, in the sight of God. It was one of my special safeguards against myself and of my supports; I could not go very wrong while I had reason to believe that I was in no respect displeasing him. It was not a mere formal obedience to rule that I put before me, but I desired to please him personally, as I considered him set over me by the Divine Hand. I was strict in observing my clerical engagements, not only because they *were* engagements, but because I considered myself simply as the servant and instrument of my Bishop. I did not care much for the Bench of Bishops, except as they might be the voice of my Church: nor should I have cared much for a Provincial Council; nor for a Diocesan Synod, presided over by my Bishop; all these matters seemed to me to be *jure ecclesiastico*, but what to me was *jure divino* was the voice of my Bishop in his own person. My own Bishop was my Pope; I knew no other; the successor of the Apostles, the Vicar of Christ. This was but a practical exhibition of the Anglican theory of Church Government, as I had already drawn it out myself. This continued all through my course; when at length in 1845 I wrote to Bishop Wiseman, in whose Vicariate I found myself, to announce my conversion [to Catholicism], I could find nothing better to say to him, than that I would obey the Pope as I had obeyed my own Bishop in the Anglican Church. My duty to him was my point of honour; his disapprobation was the one thing which I could not bear. . . .

And now in concluding my remarks on the second point on which my confidence rested, I observe that here again I have no retraction to announce as to its main outline. While I am now as clear in my acceptance of the principle of dogma, as I was in 1833 and 1816, so again I am now as firm in my belief of a visible Church, of the authority of Bishops, of the grace of the sacraments, of the religious worth of penance, as I was in 1833. I have added Articles to my Creed; but the old ones, which I then held with a divine faith, remain.

3. But now, as to the third point on which I stood in 1833, and which I have utterly renounced and trampled upon since, my view then of the Church of Rome;—I will speak about it as exactly as I can. When I was young, as I have said already, and after I was grown up, I thought the Pope to be Antichrist. At Christmas, 1824–'5, I preached a Sermon to that effect. . . . From my boyhood and in 1824 I considered, after Protestant authorities, that St. Gregory I. about A.D. 600 was the first Pope that was Antichrist, and again that he was also a great and holy man; in 1832–'3 I thought the Church of Rome was bound up with the cause of Antichrist by the Council of Trent. When it was that in my deliberate judgment I gave up the notion altogether in any shape, that some special reproach was attached to her name, I cannot tell; but I had a shrinking from renouncing it, even when my reason so ordered me, from a sort of conscience or prejudice, I think up to 1843. Moreover, at least during the Tract Movement, I thought the essence of her offence to consist in the honours which she paid to the Blessed Virgin and the Saints; and the more I grew in devotion, both to the Saints and to Our Lady, the more impatient was I at the Roman practices, as if those glorified creations of God must be gravely shocked, if pain could be theirs, at the undue veneration of which they were the objects.

21

The Revolutions of 1848

The revolutions of 1848 owed much to the liberal and nationalist heritage of the French Revolution. Revolutionary outbursts, beginning in Sicily and France in January and February, swept over central Europe in March and April, overthrowing Metternich's conservative order. In France, King Louis Philippe and his prime minister, Guizot, were replaced by a republican government. Elsewhere, the revolutionists preserved monarchy but insisted upon written constitutions. In Italy and Germany, liberals and nationalists sought unsuccessfully to achieve national unity. By mid-summer, conservative forces (army, clergy, nobility, and peasantry) rallied so effectively that by the end of the year 1848 the revolts were largely crushed.

[124] *THE FEBRUARY REVOLUTION SWEEPS AWAY THE JULY MONARCHY* *

Opposition within France to the July Monarchy of Louis Philippe included such discontented groups as Legitimists, Catholics, Bonapartists, Liberal Reformers,

* *The Recollections of Alexis de Tocqueville,* trans. by Alexander Teixeira de Mattos and ed. by J. P. Mayer (London: The Harvill Press, Ltd., 1948), pp. 37–38, 58–59, 67. Used by permission of the publisher.

Republicans, and Socialists. As these parties were prevented from airing their views in the press, they staged a series of political banquets. When the government forbade a banquet scheduled for February 22, 1848, the revolution began. In this selection, Alexis de Tocqueville recalls the first few hours of the revolution.

The next morning was the 24th of February. On leaving my bedroom, I met the cook, who had been out; the good woman was quite beside herself, and poured out a sorrowing rigamarole, of which I failed to understand a word except that the Government was massacring the poor people. I went downstairs at once, and had no sooner set foot in the street than I breathed for the first time the atmosphere of revolutions. The roadway was empty; the shops were not open; there were no carriages nor pedestrians to be seen; none of the ordinary hawkers' cries were heard; neighbors stood talking in little groups at their doors, with subdued voices, with a frightened air; every face seemed distorted with fear or anger. I met a National Guard hurrying along, gun in hand, with a tragic gait; I accosted him, but could learn nothing from him, save that the Government was massacring the people (to which he added that the National Guard would know how to put that right). It was the same old refrain; it is easily understood that this explanation explained nothing. I was too well acquainted with the vices of the Government of July not to know that cruelty was not one of them. I considered it one of the most corrupt, but also one of the least bloodthirsty, that had ever existed, and I only repeat this observation in order to show the sort of rumour that assists the progress of revolutions.

M. de Corcelles, whom I met in the street, gave me his account of what was happening, but in a very confused manner; for, in a city in a state of revolution, as on a battle-field, each one readily regards the incidents of which himself is a witness as the events of the day. He told me of the firing on the Boulevard des Capucines, and of the rapid development of the insurrection of which this act of unnecessary violence was the cause or the pretext; . . .

I returned to the House and resumed my seat. Almost all the members had left; the benches were occupied by men of the populace. Lamartine was still in the tribune between the two banners, continuing to address the crowd, or rather conversing with them; for there seemed to be almost as many orators as listeners. The confusion was at its height. In a moment of semi-silence, Lamartine began to read out a list containing the names of the different people proposed by I don't know whom to take share in the Provisional Government that had just been decreed, nobody knows how. Most of these names were accepted with acclamations, some rejected with groans, others received with jest, for in scenes in which the people take part, as in the plays of Shakespeare, burlesque often rubs shoulders with tragedy, and wretched jokes sometimes come to the relief of the ardour of revolution. . . .

M. de Lamartine, I think, was beginning to grow greatly embarrassed at his position; for in a rebellion, as in a novel, the most difficult part to invent is the end. When, therefore, someone took it into his head to cry, "To the Hôtel de Ville!" Lamartine echoed, "Yes, to the Hôtel de Ville," and went out forthwith taking half the crowd with him; the others remained with Ledru-Rollin, who, in order, I suppose, to retain a leading part for himself, felt called upon in his turn to go through the same mock election, after which he too set out for the Hôtel de Ville. There the same electoral display was gone through once more; . . .

And so the Monarchy of July was fallen, fallen without a struggle, and before rather than beneath the blows of the victors, who were as astonished at their triumph as were the vanquished at their defeat.

[125] *KING FREDERICK WILLIAM IV ADDRESSES HIS BELOVED BERLINERS* *

Frederick William IV, king of Prussia from 1840 to 1861, was a vaguely liberal dreamer, irresolute even in the calmest of circumstances. In the confusion of March 18, 1848, when barricades appeared in Berlin, he lost his courage entirely and made this ill-timed effort to win the affection of his subjects.

To My Beloved Berliners, . . . By my patent of convocation this day, you have received the pledge of the faithful sentiments of your King towards you and towards the whole of the German nation. The shout of joy which greeted me from unnumbered faithful hearts still resounded in my ears, when a crowd of peace-breakers mingled with the loyal throng, making seditious and bold demands, and augmenting in numbers as the well-disposed withdrew.

As their impetuous intrusion extended to the very portals of the Palace with apprehended sinister views, and insults were offered to my valiant and faithful soldiers, the court-yard was cleared by the cavalry, *at walking pace and with their weapons sheathed;* and two guns of the infantry went off of themselves, without, thanks be to God! causing any injury. A band of wicked men, chiefly consisting of foreigners, who, although searched for, have succeeded in concealing themselves for more than a week, have converted this circumstance into a palatable untruth, and have filled the minds of my

* "History," *The Annual Register, 1848* (London, 1849), pp. 378–379.

faithful and beloved Berliners with thoughts of vengeance for supposed bloodshed; and thus have they become the fearful authors of bloodshed themselves. My troops, your brothers and fellow country-men, did not make use of their weapons till forced to do so by several shots fired at them from the Königs Strasse. The victorious advance of the troops was the necessary consequence.

It is now yours, inhabitants of my beloved native city, to avert a fearful evil. Acknowledge your fatal error; your King, your trusting friend, enjoins you, by all that is most sacred, to acknowledge your fatal error. Return to peace; remove the barricades which are still standing; and send to me men filled with the genuine ancient spirit of Berlin, speaking words which are seemly to your King; and I pledge you my royal truth that all the streets and squares shall be instantaneously cleared of the troops, and the military garrisons shall be confined solely to the most important buildings—to the Castle, the Arsenal, and a few others—and even here only for a brief space of time. Listen to the paternal voice of your King, ye inhabitants of my true and beautiful Berlin; and forget the past, as I shall forget it, for the sake of that great future which, under the peace-giving blessing of God, is dawning upon Prussia, and through Prussia upon all Germany.

Your loving Queen, and truly your genuine mother and friend, who is lying on a sick bed, joins her heartfelt and tearful supplications to mine.

Written during the night of the 18th and 19th March, 1848.

FREDERICK WILLIAM

[126] *VIENNESE RIOTERS FORCE METTERNICH'S DISMISSAL* *

In early March, 1848, when news of the February Revolution in Paris reached Austria, a wave of excitement swept over Viennese students. Middle-class businessmen, who were disturbed by the economic depression, and factory workers, who were close to starvation, joined a crowd of students on the morning of March 13 outside the Landhaus *where the Estates of Lower Austria were meeting.*

Just then a young man came plunging through the mob, joy beaming from his face, waving a paper and crying "Kossuth's speech. Kossuth's speech." The moment was electric. For ten days rumors had been going about town concerning a speech which the great Hungarian had given to his countrymen at the moment when he was inspired by the news of the

* Priscilla Robertson, *Revolutions of 1848: A Social History* (Princeton, N.J.: Princeton University Press, 1952), pp. 210–212, 215–216. Copyright 1952 by Princeton University Press. Used by permission of the publisher and Oxford University Press.

Paris revolution. Everyone had heard of this speech, but very few had actually read the copies which were smuggled in and translated and passed from hand to hand. Now the mob hushed so that people as far away as possible could hear the magic words. For Kossuth was not afraid to use the word liberty. Hungary was a free country, he said, with an age-old constitution, and he demanded that the Hapsburgs should give her back her ancient rights. But Hungary could never count on her freedom, he insisted, under a king who was at the same time an absolute emperor to the rest of his dominions. Austria must have a constitution, too. (Hungary persisted in this demand right through 1867, when the system of the dual monarchy was set up and Austria then received a constitution at the hands of her sister nation.)

When they heard this part of the speech, the people began yelling in spite of themselves. A constitution—hardly anyone in Vienna had dared to think of such a thing, not even the students. Here was courage, here was progress, pushing them beyond their dreams. As the young reader drew toward the end of his paper, a voice from a window in the *Landhaus* cried "From the Estates," and a hundred arms passed a piece of paper toward the young man who was standing on a fountain. But the mob would not let him read the news from the Estates until he had finished every last word from Kossuth. Then he opened the new paper and read a somewhat humble request to the Emperor to call a united diet (like Prussia's) to consider reform.

"That's nothing. Tear it up," people yelled, and the Estates' document was torn into a hundred pieces and scattered down on the heads of the crowd. "We want deeds, not words. No wishes, no prayers. We *demand.* We have the right to do it." A young man with dark face and flaming eyes climbed arrogantly on the fountain. "Dismiss the minister everyone hates," he cried. "What's his name? Tell us his name," roared the people below. "Metternich." This sally was met with bravos. . . .

All this time the press outside was getting thicker, if that were possible, and the good citizens who hoped for peaceful reforms were considerably surprised to find themselves mingling with a number of those workers from the suburbs whom the students had engaged to come and help them. With sudden shrinking, many burghers felt they would rather keep on with tyranny from above than be caught fighting on the same side as the rabble from the factories.

Ordinarily, the two classes never mixed, for the inner city of Vienna was still surrounded by its ancient walls and moat, and outside was a broad grass-covered glacis which separated it from the suburbs where the workers lived.

During the morning of March 13, the city gates were ordered shut, so that all but a few hundred workmen were successfully kept out of the city. Some students who happened to be shut out too were almost frantic at missing the excitement. One bribed a mail coach to let him hang on an axle and rode inside that way. But even the few workers who got in heartened the radicals and students and terrified the milder citizens to the point where they began shrieking for arms, a national guard to protect property. Up to this point, the national guard had seemed a very radical demand, stemming straight from Paris, but now it became one the government was almost eager to gratify. For the government was losing self-confidence rapidly and hoped the burghers would forget their other wishes in their excitement of being under arms. . . .

Just at the time when the students were winning their arms, their arch enemy, Prince Metternich, quit his office. He had known for a long time that the country suffered from incurable ailments—"I am too old a physician to be deceived"—and the news of Guizot's fall in Paris struck him like the death knell.

Not for a minute, though, did he lose his perfect composure. During the morning of March 13, he had telegraphed Pressburg that by evening all would be quiet. Later on in the day, he appeared at a state conference fastidiously dressed in a green morning coat and brightly colored trousers. Glancing out of the window, he made a comment about the rabble outdoors, and when someone observed that there were many well-dressed people in the street, he said, "If my son were among those people, I would still call them rabble." Towards evening his enemies proposed to his face that he resign. Metternich only bowed courteously, saying that he did not want his term of office to outlast his usefulness to the state, but that he had promised the Emperor's father never to abandon Ferdinand. That remark only sent people scurrying, with the natural bad manners of the court, to get poor Ferdinand to give an official kick to his old servant; it was not hard to do, and with perfect *sang-froid* Prince Metternich withdrew. Let no one think, he gently reminded protesting friends, that the fate of Austria depended on any one man. The country could be lost only if it gave itself up.

Outside the palace the crowds were yelling so fiercely against Metternich that Archduke Louis said he could not be responsible for his life—a fine admission from the very Hapsburg who had served with the great minister as a regent of the Empire for thirteen years. And the state treasury would not even advance him cash for a trip to England. The Prince finally got a loan from his friends, the Rothschilds, and made his way out of Vienna in a common cab. After various adventures, he succeeded in settling in England, from whence he watched the Empire he had held together so long, fall swiftly, though temporarily, to pieces.

[127] *THE MILANESE RISE AGAINST AUSTRIA* *

Five days after the student outburst in Vienna, revolutionaries seized Milan, the prosperous industrial and commercial center of the rich Lombard plain. The struggle of the Milanese against the Austrians included a mixture of comedy and tragedy. Before the end of 1848, however, Marshal Radetzky's Austrian forces reoccupied all of Lombardy and Venice.

. . . a professor at the university told the Milanese the story of the Boston tea party, and he urged that his fellow citizens copy American tactics. He thought they might stop using tobacco or playing the imperial lottery, for the tobacco monopoly brought in millions of lire to the imperial treasury, and the lottery was even more profitable. In answer the Milanese agreed to give up these pleasures beginning on New Year's Day, 1848.

For the first two days of the year things stayed fairly quiet, and Radetzky's impatience grew when he perceived that the citizens' boycott was a success. To provoke trouble, on January 3, every Austrian soldier was issued six cigars and a ration of brandy. Until this moment their manners had been impeccably correct, but now they swaggered around in groups of twenty or more, blowing smoke in civilians' faces and sometimes flaunting two cigars at once. Finally a civilian snatched a cigar from a soldier, and the fight for which both sides were spoiling was on. The results were tragic. Infantry cut down civilians, cavalry trampled them. At the end of the day there were 61 dead, including six children under eight and five old people over sixty. A man in a cafe who tried to shield his little girl with his own body was cut down along with the child. Soldiers fell on a group of workmen coming out of a factory and tried to force them to smoke; the workmen refused and some of them were killed. Hospitals, which incidentally had been warned to get beds ready, were crowded with wounded.

Radetzky may have been pleased with this result. At any rate he refused for a whole week the civilian governor's request to hold his soldiers in their barracks. All the time he told the Milanese proletariat that the nobility started all the trouble—it was the work of a small party only.

Even though you call us twice a party, said the Marquis Massimo d'Azeglio in his report to the civilized world on the massacre, we will answer three times, "We are a nation, a nation, a nation." . . . To prove to the common people that they were not a separate party, Milanese nobles raised a sub-

* Priscilla Robertson, *Revolutions of 1848: A Social History* (Princeton, N.J.: Princeton University Press, 1952), pp. 338–341.

scription for the wounded and for the families of the dead. Fifty-two gentlemen took the unusual step of soliciting from door to door to give the lie to the Austrian assertions and show that Italians of all classes were united.

From that time until March the Milanese led their Austrian masters a dizzy dance. One day all patriots appeared with their hat bands buckled in front. When the bureaucracy caught on to this and passed an ordinance forbidding it, the same gentlemen came out the next day with the beaver fur of their hats brushed against the nap, and next another unusual fashion, and then another. Ladies too seemed under the sway of some powerful organization which told them what to do. Often La Scala was empty, except for the rows of white-coated Austrian officers, but on the night when Milan heard that the King of Naples had granted a constitution to his people, every great lady attended the performance in a gala gown. On the same day the poorer classes of people celebrated by eating Neapolitan spaghetti. "Here is a police far stronger than our own," complained a harassed Austrian who could not keep up with such tactics.

Some explosion would have come soon to any city so tense with feeling. As it happened, the news of the Vienna revolution reached Milanese patriots just as they were wondering what sort of a demonstration to make; as soon as they heard it Milan's date was moved up to March 18.

The night before, many Milanese youths took the sacrament. Afterwards, with glowing faces, they pulled out their strange and rusty assortment of hidden arms, even though their first orders were only to form a procession.

. . . 15,000 men answered the call to march to the Austrian government house. . . .

The highest Austrian official whom these patriots could find at his office was terrified, and he signed at once the order they asked for, an order to establish a civic guard for all citizens not living by their daily work. . . .

The barricades of Milan were the most fantastic of all the impromptu structures of 1848. Not only viceregal coaches and omnibusses, but sofas and pianos went into them. Rich merchants opened their warehouses and the people carried out bales of silk or coops of hens. Schools were emptied of their benches, churches of their confessionals. Rich citizens and factory workers helped each other in this work while children carried stones and tiles and boiling water to the roofs to hurl on any unlucky Austrian uniform below. Young girls pulled up the two white rows of flagstones which ran down the middle of each street for carriage wheels to pass over. Though a dozen chemists worked night and day to make powder, this item was so scarce that it was rationed out as if it were tobacco. Only men who knew how to shoot were allowed to use it, and they were happy whenever they got enough to charge their guns once or twice. They all felt that they could not afford two shots to kill a single Croat, so the young men shot in turn instead of simultaneously. Astronomers on a tower scanned the country-side with their telescopes and passed news down a wire on a little ring. University students, who were in charge of prisoners and of attacking the gates of the city, were the happiest of all. They hurried along the streets or over the roofs or through windows, intent on their business until they lost all idea of time. When they were hungry they begged a bit of bread at any doorway; if they were wounded all homes were open to them.

Radetzky's highly trained army was not prepared to deal with this sort of an insurrection, where cavalry and artillery were useless and his infantry patrols were all too easily picked off. So he decided to retire his foodless, sleepless troops from the interior of the city and make an iron ring outside from which he might starve the town and bombard it if it refused to come to terms.

[128] *THE TIDE TURNS AGAINST THE REVOLUTIONISTS* *

The first real defeat for the revolutionists of 1848 occurred in Prague, where a pan-Slavic congress had gathered to discuss Slavic autonomy within the Hapsburg empire. Prince Windischgrätz's capture of Prague, described below, heralded the end of the liberal movement in central Europe.

In the mean time national antipathies between the German and Slavonic races had broken out into open hostilities in Bohemia. Early in March a meeting had been held at Prague, for the purpose of petitioning the Austrian Government to grant certain demands upon which both the Czechs and Germans were agreed. They were principally these:—political equality of the two races (Czech or Slavonic and German); obligation on all public functionaries to speak both languages; union of Bohemia, Moravia, and Silesia, guaranteed by a Diet which was to meet alternatively at Prague and Bruun; representative and municipal reform; liberty of the press; publicity of proceedings in courts of justice; arming of the people; suppression of feudal seignories and jurisdictions; security for personal liberty; impartiality in the demands of military service; and equality of all religious sects.

After considerable delay, the whole of these demands were, on the 8th of April, granted by a royal rescript of the Emperor, and the young Archduke Francis Joseph, the nephew of Ferdinand and heir presumptive of the throne, was nominated Viceroy of the kingdom of Bohemia.

* "History," *The Annual Register, 1848* (London, 1849), pp. 408–410.

The effect of this concession, however, was very different from what had been anticipated. Hitherto the German element of the population, though numerically inferior in the proportion of 1,830,000 to 2,558,000, had been the dominant body; but now in consequence of the new constitution granted at their own request, they found themselves in a position of disadvantage. They had despised the Slavonic race too much to take the trouble to acquire a knowledge of their language, and owing much to the provision which required all public officers to speak with both tongues, they were suddenly incapacitated for state employment, and the Czechs became at once the powerful and dominant party. Count Leo Thun was elected by the latter as Burgrave of Prague, and it was resolved to convoke a great Panslavonic Congress, to meet at Prague on the 31st of May, in order to determine upon the measures necessary to protect Slavonic independence against the aggressive attempts of Teutonic supremacy.

Two days before this Assembly met, Count Leo Thun and the other leaders of the Czechs at Prague determined to establish a Provisional Government there, which should be independent of the Government at Vienna. Accordingly, eight of the most conspicuous members of that party were chosen and invested with the direction of affairs, and two of the number left Prague for Innsbruck, in order to obtain the formal sanction of the Emperor to their proceedings. . . .

In obedience to the summons issued by the Czechs of Prague, three hundred deputies from the different Slavonic States met there on the 2nd of June, when the Congress was formally opened. Their first act was to frame and publish a manifesto to the whole of Europe, in which they declared that their object was to claim and assert full justice for the whole Slavonic family; and to effect this they demanded that a great European Congress should meet, and settle the various conflicting interests of the States in which Slavs formed part of the population. But a sterner arbitrament was at hand. The Viennese ministry refused to recognize the Provisional Government at Prague, and declared that its constitution was illegal, and its acts void. At this time the Austrian Governor of Prague was Prince Windischgrätz (a lineal descendant of the great Wallenstein), and he took active measures to prepare for the struggle which he saw approaching. On the 12th of June a public meeting of the Czechs was held, to protest against the removal of artillery to points where it could be directed against the city. A tumult ensued, and the crowd rushed to the house of Prince Windischgrätz, where they gave vent to their feelings of hatred by abusive cries. The rioters were ordered to disperse, but they refused to quit the place, and some shots were fired by the mob, one of which, from a rifle, by a melancholy fatality, killed the Princess Windischgrätz, who was in an apartment of the house. The bereaved husband immediately came forward, and expostulated with the crowd in mild and dignified language, but in vain; at last an attempt was made to seize him, but the soldiers promptly interfered, and a general fight between them and the populace commenced. The contest raged with fury until the evening of the 14th, when Count Mensdorff arrived from Vienna, and assumed the command of the troops. This produced no cessation of the struggle, and on the following day the military quitted the town, and, taking up a position in the heights, began to bombard it with cannon. Even then the infuriated Czechs refused to yield; and it was not until the evening of the 17th, when a great part of the city had been destroyed, that the troops gained possession of Prague, and the insurrection was put down. The Slavonic Congress was of course at once dissolved and the revolutionary Government overthrown.

[129] *LOUIS NAPOLEON BONAPARTE INTRODUCES HIMSELF TO FRENCH VOTERS* *

Louis Napoleon Bonaparte (1808–1873), nephew of Napoleon I, was living in England when the February Revolution broke out. Although he was elected to the National Assembly in the summer of 1848, most Frenchmen knew little about him. Hence, Louis Napoleon issued the following manifesto during the presidential campaign in the fall of 1848. The second selection is from a speech delivered at Bordeaux in October, 1852, by President Louis Napoleon Bonaparte shortly before the Second French Republic became the Second Empire.

Louis Napoleon to His Fellow-Citizens: In order to recall me from exile, you have elected me a representative of the people; on the eve of choosing a chief magistrate for the republic my name presents itself to you as a symbol of order and security.

Those proofs of so honorable a confidence are, I am well aware, addressed to my name rather than to myself, who, as yet, have done nothing for my country; but the more the memory of the Emperor protects me and inspires your suffrages, the more I feel compelled to acquaint you with my sentiments and principles. There must be no equivocation between us.

I am moved by no ambition which dreams one day of empire and war, the next of the application of subversive theories. Brought up in free countries, disciplined in the school of misfortune, I shall ever remain faithful to

* James Harvey Robinson, *Readings in European History* (New York: Ginn and Company, 1904), Vol. II, p. 562.

the duties which your suffrages and the will of the Assembly impose upon me.

If elected president, I shall shrink from no danger, from no sacrifice, in the defense of society, which has been so outrageously assailed. I shall devote myself wholly and without reservation to the consolidation of the republic, so that it may be wise in its laws, honest in its aims, great and strong in its deeds. My greatest honor would be to hand on to my successor, after four years of office, the public power consolidated, its liberties intact, and a genuine progress assured. . . .

LOUIS NAPOLEON BONAPARTE

[130] *LOUIS NAPOLEON SUGGESTS THAT THE FRENCH REPUBLIC BECOME AN EMPIRE* *

The purpose of this journey, as you know, was to see for myself our beautiful provinces of the south and familiarize myself with their needs. It has, however, given rise to a much more important result. Indeed,—and I say it with a candor as far removed from arrogance as from false modesty, —never has a people testified in a manner more direct, spontaneous, and unanimous, the longing to be freed from anxiety as to the future by concentrating in a single person an authority which shall accord with their desires. They realize now both the false hopes with which they have been deluded and the dangers which threaten them. . . .

France to-day encompasses me with her sympathies because I do not belong to the group of dreamers. In order to benefit the country it is not necessary to resort to new systems, but, above all, to establish confidence in the present and security for the future. This is why France seems to wish to revert to the empire.

There is, nevertheless, one apprehension, and that I shall set at rest. A spirit of distrust leads certain persons to say that the empire means war. I say, the empire means peace. France longs for peace, and if France is satisfied the world is tranquil. Glory is rightly handed down hereditarily, but not war. . . .

I concede, nevertheless, that, like the Emperor, I have many conquests to make. I would, like him, conquer, for the sake of harmony, the warring parties and bring into the great popular current the wasteful and conflict-

* James Harvey Robinson, *Readings in European History* (New York: Ginn and Company, 1904), Vol. II, pp. 563–564.

ing eddies. I would conquer, for the sake of religion, morality, and material ease, that portion of the population, still very numerous, which, in the midst of a country of faith and belief, hardly knows the precepts of Christ; which, in the midst of the most fertile country of the world, is hardly able to enjoy the primary necessities of life. We have immense uncultivated districts to bring under cultivation, roads to open, harbors to construct, rivers to render navigable, canals to finish, and our network of railroads to bring to completion. . . .

This is what I understand by the empire, if the empire is to be re-established. These are the conquests which I contemplate, and all of you who surround me, who, like myself, wish the good of our common country, you are my soldiers.

22

The Unification of Italy and Germany

The failure of idealistic liberals in both Italy and Germany to unify their lands in 1848 led to the more violent methods adopted by Cavour and Bismarck. Cavour, realizing the inability of Sardinia to overthrow Austrian domination of Italy unaided, pursued an elaborate plan to gain the support of Napoleon III and his French forces. Bismarck created a unified German Empire by utilizing Prussian military power and his own adroit diplomacy to achieve successive victories over Denmark, Austria, and France. In both Italy and Germany, unification brought new problems of adjustment, including the relations of church and state.

[131] *CAVOUR AND NAPOLEON III CONSPIRE AGAINST AUSTRIA* *

Count Camillo Cavour (1810–1861), of a noble Piedmontese family, became prime minister of Sardinia in 1852 and worked tirelessly thereafter for Italian

* A. J. Whyte, *The Political Life and Letters of Cavour, 1848-1861* (London: Oxford University Press, 1930), pp. 255–257. Used by permission of The Clarendon Press, Oxford.

unity. By entering Sardinia in the Crimean War, Cavour was able to present the case for Italian unity at the Paris peace conference. In 1858, Napoleon III decided to work with Cavour to bring about a war with Austria. The details of the forthcoming conflict were cold-bloodedly arranged at a secret meeting at Plombières, France, in July 1858, as described below.

The first interview began at 11 A.M. and lasted until 3 P.M. Napoleon commenced by saying that he had decided to support Sardinia with all his forces in a war against Austria, provided that a nonrevolutionary cause, which would justify the war in the eyes of diplomacy, and especially of public opinion in France and Europe, could be found. Cavour then suggested, first, the trouble arising from the Treaty of Commerce with Austria, and then Austria's illegal expansion of power in Italy. Neither of these reasons satisfied Napoleon. They then examined together the map of Italy and finally found in Massa-Carrara a promising centre in which to foment the necessary rebellion. Sardinia was to provoke an appeal from the inhabitants, demanding annexation to Piedmont. The King would thereupon address a threatening note to the Duke of Modena who, relying on Austria, would probably reply in a similar tone. Victor Emmanuel would then occupy the Duchy and war would commence. After deciding that Naples should be left strictly alone, and that the Pope should be left in peaceful possession of Rome and the country round it, they passed on to the object of the war and the final settlement of Italy. Austria was to be completely driven out of the Peninsula and the country divided into a confederation of four powers: the Kingdom of Upper Italy, embracing North Italy from the Alps to the Adriatic with Romagna and the Duchies added, under the House of Savoy; a Kingdom of Central Italy composed of Tuscany and the greater part of the States of the Church; Rome and the Patriarchate; and the Kingdom of Naples. The Duchess of Parma was to be offered the throne of Central Italy, and the Pope was to be President of the Confederation, which was to have a constitution based on that of Germany.

Having settled the future of Italy there came the question of the price to be paid. Napoleon demanded the cession of Savoy and Nice. Cavour, after stressing the severity of sacrificing the cradle of the race, agreed to surrender Savoy, but pointed out that to cede Nice was to infringe the principle of nationality, the people being Italian. At this the Emperor, after thoughtfully caressing his moustache several times, remarked that this was, after all, a secondary question which they could deal with later. The military aspect was next dealt with. France would provide 200,000 men and Italy half that number. To carry out their programme the complete defeat of Austria would be necessary and peace might have to be signed at Vienna before Austria would yield her Italian provinces. As to finance the Emperor agreed to furnish Piedmont with material, and facilitate the raising of a loan in France.

[132] *GARIBALDI APPEALS TO THE SICILIANS* *

Giuseppe Garibaldi (1807–1882), an early disciple of Mazzini, had followed an adventurous revolutionary career in Italy and South America. In Genoa in May, 1860, Garibaldi, with Sardinian approval, organized a volunteer force, the thousand "red shirts," for the conquest of Sicily and southern Italy. The following proclamation, issued by Garibaldi before reaching Sicily, evoked such sympathetic support in the south that all of the Kingdom of the Two Sicilies was rapidly overrun.

Italians!—The Sicilians are fighting against the enemies of Italy, and for Italy. It is the duty of every Italian to succour them with words, money, and arms, and, above all, in person.

The misfortunes of Italy arise from the indifference of one province to the fate of others.

The redemption of Italy began from the moment that men of the same land ran to help their distressed brothers.

Left to themselves, the brave Sicilians will have to fight, not only the mercenaries of the Bourbon, but also those of Austria, and the Priest of Rome.

Let the inhabitants of the free provinces lift their voices in behalf of their struggling brethren, and impel their brave youth to the conflict.

Let the Marches, Umbria, Sabina, Rome, the Neapolitan, rise to divide the forces of our enemies.

Where the cities suffice not for the insurrection, let them send bands of their bravest men into the country.

The brave man finds an arm everywhere. Listen not to the voice of cowards, but arm, and let us fight for our brethren, who will fight for us to-morrow.

A band of those who fought with me the country's battles marches with me to the fight. Good and generous, they will fight for their country to the last drop of their blood, nor ask for other reward than a clear conscience.

"Italy and Victor Emmanuel!" they cried, on passing the Ticino. "Italy and Victor Emmanuel!" shall re-echo in the blazing caves of Mongibello.

At this cry, thundering from the great rock of Italy to the Tarpeian, the

* "Public Documents," *The Annual Register, 1860* (London, 1861), pp. 281–282.

rotten Throne of tyranny shall crumble, and, as one man, the brave descendants of Vespro shall rise.

To arms! Let me put an end, once for all, to the miseries of so many centuries. Prove to the world that it is no lie that Roman generations inhabited this land.

(Signed) G. GARIBALDI

[133] *BISMARCK DISAGREES WITH THE KING ON PEACE TERMS FOR AUSTRIA* *

Otto von Bismarck (1815–1898), named by King William I as chief minister of Prussia, ignored the opposition of liberals in the legislature and proceeded with his plan of increasing the Prussian army. In 1866, Bismarck's well-planned war against Austria resulted in a quick victory for the Prussians at Sadowa on July 3, 1866.

On July 23, 1866, under the presidency of the King, a council of war was held, in which the question to be decided was whether we should make peace under the conditions offered or continue the war. A painful illness from which I was suffering made it necessary that the council should be held in my room. On this occasion I was the only civilian in uniform. I declared it to be my conviction that peace must be concluded on the Austrian terms, but remained alone in my opinion; the King supported the military majority. My nerves could not stand the strain which had been put upon them day and night; I got up in silence, walked into my adjoining bedchamber and was there overcome by a violent paroxysm of tears. Meanwhile, I heard the council dispersing in the next room. I thereupon set to work to commit to paper the reasons which in my opinion spoke for the conclusion of peace; and begged the King, in the event of his not accepting the advice for which I was responsible, to relieve me of my functions as minister if the war were continued. With this document I set out on the following day to explain it by word of mouth. In the antechamber I found two colonels with a report on the spread of cholera among the troops, barely half of whom were fit for service. . . . Besides my political anxieties, I feared that by transferring the operations to Hungary, the nature of that country, which was well known to me, would soon make the disease overwhelming. The climate, especially in August, is dangerous. . . . Armed with

* *Bismarck, the Man and the Statesman, Being the Reflections and Reminiscences of Otto Prince von Bismarck*, trans. under the supervision of A. J. Butler (Leipzig: Bernhard Tauchnitz, 1899), Vol. II, pp. 228–233.

my document I unfolded to the King the political and military reasons which opposed the continuation of the war.

We had to avoid wounding Austria too severely; we had to avoid leaving behind in her any unnecessary bitterness of feeling or desire for revenge; we ought rather to reserve the possibility of becoming friends again with our adversary of the moment, and in any case to regard the Austrian state as a piece on the European chessboard and the renewal of friendly relations with her as a move open to us. If Austria were severely injured, she would become the ally of France and of every other opponent of ours; she would even sacrifice her anti-Russian interests for the sake of revenge on Prussia.

On the other hand, I could see no future acceptable to us for the countries constituting the Austrian monarchy, in case the latter were split up by risings of the Hungarians and Slavs or made permanently dependent on those peoples. What would be put in that portion of Europe which the Austrian state from Tyrol to the Bukowina had hitherto occupied? Fresh formations on this surface could only be of a permanently revolutionary nature. German Austria we could neither wholly nor partly make use of. The acquisition of provinces like Austrian Silesia and portions of Bohemia could not strengthen the Prussian state; it would not lead to an amalgamation of German Austria with Prussia; and Vienna could not be governed from Berlin as a mere dependency. . . .

We must finish off rapidly; before France won time to bring further diplomatic action to bear upon Austria.

To all this the King raised no objection, but declared the actual terms inadequate, without, however, definitely formulating his own demands. Only so much was clear, that his claims had grown considerably since July 4. He said that the chief culprit could not be allowed to escape unpunished, and that justice once satisfied, we could let the misguided partners off more easily, and he insisted on the cessions of territory from Austria which I have already mentioned. I replied that we were not there to sit in judgment, but to pursue the German policy. Austria's conflict in rivalry with us was no more culpable than ours with her; *our task was the establishment or initiation of German national unity under the leadership of the King of Prussia.*

Passing on to the German states, he spoke of various acquisitions by cutting down the territories of all our opponents. I repeated that we were there not to administer retributive justice, but to pursue a policy; that I wished to avoid, in the German federation of the future, the sight of mutilated territories, whose princes and peoples might very easily (such is human weakness) retain a lively wish to recover their former possessions by means of foreign help; such allies would be very unreliable. . . . What seemed to me to be paramount with his Majesty was the aversion of the military party to interrupt the victorious course of the army. The resistance which I was obliged, in accordance with my convictions, to offer to the King's views with regard to following up the military successes, and to his inclination to continue the victorious advance, excited him to such a degree that a prolongation of the discussion became impossible; and, under the impression that my opinion was rejected, I left the room with the idea of begging the King to allow me, in my capacity of officer, to join my regiment. On returning to my room I was in the mood that the thought occurred to me whether it would not be better to fall out of the open window, which was four storeys high; and I did not look round when I heard the door open, although I suspected that the person entering was the Crown Prince, whose room in the same corridor I had just passed. I felt his hand on my shoulder, while he said: "You know that I was against this war. You considered it necessary, and the responsibility for it lies on you. If you are now persuaded that our end is attained, and peace must now be concluded, I am ready to support you and defend your opinion with my father." He then repaired to the King, and came back after a short half-hour, in the same calm, friendly mood, but with the words: "It has been a very difficult business, but my father has consented." This consent found expression in a note written with lead pencil on the margin of one of my last memoranda, something to this effect: "Inasmuch as my Minister-President has left me in the lurch in the face of the enemy, and here I am not in a position to supply his place, I have discussed the question with my son; and as he has associated himself with the Minister-President's opinion, I find myself reluctantly compelled, after such brilliant victories on the part of the army, to bite this sour apple and accept so disgraceful a peace."

[134] *BISMARCK "EDITS" THE EMS TELEGRAM* *

After the creation of the North German Confederation in 1867, and the exclusion of Austria from German affairs, Bismarck arranged a series of secret treaties with the independent states of South Germany, who feared French aggression. To complete German unification, Bismarck now needed only a war with France, in which the French would appear to be the aggressors. The Spanish succession problem fortuitously provided him with the opportunity for fulfilling his grand design.

* *Bismarck, the Man and the Statesman, Being the Reflections and Reminiscences of Otto Prince von Bismarck,* trans. under the supervision of A. J. Butler (Leipzig: Bernhard Tauchnitz, 1899), Vol. II, pp. 272–273, 275–276, 278–280, 282–283.

The first demands of France respecting the candidature for the Spanish throne, and they were unjustifiable, had been presented on July 4, and answered by our Foreign Office evasively, though in accordance with truth, that the *ministry* knew nothing about the matter. This was correct so far, that the question of Prince Leopold's acceptance of his election had been treated by his Majesty simply as a family matter, which in no way concerned either Prussia or the North German Confederation, and which affected solely the personal relations between the Commander-in-Chief and a German officer, and those between the head of the family and, not the royal family of Prussia but, the entire family of Hohenzollern, or all the bearers of that name.

In France, however, a *casus belli* [an event which is a cause of war] was being sought against Prussia which should be as free as possible from German national colouring; and it was thought one had been discovered in the dynastic sphere by the accession to the Spanish throne of a candidate bearing the name of Hohenzollern. In this the overrating of the military superiority of France and the underrating of the national feeling in Germany was clearly the chief reason why the tenability of this pretext was not examined with honesty or judgment. The German national outburst which followed the French declaration, and resembled a stream bursting its sluices, was a surprise to French politicians. . . .

On July 12 I decided to hurry off from Varzin to Ems to discuss with his Majesty about summoning the *Reichstag* for the purpose of the mobilisation. . . . As I entered the courtyard of my house at Berlin, and before leaving the carriage, I received telegrams from which it appeared that the King was continuing to treat with Benedetti [the French Ambassador], even after the French threats and outrages in parliament and in the press, and not referring him with calm reserve to his ministers. During dinner, at which Moltke and Roon were present, the announcement arrived from the embassy in Paris that the Prince of Hohenzollern had renounced his candidature in order to prevent the war with which France threatened us. My first idea was to retire from the service, because, after all the insolent challenges which had gone before, I perceived in this extorted submission a humiliation of Germany for which I did not desire to be responsible. This impression of a wound to our sense of national honour by the compulsory withdrawal so dominated me that I had already decided to announce my retirement at Ems. . . . I was very much depressed, for I saw no means of repairing the corroding injury I dreaded to our national position from a timorous policy, unless by picking quarrels clumsily and seeking them artificially. I saw by that time that war was a necessity, which we could no longer avoid with honour. . . .

Having decided to resign, in spite of the remonstrances which Roon made against it, I invited him and Moltke to dine with me alone on the 13th, and communicated to them at table my views and projects for doing so. Both were greatly depressed, and reproached me indirectly with selfishly availing myself of my greater facility for withdrawing from service. I maintained the position that I could not offer up my sense of honour to politics, that both of them, being professional soldiers and consequently without freedom of choice, need not take the same point of view as a responsible Foreign Minister. During our conversation I was informed that a telegram from Ems . . . was being deciphered. When the copy was handed to me it showed that Abeken had drawn up and signed the telegram at his Majesty's command, and I read it out to my guests, whose dejection was so great that they turned away from food and drink. [The telegram, handed in at Ems on July 13, 1870, at 3:50 P.M. and received in Berlin at 6:09 ran as deciphered:

His Majesty writes to me: "Count Benedetti spoke to me on the promenade, in order to demand from me, finally in a very importunate manner, that I should authorise him to telegraph at once that I bound myself for all future time never again to give my consent if the Hohenzollerns should renew their candidature. I refused at last somewhat sternly, as it is neither right nor possible to undertake engagements of this kind *à tout jamais.* Naturally I told him that I had as yet received no news, and as he was earlier informed about Paris and Madrid than myself, he could clearly see that my government once more had no hand in the matter." His Majesty has since received a letter from the Prince. His Majesty having told Count Benedetti that he was awaiting news from the Prince, has decided, with reference to the above demand, upon the representation of Count Eulenburg and myself, not to receive Count Benedetti again, but only to let him be informed through an aide-de-camp: That his Majesty had now received from the Prince confirmation of the news which Benedetti had already received from Paris, and had nothing further to say to the ambassador. His Majesty leaves it to your Excellency whether Benedetti's fresh demand and its rejection should not be at once communicated . . . to our ambassadors and to the press.]

On a repeated examination of the document I lingered upon the authorisation of his Majesty, which included a command, immediately to communicate Benedetti's fresh demand and its rejection both to our ambassadors and to the press. I put a few questions to Moltke as to the extent of his confidence in the state of our preparations, especially as to the time they would still require in order to meet this sudden risk of war. He answered that if there was to be war he expected no advantage to us by deferring its outbreak; and even if we should not be strong enough at first to protect all the territories on the left bank of the Rhine against French invasion, our preparations would nevertheless soon overtake those of the French, while at a later period this advantage would be diminished; he regarded a rapid outbreak as, on the whole, more favourable to us than delay.

In view of the attitude of France, our national sense of honour compelled us, in my opinion, to go to war; and if we did not act according to the demands of this feeling, we should lose, when on the way to its completion, the entire impetus towards our national development won in 1866, while the German national feeling south of the Main, aroused by our military successes in 1866, and shown by the readiness of the southern states to enter the alliances, would have to grow cold again. . . .

Under this conviction I made use of the royal authorisation communicated to me through Abeken, to publish the contents of the telegram; and in the presence of my two guests I reduced the telegram by striking out words, but without adding or altering, to the following form: "After the news of the renunciation of the hereditary Prince of Hohenzollern had been officially communicated to the imperial government of France by the royal government of Spain, the French ambassador at Ems further demanded of his Majesty the King that he would authorise him to telegraph to Paris that his Majesty the King bound himself for all future time never again to give his consent if the Hohenzollerns should renew their candidature. His Majesty the King thereupon decided not to receive the French ambassador again, and sent to tell him through the aide-de-camp on duty that his Majesty had nothing further to communicate to the ambassador." The difference in the effect of the abbreviated text of the Ems telegram as compared with that produced by the original was not the result of stronger words but of the form, which made this announcement appear decisive, while Abeken's version would only have been regarded as a fragment of a negotiation still pending, and to be continued at Berlin.

After I had read out the concentrated edition to my two guests, Moltke remarked: "Now it has a different ring; it sounded before like a parley; now it is like a flourish in answer to a challenge." I went on to explain: "If in execution of his Majesty's order I at once communicate this text, which contains no alteration in or addition to the telegram, not only to the newspapers, but also by telegraph to all our embassies, it will be known in Paris before midnight, and not only on account of its contents, but also on account of the manner of its distribution, will have the effect of a red rag upon the Gallic bull." . . .

This explanation brought about in the two generals a revulsion to a more joyous mood, the liveliness of which surprised me. They had suddenly recovered their pleasure in eating and drinking and spoke in a more cheerful vein. Roon said: "Our God of old lives still and will not let us perish in disgrace."

[135] *A GERMAN EMPIRE IS PROCLAIMED AT VERSAILLES* *

As Bismarck had anticipated, the enthusiasm of a common war effort by North and South Germans greatly facilitated the final step in unification. A series of treaties negotiated in the early stages of the Franco-Prussian War tied the southern states to the North German Confederation. All that remained was the formal proclamation of the German Empire. The following selection is the official account of that event.

In the palace of Louis XIV, in that ancient center of a hostile power which for centuries has striven to divide and humiliate Germany, the solemn proclamation of the German Empire was made on January 18, exactly one hundred and seventy years after the assumption of the royal dignity by the Prussian sovereigns at Königsberg. Though the German people, owing to the necessities of the times, were represented at the ceremony only by the German army, the eyes of the entire nation were gratefully turned to the place where, surrounded by sovereigns, generals, and soldiers, King William announced to the world the assumption by himself and his heirs of a title for the reëstablishment of which we have been yearning during the sixty long years it has been in abeyance.

As yet the infatuation of the enemy does not permit us to throw aside the weapons we have taken up in self-defense; and as our unity arose out of the first part of the campaign, so will our empire be strengthened by the remaining feats of arms. By the self-sacrificing devotion of all classes of society, the nation has proved that it still possesses that warlike prowess which distinguished our ancestors. It has recovered its ancient position in Europe; and, neither fearing an adversary nor envying any neighbor, discreet and temperate in its acts and aims, it accepts the destiny prophesied for it in the proclamation of its new emperor. This destiny is to add to its power not by conquest but by promoting culture, liberty, and civilization. As far as the German people are concerned, there will be no more wars in Europe after the determination of the present campaign. . . .

Owing to the unfavorable weather the festive procession which was to conduct his Majesty from the prefecture to the palace did not take place.

* James Harvey Robinson, *Readings in European History* (New York: Ginn and Company, 1904), Vol. II, pp. 594–596.

The crown prince, with Lieutenant-General Blumenthal, his chief of staff, and an escort of Prussians, Würtembergers, Badeners, and Bavarians, drove to the palace to receive his royal father at the eastern portal in front of the Princes' Stairway. In the courtyard of the palace a company of the king's own troops was drawn up as a guard of honor. . . .

At a quarter past twelve his Majesty entered the hall, when a choir consisting of men of the Seventh, Forty-Seventh, and Fifty-Eighth regiments intoned the choral, "Let all the world rejoice in the Lord." . . . When the choir ceased, the congregation sang one verse of the choral, "Praise and honor unto the Lord." The ordinary military liturgy was then read by the clergymen. . . . The *Te Deum Laudamus* closed the service.

The king then walked up to where the colors were displayed, and, standing before them, read the document proclaiming the reëstablishment of the German empire. Count Bismarck having read the king's proclamation to the German nation, the grand duke of Baden stepped forth and exclaimed, "long live his Majesty the emperor!" The cheers of the assembly were taken up by the bands playing the national anthem.

[136] *BISMARCK STRUGGLES AGAINST THE CATHOLIC CHURCH* *

In the German Empire of 1871, Catholics constituted a sizable minority which included Rhineland industrial workers and Bavarian farmers, subject Poles in the east, and conquered Alsatians in the west. Bismarck viewed Catholicism as a serious threat to the unity of the Empire and failed to understand how Catholics could be loyal both to Germany and to the pope. This struggle against the Church is known as the Kulturkampf (battle for civilization).

Before Bismarck's Empire was a year old his Kulturkampf was under way. On July 8, 1871, the Catholic section of the Prussian Ministry of Worship, which dated from 1841, was abolished and the destiny of the Church was entirely in Protestant hands. This was followed by a series of legislative acts, the first of which, on December 10 of the same year, was the "Pulpit law." . . . Accordingly penalities were laid upon any criticism of the Reich and its constitution. . . .

A crucial move was the appointment of Adalbert Falk as Minister of Worship. During eight years of persecution until his dismissal in 1879, as

* Raymond Corrigan, S.J., *The Church and the Nineteenth Century* (Milwaukee, Wis.: The Bruce Publishing Company, 1938, pp. 209–215. Copyright 1938 by The Bruce Publishing Company. Used by permission.

Bismarck's mouthpiece or his evil genius, he enjoyed an unenviable popularity and power. The "May laws," or "Falk laws" were his work. . . .

"The Kulturkampf began in friviolity, was carried through with brutality, and ended ingloriously." So concludes a recent German historian of the Church. About the reasons, the motives behind the Kulturkampf, there is some obscurity. The main lines are clear enough. Bismarck had crushed internal and external opposition to found his mighty Empire. He would brush aside any obstacle to its unity and strength. The National-Liberal party, which should have withstood the absolute State, forgot its principles, as it conveniently could do on occasion, to fight the Catholic Church. But it is not so clear how much is to be attributed to incidental factors, to Protestant convictions, to Freemasonry, to Papal Infallibility and the "Old Catholics," to Polish activities, or to the political program of the Center Party.

Bismarck was a religious-minded man, in his own way, and he regarded the *Kleindeutsch* victory over Austria and the North German victory over France as a triumph of Protestantism. Falk was a Freemason, and so also was the Emperor. The Vatican Council and its definition of Infallibility aroused much resentment in the Fatherland. The religion of the Catholic Poles made it more difficult to make good Prussians of them. The Center Party stood for States' rights in an Empire that Bismarck was determined to centralize. In the pope, the Poles, and the Center Party Bismarck saw potential, if not actual, obstruction to his dreams of absolutism. One looks in vain for light in the writings of the Iron Chancellor. His memoirs and his recorded statements in formal speeches or in private conversation present a variety of contradictory views which effectually conceal his real mind. He wrote and he talked for effect. . . .

"God" was the God of Bismarck's Prussian State, and the enemies of Prussia or of Bismarck were the enemies of God. In politico-religious matters he was ruthlessly intolerant. . . .

When Leo XIII succeeded Pius IX in 1878 the Kulturkampf was seven years old. . . . Less than twenty-four hours after his elevation to the papal throne Leo had written a kindly letter to the Emperor. Shortly after this Bismarck had an informal conversation with the Nuncio Massella. The obnoxious Minister Falk was dismissed and his work gradually undone. A sort of diplomatic hide-and-seek game went on until the last remnants of the mass of Kulturkampf legislation were swept away with the exception of the anti-Jesuit laws, the supervision of Catholic schools, and the government approval of appointments to parishes. The process was a slow one, but it was virtually complete in 1887.

23

National Consolidations Outside of Europe

During the decade of the 1860's, as Italy and Germany achieved national unification, a number of non-European nations were progressing toward national consolidation. In the United States sectional strife of north and south led to a bitter and bloody civil war (1861–1865). The United States emerged from the Civil War with a strengthened central government and a rapidly expanding industrial economy. As the nineteenth century drew to a close, Americans were becoming conscious of their position as a potential world power, and were taking increased interest in the Caribbean area. In Latin America, the former colonies of Spain and Portugal were adjusting to national independence, either with tranquility as in the case of Brazil, or with violence as in Mexico. In the Far East the Japanese achieved a remarkable transformation of their society and emerged at the end of the century as a modern national state.

[137] *LINCOLN CONDEMNS SECESSION ON THE EVE OF THE CIVIL WAR* *

Between the election of Abraham Lincoln in November, 1860, and his inauguration in March, 1861, seven southern states seceded from the Union. Lincoln, in his inaugural address, presented his own views of the unconstitutional basis of secession, offered to the South a pledge to respect the institution of slavery and enforce the fugitive slave law, but insisted on retaining federal property in the South.

Apprehension seems to exist among the people of the Southern States that by the accession of a Republican administration their property and their peace and personal security are to be endangered. There has never been any reasonable cause for such apprehension. Indeed, the most ample evidence to the contrary has all the while existed and been open to their inspection. It is found in nearly all the published speeches of him who now addresses you. I do but quote from one of those speeches when I declare that "I have no purpose, directly or indirectly, to interfere with the institution of slavery in the States where it exists. I believe I have no lawful right to do so, and I have no inclination to do so." . . .

A disruption of the Federal Union, heretofore only menaced, is now formidably attempted.

I hold that, in contemplation of universal law and of the Constitution, the Union of these States is perpetual. Perpetuity is implied, if not expressed, in the fundamental law of all national governments. It is safe to assert that no government proper ever had a provision in its organic law for its own termination. Continue to execute all the express provisions of our national Constitution, and the Union will endure forever, it being impossible to destroy it except by some action not provided for in the instrument itself.

Again, if the United States be not a government proper, but an association of States in the nature of contract merely, can it as a contract be peaceably unmade by less than all the parties who made it? One party to a contract may violate it—break it, so to speak; but does it not require all to lawfully rescind it?

Descending from these general principles, we find the proposition that in legal contemplation the Union is perpetual confirmed by the history of the Union itself. The Union is much older than the Constitution. It was formed, in fact, by the Articles of Association in 1774. It was matured and continued by the Declaration of Independence in 1776. It was further ma-

* Lincoln's First Inaugural Address, March 4, 1861," in James D. Richardson, ed., *A Compilation of the Messages and Papers of the Presidents* (New York, 1897), pp. 3206–3211.

tured, and the faith of all the then thirteen States expressly plighted and engaged that it should be perpetual, by the Articles of Confederation in 1778. And, finally, in 1787 one of the declared objects for ordaining and establishing the Constitution was "to form a more perfect union."

But if the destruction of the Union by one or by a part of the States be lawfully possible, the Union is less perfect than before the Constitution, having lost the vital element of perpetuity.

It follows from these views that no State upon its own mere motion can lawfully get out of the Union; that resolves and ordinances to that effect are legally void; and that acts of violence, within any State or States, against the authority of the United States, are insurrectionary or revolutionary, according to circumstances.

I therefore consider that, in view of the Constitution and the laws, the Union is unbroken; and to the extent of my ability I shall take care as the Constitution itself expressly enjoins upon me, that the laws of the Union be faithfully executed in all the States. Doing this I deem to be only a simple duty on my part; and I shall perform it so far as practicable, unless my rightful masters, the American people, shall withhold the requisite means, or in some authoritative manner direct the contrary. I trust that this will not be regarded as a menace, but only as the declared purpose of the Union that it will constitutionally defend and maintain itself.

In doing this there needs to be no bloodshed or violence; and there shall be none, unless it be forced upon the national authority. The power confided to me will be used to hold, occupy, and possess the property and places belonging to the Government, and to collect the duties and imposts; but beyond what may be necessary for these objects, there will be no invasion, no using of force against or among the people anywhere. . . .

If by the mere force of numbers a majority should deprive a minority of any clearly written constitutional right, it might, in a moral point of view, justify revolution—certainly would if such a right were a vital one. But such is not our case. All the vital rights of minorities and of individuals are so plainly assured to them by affirmations and negations, guaranties and prohibitions, in the Constitution, that controversies never arise concerning them. But no organic law can ever be framed with a provision specifically applicable to every question which may occur in practical administration. No foresight can anticipate, nor any document of reasonable length contain, express provisions for all possible questions. Shall fugitives from labor be surrendered by national or by State authority? The Constitution does not expressly say. *May* Congress prohibit slavery in the Territories? The Constitution does not expressly say. *Must* Congress protect slavery in the Territories? The Constitution does not expressly say.

From questions of this class spring all our constitutional controversies, and we divide upon them into majorities and minorities. If the minority will not acquiesce, the majority must, or the Government must cease. There is no other alternative; for continuing the Government is acquiescence on one side or the other.

If a minority in such a case will secede rather than acquiesce, they make a precedent which in turn will divide and ruin them; for a minority of their own will secede from them whenever a majority refuses to be controlled by such a minority. For instance, why may not any portion of a new confederacy a year or two hence arbitrarily secede again, precisely as portions of the present Union now claim to secede from it? All who cherish disunion sentiments are now being educated to the exact temper of doing this.

Is there such perfect identity of interests among the States to compose a new Union as to produce harmony only, and prevent renewed secession?

Plainly, the central idea of secession is the essence of anarchy. A majority held in restraint by constitutional checks and limitations, and always changing easily with deliberate changes of popular opinions and sentiments is the only true sovereign of a free people. Whoever rejects it does, of necessity, fly to anarchy or to despotism. Unanimity is impossible; the rule of a minority, as a permanent arrangement, is wholly inadmissible; so that rejecting the majority principle, anarchy or despotism in some form is all that is left.

[138] *AMERICA CONTEMPLATES OVERSEAS EXPANSION* *

Alfred T. Mahan (1840–1914), a Captain in the U.S. Navy, was a vigorous advocate of U.S. expansion beyond the continental boundaries. His books dealing with the inter-relationship of colonies, commerce, and naval power, were particularly influential in the period 1890–1905, when the United States turned briefly to imperialist expansion overseas.

Were our sea frontier as strong as it now is weak, passive self-defence, whether in trade or war, would be but a poor policy; so long as this world continues to be one of struggle and vicissitude. All around us now is strife; "the struggle of life," "the race of life," are phrases so familiar that we do not feel their significance till we stop to think about them. Everywhere nation is arrayed against nation; our own no less than others. What is our protective system but an organized warfare? In carrying it on, it is true, we have only to use certain procedures which all states now concede to be a

* Captain Alfred T. Mahan, *The Interest of America in Sea Power* (Boston: Little, Brown and Company, 1897), pp. 18–22.

legal exercise of the national power, even though injurious to themselves. It is lawful, they say to do what we will with our own. Are our people, however, so unaggressive that they are likely not to want their own way in matters where their interests turn on points of disputed right, or so little sensitive as to submit quietly to encroachment by others, in quarters where they long have considered their own influence should prevail?

Our self-imposed isolation in the matter of markets, and the decline of our shipping interest in the last thirty years, have coincided with an actual remoteness of this continent from the life of the world. The writer has before him a map of the North and South Atlantic Oceans, showing the direction of the principal trade routes and the proportion of the tonnage passing over each; and it is curious to note what deserted regions, comparatively, are the Gulf of Mexico, the Caribbean Sea, and the adjoining countries and islands. A broad band stretches from our northern Atlantic coast to the English channel; another as broad from the British Islands to the East, through the Mediterranean and Red Sea, overflowing the borders of the latter in order to express the values of trade. Around either cape—Good Hope and Horn—pass strips of about one-fourth the width, joining near the equator, midway between Africa and South America. From the West Indies issues a thread, indicating the present commerce of Great Britain with a region which once, in the Napoleonic wars, embraced one-fourth of the whole trade of the Empire. The significance is unmistakable: Europe has now little mercantile interest in the Caribbean Sea.

When the Isthmus is pierced, this isolation will pass away, and with it the indifference of foreign nations. From wheresoever they come, and withersoever they afterwards go, all ships that use the canal will pass through the Caribbean. . . .

Whether they will or no, Americans must now begin to look outward. The growing production of the country demands it. An increasing volume of public sentiment demands it. The position of the United States, between the two Old Worlds and the two great oceans, makes the same claim, which will soon be strengthened by the creation of the new link joining the Atlantic and Pacific.

[139] *MEXICO TURNS FROM DEMOCRACY TO DICTATORSHIP* *

Mexico, after gaining independence from Spain early in the nineteenth century, experienced several decades of turmoil under a series of unstable dictatorships.

* Henry Bamford Parkes, *A History of Mexico* (Boston: Houghton Mifflin Company, 1938), pp. 243, 277–278, 285–287. Copyright 1938 by Henry B. Parkes. Used by permission of Houghton Mifflin Company, Boston, and Methuen & Company, Ltd., London.

The Revolution of Ayutla in 1855 brought to power a group of reformers including Benito Juarez (1806–1872). The reform movement was interrupted by the French Intervention and the Empire of Maximilian (1864–1867), and superseded, after the death of Juarez, by a dictatorship under Porfirio Diaz (1830–1915).

In this crisis Benito Juarez . . . began to display a moral grandeur unequalled by any other Mexican before or since. He was surrounded by men of greater intellectual brilliance. In his cabinet sat Melchor Ocampo and Guillermor Prieto, afterwards joined by Ignacio Ramirez and by Miguel Lerdo de Tejada and his brother Sebastian. Juarez, the small, dark-skinned Indian from the mountains of Oaxaca, relied on them for advice, distrusting his own intellectual capacities; he spoke rarely and with hesitation. Yet he had, in a superlative degree, what Mexico supremely needed: undeviating honesty, and an indomitable will which would never accept compromise or defeat. To the European ideology of liberalism he brought an Indian simplicity and persistence, and the unbending courage with which, three centuries before, Cuauhtemoc had resisted Cortes. If he could never stir a crowd or dominate a cabinet, he was capable, when stirred by profound issues, of giving to his proclamations a massive eloquence which has the permanently moving quality of great literature.

In 1861 Juarez had been confronted by problems so overwhelming that, but for the French intervention, Mexico might have again dissolved into anarchy. In 1867 he assumed the leadership of an almost united people, who regarded him as the symbol not only of a liberal constitution but also of the nation. Juarez could now proceed with the task of creating a modern and efficient administration. Mexico, as Justo Sierra said, was never really governed until Juarez governed it after the intervention. . . . Juarez himself was surer of his purposes and more confident of his abilities than in 1861. He still had faith in liberalism and in democracy, but he was now less reluctant to exercise executive authority and to give Mexico a strong government. He faced his task without illusions, knowing that it must be slow and difficult. "When a society like ours," he declared, "has had the misfortune to pass through years of intense upheavals, it is seamed through with vices whose profound roots cannot be extirpated either in a single day or by any single measure." In his ultimate objectives he failed; liberalism in a country of illiterate Indians was, perhaps, certain to fail. Yet Juarez had sufficient wisdom to avoid any too dogmatic application of the liberal creed. . . .

Juarez was re-elected to the presidency in 1867. Throughout his term he was obstructed by a factious and irresponsible opposition in congress. Unwilling to violate congressional liberties, he was compelled to safeguard himself by interfering with elections. His opponents called him a dictator, yet in reality a genuinely free election was impossible. The question was not whether voting should be free but whether it should be controlled by the federal government or by the local *caciques* (chieftains) and the state governments. As long as the reactionaries had controlled the central government, the local *caciques* had represented an element of democracy; now that the liberals governed Mexico, caciquism was an anachronism which threatened disintegration and civil war. Henceforth it was the function of the president to be the national *cacique*.

The alleged intention of the Plan of Tuxapec had been to protect constitutional government; intellectuals of the calibre of Ignacio Ramirez and Riva Palacio had supported it, in the belief that Diaz was the embodiment of Mexican democracy. Yet its result was to give Mexico a master more powerful than any she had ever known before. Porfirio Diaz was to govern the country—save for one four year interlude—for the next thirty-four years and to transform the constitution into a personal dictatorship.

The Reform had had two purposes: to establish a democratic form of government; and to stimulate economic development. Under Juarez these purposes had been combined; under Diaz the first was sacrificed for the sake of the second. According to the apologists of the Diaz regime democracy was impossible in Mexico; it meant, in practice, anarchy and the domination of the provincial *caciques*. Diaz set himself to enforce peace by making himself the national *cacique*, binding together the various discordant elements in the Mexican population through a common bond of loyalty to himself. Only a dictator, it was argued, could enforce peace, while without peace Mexico's natural resources could not be developed, and without economic development, education and social reform and the protection of national sovereignty from the encroachments of the United States were impossible.

Diaz could easily persuade himself that Mexico needed a master. Even Juarez had been compelled to interfere with elections. But Diaz had little of the enlightenment which had characterized the leaders of the Reform. A Mixtec Indian with a little Spanish blood, half educated—to the end of his life he could not write Spanish correctly—and with the crude manners of a guerrilla chieftain, he had now allowed himself to be dominated by greed for power. He was loyal, even when his control of Mexico was absolute, to a certain sense of morality. Though he killed his enemies, he did not kill wantonly or unnecessarily; and considering his opportunities, he showed a remarkable degree of financial integrity. But though he was neither a murderer nor a thief, he tolerated such crimes in others, and he was responsible for blunders which were worse than crimes. With all his extraordinary subtlety in the handling of men, Diaz retained to the end of his life the simple and unsophisticated outlook of an Indian warrior. He was too insensitive to realize that the suppression of political freedom and the enslavement of the masses might be too high a price to pay for material prosperity, and too ignorant to understand the economic forces which, during his regime, were sweeping across Mexico. Diaz himself, like a power of nature, can scarcely be judged in moral terms; but the nation which has not learned how to control such men pays a heavy penalty.

The guiding principle of the Diaz dictatorship was expressed in the phrase, *pan o palo,* bread or the club. To all dangerous elements, even to men whom he knew to be his personal enemies, Diaz offered power, prestige, and the opportunity of enriching themselves; as Diaz himself cynically remarked, a dog with a bone in its mouth neither kills nor steals. If they refused the offer, then he crushed them mercilessly. He stimulated rivalries and quarrels between the different groups whom he had attached to his government, so that they would never unite in a palace conspiracy or a *coup d'état,* while at the same time he maintained his own popularity with the Mexican people by allowing his subordinates to take the blame for tyranny and injustice. Such a program necessarily meant a cessation of social reform. Juarez had wished to lead Mexico toward democracy; Diaz proposed merely to enforce peace. In Diaz's "policy of conciliation" what was considered was not the permanent well-being of the Mexican nation but how far any particular faction might become dangerous to the dictatorship. The various groups who for the past half-century had been instigating plans and *pronunciamentos*—the landowners, the clergy, the generals, the *caciques,* the foreign-born capitalists, the office-hunting middle classes, the intelligentsia, even the brigand chieftains—all these people were converted into faithful adherents of Don Porfirio. The people who were ignored in the distribution of favors were the peasant and proletarian masses who—without leadership—had no means of asserting their interests. The meaning of the Porfirian dictatorship was that the bands of wolves, instead of fighting each other as they had been doing ever since the establishment of independence, were now invited to join each other in an attack on the sheepfolds. Peace achieved by such methods could scarcely be permanent; and when senile decay brought about the fall of the dictator, the accumulated resentment of the masses burst out into social revolution.

Whether a more enlightened and less cynical statesmanship could have given Mexico peace is questionable. Diaz had found a formula for ending civil war, and, for the first time since the establishment of the Republic, Mexico was able to devote herself to economic development. It was in the methods by which he stimulated that development, rather than in his political program, that Diaz committed his most disastrous blunders. Wishing to encourage the investment of money from abroad, he gave away Mexico's national resources to foreign entrepreneurs. Proposing to transform Mexico into a capitalistic nation, he allowed the Indians to be robbed of such lands as they still possessed. Industrialization was imposed mercilessly and recklessly, without plan or forethought, and with no attempt to mitigate the evils, upon a country which was not ready for it. The national income and the revenues of the government enormously increased; but Diaz's successors had to undertake the complex and delicate task of undoing much of what Diaz had done. They had to regain national ownership of the wealth which Diaz had lavished upon foreigners; and they had to change the Indians from peons back again into independent peasants.

[140] *EMPEROR PEDRO II GUIDES THE BRAZILIAN SHIP OF STATE* *

Brazil, the largest country of Latin America, established its independence from Portugal in 1822 as a constitutional empire, ruled by a branch of the Portuguese royal family. The long reign of Pedro II, 1831–1889, was notable for internal peace, material progress, the abolition of slavery, and the rise of immigration.

The commanding figure of the Second Empire was that of the Emperor himself. To be sure, he did not govern directly and by himself; he respected the Constitution and the forms of the parliamentary system. But since he determined the fate of every party and every statesman, making or unmaking ministries at will, the sum of power was effectively his. Cabinets had short and precarious lives, holding office only as long as it pleased the Emperor. Under these conditions, there was but one way to govern, and that was in agreement with him. To oppose his plans, his policies, was to invite dismissal. One or another minister might be ready to quit the government and the office on whose duties he had just entered, but cabinets clung to life, and the party imposed obedience to the royal will from love of offices, or patronage. So the ministers passively assented to the role that the Emperor assigned to them. The Senate, the Council of State, lived by his favor and grace. No leader wished to be "incompatible." He alone represented tradition and continuity in government. Since cabinets were short-

* Benjamin Keen, *Readings in Latin American Civilization: 1492 to the Present* (Boston: Houghton Mifflin Company, 1955), pp. 326–328. Copyright 1955 by Benjamin Keen. Used by permission of the publisher.

lived and he was permanent, only he could formulate policies that required time to mature. He alone could wait, temporize, continue, postpone, sowing in order to reap in due season. Whenever he needed to display his own unquestioned authority, he shunted the most important statesmen away from the throne.

The Emperor always exercised his power: (1) within the limits of the Constitution; (2) in accord with the fictions and usages of the English parliamentary system as adapted to public sentiment and opinion. . . . The distinguishing feature of his government was the sacrament of form; from the day on which his majority was proclaimed to that of his abdication he never abandoned his role of constitutional monarch. Then, too, the progress of affairs in his reign was not his work; he was only the clock, the regulator, that marked the time or gave the rhythm. In matters of politics, to be sure, the minister never proposed and the chambers never approved any measure that he had not sanctioned; it was he who sounded both sides of the channel that was being navigated.

Throughout his reign, from 1840 to 1889, all the statesmen who served under him were conscious that their mandates were not final, their positions uncertain and dependent. . . . But even if their mandates were precarious, even if they entered upon their duties knowing that the first serious disagreement with the monarch must lead to their dismissal, nevertheless the Emperor scrupulously respected the sphere of ministerial action. Nor could the ministers complain of the observations made by the Emperor in the council, for in his role of devil's advocate he elucidated questions, clarified his nominations, deduced precedents, compared the reports brought to him from all quarters, . . . lending to each administration the prestige of his high position and the assistance of his vast experience. At the same time he left to the ministers the political patronage, the distribution of jobs among their partisans, and the administration of affairs, including the realization of the ideas they had advocated while in the opposition. In many branches he hardly intervened at all—in the fields of justice and finance, for example.

That is why the most eminent men of the period were proud to hold those positions and competed for them, despite their uncertain tenure and the qualified nature of their mandates. It was from their number, from a small circle in parliament, that the Emperor always made his choices. He was, in fact, free only to alternate the parties, to pass from one group to the group in opposition, on the same conditions, choosing from what was often a league of chieftains the name that best pleased him at that juncture. Thus they were not royal ministers, creatures of the Palace; they were parliamentary ministers, like those in France in the reign of Louis Philippe, not like those of England in the reign of Queen Victoria. The Emperor could dismiss them, as the electorate dismisses them in the United Kingdom, but aside from this difference—that there was no electoral power capable of sustaining its representatives in the case of an appeal to the country—the ministerial mandate was the same. . . . The monarch did not degrade his ministers; he respected them, treated them with dignity. As a governor he sought only one glory for himself; to make Brazil a model of liberty among the nations.

The truth about his reign is summed up in the epigram attributed to Ferreira Vianna: "The Emperor passed fifty years in maintaining the pretense that he ruled over a free people"—that is, in upholding Brazil's reputation before the world, concealing the general indifference of its citizenry toward public affairs, toward their rights and liberties; in practicing and cherishing the cult of the Constitution as the political divinity of the Empire.

[141] *JAPAN EMERGES AS A GREAT POWER* *

In 1854 when Commodore Matthew C. Perry with an American fleet forced the Japanese to open trade with the West, a long era of Japanese isolation ended. The feudal social structure, headed by the Shogun, gave way in 1868 to "restoration" of rule under an Emperor, the Meiji Restoration.

National consciousness, which had been awakened in the struggle for the Restoration and by the threat of foreign encroachment, gradually permeated all layers of society in the early years of the Meiji and was sharpened by the arduous attempts at revision of the unequal treaties which were finally crowned with success in 1899. In the meantime, Japanese capitalism had passed through its formative stage, deprived from the first of tariff autonomy and hence forced to labor simultaneously on two fronts. *Internally,* its task was to hasten industrialization and the development of a home market, and *internationally,* to win recognition as a Great Power—a consummation which would automatically bring treaty revision, better trading privileges, even alliance with some of the Great Powers. These two problems, the internal and external, were so closely interwoven that it does violence to historical science to discuss them independently with no attempt to inter-relate them, as if such and such a foreign policy could have been arbitrarily adopted or discarded according to the fancies or ambitions of

* E. Herbert Norman, *Japan's Emergence as a Modern State: Political and Economic Problems of the Meiji Period* (New York: Institute of Pacific Relations, 1940), pp. 197–201. Copyright 1940 by the Secretariat, Institute of Pacific Relations. Used by permission of the publisher.

statesmen and generals. Actually the evolution of Japan's social organization, together with the constant pressure of international power politics, compelled Japan in the 19th century to expand in search of the foreign markets so desperately needed to realize the profits which could not be obtained from the narrow home market, and in search of cheap essential raw materials which were denied her through the accident of geography. Thus those nations which had compelled Japan during the turbulent years of the Restoration to put her house in order, to look after her defences first and last as a guarantee of her own independence, and to build up around these defences industries which were to become the blood and sinews of a modern military system, now had to witness her emergence from incipient colonial subjection to a position of demanding equal status with themselves. Having once entered upon the path of modernization and industrialization, the molders of Japanese policy saw that if they were to escape the fate of China or Egypt, they must adopt the political methods and economic policy of those powers who had been responsible for Japan's rude awakening and for the partial colonization of China. History is a relentless task-master, and all its lessons warned the Meiji statesmen that there was to be no half-way house between the status of a subject nation and that of a growing, vigorous empire whose glory, to paraphrase that gloomy realist, Clemenceau, is not unmixed with misery.

Consequently the primary task in Japanese foreign policy during the first thirty years of the Meiji period was to abolish that symbol of a nation destined for foreign domination, the unequal treaties. To turn back before they had reached the status of an independent power would spell humiliation, disaster, and possibly submission to foreign rule, while to continue along the course so brilliantly charted by the Meiji leaders meant expansion in the only direction permitted by history and geography, namely the Asiatic mainland where half-awakened peoples were stirring uneasily under the menace of the Western Powers. The leaders of Meiji Japan saw no reason to abstain from the scramble for the partition of China, and if economic pressure, a narrow home market and scarcity of essential raw materials are to be considered as justification, Japan had more of it than the other powers. So through a complex set of motives, including the necessity for foreign markets and raw materials, the fear of the uncomfortable proximity of Russian influence, and the desire to gain status as a Great Power, Japan successfully emerged from this first trial of strength as a modern nation.

That there was no halting place mid-way between a conquering and conquered nation, as far as Japan at any rate was concerned, and that the bitter struggle for national independence logically led to expansionism is strikingly shown by the fact that Japan acquired extraterritorial rights in

China before she had shaken herself free of similar foreign privileges on her own land. Viewed from another point of view, this brings into sharp relief another thesis of this study, that the *lateness* of Japan's entry into the comity of Great Powers left indelible marks on her national structure, her society and government, and hence upon her foreign policy. A modern state was established, and industries were started on the foundation of a very narrow home market at a time when other nations, having long reaped the profits of the old mercantile-colonial period, had progressed through the early morning of *laissez-faire* trading capitalism and were now entering the noontide of an imperialist epoch marked by the acquisition of colonies and spheres of influence. We have seen how Japan telescoped a whole century or more of her development as a capitalist power, passing from her restricted type of town-against-country mercantilism to a social organization compounded of monopoly control in private industry and state control of vital industries, thus permitting no economic freedom of the *laissez-faire* variety and consequently very little political freedom. There were circumstances over which the leaders had only partial control; too much had been conditioned by the preceding, complex history of Japan for them to attempt a point of departure parallel to the development, for instance, of the United States or the Scandinavian countries. Entering the race for empire with all the disadvantages of the late comer, Japan had to prove to the Western Powers her own abilities to undertake the responsibilities and tasks expected of great powers. Hence the struggle for the revision of treaties was an integral part of the struggle for recognition as a world power and for the fruits which such recognition brings. The Sino-Japanese War of 1894–95 was the first overt step in a direction which had been apparent before then. . . .

The national consciousness which had been forced into existence by events surrounding the Restoration, matured in the heated struggle for treaty revision, was to be strengthened a hundred-fold by the famous Triple Intervention, of April 23, 1895. . . . Although the intervention did not come as a complete surprise to the government, it aroused a feeling of national humiliation which was turned into rage by the unnecessary brutality of the German Minister at Tokyo who openly threatened war if Japan did not comply with the *démarche* of the East Asiatic *Dreibund* (Russia, France and Germany). Aside from the immediate sequel to this intervention, which was the retrocession of the Liaotung Peninsula and the imposition of a heavy indemnity in its place, the effect in Japan was to make national sentiment hyper-sensitive to foreign actions. Thus the adoption of a strong foreign policy came to be not only feasible but popular.

The war of 1894–95, therefore, marked a definite turning-point in Japanese foreign policy along the path of expansion, and enormously strengthened the position of the advocates of such a policy. Despite the Three Power Intervention the rewards from the war were such as to strengthen the arguments of these same advocates. The cession of the rich island of Formosa and of the Pescadores, the indemnity of 230 million Kuping taels (about 36 million pounds sterling) which became the basis for introducing the gold standard into Japan, these tangible results together with the diplomatic prestige which Japan gained were rich prizes for a nation which twenty short years earlier had just emerged from feudal isolation. The full recognition of Japan as a power on equal terms with the other nations automatically followed. Thus in 1899 the Anglo-Japanese agreement to abolish consular jurisdiction became the signal for other countries to reach a similar agreement. The participation of Japanese troops with those of the Great Powers in the suppression of the Boxer uprising in 1900 symbolized this entry of Japan into the ranks of the imperialist powers, and the Anglo-Japanese Alliance of 1902 signified that Japan had been singled out by the most experienced Empire builder, Great Britain, as the most effective counter-balance to its rival, Imperialist Russia. It is indisputable that this Anglo-Japanese Alliance, while benefiting England in its attempts to block Russian monopolistic ambitions in Manchuria and North China, was at the same time an invaluable diplomatic weapon in Japan's victory over Russia. Following this victory Japan replaced Russia as the greatest power either actual or potential in Eastern Asia. These rapid steps leading to the recognition of Japan as a world power were a logical outcome of Japan's victory in the war of 1894–95. What twenty years of peaceful negotiation had failed to do was accomplished forcefully almost overnight. This was at least the superficial explanation of success which greatly strengthened the prestige of the expansionist camp.

24

The Industrial Revolution

The term "Industrial Revolution" refers to the economic and social changes that transformed an agricultural and commercial world into a modern industrial society. Beginning in England in the middle of the eighteenth century, the Industrial Revolution had spread by 1840 to France and Belgium, and to the northeastern section of the United States. Germany remained relatively backward until economic unity was achieved by the *Zollverein* and the railroads. Watt's steam engine furnished power to heavy, expensive machinery installed in factories. With the factory system arose the industrial city, unattractive and unsanitary. Despite unhealthy working and living conditions, the population of Europe increased greatly as industrialization spread. In the course of time the Industrial Revolution brought to millions of workers a higher standard of living than nobles of earlier ages had known.

[142] *INVENTORS PLAY A LEADING ROLE IN THE INDUSTRIAL REVOLUTION* *

In eighteenth century England, wealth gained from overseas trade led to an increasing demand for goods, particularly cotton cloth, which exceeded the productive capacity of the cotton industry. Production was increased despite a labor shortage by means of a series of remarkable inventions in cotton spinning, weaving, bleaching, and printing. In the iron industry a shortage of wood led to use of coke as a smelting fuel, while the quality of wrought iron was improved by a series of inventions.

Some accounts of the technological revolution begin with the story of a dreamy boy watching the steam raise the lid of the kettle on the domestic hearth, or with that of a poor weaver gazing with stupefaction at his wife's spinning wheel, overturned on the floor but still revolving. These, needless to say, are nothing but romantic fiction. Other accounts leave the impression that the inventions were the work of obscure millwrights, carpenters, or clock-makers, untutored in principles, who stumbled by chance on some device that was destined to bring others to fame and fortune and themselves to penury. It is true that there were inventors—men like Brindley and Murdoch—who were endowed with little learning, but with much native wit. It is true that there were others, such as Crompton and Cort, whose discoveries transformed whole industries, but left them to end their days in relative poverty. It is true that a few new products came into being as the result of accident. But such accounts have done harm by obscuring the fact that scientific thought lay behind most of the innovations in industrial practice, by making it appear that the distribution of rewards and penalties in the economic system was wholly irrational, and above all, by overstressing the part played by chance in technical progress. "Chance," as Pasteur said, "favours only the mind which is prepared": most discoveries are achieved only after repeated trial and error. Many involve two or more previously independent ideas or processes, which, brought together in the mind of the inventor, issue in a more or less complex and efficient mechanism. In this way, for example, the principle of the jenny was united by Crompton with that of spinning by rollers to produce the mule; and the iron rail, which had long been in use in the coal mine, was joined to the locomotive to create the railway. In such cases of what has been called cross-mutation the part played by chance must have been very small indeed.

* Thomas S. Ashton, *The Industrial Revolution, 1760–1830,* Home University Library No. 204 (London: Oxford University Press, 1948), pp. 13–15. Used by permission of the publisher.

Yet other accounts of the industrial revolution are misleading because they present discovery as the achievement of individual genius, and not as a social process. "Invention," as a distinguished modern scientist, Michael Polanyi, has remarked, "is a drama enacted on a crowded stage." The applause tends to be given to those who happen to be on the boards in the final act, but the success of the performance depends on the close cooperation of many players, and of those behind the scenes.

[143] *A SURGEON DESCRIBES SANITARY CONDITIONS IN MANCHESTER* *

As factories tended to concentrate in certain favorable locations with advantages of water power, coal, mineral deposits, or transportation, a new type of urban community emerged—the industrial city. Manchester, center of the cotton spinning industry, was England's fastest growing factory town in the early nineteenth century.

Until twelve years ago there was no paving and sewering Act in any of the townships; even in the township of Manchester, containing in the year 1831 upwards of 142,000 inhabitants, this was the case; and the disgraceful condition of the streets and sewers on the invasion of the cholera you have no doubt learned from Dr. Kay's able and valuable pamphlet. At the present time the paving of the streets proceeds rapidly in every direction, and great attention is given to the drains. On the whole it is gratifying to bear testimony to the zeal of the authorities in carrying on the salutary improvements, especially when it is known that no street can be paved and sewered without the consent of the owners of property, unless a certain large proportion of the land on either side is built upon. Owing to this cause several important streets remain to this hour disgraceful nuisances.

Manchester has no Building Act, and hence, with the exception of certain central streets, over which the Police Act gives the Commissioners power, each proprietor builds as he pleases. New cottages, with or without cellars, huddled together row behind row, may be seen springing up in many parts, but especially in the town of Manchester, where the land is higher in price than the land for cottage sites in other townships is. With

* "Description of the Condition of Manchester by John Robertson, Surgeon," from *Report of Committee on Health of Towns* (1840), Vol. XI, pp. 221–222, App. II, as found in A. E. Bland, P. A. Brown, and R. H. Tawney, eds., *English Economic History: Select Documents* (London: G. Bell & Sons, Ltd., 1925), pp. 519–521. Used by permission of the publisher.

such proceedings as these the authorities cannot interfere. A cottage row may be badly drained, the streets may be full of pits, brimful of stagnant water, the receptacle of dead cats and dogs, yet no one may find fault. The number of cellar residences, you have probably learned from the papers published by the Manchester Statistical Society, is very great in all quarters of the town; and even in Hulme, a large portion of which consists of cottages recently erected, the same practice is continued. That it is an evil must be obvious on the slightest consideration, for how can a hole underground of from 12 to 15 feet square admit of ventilation so as to fit it for a human habitation?

We have no authorized inspector of dwellings and streets. If an epidemic disease were to invade as happened in 1832, the authorities would probably order inspection, as they did on that occasion, but it would be merely by general permission, not of right.

So long as this and other great manufacturing towns were multiplying and extending their branches of manufacture and were prosperous, every fresh addition of operatives found employment, good wages, and plenty of food; and so long as the families of working people are well fed, it is certain they maintain their health in a surprising manner, even in cellars and other close buildings. Now, however, the case is different. Food is dear, labour scarce, and wages in many branches very low; consequently, as might be expected, disease and death are making unusual havoc. In the years 1833, 1834, 1835, and 1836 (years of prosperity), the number of fever cases admitted into the Manchester House of Recovery amounted only to 1,685 or 421 per annum; while in the two pinching years, 1838 and 1839, the number admitted was 2,414, or 1,207 per annum. It is in such a depressed state of the manufacturing districts as at present exists that unpaved and badly sewered streets, narrow alleys, close, unventilated courts and cellars, exhibit their malign influence in augmenting the sufferings which that greatest of all physical evils, want of sufficient food, inflicts on young and old in large towns, but especially on the young.

Manchester has no public park or other grounds where the population can walk and breathe the fresh air. New streets are rapidly extending in every direction, and so great already is the expanse of the town, that those who live in the more populous quarters can seldom hope to see the green face of nature. . . . In this respect Manchester is disgracefully defective; more so, perhaps, than any other town in the empire. Every advantage of this nature has been sacrificed to the getting of money in the shape of ground-rents.

[144] *ROBERT OWEN AND SIR ROBERT PEEL REPORT ON CHILDREN IN FACTORIES* *

Robert Owen (1771–1858) rose from humble origins to become a factory owner, humanitarian, and social reformer. Owen's factory community was a model of the best working and living conditions possible at that time. Sir Robert Peel (1788–1850), a parliamentary leader of the Conservative Party, came from a newly rich family of cotton manufacturers. Both Owen and Peel were familiar with child labor in factories, one of the most depressing aspects of the early Industrial Revolution.

Mr. Robert Owen, Again Called in and Examined

Have you anything to add to your evidence of yesterday?—Some questions were put to me yesterday respecting the early age at which children are employed at Stockport; I knew I had made a memorandum at the time, but I could not then put my hand upon it; I have since found it; and I can now reply to the questions regarding those cases. Mr. George Oughton, secretary of the Sunday school in Stockport, informed me about a fortnight ago, in the presence of an individual, who will probably be here in the course of the morning, that he knows a little girl of the name of Hannah Downham, who was employed in a mill at Stockport at the age of four. Mr. Turner, treasurer to the Sunday school, knows a boy that was employed in a mill at Stockport when he was only three years old. . . .

They were mentioned to you as a rare instance?—They were mentioned to me in the midst of a very numerous assembly of very respectable people; I inquired of them whether they knew, as they were surrounded with, I believe, two or three thousand children at the time, what was the age at which children were generally admitted into cotton mills; their answer was, Some at five, many at six, and a greater number at seven. I have also received very important information from a very respectable individual at Manchester, relative to the age at which children are employed, the hours they are kept to work, and a variety of other particulars from very authentic sources. . . .

Does the information you propose to give come from the manufactory to which it relates?—No manufacturer would give information against himself.

State what you know relative to the number of hours which children

* *Report of Committee on Children in Manufactories* (1816), Vol. III, pp. 89, 132–133, as found in A. E. Bland, P. A. Brown, and R. H. Tawney, eds., *English Economic History: Select Documents* (London: G. Bell & Sons, Ltd., 1925), pp. 502–504. Used by permission of the publisher.

and others are employed in their attendance on mills and manufactories?—About a fortnight ago I was in Leeds; and in conversation with Mr. Gott, whose name is well-known to many gentlemen in this room, he stated to me that it was a common practice, when the woollen trade was going on well, to work sixteen hours in the day: I was also informed by Mr. Marshall, who is another principal, and considered a highly respectable manufacturer in Leeds, that it was a common practice to work at flax-mills there sixteen hours a day whenever the trade went well: I was also informed by Mr. Gott, that when the Bill, generally known by the name of Sir Robert Peel's Bill, was brought in last session of Parliament, the night-work at Leeds was put an end to. In Stockport, on Sunday fortnight, I saw a number of small children going to the church; they appeared to me to be going from a Sunday school; the master was with them; I stopped the master, and asked him what he knew of the circumstances of the manufacturers in Stockport; he said he knew a great deal, because he himself had formerly, for many years, been a spinner in those mills; his name is Robert Mayor, of the National School in Stockport; he stated that he was willing to make oath that mills in Stockport, within the last twelve months, had been worked from three and four o'clock in the morning until nine at night, that he himself has frequently worked those hours.

Sir Robert Peel, Bart.

The house in which I have a concern gave employment at one time to near to one thousand children of this description. Having other pursuits, it was not often in my power to visit the factories, but whenever such visits were made, I was struck with the uniform appearance of bad health, and, in many cases, stinted growth of the children; the hours of labour were regulated by the interest of the overseer, whose remuneration depending on the quantity of the work done, he was often induced to make the poor children work excessive hours, and to stop their complaints by trifling bribes. Finding our own factories under such management, and learning that the like practices prevailed in other parts of the kingdom where similar machinery was in use, the children being much over-worked, and often little or no regard paid to cleanliness and ventilation in the buildings; having the assistance of Dr. Percival and other eminent medical gentlemen of Manchester, together with some distinguished characters both in and out of Parliament, I brought in a Bill . . . for the regulation of factories containing such parish apprentices. The hours of work allowed by that Bill being fewer in number than those formerly practised, a visible improvement in the health and general appearance of the children soon became evident, and since the complete operation of the Act contagious disorders have rarely occurred.

[145] *DAVY CROCKETT VISITS A TEXTILE MILL* *

The factory method of producing cotton textiles was transmitted from England to America by adventurous entrepreneurs such as Samuel Slater and Francis Cabot Lowell, who circumvented English laws prohibiting the export of machinery, models, and designs. Lowell in 1812–1816 established the first American factory for cotton cloth based on power-looms.

Next morning I rose early, and started for Lowell in a fine carriage, with three gentlemen who had agreed to accompany me. I had heard so much of this place that I longed to see it; not because I had heard of the "mile of gals"; . . . but I wanted to see the power of machinery, wielded by the keenest calculations of human skill; I wanted to see how it was that these northerners could buy our cotton, and carry it home, manufacture it, bring it back, and sell it for half nothing; and in the meantime, be well to live, and make money besides.

We stopped at the large stone house at the head of the falls of the Merrimac river, and having taken a little refreshment, went down among the factories. The dinner bells were ringing, and the folks pouring out of the houses like bees out of a gum. I looked at them as they passed, all well dressed, lively, and genteel in their appearance; indeed, the girls looked as if they were coming from a quilting frolic. We took a turn around, and after dining on a fine salmon, again returned, and entered the factories.

The out-door appearance was fully sustained by the whole of the persons employed in the different rooms. I went in among the young girls, and talked with many of them. Not one expressed herself as tired of her employment, or oppressed with work; all talked well, and looked healthy. Some of them were very handsome; and I could not help observing that they kept the prettiest inside, and put the homely ones on the outside rows.

I could not help reflecting on the difference of condition between these females, thus employed, and those of other populous countries, where the female character is degraded to abject slavery. Here were thousands, useful to others, and enjoying all the blessings of freedom, with the prospect before them of future comfort and respectability; and however we, who only hear

* David Crockett, *An Account of Col. Crockett's Tour to the North and Down East* (Philadelphia: E. L. Carey and A. Hart, 1835), pp. 91–99.

of them, may call their houses workshops and prisons, I assure my neighbors there is every enjoyment of life realized by these persons, and there can be but few who are not happy. It cannot be otherwise: respectability depends upon being neighbor-like; here everybody works, and therefore no one is degraded by it; on the contrary, those who don't work are not estimated.

There are more than five thousand females employed in Lowell; and when you come to see the amount of labour performed by them, in superintending the different machinery, you will be astonished.

Twelve years ago, the place where Lowell now rises in all its pride was a sheep pasture. It took its name from Francis C. Lowell, the projector of its manufactories, and was incorporated in 1826—then a mere village. The fall, obtained by a canal from the Merrimac river, is thirty-two feet, affording two levels for mills, of thirteen and seventeen feet; and the whole water of the river can be used.

There are about fourteen thousand inhabitants. It contains nine meeting-houses; appropriates seven thousand five hundred dollars for free schools; provides instruction for twelve hundred scholars, daily; and about three thousand annually partake of its benefits. It communicates with Boston by the Middlesex canal (the first ever made in the United States); and in a short time the rail-road to Boston will be completed, affording every facility of intercourse to the seaboard.

This place has grown by, and must depend on, its manufactures. Its location renders it important, not only to the owners, but to the nation. Its consumption not only employs the thousands of its own population, but many thousands far away from them. It is calculated not only to give individual happiness and prosperity, but to add to our national wealth and independence; and instead of depending on foreign countries, to have our own material worked up in our own country.

Some of the girls attended three looms; and they make from one dollar seventy-five cents to three dollars per week, after paying their board. These looms weave fifty-five yards per day; so that one person makes one hundred and sixty-five yards per day. Every thing moves on like clockwork, in all the variety of employments; and the whole manufacture appears to be of the very best. . . .

The owner of one of the mills, Mr. Lawrence, presented me with a suit of broadcloth, made out of wool bought from Mark Cockral, of Mississippi, who sold them about four thousand pounds; and it was as good cloth as the best I ever bought for best imported.

The calico made here is beautiful, and of every variety of figure and colour. To attempt to give a description of the manner in which it is stamped and coloured is far beyond my abilities. One thing I must state, that after the web is wove, and before they go further, it is actually passed over a red-hot cylinder, to scorch off the furze. The number of different operations is truly astonishing; and if one of my countrywomen had the whole of the persons in her train that helped to make her gown, she would be like a captain on a field-muster: and yet, when you come to look at the cost, it would take a trunk full of them to find these same people in living for one day.

I never witnessed such a combination of industry, and perhaps never will again. I saw the whole process, from the time they put in the raw material, until it came out completely finished. In fact, it almost came up to the old story of a fellow walking into a patent machine with a bundle of wool under his arm, and coming out at the other end with a new coat on.

Nothing can be more agreeable than the attention that is paid by every one connected with these establishments. Nothing appears to be kept secret; every process is shown, and with great cheerfulness. I regret that more of our southern and western men do not go there, as it would help much to do away with their prejudices against these manufactories.

[146] *ENGLAND EXPORTS ITS MACHINERY AND TECHNOLOGY* *

In the period 1815–1850 Belgium followed the pace of English industrialization more closely than other European countries. A key figure in Belgium's Industrial Revolution was the English-born John Cockerill, who used English technology in developing his metallurgical and machine-building plant at Seraing. The following is a letter from Cockerill to his friend, Henry Maudslay, English machine tool inventor and designer.

Seraing, October 5, 1819

Messrs. Maudslay & Cie.

Your price of the oil mill includes engine and every thing, but as we have already in the establishment where we intend fixing the mill a 30 horse power (engine), we should wish to have the price of the mill without engine.

As to the machine for making boilers we do not require it so extensive as yours, neither do we want an engine for that purpose. What we are in need of is the leaver [*sic*] and for punching the bottom and top plates, with cutters and requisite for making one boiler per month. We have received

* Letter from John Cockerill, Seraing, Belgium, to Henry Maudslay, Lambeth, London, England, 5 October, 1819, in Archives of Société Anonyme John Cockerill, Seraing, as found in Theodore B. Hodges, "The Iron King of Liège: John Cockerill," unpublished doctoral dissertation. Copyright 1960 by Theodore B. Hodges.

one of the boilers and wish you to send the other as soon as convenient to the same address as before—Mr. E. B. Govarts, Antwerp.

We give you an order for one patent barrel fire engine, the price of 100 pounds. If there is no leather pipe included with the engine we wish you to send 20 or 30 yards also.

The chipping plate is to be worked by a 4 horse power, and as far as we learn there are 4 or 6 cutters. We require every thing compleat [*sic*]—the same with regard to the rasping barrel.

We could wish you to send the price of a threshing machine and for cutting of straw—also the best method of distilling gin, and the price of a machine for threading bolts. In our next we will write you respecting the powder mill, but in the meanwhile will thank you for any information you may be pleased to favor us with.

We could also wish to be informed [about] the price of machinery for manufactoring [*sic*] tobacco and snuff, specifying the different articles required,—also the price of rollers or what is used for making of angle irons for boilers.

As soon as we are favored with an answer to the different articles, we will give you the necessary orders. . . .

CHARLES JAMES and JOHN COCKERILL

[147] *MALTHUS VIEWS WITH ALARM THE RISE OF POPULATION* *

Thomas Robert Malthus (1766–1834) published his first Essay on Population *in 1798, when the Industrial Revolution was gaining momentum, and when the population of England was rapidly increasing. His pessimistic view that population tends to increase faster than available food supplies led many to the conclusion that charity or higher wages served only to increase the population and bring renewed poverty and distress.*

I have read some of the speculations on the perfectability of man and of society with great pleasure. I have been warmed and delighted with the enchanting picture which they hold forth. I ardently wish for such happy improvements. But I see great, and, to my understanding, unconquerable difficulties in the way to them. . . .

I think I may fairly make two postulata.

* T. R. Malthus, *Parallel Chapters from the First and Second Editions of an Essay on the Principle of Population* (New York: The Macmillan Company, 1906), pp. 4, 6–8.

First, That food is necessary to the existence of man.

Secondly, That the passion between the sexes is necessary, and will remain nearly in its present state.

These two laws ever since we have had any knowledge of mankind, appear to have been fixed laws of our nature; and, as we have not hitherto seen any alteration in them, we have no right to conclude that they will ever cease to be what they are now, without an immediate act of power in that Being who first arranged the system of the universe; and for the advantage of his creatures, still executes, according to fixed laws, all its various operations. . . .

Assuming, then, my postulata as granted, I say, that the power of population is indefinitely greater than the power in the earth to produce subsistence for man.

Population, when unchecked, increases in a geometrical ratio. Subsistence only increases in an arithmetical ratio. A slight acquaintance with numbers will show the immensity of the first power in comparison of the second.

By that law of nature which makes food necessary to the life of man, the effects of these two unequal powers must be kept equal.

This implies a strong and constantly operating check on population from the difficulty of subsistence. This difficulty must fall some where; and must necessarily be severely felt by a large portion of mankind.

Through the animal and vegetable kingdoms, nature has scattered the seeds of life abroad with the most profuse and liberal hand. She has been comparatively sparing in the room, and the nourishment necessary to rear them. The germs of existence contained in this spot of earth, with ample food, and ample room to expand it, would fill millions of worlds in the course of a few thousand years. Necessity, that imperious, all-pervading law of nature, restrains them within the prescribed bounds. The race of plants, and the race of animals shrink under this great restrictive law. And the race of man cannot, by any efforts of reason, escape from it. Among plants and animals its effects are waste of seed, sickness, and premature death. Among mankind, misery and vice. The former, misery, is an absolutely necessary consequence of it. Vice is a highly probable consequence, and we therefore see it abundantly prevail; but it ought not, perhaps to be called an absolutely necessary consequence. The ordeal of virtue is to resist all temptation to evil.

This natural inequality of the two powers of population, and of production in the earth, and that great law of our nature which must constantly keep their effects equal, form the great difficulty that to me appears insurmountable in the way to perfectability of society.

[148] *THE INDUSTRIAL REVOLUTION IS ACCOMPANIED BY AN UNPRECEDENTED POPULATION GROWTH* *

Malthus' fears that increasing poverty would result from population growth failed to materialize. However, Europe would have experienced a lowering of the standard of living, had it not been for the technological advances, increasing agricultural production, and improvements in transportation.

The outstanding feature of the social history of the period—the thing that above all others distinguishes the age from its predecessors—is the rapid growth of population. Careful estimates, based on figures of burials and christenings, put the number of people in England and Wales at about five and a half millions in 1700, and six and a half millions in 1750: when the first census was taken in 1801 it was around nine millions, and by 1831 had reached fourteen millions. In the second half of the eighteenth century population had thus increased by 40 per cent, and in the first three decades of the nineteenth century by more than 50 per cent. For Great Britain the figures are approximately eleven millions in 1801, and sixteen and a half millions in 1831.

The growth of population was not the result of any marked change in the birth rate. During the first four decades of the eighteenth century, it is true the number of births per thousand people seems to have risen a little. Farm labourers tended to set up households of their own instead of boarding with their employers, and a decline of the system of apprenticeship in industry also led to earlier marriages and larger families. But from 1740 to 1830 the birth rate appears to have fluctuated only very slightly; for no decade does the estimate rise above 37.7, or fall below 36.6. Throughout the industrial revolution fertility was high but steady.

Nor can the increase of people be attributed to an influx from other countries. In every decade men and women took ship from Ireland to England and Scotland, and at times of dearth the trickle became a stream. But there was no such torrent of Irish immigration as was to come in the last five years of the eighteen-forties. On the other hand, during the eighteenth century perhaps a million people left Britain to seek a living overseas, mainly in the colonies. Among them were some 50,000 criminals transported to Maryland [*sic*] or Botany Bay, and a number of artisans who defied the law by carrying their technical knowledge and skill to

* Thomas S. Ashton, *The Industrial Revolution, 1760–1830,* Home University Library No. 204 (London: Oxford University Press, 1948), pp. 2–5. Used by permission of the publisher.

Europe—not in the long run, it may be guessed, to the disadvantage of their native land. On balance, Britain was not a receiving center but a breeding ground for new communities across the seas.

It was a fall of mortality that led to the increase of numbers. In the first four decades of the eighteenth century excessive indulgence in cheap gin and intermittent periods of famine took a heavy toll of lives; but between 1740 and 1820 the death rate fell almost continuously—from an estimated 35.8 for the ten years ending in 1740 to one of 21.1 for those ending in 1821. Many influences were operating to reduce the incidence of death. The introduction of root crops made it possible to feed more cattle in the winter months, and so to supply fresh meat throughout the year. The substitution of wheat for inferior cereals, and an increased consumption of vegetables, strengthened resistance to disease. Higher standards of personal cleanliness, associated with more soap and cheaper cotton underwear, lessened the dangers of infection. The use of brick in place of timber in the walls, and of slate or stone instead of thatch in the roofs, of cottages reduced the number of pests; and the removal of many noxious processes of manufacture from the homes of the workers brought greater domestic comfort. The larger towns were paved, drained, and supplied with running water; knowledge of medicine and surgery developed; hospitals and dispensaries increased; and more attention was paid to such things as the disposal of refuse and the proper burial of the dead.

Since there are no reliable statistics it is not possible to say which age groups of the population benefited most from these improvements. In a well-known passage of his *Autobiography* Edward Gibbon says:

> The death of a new-born child before that of its parents may seem an unnatural, but it is strictly a probable event; since of any given number, the greater part are extinguished before their ninth year, before they possess the faculties of mind or body. Without accusing the profuse waste or imperfect workmanship of Nature, I shall only observe that this unfortunate chance was multiplied against my infant existence. So feeble was my constitution, so precarious my life, that in the baptism of each of my brothers, my father's prudence repeated my Christian name of Edward, that in case of the departure of the eldest son, this patronymic appellation might be still perpetuated in the family.

This was written in 1792–3. By that time it is probable that the profuse waste of infant life was a little less than at the date of Gibbon's birth, and, if so, there would be a higher percentage of children and young people in the population. It is a matter to be borne in mind in considering the constitution of the labour force of the early factories.

25

Democracy in Western Europe and America

While Germany and Italy were emerging as unified nations, England and France, after centuries of national unity, appeared in the late nineteenth century as strongholds of liberalism, in which a considerable degree of political democracy had been attained. England's internal problems were ably handled in her Parliament, led by two outstanding party leaders, William E. Gladstone and Benjamin Disraeli. France, after a painful transition from the Second Empire to the Third Republic, was predominantly liberal and increasingly democratic. In the United States the democratic tradition of Jefferson and Jackson was given new vigor in the direction of political and social reform by the Progressive movement.

[149] *GLADSTONE REVIEWS THE PROGRESS OF THE WORKING CLASS* *

William Ewart Gladstone (1809–1898), leader of the British Liberal Party, served as prime minister on four occasions between 1868 and 1894. The speech

* *Parliamentary Debates,* Third Series, CLXXXII, p. 1132f., as found in Carl Stephenson and Frederick George Marcham, eds. and trans., *Sources of English Constitutional History* (New York: Harper & Brothers, 1937), pp. 775–776. Copyright 1937 by Harper & Brothers. Used by permission.

below was delivered in Parliament in 1866 to support his own proposal to widen the suffrage sufficiently to include the urban working class. Gladstone's proposals served as a basis for the Reform Act of 1867, sponsored by Disraeli's Conservative cabinet.

Since 1832 every kind of beneficial change has been in operation in favour of the working classes. There never was a period in which religious influences were more active than in the period I now name. It is hardly an exaggeration to say that within that time the civilizing and training powers of education have for all practical purposes been not so much improved as, I might almost say, brought into existence, as far as the mass of the people is concerned. As regards the press, an emancipation and extension have taken place to which it would be difficult to find a parallel. I will not believe that the mass of gentlemen opposite are really insensible to the enormous benefit that has been effected by that emancipation of the press—when, for the humble sum of a penny or for even less, newspapers are circulated from day to day by the million rather than by the thousand, in numbers almost defying the powers of statistics to follow, and carrying home to all classes of our fellow-countrymen accounts of public affairs; enabling them to feel a new interest in the transaction of those affairs and containing articles which, I must say, are written in a spirit, with an ability, with a sound moral sense, and with a refinement that have made the penny press of England the worthy companion—indeed say the worthy rival—of those dearer and older papers which have long secured for British journalism a renown perhaps without parallel in the world. By external and material as well as by higher means, by measures relating to labour, to police, and to sanitary arrangements, parliament has been labouring, has been striving with admitted success. And there is not a call which has been made upon the self-improving powers of the working community which has not been fully answered. Take, for instance, the working men's free libraries and institutes throughout the country. Take, as an example of the class, Liverpool. Who are the frequenters of that institution? I believe that the majority of the careful, honest, painstaking students who crowd that library are men belonging to the working classes, a large number of whom cannot attend without making some considerable sacrifice. Then again, sir, we called upon them to be provident; we instituted for them post-office savings banks, which may now be said to have been in full operation for four years. And what has been the result? During these four years we have received these names at the rate of thousands by the week, and there are now 650,000 depositors in those savings banks. This, then, is the way in which parliament has been acting towards the working classes. But what is the meaning of all this? Parliament has been striving to make the working classes progressively fitter and fitter for the franchise. And can anything be more unwise, not to say more senseless, than to persevere from year to year in this plan, and then blindly to refuse to recognize its legitimate upshot—namely, the increased fitness of the working classes for the exercise of political power?

[150] *PARNELL URGES HOME RULE FOR IRELAND* *

Charles Stewart Parnell (1846–1891), an Irish Protestant landowner, was elected in 1875 to Parliament, where he organized the Irish Nationalist Party, advocating "home rule" for Ireland. Following the 1885 elections, during which Parnell delivered the speech below at Cork, the Irish Nationalists held the balance of power in Parliament. Gladstone gained the support of the Irish by accepting Parnell's home rule program, but the bill failed to pass in 1886.

At the election of 1880 I laid certain principles before you, and you accepted them (applause, and cries of 'we do'). I said and I pledged myself, that I should form one of an independent Irish party to act in opposition to every English government which refused to concede the just rights of Ireland (applause). And the longer time which is gone by since then, the more I am convinced that that is the true policy to pursue so far as parliamentary policy is concerned, and that it will be impossible for either or both of the English parties to contend for any long time against a determined band of Irishmen acting honestly upon these principles, and backed by the Irish people (cheers). But we have not alone had that object in view—we have always been very careful not to fetter or control the people at home in any way, not to prevent them from doing any thing by their own strength which it is possible for them to do. Sometimes, perhaps, in our anxiety in this direction we have asked them to do what is beyond their strength, but I hold that it is better even to encourage you to do what is beyond your strength even should you fail sometimes in the attempt than to teach you to be subservient and unreliant (applause). You have been encouraged to organize yourselves, to depend upon the rectitude of your cause for your justification, and to depend upon the determination which has helped Irishmen through many centuries to retain the name of Ireland and to retain her nationhood. Nobody could point to any single action of ours in the house of commons or out of it which was not based upon the knowledge that behind us existed a strong and brave people, that without the help of the people our exertions would be as nothing, and that with their help and with their confidence we should be, as I believe we shall prove

* *The Freeman's Journal,* January 22, 1885, as found in Edmund Curtis and R. B. McDowell, eds., *Irish Historical Documents, 1172–1922* (London: Methuen & Company, Ltd., 1943), pp. 282–284. Used by permission of the publisher.

to be in the near future, invincible and unconquerable (great applause). . . . We shall struggle, as we have been struggling, for the great and important interests of the Irish tenant farmer. We shall ask that his industry shall not be fettered by rent. We shall also ask from the farmer in return that he shall do what in him lies to encourage the struggling manufactures of Ireland, and that he shall not think it too great a sacrifice to be called upon when he wants anything, when he has to purchase anything, to consider how he may get it of Irish material and manufacture (hear, hear), even supposing he has to pay a little more for it (cheers). . . . Well, but gentlemen, I go back from the consideration of these questions to the land question, in which the labourers' question is also involved and the manufacturers' question. I come back, and every Irish politician must be forcibly driven back, to the consideration of the great question of national self-government for Ireland (cheers). I do not know how this great question will be eventually settled. I do not know whether England will be wise in time and concede to constitutional arguments and methods the restitution of that which was stolen from us towards the close of the last century (cheers). It is given to none of us to forecast the future, and just as it is impossible for us to say in what way or by what means the national question may be settled, in what way full justice may be done to Ireland, so it is impossible for us to say to what extent that justice should be done. . . . But, gentlemen, while we leave these things to time, circumstances and the future, we must each one of us resolve in our own hearts that we shall at all times do everything that within us lies to obtain for Ireland the fullest measure of her rights (applause). In this way we shall avoid difficulties and contentions amongst each other. In this way we shall not give up anything which the future may put in favour of our country; and while we struggle to-day for that which may seem possible for us with our combination, we must struggle for it with the proud consciousness that we shall not do anything to hinder or prevent better men who may come after us from gaining better things than those for which we now contend (prolonged applause).

[151] *THE PARIS COMMUNE BECOMES DISTORTED BY MARXIST HISTORIANS* *

Few historical episodes have been so misinterpreted and misunderstood as the Paris Commune of 1871. Following the humiliating defeat of France by Bismarck's

* Edward S. Mason, *The Paris Commune* (New York: The Macmillan Company, 1930), pp. vii-viii, x-xi. Copyright 1930 by the Bureau of International Research of Harvard University and Radcliffe College.

Prussian Army, a new provisional government at Versailles seemed ready to accept an equally humiliating peace treaty. In March, 1871, the communal government of Paris revolted against the Versailles group. Although the Commune contained a number of radicals and a few socialists, it had no intention of setting up a communist regime. The siege of Paris by the Versailles army was marked by extreme ferocity, with the final assault on the city culminating in a gigantic massacre.

The close of the Franco-Prussian War, foreshadowed by the capitulation of Paris on January 28th, 1871, after four months of heroic resistance, was quickly followed by an uprising which has long ago taken its place beside the revolutions of 1830 and 1848. The radical republicans of Paris, among whom were mingled socialists of all shades of opinion, established a government which for two months ruled the capital and gave battle to established authority in France. This government collapsed during the last week of May in the bloodiest bit of street fighting of the century.

The Commune is often lost sight of in the larger panorama of the Franco-Prussian War. Despite the profound impression which it made upon contemporaries with its bombardment of Paris, its summary executions, the massacres in the streets, and the eccentricities of its revolutionary government, it quickly lost its separate identity. For a while conservatives in France and in Europe saw in the revolution of March 18th the hand of socialism. The Commune made the reputation of Karl Marx in France and generated in Europe a remarkable fear of the First International. But soon, as the real weakness of this organization became evident, opinion turned the other way and students of the Commune were inclined to regard it as a regrettable but inevitable by-product of the war. Its socialist origins were vague and its socialist intentions, dubious. Fifteen thousand men were dead, another fifteen thousand imprisoned, and a considerable part of the most beautiful city in Europe destroyed for apparently indefinable reasons and with inappreciable results. The Commune disappeared, leaving scarcely a trace on the institutional life or development of France.

It has been rescued, however, from its somewhat insignificant position as an incident in the history of France, by the activity of the socialists and the communists. In their hands it has become an event of world-shaking importance, a proletarian and socialist revolution par excellence, and the first real government of the working class. The Commune of Paris is, in the opinion of the communists, the immediate forbear of the Russian Soviet. . . .

In the light of this fact the history of the revolution of 1871 must be reconsidered. Was it proletarian and was it socialist? Was it a revolutionary class struggle or something quite other than this? The Marxian version has it that the Commune was socialist because proletarian, "for the proletariat can fight for no other cause than socialism." But this is a complete *non sequitur* to any other than a believer in the Marxian theory of an economically determined class struggle in which the participants are a class-conscious proletariat and a class-conscious bourgeoisie.

The Commune of Paris, as a matter of fact, sprang from an exceedingly complicated historical situation. Irritation and disgust at the loss of the war, the misery of the four-month siege of Paris, the struggle of republicanism against monarchy, socialist desires and aspirations clothed in the ideas of Proudhon and Blanqui, all mingled inextricably in the causes of the revolution. No simple explanation such as that implied in the socialist theory of the class struggle can be accepted.

[152] *THE FRENCH REPUBLIC EXPERIENCES MINISTERIAL INSTABILITY* *

With the collapse of Napoleon III's Empire in 1870, a hastily assembled group of political leaders formed a provisional government, vaguely termed a "republic." However, the National Assembly of 1871 contained a large number of monarchists, who regarded the "republic" as a temporary device. Unable to agree upon details for restoring a king, the royalists acquiesced in 1875 to a republican constitution. Designed as a temporary, stop-gap measure, this constitution became the foundation of the Third Republic.

The Third Republic's constitution was monarchist by birth, republican only by adoption. Its drafters in 1875 had been inspired both by French royalist tradition and by the example of the British parliamentary monarchy; they had designed their makeshift constitution to serve as the framework for a restored monarchy in France. The structure proved flexible enough, however, to adapt itself to republican needs; and so France unintentionally furnished the world with history's first example of the parliamentary republic.

The essence of the parliamentary system lay in the dominant role of the Chamber of Deputies, which could overthrow and replace the executive organ (the cabinet) at will. In contrast to the so-called presidential form of government, there was no attempt at a clear-cut separation of powers, with the executive and legislative branches both stemming directly from the people and kept in equilibrium by a series of checks and balances. At most, there was a separation of functions between the executive and legisla-

* Gordon Wright, *The Reshaping of French Democracy* (New York: Reynal and Hitchcock, 1948), pp. 8–10. Copyright 1948 by Gordon Wright. Reprinted by permission of Harcourt, Brace and Company and of Methuen & Company, Ltd.

tive organs. The seat of national sovereignty, the source of executive authority lay in the Chamber of Deputies alone.

Between 1875 and 1940, practice altered certain aspects of the government's operation. The most significant change was a relative weakening of the executive organs in favor of the legislature. Above all, the executive's chief weapon against the legislature—the right to dissolve the Chamber and to order new elections—fell into complete disuse. The dissolution mechanism rusted for two reasons: because it was once utilized for partisan ends by the monarchist President MacMahon in 1877 (so that thereafter it bore an anti-republican odor), and because dissolution required the Senate's consent, which became more and more unlikely as the Senate fell under the control of the same parties which dominated the Chamber.

The decay of dissolution did much to produce that famous French phenomenon, cabinet instability. During the sixty-five-year life of the Third Republic, France had a sequence of 102 cabinets, which scarcely made for executive strength or authority. The changes became increasingly kaleidoscopic as time passed; calculators have figured that from 1875 to 1920, governments lasted an average of less than ten months each; but that from 1920 to 1940, the speed of rotation just about doubled. If the deputies had been faced by the prospect of dissolution and a subsequent campaign for re-election, they might have been much more cautious before putting the skids under a set of ministers.

A second factor which contributed heavily to cabinet instability was the multi-party system. Once the Republic got well under way, no party ever approached a clear majority in the Chamber; a coalition of from two to a half-dozen groups was always necessary in order to form a cabinet, and the life of such a coalition was at the mercy of each component group. Furthermore, the parties themselves were fluid and ill-disciplined, which added to the structural instability of cabinets. The largest single group, the Radical Socialist, was once described as "not a party but only a state of mind"; and the same was true of all groups except the Socialists and Communists, who arrived late on the scene. The average politician, it was sometimes said, felt that an ideal party would be one which included only himself plus enough voters to elect him to office.

A final aspect of executive decline was the creeping paralysis which afflicted the formal head of the state, the president of the republic. A series of presidents beginning with Jules Grévy consciously limited the scope of their office, and parliament helped this process along by usually electing men of distinctly second-rate qualities. Clemenceau was thinking of the presidency when he coined the caustic epigram, "I vote for the most stupid." It was not long before the president became the butt of French witticisms rather than the symbol of governmental authority. His role was sometimes important as a behind-the-scenes adviser, but in general he spent his time receiving ambassadors and presiding at cattle shows. He emerged into the limelight briefly when cabinets fell, for it was his important duty to name a new premier. Critics sometimes compared the president to the pin boy in a bowling alley, whose only function it was to pick up fallen cabinets as the Chamber knocked them down.

[153] *THE WARD POLITICIAN ASSUMES A KEY ROLE IN AMERICAN DEMOCRACY* *

Lord Bryce (1838–1922), a distinguished English scholar and political leader, wrote his classic study of American political life, The American Commonwealth, *after an extensive tour of the United States. Lord Bryce describes in this selection some of the strengths and weaknesses of American democratic practice in the post-Civil War period.*

As there are weeds that follow human dwellings, so this species thrives best in cities, and even in the most crowded parts of cities. It is known to the Americans as the "ward politician," because the city ward is the chief sphere of its activity, and the ward meeting the first scene of its exploits. A statesman of this type usually begins as a saloon or bar-keeper, an occupation which enables him to form a large circle of acquaintances, especially among the "loafer" class who have votes but no reason for using them one way more than another, and whose interest in political issues is therefore as limited as their stock of political knowledge. But he may have started as a lawyer of the lowest kind, or lodging-house keeper, or have taken to politics after failure in store-keeping. The education of this class is only that of the elementary schools: if they have come after boyhood from Europe, it is not even that. They have of course no comprehension of political questions or zeal for political principles; politics mean to them merely a scramble for places or jobs. They are usually vulgar, sometimes brutal, not so often criminal, or at least the associates of criminals. They it is who move about the populous quarters of the great cities, form groups through whom they can reach and control the ignorant voter, pack meetings with their creatures. . . .

* James Bryce, *The American Commonwealth,* in two volumes, new edition, completely revised with additional chapters (New York: The Macmillan Company, 1924), Vol. II, pp. 64–67. Copyright 1893 by Macmillan and Company; copyright 1910, 1914 by The Macmillan Company; copyright 1920 by Rt. Hon. Viscount Bryce.

English critics, taking their cue from American pessimists have often described these men as specimens of the whole class of politicians. This is misleading. These men are bad enough both as an actual force and as a symptom. But they are confined to a few great cities, those eleven or twelve I have already mentioned; it is their achievements there, and particularly in New York, where the mass of ignorant immigrants is largest, that have made them famous.

In the other cities, and in the country generally, the minor politicians are mostly native Americans, less ignorant and more respectable than these last-mentioned street vultures. The bar-keeping element is represented among them, but the bulk are petty lawyers, officials, Federal as well as State and county, and people who for want of a better occupation have turned office-seekers, with a fair sprinkling of store-keepers, farmers, and newspaper men. The great majority have some regular avocation, so that they are by no means wholly professionals. Law is of course the business which best fits in with politics. They are only a little below the level of the class to which they belong, which is what would be called in England the lower middle, or in France the *petite bourgeoisie,* and they often suppose themselves to be fighting for Republican or Democratic principles, even though in fact concerned chiefly with place hunting. It is not so much positive moral defects that are to be charged on them as a sordid and selfish view of politics and a laxity, sometimes amounting to fraud, in the use of electioneering methods.

These two classes do the local work and dirty work of politics. They are the rank and file. Above them stand the officers in the political army, the party managers, including the members of Congress and chief men in the State legislatures, and the editors of the influential newspapers. Some of these have pushed their way up from the humbler ranks. Others are men of superior ability and education, often college graduates, lawyers who have had practice, less frequently merchants or manufacturers who have slipped into politics from business. There are all sorts among them, creatures clean and unclean, as in the sheet of St. Peter's vision, but that one may say of politicians in all countries. What characterizes them as compared with the corresponding class in Europe is that their whole time is more frequently given to political work, that most of them draw an income from politics and the rest hope to do so, that they come more largely from the poorer and less cultivated than from the higher ranks of society, and that they include but few men who have pursued any of those economical, social, or constitutional studies which form the basis of politics and legislation, although many are proficient in the arts of popular oratory, of electioneering, and of party management.

They show a high average level of practical cleverness and versatility, and often some legal knowledge. They are usually correct in life, for intoxication as well as sexual immorality is condemned by American more severely than by European opinion, but are often charged with a low tone, with laxity in pecuniary matters, with a propensity to commit or to excuse jobs, with a deficient sense of the dignity which public office confers and the responsibility it implies. I shall elsewhere discuss the validity of these charges, and need only observe here that even if the years since the Civil War have furnished some grounds for accusing the class as a whole, there are many brilliant exceptions, many leading politicians whose honour is as stainless and patriotism as pure as that of the best European statesmen. In this general description I am simply repeating what non-political Americans themselves say. It is possible that with their half-humorous tendency to exaggerate they dwell too much on the darker side of their public life. My own belief is that things are healthier than the newspapers and common talk lead a traveller to believe, and that the blackness of the worst men in the large cities has been allowed to darken the whole class of politicians as the smoke from a few factories will darken the sky over a whole town. However, the sentiment I have described is no doubt the general sentiment. "Politician" is a term of reproach, not merely among the "super-fine philosophers" of the New England colleges, but among the better sort of citizens over the whole Union. "How did such a job come to be perpetuated?" I remember once asking a casual acquaintance who had been pointing out some scandalous waste of public money. "Why, what can you expect from the politicians?" was the surprised answer.

[154] *A PROGRESSIVE SURVEYS ACHIEVEMENTS IN AMERICAN DEMOCRACY* *

The Progressive Movement in the United States in the early years of the twentieth century was a revolt of the middle classes, advocating a greater degree of social justice and political reform in opposition to the economic and political power of the wealthy classes. Herbert D. Croly, a New York journalist, became the intellectual leader of the Progressive Movement with the publication of his influential work, The Promise of American Life.

There can be no democracy where the people do not rule; but government by the people is not necessarily democratic. The popular will must in

* Herbert D. Croly, *The Promise of American Life* (New York: The Macmillan Company, 1909), pp. 179–180, 341–342. Copyright 1909 by The Macmillan Company.

a democratic state be expressed somehow in the interest of democracy itself; and we have not travelled very far towards a satisfactory conception of democracy until this democratic purpose has received some definition. In what way must a democratic state behave in order to contribute to its own integrity?

The ordinary American answer to this question is contained in the assertion of Lincoln, that our government is "dedicated to the proposition that all men are created equal." Lincoln's phrasing of the principle was due to the fact that the obnoxious and undemocratic system of negro slavery was uppermost in his mind when he made his Gettysburg Address; but he meant by his assertion of the principle of equality substantially what is meant to-day by the principle of "equal rights for all and special privileges for none." Government by the people has its natural and logical complement in government for the people. Every state with a legal framework must grant certain rights to individuals; and every state, in so far as it is efficient, must guarantee to the individual that his rights, as legally defined, are secure. But an essentially democratic state consists in the circumstance that all citizens enjoy these rights equally. If any citizen or any group of citizens enjoys by virtue of the law any advantage over their fellow-citizens, then the most sacred principle of democracy is violated. On the other hand, a community in which no man or group of men are granted by law any advantage over their fellow citizens is the type of the perfect and fruitful democratic state. Society is organized politically for the benefit of all the people. Such an organization may permit radical differences among individuals in the opportunities and possessions they actually enjoy; but no man would be able to impute his own success or failure to the legal framework of society. Every citizen would be getting a "Square Deal."

It was expected . . . that the secret Australian ballot would do much to undermine the power of the professional politician. He would be prevented thereby from controlling his followers and, in case of electoral trades, from "delivering the goods." Well! The Australian ballot has been adopted more or less completely in the majority of the states; and it has undoubtedly made open electoral corruption now more difficult and less common than it once was. But it has not diminished the personal and partisan allegiance on which the power of the local "Boss" is based; and it has done the professional politician as little serious harm as have the civil service laws. Neither can it be considered an ideal method of balloting for the citizens of a free democracy. Independent voting and the splitting of tickets is essential to a wholesome expression of public opinion; but in so far as such independence has to be purchased by secrecy its ultimate value may be doubted.

American politics will never be "purified" or its general standards improved by an independence which is afraid to come out into the open; and it is curious that with all the current talk about the wholesome effects of "publicity," the reformed ballot sends a voter sneaking into a closet in order to perform his primary political duty. If American voters are more independent than they used to be, it is not because they have been protected by the state against the penalties of independence, but because they have been aroused to more independent thought and action by the intrusion and the discussion of momentous issues. In the long run that vote which is really useful and significant is the vote cast in the open with a full sense of conviction and responsibility.

Another popular reforming device which belongs to the same class and which will fail to accomplish the expected result is the system of direct primaries. It may well be that this device will in the long run merely emphasize the evil which it is intended to abate. It will tend to perpetuate the power of the professional politician by making his services still more necessary. Under it the number of elections will be very much increased, and the amount of political business to be transacted will grow in the same proportion. In one way or another the professional politician will transact this business; and in one way or another he will make it pay.

26

Resistance to Change in Eastern Europe and Asia

In contrast to the increasing industrialization and democratization of Western Europe and America, the great empires of Eastern Europe and Asia retained much of their traditional social and political structure until the second decade of the twentieth century. The multi-national Habsburg Empire of Austria-Hungary, excluded from participation in German and Italian affairs, changed its constitutional structure into a dual monarchy, and turned its attention to the East and South. Russia remained a thoroughly autocratic state throughout the last half of the nineteenth century, although serfdom was abolished by decree in 1861. In the Turkish Empire corruption and incompetence in government seemed to be symptomatic of impending collapse. Far to the East, in China, the intrusion of foreign merchants led to a series of humilitating treaties and internal disorders.

[155] *FRANCIS JOSEPH KEEPS TIGHT CONTROL OVER THE AUSTRO-HUNGARIAN EMPIRE* *

The Habsburg Empire, following defeats by the French and Italians in 1859 and by the Prussians in 1866, underwent an internal reorganization and emerged as

* Joseph Redlich, *Emperor Francis Joseph of Austria* (New York: The Macmillan Company, 1929), pp. 381–384, 445–448. Used by permission of Mrs. Joseph Redlich.

a dual monarchy based upon political dominance of Germans and Magyars. While the rising tide of Slavic nationalism posed a threat of dissolution in both Austria and Hungary, a measure of unity, continuity, and stability was provided for 68 years by Emperor Francis Joseph.

Francis Joseph's main preoccupation during the first decade of dualism was to subordinate the King of Hungary and the sovereign of Austria, the western half of the realm, to the Emperor, as common monarch over both. This role once imposed on him, he was, to the end of his days, to regard it as his most difficult and most important task. It was to dominate his domestic policy, in Hungary and in Austria. In either state, governments had to remember that beyond their immediate legislative and administrative tasks were other tasks, aims, and political considerations arising out of the fact that Austria and Hungary formed a common empire, and, in consequence, had to meet common obligations, transmitted to them through the instrumentality of common ministers. There was a great area which had to be covered by team work between the three ministries, an area covering the development of the army, the direction of foreign policy, and all the vital economic issues committed to the cooperation of the governments and parliaments of the two states by the decennial customs union, including as it did questions of currency and credit, railways and shipping. Here the common ministry—the imperial chancellor, the war minister, and the common finance minister—naturally had a sort of leadership, since, as imperial cabinet, they constituted the immediate and decisive advisers of the Emperor and King.

To complete the picture of the highly complex governmental machine, it must be noted, further, that, under the terms of the 1867 Act, it was incumbent upon the Hungarian premier to keep himself constantly informed about foreign policy; a proviso which, in course of time, was bound to give a similar function to the Austrian premier. This was the machinery Francis Joseph had to rely upon for the conduct of foreign and domestic policy involving interests represented by two parliaments and their respective delegations, seventeen Austrian Provincial Diets and the Croatian Sabor.

It was the so-called informal crown council, composed of the common ministers, the prime ministers of the two states, and, at times, their finance ministers, and presided over by the Emperor, which actually discussed and settled major questions of foreign policy and the relations between Austria and Hungary. That it could and did intervene, with drastic effect, in Austrian home politics was demonstrated by the fall of the Hohenwart ministry in 1871. It was brought down by Beust and Andrassy, who pressed the Emperor to dismiss the Austrian government.

Striking proof of Francis Joseph's gifts as a ruler, of his skill in handling the men with whom he had to deal, and of his inflexible patience and watchfulness as guardian of his realm, is afforded by the fact that the vast machine of dualism did actually work smoothly from the date of its establishment down to the fall of the monarchy, and that no essential part of the driving gear of constitutional government was ever put out of action, even by the crises, often of years' duration, that developed between Austria and Hungary. His great contribution to the vast work of the two governments and of the common ministers was really his constant care for the maintenance of imperial interests, his constant attention to common concerns in so far as they affected army and navy; that is, in the main, to every point at which the internal policy of the two states affected his policy and vice versa.

From the first Francis Joseph set his will to establishing personal authority over foreign policy and military matters. He knew from the outset that, even under dualism, notwithstanding all the ingenuities of Hungarian constitutional law, and the incalculable turns of party strife in Austria, he retained, in these spheres, great monarchical powers. To be, here, an authentic ruler, an absolute ruler such as he had been in the first years of his reign, was the aim of his personal life and of his activity as a monarch, and remained its aim up to extreme old age.

Here he was greatly helped by a singular institution—that of the delegation. The twenty members from the upper house in Vienna, constituting a third of the Austrian delegation, were a sort of reliable political bodyguard for him. In Hungary a similar arrangement was guaranteed him by the prime minister. The foreign minister was, formally, responsible to parliament, but within the first decade of royal and imperial government it had become a matter of common knowledge that so long as the minister enjoyed the confidence of the Emperor his policy had got to be endorsed by the two governments. The constitutional King and Emperor never changed his foreign ministers readily; they were apt to be his most permanent advisers. He had two foreign ministers only during a period extending beyond the first ten years of dualism—Count Andrassy and Count Beust.

Next came . . . the introduction of the new trade and tariff union, agreed upon with Hungary. To find a parliamentary majority for this was indispensable. Count Badeni [Prime Minister of Austria] sought to create one with the aid of the Czechs, at the price of a new language ordinance for the Sudetic lands. This went much further than its predecessor of 1880, since in these provinces it put Czech on a footing almost of equality with German, except for the purpose of the central offices in Vienna.

Calmly considered, this could hardly be regarded as a flagrant injustice to the Germans. At the same time, it definitely contravened the German view, a view which certainly had never been given legal sanction, that German was the Austrian "state language." The ordinance certainly did represent a notable encouragement to the rising Czech civil servant and intellectual. For the same reason, it was felt by the German middle class in Bohemia, Moravia, and Silesia as a serious infringement of their interests and their position in the service of the state. The storm that now broke out, in the first instance in the press and innumerable public meetings, gave striking proof, not only of the real and deep excitement among the Germans in those regions, but of the great advance made by party politics there. There was little talk, now, of material interests; far more of the irremediable wounds dealt at the whole "Austrian state idea" by the Polish count.

In autumn, the session opened with the submission to the members of the draft of a Trade and Tariff Union with Hungary. The German parties at once offered the most strenuous parliamentary opposition. After months of turmoil and agitation, through the length and breadth of German Austria, there was no one on the German side with any pretence of calm—a fact soon hideously evidenced in the parliamentary arena. After a few meetings of the House of Deputies, the parliamentary situation was critical. The Germans now made the fullest use of the weapon of obstruction, on the model employed against the coalition, two years earlier, by the Czechs. But the *furor Teutonicus* went incomparably beyond its Slav prototype.

An unskilful attempt on the part of the Polish vice-president, to break down legal obstruction by the use of his authority as chairman led to really alarming scenes—physical resistance on the part of the opposition and attacks on the chair. Attempts then made by the Czech vice-president, Dr. Kramarz, and Count Badeni, to clear the obstructive members from the chamber by police force, transformed parliament temporarily into a madhouse. The temper of the German members, raised to boiling point by this procedure, very soon spread to the whole population of the capital, and showed itself in the streets of Vienna. Police and then soldiers had to be called out to check first student demonstrations, and then the general populace, roused to action by the social democrats.

By November 27, 1897, conditions in Vienna were almost revolutionary. . . . Two days later, on his return journey from a visit to his daughter in Upper Austria, Francis Joseph saw the mass demonstrations in the streets. Within the space of an hour or two he had countersigned the formal request to be released from office which Count Badeni had proferred some months earlier. . . . The Emperor had simply dropped him. Francis Joseph regarded no minister as irreplaceable! Not that he believed in "revolutionary" Viennese, or any Germans; when his ministers talked so, he merely smiled.

Victorious German obstruction certainly had not saved the "Austrian state idea": the language ordinance remained in force. Equally certain was it that the constitutional principle had been smashed, in parliament, and by the Germans. Obviously, the reaction of this on the Emperor's authority was bound to be bad. Looking back on these days their meaning is clear: no one saw it at the time. *From this moment the Habsburg realm was doomed.*

[156] *THE RUSSIAN SERF LOOKS TOWARD LIBERATION* *

Although the peasants of western Europe had progressed since the thirteenth century from serfdom to freedom, the rural population of Russia from the reign of Peter the Great at the end of the seventeenth century had been forced into a miserable, degrading serfdom. Nowhere else in Europe was the social gulf between noble and peasant so great.

It is difficult to-day to realise even approximately the nature of Russian serfdom. Those familiar with the history of the institution are apt to confine their attention to its legal and economic aspects. It is necessary to grasp the moral and social implications of serfdom as it affected concrete life. We have to understand that the peasant was in actual fact another's property, soul and body; that the lord could sell his serfs; that down to the year 1833 he could at will break up the serf's family as irrevocably as death breaks it up, by selling an individual member apart from the family—for the serf, bound to the soil, could not follow the one who was sold, as the wives of aristocrats were able at their own charges to follow husbands exiled to Siberia. The serf was money, was part of the natural economy. The landowner could gamble away his "souls" at the card-table, or could make his mistress a present of them. The slaves were at the absolute disposal of the lord, who was free to settle whether a gifted child should become cook, musician, or surgeon. The lord disposed likewise of his slaves' wives and daughters, deciding what couples might marry and what couples might not; . . . Terrible is the picture of serfdom given by the best authors in their reminiscences. An attentive reader of the older Russian literature will discern everywhere this peculiar moral and social background. Those who have observed and described Russian village and rural life make express references to the matter. " 'Gryzlov,' said D.S., 'Mariya Theodorova is making ready to go to Moscow. We need money. When I was driving through

* Thomas G. Masaryk, *The Spirit of Russia*, trans. by Eden and Cedar Paul (London: George Allen & Unwin Ltd., 1919), Vol. I, pp. 134–135, 141–142. Used by permission of the publisher.

the villages I saw a number of children; our chattels have been increasing in number; take measures accordingly!' This signified that Gryzlov was commissioned to visit the villages of D.S., to seize some of the superfluous boys and girls, sell them, and hand the proceeds to the land-owner. . . ."

The liberation of the peasantry, as actually carried out, was the result of a compromise between the opponents and the supporters of serfdom and between the conflicting plans of the various parties. Whereas the peasants naturally desired their liberation to be accompanied by the assignment to them of the soil they tilled, no more than an infinitesimal minority of land-owners favored this idea. The best of the land-owners proposed that liberation, if it was to be effected, should be accompanied by the granting of land to the peasants in return for compensation payable to the land-owner by the peasant, by the state, or by both. In the Baltic provinces, liberation was effected without any grant of land, and the peasants had to rent whatever land they needed. Many land-owners in other parts would doubtless have agreed to an arrangement of the kind, but even upon this matter there were conflicting currents. Some desired that the enfranchised peasant should have no land of his own at all; others were willing that he should be granted a small allotment; others proposed a partial enfranchisement with a definite legal formulation of peasant right. The manifesto of 1861 aimed at meeting the land-owners' wishes as far as possible.

Serfdom was abolished, and agrarian difficulties, which still persist, were the sequel of enfranchisement.

[157] *CZAR ALEXANDER II EMANCIPATES THE SERFS* *

At the accession of Alexander II in 1855, nine-tenths of the Russian land was owned by the imperial family and 100,000 noble families. Except for a few small areas of free peasantry, serfs tilled the soil and served in the nobles' households. Alexander began a series of reforms by freeing the serfs on the imperial estates. This action was followed by the emancipation decree of March, 1861.

By the grace of God, we, Alexander II., Emperor and Autocrat of all the Russias, King of Poland, Grand Duke of Finland, etc., to all our faithful subjects make known: . . .

In considering the various classes and conditions of which the State is composed we came to the conviction that the legislation of the empire having wisely provided for the organization of the upper and middle classes

* "History," *The Annual Register, 1861* (London, 1862), pp. 207–212.

and having defined with precision their obligations, their rights, and their privileges, has not attained the same degree of efficiency as regards the peasants attached to the soil, thus designated because either from ancient laws or from custom they have been hereditarily subjected to the authority of the proprietors, on whom it was incumbent at the same time to provide for their welfare. . . .

Having invoked the Divine assistance, we have resolved to carry this work into execution. . . .

The peasants attached to the soil will be invested within a term fixed by the law with all the rights of free cultivators.

The proprietors retaining their rights of property on all the land belonging to them, grant to the peasants for a fixed regulated rental the full enjoyment of their close; and, moreover, to assure their livelihood and to guarantee the fulfilment of their obligations towards the Government, the quality of arable land is fixed by the said dispositions, as well as other rural appurtenances.

But, in the enjoyment of these territorial allotments, the peasants are obliged, in return, to acquit the rentals fixed by the same dispositions to the profit of the proprietors. In this state, which must be a transitory one, the peasants shall be designated as "temporarily bound."

At the same time, they are granted the right of purchasing their close, and, with the consent of the proprietors, they may acquire in full property the arable lands and other appurtenances which are allotted to them as a permanent holding. By the acquisition in full property of the quantity of land fixed, the peasants are free from their obligations towards the proprietors for land thus purchased, and they enter definitely into the condition of free peasants—landholders.

By a special disposition concerning the domestics, a transitory state is fixed for them, adapted to their occupations and the exigencies of their position. On the expiration of a term of two years, dating from the day of the promulgation of these dispositions, they shall receive their full enfranchisement and some temporary immunities. . . .

For which end, we have deemed it advisable to ordain—

1. To establish in each district a special court for the question of the peasants; it will have to investigate the affairs of the rural communes established on the land of the lords of the soil.

2. To appoint in each district justices of the peace to investigate on the spot all misunderstandings and disputes which may arise on the occasion of the introduction of the new regulation, and to form district assemblies with these justices of the peace. . . .

6. Up to the expiration of this term, the peasants and domestics are to

remain in the same obedience towards their proprietors, and to fulfil their former obligations without scruple. . . .

To render the transactions between the proprietors and the peasants more easy, in virtue of which the latter may acquire in full property their close (homestead) and the land they occupy, the Government will advance assistance, according to a special regulation, by means of loans or a transfer of debts encumbering an estate. . . .

Given at St. Petersburg, the 19th day of February (March 3 of the western calendar), of the year of Grace 1861, and the seventh of our reign.

ALEXANDER

[158] *AN ENGLISHMAN DESCRIBES THE SULTAN OF TURKEY* *

The Turkish Empire in the late nineteenth century was looked upon by westerners as a decadent and decrepit survivor of the past. With its finances controlled by foreigners, its army often defeated, its administration corrupt, and its subject peoples in chronic revolt, Turkey maintained a precarious existence. Sir Edwin Pears, author of the selection below, was an English lawyer and newspaper correspondent who lived for over forty years in the Turkish capital.

When I arrived in the country Abdul Aziz was on the throne. He was a harmless sort of Eastern sovereign, who was not generally disliked by his subjects, and who probably thought of his own pleasures more than anything else. His hobby was building. The beautiful palace of Dolma Bagsche, about two miles from Seraglio Point and one of the most conspicuous objects on the Bosporus, was completed in his reign. It was rumored that the Sultan was unwilling to occupy it on account of some superstitious fear. . . .

Public opinion in Turkey could hardly be said at any time to have existed outside Constantinople. But in that city there was a strong party opposed to the Sultan on account of his extravagance, and the show of palaces was the ever-present evidence of his failing. There was also a small group of men who wished to transform the absolutism of the Government into a limited monarchy, and to establish a Constitution. Amongst them Midhat Pasha was the leader. They succeeded in bringing about the revolution which placed Murad on the throne, which deposed him and appointed Abdul Hamid as his successor. It was not a military revolution, and though both soldiers and sailors took part in it, the movement was as spontaneous as such a change could be. After the short attempt at parliamentary govern-

* Sir Edwin Pears, *Forty Years in Constantinople* (London: Herbert Jenkins Ltd., 1916), pp. 102–106. Used by permission of the publisher.

ment and the packing off of the members from the capital, Sultan Abdul Hamid soon showed himself bitterly hostile to all projects of parliamentary government, or to anything which should tend to diminish his absolute power. He is a man of a certain amount of cunning, but also of a meanness of character which is not Turkish. . . .

The moderate party amongst the Turks, reasonable men, even those who wished the government to be conducted on the old lines and to be reformed quietly upon such lines, never had a hearing from him. They soon learned to distrust him, and he on his part became surrounded either by sycophants, working to fill their own pockets, or by unscrupulous adventurers. He had begun by believing that he was surrounded by enemies, and he ended by a general distrust of everybody with whom he came in contact, and with the conviction that he alone knew how to govern the country. Gradually we learned that the chief weapon for his own defence was a system of espionage which, limited at first to men in office, was gradually extended to comprise almost everybody of note in the country.

His surroundings had never been favourable to manliness or to the development of the talents required by a successful ruler. In this he was subject to the same disabilities that for upwards of three centuries have always weighed upon heirs to the Turkish throne. They are largely the results of the Turkish law of succession. Instead of following the European rule, the Crown Prince as already mentioned is the eldest surviving male member belonging to the Imperial family. . . .

The occupant of the throne in Turkey, and especially perhaps the mother of such occupant, desires that her son shall succeed. But in front of him there will probably stand half a dozen members of the family who are his seniors. Fourteen such members ranked before the present Sultan Mahomet V and the eldest son of the deposed Murad. A century and a half ago children of the Royal family who were likely to stand in the way of a succession were often murdered, and some of the most pathetic passages in Turkish history relate to the intrigues which took place either to kill the heir to the throne, or to prevent an infant attaining to that position. The reigning sovereign has usually regarded the Crown Prince with suspicion, and has prevented him becoming acquainted with the Ministers or having any but strictly formal communication with the representatives of foreign states.

It was under this system that Abdul Hamid had been brought up. He was never allowed to see foreign Ambassadors or to take any part in discussing the affairs of the empire. His youthful want of training and his limited environment give the key to his subsequent characteristics, unconsidered action, and above all, suspicion. When on the deposition of Murad,

Abdul Hamid was girded with the sword of Osman, he was the nominee of the party which had brought about two revolutions. That party had great hopes in him and his pliability. They were soon undeceived. . . .

From that time the Sultan turned his attention to removing from the capital all who had aided in placing him on the throne, with one exception. The exception was the Minister of Marine, who lived on and retained his office until his death in 1902. It was only towards the end of his life that I met with him, but he had the reputation of being a brave, bluff sailor who feared neither the Sultan nor anybody else. When he was reproached by Abdul for having pocketed £200,000 in one operation, he corrected his imperial master by saying that it was £300,000. None of us could understand why amidst the dismissal of so many ministers, and of everybody connected with the deposition of his predecessors, Abdul Hamid did not get rid of the Minister of Marine. It was in vain that, in the long interval between 1876 and 1902, everyone knew that the fleet had been allowed to rot and rust, and that with one insignificant exception none of the really magnificent ironclads which the Sultan had found on his accession ever went out of the harbour of the Golden Horn.

Everyone saw that the naval school languished; though torpedo boats and new ironclads had been bought. They knew that the Minister was currently reported to do nothing unless he were heavily bribed, but throughout these long years Abdul Hamid retained him at his post.

[159] *THE MANCHU DYNASTY CLINGS TO THE PAST* *

The Chinese Empire under the Manchus was already in a state of decline when European traders arrived in force about 1840. The Manchus, confronted with superior military and naval power, were forced into a series of humiliating treaties. The Europeans found it advantageous to preserve and even to defend the Manchu Dynasty, hoping to extract further concessions.

It was soon after the last of the T'ang Dynasty had disappeared that the northern barbarians, after being quiet for some centuries, began anew their series of great raids which, after lasting for centuries and sometimes succeeding in planting dynasties on Chinese soil for lengthy periods, culminated in the firm establishment of the Manchu Tartars in Peking in 1644.

The first task of the Manchus was to subdue completely the eighteen

* B. L. Putnam Weale, pseud. for Bertram Lenox Simpson, *The Re-Shaping of the Far East* (New York: The Macmillan Company, 1911), Vol. I, pp. 215–219. Copyright 1905 by The Macmillan Company.

provinces of China; to place the government of Manchuria and Mongolia on a firm military basis; to exact tribute from all neighboring countries, such as Burma and Indo-China; and to revive all the Chinese methods for carrying on the government of the country they had conquered. . . .

No sooner did they enter Peking than they accepted, practically without modifications, the Chinese system as they found it, and set to work not to destroy, but to strengthen with all the means at their disposal the bonds which bound the throne to the Chinese people. . . .

The Chinese system of government is at once patriarchal and democratic. Beginning with the Emperor, it is clear that he simply stands *in loco parentis* to his people and symbolizes in his person the highest authority on earth. In the simple heaven-worship of the ruler is found the dominant note of the Chinese system. By divine providence the Emperor is seated on the throne. Once placed there he is the sire, and his officers are the responsible elders of the provinces, the departments and the districts, as every father of a household is the ruler of its inmates. In theory, therefore, the two leading principles by which the Chinese administration preserves its power over the people are: the exercising of a strict surveillance; and the imposing of mutual responsibility on all classes. But in practice it is government by equipoise and compromise and nothing else; . . .

Supreme in Peking, and possessing the privilege of daily audiences with the throne, are two bodies, to be numbered in whose ranks is the dearest privilege of Chinese officialdom. These two bodies are the *Chun Chi Ch'u,* or Grand Council, and the *Nei-ko,* or Grand Secretariat. Which is the more important body? It is hard to say, because the Grand Council has somewhat superseded the Grand Secretariat in active importance, yet to be styled a *Ta Hsueh shih,* or Grand Secretary, confers the highest distinction attainable by Chinese officials, and possesses a greater literary magnificence than to be a *Chun Chi ta-ch'en,* or member of the Grand Council. Expressed differently, it may be said that the Grand Council, composed of Ministers holding other substantive offices, transacts the real business of the Empire, whilst the Grand Secretariat confines itself to purely internal matters, which involve principles which may be dear to *literati,* but which in reality are unessential to the welfare of the Empire. In 1900 it was the Grand Council, with its numbers temporarily greatly swelled by the presence of all the Manchu princes and nobles and by all the important Presidents and Vice-Presidents of the great Peking Boards, which decided the throne's course of action, whilst the thunder of the Boxers was at its worst and the Court did not know how to act.

Under these two deliberative or advisory bodies are the great government offices through whose hands pass the daily business of the Empire, and whose suggestions, complaints, reports, and plans are handed to the throne by members of the Grand Council and others at the Daybreak Audiences. There are now seven of these great Government Boards,—the Boards of Civil Office, Revenue, Ceremonies, War, Punishments, Works, and Foreign Affairs. An eighth, the Board of Commerce, whose creation has been recently sanctioned by Imperial Edict, as yet possesses an importance too trivial to be seriously considered.

These seven Boards, therefore, correspond to the Ministries of other countries. But their organization is peculiar and gives the first evidence of the equipoise so essential in Chinese affairs. Each Board has two Presidents, one being Manchu and the other Chinese, and four Vice-Presidents, two of whom are Manchu and two Chinese. Here the principle of equipoise is well illustrated. Any trouble that an energetic man might cause is certain to be promptly checked . . . under the system in force; for by pairing officials cleverly, the well-known propensities of each are so hedged round that all danger of inconvenient action is removed.

But in addition there is another safeguard. The obnoxious Court of Censors, a species of degenerate Star Chamber, with two presidents (Manchu and Chinese) directing it, and with a host of minor members scattered over the Empire, has the power of denouncing everybody in the country, and even of directly criticising all the actions of the sovereign. In these degenerate times, unless subsidies are regularly paid to the whole Court of Censors, both metropolitan and provincial officers have an unhappy time of it, and are constantly impeached.

27

Diplomacy and Imperialism

From 1870 to 1914 there were no wars among the major powers. Peace was preserved by a system of long-term military alliances, inaugurated by Bismarck and continued by his successors. With relative stability in Europe, with economic pressures from the increased industrialization, and with an upsurge of intense nationalism, a new imperialism emerged. In the 1880's following Stanley's well-publicized explorations, a mad scramble for African colonies began. British imperialist expansion in South Africa, stimulated by discoveries of gold and diamonds, encountered stiff resistance from the Boers. Simultaneously, in the Far East another scramble for colonies, concessions, and special privileges led to imperialist wars, such as the Russo-Japanese War, and to attempts like the "open door" notes to regulate and equalize the opportunities for imperialism.

[160] *BISMARCK'S DUAL ALLIANCE BECOMES A TRIPLE ALLIANCE* *

For twenty years after the Franco-Prussian War of 1870, Bismarck worked hard to keep the peace of Europe. In 1879 he concluded a secret defensive treaty with

* F. Pribram, *The Secret Treaties of Austria-Hungary,* trans. by Denys P. Myers and J. G. D'Arcy Paul (Cambridge, Mass.: Harvard University Press, 1920), Vol. I, pp. 65–71. Copyright 1920 by The President and Fellows of Harvard College. Reprinted by permission of the publishers.

Austria-Hungary. Two years later France, with Bismarck's blessings, seized Tunis, a land which the Italians had looked on as their future colony. Feeling isolated in a hostile world, Italy sought an alliance with Germany. Bismarck agreed, on condition that Italy join in a three-way treaty which would include her traditional foe, Austria.

Their Majesties the Emperor of Austria, King of Bohemia, etc., and Apostolic King of Hungary, the Emperor of Germany, King of Prussia, and the King of Italy, animated by the desire to increase the guaranties of the general peace, to fortify the monarchical principle and thereby to assure the unimpaired maintenance of the social and political order in Their respective States, have agreed to conclude a Treaty which, by its essentially conservative and defensive nature pursues only the aim of forestalling the dangers which might threaten the security of Their States and the peace of Europe. . . .

Article 1. The High Contracting Powers mutually promise peace and friendship, and will enter into no alliance or engagement directed against any one of their States.

They engage to proceed to an exchange of ideas on political and economic questions of a general nature which may arise, and they further promise one another mutual support within the limits of their own interests.

Article 2. In case Italy, without direct provocation on her part, should be attacked by France for any reason whatsoever, the two other Contracting Parties shall be bound to lend help and assistance with all their forces to the Party attacked.

The same obligation shall devolve upon Italy in case of any aggression without direct provocation by France against Germany.

Article 3. If one, or two, of the High Contracting Parties, without direct provocation on their part, should chance to be attacked and to be engaged in a war with two or more Great Powers nonsignatory to the present Treaty, the *casus foederis* will arise simultaneously * for all the High Contracting Parties.

Article 4. In case a Great Power nonsignatory to the present Treaty should threaten the security of the states of one of the High Contracting Parties, and the threatened Party should find itself forced on that account to make war against it, the two others bind themselves to observe towards their Ally a benevolent neutrality. Each of them reserves to itself, in this case, the right to take part in the war, if it should see fit, to make common cause with its Ally.

Article 5. If the peace of any of the High Contracting Parties should chance to be threatened under the circumstances foreseen by the preceding Articles, the High Contracting Parties shall take counsel together in ample

* That is, the other parties in this alliance would come to the aid of one attacked.

time as to the military measures to be taken with a view to eventual cooperation.

They engage, henceforward, in all cases of common participation in a war, to conclude neither armistice, nor peace, nor treaty, except by common agreement among themselves.

Article 6. The High Contracting Parties mutually promise secrecy as to the contents and existence of the present Treaty.

Article 7. The present Treaty shall remain in force during the space of five years, dating from the day of the exchange of ratifications.

Article 8. . . . Done at Vienna, the twentieth day of the month of May of the year one thousand eight hundred and eighty-two.

Additional Declaration of Italy.

The Royal Italian Government declares that the provisions of the secret Treaty concluded May 20, 1882, between Italy, Austria-Hungary, and Germany, cannot, as has been previously agreed, in any case be regarded as being directed against England. . . .

Rome, May 22, 1882.

[161] *FRANCE AND RUSSIA AGREE TO A MILITARY CONVENTION* *

Bismarck's great success in keeping France isolated barely outlasted his term in office as both France and Russia felt isolated and threatened by the Triple Alliance. Despite the extreme differences between Russian absolutism and French republicanism, the two powers drew together. Both parties were anxious to form an alliance; but to ensure complete secrecy, it took the form of a military convention rather than a formal treaty.

France and Russia, animated by a common desire to preserve the peace, and having no other aim than to prepare for the necessities of a defensive war, provoked against either of them by an attack by the forces of the Triple Alliance have agreed upon the following provisions:

1. If France is attacked by Germany, or by Italy supported by Germany, Russia shall employ all her available forces to fight Germany.

If Russia is attacked by Germany, or by Austria supported by Germany, France shall employ all her available forces to fight Germany.

* Sidney B. Fay, *The Origins of the World War,* Second Edition, Revised (New York: The Macmillan Company, 1943), Vol. I, pp. 118–119.

2. In case the forces of the Triple Alliance or of one of the Powers which compose it should be mobilized, France and Russia, at the first indication of the event, and without a previous agreement being necessary, shall mobilize all their forces immediately and simultaneously, and shall transport them as near to the frontiers as possible.

3. The forces available which must be employed against Germany shall be for France, 1,300,000 men; for Russia, from 700,000 to 800,000 men. These forces shall begin complete action with all speed, so that Germany will have to fight at the same time in the east and in the west.

4. The Staffs of the armies of the two countries shall constantly plan in concert in order to prepare for and facilitate the execution of the above measures. They shall communicate to each other in time of peace all the information regarding the armies of the Triple Alliance which is in or shall come into their possession. The ways and means of corresponding in time of war shall be studied and arranged in advance.

5. France and Russia shall not conclude peace separately.

6. The present Convention shall have the same duration as the Triple Alliance.

7. All the clauses enumerated above shall be kept absolutely secret.

[162] *STANLEY FINDS LIVINGSTONE* *

Henry Morton Stanley (1841–1904), born in Wales as John Rowlands, emigrated to America and fought on both sides in the Civil War. His war reporting won him such fame as a journalist that in 1871 he was sent by the New York Herald *to find David Livingstone in Africa. Livingstone, a Scottish missionary and explorer, was found by Stanley at Ujiji, on the shores of Lake Tanganyika. Stanley's stories from "Darkest Africa" stirred the imaginations of millions, while Livingstone became a national hero of Britain and was buried in the shrine of heroes, Westminster Abbey.*

. . . The news had been conveyed to the Doctor that it was surely a white man that was coming, whose guns were firing and whose flag could be seen; and the great Arab magnates of Ujiji . . . had gathered together before the Doctor's house, and the Doctor had come out from his veranda to discuss the matter and await my arrival.

In the meantime, the head of the Expedition had halted . . . and Selim said to me, "I see the Doctor, sir. Oh, what an old man! He has got a white

* Henry M. Stanley, *How I Found Livingstone* (New York: Scribner, Armstrong and Company, 1872), pp. 410–413.

beard." And I—what would I not have given for a bit of friendly wilderness, where, unseen, I might vent my joy in some mad freak, such as idiotically biting my hand, turning a somersault, or slashing at trees, in order to allay those exciting feelings that were well-nigh uncontrollable. My heart beats fast, but I must not let my face betray my emotions, lest it shall detract from the dignity of a white man appearing under such extraordinary circumstances.

So I did that which I thought was the most dignified. I pushed back the crowds, and, passing from the rear, walked down a living avenue of people, until I came in front of the semicircle of Arabs, in front of which stood the white man with the grey beard. As I advanced slowly toward him I noticed he was pale, looked wearied, had a grey beard, wore a bluish cap with a faded gold band round it, had on a red-sleeved waistcoat, and a pair of grey tweed trousers. I would have run to him, only I was a coward in the presence of such a mob—would have embraced him, only, he being an Englishman, I did not know how he would receive me; so I did what cowardice and false pride suggested was the best thing—walked deliberately to him, took off my hat, and said:

"Dr. Livingstone, I presume?"

"YES," said he, with a kind smile, lifting his cap slightly.

I replace my hat on my head, and he puts on his cap, and we both grasp hands, and I then say aloud:

"I thank God, Doctor, I have been permitted to see you."

He answered, "I feel thankful that I am here to welcome you."

I turn to the Arabs, take off my hat to them in response to the saluting chorus of "Yambos" I receive, and the Doctor introduces them to me by name. Then, oblivious of the crowds, oblivious of the men who shared with me my dangers, we—Livingstone and I—turn our faces towards his tembe. He points to the veranda, or, rather, mud platform, under the broad overhanging eaves; he points to his own particular seat, which I see his age and experience in Africa has suggested, namely a straw mat, with a goatskin over it, and another skin nailed against the wall to protect his back from contact with the cold mud. I protest against taking this seat, which so much more befits him than me, but the Doctor will not yield: I must take it.

We are seated—the Doctor and I—with our backs to the wall. The Arabs take seats on our left. More than a thousand natives are in our front, filling the whole square densely, indulging their curiosity, and discussing the fact of two white men meeting at Ujiji—one just come from Manyuema, in the west, the other from Unyanyembe, in the east.

Conversation began. What about? I declare I have forgotten. Oh! we mutually asked questions of one another, such as:

"How did you come here?" and "Where have you been all this long time? —the world had believed you to be dead." Yes, that was the way it began; but whatever the Doctor informed me, and that which I communicated to him, I cannot correctly report, for I found myself gazing at him, conning the wonderful man at whose side I now sat in Central Africa. Every hair of his head and beard, every wrinkle of his face, the wanness of his features, and the slightly wearied look he wore, were all imparting intelligence to me—the knowledge I craved for so much ever since I heard the words, "Take what you want, but find Livingstone."

[163] *SIR HARRY JOHNSTON ASCENDS THE CROSS RIVER* *

Sir Harry Johnston, a highly successful agent of the Royal Niger Company, became an empire builder by following a standard pattern of flag raising and treaty making. Using identical tactics, Carl Peters, an enthusiastic German adventurer, secured for Germany a vast territory in East Africa.

In a long native canoe Johnston and his forty Kruboys (negro porters) and Callabars paddled up the Cross River, through lonely glades, startling an occasional chimpanzee or elephant herd, but seeing no human beings, until they neared a large negro village. Savages rushed out into the water, dragged Johnston from his canoe, and carried him off to a native hut. There, with a hundred human skulls grinning at him from the walls, he had to sit, while a crowd of savages stared at his strange complexion and clothes. At length his captors question him, through his native interpreter. He came, he said, on a friendly mission from "a great white Queen who was the ruler of the White People." He wished to "make a book" with the ruler of the village —that is, a treaty—to "take home to the Woman Chief" who had sent him out. The natives, fortunately, were agreeable. A burly individual carried him back to the canoe, and there Johnston took a treaty form (he had a stock ready for such contingencies) from his dispatch box, while three or four negroes, apparently persons of authority, crowded into the canoe to make crosses on the treaty. The natives, it seemed, had consumed enough palm-wine to be genial, even boisterous. Seeing their condition, Johnston "was longing to get away." Accordingly, "after the crosses had been splodged on the treaty-form" and he had given them a present of beads and cloth, he made his adieux, but not before the villagers had generously compelled him to accept a hundred

* Parker T. Moon, *Imperialism and World Politics* (New York: The Macmillan Company, 1926), pp. 101–102. Copyright 1926 by The Macmillan Company. Used by permission.

yams and two sheep—and "a necklace of human knuckle bones." Then, fearing that the natives might kill and eat his servants, Johnston made "a judicious retreat."

Such in a general way was the process of treaty-making by which the negro tribes accepted Great Britain's protectorate. A courageous but nervous explorer, bravely concealing his fears; a half-explained treaty of "friendship"; presents of beads and cloth (and of liquor in the case of less high-minded explorers)—these were the typical elements in the situation.

[164] *BRITONS AND BOERS FACE A CRISIS IN SOUTH AFRICA* *

The Boers, a farming people of Dutch descent in the republics of Transvaal and the Orange Free State, developed a strong anti-British feeling in the 1890's as Uitlanders (foreigners, mainly British) swarmed into gold and diamond mining camps. The following statement of British attitude toward the Boers was drawn up by Joseph Chamberlain, British Foreign Minister, a few days after the failure of an ill-timed raid into the Transvaal Republic by British adventurers, led by Dr. Leander Jameson.

Mr. Chamberlain (Foreign Minister of Great Britain) to Sir Hercules Robinson (High Commissioner for South Africa), January 4, 1896. Telegram.

The following are . . . generally the views of Her Majesty's Government, which you should put before the President of the South African Republic. Her Majesty's Government need hardly assure President Krüger of their friendly feelings towards him and their desire to promote the best interests of the Republic, nor of their loyal adherence to the provisions of the London Convention. They feel, however, that the large interests with which they are charged in South Africa justify them in making friendly representations to the President in regard to matters outside the Convention in which persons of British nationality, who have for some time cast in their lot with the South African Republic are deeply concerned.

The principal of these questions is that of the electoral franchise, and that of naturalisation generally. . . . The claim for full citizenship for all persons born in the Republic and also for Uitlanders who have resided for a reasonable period in the Transvaal, and, who have fulfilled all other usual conditions, appears to them to be not unreasonable and justified by the precedents in all civilized States. In connection with this subject I wish you to represent to the President that the form of the oath of allegiance is unusual

* Great Britain, Foreign Office, *British and Foreign State Papers, 1896-1897*, (London, 1901), Vol. LXXXIX, pp. 283–285.

and humiliating. . . . I need only add that, once the way to naturalisation is made easy, and the electorate thus enlarged, an addition to the numbers of the Volksraad * would seem to follow as a necessary corollary, so that votes may have something approaching to an equality of value.

The next point is the taxation. Her Majesty's Government understand that the Uitlanders do not deny that public burdens should be proportionate to ability to pay, and that the Republic is entitled to take toll on the mineral wealth of those to whom the right of working the minerals has been conceded. But, for reasons with which you are familiar, they allege that the existing taxation is unequal, and more especially oppressive to that part of the community by whose toil the South African Republic has been raised to its present prosperity. . . .

The other chief causes of complaint as to which I hope that redress will be granted are (1) the absence of all provision for education for the children whose mother-tongue is other than Dutch, given, when their numbers are sufficient to make establishment of separate schools possible, in their own language; (2) want of efficient civil police in centres of population, especially in connection with detection of crime; and (3) the inefficiency of the present system of mine inspection.

I leave to you, in exercise of the discretion already intrusted to you, to bring forward and press other points as you may deem it advisable; but I should be glad if you could see your way to the inclusion of the very important question of the granting, in due course, of full municipal privileges to Johannesburg. The next matter with which I have to deal is the degree of urgency with which you are to press these points on the attention of the President and other authorities. I am aware that victory of Transvaal Government over Administrator of Mashonaland (Jameson) may possibly find them not willing to make any concessions. If this is the attitude they adopt, they will, in my opinion, make a great mistake; for danger from which they have just escaped was real, and one which, if the causes which led up to it are not removed, may recur, although in a different form.

I have done everything in my power to undo and to minimise the evil caused by late unwarrantable raid by British subjects into the territory of the South African Republic, and it is not likely that such action will be ever repeated; but the state of things of which complaint has been made cannot continue for ever. If those who are now a majority of inhabitants of the Transvaal, but are excluded from all participation in its government were, of their own initiative, and without any interference from without, to attempt to reverse that state of things, they would, without doubt, attract much sympathy from all civilised communities who themselves live under a free Gov-

* The Parliament of the Transvaal Republic.

ernment, and I cannot regard the present state of things in the South African Republic as free from danger to the stability of its institutions. The Government of the South African Republic cannot be indifferent to those considerations; and President of South African Republic himself has on more than one occasion expressed his willingness to inquire into and to deal with just reasons for discontent; and the Volksraad have now the opportunity to show magnanimity in the hour of their success, and to settle all differences by moderate concessions.

[165] *HAY PROPOSES AN OPEN DOOR POLICY TOWARDS CHINA* *

At the end of the nineteenth century China seemed to be on the verge of partition among the Great Powers. United States Secretary of State John Hay, following the suggestions of several influential Englishmen and Americans, proposed to the other powers an "open door" policy towards China (selection 1). Hay subsequently announced the universal acceptance of the "open door" principles (selection 2), despite the vague and evasive nature of the replies. Following the Boxer Rebellion of 1900, Hay reiterated the "open door" policy (selection 3).

1. Secretary to the Ambassador in Great Britain (Choate), Washington, September 6, 1899.

Sir: The Government of Her Britannic Majesty has declared that its policy and its very traditions precluded it from using any privileges which might be granted it in China as a weapon for excluding commercial rivals, and that freedom of trade for Great Britain in that Empire meant freedom of trade for all the world alike. While conceding by formal agreements, first with Germany and then with Russia, the possession of "spheres of influence or interest" in China in which they are to enjoy special rights and privileges, more especially in respect of railroads and mining enterprises, Her Britannic Majesty's Government has therefore sought to maintain at the same time what is called the "open-door" policy, to insure to the commerce of the world in China equality of treatment within said "spheres" for commerce and navigation. This latter policy is alike urgently demanded by the British mercantile communities and by those of the United States, as it is justly held by them to be the only one which will improve existing conditions, enable them to maintain their positions in the markets of China, and extend their

* U.S. Department of State, *United States Relations with China,* Publication No. 3573 (Washington, D.C., 1949), pp. 414–417.

operations in the future. While the Government of the United States will in no way commit itself to a recognition of exclusive rights of any power within or control over any portion of the Chinese Empire under such agreements as have within the last year been made, it cannot conceal its apprehension that under existing conditions there is a possibility, even a probability, of complications arising between the treaty powers which may imperil the rights insured to the United States under our treaties with China.

This Government is animated by a sincere desire that the interests of our citizens may not be prejudiced through exclusive treatment by any of the controlling powers within their so-called "spheres of interest" in China, and hopes also to retain there an open market for the commerce of the world, remove dangerous sources of international irritation, and hasten thereby united or concerted action of the powers at Pekin in favor of the administrative reforms so urgently needed for strengthening the Imperial Government and maintaining the integrity of China in which the whole western world is alike concerned. It believes that such a result may be greatly assisted by a declaration by the various powers claiming "spheres of interest" in China of their intentions as regards treatment of foreign trade therein. The present moment seems a particularly opportune one for informing Her Britannic Majesty's Government of the desire of the United States to see it make a formal declaration and to lend its support in obtaining similar declarations from the various powers claiming "spheres of influence" in China, to the effect that each in its respective spheres of interest or influence

First. Will in no wise interfere with any treaty port or any vested interest within any so-called "sphere of interest" or leased territory it may have in China.

Second. That the Chinese treaty tariff of the time being shall apply to all merchandise landed or shipped to all such ports as are within said "sphere of interest" (unless they be "free ports"), no matter to what nationality it may belong, and that duties so leviable shall be collected by the Chinese Government.

Third. That it will levy no higher harbor duties on vessels of another nationality frequenting any port in such "sphere" than shall be levied on vessels of its own nationality, and no higher railroad charges over lines built, controlled, or operated within its "sphere" on merchandise belonging to citizens or subjects of other nationalities transported through such "sphere" than shall be levied on similar merchandise belonging to its own nationals transported over equal distances.

The recent ukase of His Majesty, the Emperor of Russia, declaring the port of Ta-lien-wan open to the merchant ships of all nations during the whole of the lease under which it is to be held by Russia, removing as it does all uncertainty as to the liberal and conciliatory policy of that power, together with the assurances given this Government by Russia, justifies the expectation that His Majesty will cooperate in such an understanding as is here proposed, and our ambassador at the court of St. Petersburg has been instructed accordingly to submit the propositions above detailed to His Imperial Majesty, and ask their early consideration. . . .

The action of Germany in declaring the port of Kiaochao a "free port," and the aid the Imperial Government has given China in the establishment there of a Chinese custom-house, coupled with the oral assurance conveyed to the United States by Germany that our interests within its "sphere" would in no wise be affected by its occupation of this portion of the province of Shantung, tend to show that little opposition may be anticipated from that power to the desired declaration.

The interests of Japan, the next most interested power in the trade of China, will be so clearly served by the proposed arrangement, and the declaration of its statesmen within the last year are so entirely in line with the views here expressed, that its hearty cooperation is confidently counted on. . . .

2. Secretary Hay to American Diplomatic Representatives at London, Paris, Berlin, St. Petersburg, Rome and Tokyo.

Washington, March 20, 1900

Sir: The ——— Government having accepted the declaration suggested by the United States concerning foreign trade in China, the terms of which I transmitted to you in my instruction No. ——— of ———, and like action having been taken by all the various powers having leased territory or so-called "spheres of interest" in the Chinese Empire, as shown by the notes which I herewith transmit to you, you will please inform the Government to which you are accredited that the condition originally attached to its acceptance—that all other powers concerned should likewise accept the proposals of the United States—having been complied with, this Government will therefore consider the assent given to it by ——— as final and definitive.

You will also transmit to the minister for foreign affairs copies of the present inclosures, and by the same occasion convey to him the expression of the sincere gratification which the President feels at the friendly spirit which animates the various powers interested in the untrammeled development of commerce and industry in the Chinese Empire, and a source of vast benefit to the whole commercial world.

3. Secretary Hay to American Diplomatic Representatives at Berlin, Paris, London, Rome, St. Petersburg, Vienna, Brussels, Madrid, Tokyo, The Hague, and Lisbon.

Washington, July 3, 1900

In this critical posture of affairs in China it is deemed appropriate to define the attitude of the United States as far as present circumstances permit this to be done. We adhere to the policy initiated by us in 1857 of peace with the Chinese nation, of furtherance of lawful commerce, and of protection of lives and property of our citizens by all means guaranteed under extraterritorial treaty rights and by the law of nations. If wrong be done to our citizens we propose to hold the responsible authors to the uttermost accountability. We regard the condition at Pekin as one of virtual anarchy, whereby power and responsibility are practically devolved upon the local provincial authorities. So long as they are not in overt collusion with rebellion and use their power to protect foreign life and property, we regard them as representing the Chinese people, with whom we seek to remain in peace and friendship. The purpose of the President is, as it has been heretofore, to act concurrently with the other powers; first, in opening up communication with Pekin and rescuing the American officials, missionaries, and other Americans who are in danger; secondly, in affording all possible protection everywhere in China to American life and property; thirdly, in guarding and protecting all legitimate American interests; and fourthly, in aiding to prevent a spread of the disorders to the other provinces of the Empire and a recurrence of such disasters. It is of course too early to forecast the means of attaining this last result; but the policy of the Government of the United States is to seek a solution which may bring about permanent safety and peace to China, preserve Chinese territorial and administrative entity, protect all rights guaranteed to friendly powers by treaty and international law, and safeguard for the world the principle of equal and impartial trade with all parts of the Chinese Empire.

28

Science, Socialism, and Religion in the Late Nineteenth Century

Science in the last half of the nineteenth century made enormous strides in many fields. The most startling and controversial discoveries were those of Charles Darwin, who proposed the theory of evolution by "natural selection." Darwinian ideas profoundly influenced literature in the direction of realism and turned philosophy toward materialism. Increasing industrialization and the social evils of the factory system led to the growth of various types of anarchism, syndicalism, and socialism, particularly the "scientific socialism" of Karl Marx. In this welter of confusion the Christian churches, Protestant and Catholic, were assailed from many sides by anti-clerical liberalism, Marxian Socialism, Darwinism, and an increasing amount of indifference to religion.

[166] *DARWIN EXPLAINS EVOLUTION BY NATURAL SELECTION* *

Early in the nineteenth century there had been considerable speculation by scientists on the evolution of complex species of life from simpler forms. Charles

* Charles Darwin, *On the Origin of Species* (New York: D. Appleton and Company, 1873), pp. 1, 3, 61, 103.

Darwin (1809–1882), in his famous work Origin of Species, *carried the concept further than any of his predecessors by proposing a plausible theory of the evolutionary process, by supporting the theory with an impressive accumulation of facts, and by suggesting in the idea of natural selection an easy and universal explanation. Darwin's* Descent of Man *extended the theory from the world of plants and animals to man himself.*

When on board H.M.S. "Beagle," as naturalist, I was much struck with certain facts in the distribution of the organic beings inhabiting South America, and in the geological relations of the present to the past inhabitants of that continent. These facts, as will be seen in the latter chapters of this volume, seemed to throw some light on the origin of species—that mystery of mysteries, as it has been called by one of our greatest philosophers. On my return home, it occurred to me, in 1837, that something might perhaps be made out of this question by patiently accumulating and reflecting on all sorts of facts which could possibly have any bearing on it. After five years' work I allowed myself to speculate on the subject, and drew up some short notes; these I enlarged in 1844 into a sketch of the conclusions, which then seemed to me probable: from that period to the present day I have steadily pursued the same object. I hope that I may be excused for entering on these personal details, as I give them to show that I have not been hasty in coming to a decision. . . .

I shall devote the first chapter of this Abstract to Variation under Domestication. We shall thus see that a large amount of hereditary modification is at least possible; and, what is equally or more important, we shall see how great is the power of man in accumulating by his Selection successive slight variations. I will then pass on to the variability of species in a state of nature; but I shall, unfortunately, be compelled to treat this subject far too briefly, as it can be treated properly only by giving long catalogues of facts. We shall, however, be enabled to discuss what circumstances are most favourable to variation. In the next chapter the Struggle for Existence amongst all organic beings throughout the world, which inevitably follows from the high geometrical ratio of their increase, will be considered. This is the doctrine of Malthus, applied to the whole animal and vegetable kingdoms. As many more individuals of each species are born than can possibly survive; and as, consequently, there is a frequently recurring struggle for existence, it follows that any being, if it vary however slightly in any manner profitable to itself, under the complex and sometimes varying conditions of life, will have a better chance of surviving, and thus be *naturally selected.* From the strong principle of inheritance, any selected variety will tend to propagate its new and modified form. . . .

All that we can do, is to keep steadily in mind that each organic being is striving to increase in a geometrical ratio; that each at some period of its life, during some season of the year, during each generation or at intervals, has to struggle for life and to suffer great destruction. When we reflect on this struggle, we may console ourselves with the full belief that the war of nature is not incessant, that no fear is felt, that death is generally prompt, and that the vigorous, the healthy, and the happy survive and multiply. . . .

We have seen that it is the common, the widely-diffused, and widely-ranging species, belonging to the larger genera within each class, which vary most; and these tend to transmit to their modified offspring that superiority which now makes them dominant in their own countries. Natural selection, as has been marked, leads to divergence of character and to much extinction of the less improved and intermediate forms of life.

[167] *DARWIN LINKS MAN TO LOWER ANIMALS* *

The main conclusion here arrived at, and now held by many naturalists who are well competent to form a sound judgment, is that man is descended from some less highly organised form. The grounds upon which this conclusion rests will never be shaken, for the close similarity between man and the lower animals in embryonic development, as well as in innumerable points of structure and constitution, both of high and of the most trifling importance, —the rudiments which he retains, and the abnormal reversions to which he is occasionally liable,—are facts which cannot be disputed. They have long been known, but until recently they told us nothing with respect to the origin of man. Now when viewed by the light of our knowledge of the whole organic world, their meaning is unmistakable. The great principle of evolution stands up clear and firm, when these groups of facts are considered in connection with others, such as the mutual affinities of the members of the same group, their geographical distribution in past and present times, and their geological succession. . . .

The main conclusion arrived at in this work, namely that man is descended from some lowly organised form, will, I regret to think, be highly distasteful to many. But there can hardly be a doubt that we are descended from barbarians. . . . For my own part I would as soon be descended from that heroic little monkey, who braved his dreaded enemy in order to save the life of his keeper, or from that old baboon, who descending from the mountains, carried away in triumph his young comrade from a crowd of

* Charles Darwin, *The Descent of Man* (New York: D. Appleton and Company, 1896), pp. 606–607, 618–619.

astonished dogs—as from a savage who delights to torture his enemies, offers up bloody sacrifices, practices infanticide without remorse, treats his wives like slaves, knows no decency, and is haunted by the grossest superstitions. . . .

We must, however, acknowledge, as it seems to me, that man with all his noble qualities, with sympathy which feels for the most debased, with benevolence which extends not only to other men but to the humblest living creature, with his god-like intellect which has penetrated into the movements and constitution of the solar system—with all these exalted powers—Man still bears in his bodily frame the indelible stamp of his lowly origin.

[168] *NIETZSCHE INVOKES THE SUPERMAN* *

Friedrich Nietzsche (1844–1900) developed a brutal, pessimistic type of realism with his violent attacks on traditional morality. Nietzsche, greatly influenced by Darwin's concept of the struggle for existence, called on the will of man to create a race of supermen. Nietzsche despised Christianity and the Golden Rule and sought a victory of strength and will over humility and charity.

And Zarathustra spake thus unto the people:

I teach you the Superman. Man is something that is to be surpassed. What have ye done to surpass man?

All beings hitherto have created something beyond themselves: and ye want to be the ebb of that great tide, and would rather go back to the beast than surpass man?

What is the ape to man? A laughing-stock, a thing of shame. And just the same shall man be to the Superman: a laughing-stock, a thing of shame.

Ye have made your way from the worm to man, and much within you is still worm. Once ye were apes, and even yet man is more of an ape than any of the apes.

Even the wisest among you is only a disharmony and hybrid of plant and phantom. But do I bid you become phantoms or plants?

Lo, I teach you the Superman!

The Superman is the meaning of the earth. Let your will say: The Superman *shall be* the meaning of the earth!

For to-day have the petty people become master: they all preach submis-

* Friedrich Nietzsche, *Thus Spake Zarathustra,* trans. by Thomas Common (New York: The Modern Library, n.d.), pp. 27–28, 286–287. Used by permission of the publishers, George Allen and Unwin Ltd., London.

sion and humility and policy and diligence and consideration and the long *et cetera* of petty virtues.

Whatever is of the effeminate type, whatever originateth from the servile type, and especially the populace-mish-mash:—*that* wisheth now to be master of all human destiny—O disgust! Disgust! Disgust! . . .

These masters of to-day—surpass them, O my brethren—these petty people: *they* are the Superman's greatest danger!

[169] *KARL MARX CALLS FOR A COMMUNIST REVOLUTION* *

Karl Marx (1818–1883), in collaboration with Friedrich Engels, issued the inflammatory pamphlet The Communist Manifesto *early in 1848. This publication exerted almost no influence on the wave of revolutions of 1848, however. The* Manifesto *contains nearly all the basic doctrines of Marxian Socialism, and was widely circulated and read in the last half of the nineteenth century.*

A spectre is haunting Europe—the spectre of Communism. All the Powers of old Europe have entered into a holy alliance to exorcise this spectre; Pope and Czar, Metternich and Guizot, French Radicals and German police-spies.

Where is the party in opposition that has not been decried as communistic by its opponents in power? Where the Opposition that has not hurled back the branding reproach of Communism against the more advanced opposition parties, as well as against its revolutionary adversaries?

Two things result from this fact.

I. Communism is already acknowledged by all European Powers to be itself a Power.

II. It is high time that Communists should openly, in the face of the whole world, publish their views, their aims, their tendencies, and meet this nursery tale of the spectre of Communism with a Manifesto of the party itself. . . .

The history of all hitherto existing society is the history of class struggles.

Freeman and slave, patrician and plebeian, lord and serf, guild-master and journeyman, in a word, oppressor and oppressed, stood in constant opposition to one another, carried on uninterrupted, now hidden, now open fight, a fight that each time ended, either in a revolutionary re-constitution of society at large, or in the common ruin of the contending classes.

In the earlier epochs of history we find almost everywhere a complicated

* Karl Marx, "The Communist Manifesto," in *Capital, the Communist Manifesto, and Other Writings* (New York: The Modern Library, 1932), pp. 320–324, 326, 327 329, 330, 332, 333, 335, 343, 355.

arrangement of society into various orders, a manifold gradation of social rank. In ancient Rome we have patricians, knights, plebeians, slaves; in the middle ages, feudal lords, vassals, guild-masters, journeymen, apprentices, serfs; in almost all of these classes, again, subordinate gradations.

The modern bourgeois society that has sprouted from the ruins of feudal society, has not done away with class antagonisms. It has but established new classes, new conditions of oppression, new forms of struggle in place of the old ones.

Our epoch, the epoch of the bourgeoisie, possesses, however, this distinctive feature; it has simplified the class antagonisms. Society as a whole is more and more splitting up into two great hostile camps, into two great classes directly facing each other: Bourgeoisie and Proletariat.

The bourgeoisie has at last, since the establishment of Modern Industry and of the world-market, conquered for itself, in the modern representative State, exclusive political sway. The executive of the modern State is but a committee for managing the common affairs of the whole bourgeoisie. . . .

The bourgeoisie has stripped of its halo every occupation hitherto honored and looked up to with reverent awe. It has converted the physician, the lawyer, the priest, the poet, the man of science, into its paid wage laborers.

The bourgeoisie has torn away from the family its sentimental veil, and has reduced the family relation to a mere money relation. . . .

The need of a constantly expanding market for its products chases the bourgeoisie over the whole surface of the globe. It must nestle everywhere, settle everywhere, establish connections everywhere. . . .

The bourgeoisie, during its rule of scarce one hundred years, has created more massive and more colossal productive forces than have all preceding generations together. . . .

The weapons with which the bourgeoisie felled feudalism to the ground are now turned against the bourgeoisie itself.

But not only has the bourgeoisie forged the weapons that bring death to itself; it has also called into existence the men who are to wield those weapons —the modern working-class—the proletarians.

In proportion as the bourgeoisie, *i.e.*, capital, is developed, in the same proportion is the proletariat, the modern working-class, developed, a class of laborers who live only so long as they find work, and who find work only so long as their labor increases capital. These laborers, who must sell themselves piecemeal, are a commodity, like every other article of commerce, and are consequently exposed to all the vicissitudes of competition, to all the fluctuations of the market. . . .

The lower strata of the middle class—the small trades-people, shopkeepers and retired tradesmen generally, the handicraftsmen and peasants—

all these sink gradually into the proletariat, partly because their diminutive capital does not suffice for the scale on which Modern Industry is carried on, and is swamped in the competition with the large capitalists, partly because their specialized skill is rendered worthless by new methods of production. Thus the proletariat is recruited from all classes of the population. . . .

But with the development of industry the proletariat not only increases in number; it becomes concentrated in greater masses, its strength grows and it feels that strength more. The various interests and conditions of life within the ranks of the proletariat are more and more equalized, in proportion as machinery obliterates all distinctions of labor, and nearly everywhere reduces wages to the same low level. . . .

The proletarian is without property; his relation to his wife and children has no longer anything in common with the bourgeois family relations; modern industrial labor, modern subjection to capital, the same in England as in France, in America as in Germany, has stripped him of every trace of national character. Law, morality, religion, are to him so many bourgeois prejudices, behind which lurk in ambush just as many bourgeois interests.

The modern laborer, on the contrary, instead of rising with the progress of industry, sinks deeper and deeper below the conditions of existence of his own class. He becomes a pauper, and pauperism develops more rapidly than population and wealth. And here it becomes evident that the bourgeoisie is unfit any longer to be the ruling class in society, and to impose its conditions of existence upon society as an over-riding law. It is unfit to rule, because it is incompetent to assure an existence to its slave within his slavery, because it cannot help letting him sink into such a state that it has to feed him, instead of being fed by him. Society can no longer live under this bourgeoisie; in other words, its existence is no longer compatible with society. . . .

The theory of the Communists may be summed up in the single sentence: Abolition of private property. . . .

If the proletariat during its contest with the bourgeoisie is compelled, by the force of circumstances, to organize itself as a class, if, by means of a revolution, it makes itself the ruling class, and, as such, sweeps away by force the old conditions of production, then it will, along with these conditions, have swept away the conditions for the existence of class antagonism, and of classes generally, and will thereby have abolished its own supremacy as a class.

In place of the old bourgeois society, with its classes and class antagonisms, we shall have an association in which the free development of each is the condition for the free development of all. . . .

In short, the Communists everywhere support every revolutionary movement against the existing social and political order of things.

In all these movements they bring to the front, as the leading question in each, the property question, no matter what its degree of development at the time.

Finally, they labor everywhere for the union and agreement of the democratic parties of all countries.

The Communists distain to conceal their views and aims. They openly declare that their ends can be attained only by the forcible overthrow of all existing social conditions. Let the ruling classes tremble at a Communistic revolution. The proletarians have nothing to lose but their chains. They have a world to win.

Working men of all countries, unite!

[170] *POPE PIUS IX CONDEMNS LIBERALISM IN THE SYLLABUS OF ERRORS* *

At the end of the encyclical Quanta Cura, *issued by Pius IX in 1864, appeared a list of eighty erroneous propositions, the* Syllabus of Errors. *Therein the Pope reaffirmed earlier condemnations of liberalism, rationalism, and indifference. The Syllabus was generally misunderstood by its critics. Anti-clerical liberals pointed with glee at the last proposition, in which the Pope seemed to be condemning all modern civilization. It should be borne in mind by the reader that the following are propositions to which the Pope was opposed.*

1. There exists no supreme, all wise, most provident divine Being, distinct from the universe; God and nature are one, and God is therefore subject to change; actually, God is produced in man and in the world; God and the world are identical, as are spirit and matter, true and false, good and evil, just and unjust. . . .

4. All truths of religion derive from the natural force of human reason; hence reason is the principal rule by which man can and should attain the knowledge of all truths of whatever kind. . . .

7. Prophecies and miracles, set forth and narrated in Holy Scripture, are poetical fictions; the mysteries of Christian faith are the results of philosophic investigations; in the books of both Testaments are contained mythical inventions; and Jesus Christ Himself is a mythical fiction. . . .

9. Without exception, all the dogmas of the Christian religion are the

* *The Syllabus of Errors,* in Raymond Corrigan, S.J., *The Church and the Nineteenth Century* (Milwaukee, Wis.: The Bruce Publishing Company, 1938), pp. 289–295.

object of natural science or philosophy; and human reason, developed solely by history, can by its own natural strength and principles arrive at the true knowledge of even the more abstruse dogmas, provided these dogmas be proposed as the object of reason. . . .

15. Every man is free to embrace and profess that religion which, guided by the light of reason, he shall believe true. . . .

20. The Ecclesiastical power must not exercise its authority without the permission and assent of civil government. . . .

26. The Church has no natural and legitimate right to acquire and possess property.

27. The ministers of the Church and the Roman Pontiff ought to be absolutely excluded from all care and dominion over temporal things. . . .

55. The Church should be separated from the State, and the State from the Church.

56. Moral laws do not require a divine sanction, nor is there any need for human laws to be conformable to the law of nature or to receive their binding force from God.

57. The science of philosophy and morals, and likewise of civil laws may and should be withdrawn from divine and ecclesiastical authority. . . .

67. The marriage bond is not indissoluble according to the natural law, and in certain cases divorce, properly so called, may be sanctioned by civil authority. . . .

77. In our times it is no longer necessary that the Catholic religion should be the only religion of the State to the exclusion of all others whatsoever. . . .

80. The Roman Pontiff can and should reconcile and align himself with progress, liberalism, and modern civilization.

[171] *LEO XIII IN* RERUM NOVARUM *ENCOURAGES A CATHOLIC SOCIAL MOVEMENT* *

Leo XIII, greatest of the modern popes, issued his famous encyclical On the Condition of the Workers (Rerum Novarum) *in 1891. The encyclical denied the Marxian concept of class warfare, defended the rights of private property, and called for a "living family wage" for the working man. In the years following, a number of Catholic political parties and Catholic labor unions arose to pursue a social program based on Christian principles, in opposition to Marxian Socialism and economic liberalism.*

* *Two Basic Social Encyclicals: On the Condition of Workers, Leo XIII and Forty Years After, On Reconstructing Social Order, Pius XI.* Latin text with English translation approved by the Holy See, pp. 3–81, *passim.* Copyright 1943 by Benziger Brothers, Inc. Quoted with the permission of Benziger Brothers, Inc., publishers and copyright owners.

1. Once the passion for revolutionary change was aroused—a passion long disturbing governments—it was bound to follow sooner or later that eagerness for change would pass from the political sphere over into the related field of economics. In fact, new developments in industry, new techniques striking out on new paths, changed relations of employer and employee, abounding wealth among a very small number and destitution among the masses, increased self-reliance on the part of the workers as well as a closer bond of union with one another, and, in addition to all this, a decline in morals have caused conflict to break forth.

2. The momentus nature of the questions involved in this conflict is evident from the fact that it keeps men's minds in anxious expectation, occupying the talents of the learned, the discussions of the wise and experienced, the assemblies of the people, the judgment of law makers, and the deliberations of rulers, so that now no topic more strongly holds men's interests.

3. Therefore, Venerable Brethren, with the cause of the Church and the common welfare before Us, We have thought it advisable, following Our custom on other occasions when We issued to you the Encyclicals *On Political Power, On Human Liberty, On the Christian Constitution of States,* and others of similar nature, which seemed opportune to refute erroneous opinions, that We ought to do the same now, and for the same reasons, *On the Condition of Workers.* We have on occasion touched more than once upon this subject. In this Encyclical, however, consciousness of Our Apostolic office admonishes Us to treat the entire question thoroughly, in order that the principles may stand out in clear light, and the conflict may thereby be brought to an end as required by truth and equity.

4. The problem is difficult to resolve and is not free from dangers. It is hard indeed to fix the boundaries of the rights and duties within which the rich and the proletariat—those who furnish material things and those who furnish work—ought to be restricted in relation to each other. The controversy is truly dangerous, for in various places it is being twisted by turbulent and crafty men to pervert judgment as to truth and seditiously to incite the masses.

5. In any event, We see clearly, and all agreed that the poor must be speedily and fittingly cared for, since the great majority of them live undeservedly in miserable and wretched conditions.

6. After the old trade guilds had been destroyed in the last century, and no protection was substituted in their place, and when public institutions and legislation had cast off traditional religious teaching, it gradually came about that the present age handed over the workers, each alone and defenseless, to the inhumanity of employers and the unbridled greed of competitors. A devouring usury, although often condemned by the Church, but practiced nevertheless under another form by avaricious and grasping men, has in-

creased the evil; and in addition the whole process of production as well as trade in every kind of goods has been brought almost entirely under the power of a few, so that a very few rich and exceedingly rich men have laid a yoke almost of slavery on the unnumbered masses of non-owning workers.

7. To cure this evil, the Socialists, exciting the envy of the poor toward the rich, contend that it is necessary to do away with private possession of goods and in its place to make the goods of individuals common to all, and that the men who preside over a municipality or who direct the entire State should act as administrators of these goods. They hold that, by such a transfer of private goods from private individuals to the community, they can cure the present evil through dividing wealth and benefits equally among the citizens.

8. But their program is so unsuited for terminating the conflict that it actually injures the workers themselves. Moreover, it is highly unjust, because it violates the rights of lawful owners, perverts the functions of the State, and throws governments into utter confusion. . . .

Inasmuch as the Socialists seek to transfer the goods of private persons to the community at large, they make the lot of all wage earners worse, because in abolishing the freedom to dispose of wages they take away from them by this very act the hope and the opportunity of increasing their property and of securing advantages for themselves. . . .

10. But, what is of more vital concern, they propose a remedy openly in conflict with justice, inasmuch as nature confers on man the right to possess things privately as his own. . . .

21. The desire . . . that the civil power should enter arbitrarily into the privacy of homes is a great and pernicious error. If a family perchance is in such extreme difficulty and is so completely without plans that it is entirely unable to help itself, it is right that the distress be remedied by public aid, for each individual family is a part of the community . . . for the very reason that children "are by nature part of their father . . . before they have the use of free will, they are kept under the care of their parents." Inasmuch as the Socialists, therefore, disregard care by parents and in its place introduce care by the State, they act *against natural justice* and dissolve the structure of the home. . . .

28. It is a capital evil with respect to the question We are discussing to take for granted that the one class of society is of itself hostile to the other, as if nature had set rich and poor against each other to fight fiercely in implacable war. This is so abhorrent to reason and truth that the exact opposite is true; for just as in the human body the different members harmonize with one another, whence arises that disposition of parts and proportion in the human figure rightly called symmetry, so likewise nature has commanded in

the case of the State that the two classes mentioned should agree harmoniously and should properly form equally balanced counterparts to each other. Each needs the other completely: neither capital can do without labor, nor labor without capital. Concord begets beauty and order of things. Conversely, from perpetual strife there must arise disorder accompanied by bestial cruelty. But for putting an end to conflict and for cutting away its very roots, there is wondrous and multiple power in Christian institutions.

29. And first and foremost, the entire body of religious teaching and practice, of which the Church is the interpreter and guardian, can pre-eminently bring together and unite the rich and the poor by recalling the two classes of society to their mutual duties, and in particular to those duties which derive from justice.

30. Among these duties the following concern the poor and the workers: To perform entirely and conscientiously whatever work has been voluntarily and equitably agreed upon; not in any way to injure the property or to harm the person of employers; in protecting their own interests, to refrain from violence and never to engage in rioting. . . .

31. The following duties, on the other hand, concern rich men and employers: Workers are not to be treated as slaves; justice demands that the dignity of human personality be respected in them, ennobled as it has been through what we call the Christian character. If we harken to natural reason and to Christian philosophy, gainful occupations are not a mark of shame to man, but rather of respect, as they provide him with an honorable means of supporting life. It is shameful and inhuman, however, to use men as things for gain and to put no more value on them than what they are worth in muscle and energy. . . .

37. Those who lack fortune's goods are taught by the Church that, before God as Judge, poverty is no disgrace, and that no one should be ashamed because he makes his living by toil. . . .

49. . . . the State has one basic purpose for existence, which embraces in common the highest and the lowest of its members. Non-owning workers are unquestionably citizens by nature in view of the same right as the rich, that is, true and vital parts whence, through the medium of families, the body of the State is constituted; and it hardly need be added that they are by far the greatest number in every urban area. Since it would be quite absurd to look out for one portion of the citizens and to neglect another, it follows that public authority ought to exercise due care in safe-guarding the well-being and the interests of non-owning workers. . . .

59. Now as concerns the protection of corporeal and physical goods, the oppressed workers, above all, ought to be liberated from the savagery of greedy men, who inordinately use human beings as things for gain. Assur-

edly, neither justice nor humanity can countenance the exaction of so much work that the spirit is dulled from excessive toil and that along with it the body sinks crushed from exhaustion. . . .

69. In our present age of greater culture, with its new customs and ways of living, and with the increased number of things required by daily life, it is most clearly necessary that workers' associations be adapted to meet the present need. It is gratifying that societies of this kind composed either of workers alone or of workers and employers together are being formed everywhere, and it is truly to be desired that they grow in number and in active vigor. . . .

81. The condition of workers is a subject of bitter controversy at the present time; and whether this controversy is resolved in accordance with reason or otherwise, is in either event of utmost importance to the State. But Christian workers will readily resolve it in accordance with reason, if, united in associations and under wise leaders, they enter upon the path which their fathers and their ancestors followed to their own best welfare as well as to that of the State.

IV

The Contemporary Age

THE YEAR 1914 PROVIDES a convenient historical dividing line, separating a long era of relative peace from the contemporary world, in which violence and bloodshed have become commonplace. The years since 1914 have differed markedly from earlier historical periods in (1) the amount of destruction and disruption caused by two world wars and a number of lesser wars and revolutions; (2) the bitterness and intensity of the confrontation of mutually incompatible ideologies; (3) the rapidity of scientific and technological change; and (4) the spread of nationalism to the peoples of Asia and Africa.

The initial tragedy of this period was that none of the Great Powers in 1914 had a compelling or even a justifiable reason for going to war. Probably none, with the exception of Austria-Hungary, really wanted war. Yet, when the leaders faced the alternatives of war or the probable breakdown of the alliance system, on which they believed their security to be based, they chose the former.

World War I, despite the global implication of the name, was essentially a European conflict, like the earlier "world wars" of the eighteenth and early nineteenth centuries. The bitterness of feeling engendered by the intensity and length of World War I carried over to the Peace Conference of 1919. Unlike the earlier Congress of Vienna, in which the vanquished party, France, participated, the peacemakers of the Paris Conference excluded Germany from the discussions. The terms were harsh for the losers, particularly in loss of territory and in the reparations clauses. The new German Republic, founded in 1918, flourished for a few years, but collapsed in 1933 under the double impact of the economic depression and pressure exerted by Hitler's Nazi Party. With the Nazis in power, the Jews were blamed for Germany's past misfortunes, the terms of the Versailles Treaty were openly violated, and an aggressive foreign policy was adopted, which led directly to World War II.

World War II was a truly global conflict; much of the fighting took place in the western Pacific region, in North Africa, and in Southeast Asia, as well as Europe. The development of long-range aircraft brought heavy destruction to cities far from the front. An added tragedy of World War II was Hitler's "Final solution of the Jewish problem"—mass extermination. An estimated six million Jews were slaughtered in this deliberate attempt to wipe out an entire socio-religious group. The end of World War II brought a double challenge to the post-war generation: the problem of controlling atomic weapons, and an intense ideological conflict, the Cold War.

Political ideology had played little part in World War I until Woodrow Wilson asserted that the Allies were fighting to make the world safe for democracy. The expression became immensely popular, and a number of new "democracies" were established in 1918 and the years following. The writing of democratic constitutions proved to be much simpler than the practical application of democratic principles among people who had had little previous experience in active participation in political life. Nations with highly stratified social structures and with concentrations of wealth in a few hands rarely achieved democracy.

During 1925–1939 dictatorships and authoritarian rule supplanted democracy in many of the nations of Europe. Most of the dictatorships were of the "right," following in general the pattern of Mussolini, who stressed nationalism, exalted the concept of the State, and preserved under tight control the institutions of capitalism.

In Russia the revolution of March, 1917, had brought to power a liberal, democratic regime in place of the autocracy of the Czars. This Provisional Government was overthrown in November, 1917, by a tightly organized Communist group under Lenin, who established a "dictatorship of the proletariat" according to the principles of Karl Marx. The Communists defended their regime through a period of civil war, and proceeded to eliminate the middle classes, abolish private capital and organized religion, and adopt a planned economy.

From the start, Lenin's Communism was a militant proselyting movement, controlling an international network of dedicated sympathizers in all countries of the world. The avowed and unchanged aim was the attainment of a Communist world, directed by Moscow. During and after World War II, Soviet-sponsored Communist governments were installed in most of the countries of Eastern Europe which were under occupation by the Red Army. Soviet occupation zones in Germany and Korea were turned into satellite Communist states, and the Communist Party of China gained control of that country by driving out the Nationalist regime.

Confronting this monolithic organization were: the United States, the wealthiest and most powerful nation of the world in the post-war period; the traditional democracies of the West; the newly democratic states of Japan and West Germany; and a number of lesser nations. It is another of the tragedies of modern times that the development of atomic energy occurred at a moment when the world was sharply divided ideologically. With both camps in possession of nuclear weapons and missiles, each had the power to obliterate the other.

Aside from the spectacular discoveries of atomic physics, progress in physics and chemistry and in related technological fields transformed the everyday lives of millions, particularly in the "advanced" countries of Europe and North America. New drugs and vaccines and better diets increased longevity. New fertilizers and better mechanical equipment increased agricultural yields, especially in the United States, where huge food surpluses became for the first time in history a major problem. Use of machinery, particularly automated equipment in industry, released workers from long hours of toil. New applications of electricity and new electronic devices brought revolutionary changes in communications.

The concentration of these achievements within the advanced countries of the West emphasized the increasing gulf separating the economically mature nations from the backward or underdeveloped countries. Most of these underdeveloped countries, particularly in Africa and Asia, were swept up in a wave of intense nationalism, in which a movement toward independence from colonial domination was merged with the desire for industrialization and economic betterment. By the early 1960's the emergence of the backward peoples was becoming an important element in the global struggle between Communism and the Free World.

29

World War I and the Russian Revolution

In the decade from 1905 to 1914 a succession of crises increased tension between the Triple Entente and the Triple Alliance. Compromise became impossible as each of the great powers felt that its national interests were at stake. When war came, Germany found herself fighting a two-front war against Russia in the east and against England and France, later joined by Italy and America, in the west. The entry of America on the Allied side in 1917 compensated for the near-exhaustion of England and France, and the collapse of Russia. In Russia the liberal, democratic elements which had overthrown the Czarist government in March, 1917, were in turn replaced by the Communists in November of the same year. The Communists quickly made a separate peace with Germany and began to consolidate their regime.

[172] *A RUSSIAN DIPLOMAT REVIEWS THE BOSNIAN CRISIS OF 1908* *

Austria-Hungary in 1908 took the dangerous step of annexing Bosnia and Herzegovina, Serb-speaking provinces nominally a part of the Turkish Empire but

* Serge Sazonov, *Fateful Years, 1909–1916* (London: Jonathan Cape Limited, 1928), pp. 14–15, 17, 19, 20. Used by permission of Jonathan Cape Limited.

administered by Austria-Hungary since 1878. Serbia, enraged by this crushing blow to her expansion plans, appealed to Russia. The Russians, however, were too exhausted by their recent war with Japan to furnish aid. Germany, on the other hand, offered full military support to Austria. Serge Sazonov, author of this selection, was an able diplomat, serving as Russia's foreign minister from 1910 to 1916.

From this political rivalry in the Balkans sprang a perpetual enmity between Vienna and St. Petersburg, fated to lead sooner or later to open war—the inevitable outcome of the irreconcilable antipathy. It was always improbable, on account of the general European character which Balkan questions had long since assumed, that Russia and Austria-Hungary would be able to settle accounts with regard to the Balkans without drawing the other Powers into the struggle; but when Bismarck concluded an alliance with Austria in 1879 there was no longer any hope of confining the matter to a mére duel between the two rivals. This was recognized by all the European Cabinets. Nevertheless, up to 1909 Germany refrained from openly avowing her full solidarity with Austria-Hungary's Balkan policy; . . . The Bosnia and Herzegovina crisis in 1908–9 revealed the true state of affairs to the whole of Europe. Aehrenthal's unscrupulous conduct in converting the actual control of Bosnia and Herzegovina, which entailed no danger for the Austro-Hungarian Monarchy, into a juridical possession by means of a gross infringement of all law, was a challenge to the whole Serbian people and also to Russia; not only did it fail to evoke any expression of disapproval from the German Government—it actually received the support and protection of Germany's Imperial power. Europe was confronted with a *fait accompli,* and was forced either to accept it as such, or to engage in an armed struggle with Austria-Hungary, and possibly with the whole of the Triple Alliance.

The public opinion of Europe condemned the methods of Austrian diplomacy, recognizing in them a threat to the legal stability of international State life; but no one was eager to oppose them by force of arms. The direct interests of Western Europe were not affected by the Austrian *coup,* and the danger of provoking a European war, with its disastrous consequences, was apparent to all. Consequently, neither France nor England could be expected to concern themselves with this question, beyond according their diplomatic support to the wronged party.

In Serbia and Russia, however, the Bosnia-Herzegovina crisis called forth very different feelings. For Serbia the absorption by Austria-Hungary of a considerable portion of the Serbian race was not only a heavy blow to her national pride, it was also an ominous forecast of the ulterior designs of the Viennese policy. Russia, although her interests were not directly affected, nevertheless felt insulted by the methods adopted by Count Aehrenthal in dealing with [Isvolsky] the Russian Minister for Foreign Affairs. By means of a palpable concealment he allowed himself to interpret certain general conversations between himself and Isvolsky as a consent on the part of the Russian Government to the immediate annexation of the occupied Turkish provinces. . . .

In order to paralyse any active opposition on the part of Russia, it was necessary to have recourse to extreme measures; and Aehrenthal, not relying upon his own strength, sought the aid of his ally, Germany. Assistance was accorded him without stint. . . .

The Russian Government was called upon to choose between two weighty decisions: to sacrifice Serbia, or to renounce its openly-expressed opinion as to the legality of the Austrian seizure. It chose the latter course, at the price of its own self-respect. . . .

Serbia obeyed the friendly advice of Russia and the Western Powers, and prudently refrained from kindling a European conflagration under political circumstances unfavourable to her own future. The diplomatic incident was closed; but the bad seed sown by Aehrenthal bore poisonous fruit in the injured sense of national dignity of which the Serbs remained conscious.

[173] *DEATH COMES TO ARCHDUKE FRANCIS FERDINAND* *

Archduke Francis Ferdinand of Austria was the nephew and heir to the throne of the aged Habsburg Emperor Francis Joseph. The announcement of the Archduke's intention of visiting Sarajevo, the Bosnian capital, led to a plot by a group of Bosnian youths to assassinate him. Trained and armed in Serbia by the "Black Hand" organization, three assassins returned to Sarajevo to await their victim.

Sarajevo, for some five hundred years, had been the capital of Bosnia and is still its principal city. It is crowded into a narrow valley at the foot of high hills. Through its center runs a little river, the Miljachka, half dry in summer. In the older parts of the city toward the cathedral the streets are crooked and narrow. But the Appel Quay, now known as the Stepanovitch Quay, is a fairly wide straight avenue lined with houses on one side, and with a low wall on the other, where the Quay follows the Miljachka. . . . Along the

* Sidney B. Fay, *The Origins of the World War,* Second Edition, Revised (New York: The Macmillan Company, 1943), Vol. II, pp. 121–126.

Appel Quay, which was the route the Archduke and his wife were to follow, Ilitch had placed the various murderers to whom he had distributed the bombs and revolvers a few hours before the assassination. . . .

On Vidov-Dan, Sunday, June 28, 1914, the day opened with glorious summer weather. The streets, at the request of the Mayor, had been beflagged in the Archduke's honor. His portrait stood in many windows. Considerable crowds were abroad in the streets to see him pass. No effort was made to keep them back, by forming a line of soldiers, as had been done in 1910 when Francis Joseph visited the city. Several of the loyal newspapers welcomed the Archduke's presence, but the leading Serb newspaper, *Narod,* contented itself with the bare announcement of his visit, and devoted the rest of its issue to a patriotic account of the significance of Vidov-Dan, an account of the Battle of Kossovo, and a picture of King Peter of Serbia framed in the national Serbian colors.

Franz Ferdinand and his party reached Sarajevo . . . about 10 A.M. After reviewing local troops, they started in autos toward the Town Hall for the formal reception in accordance with the announced program. The Heir to the Throne was in full uniform, wearing all his decorations. His wife, in a white gown and large hat, sat beside him. On the seat facing them was General Potiorek, the military Governor of Bosnia, who pointed out the objects of interest as they drove along. In front of them, in another car, the Mayor and Chief of Police led the way. Then followed two other autos bearing various persons belonging to the Archduke's suite or General Potiorek's staff.

Just as they were approaching the Cumurja Bridge and Potiorek was calling the Archduke's attention to some new barracks, Chabrinovitch knocked off the cap of his bomb against a post, stepped forward, and hurled it at the Archduke's car. The chauffeur, observing him, put on speed, so that the missile fell onto the folded hood of the uncovered car and bounced off; or, according to another account, Franz Ferdinand, with extraordinary coolness, seized it and threw it back of him into the road. There it exploded with a heavy detonation, partly wrecking the following auto and seriously wounding Lieut.-Col. Merizzi and several bystanders. Chabrinovitch sprang over the wall into the river-bed, which was nearly dry at this season of the year, and tried to escape; but police agents quickly seized him and marched him off for examination. Meanwhile the fourth auto, uninjured except for a broken windshield, passed the wrecked car and closed up quickly to that of the Archduke, none of whose occupants had been hurt, except for a scratch on the Archduke's face, probably caused by the flying cap of the bomb. The Archduke ordered all the cars to stop, in order to learn what damage had been done. Having seen that the wounded men were dispatched to a hospital, he remarked with characteristic coolness and courage: "Come on. The fellow is insane. Gentlemen, let us proceed with our program."

So the party drove on to the Town Hall, at first rapidly, and then, at the Archduke's order, more slowly so that the people could see him better. The Archduke's wife met a deputation of Mohammedan women, while the Archduke was to receive the city officials. The Mayor, who had written out his speech of welcome, started to read it, as if nothing had happened. But it hardly suited the occasion. It dilated upon the loyalty of the Bosnian people and the overwhelming joy with which they welcomed the Heir to the Throne. Franz Ferdinand, by nature quick-tempered and outspoken, roughly interrupted the Mayor, saying: "Enough of that. What! I make you a visit, and you receive me with bombs." Nevertheless, he allowed the Mayor to finish his address. This terminated the formalities at the Town Hall.

The question then arose whether the party should still follow the prearranged program which provided for a drive through the narrow Franz Josef Street in the crowded part of the city, and a visit to the Museum; or whether, in view of another possible attack, they should drive straight to the Governor's residence on the other side of the river for luncheon. The Archduke insisted that he wanted to visit the hospital to inquire after the officer who had been wounded by Chabrinovitch's bomb. General Potiorek and the Chief of Police thought it very unlikely that any second attempt at murder would be made on the same day. But as a punishment for the first, and for the sake of safety, it was decided that the autos should not follow the prearranged route through the narrow Franz Josef Street, but should reach the hospital and Museum by driving rapidly straight along the Appel Quay. Therefore the Archduke and his wife and the others entered the cars in the same order as before, except that Count Harrach stood on the left running-board of the Archduke's car, as a protection from any attack from the Miljachka side of the Quay. On reaching the Franz Josef Street the Mayor's car in the lead turned to the right into it, according to the original program. The Archduke's chauffeur started to follow it, but Potiorek called out. "That's the wrong way! Drive straight down the Appel Quay!" The chauffeur put on the brakes in order to back up. It happened that it was precisely at this corner, where the car paused for a fatal moment, that Princip was now standing, having crossed over from his original position on the river side of the Quay. These chance occurrences gave him the best possible opportunity. He stepped forward and fired two shots point blank. One pierced the Archduke's neck so that blood spurted from his mouth. The other shot, aimed perhaps at Potiorek, entered the abdomen of Sophie Chotek [wife of the Archduke].

The car turned and sped over the Latin Bridge to the Konak. The Archduke's last words to his wife were: "Sophie, Sophie, do not die. Live for our children." But death overtook them both within a few minutes. It was about 11:30 A.M., St. Vitus's Day, Sunday, June 28, 1914.

[174] *WILSON PRESENTS A FOURTEEN POINT PROGRAM FOR PEACE* *

President Woodrow Wilson's Fourteen Points, presented in January, 1918, became a potent propaganda weapon for the Allied cause. Germany in November, 1918, agreed to an armistice on the understanding that the Fourteen Points would be taken as the basis for a peace settlement.

. . . We entered this war because violations of right had occurred which touched us to the quick and made the life of our own people impossible unless they were corrected and the world secured once for all against their recurrence. What we demand in this war, therefore, is nothing peculiar to ourselves. It is that the world be made fit and safe to live in; and particularly that it be made safe for every peace-loving nation which, like our own, wishes to live its own life, determine its own institutions, be assured of justice and fair dealing by the other peoples of the world as against force and selfish aggression. All the peoples of the world are in effect partners in this interest, and for our own part we see very clearly that unless justice be done to others it will not be done to us. The programme of the world's peace, therefore, is our programme; and that programme, the only possible programme, as we see it, is this:

I. Open covenants of peace, openly arrived at, after which there shall be no private international understandings of any kind but diplomacy shall proceed always frankly and in the public view.

II. Absolute freedom of navigation upon the seas, outside territorial waters, alike in peace and in war, except as the seas may be closed in whole or in part by international action for the enforcement of international covenants.

III. The removal, so far as possible, of all economic barriers and the establishment of an equality of trade conditions among all the nations consenting to the peace and associating themselves for its maintenance.

IV. Adequate guarantees given and taken that national armaments will be reduced to the lowest point consistent with domestic safety.

* "Address of the President of the United States Delivered at a Joint Session of the Two Houses of Congress, January 8, 1918," U.S. Department of State, *Papers Relating to the Foreign Relations of the United States, 1918,* Supplement I, pp. 12–17.

V. A free, open-minded, and absolutely impartial adjustment of all colonial claims, based upon a strict observance of the principle that in determining all such questions of sovereignty the interests of the populations concerned must have equal weight with the equitable claims of the government whose title is to be determined.

VI. The evacuation of all Russian territory and such a settlement of all questions affecting Russia as will secure the best and freest cooperation of the other nations of the world in obtaining for her an unhampered and unembarrassed opportunity for the independent determination of her own political development and national policy and assure her of a sincere welcome into the society of free nations under institutions of her own choosing; and, more than a welcome, assistance of every kind that she may need and may herself desire. The treatment accorded Russia by her sister nations in the months to come will be the acid test of their good will, of their comprehension of her needs as distinguished from their own interests, and of their intelligent and unselfish sympathy.

VII. Belgium, the whole world will agree, must be evacuated and restored, without any attempt to limit the sovereignty which she enjoys in common with all other free nations. No other single act will serve as this will serve to restore confidence among the nations in the laws which they have themselves set and determined for the government of their relations with one another. Without this healing act the whole structure and validity of international law is forever impaired.

VIII. All French territory should be freed and the invaded portions restored, and the wrong done to France by Prussia in 1871 in the matter of Alsace-Lorraine, which has unsettled the peace of the world for nearly fifty years, should be righted in order that peace may once more be made secure in the interest of all.

IX. A readjustment of the frontiers of Italy should be effected along clearly recognizable lines of nationality.

X. The peoples of Austria-Hungary, whose place among the nations we wish to see safeguarded and assured, should be accorded the freest opportunity of autonomous development.

XI. Rumania, Serbia, and Montenegro should be evacuated; occupied territories restored; Serbia accorded free and secure access to the sea; and the relations of the several Balkan states to one another determined by friendly counsel along historically established lines of allegiance and nationality; and international guarantees of the political and economic independence and territorial integrity of the several Balkan states should be entered into.

XII. The Turkish portions of the present Ottoman Empire should be assured a secure sovereignty, but the other nationalities which are now under Turkish rule should be assured an undoubted security of life and an absolutely unmolested opportunity of autonomous development, and the Dardanelles should be permanently opened as a free passage to the ships and commerce of all nations under international guarantees.

XIII. An independent Polish state should be erected which should include the territories inhabited by indisputably Polish populations, which should be assured a free and secure access to the sea, and whose political and economic independence and territorial integrity should be guaranteed by international covenant.

XIV. A general association of nations must be formed under specific covenants for the purpose of affording mutual guarantees of political independence and territorial integrity to great and small states alike.

[175] *THE SOVIET OF WORKERS' DEPUTIES APPEALS TO THE RUSSIAN PEOPLE.* *

Conditions in Russia by 1917 were becoming impossible. Food shortages in the cities, munitions shortages at the front, the breakdown of rail transport, and the incompetence of the Czar's government led to a revolution in Petrograd, the capital, in which soldiers and workers formed "soviets" or councils. The soviets joined with the Duma, the Russian parliament, to form a provisional government. The next day Czar Nicholas II abdicated.

The old regime has brought the country to ruin and the population to famine. It was impossible to bear this longer, and the inhabitants of Petrograd came out on the street to express their dissatisfaction. They were greeted with a volley of bullets. In place of bread, the Czar's Ministers gave them lead.

But the soldiers would not act against the people and turned against the Government. Together with the people they seized guns, arsenals, and important governmental institutions.

The fight is still on and must go on to the end. The old power must be completely crushed to make way for popular government. In that lies the salvation of Russia.

In order to succeed in this struggle for democracy, the people must create their own governmental organ. Yesterday, March 12, there was formed

* *Izvestiya,* No. 1, March 13, 1917, Soviet of Workers' Deputies, as found in Frank Alfred Golder, *Documents of Russian History, 1914–1917,* trans. by Emanuel Aronsberg, pp. 287–288. Copyright 1927 by The Century Co. Reprinted by permission of Appleton-Century-Crofts, Inc.

at the capital a Soviet of Workers' Deputies, made up of representatives of factories, mills, revolted troops, and democratic and socialistic parties and groups. The Soviet, sitting in the Duma, has set for itself as its main task to organize the popular forces, and to fight for the consolidation of political freedom and popular government.

The Soviet has appointed commissars to establish the people's authority in the wards of Petrograd. We invite the entire population of the capital to rally at once to the Soviet, to organize local committees in their wards and take into their hands the management of local affairs.

All together, with our forces united, we will fight to wipe out completely the old Government and to call a constituent assembly on the basis of universal, equal, direct, and secret suffrage.

[176] *LENIN AND THE BOLSHEVIKS OVERTHROW THE KERENSKY REGIME* *

The provisional government which emerged from the first Russian Revolution of March, 1917, attempted, under Alexander Kerensky, to continue the unpopular war against Germany. As Kerensky failed to provide determined, effective leadership, a small group of Bolsheviks (Communists) won the support of soldiers, sailors, and workers in Petrograd. The Bolsheviks, ably led by Nicolai Lenin, who had returned from exile with German assistance, seized control from the Kerensky Regime on November 7, 1917.

Meeting of the Petrograd Soviet

The meeting opened at 2:35 P.M. with Trotzky in the chair. He said: "In the name of the War-Revolutionary Committee, I announce that the Provisional Government no longer exists. (Applause.) Some of the Ministers are already under arrest. (Bravo.) Others soon will be. (Applause.) The revolutionary garrison, under the control of the War-Revolutionary Committee, has dismissed the Assembly of the Pre-Parliament Council of the Republic. (Loud applause. "Long live the War-Revolutionary Committee.") . . . The railway stations, post and telegraph offices, the Petrograd Telegraph Agency, and State Banks are occupied. . . ."

Trotzky continued by saying: "In our midst is Vladimir Ilich Lenin, who, by force of circumstances, had not been able to be with us all this time. . . . Hail the return of Lenin!" The audience gave him a noisy ovation. . . .

* *Izvestiya,* No. 207, November 8, 1917, as found in Frank Alfred Golder, *Documents of Russian History, 1914–1917,* trans. by Emanuel Aronsberg, pp. 617–619.

Lenin's Speech

Comrades, the workmen's and peasants' revolution, the need of which the Bolsheviks have emphasized many times, has come to pass.

What is the significance of this revolution? Its significance is, in the first place, that we shall have a soviet government, without the participation of bourgeoisie of any kind. The oppressed masses will of themselves form a government. The old state machinery will be smashed into bits and in its place will be created a new machinery of government by the soviet organizations. From now on there is a new page in the history of Russia, and the present, third Russian revolution shall in its final result lead to the victory of Socialism.

One of our immediate tasks is to put an end to the war at once. But in order to end the war, which is closely bound up with the present capitalistic system, it is necessary to overthrow capitalism itself. In this work we shall have the aid of the world labor movement, which has already begun to develop in Italy, England, and Germany.

A just and immediate offer of peace by us to the international democracy will find everywhere a warm response among the international proletariat masses. In order to secure the confidence of the proletariat, it is necessary to publish at once all secret treaties.

In the interior of Russia a very large part of the peasantry has said: Enough playing with the capitalists; we will go with the workers. We shall secure the confidence of the peasants by one decree, which will wipe out the private property of the landowners. The peasants will understand that their only salvation is in union with the workers.

We will establish a real labor control on production.

We have now learned to work together in a friendly manner, as is evident from this revolution. We have the force of mass organization which has conquered all and which will lead the proletariat to world revolution.

We should now occupy ourselves in Russia in building up a proletarian socialist state.

Long live the world-wide socialist revolution.

[177] *TROTZKY ORGANIZES THE RED ARMY* *

Leon Trotzky (real name—Lev Bronstein) returned to Russia from exile in 1917 to join Lenin in overthrowing the Kerensky government. As Commissar of War under

* William Henry Chamberlin, *The Russian Revolution, 1917–1921* (New York: The Macmillan Company, 1935), Vol. II, pp. 38–40. Copyright 1935 by The Macmillan Company.

Lenin, Trotzky faced a formidable situation in 1918. Allied troops occupied several Russian seaports, and minority nationalities and anti-Bolshevik Russians were in open revolt against the Reds.

It was Leon Trotzky who made by far the greatest individual contribution to the victory of the Red Army. The systematic campaign of defamation and ignoring which has been carried on against him in the decidedly colored works about the civil war which were written in Russia after his fall cannot obscure this fact. What Trotzky did in rallying the demoralized Red forces at Sviazhsk, the little town to which they had retreated after the fall of Kazan is vividly summarized by a subsequent political enemy and critic, who was with him at the time, as follows:

"The general condition of the Sviazhsk group of troops at the beginning of August could be briefly described as lack of confidence in their own strength, absence of initiative, passivity in all work and absence of discipline from top to bottom. The arrival of Trotzky brought a decisive change into the state of affairs. In the train of Trotzky arrived at the backwoods station, Sviazhsk, firm will to victory, initiative, and decisive exertion in all sides of army work."

This trip to Sviazhsk was only the first of thirty-six long journeys to the widely separated fronts of the civil war which Trotzky made in the special train from which he guided much of the conduct of the civil war and which was a symbol of his restless, consuming physical and mental energy. On the train, which was so heavy that it had to be pulled by two locomotives, were a library, a printing-press, an electrical station, a radio and telegraph station and a small garage for the automobiles in which the indefatigable War Commissar sometimes dashed off over the muddy steppe roads in order to visit places far away from the railroad. A detachment of machine-gunners and sharpshooters accompanied the train; it was never quite safe from attack by roving guerrilla bands, especially near the front.

At the time when the White General Yudenitch made a dash for Petrograd and very nearly captured it, in the autumn of 1919, the guards on Trotzky's train took an active part in the fighting and the train received the Order of the Red Banner, the newly created highest Soviet military decoration. In the few spare moments which remained from receiving reports, dictating orders, inspecting units, making speeches, awarding gold watches and other signs of distinction to officers and soldiers who had distinguished themselves, Trotzky dashed off articles for the little newpaper, *On the Road,* which was published on the train. Many of these articles referred to phases of the political and military struggle through which Russia was passing, denouncing Mensheviki and Socialist Revolutionaries, defending pre-revolutionary officers against the violent attacks of unreconciled Communists, threatening deserters and mutineers that they would be "wiped off the face of the earth" if they did not immediately submit, analyzing the weaknesses in the position of the Whites. On one occasion, in a dreary little station in Southeastern Russia, Trotzky gave his revolutionary fantasy free play and wrote an article predicting the triumph of Bolshevism all over Europe, to be followed by a triumphant onset of the European workers on the last stronghold of capitalism, the United States.

Trotzky was not an infallible leader. He was not, and did not imagine that he was, a Napoleon or a Marlborough; he left matters of strategy to the judgment of military experts. Some defects of his character and temperament left their impression on his work as War Commissar. In the autumn of 1918 two Communist members of the revolutionary military council of the Third Army, Smilga and Lashevitch, protested to the Party Central Committee against "Trotzky's extremely light-hearted attitude toward such things as shooting." The occasion for this protest was a peremptory demand from Trotzky that the commissars attached to a division from which some officers had deserted to the Whites should be promptly shot. Among these Commissars were old Bolsheviki with long revolutionary records, and Smilga and Lashevitch flatly refused to carry out the order, declaring that there were cases of treachery in every division, and that there would be no end of executions if the death penalty were applied in every such case.

To say that Trotzky was cruel is merely to say that the Revolution was cruel. Every Bolshevik leader, from Lenin down, was prepared to use as much "frightfulness" as was necessary to win the war and to confirm the new regime in power. But Trotzky's passionate, impetuous nature sometimes led him to order measures, such as the shooting of the commissars, which would have been not only inhuman, but inexpedient.

The War Commissar's habit of racing from front to front had its disadvantages as well as its advantages; it upset the regular functioning of the administrative apparatus to some extent. Trotzky's intense individualism made him a difficult man to work with; in the summer of 1919 he resigned his post as War Commissar as a result of sharp differences of opinion with the Party Central Committee; he was finally induced to withdraw it, however.

But when one has made all allowances for the weak sides of Trotzky's military activity, he still remains the outstanding hero of the civil war, from the Soviet standpoint. All the conditions of Russian life at that time tended to eliminate the possibility of a precise, mechanically perfect functioning of the improvised Soviet war machine; what was necessary above everything else was to galvanize the huge amorphous body of the Red Army with spirit and will to victory, to stiffen morale, to give new drive to the nucleus of

Communists which was driving into action the wavering and uncertain peasant masses of soldiers. Here Trotzky's service was unique and unquestionable. And, so far as one can judge from the imperfect available evidence, his judgment on military matters was at least as good as Lenin's. If Trotzky was wrong in his desire to stop the offensive against Kolchak in the summer of 1919 he was certainly right in rejecting Lenin's hasty suggestion that Petrograd should be abandoned before the drive of Yudenitch in October, 1919.

The Russian civil war differed very greatly in character both from the World War and from the American Civil War. It was a struggle not so much between sections of the country as between classes of the population, and it took place in a country which was already exhausted and war-weary after the years of unequal struggle against the technically superior German armies. Consequently its history is full of revolts behind the lines on both sides, of wholesale desertions, of mutinies, of spectacularly successful raids, of sudden breakdowns on the fronts which are attributable more to political than to military causes. In that vast panorama of confusion and disorder the cometlike figure of Trotzky, storming up and down the Red lines, distributing new revolutionary military honors and orders for execution with equal prodigality, exhorting and denouncing, always organizing for victory, was certainly one of the decisive factors in finally bringing the whole Russian land under the red flag of the Soviets.

30

Versailles and the New Democracies

The major decisions of the Paris Peace Conference were made by the leaders of the three major Allied and Associated governments: Clemenceau of France, Wilson of the United States, and Lloyd George of Great Britain. The peace treaties, based more upon previous secret treaties of the Allies than upon Wilson's Fourteen Points, were generally harsh and punitive. Wilson's contention that the war had been fought "to make the world safe for democracy," seemed affirmed, as all of the new states of Europe adopted the republican form of government, and most of them followed democratic principles. Even in the older states, less shaken politically by the war, electoral reforms, the enfranchisement of women, and guarantees of individual liberties were adopted. Democracy proved to be a temporary phenomenon, however, which was soon replaced by authoritarian rule in most of Central and Eastern Europe and in the Middle East.

[178] *THE ALLIES DRAW UP PEACE TERMS FOR GERMANY* *

At the Paris Peace Conference in 1919, the bitterness of Clemenceau dominated the proceedings. The Fourteen Points, on the basis of which the Germans had

* Great Britain, Foreign Office, *British and Foreign State Papers, 1919* (London, 1922), Vol. CXII.

agreed to the Armistice, were largely abandoned by Wilson to gain support for his concept of a permanent League of Nations. The following excerpts from the lengthy document of the Treaty of Versailles are typical of the spirit and language used.

The Covenant of the League of Nations

The high contracting parties, in order to promote international co-operation and to achieve international peace and security

by the acceptance of obligations not to resort to war,

by the prescription of open, just and honourable relations between nations,

by the firm establishment of the understandings of international law as the actual rule of conduct among Governments, and

by the maintenance of justice and a scrupulous respect for all treaty obligations in the dealings of organised peoples with one another,

Agree to this Covenant of the League of Nations.

Article 11. Any war or threat of war, whether immediately affecting any of the Members of the League or not, is hereby declared a matter of concern to the whole League, and the League shall take any action that may be deemed wise and effectual to safeguard the peace of nations. . . .

Article 22. To those colonies and territories which, as a consequence of the late war, have ceased to be under the sovereignty of the States which formerly governed them, and which are inhabited by peoples not yet able to stand by themselves under the strenuous conditions of the modern world, there should be applied the principle that the well-being and development of such peoples form a sacred trust of civilisation, and that securities for the performance of this trust should be embodied in this Covenant.

The best method of giving practical effect to this principle is that the tutelage of such peoples should be entrusted to advanced nations, who, by reason of their resources, their experience, or their geographical position can best undertake this responsibility, . . .

Left Bank of the Rhine

Article 42. Germany is forbidden to maintain or construct any fortifications either on the left bank of the Rhine or on the right bank to the west of a line drawn 50 kilometres to the East of the Rhine.

Article 43. In the area defined above the maintenance and the assembly of armed forces, either permanently or temporarily, and military manoeuvres of any kind, as well as the upkeep of all permanent works for mobilisation are in the same way forbidden.

Article 44. In case Germany violates in any manner whatever the provisions of Articles 42 and 43, she shall be regarded as committing a hostile act against the Powers signatory of the present Treaty and as calculated to disturb the peace of the world.

Saar Basin

Article 45. As compensation for the destruction of the coal mines in the north of France and as part payment towards the total reparation due from Germany for the damage resulting from the war, Germany cedes to France . . . the coal mines situated in the Saar Basin. . . .

Article 49. Germany renounces in favour of the League of Nations, in the capacity of trustee, the government of the territory defined above. At the end of fifteen years . . . the inhabitants of the said territory shall be called upon to indicate the sovereignty under which they desire to be placed.

Alsace-Lorraine

Article 51. The territories which were ceded to Germany in accordance with . . . the Treaty of Frankfort of May 10, 1871, are restored to French sovereignty. . . .

Austria

Article 80. Germany acknowledges and will respect strictly the independence of Austria, . . . she agrees that this independence shall be inalienable, . . .

Poland

Article 87. Germany in conformity with the action already taken by the Allied and Associated Powers, recognizes the complete independence of Poland. . . . The boundaries of Poland not laid down in the present Treaty will be subsequently determined by the Principal Allied and Associated Powers.

Danzig

Article 102. The Principal Allied and Associated Powers undertake to establish the town of Danzig, together with the rest of the territory described in Article 100, as a Free City. It will be placed under the protection of the League of Nations.

Schleswig

Article 109. The frontier between Germany and Denmark shall be fixed in conformity with the wishes of the population. . . .

Colonies

Article 119. Germany renounces in favour of the Principal Allied and Associated Powers all her rights and titles over her oversea possessions.

Shantung

Article 156. Germany renounces, in favour of Japan, all her rights, title and privileges . . . relative to the Province of Shantung.

Military Clauses

Article 160. By a date which must not be later than March 31, 1920, the German Army must not comprise more than seven divisions of infantry and three divisions of cavalry. After that date the total number of effectives in the Army of the States constituting Germany must not exceed one hundred thousand men, including officers, . . .

Article 168. The manufacture of arms, munitions, or any war material, shall only be carried out in factories or works the location of which shall be communicated to and approved by the . . . Powers, and the number of which they retain the right to restrict.

Naval Clauses

Article 181. After the expiration of a period of two months from the coming into force of the present Treaty the German naval forces in commission must not exceed: 6 battleships of the *Deutschland* or *Lothringen* type, 6 light cruisers, 12 destroyers, 12 torpedo boats, . . . No submarines are to be included.

Air Clauses

Article 198. The armed forces of Germany must not include any military or naval air forces. . . . No dirigible shall be kept.

Penalties

Article 227. The . . . Powers publicly arraing William II of Hohenzollern, formerly German Emperor, for a supreme offence against international morality and the sanctity of treaties.

A special tribunal will be constituted to try the accused . . .

The . . . Powers will address a request to the Government of the Netherlands for the surrender to them of the ex-Emperor in order that he may be put on trial.

Reparations

Article 231. The Allied and Associated Governments affirm and Germany accepts the responsibility of Germany and her allies for causing all the loss and damage to which the Allied and Associated Governments and their nationals have been subjected as a consequence of the war imposed upon them by the aggression of Germany and her allies.

Article 232. The Allied and Associated Governments recognize that the resources of Germany are not adequate, after taking into account permanent diminutions of such resources which will result from other provisions of the present Treaty, to make complete reparation for all such loss and damage.

The Allied and Associated Governments, however, require, and Germany undertakes, that she will make compensation for all damage done to the civilian population of the Allied and Associated Powers and to their property during the period of the belligerency of each as an Allied or Associated Power against Germany by such aggression by land, sea, and from the air, and in general all damage as defined in Annex 1, hereto.

Article 233. The amount of the above damage for which compensation is to be made by Germany shall be determined by an Inter-Allied Commission, to be called the *Reparation Commission,* . . . The findings of the Commission as to the amount of damage defined as above shall be concluded and notified to the German Government on or before May 1, 1921, as representing the extent of that Government's obligations.

The Commission shall concurrently draw up a schedule of payments prescribing the time and manner for securing and discharging the entire obligation within a period of thirty years from May 1, 1921.

Guarantees

Article 428. As a guarantee for the execution of the present Treaty by Germany, the German territory situated to the west of the Rhine together with the bridge-heads, will be occupied by Allied and Associated troops for a period of fifteen years from the coming into force of the present Treaty.

[179] *THE TREATY OF VERSAILLES IS REVEALED TO THE GERMANS* *

The peacemakers at the Paris Conference at no time consulted with the Germans while drawing up the Treaty of Versailles. Only after the Treaty was completed were German delegates summoned to Paris.

The Treaty of Versailles was formally presented to the German representatives on May 7, 1919, by coincidence the fourth anniversary of the sinking of the *Lusitania.*

The scene was the Trianon Palace at Versailles. The day was one of surpassing loveliness, and brilliant spring sunlight flooded the room. Dr.

* Thomas A. Bailey, "Woodrow Wilson and the Lost Peace," in *Wilson and the Peacemakers* (New York: The Macmillan Company, 1947), pp. 288–290. Copyright 1944 by Thomas A. Bailey. Used by permission of the publisher.

Walter Simons, Commissioner-General of the German delegation, noted that "outside of the big window at my right there was a wonderful cherry tree in bloom, and it seemed to me the only reality when compared with the performance in the hall. This cherry tree and its kind will still be blooming when the states whose representatives gathered here exist no longer."

The crowd was small, for the room was small—merely the delegates of both sides, with their assistants, and a few carefully selected press representatives. The grim-visaged Clemenceau sat at the center of the main table: Wilson at his right, Lloyd George at his left.

The air was surcharged with electricity: German and Allied diplomats had not met face to face since the fateful summer of 1914. Would the Germans do something to offend the proprieties?

When all were seated, the doors swung open. At the cry, "*Messieurs les plénipotentiaires allemands!*" the whole assembly rose and stood in silence while the German delegates filed in before their conquerors and sat at a table facing Clemenceau.

The Tiger rose to his feet, and, his voice vibrant with the venom of 1871, almost spat out his speech with staccato precision: "It is neither the time nor the place for superfluous words. . . . The time has come when we must settle our accounts. You have asked for peace. We are ready to give you peace."

Already a secretary had quietly walked over to the table at which the Germans sat, and laid before them the thick, two-hundred-odd-page treaty—"the book."

With Clemenceau still standing, the pale, black-clad Count Brockdorff-Rantzau, head of the German delegation, began reading his reply—*seated.*

An almost perceptible gasp swept the room, for the failure of the German to rise was taken as a studied discourtesy. Some felt that he was too nervous and shaken to stand. Others felt that he wanted to snub his "conquerors." The truth is that he planned to sit, not wishing to stand like a culprit before a judge to receive sentence.

Nothing could better reflect the spirit of the Germans. They felt that the war had been more or less a stalemate; they had laid down their arms expecting to negotiate with a chivalrous foe. As equals, why should they rise like criminals before the Allied bar?

If Brockdorff-Rantzau's posture was unfortunate, his words and the intonation of his words were doubly so.

The Germans had not yet read the Treaty, but they had every reason to believe that it would be severe. They had not been allowed to participate in its negotiation; they would not be allowed to discuss its provisions *orally* with their conquerors. Brockdorff-Rantzau decided to make the most of this,

his only opportunity to meet his adversaries face to face and comment on the unread Treaty. Both his manner and his words were sullen, arrogant, unrepentant.

Speaking with great deliberation and without the usual courteous salutation to the presiding officer, he began by saying that the Germans were under "no illusions" as to the extent of their defeat and the degree of their "powerlessness." This was not true, for both he and his people were under great illusions.

Then he referred defiantly but inaccurately to the demand that the Germans acknowledge that "we alone are guilty of having caused the war. Such a confession in my mouth would be a lie." And the word "lie" fairly hissed from between his teeth.

Bitterly he mentioned the "hundreds of thousands" of German noncombatants who had perished since Armistice Day as a result of Allied insistence on continuing the blockade during the peace negotiations. This shaft struck home, especially to the heart of Lloyd George.

When the echo of Brockdorff-Rantzau's last tactless word had died away, Clemenceau spoke. His face had gone red during the harangue, but he had held himself in check with remarkable self-restraint. Harshly and peremptorily he steam-rolled the proceedings to an end: "Has anybody any more observations to offer? Does no one wish to speak? If not, the meeting is closed."

The German delegates marched out, facing a battery of clicking moving picture cameras. Brockdorff-Rantzau lighted a cigarette with trembling fingers.

Lloyd George, who had snapped an ivory paper knife in his hands, remarked angrily: "It is hard to have won the war and to have to listen to that."

Thus, within a half-hour, was compressed one of the greatest dramas of all time.

[180] *GERMANY EXPERIENCES A RUNAWAY INFLATION* *

The German Republic (the so-called Weimar Republic) was handicapped economically from the start by an enormous reparation burden. When the Germans indicated their inability to meet future payments, the French and Belgians in 1923 occupied the mining and industrial area of the Ruhr. Meanwhile, the inflation of German currency, already advanced, now proceeded unchecked.

* Shepard B. Clough and Charles W. Cole, *Economic History of Europe*, Revised Edition (Boston: D. C. Heath and Company, 1946), pp. 743–746. Copyright 1946 by D. C. Heath and Company. Used by permission of the publisher.

At the conclusion of the war the amount of money in circulation in Germany was about five times what it had been in 1914; the public debt, owed almost entirely within the country, was twenty-fold what it had been before the conflict; and the price index showed an increase of about 100 per cent—all of which were conditions not materially worse than those in France. What made the German financial position much less healthy than the French was that it was faced with enormous reparation payments. From the time when the Versailles treaty became effective (May 10, 1920) to May 1, 1921, the Germans had to make payments in goods which the Allies valued at less than the cost of supporting the Allied armies of occupation—costs which the Germans had to assume. Then on May 1, 1921, the Reparations Commission fixed its bill at the tremendous figure of 132,000,000,000 gold marks ($33,000,000,000) or more than four times the amount which the British and American experts at Paris had deemed feasible to collect. This huge bill was to be paid over a period of thirty years in annual installments of 2,000,000,000 gold marks plus about 26 per cent of the proceeds of German exports and reparations in kind.

By May, 1921, the German budget had been brought nearly to a balance, the value of the mark was being maintained in foreign exchange, and paper money was not being printed in very large quantities. The reparation payments in cash, however, threw a monkey wrench into the machinery. It became necessary to sell marks in order to buy foreign moneys with which to pay reparations, and these sales forced the foreign-exchange value of the mark down. It fell from 14.8 marks to the dollar in May, 1921, to 62.6 marks in November, and wholesale prices in these months tripled. This situation meant that a larger number of marks than formerly were needed to meet reparation payments in gold marks, and it also meant that the cost of running the government increased. Taxes could not be increased fast enough to offset the increased number of marks needed; so more paper money was printed and the government issued treasury notes.

Before the end of 1921 Germany notified the Reparations Commission that it could not meet its 1922 payments and so the commission reduced the sum to be paid in 1922 to 72,000,000 gold marks. Even this sum could not be found, and on August 31, 1921, the Reparations Commission agreed to a complete suspension of cash payments for six months. The mark fell to one-third of an American cent on June 1, 1922, and then to one one-hundreth of an American cent in December, while for the entire year prices went from an index of 36.7 to 1,475. The printing presses were now put to work with a vengeance, pouring out currency and treasury notes, for although no reparation payments were being made, governmental expenditures and the need of banks to extend credit necessitated more money. Then in January, 1923, the French and Belgians occupied the Ruhr as punishment for the German defaults, and this not only disrupted German economy but led to heavy German expenditures in financing passive resistance in the Ruhr. Finally, the printing presses were turning out 400,000,000,000,000,000 marks a day, and it took on October 30, 1923, 15,483,564,000 paper marks to equal one gold mark.

Thus inflation ran its course. It had begun with the great expenses of the war and the issuing of paper money and treasury bills to help meet those expenses. After the conflict, when the nation's finances and currency systems might have been put in order, the necessity of making cash reparation payments started the mark on its downward journey. . . . As the mark fell lower and lower, the printing presses seemed to have taken the initiative in carrying the currency to utter ruin. That this was a premeditated policy is not true. It began as the result of circumstances from which the Germans found it impossible to escape. It continued to its end because an attitude of inertia or a feeling of futility seized German statesmen.

The effects of this greatest of all post-war inflations were tremendous. In the field of production, the inflationary movement acted as a stimulant. Within Germany persons hastened to spend what money they had—before it became worthless. A laborer, paid in the morning, would hurry to make his purchases, for fear that by nightfall the purchasing power of his wages would be cut in half. . . . Thus purchasing and extension of plants increased German industrial production from an index of 61 in 1920 to 77 in 1921, and to 86 in 1922, when other countries were experiencing a decline in production because of the business depression. There was practically full employment in 1922, but real wages per worker fell, because prices rose faster than wages.

While inflation had reacted favorably on production, it played antics with debtor-creditor relationships. As the value of the mark decreased and prices soared, it was not difficult to obtain enough marks to pay off one's debts. Thus the mortgage indebtedness of Germany, which was 40,000,000,000 marks in 1913 and amounted to one-sixth of the national wealth, was worth less in 1923 than one American cent. . . . The German national debt resulting from the war was virtually wiped out as were practically all other private or public debts. Bonds, mortgages, insurance policies, savings-bank accounts, and promises to pay became hardly more than scraps of paper. Thus, the holders of such securities suffered—and many of these holders were members of the middle class. Inflation forced this class to the wall and deprived Germany for a time of one of its most important social stabilizers.

The groups that profited most from the inflation were the big landowners (particularly those who had mortgages to pay off), big industrialists, and merchants. . . .

With the temporary elimination of the middle class, with the concentration of more wealth in the hands of very rich industrialists, and with the loss of real wages on the part of labor, inflation made a deep mark on society. With increased concentration of plants, with increased production, and with the wiping out of debts, it had its effect in the field of economics. From the national point of view, the gains from inflation seem to have offset the losses. During the flight from the mark, when Germans sold marks for foreign exchange, foreigners bought the marks with the hope that this currency would return to a higher value. When the mark continued to fall, the German nation was, of course, the net gainer. There was some national loss probably in the exportation of goods at ridiculously low prices, but it was not great. The greatest national losses were of a social and psychological nature—losses from which Germany probably did not recover before it became engaged in another war.

The end of inflation came rather abruptly as a "result of a dramatic though legitimate confidence trick." In October, 1923, a new bank, the Rentenbank, was established for the purpose of issuing new paper bank notes based on large agricultural holdings and business enterprises. Each new Rentenmark was declared the equivalent of 1,000,000,000,000 old marks or approximately $.24. That this new money was accepted by Germans at its face value is remarkable, for it was convertible only in land or buildings and, as these could not actually be had, it was really inconvertible. It was, in fact, little more than paper. Yet the Rentenmark obtained the confidence of the people and remained nearly at par until the government could balance its budget, could bring, through the Dawes Plan of 1924, some order out of the chaos of reparations, and could see the Reichsbank secure loans to provide a backing for a new currency.

[181] *MASARYK REVIEWS THE PROGRESS OF THE CZECHOSLOVAK REPUBLIC* *

Czechoslovakia, founded in 1918, and established as a democratic republic in 1920 under President Thomas G. Masaryk, was noteworthy as the most successful new democracy of the many established after World War I, despite cultural and economic differences between Czechs and Slovaks, conflicts between Catholics and Socialists, and the disruptive presence of Sudeten Germans and other minority peoples.

* "Speech of T. G. Masaryk, President of the Czechoslovak Republic, on the Tenth Anniversary of the Attainment of the Country's Independence, 28th October, 1928," *Czechoslovak Sources and Documents* (Prague, 1928), No. 4, pp. 9–23, *passim.*

Ten years is a brief span in history, but means much in the life of men. When I returned here ten years ago to the emancipated Republic, I used words which forced themselves to my lips—I said that it was like a fairy tale. As I look back today on those first ten years, I would say again that it is like a fairy tale—a miracle. We began with empty hands, without an army, without constitutional traditions, with a rapidly falling currency, in the midst of economic chaos and the universal decline of discipline, with the heritage of Dualism, with irredentism within our frontiers, unaccustomed to govern, little inclined to obey, and almost unknown to the world. And yet, we have stood the test and acquitted ourselves with honour; we gave the restored State a Constitution, we organized the administration and the army; we faced the economic depression, the nationalist struggle, and the international conflicts. Our tasks were heavier than we admitted to ourselves; and yet we have built up a State which enjoys the confidence of foreign countries and,—what is still more important—of ourselves, of us all. After this testing time of ten years we can quietly continue our creative political work. It has been a successful period of development; it has involved much patient work and therefore let us remember with gratitude all those who have given their collaboration and have not been afraid to take upon themselves responsibilities. . . .

Our political task is to build up a democratic Republic. People are speaking and writing all over the world about a crisis in democracy, a crisis in parliamentarism. What does it all mean? What is the course of political events in Europe after the World War?

The World War became a profound revolution which continued the great political change begun by the revolutions of the 18th century. Everywhere was accelerated the transition from aristocratism and absolutist monarchism through constitutional monarchism to democratism. In a word: government by all takes the place of government by one individual.

Properly speaking, one individual can never govern alone and cannot govern without political training and a knowledge of the art of administration. Thus, in addition to the monarch there arose various bodies of trained officials. In a monarchy the power was inherited; the officials were appointed by the monarch or inherited their office; in a democracy the government is decided by election. Hence the importance today of the electoral system. According to it, and of course according to the general cultural level of the citizens, democracies are of various kinds, such as the British, American, French and Swiss democracies, and the Germanic and Latin national and racial types. Which type do we Slavs form?

Government of all by all, so that every citizen can repeat the phrase of the French despot, "*L'Etat c'est moi*", or more modestly, "I am also the State"—this is the problem of democracy. . . .

The chief fact is that we are a mixed State from the point of view of nationalities and languages; other States, indeed all States, have national minorities, but in Czechoslovakia the minorities are of another character. There is no uniform solution for the problem of national minorities; each minority presents a special problem of its own. With us it is a question above all of the relation of the Czechoslovak majority to our German citizens. If this problem is solved, it will be easy to solve the remaining language and national problems. Fate ordained that in addition to the Czechs and Slovaks in our State there should be a considerable German population which has long been settled in this territory. There are States whose total population does not exceed that of our German minority, and our German fellow citizens are on a high cultural and economic level. I have often spoken and written on our German problem, and it is one of the most important problems with which we have to deal. I repeat and emphasize what I have said before, namely, that everything in the nature of Chauvinism must be excluded from our political life—of course, on both sides.

In a democracy the representation of minorities is a necessity. In any case, it is the duty of the majority, which according to the democratic principle of the majority gives its character to the State, to win over the minority to the State. I regard the entry into the Government of two German Ministers as a happy beginning of a definitive agreement.

[182] *TURKEY BECOMES A WESTERNIZED NATION* *

The Republic of Turkey, which emerged during 1920–1923 from the ruins of the old Ottoman Empire, owed its existence and much of its vitality to its founder, Mustafa Kemal Atatürk. Nominally a democratic republic, Turkey was in actuality a nationalist dictatorship. Under Atatürk's vigorous direction, the Turkish nation was rapidly westernized and secularized.

Although the whole world has heard of Atatürk and admired his great work, the meaning and scope of his accomplishments have not been fully understood. They deserve to be more widely known because they constitute a remarkable experiment for any nation, demonstrating how seemingly impossible things can be achieved according to a plan; how possible it is to do away with prejudice, fanaticism, and conceit; and how decency in international politics can be a profitable course.

Atatürk had seen his nation almost dead, exhausted by continual military

* Ahmed Emin Yalman, *Turkey in My Time* (Norman, Oklahoma: University of Oklahoma Press, 1956), pp. 172–177. Copyright 1956 by the University of Oklahoma Press and used by their permission.

defeats, migrations, losses of territory, and the unbearable drain of a world war, and finally by a foreign occupation which had almost led to the dissection of Turkey into small pieces. Turkey was truly the "Sick Man." The obvious thing for any Turkish patriot had been to salvage from the ashes as much unity and autonomy as possible, and to try to revive even an instinct of survival in the Turkish nation. It was not so with Atatürk. He believed in the Turks, and he resolved to secure for his people their full heritage and re-endow them with the vitality of their ancestors. For this bold man, the collapse of the edifice of the recent past was no reason to mourn; he could see in this seeming tragedy an opportunity to launch constructive innovations and reforms which would have been completely impossible under normal circumstances.

I have already described the manner in which he abolished the khalifate and the temporal authority of religion, opening wide the avenues of reason for the advance of science, education, and justice, hitherto saddled with religious dogma. He made secularism a going policy in Turkey, more so than in most advanced countries, leaving religion its proper function as a source of altruism and love, but preventing it from being used as an unfair and reactionary tool in politics.

Religion had hampered the freedom and equality of women by depriving them of opportunities for public activity. Atatürk gave them equal political rights with men and opened all professions and offices to them. The result was that Turkey swung, within a few years, from one extreme to the other. In Turkey today there is a larger proportion of women judges, lawyers, architects, engineers, chemists, and high-ranking government officials than anywhere else in the world. Usually people are surprised to learn that the assistant head of the aviation school run by the Turkish Air League, confined exclusively to military aviators during World War I, was for some time a woman pilot with an iron sense of discipline and duty.

After the reforms in religion and the status of women, a sweeping change in personal attire, itself a symbol of the old narrow life, was introduced. The Turks had adopted European dress for men about one hundred years earlier, but had kept the red fez as a sign of Ottoman distinction. The conservative mind clung to it as its last symbol of religious and political difference from the Christian West. Atatürk, on the contrary, thought that there should be no symbol of difference. The fez had to go.

Resistance rooted in habit and prejudice is always strong. No Muslim, and no man of any religion in government service, would have dared to wear a hat in Turkey, though he would do so as a matter of course when he left the country. If a Muslim Turk had worn a hat in old Turkey, public opinion would have taken it as an open divorce from both religious and national bonds, and would have resented it bitterly. Only to the *kalpak*, a brimless tall hat made of sheepskin, was any tolerance shown. Atatürk chose a remarkable way for eliminating the fez. He singled out Kastamonu, a town north of Ankara reputed to be the most conservative community in Turkey, as the place to inaugurate this phase of his program and arranged there a meeting with noted reactionaries of the town.

"I have brought you some nice presents," he told them, on arrival. "Look at them. They are called hats, a much more suitable headgear than the fez as protection against sun and rain."

The men were startled and terrified at the prospect of wearing hats. All of them said they could not accept the gifts. "But why?" asked Atatürk. They gave reasons easy to repudiate. Atatürk told them that the fez was of Venetian origin, that when Sultan Mahmud II had introduced it as a radical reform to do away with the turban, there had been a full revolution against that innovation in Bosnia, then a part of Turkey.

Contrary to expectations, the reactionaries were easily defeated in the discussion. One by one they had to admit that their opposition was based on prejudice. Then Atatürk said, "Let us separate into two groups; one favoring prejudice; the other, the dictates of free reason."

There was just one group. Everybody accepted the hat. When a group of pious conservatives led by Atatürk, all wearing hats, took a stroll through the main street of the town, people could not believe their eyes. Such was the case with the entire population in Turkey when they read an Anatolian News Agency dispatch in their papers the next day, saying that the conservative men of Kastamonu had accepted the hats given to them by Atatürk and had begun to wear them as more practical headgear. In all communities the radicals started to wear hats that very day. Others followed. Then a law was passed forbidding the wearing of the fez. Here and there the law met silent resistance, but there was no open manifestation of it. A reform thought impossible had taken place simply and smoothly.

"Now we need a new law to do the same thing with the veils of women," Atatürk was told by his political friends.

"Oh no," he said. "You can't catch me doing that. When religious prejudice and men's jealousy over their women's faces being seen in public are coupled in this problem, it becomes most difficult to cope with. No legislation about veils! There is a natural law which will take care of it more easily than any written law. It is called 'fashion'."

He proved to be right again. Some women discarded the veil; others followed. Those in government service were obliged to discard it at work in the offices. After a short time only a limited number of veiled women could be seen in the streets. Nobody cared. It had ceased to be a public issue and a crucial factor of conservatism and prejudice.

The change in the alphabet was another sweeping reform by Atatürk.

The complicated Arabic characters, so long used by the Turks, were one of the main causes of illiteracy. Adoption of the Latin alphabet had been a wish in the hearts of a few radicals, perhaps, but it was hardly a subject for public discussion. To change the alphabet would be a tremendously difficult and unpopular job. But Atatürk called a conference of writers and leading authorities to consider language problems. The majority approved the adoption of Latin characters.

"How long a period of transition do you foresee?" Atatürk asked them.

"About fifteen years," was the almost unanimous answer.

"No," said Atatürk. "It must be completed in six months."

The entire country became a school to teach the new alphabet. Evening classes were compulsory for men up to sixty and women up to fifty years old. Atatürk was one of the teachers. From partly Arabic and partly Latin, the newspapers went, in a few months, to entirely Latin characters. Circulation fell; the government had to subsidize some papers so that they might survive. The clever papers used many pictures and the new characters in very large type for some time. Then circulation began to rise and soon passed the old sales limits of papers in Arabic letters.

As a rule, Turks had no family names and were called by their given names. There were no surnames to denote a common family bond except in a few families in large cities—mostly families with historical backgrounds—and more frequently in small towns and villages. Even in such instances, the family name was not officially registered. To differentiate a man from others with the same given name, it was necessary to add detailed information about him, such as "son of," "native of," and so on. In military schools, where thousands of students enrolled each year, it was quite a problem for teachers to distinguish between hundreds of Mehmets, Ahmeds, Hasans, Mustafas, and Ismails in the same class. Ordinarily the name of the district or the town where a man lived was mentioned with his name. Some men were known by colorful nicknames.

A law passed in 1935 made it compulsory for every Turk to adopt and register a family name. Mustafa Kemal was given the name of Atatürk by the Grand National Assembly. Atatürk gave General Ismet the surname "Inönü" in honor of his victory in the battles of Inönü. Everyone used his imagination and wits in selecting his own name. I spent hours searching in a dictionary for a euphonious name without a poor meaning. "Yalman," meaning "the highest summit of a mountain," seemed to be all right. It sounded pretentious, but most people were taking pretentious names. As long as they could choose, they took the best.

31

Science and Humanity in the Twentieth Century

Man's acquisition of scientific knowledge and mastery of technology increased at an ever accelerating rate in the twentieth century. Progress was particularly impressive in the fields of medicine, psychology, chemistry and physics. Sigmund Freud's pioneering work in psychoanalysis opened a new field of scientific investigation and inspired a generation of authors and artists. On the eve of World War II a series of remarkable discoveries in atomic physics, based in part upon earlier scientific works of Albert Einstein, A. H. Becquerel, and the Curies, led to the intense collaborative efforts of the early 1940's to develop an atomic bomb. Use of the bomb against Japan in the summer of 1945 led to the sobering realization that man had acquired the means to total self-destruction before learning to live in peace. In a fearful and confused world, the selfless dedication of a few great humanitarians, such as Albert Schweitzer, Dr. Thomas Dooley, and Fr. Dominique Pire, offered a hope and a challenge.

[183] *FREUD DEVELOPS THE THEORY OF PSYCHOANALYSIS* *

Sigmund Freud (1856–1939) began his scientific career as a clinical neurologist in Vienna. After achieving some success in the use of hypnosis as a theraputic technique in the treating of mental illness, Freud turned to the "free association" method and to the study of the unconscious, which was to become his life work. As the following autobiographical excerpt indicates, Freud's psychoanalytic theories were not readily accepted at the start by the medical profession.

The interpretation of dreams became a solace and a support to me in those arduous first years of analysis, when I had to master the technique, clinical phenomena and therapy of the neuroses all at the same time. At that period I was completely isolated and in the network of problems and accumulation of difficulties I often dreaded losing my bearings and also my confidence. There were often patients with whom an unaccountably long time elapsed before my hypothesis, that a neurosis was bound to become intelligible through analysis, proved true; but these patients' dreams, which might be regarded as analogues of their symptoms, almost always confirmed the hypothesis.

It was only my success in this direction that enabled me to persevere. The result is that I have acquired a habit of gauging the measure of a psychologist's understanding by his attitude to dream-interpretation; and I have observed with satisfaction that most of the opponents of psycho-analysis avoid this field altogether or else display remarkable clumsiness if they attempt to deal with it. Moreover, I soon saw the necessity of carrying out a self-analysis, and this I did with the help of a series of my own dreams which led me back through all the events of my childhood; and I am still of the opinion today that this kind of analysis may suffice for anyone who is a good dreamer and not too abnormal.

I think that by thus unrolling the story of the development of psychoanalysis I have shown what it is better than by a systematic description of it. I did not at first perceive the peculiar nature of what I had discovered. I unhesitatingly sacrificed my growing popularity as a doctor, and the increase in attendance during my consulting hours, by making a systematic enquiry into the sexual factors involved in the causation of my patients'

* *The Standard Edition of the Complete Psychological Works of Sigmund Freud,* trans. from the German under the general editorship of James Strachey, in collaboration with Anna Freud, assisted by Alix Strachey and Alan Tyson. Vol. XIV (1914–1916) *On the History of the Psycho-Analytic Movement* (London: The Hogarth Press and the Institute of Psycho-Analysis, 1957), pp. 20–24. Used by permission of The Hogarth Press.

neuroses; and this brought me a great many new facts which finally confirmed my conviction of the practical importance of the sexual factor. I innocently addressed a meeting of the Vienna Society for Psychiatry and Neurology with Krafft-Ebing in the chair, expecting that the material losses I had willingly undergone would be made up for by the interest and recognition of my colleagues. I treated my discoveries as ordinary contributions to science and hoped they would be received in the same spirit. But the silence which my communications met with, the void which formed itself about me, the hints that were conveyed to me, gradually made me realize that assertions on the part played by sexuality in the aetiology * of the neuroses cannot count upon meeting with the same kind of treatment as other communications. I understood that from now onwards I was one of those who have "disturbed the sleep of the world," as Hebbel says, and that I could not reckon upon objectivity and tolerance. Since, however, my conviction of the general accuracy of my observations and conclusions grew even stronger, and since neither my confidence in my own judgment nor my moral courage were precisely small, the outcome of the situation would not be in doubt. I made up my mind to believe that it had been my fortune to discover some particularly important facts and connections, and I was prepared to accept the fate that sometimes accompanies such discoveries.

I pictured the future as follows:—I should probably succeed in maintaining myself by means of the therapeutic success of the new procedure, but science would ignore me entirely during my lifetime; some decades later, someone else would infallibly come upon the same things—for which the time was not now ripe—would achieve recognition for them and bring me honour as a forerunner whose failure had been inevitable. Meanwhile, like Robinson Crusoe, I settled down as comfortably as possible on my desert island. When I look back to those lonely years, away from the pressures and confusions of today, it seems like a glorious heroic age. My "splendid isolation" was not without its advantages and charms. I did not have to read any publications, nor listen to any ill-informed opponents; I was not subject to influence from any quarter; there was nothing to hustle me. I learnt to restrain speculative tendencies and to follow the unforgotten advice of my master, Charcot: to look at the same things again and again until they themselves begin to speak. My publications, which I was able to place with a little trouble, could always lag far behind my knowledge, and could be postponed as long as I pleased, since there was no doubtful "priority" to be defended. *The Interpretation of Dreams,* for instance, was finished in all essentials at the beginning of 1896 but was not written out until the summer of 1899. The analysis of "Dora" was over at the end of 1899; the case history

* The causes or investigation of causes of a disease.

was written in the next two weeks, but was not published until 1905. Meanwhile my writings were not reviewed in the medical journals, or, if as an exception they *were* reviewed, they were dismissed with expressions of scornful or pitying superiority. Occasionally a colleague would make some reference to me in one of his publications; it would be very short and not at all flattering—words such as "eccentric," "extreme," or "very peculiar" would be used. It once happened that an assistant at the clinic in Vienna where I gave my University lectures asked me for permission to attend the course. He listened very attentively and said nothing; after the last lecture was over he offered to join me outside. As we walked away, he told me that with his chief's knowledge he had written a book combatting my views; he regretted very much, however, that he had not first learnt more about them from my lectures, for in that case he would have written much of it differently. He had indeed enquired at the clinic whether he had not better first read *The Interpretation of Dreams,* but had been advised against doing so—it was not worth the trouble. He then himself compared the structure of my theory, so far as he now understood it, with that of the Catholic Church as regards its internal solidity. In the interests of the salvation of his soul, I shall assume that this remark implied a certain amount of appreciation. But he concluded by saying that it was too late to alter anything in his book, since it was already in print. Nor did my colleague think it necessary later to make any public avowal of his change of views on the subject of psycho-analysis; but preferred, in his capacity as a regular reviewer for a medical journal, to follow its development with flippant comments.

Whatever personal sensitiveness I possessed became blunted during those years, to my advantage. I was saved from becoming embittered, however, by a circumstance which is not always present to help lonely discoverers. Such people are as a rule tormented by the need to account for the lack of sympathy or the aversion of their contemporaries, and feel this attitude as a distressing contradiction of the security of their own sense of conviction. There was no need for me to feel so; for psychoanalytic theory enabled me to understand this attitude in my contemporaries and to see it as a necessary consequence of fundamental analytic premises. If it was true that the set of facts I had discovered were kept from the knowledge of patients themselves by internal resistances of an affective kind, then these resistances would be bound to appear in healthy people too, as soon as some external source confronted them with what was repressed. It was not surprising that they should be able to justify this rejection of my ideas on intellectual grounds though it was actually affective in origin. The same thing happened equally often with patients; the arguments they advanced were the same and were not precisely brilliant. In Falstaff's words, reasons are "as plenty as blackberries." The only difference was that with patients one was in a position to bring pressure to bear on them so as to induce them to get insight into their resistances and overcome them, whereas one had to do without this advantage in dealing with people who were ostensibly healthy. How to compel these healthy people to examine the matter in a cool and scientifically objective spirit was an unsolved problem which was best left to time to clear up. In the history of science one can clearly see that often the very proposition which has at first called out nothing but contradictions has later come to be accepted, although no new proofs in support of it have been brought forward.

It was hardly to be expected, however, that during the years when I alone represented psycho-analysis I should develop any particular respect for the world's opinion or any bias towards intellectual appeasement.

[184] *NUCLEAR FISSION COMES TO AMERICA* *

In 1938–1939 two noted physicists, Lise Meitner and O. R. Frisch, refugees from Nazi Germany, worked with Niels Bohr, a Danish physicist in Copenhagen, continuing experiments with uranium atoms, which had begun in Germany. Early in 1939 Bohr came to America, where he, Enrico Fermi, a refugee from Fascist Italy, and several American physicists further developed the Meitner-Frisch theories.

Bohr sailed for the United States from Göteborg, Sweden, the following day, January 7, 1939, on the Swedish-American liner *Drottningholm.* He planned to spend several months with Einstein at the Institute for Advanced Study at Princeton, New Jersey, where Einstein was elaborating his most ambitious theory of the cosmos. Neither Bohr nor Einstein could even remotely suspect that much more immediate problems involving this little earth of ours would soon require them to postpone their contemplations of the cosmos at large.

It was on Sunday, January 15, as Bohr was approaching New York Harbor, that Frisch performed in Bohr's laboratory the crucial experiment that proved beyond doubt that his and Lise Meitner's interpretation of Hahn's experiment—uranium fission—was correct beyond any shadow of doubt. With surprisingly simple apparatus, a bit of uranium in an ionization chamber, a tube of radium and beryllium as a source of neutrons, a

* William L. Laurence, *Men and Atoms: The Discovery, the Uses and the Future of Atomic Energy* (New York: Simon and Schuster, 1959), pp. 31–36. Copyright © 1959 by William L. Laurence. Used by permission of Simon and Schuster, New York, and Hodder & Stoughton Ltd., London.

pair of headphones and one valve for amplification, he soon demonstrated that the bombardment of uranium with neutrons led to the registration on a television screen of the most intense electrical pulses ever observed.

The height of these pulses served as an atomic thermometer, as it were, recording the amount of energy liberated inside the chamber. And, as he stood there watching with that sense of elation and awe that can be experienced only by one privileged to lift the veil for the first time from one of nature's secrets, he saw the atomic thermometer indicate an energy 100 million times as great as the energy released in the burning of one hydrogen atom in oxygen.

That was exactly the amount of energy he and Lise Meitner had calculated would be liberated if the nucleus of a uranium atom were to split in two nearly equal parts. Uranium fission had thus been demonstrated for the first time as a fact on this earth, and it may therefore be said that January 15, 1939, was the day the atomic age was born.

Essentially, Frisch's experiment was the same one first performed by Fermi and his co-workers. But the experiment in Copenhagen in 1939 differed in one highly important respect from the one in Rome in 1934. This time there was no three-mil strip of aluminum foil to blot out from view the atomic volcano that was erupting within the chamber.

On the following day, Monday, January 16, 1939, two weeks to the day after Fermi's arrival in the United States, Meitner and Frisch sent a historic report to the British scientific journal, *Nature,* which bore the title "Disintegration of Uranium by Neutrons: A New Type of Nuclear Reaction." The report was laboriously composed by long-distance telephone between Meitner in Stockholm and Frisch in Copenhagen, and its publication marked a milestone in the history of science.

After outlining the basic scientific reasons for their conclusions, they wrote the lines that have since become famous:

> It seems therefore possible that the uranium nucleus has only small stability of form, and may, after neutron capture, divide itself into two nuclei of roughly equal size. . . . These two nuclei will repel each other (because they both carry large positive charges) and should gain a total of kinetic energy of about 200,000,000 electron volts, as calculated from nuclear radius and charge.

That energy is three million times the heat energy content of coal and twenty million times the explosive energy of TNT, in terms of equal weights. In this same report, which appeared in *Nature* on February 11, 1939, Meitner and Frisch also christened the "new type of nuclear reaction" as "nuclear fission," because, as Frisch explained later, "of the striking similarity of that picture with the process of fission by which bacteria multiply."

That same Monday, January 16, Frisch sent *Nature* a second report, describing his experiment of the day before demonstrating the reality of nuclear fission. That report, entitled "Physical Evidence for the Division of Heavy Nuclei under Neutron Bombardment," was published in a supplement to *Nature* of February 18, a week after the publication of the original Meitner-Frisch report.

It was on that historic Monday that Bohr landed in New York. But when he arrived in Princeton that afternoon he did not go to see Einstein to discuss abstract theories of the cosmos. Instead he called on his former pupil John Archibald Wheeler, then an assistant professor of physics at Princeton University, to tell him about the Hahn-Strassmann experiment and its interpretation by Meitner and Frisch. Together they talked about the potential significance of the discovery, and young Wheeler, who was then twenty-seven, laid plans for a special meeting to be called at Princeton to which a select number of American physicists would be invited to hear Bohr tell the story in detail. One of these was Willis Lamb, a twenty-five-year-old physics instructor at Columbia, who was to win the Nobel Prize in physics sixteen years later.

So it came to pass on the afternoon of Wednesday, January 25, 1939, that Willis Lamb dashed, breathless, into Fermi's laboratory at Pupin Hall, Columbia University.

"Bohr has leaked out great news," he said. Lamb was "very excited," Fermi reminisced fifteen years later.

Fermi himself was stunned at the news. It was nearly five years since he had performed the first experiment, and all that time he, and all the others who followed him, had been lost in a scientific dream world. There is no record that, like Bohr, he slapped himself on the forehead. But, as history records, he more than made up for his failure to recognize the great new domain of knowledge of which he had been the discoverer.

At the time, Fermi had been in the United States about three weeks. That day his course for the next seven years was set by destiny.

With Professors George B. Pegram and John R. Dunning he discussed an experiment that would demonstrate fission. But Fermi did not wait for the experiment to take place. He had an important date with Bohr in Washington for the following morning, Thursday, January 26, when a meeting on theoretical physics was scheduled to begin at George Washington University.

At about seven o'clock that Wednesday evening, Dunning went down to the cyclotron laboratory in the basement of Pupin Hall. There he found Dr. Francis G. Slack, then a visiting professor of physics from Vanderbilt University, and Dr. Eugene T. Booth. Together they began setting up the apparatus that was to make uranium fission a reality for the first time in the New World.

Inside a metal chamber Dunning arranged two metal plates parallel to each other with a gap between. One plate was coated with uranium oxide and the second was to catch any particles shooting off the uranium-coated plate. This plate was connected to the grid of the first vacuum tube in a multistage amplifier and the output of the amplifier led to a television tube.

Inside the chamber was also a tiny glass vessel containing beryllium powder and radium, the combination used as the standard source of neutrons. It was the same type of neutron gun used by Fermi.

Then Dunning moved the neutron gun close to the plate coated with the uranium and watched the dancing line on the television tube. In the darkness of the basement they watched a strange ominous green line, shooting upward to unprecedented heights. And the closer to the uranium he moved his neutron gun the greater was the height of the green line.

The dancing green line was telltale evidence of the fission of the uranium on the metal plate. It was, in fact, the explosion of a miniature atomic bomb, though they did not think of it at that time in terms of a bomb.

Dunning, Booth and Slack were elated, but Dunning wanted to make sure. Again and again he moved the neutron gun close to the uranium plate. Again and again the dancing green line on the television screen rose sharply.

It was eleven o'clock when the three Columbia scientists, tired but elated, called it a day. At that time they did not know that Frisch had preceded them by ten days.

Early the next morning Fermi and Bohr entered a George Washington University classroom where a meeting on the properties of helium at very low temperatures had just started. Oblivious to their surroundings, they sat in one of the back rows talking, gesticulating, now the one, now the other, and scribbling symbols on the backs of envelopes. Word was passed around that the two Nobel laureates were about to report a new discovery. Soon the entire room was in a state of excitement. The speaker on the platform continued talking about the strange behavior of helium at a temperature near absolute zero, but no one paid any attention. All present waited impatiently for the ringing of the bell signaling the end of the speaker's time.

And when the bell did ring at last, and the chairman politely asked for the customary discussion of the subject just presented, all eyes turned to the great Bohr as he walked to the platform. And the tale he told them made them sit up in amazement, every one of them figuratively slapping himself resoundingly on the forehead.

They had all been like Molière's M. Jourdain, who discovered that he had been speaking prose all his life without knowing it. Ever since Fermi's first experiment in 1934 they had been splitting uranium atoms without realizing what they had been doing.

Fermi grinned when his turn came, and his audience grinned with him. Though he had learned of nuclear fission only the day before, he now recognized the true meaning of the elusive, puzzling phenomena he had seen during his five years of wandering in the atomic wilderness. In a flash of recognition, the pieces of the jigsaw puzzle all fell into their proper places and the true picture stood revealed at last.

In the course of his talk, Fermi mentioned the possibility that neutrons might be emitted in the process of nuclear fission. At the time it was only a guess, but its implication of the possibility of a chain reaction was obvious, though the term "chain reaction" was not mentioned that Thursday morning.

One by one, the youthful physicists were seen hurriedly leaving the room, some doing so even before Bohr had finished speaking. Those from the Carnegie Institution of Washington and Johns Hopkins University rushed off directly to their laboratories, hoping to be the first to perform the fission experiment. Those from farther away rushed to the nearest telephone to tell the great news to their co-workers in hopes that they would be the first to split uranium atoms. For Bohr had not yet been informed that Frisch had already performed his classic experiment, nor did anyone yet know about the experiment at Columbia the night before.

It was not until about a week later that Bohr was informed in a letter from one of his sons in Copenhagen that Frisch had found the large electrical pulses on January 15, ten days ahead of Columbia. "I had not written to him (Bohr) myself," Frisch related some years later, "wanting to make sure and to follow up various questions, but I had told his son."

The news brought by Bohr was the biggest bombshell ever exploded at a scientific meeting. It was the intellectual forerunner of the atomic bomb, in the development of which Fermi and Bohr were to play leading roles.

[185] *UNITED STATES DEVELOPS AN ATOMIC BOMB* *

Henry L. Stimson (1867–1950) had a long and distinguished career in law and government before becoming Secretary of War in 1940 in the Cabinet of Franklin D. Roosevelt. Stimson, a lifelong Republican, had served as Secretary of War under President Taft, as Secretary of State under President Hoover, and as Gov-

* Henry L. Stimson and McGeorge Bundy, *On Active Service in Peace and War* (New York: Harper & Brothers, 1948), pp. 612–613, 615, 617–619, 624–626. Copyright, 1947, 1948 by Henry L. Stimson. Reprinted by permission of Harper & Brothers, and of Hutchinson & Company Ltd., London.

ernor-General of the Philippines under President Coolidge. During 1941–1945, he held the additional post of co-ordinator of the atomic energy program, the "Manhattan Project."

It was in the fall of 1941 that the question of atomic energy was first brought directly to my attention. At that time President Roosevelt appointed a committee consisting of Vice President Wallace, General Marshall, Dr. Vannevar Bush, Dr. James B. Conant, and myself. The function of this committee was to advise the President on questions of policy relating to the study of nuclear fission which was then proceeding both in this country and in Great Britain. For nearly four years thereafter I was directly connected with all major decisions of policy on the development and use of atomic energy, and from May 1, 1943, until my resignation as Secretary of War on September 21, 1945, I was directly responsible to the President for the administration of the entire undertaking; my chief advisers in this field were General Marshall, Dr. Bush, Dr. Conant, and Major General Leslie R. Groves, the officer in charge of the project. At the same time I was the President's senior adviser on the military employment of atomic energy.

The policy adopted and steadily pursued by President Roosevelt and his advisers was a simple one. It was to spare no effort in securing the earliest possible successful development of an atomic weapon. The reasons for this policy were equally simple. The original experimental achievement of atomic fission had occurred in Germany in 1938, and it was known that the Germans had continued their experiments. In 1941 and 1942 they were believed to be ahead of us, and it was vital that they should not be the first to bring atomic weapons into the field of battle. Furthermore, if we should be the first to develop the weapon, we should have a great new instrument for shortening the war and minimizing destruction. At no time, from 1941 to 1945, did I ever hear it suggested by the President, or by any other responsible member of the government, that atomic energy should not be used in the war. All of us of course understood the terrible responsibility involved in our attempt to unlock the doors to such a devastating weapon; President Roosevelt particularly spoke to me many times of his own awareness of the catastrophic potentialities of our work. But we were at war, and the work must be done. I therefore emphasize that it was our common objective, throughout the war, to be the first to produce an atomic weapon and use it. The possible atomic weapon was considered to be a new and tremendously powerful explosive, as legitimate as any other of the deadly explosive weapons of modern war. The entire purpose was the production of a military weapon; on no other ground could the wartime expenditure of so much time and money have been justified. The exact circumstances in which that weapon might be used were unknown to any of us until the middle of 1945, and when that time came, as we shall presently see, the military use of atomic energy was connected with larger questions of national policy. . . .

As time went on it became clear that the weapon would not be available in time for use in the European theater, and the war against Germany was successfully ended by the use of what are called conventional means. But in the spring of 1945 it became evident that the climax of our prolonged atomic effort was at hand. By the nature of atomic chain reactions, it was impossible to state with certainty that we had succeeded until a bomb had actually exploded in a full-scale experiment; nevertheless it was considered exceedingly probable that we should by midsummer have successfully detonated the first atomic bomb. This was to be done at the Alamogordo Reservation in New Mexico. It was thus time for detailed consideration of our future plans. What had begun as a well-founded hope was now developing into a reality. . . .

The principal political, social, and military objective of the United States in the summer of 1945 was the prompt and complete surrender of Japan. Only the complete destruction of her military power could open the way to lasting peace.

Japan in July, 1945, had been seriously weakened by our increasingly violent attacks. It was known to us that she had gone so far as to make tentative proposals to the Soviet Government, hoping to use the Russians as mediators in a negotiated peace. These vague proposals contemplated the retention by Japan of important conquered areas and were therefore not considered seriously. There was as yet no indication of any weakening in the Japanese determination to fight rather than accept unconditional surrender. If she should persist in her fight to the end, she had still a great military force. . . .

As we understood it in July, there was a very strong possibility that the Japanese Government might determine upon resistance to the end, in all the areas of the Far East under its control. In such an event the Allies would be faced with the enormous task of destroying an armed force of five million men and five thousand suicide aircraft, belonging to a race which had already amply demonstrated its ability to fight literally to the death.

The strategic plans of our armed forces for the defeat of Japan, as they stood in July, had been prepared without reliance upon the atomic bomb, which had not yet been tested in New Mexico. We were planning an intensified sea and air blockade, and greatly intensified strategic air bombing, through the summer and early fall, to be followed on November 1 by an invasion of the southern island of Kyushu. This would be followed in turn by an invasion of the main island of Honshu in the spring of 1946. The total U.S. military and naval force involved in this grand design was of the order of 5,000,000 men; if all those indirectly concerned are included, it was larger still. . . .

We estimated that if we should be forced to carry this plan to its conclusion, the major fighting would not end until the latter part of 1946, at the earliest. I was informed that such operations might be expected to cost over a million casualties, to American forces alone. Additional large losses might be expected among our allies and, of course, if our campaign were successful and if we could judge by previous experience, enemy casualties would be much larger than our own.

It was already clear in July that even before the invasion we should be able to inflict enormously severe damage on the Japanese homeland by the combined application of "conventional" sea and air power. The critical question was whether this kind of action would induce surrender. It therefore became necessary to consider very carefully the probable state of mind of the enemy, and to assess with accuracy the line of conduct which might end his will to resist. . . .

I find that I stated in my diary, as early as June 19, that "the last chance warning . . . must be given before an actual landing of the ground forces in Japan, and fortunately the plans provide for enough time to bring in the sanctions to our warning in the shape of heavy ordinary bombing attack and an attack of S-1." S-1 was a code name for the atomic bomb.

There was much discussion in Washington about the timing of the warning to Japan. The controlling factor in the end was the date already set for the Potsdam meeting of the Big Three. It was President Truman's decision that such a warning should be solemnly issued by the U.S., and the U.K. from this meeting, with the concurrence of the head of the Chinese Government, so that it would be plain that *all* of Japan's principal enemies were in entire unity. This was done, in the Potsdam ultimatum of July 26, . . .

On July 28 the Premier of Japan, Suzuki, rejected the Potsdam ultimatum by announcing that it was "unworthy of public notice." In the face of this rejection we could only proceed to demonstrate that the ultimatum had meant exactly what it said when it started that if the Japanese continued the war, "the full application of our military power, backed by our resolve, will mean the inevitable and complete destruction of the Japanese armed forces and just as inevitably the utter devastation of the Japanese homeland."

For such a purpose the atomic bomb was an eminently suitable weapon. The New Mexico test occurred while we were at Potsdam, on July 16. It was immediately clear that the power of the bomb measured up to our highest estimates. We had developed a weapon of such a revolutionary character that its use against the enemy might well be expected to produce exactly the kind of shock on the Japanese ruling oligarchy which we desired, strengthening the position of those who wished peace, and weakening that of the military party.

Because of the importance of the atomic mission against Japan, the detailed plans were brought to me by the military staff for approval. With President Truman's warm support I struck off the list of suggested targets the city of Kyoto. Although it was a target of considerable military importance, it had been the ancient capital of Japan and was a shrine of Japanese art and culture. We determined that it should be spared. I approved four other targets including the cities of Hiroshima and Nagasaki.

Hiroshima was bombed on August 6, and Nagasaki on August 9. These two cities were active working parts of the Japanese war effort. One was an army center; the other was naval and industrial. Hiroshima was the headquarters of the Japanese army defending southern Japan and was a major military storage and assembly point. Nagasaki was a major seaport and it contained several large industrial plants of great wartime importance. We believed that our attacks had struck cities which must certainly be important to the Japanese military leaders, both Army and Navy, and we waited for a result. We waited one day.

[186] *ALBERT SCHWEITZER CHOOSES A CAREER* *

Albert Schweitzer, born in 1875 in Alsace, one of the most versatile scholars of the twentieth century, attained an early reputation as an accomplished organist, as the foremost authority on J. S. Bach, and as a Christian theologian. Since 1913 Schweitzer has served as a medical missionary in Central Africa, and has developed an original system of universal ethics. In 1952 he was awarded the Nobel Peace Prize.

On October 13th, 1905, a Friday, I dropped into a letter box in the Avenue de la Grande Armée in Paris, letters to my parents and to some of my most intimate acquaintances, telling them that at the beginning of the winter term I should enter myself as a medical student, in order to go later on to Equatorial Africa as a doctor. In one of them I sent in the resignation of my post as principal of the Theological College of St. Thomas', because of the claim on my time that my intended course of study would make.

The plan which I meant now to put into execution had been in my mind

* Albert Schweitzer, *Out of My Life and Thought: An Autobiography*, trans. by C. T. Campion, original title, "Aus Meinem Leben und Denken" (New York: Henry Holt and Company, Inc., 1949), pp. 84–88. Copyright 1933, 1949, by Henry Holt and Company, Inc. Used by permission of Holt, Rinehart and Winston, Inc. and of George Allen & Unwin Ltd., London.

for a long time, having been conceived so long ago as my student days. It struck me as incomprehensible that I should be allowed to lead such a happy life, while I saw so many people around me wrestling with care and suffering. Even at school I had felt stirred whenever I got a glimpse of the miserable home surroundings of some of my schoolfellows and compared them with the absolutely ideal conditions in which we children of the parsonage at Günsbach lived. While at the university and enjoying the happiness of being able to study and even to produce some results in science and art, I could not help thinking continually of others who were denied that happiness by their material circumstances or their health. Then one brilliant summer morning at Günsbach, during the Whitsuntide holidays—it was in 1896—there came to me, as I awoke, the thought that I must not accept this happiness as a matter of course, but must give something in return for it. Proceeding to think the matter out at once with calm deliberation, while the birds were singing outside, I settled with myself before I got up, that I would consider myself justified in living till I was thirty for science and art, in order to devote myself from that time forward to the direct service of humanity. Many a time already had I tried to settle what meaning lay hidden for me in the saying of Jesus: "Whosoever would save his life shall lose it, and whosoever shall lose his life for My sake and the Gospels shall save it." Now the answer was found. In addition to the outward, I now had inward happiness.

What would be the character of the activities thus planned for the future was not yet clear to me. I left it to circumstances to guide me. One thing only was certain, that it must be directly human service, however inconspicuous the sphere of it.

I naturally thought first of some activity in Europe. I formed a plan for taking charge of abandoned or neglected children and educating them, then making them pledge themselves to help later on in the same way children in similar positions. When in 1903, as warden of the theological hostel, I moved into my roomy and sunny official quarters on the second floor of the College of St. Thomas, I was in a position to begin the experiment. I offered my help now here, now there, but always unsuccessfully. The constitutions of the organizations which looked after destitute and abandoned children made no provision for the acceptance of such voluntary co-operation. For example, when the Strasbourg orphanage was burnt down, I offered to take in a few boys, for the time being, but the superintendent did not even allow me to finish what I had to say. Similar attempts which I made elsewhere were also failures.

For a time I thought I would some day devote myself to tramps and discharged prisoners. In some measure as a preparation for this I joined the

Rev. Augustus Ernst at St. Thomas' in an undertaking which he had begun. He was at home from one to two P.M. and ready to speak to anyone who came to him asking for help or for a night's lodging. He did not, however, give the applicant a trifle in money, or let him wait till he could get information about his circumstances. He would offer to look him up in his lodging house that very afternoon and test the statements he had volunteered about his condition. Then, and only then, would he give him help, but as much and for as long a time as was necessary. What a number of bicycle rides we made with this object in the town and the suburbs, and very often with the result that the applicant was not known at the address he had given. In a great many cases, however, it provided an opportunity for giving, with knowledge of the circumstances, very seasonable help. I had some friends, too, who kindly placed a portion of their wealth at my disposal.

Already as a student I had been active in social service as a member of the student association known as the Diaconate of St. Thomas, which held its meetings in St. Thomas' College. Each of us had a certain number of poor families assigned to him, which he was to visit every week, taking to them the help allotted to them, and making a report on their condition. The money we thus distributed we collected from members of the old Strasbourg families who supported this undertaking, begun by former generations and now carried on by us. Twice a year, if I remember right, each of us had to make his definite number of such begging appeals. To me, being rather shy and rather awkward in society, these visits were a torture. I believe that in these preparatory studies for the begging I have had to do in later years I sometimes showed myself extremely unskillful. However, I learned through them that begging with tact and restraint is better appreciated than any sort of stand-and-deliver approach, and also that the correct method of begging includes the good tempered acceptance of a refusal.

In our youthful inexperience we no doubt often failed, in spite of the best intentions, to use all the money entrusted to us in the wisest way, but the intentions of the givers were nevertheless fully carried out in that it pledged young men to take an interest in the poor. For that reason I think with deep gratitude of those who met with so much understanding and liberality our efforts to be wisely helpful, and hope that many students may have the privilege of working, commissioned in this way by the charitable, as recruits in the struggle against poverty.

While I was concerned with tramps and discharged prisoners it had become clear to me that they could only be effectively helped by a number of individuals who would devote themselves to them. At the same time, however, I had realized that in many cases these could only accomplish their best work in collaboration with organizations. But what I wanted was an absolutely personal and independent activity. Although I was resolved to put my services at the disposal of some organization, if it should be really necessary, I nevertheless never gave up hope of finding a sphere of activity to which I could devote myself as an individual and as wholly free. That this longing of mine found fulfillment I have always regarded as a signal instance of the mercy which had again and again been vouchsafed to me.

One morning in the autumn of 1904 I found on my writing table in the college one of the green-covered magazines in which the Paris Missionary Society reported every month on its activities. A certain Miss Scherdlin used to put them there knowing that I was specially interested in this society on account of the impression made on me by the letters of one of its earliest missionaries, Casalis by name, when my father read them aloud at his missionary services during my childhood. That evening, in the very act of putting it aside that I might go on with my work, I mechanically opened this magazine, which had been laid on my table during my absence. As I did so, my eye caught the title of an article: *Les besoins de la Mission du Congo* ("The Needs of the Congo Mission").

It was by Alfred Boegner, the President of the Paris Missionary Society, an Alsatian, and contained a complaint that the mission had not enough workers to carry on its work in the Gaboon, the northern province of the [French] Congo Colony. The writer expressed his hope that his appeal would bring some of those "on whom the Master's eyes already rested" to a decision to offer themselves for this urgent work. The conclusion ran: "Men and women who can reply simply to the Master's call, 'Lord, I am coming,' those are the people whom the Church needs." Having finished the article, I quietly began my work. My search was over.

32

The Rise of Totalitarianism

America had entered World War I to "make the world safe for democracy," in the words of Woodrow Wilson. Yet, within a few years democracy was in full retreat as new types of authoritarian rule emerged. The first of these totalitarian dictatorships appeared in Russia in November, 1917, when Lenin overthrew the shaky liberal, democratic government. In Italy, Mussolini replaced a weak parliamentary government with a Fascist dictatorship. Similarly, in Germany economic distress and political confusion were skillfully exploited by Adolf Hitler to establish a Nazi dictatorship. Other types of dictatorial or authoritarian rule emerged in Hungary under Horthy, in Poland under Pilsudski, in Portugal under Salazar, and in Spain under Franco.

[187] *MUSSOLINI EXPLAINS FASCISM* *

Italy, although victorious in World War I, had experienced serious losses and deep humiliation in the war, and had failed to gain the expected fruits of victory. Riots and strikes, and the inability of an unstable parliamentary government to cope

* Benito Mussolini, *Fascism: Doctrine and Institutions* (Rome: Ardita Publishers, 1935), pp. 18–27, *passim*. Copyright 1935 by "Ardita," Rome.

with violence, left the way open for the rise of a nationalist movement, Fascism, led by a former Socialist, Benito Mussolini (1883–1945). Before Mussolini's seizure of power in 1922, Fascism contained little coherent political theory. Its political philosophy was added in the following years.

First of all, as regards the future development of mankind,—and quite apart from all present political considerations—Fascism does not, generally speaking, believe in the possibility or utility of perpetual peace. It therefore discards pacifism as a cloak for cowardly supine renunciation in contradistinction to self-sacrifice. War alone keys up all human energies to their maximum tension and sets the seal of nobility on those peoples who have the courage to face it. . . .

Such a conception of life makes Fascism the resolute negation of the doctrine underlying so-called scientific and Marxian socialism, the doctrine of historic materialism which would explain the history of mankind in terms of the class-struggle and by changes in the processes and instruments of production, to the exclusion of all else. . . .

After socialism, Fascism trains its guns on the whole block of democratic ideologies, and rejects both their premises and their practical applications and implements. Fascism denies that numbers, as such, can be the determining factor in human society; it denies the right of numbers to govern by means of periodic consultations; it asserts the irremediable and fertile and beneficent inequality of men who cannot be levelled by any such mechanical and extrinsic device as universal suffrage. . . .

Fascism is definitely and absolutely opposed to the doctrines of liberalism, both in the political and the economic sphere. The importance of liberalism in the XIXth century should not be exaggerated for present-day polemical purposes, nor should we make of one of the many doctrines which flourished in that century a religion for mankind for the present and for all time to come. . . .

A party governing a nation "totalitarianly" is a new departure in history. There are no points of reference nor of comparison. From beneath the ruins of liberal, socialist, and democratic doctrines, Fascism extracts those elements which are still vital. . . . We are free to believe that this is the century of authority, a century tending to the "right," a Fascist century. If the XIXth century was the century of the individual (liberalism implies individualism) we are free to believe that this is the "collective" century, and therefore the century of the State. . . .

The key-stone of the Fascist doctrine is its conception of the State, of its essence, its functions, and its aims. For Fascism the State is absolute, individuals and groups relative. Individuals and groups are admissable in so far as they come within the State.

[188] *STALIN REVEALS THE PURPOSE OF THE FIRST FIVE-YEAR PLAN* *

Joseph Stalin (1879–1953), Lenin's successor as dictator of Communist Russia, sought to establish the basis for a socialist economy by means of a Five-Year Plan (1928–1932). As he explains below, one of the goals was the elimination of capitalism which Lenin had permitted in the form of the NEP (New Economic Policy) in small businesses and in agriculture.

What was the fundamental task of the Five-Year Plan?

The fundamental task of the Five-Year Plan was, in converting the U.S.S.R. into an industrial country, fully to eliminate the capitalist elements, to widen the front of socialist forms of economy, and to create the economic base for the abolition of classes in the U.S.S.R., for the construction of socialist society.

The fundamental task of the Five-Year Plan was to create such an industry in our country as would be able to re-equip and reorganize, not only the whole of industry, but also transport and agriculture—on the basis of socialism.

The fundamental task of the Five-Year Plan was to transfer small and scattered agriculture to the lines of large-scale collective farming, so as to ensure the economic base for socialism in the rural districts and thus to eliminate the possibility of the restoration of capitalism in the U.S.S.R.

Finally, the task of the Five-Year Plan was to create in the country all the necessary technical and economic prerequisites for increasing to the utmost the defensive capacity of the country, to enable it to organize determined resistance to any and every attempt at military intervention from outside, to any and every attempt at military attack from without.

[189] *STALIN BUILDS A COMMUNIST DICTATORSHIP* †

Lenin, the creator of the Communist state in Russia, held dictatorial powers from 1917 to 1924. In the last two years of this period, with Lenin incapacitated by illness, a struggle for succession broke out between Trotsky, organizer of the Red Army, and Stalin, secretary of the Central Committee of the Communist party.

* Joseph Stalin, *Selected Writings* (New York: International Publishers, 1942), p. 242.

† Waldemar Gurian, *Bolshevism: An Introduction to Soviet Communism* (Notre Dame, Ind.: University of Notre Dame Press, 1952), pp. 46–48, 51, 55–57. Copyright 1952 by the University of Notre Dame Press. Used by permission.

Control of the party proved to be the decisive factor, giving Stalin a complete victory over Trotsky and a firm grip on the Soviet government.

The Bolshevik regime had to maneuver in order to survive until proper conditions—namely, its own strength and the weakness of the other powers —would permit a new advance. . . .

The whole period of 1921–1927 can be characterized as a period in which the Soviet regime tried to gain strength for such a new advance. This period opened with Lenin's introduction of the New Economic Policy (NEP), designed to make concessions to the tired and exhausted masses. A limited free market and private trade were admitted in the interest of the peasants. Lenin even offered "concessions" to foreign capitalists in order to make investments in Soviet Russia attractive to them—a policy which did not have the success expected. Principles of calculation and the stringencies of legalistic rules were emphasized and introduced, replacing the former policies of confiscation without regulations, which had aided in winning the civil war. But the "commanding positions" remained in the hands of the party. The nationalized economy controlled the sector into which private initiative was admitted. Banks, big enterprises, and foreign trade remained under the control of the Soviet state. No other parties were permitted alongside the Bolshevik party. A committee which was organized in the hunger-catastrophe of 1922 was dissolved when its non-Bolshevik members tried to gain independent influence. The Che-Ka [secret police] was rechristened G-P-U; but even under formal legal supervision, it retained its basically unlimited powers. The consolidation of the regime advanced.

The loose confederation of Soviet Republics—of which the Russian and Ukrainian were the most important ones—was held together by the solidarity and unity of the Communists; it was replaced in 1922 by the Soviet Union. The U.S.S.R. was nominally a federation, but in reality, despite the explicit statement of the constitution about the right of secession, it continued to concentrate power in Moscow. . . .

During Lenin's illness (he was incapacitated in 1922 and died in 1924), an internal struggle about who was to succeed him developed within the party leadership. Upon Zinoviev's suggestion Stalin had been made secretary general of the party in 1922. He used this office to bring the party machine, step by step, under his control. Together with Kamenev and Zinoviev, two typical Bolshevik intellectuals, he prevented Trotsky from becoming Lenin's heir and helped reduce his influence in the party. Then Stalin turned against his allies of the first hour and in their turn deprived them of power. Now they joined with Trotsky, opposing Stalin in a bloc. But it was too late. Stalin could use the party machine against the opposition; the party voted always in Stalin's favor and did not listen to the arguments of the opposition. Of course, all competitors in the fight for power cited Lenin as the highest infallible authority. . . . In 1927 the opposition was expelled from the party; its leaders submitted more or less eagerly to the official line; and Trotsky was exiled (1929) from the Soviet Union. . . .

The Bolsheviks under Stalin organized and consolidated their complete control of the Soviet Union according to a definite totalitarian pattern. The Five Year plans for the organization of production and the acceleration of industrialization were put into operation. After 1929, Stalin carried out the collectivization of agriculture from above, using every form of compulsion. For millions of people, this policy resulted in death through hunger, or in deportation to labor camps. For Stalin was determined to destroy the independence of the peasants who had threatened the process of industrialization by their refusal to supply cities with foodstuffs. The peasants were forced into kolhozes controlled by party officials and had to fulfill production quotas imposed from above. They were forced to adopt agricultural machinery in order to form a market for the products of the industrial plants; the government organized and controlled the centers (stations) for the machines.

The millions deported as forced labor brought a change in the activities of the GPU. Its concentration camps had served to isolate active or potential enemies of the regime; now these camps became enterprises for economic and colonizing purposes. The Volga-White Sea canal had served as a preparatory experiment for the exploitation of forced labor; now deportees, political and criminal prisoners, could be used on a much larger scale in the almost unpopulated regions of Northern Europe as well as of Asiatic Russia. In other words, terror was now combined with economic planning. . . .

The great purge from 1936 to 1938 definitely established Stalin's absolute control over the party. . . .

The great purge stabilized definitely a totalitarian rule by an omnipotent Soviet leadership. Perpetuating itself by controlling everything with the help of a subservient bureaucracy, it pretended (and still pretends) to fulfill and interpret authoritatively an absolutely true doctrine. But, as we have seen, this development was not a break with Lenin's principles; Stalin's extension of terroristic methods to the party was only an application of these principles. Stalin had instruments for establishing the regime which Lenin, fighting for a conquest of power, obviously did not yet have. . . .

The Bolshevik regime construes itself to have started as a dictatorship founded upon an alliance between the proletariat and the poor peasants. . . . Today the official doctrine explains that socialism is realized in the Soviet Union: the economy is entirely socialized; private ownership of the means of production (and therefore the division of society into classes) has been abolished; all-out planning, extending to agriculture, has been introduced. True, a Communism in which everybody will be rewarded according to his needs has not yet been achieved. In the present phase the principle prevails that rewards are differentiated according to the individual's contribution to society. . . .

Contrary to Lenin's original expectations and announcements, formulated particularly in his *State and Revolution* (1917), the alleged realization of socialism was not accompanied by a corresponding withering away of the state (the instrument of coercion in the interest of one class). Lenin had hoped that with the advance of the dictatorship of the proletariat, the organs of the state separated from the people, like the army and the bureaucracy, would disappear. All these announcements, expectations and hopes have not come true. . . . Stalin emphasizes the necessity for the state's continuing existence even after the realization of socialism in the Soviet Union. This acceptance of the state as official doctrine has increased tremendously the employment of power and violence. Pressure is applied in order to accomplish the transformation of society and the education of the masses; the doctrine of the necessary development of society towards the aims of socialism and communism justifies this systematic, ruthlessly cool pressure. Terrorism is unavoidable in order to force the masses in the right direction. Here Bolshevist policies rejoin typical traditions of Russian Muscovite history where brutal power is applied from above to shape society (Ivan the Terrible, Peter the Great). Industrial backwardness must be overcome by promoting an artificial acceleration of economic developments through constant compulsion from above, disregarding, as the forced collectivization of agriculture and the large masses in the labor camps show, the will and welfare of the people and society.

[190] *HILTER EXPLAINS NATIONAL SOCIALISM* *

Adolf Hitler (1889–1945) joined the newly formed National Socialist Party (Nazis) in 1919 and soon became its leader. Mein Kampf *was written by Hitler in prison, following his arrest in 1923 in an attempt to overthrow the government of Bavaria. The book is crudely written and repetitious and features racism and anti-Semitism as the main themes.*

* Adolf Hitler, *Mein Kampf,* trans. by Ralph Manheim (Boston: Houghton Mifflin Company, 1943), pp. 3, 296, 302, 339, 389, 427, 611, 624–625, 654. Copyright 1943 by Houghton Mifflin Company. The selections from *Mein Kampf,* trans. by Ralph Manheim, are reprinted by permission of and arrangement with Houghton Mifflin Company, the authorized publishers, and by Hutchinson & Company Ltd., London.

One blood demands one Reich. Never will the German nation possess the moral right to engage in colonial politics until, at least, it embraces its own sons within a single state. Only when the Reich borders include the very last German, but can no longer guarantee his daily bread, will the moral right to acquire foreign soil arise from the distress of our own people. Their sword will become our plow, and from the tears of war the daily bread of future generations will grow. . . .

Blood mixture and the resultant drop in the racial level is the sole cause of the dying out of old cultures; for men do not perish as a result of lost wars, but by the loss of that force of resistance which is contained only in pure blood.

All who are not of good race in this world are chaff.

And all occurrences in world history are only the expression of the races' instinct of self-preservation, in the good or bad sense. . . .

If the Jews were alone in this world, they would stifle in filth and offal; they would try to get ahead of one another in hate-filled struggle and exterminate one another, in so far as the absolute absence of all sense of self-sacrifice, expressing itself in their cowardice, did not turn battle into comedy here too.

So it is absolutely wrong to infer any ideal sense of sacrifice in the Jews from the fact that they stand together in struggle, or, better expressed, in the plundering of their fellow men. . . .

Without the clearest knowledge of the racial problem and hence of the Jewish problem there will never be a resurrection of the German nation.

The racial question gives the key not only to world history, but to all human culture. . . .

Since nationality or rather race does not happen to lie in language but in the blood, we would only be justified in speaking of a Germanization if by such a process we succeeded in transforming the blood of the subjected people. But this is impossible. Unless a blood mixture brings about a change, which, however, means the lowering of the level of the higher race. The final result of such a process would consequently be the destruction of precisely those qualities which had formerly made the conquering people capable of victory. Especially the cultural force would vanish through a mating with the lesser race, even if the resulting mongrels spoke the language of the earlier, higher race a thousand times over. . . .

The crown of the folkish state's entire work of education and training must be to burn the racial sense and racial feeling into the instinct and the intellect, the heart and brain of the youth entrusted to it. No boy and no girl must leave school without having been led to an ultimate realization of the necessity and essence of blood purity. . . .

The presupposition for the gaining of lost territories is the intensive promotion and strengthening of the remaining remnant state and the unshakable decision slumbering in the heart to dedicate the new force thus arising to the freedom and unification of the entire nationality in the proper hour: therefore, *subordination* of the interests of the separated territories to the single interest of winning for the remaining remnant that measure of political power and strength which is the precondition for a correction of the will of hostile victors. *For oppressed territories are led back to the bosom of a common Reich, not by flaming protests, but by a mighty sword.*

To forge this sword is the task of a country's internal political leadership; to safeguard the work of forging and seek comrades in arms is the function of diplomatic leadership. . . .

What France, spurred on by her own thirst for vengeance and systematically led by the Jew, is doing in Europe today is a sin against the existence of white humanity and some day will incite against this people all the avenging spirits of a race which has recognized racial pollution as the original sin of humanity.

For Germany, however, the French menace constitutes an obligation to subordinate all considerations of sentiment and hold out a hand to those who, threatened as much as we are, will neither suffer nor tolerate France's desires for domination.

In the predictable future there can be only two allies for Germany in Europe: England and Italy. . . .

And so we National Socialists consciously draw a line beneath the foreign policy tendency of our pre-War period. We take up where we broke off six hundred years ago. We stop the endless German movement to the south and west, and turn our gaze toward the land in the east. At long last we break off the colonial and commercial policy of the pre-War period and shift to the soil policy of the future.

If we speak of soil in Europe today, we can primarily have in mind only *Russia* and her vassal border states.

[191] *THE GERMAN PEOPLE ACCEPT HITLER'S POLICE STATE* *

By 1932, German democracy as practiced under the Weimar Constitution had virtually ceased to exist. Although the chancellors of that year ruled by decree, they were unable to achieve a stable government. In January, 1933, Hitler became

* Allen Welsh Dulles, *Germany's Underground* (New York: The Macmillan Company, 1947), pp. 12–22, *passim*. Copyright 1947 by Allen W. Dulles.

chancellor in a constitutional manner, even though his Nazi Party did not command a parliamentary majority. Once in office Hitler began the creation of an authoritarian state.

Throughout the decade before Hitler came to power, the National Socialist German Workers Party (NSDAP) appealed to both the nationalists on the right and the workers on the left. It also gathered in elements of the population that lacked sufficient interest to vote or had no definite party affiliations—many youths as they came to voting age, and disillusioned veterans of the First World War. Hitler also profited from the world-wide depression which set in after 1929. But in the elections of November, 1932, the Nazi party's voting strength, for the first time, declined. Many Germans who had viewed its uninterrupted progress with growing alarm felt that at last the tide was receding, the danger was over. But in those same elections the Communist party gained as much as the Nazis lost. Old and decrepit President Hindenburg, influenced by reactionary advisers—especially his son Oskar and his favorite Papen—was persuaded that the choice lay between Communism and Fascism, that with one more election the Communists would be in power. In a panic, he made Hitler Chancellor. This was done in such a constitutional and, to the Germans, orderly manner, that the majority in Germany failed to realize the significance of what was happening.

Many German industrialists, equally fearful of Communism, shared the view of the conservatives who helped Hitler into power and gave the Nazi party financial backing. . . .

Hitler then proceeded to destroy his opponents, playing them off against one another, and to wreck the institutions on which liberty and democratic government are based. At the outset he pleased the nationalists by his unconstitutional exclusion of the Communists from the Reichstag and his suppression of the Socialist party. Then he turned on the junkers—Hugenberg, Papen, and associates. He lured them into acquiescence by letting them keep their freedom, their property, and sometimes even their official positions, but saw to it that they were mere figureheads. He pleased the industrialists by destroying the labor unions, and then harnessed industry to the Nazi military machine. But he left the industrialists at least ostensible control of their properties. Then followed the destruction of *all* political parties, the suppression of the freedom of the press, the cruel extermination of the Jews and the creation of one of the most ruthlessly efficient police states in history. He even attacked the churches to prevent them from becoming an instrument for the preservation of political or personal liberty.

Finally, Hitler turned his attention to the High Command of the German army and to those generals who had leadership potentialities. The army tried to remain immune from Nazi influence, but its independence was slowly undermined. Some generals were won over when Hitler repudiated the provision of the Versailles Treaty that restricted the size of the German army; others, who remained hostile, were ousted—simply or deviously. . . .

Hitler could not have accomplished all these things without the support of the German people, including, at the end, some eight million party members. Unfortunately he also found far too many supporters in England, France, the United States, and elsewhere throughout the world. The appeal of the "strong leader" was not limited to Germany. . . .

As for the Germans themselves, it was a commonplace, just after Hitler came to power, to hear even intelligent people say: "Let him have a taste a power. Six months of it will show up his inability to run a state—the responsibilities of government will ruin the Nazis and then we Germans will be rid of them forever." Intellectuals particularly succumbed to the illusion that Hitler and his crowd were too uncouth and too ignorant to direct the complicated mechanism of government. The experiences of the last few decades should teach all future intellectuals that it does not take "culture" to rule a state.

Even today we tend to fall into the smug and dangerous habit of dismissing Hitler as a mountebank and fool, a crazy fanatic. The truth is he was one of the smartest tyrants who ever hypnotized a people. He understood his Germans thoroughly. He bemused the common man and gave hope and confidence to millions who, under the Weimar government, had seen no way to escape from their frustrations. Hitler's firsthand knowledge of these frustrations and illusions of the masses equipped him well for the task of deceiving and leading the declassed, the uprooted and the unhappy of Germany. He had learned the secret of the demagogue, which is to proffer some explanation, no matter how specious, for mass discontent, and then to promise to ameliorate it. Hitler asserted, over and over until the least literate understood him, that the plight of the German nation and the unhappiness of the individual German were the result of the Versailles Treaty, the Jews, and the Weimar Republic, i.e., democracy. To the unemployed he promised jobs, to the veterans he promised a revival of militarism (though at first it was only the pseudo militarism of the S.A.), and to the hopeless he promised a renaissance of German glory.

Under Hitler there was a feeling of resurgence, and the average middle- and working-class German, the "little man," felt he had a better chance in the world and a new self-respect. Compared to these advantages, what, after all, were the liberties he had sacrificed? So thought the average German. . . .

National Socialism was in reality a revolt against the principles of civil rights and responsibilities, against enlightenment and human progress, against the achievements of the French and American revolutions. . . .

The German intelligentsia, with its cultural tradition, should have done far more than it did. Its misfortune was that it did not have political experience and had lost contact with the people. The intellectuals failed to realize that democracy must never be taken for granted. They did not see the vital need for coming to its defense. To the staid and aloof professors in the German universities Hitler's movement, exemplified in an incoherent book like *Mein Kampf*, was so ridiculous that they did not take it seriously. Before they knew it, many were removed, imprisoned, or, at best, forced into silence or exile.

It was under the guise of national and moral rebirth that Hitler built up his dictatorship. There is an almost unbelievable paradox here. Many Germans, and not a few foreigners, years after Hitler came to power, still believed that a system built on the vilest intrigue and unprecedented sadism was highly moral and virtuous. What impressed them was not that the Reichstag was burned, but that Nazi decrees legislated a new kind of morality—outlawed the use of lipstick, closed shady night clubs—and that the statistics showed that criminality had declined in the Third Reich. The height of hypocrisy was reached when the Nazi writers' association . . . decreed that no more than two murders were to occur in any mystery novel, so that "the low instincts are not incited."

By the time the German people realized what their "national rebirth" and "moral awakening" actually meant, one of the most ruthless police states the world has seen was firmly established. The Nazi leaders had studied the prototype of totalitarianism in Russia. . . .

Modern technology—the radio, telephotography, the concealed dictaphone—and the most efficient methods of detection and of torture were devoted to suppressing freedom and ferreting out any who dared to oppose the Nazi dictatorship. In a police state equipped with machine guns, tear gas, tanks and aircraft, revolutions are not made by aroused masses with their bare hands. . . .

As Hitler gained one political and diplomatic victory after another, his popularity and power increased to the point where only a very small band of Germans dared to carry on a clandestine resistance. Those who opposed openly or whose secret opposition was discovered were relegated to concentration camps, of which some seventy to eighty existed even before the war. . . .

A people that accepts regimentation is not likely to develop the virtue of individual initiative which a popular underground movement requires. The great majority of the German people, by 1939, either supported the Nazi regime, acquiesced in it because their livelihood depended upon it, or were terrified into silence and inaction by the political police.

33

Totalitarian Aggression

The decade of the 1930's brought to the world the double disasters of depression and aggression. The promising economic recovery of the late 1920's ended in the deepest depression the modern world has known. While America remained aloof from international controversies, a wave of aggressive acts by the totalitarian powers culminated in World War II. The Mukden Incident of 1931 presaged Japanese expansion in the Far East. Mussolini's conquests of Ethiopia and Albania were more than matched in audacity by Hitler's annexations in central Europe. France and Britain followed a policy of appeasement, dramatically demonstrated at Munich in 1938. In the next year Hitler's non-aggression pact with Russia and his subsequent attack on Poland brought on World War II.

[192] *THE GREAT DEPRESSION PARALYZES EUROPE AND AMERICA* *

The Wall Street crash in the autumn of 1929 led to a world-wide depression. In panic, each nation looked to itself: tariffs were raised, imperial preferences ar-

* Shepard Bancroft Clough and Charles Woolsey Cole, *Economic History of Europe*, Revised Edition (Boston: D. C. Heath and Company, 1946), pp. 803–808. Copyright 1946 by D. C. Heath and Company. Used by permission of the publisher.

ranged, and currencies manipulated to gain momentary advantages. In Germany, depression and unemployment aided the rise of the Nazis. In America, domestic economic troubles intensified the isolationist trend. In England and France, prolonged internal distress paralyzed any potential resistance to totalitarian aggression.

It is clear that the wave of prosperity which followed the depression of 1920–1921 was being broken down by recessionary movements before the year 1929 arrived. Yet 1929 is an important date, for it marks the crash of the stock-market boom in the United States. Speculative enthusiasm got under way in this country because people had come to believe that an increase in production and a steadiness of prices meant a long-continued period of prosperity. They therefore began to buy common stocks and to force security prices upward. As quotations of stocks rose, more people put their money in the market in order to get a profit from this rise. Before long money was being borrowed at 10 percent in order to buy stocks which, if dividends on the basis of earnings were paid, could produce only 2 percent on the purchase price. The Federal Reserve authorities contemplated raising the discount rate (1927) to stop this "race toward a fall," but did not do so until it was too late to be effective. From 1926 to September, 1929, the index of 421 common stocks in New York rose from 100 to 225, and in the twenty months ending in September, 1929, the value of stocks on the New York Exchange increased by over $51,000,000,000. In October, 1929, however, speculators discovered that the prices of stocks failed to go up; and they began to sell. Between September 3 and November 13, shares on the New York Stock Exchange fell by $30,000,000,000 and in June, 1932, reached an index of 34 (1926 equals 100).

This speculative crash . . . had far-reaching effects. Immediately stocks on the European exchanges followed those in New York in their downward plunge. People began to withdraw their money from banks in order to pay their usual obligations and their stock-market debts. Capital in America was no longer available for export, and consequently Europeans, who had become accustomed to borrowing from the United States, were hard put to it to meet interest payments. This stringency in the money market brought such pressure on banks that those whose assets were not liquid began to go under. The Austrian Creditanstalt, founded by the Rothschilds in 1855, became insolvent in the early part of 1931; the great German Danatbank closed its doors in July of the same year; . . . Wholesale prices fell, production declined, unemployment increased, foreign trade went to pieces, and the investment of new capital was extremely low.

The depression also led many countries to abandon the so recently acquired gold standard. The credit crisis in Austria and Germany . . . tended to freeze many of the foreign loans to these states and caused nations, insofar as they could, to withdraw their holdings from abroad. This burden fell on the shoulders of the British, for they were heavy lenders in the areas mentioned and they held large amounts of foreign capital on deposit. Then when the drain on London got under way, it was obvious that other factors were involved. Great Britain had been importing more than usual . . . at the same time, it was exporting less because of its high domestic prices. . . .

The English decided to abandon the gold standard September 20, 1931, and the pound was permitted to rest not on gold but on what businessmen would pay for it in gold or other currencies. By the end of 1931, it was about 30 percent below its former level.

England's monetary depreciation was followed by similar moves on the part of other states. . . . By the end of 1932, thirty-five countries had left the gold standard. Those remaining on it—the United States, France, Switzerland, Holland, and Belgium—formed for a time a "gold bloc."

Problems arising from this upset of currencies were numerous and complex. There was, for instance, a great amount of "hot money"—capital which took flight from a country that was on the verge of depreciation and which sought refuge in a country that appeared to have a stable currency. These flights of capital worked mischief in the money markets, for they drained gold from the country whence they came and forced interest rates down in the nation to which they went. For these reasons, capital exports were limited by laws, which also had the effect of preventing persons from buying what they wanted or from settling their foreign debts. Furthermore, prices for various goods fluctuated widely from country to country. . . . Nor could these differences be easily ironed out, because quotas or other controls restricted foreign trade.

With cheap money in the countries which had devalued, with controlled currencies in many other places, and with embargoes of various kinds on trade, the "gold bloc" nations found that their currencies were so high that foreigners would not buy their goods. Hence agitation for devaluation got under way among them. . . . This agitation soon led to action. The United States abandoned the gold standard in April, 1933, and devalued the dollar by 40.94 percent by act of 1934. . . . Those countries which did not devalue, and even some of those which did, increased their control of currencies and of prices (thirty-six countries in 1939).

The effect of these devaluations on international trade was again to give the country which had devalued an advantage in selling goods, but this advantage was usually temporary because some other state would soon devalue below the point fixed by the first nation. In international payments, the consequence was to make it easier for debtor states to pay off their obligations.

In domestic economic relationships, the cheap money was similarly advantageous to debtors, for if a rise in prices occurred, as it usually did, they could pay their creditors with less effort. In general, such conditions mean good times. Thus devaluation had its *raisons d'etre*, but to work itself out to logical ends, time, peace, and relatively free economic exchanges were required. And these conditions were not present.

[193] *THE LEAGUE OF NATIONS INVESTIGATES THE MUKDEN INCIDENT* *

Violence, the prevailing spirit of the 1930's, was ushered in by the Mukden Incident of 1931, which led to the Japanese occupation of all Manchuria. For many decades Japan had coveted the rich agricultural lands and the mineral resources of Manchuria, a province nominally under Chinese sovereignty. In 1931 a large Japanese force was already on the scene, ostensibly to protect the South Manchuria Railway. The outbreak of hostilities brought the League of Nations Commission of Inquiry to Mukden. The following excerpt is taken from the Commission's report.

According to the Japanese versions, Lieutenant Kawamoto, with six men under his command, was on patrol duty on the night of September 18th, practicing defence exercises along the track of the South Manchuria Railway to the north of Mukden. They were proceeding southwards in the direction of Mukden. The night was dark but clear and the field of vision was not wide. When they reached a point at which a small road crosses the line, they heard the noise of a loud explosion a little way behind them. They turned and ran back, and after going about 200 yards they discovered that a portion of one of the rails on the down track had been blown out. The explosion took place at the point of junction of two rails; the end of each rail had been cleanly severed, creating a gap in the line of 31 inches. On arrival at the site of the explosion, the patrol was fired upon from the fields on the east side of the line. Lieutenant Kawamoto immediately ordered his men to deploy and return the fire. The attacking body, estimated at five or six, then stopped firing and retreated northwards. The Japanese patrol at once started in pursuit, and, having gone about 200 yards, they were again fired upon by a larger body, estimated at between three and four hundred. Finding himself in danger of being surrounded by this large force, Lieutenant Kawamoto then ordered one of his men to report to the Commander

* "Report of the League of Nations Commission of Inquiry on Manchuria" (The Lytton Report), pp. 67–71, in Sara R. Smith, *The Manchurian Crisis, 1931–1932* (New York: Columbia University Press, 1948), pp. 19–21. Used by permission.

of the No. 3 Company, who was also engaged in night manoeuvres some 1500 yards to the north; at the same time, he ordered another of his men to telephone (by means of a box telephone near the spot) to Battalion Headquarters at Mukden for reinforcements.

At this moment the south-bound train from Changchun was heard approaching. Fearing that the train might be wrecked when it reached the damaged line, the Japanese patrol interrupted their engagement and placed detonators on the line in the hope of warning the train in time. The train, however, proceeded at full speed. When it reached the site of the explosion it was seen to sway and heel over to the side, but it recovered and passed on without stopping. As the train was due at Mukden at 10:30 P.M., where it arrived punctually, it must have been about 10 o'clock P.M., according to Lieutenant Kawamoto, when he first heard the explosion.

Fighting was then resumed. . . .

Lieutenant Kawamoto's patrol, reinforced by Captain Kawashima's Company, was still sustaining the fire of the Chinese troops concealed in the tall kaoliang grass, when the two Companies arrived from Mukden. Although his force was then only 500, and he believed the Chinese army in the North Barracks numbered 10,000, Lieutenant-Colonel Shinamoto at once ordered an attack on the Barracks. . . . When the Japanese reached the North Barracks, which were described as glittering with electric light, an attack was made by the 3rd Company, which succeeded in occupying a corner of the left wing. The attack was vigorously contested by the Chinese troops within, and there was fierce fighting for some hours. . . . by 6 o'clock A.M. the entire barracks were captured at the cost of two Japanese privates killed, and twenty-two wounded. . . .

According to the Chinese version, the Japanese attack on the Barracks . . . was entirely unprovoked and came as a complete surprise. On the night of September 18th, all the soldiers of the 7th Brigade, numbering about 10,000 were in the North Barracks. As instructions had been received from Marshal Chang Hsueh-liang on September 6th that special care was to be taken to avoid any clash with Japanese troops in the tense state of feeling existing at the time, the sentries at the walls of the Barracks were armed only with dummy rifles. For the same reason the west gate in the mud wall surrounding the camp which gave access to the railway had been closed. The Japanese had been carrying out night manoeuvres around the barracks on the nights of September 14th, 15th, 16th, and 17th. . . . At 10 P.M. (of the 18th) the sound of a loud explosion was heard, immediately followed by rifle fire. This was reported over the telephone by the Chief of Staff to the Commanding Officer, General Wang I-Cheh. . . . While the Chief of Staff was still at the telephone, news was brought to him that the Japanese were attacking the Barracks. . . . As soon as the attack began, the Chief of Staff . . . again reported to General Wang I-Cheh by telephone. The latter replied that no resistance was to be offered. . . .

The Commission has come to the following conclusions:

Tense feeling undoubtedly existed between the Japanese and Chinese military forces. The Japanese, as was explained to the Commission in evidence, had a carefully prepared plan to meet the case of possible hostilities between themselves and the Chinese. On the night of September 18th–19th, this plan was put into operation with swiftness and precision. The Chinese . . . had no plan of attacking the Japanese troops, or of endangering the lives or property of Japanese nationals at this particular time or place. They made no concerted or authorised attack on the Japanese forces and were surprised by the Japanese attack and subsequent operations. An explosion undoubtedly occurred on or near the railroad between 10 and 10:30 P.M. on September 18th, but the damage, if any, to the railroad did not in fact prevent the punctual arrival of the south-bound train from Changchun, and was not in itself sufficient to justify military action. The military operations of the Japanese troops during this night, which have been described above cannot be regarded as measures of legitimate self-defence.

[194] *A DEFENDER OF THE REPUBLIC REVIEWS THE SPANISH CIVIL WAR* *

In July, 1936, in response to chaotic conditions in Spain, General Franco led a military uprising against the leftist popular-front government. The civil war dragged on for nearly three years amid conditions of shocking barbarity. France and England maintained neutrality, while Germany and Italy intervened directly on behalf of Franco's insurgents, or Nationalists. The Republican forces, or Loyalists, received considerable aid from Soviet Russia.

The rebels counted on a short war. The confusion and disorder prevailing in the democratic camp, the mutual suspicion between the parties, the hostility between the leaders, the indiscipline of the masses, the weakness of the Government—all led them to believe that the rebellion would not encounter any serious obstacle. . . .

The lack of weapons of war from which Republican Spain suffered, due to the backwardness of the nation, led naturally to a display of great virtues

* A. Ramos Oliveira, *Politics, Economics, and Men of Modern Spain, 1808–1946,* trans. by Teener Hall (London: Victor Gollancz, Ltd., 1946), pp. 567, 568, 579–580, 582, 594, 598–599. Copyright 1946 by A. Ramos Oliveira. Used by permission of Crown Publishers, Inc., New York, and Victor Gollancz, Ltd., London.

by the people. Individual man, natural man, still counted in Spain. Six months afterwards, he was to count less, because the war would be waged on modern methods, when with foreign aid, mechanized warfare superseded the period of street barricades. But in the meantime, the proletariat of Madrid and Barcelona did memorable things and saved the Republic. . . .

In a matter of a few days, Spain split up into rebel territory and loyal territory. Two Spains, each hating the other, were locked in combat. . . . The two Spains which were tearing each other to pieces were the Spain that was sick, where the structure of property and the character of economic life were concerned, and the Spain that was healthy. . . . The industrial and commercial regions, the regions of the middle class and modern proletariat, rose then, spontaneously, for the Republic.

On the other side, the insurgents made themselves master with hardly any opposition (which makes the opposition they did encounter all the more honourable and heroic), of the whole of the Spain which was socially sick. . . .

This peculiar division of the country into rebel and loyal, absolutist and Liberal, even were it not so nicely adjusted to social conditions, certainly affords, in my opinion, the most profound historical lesson to be learned from the civil war. It uncovers the root of the national problem of our days and confirms the fact that a Republic or a parliamentary democracy can only flourish where the middle classes predominate, preferably in regions where industry and commerce are fairly well developed. . . .

. . . the insurgents were in a desperate situation. They were rising against the State—an always risky enterprise—they had the people against them, and to complete their discomfiture, the country's important industry, an indispensable factor in war, was located in regions which remained under the legitimate Government. . . . The confidence or faith of the rebels could only be explained by the negotiations they had concluded with foreign Powers.

The military uprising had been mastered; that it finally triumphed was due entirely to the favour, expressed in aid of every shape and form, of the great Fascist and parliamentary Powers. . . .

Towards the end of 1936, when German, Italian and Portuguese intervention had already lasted three months, the first Russian aeroplanes and war material appeared in Spain. But the Republic never succeeded in solving the problem of war material and this spelt its doom. Franco had armaments and to spare, but he was always short of men; the Republic, on the other hand, had plenty of soldiers, but no arms. But the rebels could import Italian troops and German technicians without let or hindrance, and the Republican Government encountered insuperable obstacles in obtaining war material. . . .

The Communist Party, which had only a few thousand members in 1931, the year of the Republic, had been adding to its numbers in proportion as the proletariat veered towards radicalism as a result of the opposition of the oligarchy to all reform. . . . For the rest, internal unanimity, enthusiasm, and a facility for expounding without prolixity constructive formulas of action, made the Communist Party a group which was more important for its methods of combat than for its numbers. . . .

That meant that, at the outbreak of the military rising, no party of the Republic was better placed for the struggle than the Communist Party. None was so coherent, so disciplined or so sure of itself. And when the parliamentary democracies—the inspiration of all the other parties of the regime—abandoned the Spanish people, and the U.S.S.R. fulfilled its obligations under international law, the Communist Party inevitably came to the fore in the moral leadership of the regime. The people, contrasting the war material and supplies of all kinds arriving from Russia, with the blockade maintained by France and England, ascribed their salvation to the Soviet State. The Republican middle class, surprised by the moderate tone of Communist propaganda and impressed by the unity and realism which prevailed in this party, flocked in large numbers to join its ranks. Nothing succeeds like success; and the Communists, at home and abroad, were a force to be reckoned with.

[195] *HITLER AND GOERING SEIZE AUSTRIA BY TELEPHONE* *

In 1934, Hitler's attempt to annex German-speaking Austria had failed because Austrian Nazis were poorly prepared, and because Mussolini firmly backed Austria. Four years later in more favorable circumstances Hitler applied pressure to Austrian Chancellor Schuschnigg to surrender his nation to the Nazis. Schuschnigg defiantly called for a plebiscite by which Austrians might present their views on annexation to the world. The plebiscite was never held, for Hitler, Goering, and the Austrian Nazis acted quickly to seize control, as revealed in these transcriptions of telephone conversations.

Keppler [Goering's Agent] in Vienna and Goering in Berlin, March 11, 1938, 8:48 P.M.

KEPPLER: I want to inform you shortly: Federal President Miklas has refused to do anything. But nevertheless, the government has ceased to function. . . . The old government has ordered the Army not to put up any resistance. Therefore, shooting is not allowed.

* *Nazi Conspiracy and Aggression,* compiled by Office of United States Chief of Counsel for Prosecution of Axis Criminality, International Military Trials—Nurnberg (Washington, D.C.: U.S. Government Printing Office, 1946), Vol. V, pp. 639–642.

GOERING: Listen: The main thing is, that Seyss- (Inquart) [leader of the Austrian Nazis] takes over all powers of the Government, that he keeps the radio stations occupied.

K: Well, we represent the Government now.

G: Yes, that's it. You are the Government. Listen carefully: The following telegrams should be sent here by Seyss-Inquart: Take the notes, "The provisional Austrian Government which after the dismissal of the Schuschnigg Government, considers it its task to establish peace and order in Austria, sends to the German Government the urgent request, to support it in its task and to help it to prevent bloodshed. For this purpose it asks the German Government to send German troops as soon as possible."

K: Well, SA and SS are marching through the streets, . . .

G: Now listen: He has to guard the borders, so that they cannot disappear with their fortunes.

K: Yes, indeed.

G: And then—above all, he also is responsible for the foreign policy.

K: Yes, we still do need some one for this post.

G: Well, that does not matter. Now, Seyss-Inquart has to take it over and he has to appoint a few people. He should call upon the people we recommend to him. He should form now a provisional government. It is absolutely unimportant what the Federal President may have to say.

K: Yes, they are not doing anything!

G: No, no, he has to form the Government right now as he intended to do, and he should inform the people abroad about it.

K: Yes.

G: He is the only one who still has power in Austria.

K: Yes.

G: Then our troops will cross the border today.

K: Yes.

G: Well. And he should send the telegram as soon as possible.

K: Will send the telegram to Seyss-Inquart in the office of the Federal Chancellery.

G: Please. Show him the text of the telegram and do tell him that we are asking him—well, he does not even have to send the telegram—all he needs to do, is to say: agreed.

K: Yes.

G: Either call me at the Fuehrer's or at my place. Well, good luck. Heil Hitler!

Prince Philipp of Hesse, German Ambassador in Rome, and Hitler in Berlin, March 11, 1938, 10:25 P.M.

HESSE: I have just come back from Palazzo Venezia. The Duce accepted the whole thing in a very friendly manner. He sends you his regards. He has been informed from Austria. Schuschnigg gave him the news. He had then said it would be a complete impossibility, it would be a bluff, such a thing could not be done. So he was told that it was unfortunately arranged thus, and it could not be changed any more. Then Mussolini said that Austria would be immaterial to him.

HITLER: Then, please, tell Mussolini, I will never forget him for this.

HESSE: Yes.

HITLER: Never, never, never, whatever happens. I am still ready to make a quite different agreement with him.

HESSE: Yes, I told him that, too.

HITLER: As soon as the Austrian affair has been settled, I shall be ready to go with him through thick and thin, nothing matters.

HESSE: Yes, my fuehrer.

HITLER: Listen, I shall make any agreement—I am no longer in fear of the terrible position which would have existed militarily in case we had gotten into a conflict. You may tell him that I do thank him ever so much. Never, never, shall I forget that.

HESSE: Yes, my fuehrer.

HITLER: I will never forget it, whatever will happen. If he should ever need any help or be in any danger, he can be convinced that I shall stick to him whatever might happen, even if the whole world were against him.

HESSE: Yes, my fuehrer.

[196] *CHAMBERLAIN AND DALADIER SEEK TO APPEASE HITLER AT MUNICH* *

In the summer of 1938, Hitler launched a violent propaganda attack against the Czechoslovak Republic, claiming that Sudetan Germans living in Czechoslovakia were being brutally persecuted. By September, as Hitler was clearly preparing for war, British Prime Minister Chamberlain made three dramatic flights to Germany. At the last of these, at Munich, Chamberlain and Daladier of France, meeting with Hitler and Mussolini, agreed to the German demands for occupation of the Sudetenland.

Agreement Concluded at Munich on September 29, 1938.

Germany, the United Kingdom, France and Italy, taking into consideration the agreement, which has been already reached in principle for the

* *Nazi Conspiracy and Aggression,* compiled by Office of United States Chief of Counsel for Prosecution of Axis Criminality, International Military Trials—Nurnberg (Washington, D.C.: U.S. Government Printing Office, 1946), Vol. VIII, pp. 370–373.

cession to Germany of the Sudeten German territory, have agreed on the following terms and conditions. . . .

1. The evacuation will begin on the 1st October.

2. The United Kingdom, France and Italy agree that the evacuation of the territory shall be completed by the 10th October, without any existing installations having been destroyed and that the Czechoslovak Government will be held responsible for carrying out the evacuation without damage to the said installations.

3. The conditions governing the evacuation will be laid down in detail by an international commission composed of representatives of Germany, the United Kingdom, France, Italy and Czechoslovakia. . . .

6. The final determination of the frontiers will be carried out by the international commission.

7. There will be a right of option into and out of the transferred territories, the option to be exercised within six months from the date of this agreement. A German-Czechoslovak commission shall determine the details of the option, consider ways of facilitating the transfer of population and settle questions of principles arising out of the said transfer.

8. The Czechoslovak Government will within a period of four weeks from the date of this agreement release from their military and police forces any Sudeten Germans who may wish to be released, and the Czechoslovak Government will within the same period release Sudeten German prisoners who are serving terms of imprisonment for political offences.

Annex to the Agreement

His Majesty's Government in the United Kingdom and the French Government have entered into the above agreement on the basis that they stand by the offer . . . of the 19th September, relating to an international guarantee of the new boundaries of the Czechoslovak State against unprovoked aggression.

When the question of the Polish and Hungarian minorities in Czechoslovakia has been settled, Germany and Italy for their part will give a guarantee to Czechoslovakia.

Declaration

The Heads of Governments of the four Powers declare that the problems of the Polish and Hungarian minorities in Czechoslovakia, if not settled within three months by agreement between the respective Governments, shall form the subject of another meeting of the Heads of Government of the four Powers here present.

[197] *GERMANY AND RUSSIA AGREE TO A NON-AGGRESSION PACT* *

In the spring and summer of 1939, Hitler launched a bitter propaganda attack on Poland, obviously the next victim. In August, Nazi Foreign Minister Ribbentrop, acting upon a previous informal suggestion of the Soviets, proposed to Moscow an ending of the long-standing mutual hostility (selection 1, below). The resulting non-aggression pact (selection 2), containing a secret protocol on the territorial division of Eastern Europe, was signed at Moscow on August 23, 1939. On September 1, 1939, Hitler invaded Poland.

1. Telegram, from Ribbentrop, German Foreign Minister, to Schulenburg, German Ambassador in Moscow, August 14, 1939

I request you to call upon M. Molotov and communicate to him the following:

1. The contradiction between the national idea, exemplified by National Socialist Germany, and the idea of world revolution, exemplified by the U.S.S.R., has in past years been the sole cause for the alignment of Germany and Russia in ideologically separate and hostile camps. The developments of the recent period seem to show that differing philosophies do not prohibit a reasonable relationship between the two States, and the restoration of new, friendly cooperation. The period of opposition in foreign policy could therefore be brought to an end once and for all and the way opened to a new future for both countries.

2. There exist no real conflicts of interests between Germany and Russia. The living spaces of Germany and Russia touch each other, but in their natural requirements they do not overlap. Thus there is lacking all cause for an aggressive attitude on the part of one country against the other. Germany has no aggressive intentions against the U.S.S.R. The Reich Government are of the opinion that there is no question between the Baltic Sea and the Black Sea which cannot be settled to the complete satisfaction of both countries. Among these are such questions as: the Baltic Sea, the Baltic States, Poland, South-Eastern questions, etc. Over and above such matters political cooperation between the two countries can only have a beneficial effect. The same applies also to the German and Russian economies, which are complementary in every sphere.

3. There is no doubt that German-Russian policy today has come to an historic turning-point. The decisions with respect to policy to be made in

* U.S. Department of State, *Documents on German Foreign Policy, 1918–1945* (Washington, D.C.: U.S. Government Printing Office, 1956), Series D, Vol. VII, State Publication No. 6462, pp. 62–64, 245–247.

the immediate future in Berlin and Moscow will be of decisive importance for the development of relations between the German and Russian peoples for generations. On these decisions will depend whether the two peoples will some day, again and without any compelling reason, take up arms against each other, or whether they pass again into a new friendly relationship. It has gone well with both countries previously when they were friends and badly when they were enemies.

4. It is true that Germany and Soviet Russia, as a result of years of ideological opposition, today face each other distrustfully. A great deal of accumulated rubble will have to be cleared away. It must be said, however, that even during this period the natural sympathy of the Germans for the Russians never disappeared. The policy of both States can be built anew on that basis.

5. The Reich Government and the Soviet Government must, judging from past experience, take into account that the capitalistic Western democracies are the implacable enemies of both National Socialist Germany and Soviet Russia. They are today trying again, by the conclusion of a military alliance, to drive Russia into war against Germany. In 1914 the Russian regime collapsed as a result of this policy. It is the compelling interest of both countries to avoid for all future time the destruction of Germany and of Russia in the interests of Western democracies.

6. The crisis which has been produced in German-Polish relations by English policy, as well as English agitation for war and the attempts at an alliance which are bound up with that policy, make a speedy clarification of German-Russian relations necessary. Otherwise matters might, without Germany contributing thereto, take a turn which would deprive both Governments of the possibility of restoring German-Russian friendship and in due course clarifying jointly territorial questions in Eastern Europe. The leadership of both countries, therefore, should not allow the situation to drift, but should take action at the proper time. It would be fatal if, through mutual ignorance of views and intentions, the two peoples should finally drift apart.

As we have been informed, the Soviet Government also feel the desire for a clarification of German-Russian relations. Since, however, according to previous experience this clarification can be achieved only slowly through the usual diplomatic channels, I am prepared to make a short visit to Moscow in order, in the name of the Fuehrer, to set forth the Fuehrer's views to M. Stalin. In my view only through such a direct discussion can a change be brought about, and it should not be impossible thereby to lay the foundations for a final settlement of German-Russian relations.

RIBBENTROP

2. Treaty of Non-Aggression between Germany and the Union of Soviet Socialist Republics

The Government of the German Reich and the Government of the Union of Soviet Socialist Republics, desirous of strengthening the cause of peace between Germany and the U.S.S.R., and proceeding from the fundamental provisions of the Treaty of Neutrality, which was concluded between Germany and the U.S.S.R. in April 1926, have reached the following agreement:

ARTICLE I

The two Contracting Parties undertake to refrain from any act of violence, any aggressive action and any attack on each other either severally or jointly with other Powers.

ARTICLE II

Should one of the Contracting Parties become the object of belligerent action by a third Power, the other Contracting Party shall in no manner lend its support to this third Power.

ARTICLE III

The Governments of the two Contracting Parties will in future maintain continual contact with one another for the purpose of consultation in order to exchange information on problems affecting their common interests. . . .

ARTICLE VI

The present Treaty shall be concluded for a period of ten years with the proviso that, in so far as one of the Contracting Parties does not denounce it one year before the expiry of this period, the validity of this Treaty shall be deemed to be automatically prolonged for another five years.

ARTICLE VII

The present Treaty shall be ratified within the shortest possible time. The instruments of ratification will be exchanged in Berlin. The Treaty shall enter into force immediately upon signature.

Done in duplicate in the German and Russian languages.

Moscow, August 23, 1939.

For the Government of the German Reich: v. RIBBENTROP

With full power of the Government of the U.S.S.R.: V. MOLOTOV.

Secret Additional Protocol

On the occasion of the signature of the Non-Aggression Treaty between the German Reich and the Union of Soviet Socialist Republics, the undersigned plenipotentiaries of the two Parties discussed in strictly confidential conversations the question of the delimitation of their respective spheres of influence in Eastern Europe. These conversations led to the following result:

1. In the event of a territorial and political transformation in the territories belonging to the Baltic States (Finland, Estonia, Latvia, Lithuania), the northern frontier of Lithuania shall represent the frontier of the spheres of interest both of Germany and the U.S.S.R. In this connection the interest of Lithuania in the Vilna territory is recognized by both Parties.

2. In the event of a territorial and political transformation of the territories belonging to the Polish State, the spheres of interest of both Germany and the U.S.S.R. shall be bounded approximately by the line of the rivers Narev, Vistula, and San.

The question whether the interests of both Parties make the maintenance of an independent Polish State appear desirable and how the frontiers of this State should be drawn can be definitely determined only in the course of further political developments.

In any case both Governments will resolve this question by means of a friendly understanding.

3. With regard to South-Eastern Europe, the Soviet side emphasizes its interest in Bessarabia. The German side declares complete political *desintéressement* in these territories.

4. This Protocol will be treated by both parties as strictly secret.

Moscow, August 23, 1939.

For the Government of the German Reich: v. RIBBENTROP
With full power of the Government of the U.S.S.R.: V. MOLOTOV.

34

World War II

In the first two years of World War II, Hitler's mighty war machine overran Poland and Western Europe, except for the British Isles, rescued Italy from an impending defeat by the Greeks, and finally launched an attack on Russia. Japan's early successes in the Pacific area were equally startling, as she followed the Pearl Harbor attack with conquest of Southeast Asia. However, Allied victories in North Africa, the South Pacific, and Stalingrad turned the tide by early 1943. In the final two years, Allied landings in Normandy, a massive air attack on Germany, and the Russian advance from the east brought victory over Nazi Germany; while in the Pacific an island-hopping campaign, combined with naval and air assaults and the dropping of an atomic bomb on Hiroshima (selection no. 185 in Chapter 31), defeated Japan.

[198] *THE MAGINOT LINE FAILS TO PROTECT FRANCE* *

France's Maginot Line, built in the 1930's to defend the northeast frontier facing Germany, was the world's most elaborate fortification system. It reflected the

* Pertinax, *The Gravediggers of France* (Garden City, N.Y.: Doubleday & Company, Inc., 1942), pp. 11–15. Copyright 1942, 1944 by Doubleday & Company, Inc. Used by permission of the publisher and the author.

defensive strategy of French military leaders after World War I, and lulled the French people into a false sense of security. Hitler's blitzkrieg attack on the West on May 10, 1940, was directed against the Low Countries, so that the Maginot Line was outflanked as the Nazis poured into France from the north.

How can one explain the immovable calm of the generalissimo, the confidence with which he looked forward to a future of flame, steel, and blood? The answer is that General Gamelin had settled down into the certainties of what may be called the *Credo* of the Maginot Line. Here are the central articles of this faith:

1. Men defending fieldworks can hold out against an offensive, even if they are outnumbered three to one, or if the attack is carried out with bombers and tanks in massive quantities. This is even more true of the defense of concrete and steel fortifications. In order to do this successfully, they need only know how to handle their automatic rifles, machine guns, mortars, grenades, trench cannon, anti-tank and anti-aircraft cannon, avail themselves of the various types of artillery, and, in counter-attacks, combine planes and tanks with all other arms.

The French Command was well aware that tanks would be launched against our lines in a density of one hundred units to the kilometer. . . . But this avalanche of steel did not worry the High Command. Besides, they ignored that there was such a thing as air artillery which was to work in conjunction with fortresses on wheels. . . .

2. The ground gained by an enemy attack will always be limited, since it will be easier for the defense to organize resistance than for the attack to assemble the fresh troops required to widen the breach it has made. . . .

3. Besides, the Maginot Line has replaced the fieldworks of twenty-five years ago. These works were continuous; the Maginot Line is not only continuous, it has a strength far above anything we have ever seen. True enough, it lacks depth and elasticity. The lack of these is the price we paid for building strength into continuity and permanence. All in all, nevertheless, this combination probably excludes the possibility even of a minor breakthrough. . . .

The Maginot Line ends at Montmédy; from the Meuse to the Pas-de-Calais the terrain is open or slightly protected. How were we to ward against the dangers which arose from this solution of continuity, supposing that we did not get the hoped-for chance to attack along the Belgian-German frontier? Various answers were given. They amounted to this: fieldworks will be constructed. The natural obstacle which consists of the Ardennes Forest and the Meuse River rules out a break-through in that area. And the French-British-Belgian armies will be able to get to the relatively narrow stretch of territory between Givet and Antwerp quickly enough to prevent an enemy outflanking action. In the defensive credo here was the point which remained ill defined and vague. But this must be emphasized: Under the military philosophy which goes by the name of Maginot an appendix was set apart for strategy in open space. The "Maginot" credo was not a closed one—and that was the worst of it. In May–June 1940 the fortifications were not actually stormed by the enemy. They were turned.

[199] *CHURCHILL'S SPEECHES STIFFEN BRITISH MORALE* *

On May 10, 1940, the day Hitler attacked the Low Countries, Winston S. Churchill succeeded Neville Chamberlain as British prime minister. Churchill, a master of the English language, in a series of resounding speeches found the words to inspire his people. Excerpt **A** *below is from a speech of May, 1940, on his accession as prime minister;* **B,** *after the Dunkirk evacuation;* **C,** *two weeks later at the beginning of the Battle of Britain;* **D,** *an address to the Italian people on December 23, 1940.*

[A] On Monday, May 13, I asked the House of Commons . . . for a vote of confidence in the new Administration. After reporting the progress which had been made in filling the various offices, I said, "I have nothing to offer but blood, toil, tears and sweat." In all our long history no Prime Minister had ever been able to present to Parliament and the nation a programme at once so short and so popular. I ended:

You ask, what is our policy? I will say: It is to wage war, by sea, land and air, with all our might and with all the strength that God can give us: to wage war against a monstrous tyranny, never surpassed in the dark, lamentable catalogue of human crime. That is our policy. You ask, What is our aim? I can answer in one word: Victory—victory at all costs, victory in spite of all terror; victory, however long and hard the road may be; for without victory, there is no survival. Let that be realised; no survival for the British Empire; no survival for all that the British Empire has stood for, no survival for the urge and impulse of the ages, that mankind will move forward towards its goal. But I take up my task with buoyancy and hope. I feel sure that our cause will not be suffered to fail among men. At this

* Winston S. Churchill, *Their Finest Hour,* in *The Second World War* (Boston: Houghton Mifflin Company, 1949), Vol. II, pp. 25–26, 118, 225–226, 620–621. Copyright 1949 by Houghton Mifflin Company. The selections from Winston S. Churchill, *The Second World War,* are reprinted by permission of and arrangement with Houghton Mifflin Company, the authorized publishers, and by Cassell and Company, Ltd., London.

time I feel entitled to claim the aid of all, and I say, "Come, then, let us go forward together with our united strength."

[B] Even though large tracts of Europe and many old and famous States have fallen or may fall into the grip of the Gestapo and all the odious apparatus of Nazi rule, we shall not flag or fail. We shall go on to the end, we shall fight in France, we shall fight in the seas and oceans, we shall fight with growing confidence and growing strength in the air, we shall defend our island, whatever the cost may be, we shall fight on the beaches, we shall fight on the landing grounds, we shall fight in the fields and in the streets, we shall fight in the hills; we shall never surrender, and even if, which I do not for a moment believe, this island or a large part of it were subjugated and starving, then our Empire beyond the seas, armed and guarded by the British Fleet, would carry on the struggle, until, in God's good time, the New World, with all its power and might, steps forth to the rescue and the liberation of the Old.

[C] During the first four years of the last war the Allies experienced nothing but disaster and disappointments. . . . We repeatedly asked ourselves the question "How are we going to win?" and no one was ever able to answer it with much precision, until at the end, quite suddenly, quite unexpectedly, our terrible foe collapsed before us, and we were so glutted with victory that in our folly we threw it away.

However matters may go in France or with the French Government or other French Governments, we in this island and in the British Empire will never lose our sense of comradeship with the French people. . . . If final victory rewards our toils they shall share the gains—aye, and freedom shall be restored to all. We abate nothing of our just demands; not one jot or tittle do we recede. . . . Czechs, Poles, Norwegians, Dutch, Belgians, have joined their causes to our own. All these shall be restored.

What General Weygand called the Battle of France is over. I expect that the Battle of Britain is about to begin. Upon this battle depends the survival of Christian civilization. Upon it depends our own British life, and the long continuity of our institutions and our Empire. The whole fury and might of the enemy must very soon be turned on us. Hitler knows that he will have to break us in this island or lose the war. If we can stand up to him, all Europe may be free and the life of the world may move forward into broad, sunlit uplands. But if we fail, then the whole world, including the United States, including all that we have known and cared for, will sink into the abyss of a new Dark Age, made more sinister, and perhaps more protracted, by the lights of perverted science. Let us therefore brace ourselves to our duties, and so bear ourselves that, if the British Empire and its Commonwealth last for a thousand years, men will say, "This was their finest hour."

[D] Where is it that the Duce has led his trusting people after eighteen years of dictatorial power? What hard choice is open to them now? It is to stand up to the battery of the whole British Empire on sea, in the air, and in Africa, and the vigorous counter-attack of the Greek nation; or, on the other hand, to call in Attila over the Brenner Pass with his hordes of ravenous soldiery and his gangs of Gestapo policemen to occupy, hold down, and protect the Italian people, for whom he and his Nazi followers cherish the most bitter and outspoken contempt that is on record between races.

There is where one man and one man only has led you; and there I leave this unfolding story until the day comes—as come it will—when the Italian nation will once more take a hand in shaping its own fortunes.

[200] *JAPAN DECIDES ON WAR WITH THE UNITED STATES* *

In the summer and fall of 1941, Japanese-United States relations deteriorated rapidly. With the Soviet Union and Great Britain fully occupied in the war against Nazi Germany, and with France and the Netherlands unable to defend their Asian colonies, only the United States stood in the way of a Japanese advance into Southeast Asia. The Japanese premier, Prince Konoye, attempted unsuccessfully to negotiate with the United States. The Prince resigned the premiership in October as Japan's war plans crystallized.

While the complicated and prolonged diplomatic negotiations were being conducted between Tokyo and Washington, in Tokyo itself a question of special significance was being deliberated upon by the cabinet. The question was whether to continue negotiations indefinitely with America, or whether to break them off abruptly. And more important still, they were considering whether war with America would follow upon the heels of the breaking off of negotiations.

The diplomatic negotiations for establishing a better American-Japanese understanding were being participated in by only the highest leaders of the Government, Army, Navy, and the Supreme Command. They were progressing to the absolute exclusion of lesser officials. With the sole exception of Foreign Minister Matsuoka, all the leading participants were hoping for

* "Memoirs of Prince Konoye," in United States Congress, Joint Committee on the Investigation of the Pearl Harbor Attack, *Pearl Harbor Attack* (Washington, D.C., 1946), part 20, pp. 4003–4004, 4025–4026.

the success of the negotiations, and for this very reason they were conducting it in absolute secrecy lest it encounter opposition.

Nevertheless, news began to leak out, particularly as a result of Foreign Minister Matsuoka's secret reports to the German and Italian Ambassadors. As they began to perceive the general outline of the negotiations, the lesser officials began to give evidence of their disapproval. The Army in particular stiffened in its opposition. Just at this moment the German-Soviet war suddenly broke out. Though the governmental leaders were able to set aside the insistent demands for an immediate war against the Soviets, they were obliged to decide upon the armed occupation of French Indo-China as a sort of consolation prize. At the same time, in order to be prepared for any emergency, they proceeded with full-scale preparations for a possible war against England and America. Though it was no easy task, the division between preparation for war and war itself had to be firmly borne in mind. As preparations for war progressed, opposition to American-Japanese negotiations became more vociferous.

Meanwhile the effect of Japan's armed occupation of French Indo-China was immediate and powerful. America immediately effected a breaking off of economic relations painful to Japan and without hesitation made clear that her own country's traditional policy alone was the policy conducive to peace. This strong American retaliation created a proportionate reaction in the anti-American camp in Japan. Opposition to the American-Japanese negotiations came into the open, and the course of action of the Cabinet, which had been created expressly for this purpose, became fraught with difficulties. Developments finally induced me to request a personal interview with the American President. . . . It would seem that from about August 1941, the Army General Staff, even including the highest quarters, began advocating an immediate breaking off of negotiations and an opening of American-Japanese hostilities. Seeking in every possible way to contravene these policies, from the latter half of August I repeatedly held consultations with the Army and Navy Ministers and called together countless joint conferences. To a certain degree, the "National Policy" calling for the breaking off of negotiations and the immediate opening of hostilities against England and America was brought under discussion.

Thus it came about that on September 6th, at a conference held in the Imperial presence, the "Outline for the Execution of the National Policy of the Imperial Government" was decided upon.

Plans for the Prosecution of the Policy of the Imperial Government

. . . 1. Determined not to be deterred by the possibility of being involved in a war with America (and England and Holland) in order to secure our national existence, we will proceed with war preparations so that they be completed approximately toward the end of October.

2. At the same time, we will endeavor by every possible diplomatic means to have our demands agreed to by America and England. . . .

3. If by the early part of October there is no reasonable hope of having our demands agreed to in the diplomatic negotiations mentioned above, we will immediately make up our minds to get ready for war against America (and England and Holland). . . . Special effort will be made to prevent America and Soviet Russia from forming a united front against Japan.

Annex Document

Japan's Minimum Demands in her Negotiations with America (and England)

1. America and England shall not intervene in or obstruct a settlement by Japan of the China incident. . . . America and England will close the Burma Route and offer the Chiang Regime neither military, political, nor economic assistance. . . .

2. America and England will take no action in the Far East which offers a threat to the defense of the (Japanese) Empire. . . .

3. America and England will cooperate with Japan in her attempt to obtain needed raw materials. . . .

Japan's Maximum Concessions

1. Japan will not use French Indo-China as a base for operations against any neighboring countries with the exception of China. . . .

2. Japan is prepared to withdraw her troops from French Indo-China as soon as a just peace is established in the Far East.

3. Japan is prepared to guarantee the neutrality of the Philippine Islands.

As far as Japan was concerned, since April, just about everything possible had been done to forward American-Japanese negotiations. I had taken the important step of proposing a personal interview with the President. I had sent him a message, and I had in addition explained my true feelings to Ambassador Grew. On the other hand, as a result of the important National Policy decided upon at the Imperial Conference on September 6th, as far as Japan was concerned, a point had been established beyond which negotiations could not proceed. We came more and more to feel that we were approaching a show-down. . . .

. . . The urgency of the political situation in Japan increased with oppressive force, and at last resulted in the resignation of the Cabinet en masse.

The Resignation of Premier Konoye, October 16, 1941

Recently . . . War Minister Tojo has come to believe that there is absolutely no hope of reaching an agreement with America by the time we specified. . . . He thus concludes that the time has arrived for us to make up our minds to get ready for war against America. However, careful reconsideration of the situation leads me to the conclusion that, given time, the possibility of reaching an agreement with the United States is not hopeless. In particular, I believe that even the most difficult question involved, namely, that of the withdrawal of troops, can be settled if we are willing to sacrifice our honor to some extent and agree to the formula suggested by America. To plunge into a great war, the issue of which is most uncertain, at a time when the China Incident is still unsettled would be something which I could not possibly agree to, especially since I have painfully felt my grave responsibility for the present state of affairs ever since the outbreak of the China Incident. . . . Thus I have done my utmost in stating my earnest convictions in an endeavor to persuade War Minister Tojo to accept my viewpoint. In response to this, the War Minister insisted that . . . it was impossible from the standpoint of preserving military morale for him to agree to the withdrawal of troops; that if we once gave in to America that country would become so arrogant that there would be no end of its depredations; and that even if we should be able to settle the China affair now, Sino-Japanese relations would again reach a deadlock in a mere two or three years. He pointed out that while there are certain weak points in our position, America also has its weak points and that we should therefore grasp the present opportunity and get ready for war at once.

[201] *THE NAZIS ATTEMPT TO EXTERMINATE THE JEWISH PEOPLE* *

From the start, the Nazi Movement endorsed a vicious anti-semitism. Before 1939, a series of increasingly harsh laws restricted the activities of Jews in Germany. During the war, the policy of persecution was transformed into a European-wide mass extermination of Jews.

I, Rudolf Franz Ferdinand Hoess, being first duly sworn, depose and say as follows: I am forty-six years old, and have been a member of the

* *Nazi Conspiracy and Aggression,* compiled by Office of United States Chief of Counsel for Prosecution of Axis Criminality, International Military Trials—Nurnberg (Washington, D.C.: U.S. Government Printing Office, 1946), Vol. VI, pp. 787–789.

NSDAP (Nazi Party) since 1922; a member of the SS since 1934; a member of the Waffen-SS since 1939.

I have been constantly associated with the administration of concentration camps since 1934, serving at Dachau until 1938; then as Adjutant in Sachenhausen from 1938 to May 1, 1940, when I was appointed Commandant of Auschwitz. I commanded Auschwitz until 1 December 1943, and estimate that at least 2,500,000 victims were executed and exterminated there by gassing and burning, and at least another half million succumbed to starvation and disease, making a total dead of about 3,000,000. This figure represents about 70% or 80% of all persons sent to Auschwitz as prisoners, the remainder having been selected and used for slave labor in the concentration camp industries. Included among the executed and burned were approximately 20,000 Russian prisoners of war, . . . The remainder of the total number of victims included about 100,000 German Jews, and great numbers of citizens, mostly Jewish from Holland, France, Belgium, Poland, Hungary, Czechoslovakia, Greece, or other countries. We executed about 400,000 Hungarian Jews alone at Auschwitz in the summer of 1944. . . .

Mass executions by gassing commenced during the summer of 1941 and continued until the fall of 1944. I personally supervised executions at Auschwitz until the first of December 1943. . . .

The "final solution" of the Jewish question meant the complete extermination of all Jews in Europe. I was ordered to establish extermination facilities at Auschwitz in June 1941. At that time there were already in the general government (German-occupied Poland) three other extermination camps: Belzek, Treblinka, and Wolzek. . . . The Camp Commandant at Treblinka told me that he had liquidated 80,000 in the course of one-half year. He was principally concerned with liquidating all the Jews from the Warsaw ghetto. He used monoxide gas and I did not think that his methods were very efficient. So when I set up the extermination building at Auschwitz, I used Cyclon B, which was a crystallized prussic acid which we dropped into the death chamber from a small opening. It took from 3 to 15 minutes to kill the people in the death chamber depending upon climatic conditions. We knew when the people were dead because their screaming stopped. We usually waited about one half hour before we opened the doors and removed the bodies. After the bodies were removed our special commandos took off the rings and extracted the gold from the teeth of the corpses.

Another improvement that we made over Treblinka was that we built our gas chambers to accommodate 2,000 people at one time, whereas at Treblinka their 10 gas chambers only accommodated 200 people each. The way we selected our victims was as follows: we had two SS doctors on duty at Auschwitz to examine the incoming transports of prisoners. The prisoners would be marched by one of the doctors who would make spot decisions as they walked by. Those who were fit to work were sent into the Camp. Others were sent immediately to the extermination plants. Children of tender years were invariably exterminated since by reason of their youth they were unable to work. Still another improvement we made over Treblinka was that at Treblinka the victims almost always knew that they were going to be exterminated, and at Auschwitz we endeavored to fool the victims into thinking that they were to go through a delousing process. Of course, frequently they realized our true intentions and we sometimes had riots and difficulties due to that fact. Very frequently women would hide their children under the clothes but of course when we found them we would send the children in to be exterminated. We were required to carry out these exterminations in secrecy but of course the foul and nauseating stench from the continuous burning of bodies permeated the entire area and all of the people living in the surrounding communities knew that exterminations were going on at Auschwitz. . . .

From time to time we conducted medical experiments on women inmates, including sterilization and experiments relating to cancer. Most of the people who died under these experiments had already been condemned to death by the Gestapo. . . .

I understand English as it is written above. The above statements are true; this declaration is made by me voluntarily and without compulsion.

[202] *ALLIED AIR POWER DESTROYS GERMAN INDUSTRY AND TRANSPORTATION* *

At the start of World War II, Germany possessed a superior air force which not only effectively supported the blitzkrieg tactics of ground forces, but also devastated such cities as Warsaw, Rotterdam, and London. By 1944, however, air supremacy passed to the British and Americans, who carried out a systematic bombardment of German industrial cities and communications centers. In early 1945, Allied armies entering Germany found the cities in ruins and transportation paralyzed.

The outstanding feature of the German war effort is the surprisingly low output of armaments in the first three years of the war—surprisingly low as measured not only by Germany's later achievements, but also by the

* The United States Strategic Bombing Survey, *The Effects of Strategic Bombing on the German War Economy* (Overall Economic Effects Division, October, 1945), pp. 6–14.

general expectations of the time and by the level of production of her enemy, Britain. In aircraft, trucks, tanks, self-propelled guns, and several other types of armaments, British production was greater than Germany's in 1940, 1941, and 1942.

For those early years the conclusion is inescapable that Germany's war production was not limited by her war potential—by the resources at her disposal—but by demand; in other words, by the notions of the German war leaders as to what was required for achieving their aim. The Germans did not plan for a long war, nor were they prepared for it. Hitler's strategy contemplated a series of separate thrusts and quick victories over enemies that were even less prepared than Germany; he did not expect to fight a prolonged war against a combination of major world powers. The Polish campaign, while it brought an unexpected declaration of war from France and England, went according to plan. The Norwegian and later the French campaign further justified the German faith in "Blitzkrieg." Both ended in complete victory within a very short time and with an unexpectedly small expenditure of military resources. After the occupation of France, England, though not invaded or brought to heel through aerial bombardment, was no longer considered an immediate threat. Eventual intervention by the United States was not taken seriously. The attack on Russia was started in the confident expectation that the experience of the earlier campaigns was to be repeated; Russia was to be completely subjugated in three to four months.

The underestimation of Russia's strength was the major miscalculation of this strategy. The Polish and French campaigns had shown that Germany's military preparedness, large or small, was fully adequate for achieving her strategic objectives. But in the case of Russia the same strategy would have required preparations on a far greater scale; and in the critical nine months that separated the decision to invade Russia from the actual beginning of the campaign, such preparations were not made, even though there were no serious obstacles to an all-around expansion of armaments production. The first three months of the Russian campaign did, in fact, go entirely "according to plan"; and at the end of September Hitler, believing the war about won, ordered a large scale reduction in armaments production. This order, even though only partially carried out, caused important reductions in stocks, particularly of ammunition, the effects of which were not overcome for a considerable time.

The defeat before Moscow, and the entry of the United States into the war in December 1941, brought the German leaders for the first time face to face with the prospect of a prolonged war with the three greatest powers ranged against them. From that time onward limitations of demand no longer played a role in restricting armaments production; Germany's leaders called for an all-out effort. Yet, measured by the standards of other belligerents, there was no "total mobilization" and no long-term planning to bring the war effort to its attainable maximum. The production of civilian goods was restricted only to a moderate extent; there was no further mobilization of women and no large scale transfer of labor from non-essential to essential industries.

In February 1942, Albert Speer, Hitler's personal architect, was appointed Minister of Armament Production with wide powers; and the production history of the following two and a half years bears the stamp of the "Speer Period." Speer set about replacing the existing machinery of control with a new organization (the "Rings" and "Committees"), manned by people selected from among the production managers and technicians of industry. They were charged with the task of increasing production by rationalizing German war industry; that is, by simplifying designs, standardizing components, concentrating production in the most suitable plants, reducing the number of different armaments orders given to a single firm, exchanging patents and secret processes, and generally adopting, throughout industry, the most efficient processes of production. The result of this policy was a more than threefold increase in Germany's munition production. . . .

There can be no doubt that Germany started the conversion of her economy to a wartime footing far too late. Had Germany's leaders decided to make an all-out war effort in 1939 instead of 1942, they would have had time to arm in "depth"; that is, to lay the foundations of a war economy by expanding their basic industries and building up equipment for the mass production of munitions. Starting their armanent program as late as 1942, they could only arm in "width"; that is, accept their equipment and material base as given and expand munitions production on the basis of available capacity. . . .

. . . Production capacity, except in a few special cases, of which oil was the most notable, was never really short; machinery capacity was never fully utilized. Manpower—particularly woman power—was never fully mobilized. Raw material stocks of the most important categories, such as steel, were rising up to mid-1944. The output of civilian consumption goods, after the restriction of the first two years of the war (which still left the civilian standard of living at a fairly comfortable level and above that of the depression years in the early thirties), was maintained virtually stable until the second quarter of 1944. . . .

. . . apart from the aero-engine industry and a few other exceptions, the German armament industries worked only a single shift throughout the war, and the great capacity reserve that would have been available from double or triple shift operations was largely unutilized. Furthermore, the German machine tool industry hardly expanded during the war, worked on a single shift basis throughout, and converted almost 30 percent of its capacity to direct munitions production.

Germany's easy machine tool position is in striking contrast with the experience of the United States and Great Britain, where machine tools were kept working 24 hours a day seven days a week, and the machine tool industry was very much expanded and strained to the utmost to supply requirements. . . .

Germany's experience was fundamentally different from that of the Anglo-American Allies also as far as the manpower problem is concerned. While England and America both entered the war with substantial unemployment, Germany's labor force was fully employed already in 1939. Total employment increased by 8 million, or 30 percent, between 1933 and 1939. Industrial employment nearly doubled, with most of the increase concentrated on the heavy goods industries.

The absence of unemployment does not mean, however, that Germany was fully mobilized for war in 1939. The percentage of workers in her nonagricultural population of working age was hardly greater than it was in Great Britain at the time; and what manpower she utilized was not concentrated unduly on war production. According to German statistics, civilian consumption in 1939 was above the 1929 level and had only fallen slightly by 1941. This shows that Germany entered the war with a "guns *and* butter" philosophy which was continued well after the initial defeats in Russia. . . .

Prior to the summer of 1943, air raids had no appreciable effect either on German munitions production or on the national output in general. . . .

The effects of air raids became more noticeable from the summer of 1943 onward. This was partly due to the heavier weight of the RAF attacks and partly to the appearance of the AAF in major strength. Area raids on the Ruhr caused an estimated 8 percent loss of steel output, but adequate stocks in the hands of industrial users prevented the loss from affecting armament outputs. . . .

For the first four months of 1944 the AAF, capable for the first time of carrying out repeated attacks deep into Germany, concentrated its strength on aircraft and ball bearing targets. During the attacks beginning in February, about 90 percent of German fighter production capacity was attacked and 70 percent destroyed. . . .

The attack on transportation beginning in September 1944 was the most important single cause of Germany's ultimate economic collapse. Between August and December freight car loadings fell by approximately 50 percent. The progressive traffic tie-up was found to have first affected commodities normally shipped in less than full trainload lots—finished and semifinished manufactured goods, components and perishables. The effects of the attack are best seen, however, in the figures of coal transport, which normally constituted 40 per cent of rail traffic. Shipments by rail and water fell from 7.4 million tons in August to 2.7 million tons in December. By March coal shipments were scarcely adequate even for the needs of the railroads. The operation of Germany's raw material industries, her manufacturing industries, and her power supply were all dependent on coal. By January their stocks were becoming exhausted and collapse was inevitable. . . .

From December 1944 onwards, all sectors of the German economy were in rapid decline. This collapse was due to the results of air raids working in combination with other causes. The armament index fell from 322 in July to 263 in December and to 145 in March. . . .

. . . "The German economy," Speer wrote in his report of March 15, 1945, "is heading for an inevitable collapse within 4–8 weeks." Even if the final military victories that carried the Allied armies across the Rhine and the Oder had not taken place, armament production would have come to a virtual standstill by May; the German armies, completely bereft of ammunition and motive power, would almost certainly have had to cease fighting by June or July.

35

The Rise of Communism

The foreign policy of the Soviet Union since its inception in 1917 has followed the Marxist-Leninist view of an inevitable trend toward world communism. Whenever expedient and wherever possible, the Soviet Union has attempted to hasten the progress of Communism, either directly by revolution or military conquest, or indirectly by subversion and penetration. By the end of World War II the Soviet Army occupied all of Eastern Europe to the banks of the Elbe River. In most of this territory Communist-dominated governments were placed in power, backed by Soviet military might. In China during 1946–1949, the weakness and corruption of Chiang Kai-shek's Kuomintang (Nationalist) Party provided an opportunity for the Chinese Communists under Mao Tse-tung to win control. Since 1949 Chinese influence within the Communist Bloc has grown, and Chinese acts of aggression have threatened the free countries of Asia.

[203] *POST-WAR PLANS ARE DRAWN UP AT YALTA* *

At Yalta in the Crimea, in February, 1945, preliminary arrangements were made for elections in the liberated countries of Europe. Although Stalin agreed to these

* U.S. Department of State, *Foreign Relations of the United States: The Conferences at Malta and Yalta, 1945* (Washington, D.C.: U.S. Government Printing Office, 1955), pp. 969–975, 984.

elections at the Yalta Conference, the promise was not fulfilled. Roosevelt, believing that Soviet aid in the war against Japan would shorten that conflict significantly, offered the Soviets territorial concessions in the Far East.

The Crimea Conference of the Heads of the Governments of the United States of America, the United Kingdom, and the Union of Soviet Socialist Republics which took place from February 4th to 11th came to the following conclusions:

Declaration on Liberated Europe

They jointly declare their mutual agreement to concert during the temporary period of instability in liberated Europe the policies of their three governments in assisting the peoples liberated from the domination of Nazi Germany and the peoples of the former Axis satellite states of Europe to solve by democratic means their pressing political and economic problems.

The establishment of order in Europe and the re-building of national economic life must be achieved by processes which will enable the liberated peoples to destroy the last vestiges of Nazism and Fascism and to create democratic institutions of their own choice. This is a principle of the Atlantic Charter—the right of all peoples to choose the form of government under which they will live—the restoration of sovereign rights and self-government to those peoples who have been forcibly deprived of them by the aggressor nations.

To foster the conditions in which the liberated peoples may exercise these rights, the three governments will jointly assist the people in any European liberated state or former Axis satellite state in Europe where in their judgment conditions require (a) to establish conditions of internal peace; (b) to carry out emergency measures for the relief of distressed peoples; (c) to form interim governmental authorities broadly representative of all democratic elements in the population and pledged to the earliest possible establishment through free elections of governments responsive to the will of the people; and (d) to facilitate where necessary the holding of such elections.

Dismemberment of Germany

It was agreed that Article 12a of the Surrender Terms for Germany should be amended to read as follows: The United Kingdom, the United States of America, and the Union of Soviet Socialist Republics shall possess supreme authority with respect to Germany. In the exercise of such authority they will take such steps, including the complete disarmament, demilitarization, and the dismemberment of Germany as they deem requisite for future peace and security. . . .

Reparation

The following protocol has been approved:

1. Germany must pay in kind for the losses caused by her to the Allied nations in the course of the war. Reparations are to be received in the first instance by those countries which have borne the main burden of the war, have suffered the heaviest losses, and have organized victory over the enemy.

2. Reparation in kind is to be exacted from Germany in three following forms: (a) Removals within 2 years from the surrender of Germany or the cessation of organized resistance from the national wealth of Germany located on the territory of Germany herself as well as outside her territory (equipment, machine-tools, ships, rolling stock, German investments abroad, shares of industrial, transport and other enterprises in Germany etc.) these removals to be carried out chiefly for purpose of destroying the war potential of Germany.

(b) Annual deliveries of goods from current production for a period to be fixed.

(c) Use of German labor. . . .

Poland

A new situation has been created in Poland as a result of her complete liberation by the Red Army. This calls for the establishment of a Polish Provisional Government which can be more broadly based than was possible before the recent liberation of the Western part of Poland. The Provisional Government which is now functioning in Poland should therefore be reorganized on a broader democratic basis with the inclusion of democratic leaders from Poland itself and from Poles abroad. The new Government should then be called the Polish Provisional Government of National Unity. . . .

This Polish Provisional Government of National Unity shall be pledged to the holding of free and unfettered elections as soon as possible on the basis of universal suffrage and secret ballot. In these elections all democratic and anti-Nazi parties shall have the right to take part and to put forward candidates. . . .

The three Heads of Government consider that the Eastern frontier of Poland should follow the Curzon Line with digression from it in some regions. . . . They recognize that Poland must receive substantial accessions of territory in the North and West. They feel that the opinion of the new Polish Provisional Government of National Unity should be sought in due course on the extent of these accessions and that the final delimitation of the Western frontier of Poland should thereafter await the Peace Conference.

Agreement Regarding the Entry of the Soviet Union into the War Against Japan (Top Secret)

The leaders of the three Great Powers—the Soviet Union, the United States of America and Great Britain—have agreed that in two or three months after Germany has surrendered and the war in Europe has terminated, the Soviet Union shall enter the war against Japan on the side of the Allies on condition that:

1. The *status quo* in Outer-Mongolia (The Mongolian People's Republic) shall be preserved.

2. The former rights of Russia violated by the treacherous attack of Japan in 1904 shall be restored, viz:

(a) the southern part of Sakhalin as well as all the islands adjacent to it shall be returned to the Soviet Union,

(b) the commercial port of Dairen shall be internationalized, the pre-eminent interests of the Soviet Union in this port being safe-guarded and the lease of Port Arthur as a naval base of the U.S.S.R. restored,

(c) the Chinese-Eastern Railroad and the South-Manchurian Railroad which provides an outlet to Dairen shall be jointly operated by the establishment of a joint Soviet-Chinese Company it being understood that the pre-eminent interests of the Soviet Union shall be safeguarded and that China shall retain full sovereignty in Manchuria.

3. The Kuril Islands shall be handed over to the Soviet Union.

It is understood, that the agreement concerning Outer-Mongolia and the ports and railroads referred to above will require concurrence of Generalissimo Chiang Kai-shek. The President will take measures to obtain this concurrence on advice from Marshal Stalin.

The Heads of the three Great Powers have agreed that these claims of the Soviet Union shall be unquestionably fulfilled after Japan has been defeated.

For its part the Soviet Union expresses its readiness to conclude with the National Government of China a pact of friendship and alliance between the U.S.S.R. and China in order to render assistance to China with its armed forces for the purpose of liberating China from the Japanese yoke.

J. Stalin
Franklin D. Roosevelt
Winston S. Churchill

February 11, 1945.

[204] *CHINA FALLS TO THE COMMUNISTS* *

In 1945 the Chinese Nationalists under Generalissimo Chiang Kai-shek emerged from the mountains of Southwest China, seriously weakened after 8 years of resistance to the Japanese. The Chinese Communists under Mao Tse-tung, numerically fewer and less well equipped than the Nationalists, despite the receipt from the Soviets of some surrendered Japanese military supplies, held a strong base in Northwest China. Efforts of General George C. Marshall to arrange a truce between the two groups failed in 1946, and was followed by the civil war.

The Ambassador in China (Stuart) to Secretary Marshall
Nanking, July 1, 1947

Communist military successes, the shrinkage of railway mileage in Nationalist hands, the depreciation and depletion of Nationalist equipment and supplies, the increasing friction between southern military forces and civil administrators on one hand and northern troops and the local civil population on the other, reports of a projected withdrawal of Nationalist forces to intramural China, and the abandonment of Manchuria to the Communists, rumors of the early return of Marshal Chang Hsueh-liang to Manchuria, and the expanding economic stagnation suggest the following observations:

The recent Communist drive has met with little Nationalist resistance. Northeast Combat Command sources and military observers admit that many Nationalist withdrawals were premature and without military necessity. The words "strategic retreat" have lost all significance. As a result the Communists possess almost complete initiative and are able to maneuver practically at will. . . . Nationalist military intelligence has been outstandingly deficient. The Northeast Combat Command is seemingly in almost complete ignorance of Communist plans and is therefore being constantly outwitted. . . .

Rivalry (if not enmity) between General Hsiung Shih-hui, the Generalissimo's representative, and General Tu Li-ming, commanding the Northeast Combat Command, is openly discussed and the absence of closely integrated military and economic planning in Manchuria is attributed to it.

By holding the initiative, the Communists are able to keep the Nationalists scurrying over the countryside, thereby causing depreciation of Nationalist motorized mobile equipment and depletion of sorely needed supplies. . . .

Nationalist southern military forces and civil administrators conduct themselves in Manchuria as conquerors, not as fellow countrymen, and have

* U.S. Department of State, *United States Relations with China* (Washington, D.C., 1949), Publication no. 3573, pp. 732–735, 832–834, 901.

imposed a "carpet-bag" regime of unbridled exploitation upon areas under their control. If military and civil authorities of local origin were in control, they too would probably exploit the populace, but experience has shown that Chinese authorities of local origin, in general, never quite strangle a goose laying golden eggs, and furthermore, it is a human trait to be less resentful toward exploitation by one's own than toward that by outsiders. The result of this is that the countryside is so antagonistic toward outsiders as to affect the morale of non-Manchurian troops and at the same time arouse vindictiveness in southern military officers and civil administrators.

Nationalist withdrawals toward Mukden have progressively cut off Nationalist held areas from the great food producing regions of Manchuria, thereby causing a potential Nationalist food shortage which was already apparent in extensive grain hoarding and speculation. Puerile efforts have been made toward price control and to combat hoarding, but in general, the results of these efforts have been largely to enforce the requisitioning of grain at bayonet point for controlled prices and to enable the resale of requisitioned grain at black market prices for the benefit of the pockets of rapacious military and civil officials. The common man is being crushed between the rising cost of living and the depreciating currency. (The cost of living index of May, 160 percent compared to 100 percent in April). . . .

The evidence is growing daily that the people of Manchuria not only are prepared for but are keenly desirous of a change in the government. But what change? Most are undecided even though voluble in discontent of the present way of living and the trend of events. It is safe to state that the overwhelming majority in the nation are as dissatisfied with, dislike, and would welcome freedom from the present Nationalist regime. A like majority fear and would therefore not welcome the Communist regime. . . .

There is every reason to believe that punitive military action against the Communists, unless succeeded by overwhelming military occupation will not save Manchuria to China. It is high time for Nanking to be realistic and to replace its present impotent, disliked regime in Manchuria with one which will be supported by the local population and would thereby serve to weaken the Communist movement. It may be, and some think that it is, too late to accomplish this purpose. Without some such effective measure there are many indications that it will be only a matter of some months, perhaps six to nine, before Manchuria will be lost.

The Ambassador in China (Stuart) to Secretary Marshall
Nanking, October 29, 1947

Sir: I have the honor to comment on political trends in China perhaps more as a record of my present impressions than because of any substantial objective changes. Most of this may therefore be mere repetition of what is already familiar.

COMMUNIST PARTY

There is no evidence of any weakening either in fighting power or in morale. Rather the opposite. They seem to be relatively well supplied with ammunition, money, and other material necessities, and to be confident of their ability to carry on for the two or three years which they estimate as the time required to get control of the territory north of the Yangtse River. They are steadily improving their organization and discipline. Officers and men share the same hardships and have the enthusiasm of those who are devotedly fighting for a cause which transcends all thought of selfish ambition or enjoyment. There is little if any evidence of material assistance from Moscow but there is undoubtedly very close and conscious affinity in aims, methods and objectives. This will probably become more apparent as the rift widens between the United States and the Soviet Union. . . . There is no slightest question but that they intend to carry on their destructive tactics until the present government succumbs. They will then agree to any temporary compromise or coalition that will enable them to extend their control until they achieve their goal of a thoroughly communized China. Nor is there any doubt in my mind but that their control will follow the invariable Communist pattern of a police-state, with no freedom of thought or action and with brutal slaughter or expropriation of all who seem to be in their way.

KUOMINTANG

The corruption and the reactionary forces pervading the Kuomintang are too familiar to call for further emphasis. It should be kept in mind, however, that single-party control always tends to be corrupt, that the period during which this party has been in power has been one of incessant conflict, that the mounting cost of living has greatly aggravated an age-long tradition in China, and that the mood of defeatism in an increasingly hopeless outlook has caused a creeping paralysis upon all creative effort. Even so the men at the very top are of high integrity and continue to struggle bravely against terrific difficulties. There are many more like them within and outside the Government.

OTHER PARTIES

The minority parties are rather disappointing. Those now absorbed into the Government are contributing but little and are busily seeking office for their members. The Democratic League continues to arouse suspicion of its communistic proclivities and offers little prospect of serving as a nucleus for liberal action. . . .

The Ambassador in China (Stuart) to Secretary Marshall
Nanking, December 30, 1948

Their (Communist) military forces gathered north of Nanking and already moving to encircle the city are overwhelming. Proclamations promising safety and good treatment to technicians both within and without the government and the precedent set in Tsinan and Mukden make it highly likely that sufficient government and public utility officials would remain in their jobs to ease the problem of running the government which will confront the Communists. . . .

[205] *MAO TSE-TUNG EXPLAINS THE AIMS OF COMMUNISM IN CHINA* *

The Chinese Communists' victory over the Nationalists in the civil war of 1946–1949 was achieved with much greater speed than most observers, including leaders of the Soviet Union, had anticipated. The following speech of Mao Tse-tung, delivered in June, 1949, on the 28th Anniversary of the Communist Party in China, is typical of the distorted propaganda used by Communists everywhere. The reader should note the Communists' peculiar use of the word "democratic."

The Chinese found Marxism through the introduction of the Russians. Before the October Revolution, the Chinese not only did not know Lenin and Stalin, but also did not know Marx and Engels. The gunfire of the October Revolution sent us Marxism and Leninism. The October Revolution helped the progressive elements of the world and China to use the world outlook of the proletariat as the instrument for observing the destiny of the country and reconsidering their own problems. Travel the road of the Russians—this was the conclusion.

In 1919 the May 4 Movement occurred in China, and the Communist Party of China was formed in 1921. During this period, Sun Yat-sen came across the October Revolution and the Communist Party of China. He welcomed the October Revolution, welcomed Russian help to the Chinese, and welcomed the Communist Party of China to cooperate with him.

* U.S. Department of State, *United States Relations with China* (Washington, D.C., 1949), Publication no. 3573, pp. 720–729.

Sun Yat-sen died, and Chiang Kai-shek came into power. During the long period of 22 years, Chiang Kai-shek dragged China into hopeless straits. At this period, the antifascist Second World War, with the Soviet Union as its main force, defeated three big imperialist powers, weakened two other big imperialist powers, and only one imperialist country in the world, the United States of America, suffered no loss. However, the domestic crisis of America was very grave. She wanted to enslave the entire world, and she aided Chiang Kai-shek with arms to slaughter several millions of Chinese. Under the leadership of the Communist Party of China, the Chinese people, after having driven away Japanese imperialism, fought the people's war of liberation for three years and gained a basic victory.

Twenty-four years have elapsed since Sun Yat-sen's death, and under the leadership of the Communist Party of China, Chinese revolutionary theory and practice have made big strides forward, fundamentally changing the features of China. Up to the present, the Chinese people have gained the following two basic experiences:

1. To awaken the masses in the country. This is to unite the working class, the peasant class, the petty bourgeoisie, and the national bourgeoisie into a united front under the leadership of the working class and develop into a state of the people's democratic dictatorship, led by the working class, with the alliance of workers and peasants as its basis.

2. To unite in a common struggle with those nations of the world who treat us on the basis of equality and the peoples of all countries. This is to ally with the Soviet Union, to ally with the new democratic countries of Europe, and to ally with the proletariat and masses of the people in other countries to form an international united front.

"You lean to one side." Precisely so. The 40 years' experience of Sun Yat-sen and the 28 years' experience of the Communist Party have made us firmly believe that in order to win victory and to consolidate victory, we must lean to one side. The experiences of 40 years and 28 years show that without exception, the Chinese lean either to the side of imperialism or to the side of socialism.

To sit on the fence is impossible. A third road does not exist. We oppose the Chiang Kai-shek reactionary clique who lean to the side of imperialism. We also oppose the illusion of a third road. Not only in China but also in the world, without exception, one either leans to the side of imperialism or to the side of socialism. Neutrality is a camouflage, and a third road does not exist.

"You are too provoking." We are talking of how to deal with domestic and foreign reactionaries, that is, imperialists and their running dogs, and not of any other people.

With regard to foreign and domestic reactionaries, the question of provoking does not arise, for whether there is provoking or not does not make any difference as they are reactionaries.

Only by drawing a clear line between reactionaries and revolutionaries, only by exposing the designs and plots of the reactionaries, arousing vigilence and attention within the revolutionary ranks, and only by raising our own morale and taking down the arrogance of the enemy can the reactionaries be isolated, conquered, or replaced. . . .

Internationally we belong to the anti-imperalist front, headed by the U.S.S.R., and we can only look for genuine friendly aid from that front, and not from the imperialist front.

"You are dictatorial." Yes, dear gentlemen, you are right and we are really that way. . . . The experiences of several decades amassed by the Chinese people tell us to carry out the people's democratic dictatorship, that is, the right of reactionaries to voice their opinion must be deprived, and only the people are allowed to have the right of voicing their opinions.

Who are the "people" at the present stage in China? They are the working class, the peasants, the petty bourgeoisie, and the national bourgeoisie. Under the leadership of the working class and the Communist Party, these classes unite together to form their own state and elect their own government to enact dictatorships over the lackeys of imperialism—the landlords, the bureaucratic class, and the Kuomintang reactionaries and their henchmen, representing these classes to oppress them and only allow them to behave properly and not allow them to talk and act wildly. If they talk and act wildly they will be prohibited and punished immediately.

The democratic system is to be carried out within the ranks of the people, giving them freedom of speech, assembly, and association. The right to vote is given only to the people and not to the reactionaries. These two aspects, namely democracy among the people and dictatorships over the reactionaries, combine to form the people's dictatorship.

Why should it be done this way? It is very obvious that if this is not done, the revolution will fail, the people will meet with woe and the State will perish. "Do you not want to eliminate State authority?" Yes, but not at present. We cannot eliminate State authority now. Why? Because imperialism still exists, the domestic reactionaries still exist, and classes in the country still exist. Our present task is to strengthen the people's State apparatus, which refers mainly to the People's Army, People's Police, and People's Court, for national defense and protection of the people's interests, and with this as condition, to enable China to advance steadily, under the leadership of the working class and the Communist Party, from an agricultural to an industrial country, and from a new democratic to a socialist and Communist society, to eliminate classes and to realize world Communism.

[206] *KHRUSHCHEV DENOUNCES STALIN* *

At the death of Stalin in March, 1953, leadership of the Soviet Union passed to a group of five officials, headed by G. Malenkov. Nikita Khrushchev succeeded Stalin as Secretary of the Communist Party. In less than three years Khrushchev successfully removed Malenkov and his associates, and attained dictatorial power. At the Twentieth Congress of the Communist Party of the Soviet Union in February, 1956, Khrushchev read a sensational report attacking Stalin.

Lenin used severe methods only in the most necessary cases, when the exploiting classes were still in existence and were vigorously opposing the revolution, when the struggle for survival was decidedly assuming the sharpest forms, even including civil war.

Stalin, on the other hand, used extreme methods and mass repressions at a time when the revolution was already victorious, when the Soviet state was strengthened, when the exploiting classes were already liquidated and Socialist relations were rooted solidly in all phases of national economy, when our party was politically consolidated and had strengthened itself both numerically and ideologically. It is clear that here Stalin showed in a whole series of cases his intolerance, his brutality and his abuse of power. . . .

Stalin was a very distrustful man, sickly suspicious; we knew this from our work with him. He could look at a man and say: "Why are your eyes so shifty today?" or "Why are you turning so much today and avoiding to look at me directly in the eyes?" The sickly suspicion created in him a general distrust even toward eminent Party workers whom he had known for years. Everywhere and in everything he saw "enemies, two-facers, and spies. . . ."

The power accumulated in the hands of one person, Stalin, led to serious consequences during the Great Patriotic War.

When we look at many of our novels, films, and historical "scientific studies," the role of Stalin in the Patriotic War appears to be entirely improbable. Stalin had foreseen everything. The Soviet Army, on the basis of a strategic plan prepared by Stalin long before, used the tactics of so-called "active defense," i.e., tactics which, as we all know, allowed the Germans

* U.S. Department of State, Press Release of June 4, 1956.

to come up to Moscow and Stalingrad. Using such tactics the Soviet Army, supposedly, thanks only to Stalin's genius, turned to the offensive and subdued the enemy. . . .

During the war and after the war Stalin put forward the thesis that the tragedy which our nation experienced in the first part of the war was the result of the "unexpected" attack of the Germans against the Soviet Union. But, Comrades, this is completely untrue. As soon as Hitler came to power in Germany he assigned himself the task of liquidating Communism. The Fascists were saying this openly; they did not hide their plans. In order to attain this aggressive end all sorts of pacts and blocs were created, such as the famous Berlin-Rome-Tokyo axis. Many facts from the pre-war period clearly showed that Hitler was going all out to begin a war against the Soviet State and that he had concentrated large armed units, together with armored units, near the Soviet borders.

Documents which have now been published show that by April 3, 1941, Churchill, through his ambassador to the U.S.S.R., Cripps, personally warned Stalin that the Germans had begun regrouping their armed units with the intent of attacking the Soviet Union. However, Stalin took no heed of these warnings. What is more, Stalin ordered that no credence be given to information of this sort, in order not to provoke the initiation of military operations. . . .

Had our industry been mobilized properly and in time to supply the army with the necessary material, our wartime losses would have been decidedly smaller. Such mobilization had not been, however, started in time. And already in the first days of the war it became evident that our army was badly armed, that we did not have enough artillery, tanks and planes to throw the enemy back. . . .

We must state that after the war the situation became even more complicated. Stalin became even more capricious, irritable, and brutal; in particular his suspicions grew. His persecution mania reached unbelievable dimensions. . . .

Let us recall the "Affair of the Doctor-Plotters." (Animation in the Hall) Actually there was no "Affair" outside of the declaration of the woman doctor, Timashuk, who was probably influenced or ordered by someone (after all, she was an unofficial collaborator of the organs of State security), to write to Stalin a letter in which she declared that doctors were applying supposedly improper methods of medical treatment.

Such a letter was sufficient for Stalin to reach an immediate conclusion that there are doctor-plotters in the Soviet Union. He issued orders to arrest a group of eminent Soviet medical specialists. He personally issued advice on the conduct of the investigation and the method of interrogation of the arrested persons. He said that the academician Vinogradov should be put in chains, another one should be beaten. Present at this Congress is a delegate, former Minister of State Security, Comrade Ignatiev. Stalin told him curtly, "If you do not obtain confessions from the doctors we will shorten you by a head." (Tumult in the Hall)

Stalin personally called the investigative judge, gave him instruction, advised him on which investigative methods should be used; these methods were simple—beat, beat, and once again, beat.

Shortly after the doctors were arrested we members of the Political Bureau received protocols on the doctors: confessions of guilt. After distributing these protocols Stalin told us, "You are blind like young kittens; what will happen without me? The country will perish because you do not know how to recognize enemies."

The case was so presented that no one could verify the facts on which the investigation was based. There was no possibility of trying to verify facts by contacting those who had made the confessions of guilt.

We felt, however, that the case of the arrested doctors was questionable. We knew some of these people personally because they had once treated us. When we examined this "case" after Stalin's death, we found it to be fabricated from beginning to end.

[207] *THE HUNGARIANS ATTEMPT TO THROW OFF THE SOVIET YOKE* *

During the summer and fall of 1956 unrest and sporadic rioting broke the Soviet-enforced internal peace of the satellite states of Poland and Hungary. In October 1956 the Hungarians turned to open revolt against the hated Soviet army of occupation and the Hungarian Communist leaders. The Hungarians enjoyed a few days of freedom, but no help was forthcoming from the West, and the revolt was soon brutally crushed by Soviet power.

What took place in Hungary in October and November 1956 was a spontaneous national uprising, due to long-standing grievances which had caused resentment among the people. One of these grievances was the inferior status of Hungary with regard to the U.S.S.R.; the system of government was in part maintained by the weapon of terror, wielded by the AVH or political police, whose influence was exercised at least until the end of 1955,

* United Nations. General Assembly. Special Committee on the Problem of Hungary, *Report of the Special Committee on the Problem of Hungary* (New York: U.N. General Assembly, Official Records: Eleventh Session Supplement No. 18, 1957), pp. 137–140.

through a complex network of agents and informers permeating the whole of Hungarian society. In other respects also, Soviet pressure was resented. From the stifling of free speech to the adoption of a Soviet-style uniform for the Hungarian army, an alien influence existed in all walks of life. Hungarians felt no personal animosity towards the individual Soviet soldiers on Hungarian soil, but these armed forces were symbols of something which annoyed a proud people and fed the desire to be free; . . .

The thesis that the uprising was fomented by reactionary circles in Hungary and that it drew its strength from such circles and from Western "Imperialists" failed to survive the Committee's examination. From start to finish, the uprising was led by students, workers, soldiers, and intellectuals, many of whom were Communists or former Communists. The majority of political demands put forward during the revolution included a stipulation that democratic socialism should be the basis of the Hungarian political structure and that such social achievements as the land reform should be safeguarded. At no time was any proposal made for the return to power, or to the Government, of any figure associated with pre-war days. "Fascists" and "saboteurs," heavily armed, could not have succeeded in landing on Hungarian airfields which were under Soviet supervision, or in crossing the Austrian frontier, where a closed zone was shown by the Austrian authorities to the military attachés of France, the United Kingdom, the United States of America, and the U.S.S.R.

The uprising was not planned in advance. It was the universal testimony of witnesses examined by the Committee that events took participants by surprise. No single explanation can determine exactly why the outbreak occurred just when it did. Communist spokesmen, including Mr. Kadar and the members of the present Government, have recognized the bitter grievances of the Hungarian people before 23 October. They have spoken of a "broad, popular movement" caused by the "bitterness and indignation" of the masses. Two factors would seem to have brought this resentment to a head. The first of these was the news received on 19 October of a successful move by Poland for greater independence from the U.S.S.R. This news was largely instrumental in bring the Hungarian students together in the meetings of 22 October. The second factor was the acute disappointment felt by the people when Erno Gero, First Secretary of the Central Committee of the Hungarian Workers' (Communist) Party, in his speech on the evening of 23 October failed to meet any of the popular demands and adopted what was considered a truculent tone towards his hearers.

Although no evidence exists of advance planning, and although the whole course of the uprising bears the hall mark of continuous improvisation, it would appear that the Soviet authorities had taken steps as early as 20

October to make armed intervention in Hungary possible. Evidence exists of troop movements, or projected troop movements, from that date on. It would appear that plans for action had therefore been laid some time before the students met to discuss their demands. The Committee is not in a position to say whether the Soviet authorities anticipated that the grievances of the Hungarian people, stimulated by events in Poland, could no longer be contained. Signs of opposition were evident before the 23rd; the Hungarian Government had reason to foresee that trouble was brewing. While the evidence shows that Soviet troops from outside Hungary were used even in the first intervention, no clause of the Warsaw Treaty provides for intervention by armed forces of the Soviet Union to dictate political developments within any signatory's frontiers.

The demonstrations on 23 October were at first entirely peaceable. None of the demonstrators appear to have carried arms, and no evidence has been discovered that any of those who voiced the political demands or joined the demonstrators had any intention to resort to force. While disappointment at Mr. Gero's speech may have angered the crowds, it would hardly of itself have sufficed to turn the demonstration into an armed uprising. That this happened was due to the action of the AVH in opening fire on the people outside the radio building. Within a few hours, Soviet tanks were in action against the Hungarians. This appearance of Russian soldiers in their midst not as friendly allies, but as enemies in combat, had the effect of still further uniting the people. . . .

The few days of freedom enjoyed by the Hungarian people provided abundant evidence of the popular nature of the uprising. A free Press and radio came to life all over Hungary, and the disbanding of the AVH was the signal for general rejoicing, which revealed the degree of unity achieved by the people, once the burden of fear had been lifted from them.

There were a number of lynchings and beatings by the crowds. These were, in almost all cases, confined to members of the AVH or those who were believed to have cooperated with them.

Steps were taken by the Workers' Councils during this period to give the workers real control of nationalized industrial undertakings and to abolish unpopular institutions, such as the production norms. These were widely resented as being unfair to workers and also a reflection of popularly suspected secret trade agreements with the U.S.S.R., which were said to make heavy demands on the Hungarian economy for the benefit of the Soviet Union. During the days of freedom, while negotiations continued with the Soviet authorities for the withdrawal of Russian troops, attempts were made to clear up the streets of Budapest and life was beginning to return to normal. The insurgents had agreed to amalgamate, while maintaining their identity, in a National Guard, which would have been responsible, with the Army and Police, for maintaining order.

Following the second Soviet intervention of 4 November, there has been no evidence of popular support for Mr. Kadar's Government. Mr. Kadar has successively abandoned most of the points from the revolutionary programme which he had at first promised to the Hungarian people. On the central question of the withdrawal of Soviet troops, he has moved from complete acceptance of the nation's wishes to a refusal to discuss the subject in present circumstances. Against the workers, he has proceeded step by step to destroy their power and that of the Workers' Councils. Capital punishment is applicable to strike activities. The processes of justice have been distorted by the institution of special police and special courts and by the ignoring of the rights of the accused. The Social Democratic Party has again been forcibly liquidated. General elections have been postponed for two years. Writers and intellectuals are subjected to repressive measures. The Hungarian workers have shown no sign of support for Mr. Kadar's Government or for the prospect of continuous Soviet occupation. Only a small fraction of the 190,000 Hungarians, mostly young people, who fled the country have accepted his invitation to return.

36

Defense of the Free World

With the end of World War II a new struggle began, the cold war of Communism vs. the Free World. The United States under the Marshall Plan offered extensive aid to Western Europe. With American backing, the nations of Western Europe drew closer together militarily and economically to meet the Soviet threat. West Germany and Japan experienced remarkable economic growth and adopted democratic forms of government. In 1948 the Soviet attempt to blockade free Berlin led to the Allied Airlift. In the Far East the Communist attack on South Korea brought on a protracted struggle of North Koreans and Communist Chinese, supported by the Soviet Bloc, against a United Nations force composed mainly of Americans and South Koreans.

[208] *SECRETARY MARSHALL OFFERS A PLAN FOR EUROPEAN RECOVERY* *

In June 1947, General George C. Marshall (1880–1959), Secretary of State, proposed a new type of foreign aid, an imaginative program for the rebuilding of

* "Remarks by the Honorable George C. Marshall, Secretary of State, at Harvard University on June 5, 1947," from *Congressional Record,* June 30, 1947.

Europe. In the period 1948–1951, over 13 billion dollars were spent, and by the latter year the aims of the Plan were largely fulfilled.

I need not tell you gentlemen that the world situation is very serious. That must be apparent to all intelligent people. I think one difficulty is that the problem is one of such enormous complexity that the very mass of facts presented to the public by press and radio make it exceedingly difficult for the man in the street to reach a clear appraisement of the situation. Furthermore, the people of this country are distant from the troubled areas of the earth and it is hard for them to comprehend the plight and consequent reactions of the long-suffering peoples, and the effect of those reactions on their governments in connection with our efforts to promote peace in the world.

In considering the requirements for the rehabilitation of Europe the physical loss of life, the visible destruction of cities, factories, mines, and railroads was correctly estimated, but it has become obvious during recent months that this visible destruction was probably less serious than the dislocation of the entire fabric of European economy. For the past 10 years conditions have been highly abnormal. The feverish preparation for war and the more feverish maintenance of the war effort engulfed all aspects of national economies. Machinery has fallen into disrepair or is entirely obsolete. Under the arbitrary and destructive Nazi rule, virtually every possible enterprise was geared into the German war machine. Longstanding commercial ties, private institutions, banks, insurance companies and shipping companies disappeared, through loss of capital, absorption through nationalization or by simple destruction. In many countries, confidence in the local currency has been severely shaken. The breakdown of the business structure of Europe during the war was complete. Recovery has been seriously retarded by the fact that two years after the close of hostilities a peace settlement with Germany and Austria has not been agreed upon. But even given a more prompt solution of these difficult problems, the rehabilitation of the economic structure of Europe quite evidently will require a much longer time and greater effort than had been foreseen.

There is a phase of this matter which is both interesting and serious. The farmer has always produced the foodstuffs to exchange with the city dweller for the other necessities of life. This division of labor is the basis of modern civilization. At the present time it is threatened with breakdown. The town and city industries are not producing adequate goods to exchange with the food producing farmer. Raw materials and fuel are in short supply. Machinery is lacking or worn out. The farmer or the peasant cannot find the goods for sale which he desires to purchase. So the sale of his farm produce for money which he cannot use seems to him an unprofitable transaction.

He, therefore, has withdrawn many fields from crop cultivation and is using them for grazing. He feeds more grain to stock and finds for himself and his family an ample supply of food, however short he may be on clothing and the other ordinary gadgets of civilization. Meanwhile people in the cities are short of food and fuel. So the governments are forced to use their foreign money and credits to procure these necessities abroad. This process exhausts funds which are urgently needed for reconstruction. Thus a very serious situation is rapidly developing which bodes no good for the world. The modern system of the division of labor upon which the exchange of products is based is in danger of breaking down. The truth of the matter is that Europe's requirements for the next three or four years of foreign food and other essential products—principally from America—are so much greater than her present ability to pay that she must have substantial additional help, or face economic, social and political deterioration of a very grave character.

The remedy lies in breaking the vicious circle and restoring the confidence of the European people in the economic future of their own countries and of Europe as a whole. The manufacturer and the farmer throughout wide areas must be able and willing to exchange their products for currencies, the continuing value of which is not open to question.

Aside from the demoralizing effect on the world at large and the possibilities of disturbances arising as a result of the desperation of the people concerned, the consequences to the economy of the United States should be apparent to all. It is logical that the United States should do whatever it is able to do to assist in the return of normal economic health in the world, without which there can be no political stability and no assured peace. Our policy is directed not against any country or doctrine but against hunger, poverty, desperation and chaos. Its purpose should be the revival of a working economy in the world so as to permit the emergence of political and social conditions in which free institutions can exist. Such assistance, I am convinced, must not be on a piecemeal basis as various crises develop. Any assistance that this Government may render in the future should provide a cure rather than a mere palliative. Any government which maneuvers to block the recovery of other countries cannot expect help from us. Furthermore, governments, political parties, or groups which seek to perpetuate human misery in order to profit therefrom politically or otherwise will encounter the opposition of the United States.

It is already evident that, before the United States Government can proceed much further in its efforts to alleviate the situation and help start the European world on its way to recovery, there must be some agreement among the countries of Europe as to the requirements of the situation and the part those countries themselves will take in order to give proper effect to whatever action might be undertaken by this Government. It would be neither fitting nor efficacious for this Government to undertake to draw up unilaterally a program designed to place Europe on its feet economically. This is the business of the Europeans. The initiative, I think, must come from Europe. The role of this country should consist of friendly aid in the drafting of a European program and of later support of such a program so far as it may be practical for us to do so. The program should be a joint one, agreed to by a number, if not all European nations.

[209] *THE AIRLIFT OVERCOMES THE BERLIN BLOCKADE* *

Post-war Germany, for occupation purposes, was divided into four zones under Soviet, American, British, and French control. The former capital, Berlin, was likewise divided into four zones, and both Berlin and the country as a whole came under the jurisdiction of the Allied Control Council. In 1948 General Lucius D. Clay was U.S. Commander in Germany and American representative on the Council. Berlin lay within the Soviet Zone, and was, thereby, exceedingly vulnerable to Soviet pressure.

When the order of the Soviet Military Administration to close all rail traffic from the western zones went into effect at 6:00 A.M. on the morning of June 24, 1948, the three western sectors of Berlin, with a civilian population of about 2,500,000 people, became dependent on reserve stocks and airlift replacements. It was one of the most ruthless efforts in modern times to use mass starvation for political coercion. Our food stocks on hand were sufficient to last for thirty-six days and our coal stocks for forty-five. These stocks had been built up with considerable difficulty as our transportation into Berlin was never adequate. We had foreseen the Soviet action for some months. We could sustain a minimum economy with an average daily airlift of 4000 tons for the German population and 500 tons for the Allied occupation forces. This minimum would not maintain industrial output or provide for domestic heating and normal consumer requirements, and even if coal could be brought into Berlin in unlimited quantities, the electrical generating capacity in the western sectors was limited because the Russians had removed the equipment of its most modern plant before we entered the city. Electricity from the Soviet Zone was cut off when the blockade was imposed. The capacity which remained could provide electricity for essen-

* Lucius D. Clay, *Decision in Germany* (Garden City, New York: Doubleday & Company, Inc., 1950), pp. 365–367, 374, 381–382, 386. Used by permission of Doubleday & Company, Inc., and of William Heinemann Ltd., London.

tial purposes only a few hours a day, and even these hours of use had to be staggered for the various parts of western Berlin. Despite these conditions, we had confidence that its people were prepared to face severe physical suffering rather than live again under totalitarian government, that they would endure much hardship to retain their freedom.

The resources which we had within the theater to defeat the blockade were limited. Our transport and troop carrier planes, although more than 100 in number, were C-47's, twin-engine planes of about two and a half tons cargo capacity, and many of them had seen hard war service. The British resources were even more limited. There were no French transport planes to be made available.

Nevertheless, I felt that full use of our available C-47's would prove that the job could be done. I called General LeMay on the telephone on the morning of June 24 and asked him to drop all other uses of our transport aircraft so that his entire fleet of C-47's could be placed on the Berlin run. With air commanders of the stature of General LeMay and his successor, General Cannon, you have only to state what is wanted to know that their full resources will be applied to the effort. At the same time arrangements were made for the movement of food to our airports and on the morning of June 25 the first C-47's arrived in Berlin with food for its people.

On that same day the Department of the Army called for another teleconference and suggested that the introduction of Western currency in Berlin should be slowed down if there was any possibility that it might bring armed conflict but it was too late then. I pointed out in my reply that the difficulties to be expected had been reported in full and that we had been instructed to proceed with the issue of the western zone mark unless agreement was obtained to a separate Berlin currency. I added:

> We do not expect armed conflict. . . . Principal danger is from Russian-planned German Communists groups. . . . Conditions are tense. . . . Our troops and British are in hand and can be trusted. We both realize desire of our governments to avoid armed conflicts. Nevertheless, we cannot be run over and a firm position always induces some risk.

I also pointed out that the amazingly courageous resistance of the Berlin population would drive the Soviet Administration to extreme measures and that Sokolovsky had issued a proclamation on the preceding day declaring the end of four-power government. His purpose was to frighten the Berlin population so that they would not exchange their old currency for Western currency. I stated:

> Every German leader, except SED leaders, and thousands of Germans have courageously expressed their opposition to Communism. We must not destroy their confidence by any indication of departure from Berlin. I still do not believe that

our dependents should be evacuated. Once again we have to sweat it out, come what may. If Soviets want war, it will not be because of Berlin currency issue but because they believe this the right time. I regard the probability as remote, although it cannot be disregarded entirely. Certainly we are not trying to provoke war. We are taking a lot of punches on the chin without striking back.

On the next day, June 26, the airlift became an organized operation.

A separate exchange of letters between Marshal Sokolovsky and General Robertson gave the latter the opportunity to suggest a meeting of the military governors to discuss the lifting of the blockade and the acceptance of the Eastern German currency in Berlin. I did not favor this move, because it seemed to me an indication of apprehension on our part. This time General Koenig agreed with me. While our government did not particularly desire the meeting, it was urged by the British Government to instruct me to participate. The British appeared to want agreement so badly that they believed it possible of attainment. The decision was left in my hands, and with some reluctance I agreed to attend.

On July 3 the three Western military governors proceeded separately to Sokolovsky's headquarters near Potsdam, picking up Soviet escort officers as we left the Berlin city limits. We were taken directly to Sokolovsky's anteroom and then into his office, where he greeted us politely but coldly. He had with him three attendants, none of whom we had seen before. Robertson expressed concern over the deterioration of our relationship which had culminated in the blockade and told him of our desire to reach an agreement on currency which would restore the situation. Sokolovsky interrupted to state blandly that the technical difficulties would continue until we had abandoned our plans for West German Government. This was the first admission of the real reason for the blockade. He did not even discuss the currency issue which was later given as the reason for the blockade by his government. It was evident that he was confident we would be forced to leave Berlin and that he was enjoying the situation. We were not. We had nothing further to gain from the conference so we left after a very brief discussion, and our farewell was as cold as our reception. My British and French colleagues returned with me to my office where we prepared a report. . . .

The care with which the Russians avoided measures which would have been resisted with force had convinced me that the Soviet Government did not want war although it believed that the Western Allies would yield much of their position rather than risk war. On July 10, I reported this conviction to our government, suggesting that we advise the Soviet representatives in Germany that under our rights to be in Berlin we proposed on a specific date to move in an armed convoy which would be equipped with the engineering material to overcome the technical difficulties which the Soviet representatives appeared unable to solve. I made it clear that I understood fully the risk and its implications and that this was a decision which could be made only by government. No armed convoy could cross the border without the possibility of trouble. In my view the chances of such a convoy being met by force with subsequent developments of hostilities were small. I was confident that it would get through to Berlin and that the highway blockade would be ended. When our government turned down my suggestion, I understood its desire to avoid this risk of armed conflict until the issue had been placed before the United Nations. I shall always believe that the convoy would have reached Berlin.

Berlin under blockade was like a besieged city with only one supply line linking it to the Western world, the airlift bringing food, clothing, coal, raw materials, and medicines to the 2,500,000 men, women, and children in its western sectors. Operation Vittles, as the pilots designated the airlift, grew steadily from the few outmoded planes we had in Germany to the fleet of giant flying transports which on the record day delivered almost 13,000 tons to our three airports.

At the start our C-47's had flown the clock around; pilots, plane, and ground crews worked far beyond normal hours to achieve a maximum effort. This effort showed the high number of landings which could be made, thus demonstrating that with larger planes we could sustain the Berlin population. It was a welcome sight to the pilots of the C-47's when the first C-54's began to arrive on June 30, 1948, from Alaska, Panama, and Hawaii. It was impressive to see these planes with their insignia indicating the parts of the world from which they had come to participate in the airlift. . . .

The airlift was no makeshift operation. From the beginning it was a carefully planned split-second operation. It started with the determination of priority requirements in Berlin. The next steps were the requisitioning of supplies by the Bizonal Administration in Frankfurt, then the co-ordinated movement of these supplies by ship, rail, and truck to the planes at the five airports in the western zones, the airlift delivery to the three Berlin airports, and the transfer of cargo from these airports to the German authorities.

Latest radar techniques made landings possible under almost unbelievable weather conditions, and with a remarkable safety record.

When spring came in 1949, with our British colleagues we achieved a daily average of 8,000 tons, which was as much as we had been able to bring into Berlin by rail and water prior to the blockade. Obviously, given the larger planes now coming off the production lines, this tonnage would be doubled, or, if maintained at the same figure, delivered in Berlin at from 25 to 35 percent less cost. We were gaining invaluable experience in the use of air transport to support military operations and for civil use. The cost of the airlift could well be justified in its contribution to national defense.

Volumes can be written, and perhaps will be written, to cover in detail the work of the airlift, though I doubt if they will do it justice. Mechanically, it proved the efficiency of the Western Powers in the air in a way that the Soviet Government could understand. Morally and spiritually, it was the reply of Western civilization to the challenge of totalitarianism which was willing to destroy through starvation thousands of men, women, and children in the effort to control their souls and minds.

[210] *ADENAUER REJECTS NEUTRALITY* *

In May 1949, the Federal Republic of Germany came into existence under the skillful leadership of Konrad Adenauer, head of the Christian Democratic Union. Adenauer played a major role in the phenomenal growth of the economy of West Germany in the 1950's, and in the alignment of West Germany with the NATO powers, despite constant Soviet threats and harassment.

The Federal Republic today constitutes a border land of the Western world. Should war break out between the two great power groupings, our country would inevitably become a battlefield. It is therefore self-evident that we must look for a way to shield ourselves from this dreadful doom. One such way which has been proposed, whether out of sincere conviction or for reasons of political strategy, is the neutralization of Germany. The word "neutralization" has a seductive sound, especially for a nation that has suffered so severely in the last two wars.

The idea of neutralizing Germany may well be attractive also to a good many persons in the countries of Europe which only a few years ago were fighting Germany. But we Europeans, within and outside of Germany, must not subscribe to illusions. The neutralization of the Federal Republic would make sense only if genuine armed neutrality were meant, that is, if the Fed-

* Konrad Adenauer, *World Indivisible: With Liberty and Justice for All,* introduction by Ernest Jackh, trans. from the German by Richard and Clara Winston. Volume Five of *World Perspectives,* planned and edited by Ruth Nanda Anshen (New York: Harper & Brothers, 1955), pp. 56–59. Copyright 1955 by Harper & Brothers. Used by their permission and by that of George Allen & Unwin Ltd., London.

eral Republic possessed sufficient defensive power to oppose all attempts at aggression with some prospect of success. That is not the case.

But in the case of a neutralization depending solely upon international agreement there is no assurance that the march of events might not trample ruthlessly over it. If that should happen Germany would lack any concrete defense such as she now possesses by her partnership in the free world's community of nations. The Germans would live in constant fear of future developments, and sooner or later would inevitably succumb to the suction of the East bloc. Then we would be put through the same process that has taken place in the satellite states; that is, all of Germany would be converted into a satellite state. The hope of our East Zone, that as a result of our political efforts it will eventually be reunited with us in freedom, would be blasted forever.

Some Germans, happily only a few—who are either gullible or not so gullible—see a way out in the neutralization of Germany. They imagine that this would leave the Federal Republic, withdrawn from the worldwide struggle between East and West, free to lead a peaceful existence. Such a line of thought simply ignores reality. In none of the last wars has the neutrality of any country been respected by the belligerents if the belligerent thought the occupation of the neutral country would be advantageous to him. Given Germany's geographical position in the center of the European area of tension, her neutrality would not be worth a thing if it came to hostilities. If European countries like Sweden and Switzerland believe they can preserve their neutrality even during conflicts still to come, they base this hope on the one hand on their geographical situation—a situation totally different from Germany's—and on the other hand on their having built up over many years armaments and military power commensurate to the needs of these times. Lastly they base this hope upon the fact that their countries would not be of crucial importance to the belligerent states. We must look the facts in the face: none of these conditions holds true for the German Federal Republic. Paper neutrality means nothing at all, as two world wars have amply demonstrated. But as for defending our neutrality by our own strength in case a hot war started between West and East—of that we are simply not capable either economically or in armaments in the age of atomic weapons and the commanding role of air power.

But since the tension between East and West is a fact, it would be an ostrich policy to hide our heads in the sand and remain passive as though nothing at all were happening in the world.

It is far more sensible and to the point to pitch in with all our strength so that peace may be preserved and secured. Only by so doing can we expect also to reunite all of Germany.

[211] *DEMOCRACY COMES TO JAPAN* *

The crushing defeat of Japan in 1945 discredited the old militarist clique, but left temporarily a political void. Under General MacArthur, Supreme Commander of Allied Powers (SCAP), Japanese society was profoundly altered and an attempt was made to transmit to Japan the principles of American democracy.

Demilitarization, war crime trials, and purging were all essentially negative programs. The bulk of American energy during this early period was spent on more positive measures. We again played the role of revolutionaries in Asia, and on this occasion we had the opportunity and power to implant our ideas directly into policy: to shape Japanese institutions and to select Japanese leaders. Scholars are still trying to decide how well we accomplished our objectives.

The American democratization program was certain to face a few fundamental problems. A kind of paradox is involved in attempting to establish democracy through foreign military government. In one sense, it can almost be said that Japanese politics under the Occupation reverted back to the Tokugawa period. General MacArthur's headquarters represented the *bakufu* or military administration in Tokyo, with MacArthur as the new *Shogun;* the Japanese government stood for the Imperial Court, which in the old days had resided at Kyoto and had done what it was told to do under the watchful eyes of the *bakufu.* The fact that Japan had had a long history of indirect rule and obscured responsibility may have made the American Occupation more acceptable but by the same token it made training for responsible government difficult.

On the one hand, the new Japanese political structure was to operate on the basis of the electorate's decision and in accordance with strict constitutional safeguards for individual liberties; on the other hand, SCAP had absolute power over any part of that government and did not hesitate on occasion to use it. No wonder the Japanese people were sometimes confused. Conservative Japanese governments were caused to pass the equivalent of a Wagner Labor Relations Act (much to their chagrin); but the score was evened when a later Socialist-led government was pushed into supporting the Japanese Taft-Hartley Law! Tutelage for democracy is never easy; foreign military tutelage undoubtedly complicates the problem.

The capacity of American society at this point to play a successful revo-

* Robert A. Scalapino, "The United States and Japan," in *The United States and the Far East* (New York: The American Assembly, Graduate School of Business, Columbia University, 1956), pp. 45–46, 48, 50–51. Used by permission of The American Assembly.

lutionary role in Japan and its appropriateness as a prototype have not yet become clear. It was probably inevitable that the major reforms attempted would bear the strong imprint of American institutions and patterns. More specifically, the reform era represented the American New Deal, somewhat late and somewhat altered to Japanese requirements, but still strongly colored by that famous and recent epoch in American history. The questions of whether such a program could work effectively in Japan or, if it could, of what modifications needed to be made and whether they were made are all points of vital importance. And with these questions, it is necessary to pose another: was democracy possible in Japan as we understood and knew that term, or at least, could there be a "Japanese-style democracy" that would still deserve the democratic label? The final answers to these questions cannot be given even yet. . . .

The proclivities and problems of American reform policies were also illustrated in the programs of economic and social change carried out under Occupational authority. The traditional Japanese family system was sharply attacked in a variety of ways, and equality for women was written into the new Japanese laws. Major changes in the educational system were ordered, affecting every aspect of that system including structure, curriculum, and basic objectives. The hope was that such actions would bring the home and the school into conformity with democratic values and actions.

Two additional reforms of key importance reveal some very interesting facets of American society in action in Asia. Our land-reform program was one of the most radical yet conducted in the Far East, yet it conformed in general with the American ideal of the family-owned farm. Inflation rendered the compensation formula for landlords almost meaningless, however, and the program as executed brought about a substantial change in the composition of the agrarian classes. In the so-called economic deconcentration program, another American ideal was pursued: the reduction of monopoly and encouragement of competition. But here, serious obstacles were met in the nature of Japanese society and ultimately this program settled for the reduction of certain family fortunes, a fairly strong attack upon the large cartels and trusts, and the establishment of anti-monopoly and trust laws patterned upon the American model. . . .

Two years after the war, the Japanese economy was still in the doldrums. Production was low and inflation was still rampant, producing a vicious price-wage spiral which threatened a complete collapse. In the fiscal year 1947, the index of mining and manufacturing production stood at only 43.2, the average of 1932–1936 representing 100. It must be remembered also that the population of Japan was steadily increasing. In November, 1945, the census showed a population of 72 million after the large scale repatriations and postwar marriage boom; the population figures reached 80.5 million by 1948, or 21 percent above the 1930–34 average. There were many statistical indications of the serious inflation. Perhaps the most graphic were comparative figures from the wholesale price and consumer price indices. Ministry of Finance figures using 1 as the index figure for the 1934–36 average were 128 and 171 respectively for 1948. Such figures may not be very reliable but there can be no doubting the trend or its proportions.

These developments had an obvious effect upon the democratization experiment, a fact that could not long escape American attention. They were also related to the costs that the American taxpayer had to assume in connection with keeping the Japanese people alive. Our contributions in all forms were close to four hundred million dollars a year. It is not surprising, therefore, that SCAP began somewhat belatedly to abandon its laissez-faire attitude toward the Japanese economy. At first, we had taken the position that the Japanese themselves had to straighten out an economic mess for which they were to blame. We stood by more or less idly during the early period while the situation grew progressively worse. Many wartime controls were dropped or poorly enforced. Military stockpiles were dumped on the market, and "black market" operations accounted for up to fifty percent of individual expenditures. The government engaged in deficit financing by means of an enormous increase in the amount of Bank of Japan notes in circulation. The interactive effect among these factors was cumulative, and the economic situation, bad as it was, was threatened by further deterioration.

SCAP had the authority to intervene directly in the Japanese economy, and it finally began to use that authority cautiously after Japanese government efforts proved insufficient. Beginning in 1947, we used various pressures in an effort to restore production, particularly in coal mining, and also to improve food collection from the farms. We were now exhorting the Japanese people, officials and citizens alike, to make heroic efforts to rehabilitate themselves. The new key word for American policy in Japan was "Recovery." This drive led up to the famous Nine-Point Stabilization Program, announced at the close of 1948. Through this program the United States sought to restore stability to the Japanese economy by such measures as a balanced budget, improved tax collection, credit restrictions, wage and price controls, trade expansion, production increases, and improved food collection. The Dodge Plan, as it was commonly called, achieved considerable success, and 1949 represented a year of relative price stability and accelerated recovery in many spheres of the economy, particularly in production. There were many continuing problems, to be sure, and a few were aggravated by the policy shift. Unemployment rose at first; and there was a conflict between deflation and the supply of capital for reconstruction purposes. The Korean War, in the following year, was to help the Japanese economy greatly, with Japan serving as a key center for American procurement demands. In fact, from the extremely low postwar levels, Japan was to make a phenomenal comeback, paralleling that of West Germany in Europe and proving that with sufficient technical know-how, experience, and cultural adaption to modern industrialism, amazing obstacles can be overcome in a relatively short time.

[212] *TRUMAN AND THE UNITED NATIONS DEFEND SOUTH KOREA* *

North Korean Communist forces swept south in June 1950, expecting little resistance from the South Koreans. In the first phase of the fighting, the North Koreans conquered most of South Korea; in the next phase, a United Nations Army, consisting mainly of Americans and South Koreans, under General MacArthur, swept north to the Yalu River; in the third phase, a Chinese Communist force defeated the U.N. Army; the final phase was a long, bloody stalemate.

As I discussed Korean policy with my advisers in the spring of 1948, we knew that this was one of the places where the Soviet-controlled Communist world might choose to attack. But we could say the same thing for every point of contact between East and West, from Norway through Berlin and Trieste to Greece, Turkey, and Iran; from the Kuriles in the North Pacific to Indo-China and Malaya.

Of course each commander believed that his area was in the greatest danger. It is obvious that the final decisions on the allocation of forces and materiel cannot be left to an area commander and must be made by the top-level command.

The intelligence reports from Korea in the spring of 1950 indicated that the North Koreans were steadily continuing their build-up of forces and that they were continuing to send guerilla groups into South Korea. There were continuing incidents along the 38th parallel, where armed units faced each other.

Throughout the spring the Central Intelligence reports said that the

* Harry S. Truman, *Years of Trial and Hope: Memoirs* (Garden City, New York: Doubleday & Company, Inc., 1956), pp. 331–332, 333, 335–337.

North Koreans might at any time decide to change from isolated raids to a full-scale attack. The North Koreans were capable of such an attack at any time, according to intelligence, but there was no information to give any clue as to whether an attack was certain or when it was likely to come. But this did not apply alone to Korea. These same reports also told me repeatedly that there were any number of other spots in the world where the Russians "possessed the capability" to attack.

On Saturday, June 24, 1950, I was in Independence, Missouri, to spend the weekend with my family and to attend to some personal family business.

It was a little after ten in the evening, and we were sitting in the library of our home on North Delaware Street when the telephone rang. It was the Secretary of State calling from his home in Maryland.

"Mr. President," said Dean Acheson, "I have very serious news. The North Koreans have invaded South Korea."

My first reaction was that I must get back to the capital, and I told Acheson so. He explained, however, that details were not yet available and that he thought I need not rush back until he called me again with further information. In the meantime, he suggested to me that we should ask the United Nations Security Council to hold a meeting at once and declare that an act of aggression had been committed against the Republic of Korea. I told him that I agreed and asked him to request immediately a special meeting of the Security Council, and he said he would call me to report again the following morning, or sooner if there was more information on the events in Korea.

Acheson's next call came through around eleven-thirty Sunday morning, just as we were getting ready to sit down to an early Sunday dinner. Acheson reported that the U.N. Security Council had been called into emergency session. Additional reports had been received from Korea, and there was no doubt that an all-out invasion was under way there. The Security Council, Acheson said, would probably call for a cease-fire, but in view of the complete disregard the North Koreans and their big allies had shown for the U.N. in the past, we had to expect that the U.N. order would be ignored. Some decision would have to be made at once as to the degree of aid or encouragement which our government was willing to extend to the Republic of Korea.

I asked Acheson to get working with the Service Secretaries and the Chiefs of Staff and start working on recommendations for me when I got back. Defense Secretary Louis Johnson and Chairman of the Chiefs of Staff Omar Bradley were on their way back from an inspection tour of the Far East. I informed the Secretary of State that I was returning to Washington at once. . . .

When the *Independence* landed, Secretary of State Acheson was waiting for me at the airport, as was Secretary of Defense Johnson, who himself had arrived only a short while before. We hurried to Blair House, where we were joined by the other conferees. . . .

It was late, and we went at once to the dining room for dinner. I asked that no discussion take place until dinner was served and over and the Blair House staff had withdrawn. . . .

Earlier that Sunday evening, Acheson reported, the Security Council of the United Nations had, by a vote of 9 to 0, approved a resolution declaring that a breach of the peace had been committed by the North Korean action and ordering the North Koreans to cease their action and withdraw their forces. . . .

As we continued our discussion, I stated that I did not expect the North Koreans to pay any attention to the United Nations. This, I said, would mean that the United Nations would have to apply force if it wanted its order obeyed.

General Bradley said we would have to draw the line somewhere. Russia, he thought, was not yet ready for war, but in Korea, they were obviously testing us, and the line ought to be drawn now.

I said that most emphatically I thought the line would have to be drawn. General Collins reported that he had had a teletype conference with General MacArthur. The Far East Commander, he told us, was ready to ship ammunition and supplies to Korea as soon as he received the green light.

I expressed the opinion that the Russians were trying to get Korea by default, gambling that we would be afraid of starting a third world war and would offer no resistance. I thought that we were still holding the stronger hand, although how much stronger, it was hard to tell. . . .

By Monday the reports from Korea began to sound dark and discouraging, and among the messages that arrived was one from Syngman Rhee asking for help. . . .

There was now no doubt! The Republic of Korea needed help at once if it was not to be overrun. More seriously, a Communist success in Korea would put Red troops and planes within easy striking distance of Japan, and Okinawa and Formosa would be open to attack from two sides.

I told my advisers that what was developing in Korea seemed to me like a repetition on a larger scale of what had happened in Berlin. The Reds were probing for weaknesses in our armor; we had to meet their thrust without getting embroiled in a world-wide war.

I directed the Secretary of Defense to call General MacArthur on the scrambler phone and to tell him in person what my instructions were. He was to use air and naval forces to support the Republic of Korea with air and naval elements of his command, but only south of the 38th parallel. He was also instructed to dispatch the Seventh Fleet to the Formosa Strait. The purpose of this move was to prevent attacks by the Communists on Formosa as well as forays by Chiang Kai-shek against the mainland, this last to avoid reprisal actions by the Reds that might enlarge the area of conflict.

I also approved recommendations for the strengthening of our forces in the Philippines and for increased aid to the French in Indo-China. Meanwhile the Security Council of the United Nations met again and adopted on June 27 the resolution calling on all members of the U.N. to give assistance to South Korea.

37

A World in Ferment: The Emergence of Africa and Asia

The liberation of the subject peoples of Africa and Asia from European domination, which had started before World War II, progressed at an accelerated pace after 1945. The colonial powers had lost prestige by humiliating defeats in the Far East and in the Mediterranean Area during the early years of World War II. After the war the self-serving anti-imperialist propaganda of the U.S.S.R. and the disinterested encouragement given to aspiring colonial peoples by the United States hastened the anticolonial trend. The post-war governments of Great Britain offered independence and commonwealth privileges to the more politically mature of their subject peoples. Frequently, however, violence, sporadic or sustained, resulted from the impatience of native nationalist leaders to achieve, and the reluctance of Europeans to grant, full independence.

[213] *NASSER NATIONALIZES THE SUEZ CANAL* *

In 1952 the corpulent and corrupt King Farouk of Egypt was dethroned as a result of the rising tide of nationalist feeling and the accumulated frustrations of

* Speech by President Nasser, Alexandria, July 26, 1956. (Translation transmitted by the American Embassy at Cairo, based on the Arabic press text, which in turn was checked against a tape recording of the speech itself.) U.S. Department of State, Publication 6392, *The Suez Canal Problem, July 26–September 22, 1956* (Washington, D.C., October, 1956), pp. 25–30.

military leaders who had suffered defeat in the 1948 war against Israel. Egypt became a republic under a military clique headed by General Neguib, who was succeeded by Gamal Abdel Nasser in 1954.

(Speaking of a meeting with Mr. Eugene R. Black, President of the International Bank for Reconstruction and Development, with which Egypt had been negotiating for a loan to help finance the construction of a high dam on the Nile at Aswan, Mr. Nasser said:)

I began to look at Mr. Black sitting in his chair imagining that I was sitting before Ferdinand de Lesseps.

I recalled the words which we used to read. In 1854 Ferdinand de Lesseps arrived in Egypt. He went to Mohamed Said Pasha, the Khedive. He sat beside him and told him, "We want to dig the Suez Canal. This project will greatly benefit you. It is a great project and will bring excellent returns to Egypt."

While Black was speaking to me, I felt the complexes which his words revived. I was again carried back to Ferdinand de Lesseps.

I told him we have complexes from such matters, and we do not want to see another Cromer ** governing us again. Loans and interests on these loans have ended in the occupation of our country. I requested him to take this into consideration. We have complexes from De Lesseps and from Cromer, and from political occupation through economic occupation.

That was the picture I had in mind, the picture of De Lesseps who arrived on November 7, 1854. He arrived in Alexandria and began to work cautiously and treacherously. On November 30, 1854, he had already contacted the Khedive and obtained the Concession for the Canal from him. The Concession said: "Our friend De Lesseps has drawn our attention to the benefits which will accrue to Egypt by joining the Mediterranean and the Red Sea by a waterway for the passage of ships. He informed us of the possibility of forming a company for this purpose to comprise the investors of capital. We have approved the idea and have authorized him to form and to operate a company for the digging of the Suez Canal and to exploit it between the two seas."

This was in 1854. In 1856, a hundred years ago, a Firman was issued whereby the company was formed. Egypt got 44% of the shares and bound herself with certain obligations to De Lesseps. The De Lesseps company is a private company! It has nothing to do with governments, domination, occupation or imperialism! De Lesseps told the Khedive, "I am your friend, I

** Evelyn Baring, First Earl of Cromer (1841–1917), was the British agent and Consul General in Egypt during 1883–1907. Cromer was a virtual ruler of Egypt, directing the finances and administration of the country.

have come to benefit you, and to dig a canal between the two seas for your advantage."

The Suez Canal Company was formed, and Egypt got 44% of the shares. Egypt undertook to supply labor to dig the Canal by corvée,* of whom 120,000 died without getting paid. We also paid De Lesseps in order that he might give up some concession. We gave up the 15% of the profits which we were supposed to get over and above the profits of our 44% of the shares. Thus, contrary to the statements made by De Lesseps to the Khedive in which he said that the Canal was dug for Egypt, Egypt has become the property of the Canal. . . .

The results of the words of De Lesseps in 1856, the result of friendship and loans was the occupation of Egypt in 1882.

Egypt then borrowed money. What happened? Egypt was obliged, during the reign of Ismail, to sell its 44% of the shares in the company. Immediately, England set out to purchase the shares. It bought them for 4 million pounds. Then, Ismail gave up his 5% of the company's profits against the ceding of some concessions by the Company which were granted to it.

Then Ismail was obliged to pay to Britain the 5% profit which he had relinquished. This amounted to over 4 million pounds. In other words, Britain got Egypt's 44% of the Company's shares free. This was the history which took place a century ago.

Is history to repeat itself again with treachery and deceit?

Brothers, it is impossible that history should repeat itself.

Today, we do not repeat what happened in the past. We are eradicating the traces of the past. We are building our country on strong and sound bases.

Whenever we turn backwards, we aim at the eradication of past evils which brought about our domination, and the vestiges of the past which took place despite ourselves and which were caused by imperialism through treachery and deceit.

Today, the Suez Canal where 120,000 of our sons had lost their lives in digging it by corvée, and for the foundation of which we paid 8 million pounds, has become a state within a state. It has humiliated ministers and cabinets. . . .

The income of the Suez Canal Company in 1955 reached 35 million Egyptian pounds, or 100 million dollars! This is the Suez Canal Company, which, according to the Firman was dug for the sake of Egypt and its benefit!

Do you know how much assistance America and Britain were going to

* Corvée: unpaid or poorly paid labor exacted by public authorities for construction or repair of roads, bridges, canals, etc.

offer us over 5 years? 70 million dollars. Do you know who takes the 100 million dollars, the Company's income, every year: They take them, of course.

It is no shame that I may be poor and borrow money to build my country. It is no shame that I should attempt to get aid for the sake of my country. But, it is shameful that I suck peoples' blood and rights.

We shall not repeat the past. We shall eradicate it by restoring our rights in the Suez Canal. This money is ours. This Canal is the property of Egypt because it is an Egyptian Joint Stock Company.

The Canal was dug by Egypt's sons and 120,000 of them died while working. The Suez Canal Company in Paris is an imposter company. It usurped our concessions.

When De Lesseps came over to Egypt, his arrival was the same as Black who came to Egypt to talk with me. The same action.

But history will never repeat itself. On the contrary, we shall build the High Dam. We shall restore our usurped rights. We shall build the High Dam as we want it. We are determined to do it. Thirty-five million Egyptian pounds the company gets every year; let Egypt take it. One hundred million dollars are collected every year by the company which collects them for the benefit of Egypt. Let it be so, and Egypt will collect the 100 million dollars for the benefit of Egypt.

Thus, today, citizens, when we build the High Dam, we are actually building the dam to defend our dignity, freedom and pride, and to eradicate humiliation and submission.

Egypt—the whole of Egypt—one national front—one unified and solid front—announces that it will fight to the last drop of its blood. . . . We shall all fight to the last drop of our blood for building our country, for the sake of Egypt. We shall not let war mongers, imperialists, or those who trade in human beings dominate us. We shall depend on our hands and on our blood. We are rich, but we were careless. We shall restore these rights. The battle continues. We shall restore these rights step by step. We shall realize everything. We shall build a strong and dignified Egypt, the Arab Egypt. . . .

Today, citizens, the Suez Canal Company has been nationalized. This order has been published in the Official Journal. It has become a matter of fact.

Citizens, today we say our wealth has been restored to us. . . .

We shall work, produce, and step-up production despite all these intrigues and these talks. Whenever I hear talk from Washington, I shall say "Die of your fury."

We shall build up industry in Egypt and compete with them. They do not want us to become an industrial country so that they can promote the sale of their products and market them in Egypt. I never saw any American aid directed towards industrialization as this would cause us to compete with them. American aid is everywhere directed towards exploitation.

On entering upon the fifth anniversary of the Revolution, as I said at the beginning of my speech, we feel stronger, more resolute, and faithful than during the former years.

On embarking upon the fifth year of the Revolution, as Farouk was expelled on July 26, 1952, the Suez Canal Company will depart on the very same day. We are conscious of accomplishing glories and achieving true dignity. Sovereignty in Egypt will belong only to her sons.

[214] *EDEN EXPLAINS THE SUEZ CRISIS OF 1956* *

In the summer of 1956 President Nasser of Egypt, angered at the withdrawal of an offer by the United States to build a high dam at Aswan on the Nile, decreed the nationalization of the Suez Canal. Prime Minister Eden of Great Britain, in cooperation with the French, attempted to set up a Canal Users' Association, but the Egyptians rejected it, and took control of the Canal. Eden, in this selection from his Memoirs, describes the situation on the eve of the Anglo-French-Israeli attack on Egypt.

On October 25 a report came that Israel was about to mobilize. She did so on the 27 and moved against Egypt on the evening of the 29th. I thought then, and I think now, that the Israelis had justification for their action. It is at least a grim possibility that they would not be a free nation to-day had they not taken it. The marked victim of the garrotter is not to be condemned if he strikes out before the noose is round his throat.

If we were not prepared to condemn Israel, we could not stand aside and watch events. In an Israeli-Egyptian conflict our military advisors expected the Israelis to win; their quality, intelligent training and dedicated courage outmatched the Egyptian advantage in numbers and equipment. The chief peril to us lay not in the conflict but in its extension by the intervention of other Arab states. The best way to halt that was by intervening ourselves. These considerations decided our course of action.

Ministers had already considered at several meetings the way in which the situation might develop. These had also been canvassed with the French. On October 25 the Cabinet discussed the specific possibility of conflict between Israel and Egypt and decided in principle how it would react if this occurred. The Governments of France and the United Kingdom

* *The Memoirs of Anthony Eden: Full Circle* (Boston: Houghton Mifflin Company, 1960), pp. 584–588.

should, it considered, at once call on both parties to stop hostilities and withdraw their forces to a distance from either bank of the canal. If one or both failed to comply within a definite period, then British and French forces would intervene as a temporary measure to separate the combatants. To ensure this being effective, they would have to occupy key positions at Port Said, Ismailia and Suez. Our purpose was to safeguard free passage through the canal, if it were threatened with becoming a zone of warfare, and to arrest the spread of fighting in the Middle East.

To realize this we would put into operation the plan for occupation of the Suez Canal zone, prepared by the joint Anglo-French military staff which had been studying the problem since the end of July. An advantage of this course was that we did not need to recast our military preparations. The same plan that had been intended to deal with Nasser's seizure of the Canal fitted equally well with our new objective. Critics asked why we landed so far behind the combatant area. The answer is that to land anywhere except as planned would have involved delay and we could not afford delay. We were also limited by shortage of landing craft and had to have the use of a port.

Of course there were dangers in this policy. But there were dangers in any policy which we might have chosen, not least in that of complete inaction. Political decisions, especially when they concern the Middle East, usually involved a choice of evils. I am convinced that we chose the lesser evil. . . .

On the morning of October 30 the Cabinet were informed that Israeli troops had entered Egyptian territory on the evening of the 29th and during the night had reached a point half way between their frontier and Ismailia. A second Israeli force was reported to be striking towards Suez. Other swift Israeli actions were also unrolling, though we only learnt details of these later. This was the situation the Cabinet had considered five days before.

The Cabinet was sternly conscious of the importance and urgency of the decisions it had to take. Now that the situation had actually arisen, it confirmed its readiness to act as had been decided, subject to the agreement of the French Ministers, who were flying to London for consultations. It now considered the actual terms of the note in which this demand was to be addressed to Egypt and Israel; these would be discussed with M. Mollet and M. Pineau on their arrival.

The Cabinet examined the wording of the statement I was to make in the House that afternoon and endorsed it. We also discussed the attitude of the United States. The American Administration were urgently proposing to have Israel branded as an aggressor by the Security Council. They were unmoved by the history of the dispute or Egypt's aggressive attitude and declared intentions against Israel. Our hope was that the United States would take some account of these events and be watchful of Soviet moves. The Cabinet then approved the terms of a message to President Eisenhower inviting his general support. I sent two telegrams to Washington that day. In the first I said:

We have never made any secret of our belief that justice entitles us to defend our vital interests against Nasser's designs. But we acted with you in summoning the London Conference, in despatching the abortive Menzies mission and in seeking to establish S.C.U.A.* As you know, the Russians regarded the Security Council proceedings as a victory for themselves and for Egypt. Nevertheless we continued through the Secretary-General of the United Nations to seek a basis for the continuation of the negotiations.

Egypt has to a large extent brought this attack on herself by insisting that the state of war persists, by defying the Security Council and by declaring her intention to marshal the Arab states for the destruction of Israel. The latest example of Egyptian intentions is the announcement of a joint command between Egypt, Jordan, and Syria.

We have earnestly deliberated what we should do in this serious situation. We cannot afford to see the canal closed to or lose the shipping which is daily on passage through it. We have a responsibility for the people in these ships. We feel that decisive action should be taken at once to stop hostilities. We have agreed with you to go to the Security Council and instructions are being sent this moment. Experience, however, shows that its procedure is unlikely to be either rapid or effective.

My second message was sent after our talks with the French Ministers and the delivery of our jointly agreed notes to the Egyptian Ambassador and the Israeli Chargé d'Affaires. It informed the President of the requests we were making to the belligerents, and continued:

My first instinct would have been to ask you to associate yourself and your country with the declaration. But I know the constitutional and other difficulties in which you are placed. I think there is a chance that both sides will accept. In any case it would help this result very much if you found it possible to support what we have done at least in general terms. We are well aware that no real settlement of Middle East problems is possible except through the closest cooperation between our two countries. Our two governments have tried with the best will in the world all sorts of public and private negotiations through the last two or three years and they all failed. This seems an opporunity for a fresh start.

. . . Nothing could have prevented this volcano from erupting somewhere, but when the dust settles there may well be a chance for our doing a really constructive piece of work together and thereby strengthening the weakest point in the line against communism.

A message from President Eisenhower crossed my telegrams. He expressed his disquiet upon a number of points, but considered it of the greatest importance that the United Kingdom and the United States should quickly and clearly lay out their present views and intentions before each other, so that they might not in any real crisis be powerless to act in concert

* Suez Canal Users' Association.

because of misunderstanding. That had been my purpose also at the January meeting in Washington, and all through this drawn-out business.

The question of consultation before action with the Commonwealth countries and the United States was one that troubled us greatly. Of course we would have preferred to do this. Whatever the outcome of such consultation, it would have smoothed our path. On the other hand, however sharply pressed, such consultation was not possible within a matter of hours; it must take days at least. Nor was there any chance that all concerned would take precisely the same view of what action must follow the consultation. As a result there would be attempts to modify our proposals, to reach some compromise between several divergent points of view and, before we knew where we were, we would be back at an eighteen-power conference once more. This was the last thing in the world we wanted, because we knew quite well that once palavers began, no effective action would be possible.

The chief danger, especially for us, was that the conflict would spread. A localized war between Israel and Egypt, while troublesome, should not be highly dangerous internationally. The same could not be said of a war which had spread to include Syria and Jordan, with Iraq morally compelled to take a hand too. If this were to happen, the Jordan committment would raise its head again, not in so acute a form, but alarming enough. Two events could be counted on to encourage Jordan and Syria to inaction, swift Israeli military success and the knowledge that British and French forces were on the way and would be used to localize the dispute. If that restraint was to be effective, it must be applied at once. Twenty-four hours might well be too late, forty-eight certainly would.

The choice for us was stark and inescapable, either act at once to bring about the result we sought, the localization of the conflict, or involve ourselves in consultations. This would mean the same inaction as in the last three months. We chose to act.

[215] *NKRUMAH CALLS FOR GHANA'S INDEPENDENCE* *

Kwame Nkrumah, born in 1909 in the Gold Coast Colony and educated in Catholic mission schools, spent ten years in the United States (1935–1945), completing his studies. In 1949, after returning to Africa, he founded the Convention Peoples Party (CPP). Nkrumah, in this speech to the Gold Coast Legislative Assembly in 1953, outlined the goals of the CPP, which were achieved four years later.

* Bankole Timothy, *Kwame Nkrumah: His Rise to Power* (London: George Allen & Unwin Ltd., 1955), pp. 143–147, 150–152. © George Allen & Unwin Ltd., 1955. Used by permission of George Allen & Unwin Ltd., London, and The Macmillan Company, New York.

Mr. Speaker, I beg to move that this Assembly, in adopting the Government's White Paper on Constitutional Reform, do authorise the Government to request that Her Majesty's Government, as soon as the necessary constitutional and administrative arrangements for independence are made, should introduce an Act of Independence into the United Kingdom Parliament declaring the Gold Coast a sovereign and independent State within the Commonwealth; and further, that this Assembly do authorise the Government to ask Her Majesty's Government, without prejudice to the above request, to amend as a matter of urgency the Gold Coast (Constitution) Order in Council 1950, in such a way as to provide *inter alia* that the Legislative Assembly shall be composed of members directly elected by secret ballot, and that all Members of the Cabinet shall be Members of the Assembly and directly responsible to it. . . .

In seeking your mandate, I am asking you to give my Government the power to bring to fruition the longing hopes, the ardent dreams, the fervent aspirations of the chiefs and people of our country. Throughout a century of alien rule our people have, with ever increasing tendency, looked forward to that bright and glorious day when they shall regain their ancient heritage, and once more take their place rightly as free men in the world.

Mr. Speaker, we have frequent examples to show that there comes a time in the history of all Colonial peoples when they must, because of their will to throw off the hampering shackles of Colonialism, boldly assert their God-given right to be free of a foreign ruler. Today we are here to claim this right to our independence. . . .

The right of a people to decide their own destiny, to make their way in freedom, is not to be measured by the yardstick of color or degree of social development. It is an inalienable right of peoples which they are powerless to exercise when forces, stronger than they themselves, by whatever means, for whatever reasons, take this right away from them. If there is to be a criterion of a people's preparedness for Self-government, then I say it is their readiness to assume the responsibilities of ruling themselves. For who but a people themselves can say when they are prepared? How can others judge when that moment has arrived in the destiny of a subject people? What other gauge can there be?

Mr. Speaker, never in the history of the world has an alien ruler granted self-rule to a people on a silver platter. Therefore, Mr. Speaker, I say that a people's readiness and willingness to assume the responsibilities of self-rule is the single criterion of their preparedness to undertake those responsibilities. . . .

There is no conflict that I can see between our claim and the professed policy of all parties and governments of the United Kingdom. We have here in our country a stable society. Our economy is healthy, as good as any for a country of our size. In many respects, we are very much better off than many Sovereign States. And our potentialities are large. Our people are fundamentally homogeneous, nor are we plagued with religious and tribal problems. And, above all, we have hardly any colour bar. In fact, the whole democratic tradition of our society precludes the *herrenvolk* doctrine. The remnants of this doctrine are now an anachronism in our midst and their days are numbered. . . .

In the very early days of the Christian era, long before England had assumed any importance, long even before her people had united into a nation, our ancestors had attained a great empire, which lasted until the eleventh century, when it fell before the attacks of the Moors of the North. At its height that empire stretched from Timbuctoo to Bamako, and even as far as to the Atlantic. It is said that lawyers and scholars were much respected in that empire and that the inhabitants of Ghana wore garments of wool, cotton, silk and velvet. There was trade in copper, gold, and textile fabrics, and jewels and weapons of gold and silver were carried.

Thus may we take pride in the name of Ghana, not out of romanticism, but as an inspiration for the future. It is right and proper that we should know about our past. For just as the future moves from the present, so the present has emerged from the past. Nor need we be ashamed of our past. There was much in it of glory. What our ancestors achieved in the context of their contemporary society gives us confidence that we can create, out of that past, a glorious future, not in terms of war and military pomp, but in terms of social progress and of peace. For we repudiate war and violence. Our battles shall be against the old ideas that keep men trammelled in their own greed; against the crass stupidities that breed hatred, fear, and inhumanity. The heroes of our future will be those who can lead our people out of the stifling fog of disintegration through serfdom, into the valley of light where purpose, endeavor, and determination will create that brotherhood which Christ proclaimed two thousand years ago, and about which so much is said, but so little done.

[216] *DE GAULLE ESTABLISHES THE FIFTH FRENCH REPUBLIC* *

The independence movement in Asia and Africa brought severe repercussions to the former European colonial powers, particularly France. The Fourth French

* "Radio and Television Broadcast to the French Nation by Charles De Gaulle, June 13, 1958," from "Speeches and Press Conferences No. 110, June 1958," Ambassade de France, Service de Presse et d'Information, New York. Used by permission.

Republic, shaken by the military defeat in Indo-China in 1954, collapsed in May, 1958, under the impact of the Algerian crisis. General Charles De Gaulle, wartime leader of the Free French forces, came to power with the avowed intention of revising the constitution and regenerating French national spirit.

French unity was breaking up. Civil war was about to begin. In the eyes of the world, France seemed on the verge of dissolution. It was then that I assumed responsibility for governing our country.

The tragedy of Algeria—upsetting the populations, putting the Army to a harsh test, raising a wave of indignation there for the present, and of change and fraternity for the future—started this national crisis. But, at all events, the crisis was inevitable.

Because for twelve years the party system, insecurely based on a deeply divided people, in the midst of a terribly dangerous world, showed itself totally unfit to ensure the conduct of affairs. This was by no means due to the incompetence or the unworthiness of men. Those who held positions of power under the Fourth Republic were able people, honest and patriotic.

But, as they never represented anything but small fractions of the population, these men who governed did not identify themselves with the general interest. Moreover,—divided amongst themselves, as were their own groups, struggling against the encroachments of the Parliamentary Assembly from which they received their mandates, subjected to the demands of the parties they represented—they were doomed to live, for a few months or a few weeks, faced with huge problems which they could not possibly solve.

I said huge problems. They were indeed huge, those problems which confronted them. So are those which we shall have to brave together. To pacify Algeria. To do it in such a way that it will, forever, be body and soul with France. To organize, in the federal manner, the ties between our metropolitan country and the associated countries in Africa and Madagascar. To establish on the basis of cooperation our relations with Morocco, Tunisia, and the States of Indochina.

In the Western world to which we belong—without having to confine ourselves in it—to take a place that is our own, to perform an action that is our action, with a view to serving simultaneously both peace and security.

At home, to succeed in making the very difficult, but nonetheless absolutely necessary effort to restore the equilibrium of our finances and our economy, lacking which our country would be heading for a stupid disaster, but thanks to which it will see a prosperous future opening up before it. Women and men of France, this is what we must do first of all. To start out with, I request you, yes, I request you earnestly to ensure a triumphal success for the loan which we are about to float. First phase of our recovery.

First test of national confidence that you will give to yourselves and—if I may say so—that you will grant me, who need it so very badly.

"Isn't all this too much for us?" complain those who, by dint of believing that nothing can succeed, end by hoping that it cannot, those who have, as their secret motto, that of Mephistopheles, the eloquent demon of despair; "I am the spirit which denies everything." No, it is not too much for France, for this marvellous country which, in spite of past trials and the confusion in her affairs of state, can manage to hold in her hand all the cards for an extraordinary regeneration.

A population that is growing. An economy that has, once and for all, overcome the obstacle of routine. A technology that is forging ahead. New sources of ability that are ready to spring from the deepest layers of the populations. The Sahara, which holds a fortune for us and for the territories bordering it on the north and on the south. An army that is very fine and very good. Lastly the world which wishes—even if it sometimes pretends the opposite—to see us play the part that is rightfully ours, because it feels that this will be to the advantage of all mankind. Ah, I do not pity our youth, which sees all these resources of life, all these incentives to activity offered to it.

But there is not a single Frenchman who does not know that any future is barred to us, if France does not have to guide her a state which is capable of doing so.

It is the necessary condition for everything. We have just proved this on the very brink of the abyss. It is my task, along with my Government, to propose to our people new institutions of such a kind that they will provide for the Republic powers that are strong enough, stable enough, effective enough to be responsible for its destiny. I shall do so at the beginning of the autumn. Women and men of France, it is you who will decide, at that time, through your votes, this essential reform and, thereby, the destiny of France.

The way is hard, but how glorious! The aim is difficult, but how grand! Let us go! The signal for departure is being given.

[217] *KENNEDY OUTLINES THE PROBLEMS OF DEFENDING LIBERTY IN THE 1960'S* *

John F. Kennedy, winner by an extremely narrow margin in the presidential election of 1960, enumerated in his inaugural address in January, 1961, some of the problems facing the United States and the Free World in the decade of the 1960's.

* Inaugural Address of President John F. Kennedy, January 20, 1961.

My fellow citizens:

We observe today, not a victory of party but a celebration of freedom—symbolizing an end as well as a beginning—signifying renewal as well as change. For I have sworn before you and Almighty God the same solemn oath our forebears prescribed nearly a century and three-quarters ago.

The world is very different now. For man holds in his mortal hands the power to abolish all form of human poverty and to abolish all form of human life. And yet the same revolutionary beliefs for which our forebears fought are still at issue around the globe—the belief that the rights of man come not from the generosity of the state but from the hand of God.

We dare not forget today that we are the heirs of that first revolution. Let the word go forth from this time and place, to friend and foe alike, that the torch has been passed to a new generation of Americans—born in this century, tempered by war, disciplined by a cold and bitter peace, proud of our ancient heritage—and unwilling to witness or permit the slow undoing of those human rights to which this Nation has always been committed, and to which we are committed today.

Let every nation know, whether it wishes us well or ill, that we shall pay any price, bear any burden, meet any hardship, support any friend or oppose any foe in order to assure the survival and success of liberty.

This much we pledge and more. To those old allies whose cultural and spiritual origins we share, we pledge the loyalty of faithful friends. United there is little we cannot do in a host of new co-operative ventures. Divided, there is little we can do—for we dare not meet a powerful challenge at odds and split asunder.

To those new states whom we now welcome to the ranks of the free we pledge our word that one form of colonial control shall not have passed, merely to be replaced by a far more iron tyranny. We shall not always expect to find them strongly supporting our every view. But we shall always hope to find them strongly supporting their own freedom—and to remember that, in the past, those who foolishly sought to find power by riding on the tiger's back inevitably ended up inside.

To those peoples in the huts and villages of half the globe struggling to break the bonds of mass misery, we pledge our best efforts to help them help themselves, for whatever period is required—not because the Communists are doing it, not because we seek their votes, but because it is right. If the free society cannot help the many who are poor, it can never save the few who are rich.

To the sister republics south of our border, we offer a special pledge—to convert our good words into good deeds—in a new alliance for progress—to assist free men and free governments in casting off the chains of poverty.

But this peaceful revolution of hope cannot become the prey of hostile powers. Let all our neighbors know that we shall join with them to oppose aggression or subversion anywhere in the Americas. And let every other power know that this hemisphere intends to remain the master of its own house.

To that world assembly of sovereign states, the United Nations, our last best hope in an age where the instruments of war have far outpaced the instruments of peace, we renew our pledge of support—to prevent it from becoming merely a forum for invective—to strengthen its shield of the new and weak—and to enlarge the area in which its writ may run.

Finally, to those nations who would make themselves our adversary, we offer not a pledge but a request: that both sides begin anew the quest for peace, before the dark powers of destruction unleashed by science engulf all humanity in planned or accidental self-destruction.

We dare not tempt them with weakness. For only when our arms are sufficient beyond doubt can we be certain beyond doubt that they will never be employed.

But neither can two great and powerful groups of nations take comfort from our present course—both sides overburdened by the cost of modern weapons, both rightly alarmed by the steady spread of the deadly atom, yet both racing to alter that uncertain balance of terror that stays the hand of mankind's final war.

So let us begin anew—remembering on both sides that civility is not a sign of weakness, and sincerity is always subject to proof. Let us never negotiate out of fear. But let us never fear to negotiate.

Let both sides explore what problems unite us instead of belaboring the problems which divide us.

Let both sides, for the first time, formulate serious and precise proposals for the inspection and control of arms—and bring the absolute power to destroy other nations under the absolute control of all nations.

Let both sides join to invoke the wonders of science instead of its terrors. Together let us explore the stars, conquer the deserts, eradicate disease, tap the ocean depths and encourage the arts and commerce.

Let both sides be united to heed in all corners of the earth the command of Isaiah—to "undo the heavy burdens . . . (and) let the oppressed go free."

And if a beach-head of cooperation can be made in the jungles of suspicion, let both sides join in the next task: Creating, not a new balance of power, but a new world of law, where the strong are just and the weak secure and the peace preserved.

All this will not be finished in the first 100 days. Nor will it be finished in the first 1,000 days, in the life of this administration, nor even perhaps in our lifetime on this planet. But let us begin.

In your hands, my fellow citizens, more than in mine, will rest the final success or failure of our course. Since this country was founded, each generation of America has been summoned to give testimony to its national loyalty. The graves of young Americans who answered the call to service surround the globe.

Now the trumpet summons us again—not as a call to bear arms, though arms we need—not as a call to battle, though embattled we are—but a call to bear the burden of a long twilight struggle, year in and year out, "rejoicing in hope, patient in tribulation"—a struggle against the common enemies of man: Tyranny, poverty, disease, and war itself.

Can we forge against these enemies a grand and global alliance, North and South, East and West, that can assure a more fruitful life for all mankind? Will you join in that historic effort?

In the long history of the world, only a few generations have been granted the role of defending freedom in its hour of maximum danger. I do not shrink from this responsibility—I welcome it. I do not believe that any of us would exchange places with any other people or any other generation. The energy, the faith, and the devotion which we bring to this endeavor will light our country and all who serve it—and the glow from that fire can truly light the world.

And so, my fellow Americans: Ask not what your country can do for you—ask what you can do for your country.

My fellow citizens of the world: Ask not what America will do for you, but what together we can do for the freedom of man.

Finally, whether you are citizens of America or of the world, ask of us here the same high standards of strength and sacrifice that we ask of you. With a good conscience our only sure reward, with history the final judge of our deeds, let us go forth to lead the land we love, asking His blessing and His help, but knowing that here on earth God's work must truly be our own.

...fellows do the like... the colonial... not even perhaps ...in the planet Earth or future.

...this Administration, nor even perhaps in our lifetime on this planet. But let us begin.

...not in the hands of my fellow citizens, more than mine, will rest the final success or failure of our course. Since this country was founded, each generation of Americans has been summoned to give testimony to its national loyalty. The graves of young Americans who answered the call to service surround the globe.

Now the trumpet summons us again—not as a call to bear arms, though arms we need—not as a call to battle, though embattled we are—but a call to bear the burden of a long twilight struggle, year in and year out, "rejoicing in hope, patient in tribulation"—a struggle against the common enemies of man: tyranny, poverty, disease, and war itself.

Can we forge against these enemies a grand and global alliance, North and South, East and West, that can assure a more fruitful life for all mankind? Will you join in that historic effort?

In the long history of the world, only a few generations have been granted the role of defending freedom in its hour of maximum danger. I do not shrink from this responsibility—I welcome it. I do not believe that any of us would exchange places with any other people or any other generation. The energy, the faith, and the devotion which we bring to this endeavor will light our country and all who serve it—and the glow from that fire can truly light the world.

And so, my fellow Americans: ask not what your country can do for you—ask what you can do for your country.

My fellow citizens of the world: ask not what America will do for you, but what together we can do for the freedom of man.

Finally, whether you are citizens of America or citizens of the world, ask of us here the same high standards of strength and sacrifice which we ask of you. With a good conscience our only sure reward, with history the final judge of our deeds, let us go forth to lead the land we love, asking His blessing and His help, but knowing that here on earth God's work must truly be our own.